COMPUTER GRAPHICS

COMPUTER GRAPHICS
For Scientists and Engineers

Second Revised Edition

R.G.S. ASTHANA
N.K. SINHA

PUBLISHING FOR ONE WORLD

NEW AGE INTERNATIONAL (P) LIMITED, PUBLISHERS
(formerly Wiley Eastern Limited)
New Delhi • Bangalore • Chennai • Guwahati • Hyderabad
Jalandhar • Kolkata • Lucknow • Mumbai • Ranchi
Visit us at **www.newagepublishers.com**

Published by New Age International (P) Ltd., Publishers
First Edition: 1996
Second Edition: 1998
Reprint: 2007

ISBN : 81-224-0874-5

Rs. 225.00

C-07-06-1664

9 10 11 12 13 14 15

Printed in India at Printo Pack, Delhi.

PUBLISHING FOR ONE WORLD

NEW AGE INTERNATIONAL (P) LIMITED, PUBLISHERS

(formerly Wiley Eastern Limited)

4835/24, Ansari Road, Daryaganj, New Delhi - 110002

Visit us at www.newagepublishers.com

Preface to the Second Edition

The first edition of this book was published in 1993, and is completely sold out now. The success of the first adaptation, and the feedback received from many professors has prompted the authors to add extra material to the book. In addition to minor revisions and updating of material in chapters 1 to 8, two new chapters have been added. Chapter 9 presents a brief introduction to the fascinating developments in virtual reality. Chapter 10 introduces the reader to the recent advances in the area of multimedia technology and its applications.

Several persons have been very helpful in the preparation of this book. In addition to those listed in the first edition, we would like to express our sincere appreciation to Mrs. Renu V. Kumar in preparing this edition. We are grateful to Mr. H.S. Poplai, General Manager of Wiley Eastern for his help and encouragement.

R.G.S. Asthana
Naresh K. Sinha
December 1995

Preface to the First Edition

The subject of Computer Graphics has become very important for all engineers, especially due to the availability of inexpensive personal computers. At present, most engineering students in North America as well as Europe have their own computers. As engineers use graphics extensively, most progressive engineering schools now have a required undergraduate course on Computer Graphics. This has become especially important since computer graphics can be used in an interactive fashion, enabling a designer to view, almost immediately, the effect of modifying certain parameters. Therefore, we believe that there is a great need for a suitable text-book on the subject for engineering students as well as for practicing engineers. This book is an attempt to fill this gap.

The purpose of this book is to provide an introductory text for understanding the fundamental principles of computer graphics. The book also includes a number of worked-out examples along with problems and references at the end of each chapter to act both as a tutorial and a reference source for readers interested in various aspects of computer graphics : hardware, software, data structures, manipulation of 2-D and 3-D graphical objects and surfaces, and the fundamental algorithms. Some salient features are chapters on : data structures along with examples for manipulating pictures/graphical objects; interactive graphics covering i/o devices and systems that facilitate the man-machine graphic communication with emphasis on device-independent graphic programming; 2-D and 3-D graphics, application of graphics to real-life problems with sample source programs covering areas such as business graphics, graph plotting, line drawing, image processing, animation, 3-D solid-modelling, and multi-media.

This book covers and brings collection of topics, such as, graphical hardware devices, data structures, 2-D and 3-D transformations and homogeneous co-ordinates using matrix notations, interactive graphical concepts, interpolation and approximation of curves, 3-D graphics including projections, clipping, hidden line and surface removal, algorithms for generation and display of surfaces and applications of computer graphics to engineering and allied problems, into one volume.

A floppy disk containing a large number of program examples can be obtained from the publishers at a nominal price. These will help students in writing their own programs and build their confidence. In this way it will promote self-reliance. These programs, as teaching aids, add to the utility of the book. The book is tailored mainly for IBM PC and its compatibles. However, since programs are given in both Pascal and *C* languages, these can be ported easily to other platforms, for example, the Macintosh as well as work-stations. In addition, a Solutions Manual is available for professors using this as a text book.

Most of the material in the book can be covered in a one semester course on graphics, which can be taught either at the sophomore or the junior level to students in Computer Science or Computer Engineering programs. Very little mathematical background is expected, except the knowledge of matrix algebra, normally taught to engineering students at the sophomore level. It is also expected that the reader has some familiarity with programming in a structured language like Pascal or *C*.

Acknowledgements

The final version of the book was prepared while one of the authors (Naresh K. Sinha) was visiting the Delhi Institute of Technology (January to April 1993). Special thanks are extended to Professor B.N. Mishra, Director of the Institute for providing all help and making available the computing and printing facilities of the Institute.

We also acknowledge the help received from several persons in the Centre for Railway Information Systems and other organisations in preparation of different parts of the text, especially, some of the diagrams in the text. These include Mr Ankush Krishen, Mr. Sunil Jain, Mr. Ghanshyam Sharma, Ms. Urmila Bisht and Ms Renu V. Kumar.

Just as one does not thank himself, expressing gratitude to one's wife in public is not a Hindu custom. The reason is that the wife and husband are considered one person. As such, the coauthorship of the wife is tacitly assumed in any book that the husband writes. There is little doubt that this book would not have been possible without the help, patience and encouragement of Geeta Asthana and Meena Sinha.

CONTENTS

CHAPTER 1
INTRODUCTION

1.1 THE IMPORTANCE OF COMPUTER GRAPHICS

The old Chinese saying "one picture is worth a thousand words" can be modified in this computer age into "one picture is worth many kilobytes of data." It is natural to expect that graphical communication, which is an older and more popular method of exchanging information than verbal communication, will often be more convenient when computers are utilized for this purpose. This is especially true for a large number of engineering applications where one must describe objects in two-dimensional and three-dimensional spaces. Often it is much easier to display these objects on the screen than to attempt to visualize them from many pages of computer output describing their geometrical shapes.

For example, computer graphics methods are utilized in computer-aided design (CAD) to produce the drawings of certain parts of a machine from any viewing angle while specifying all the dimensions. Another example is in the field of computer-aided manufacturing (CAM) where by employing computer graphics techniques, one may display the manufacturing layout for a given part and trace the path taken by machine tools for a given manufacturing process. This information can then be used for numerical control of the machine tool.

Architects can use computer graphics to produce layouts of buildings and utilize them for computer-aided design. The appearance of the building can be viewed through three-dimensional displays, whereas floor plans can be used for designing locations of doors and windows, arrangements of rooms and the placement of various facilities. Not only is it very straightforward to display these designs on the computer, but one can also modify them with very little effort. Virtual reality can take you one step further. Your architect can let you walk through a simulated building to see how accessible are the light switches and shelves, how good is the outside view from the terrace, and so on.

Interactive graphics can be used by engineers in most disciplines to assist in design problems. For example, electrical engineers concerned with the design of large-scale integrated circuits can utilize the computer to display in a graphical form the response of the circuit as well as its layout. The effect of modifying the values of certain components can then be viewed on the computer and utilized for improving the design. Structural engineers can use the computer with interactive graphics for efficient design of structures on the basis of the analysis of stress in various elements of the structure. The main advantage, again, is the ability to view, immediately, the effect of certain changes in the design on the overall performance in a graphical form.

It is evident from the above examples that the engineer of the future will be using computer graphics quite extensively, irrespective of the particular discipline of engineering to which he or she belongs. Furthermore, most progressive engineering schools have already made personal computers accessible to their undergraduates. Hence, it is very important for all science and engineering students to fully understand and utilize the graphics capabilities of personal computers.

1.2 COMPUTERS AND GRAPHICS HARDWARE TECHNOLOGY

Computers have been getting progressively more inexpensive, and it is envisaged that they will soon be as much the part of every household as the telephone or the television set is these days. It is of interest to review the history of their growth.

1.2.1 Brief History

In the early days of the development of computers, all the emphasis was placed on their use for number crunching for scientific applications. As computers were applied for solving engineering problems, the importance of visual presentation of the results was recognized. The high cost of the hardware for computer graphics remained the stumbling block which prevented their widespread use. The microelectronics revolution and the consequent reduction in the price of the hardware have completely changed the situation to the extent that it is now realistic to expect that all engineers of the future will be making extensive use of computer graphics.

The announcement of the IBM Personal Computer using the 16-bit Intel-8088 microprocessor on August 12, 1981, can be regarded as a historic event, which has had a profound effect in the world of computers. Prior to this date, all other personal computers were built around 8-bit microprocessors. Although such computers were very popular with hobbyists, they were not taken seriously by engineers since they did not have the computing power required for most engineering applications. The situation changed completely with the advent of the IBM Personal Computer, its more advanced versions (the PC-XT and the PC-AT) and many other "compatibles" that followed.

Computer graphics has, in the past, required sophisticated and rather expensive hardware. With the advent of inexpensive microprocessors, not only has there been a significant reduction in the cost but also a substantial increase in the graphics capabilities. It has also been recognized that it is not necessary to have a high-resolution graphics terminal to provide good visual representations for a large class of engineering design problems. In 1981, the IBM Personal Computer significantly improved the state of display technology in the world of personal computers. The first IBM PC used the Intel 8088 microprocessor, which was capable of addressing 1 M-byte in the address space and processing 16 bits internally. Two display adapters could reside in the address space: the Monochrome Display Adapter (MDA) and the Color Graphics Adapter (CGA). While the MDA could display 25 rows of 80-column text, the CGA could display graphics as well as text. Several graphics display modes were made available, including four-color graphics at a low resolution of 320 X 200 pixels and two medium resolution color graphics at 640 X 200 pixels. Since then, the 720 X 348 resolution of the Hercules Graphics Card and the 640 X 350 resolution of the Extended Graphics Adapter (EGA) have become commonplace. Several manufacturers of EGA compatible boards reached out and touched the 640 X 480 mark. IBM also released, in the fall of 1984, a Professional Graphics Controller (PGC) with resolution of 640 X 480 and with 256 simultaneous colors selectable from a palette of 4096. The PGC had support for both two- and three-dimensional drawing, and was therefore, suitable for applications in computer-aided design and drafting.

The next major change in personal computer display technology was announced by the Apple Company in 1984, when it introduced the Macintosh Personal Computer. It was the first personal computer that did not include a text-based display but provided only a graphic display. The application programs developed for the Macintosh advocated a WYSIWYG (What You See Is What You Get) style of an interface, stressing fidelity between the contents of the screen as manipulated by the user and the final hard-copy output. This concept has now become a basic requirement in the area of desktop publishing.

In 1987, IBM announced four models of their new Personal System/2 : Models 30, 50, 60 and 80. Model 30 was smaller than the IBM PC, but processed most jobs more than twice as fast as the PC or the XT. Models 50 and 60 used the 80286 microprocessor from Intel, while model 80 used the Intel 80386. Models 50, 60 and 80 used a parallel bus architecture referred to as "micro-channel" by IBM and capable of handling several jobs at once, rather than the one-at-a-time approach of the old PC's. Model 80 was a 32-bit system that did jobs up to three and a half times faster than an IBM PC/AT. The personal system/2 ran PC DOS 3.3 on Model 30 and a new multitasking operating system OS/2 in models 50, 60 and 80. This provided an environment that could run most existing DOS programs. One of the protected-mode screen groups provided a graphics based windowing system. IBM called this the Presentation Manager while Microsoft called it the Windows Presentation Manager. Applications that use graphics can be written for the presentation manager and take advantage of the built-in graphics and dialogue box logic. The IBM PS/2 line of products introduced three new video standards, as given below:

- Multi-Color Graphics Array (MCGA) built into Model 30,
- Video Graphic Array (VGA) built into models 50, 60 and 80
- 8514/A, a high resolution add-on board that is used on Models 50, 60 and 80.

The MCGA and VGA boards are capable of graphics mode of 640 X 480 pixels with 16 colors and 320 X 200 pixels with 256 colors. Text resolution is even sharper, with 720 X 400 pixels in either 16 colors or shades of gray in monochrome. The characters are constructed from a 9 X 16 matrix of screen dots. On the other hand, the 8514/A board could display 256 colors simultaneously with the resolution of 640 X 480 pixels.

The July 1992 issue of the PC Magazine described several technological issues for design of a perfect personnel computer as follows:

- A high degree of chip-set integration lowers cost and improves system reliability.
- To save space, the parallel and serial ports, and IDEA and video circuitry should be built-in on the mother board.
- To take advantage of a 32-bit operating system such as OS/2.x, or Windows one need at least 8 MB of RAM, 16 MB motherboards may prove limiting in the next couple of years.
- Metal SIMM sockets are preferred to the plastic ones.
- PC magazine mentions that a 60-Hz refresh rate is inadequate. It gives more flickery look than a monitor and video card operating at 70-72 Hz.
- Display adapters using VRAM are often twice as fast compared to DRAM-BASED boards.

The Digital Equipment Corporation (DEC) entered the PC market in September 1992 and claimed that their machines conform to the perfect PC standards as advocated by the PC Magazine. In an attempt to produce lower-cost desktops, IBM redefined its PS/2 line, which had ranged from the 386SX/20-based PS/2 model 35 to the PS/2 Server 295. The modified PS/2 exclusively supported the micro channel architecture, XGA-2 graphics on the motherboard, compliance with the existing IS specifications for the work environment, SCSI, and came with pre-installed OS/2 2.0.

The PowerPCs 6XX from IBM, Apple and other vendors may create a new standard for desktop computers in case they are accepted by the users. Apple's Power Macintosh is actually two PCs in one: a standard Macintosh 6100 desktop system powered by a PowerPC 601 processor and a 486 DX2/66 CPU card which sits into the system's processor direct slot.

Graphic user interfaces (GUIs) like A Microsoft Windows 3.x choke a video adapter sitting on an 8-MHz, 16-bit ISA (Industry Standard Architecture) expansion bus. ISA bus is now a bottleneck when it is mated with a 100-mhz Pentium processor. Local Bus technology breaks the bottleneck by getting peripherals like video controllers up to clock speed. This allows the video controller to gain access to the CPU's 32-bit bus running on full clock speed, e.g.. on a 33-MHz, 486 local bus PC a video controller could match the 33 MHz clock speed of the processor. Nevertheless, the video performance is enhanced two to 15 times as compared with a standard VGA adapter. Local bus design is available easily on 486 mother boards

Two local bus standards are: VL-Bus, a standard proposed by VESA (Video Electronic Standard Association) Committee and PCI (Peripherals Component Interconnect) - a brain child of Intel Corp. EISA (Extended industry standard architecture) and MCA (IBM's Micro Channel Architecture) are similarly limited regarding the rate at which peripherals on the expansion bus can operate. The EISA expansion bus operates up to 8.33 MHz and the MCA up to 10 MHz. In special mode, MCA can operate up to 16 MHz EISA and MCA cannot, however, run at the speed of the local bus.

A number of devices like LAN Cards, Fax/modem, CD-ROM interfaces, stereo sound cards, and multimedia video support are put in expansion slots to add functionality to personal computers. Users find it very difficult to handle the complexities of IRQs, DIP switches, jumpers, and drivers. Apple has Plug and Play (PnP) as standard since 1987 to keep users free from configuration problems. This idea is being applied to the new interface devices such as PCI and PCMCIA. PnP as proposed by Microsoft and Intel will make PCs easy to set up and configure, ease the task of installing new hardware and software, and bestow a PC with new features such as the ability to change configurations on the fly and to react and change its set up dynamically on a configuration event.

Video/graphic processing can be made faster in two ways: by using (1) a graphic co-processor and (2) a graphic accelerator. The graphic co-processor boosts video performance by assuming tasks normally handled by the CPU. These are programmable and can execute even a high-level *C* program An accelerator takes control of a graphic task otherwise performed by the CPU but it is not programmable. It is a fixed function processor and carries out specific tasks hard-coded into the chip. While an accelerator may excel in one application, it can get bogged down in another.

The new video adapters and monitors used analog signals and could generate 64 values for each of the primary colors, red, green and blue. The result is that these systems can present 256 colors simultaneously on the screen from a palette of 262144 colors. The Apple Macintosh II can also provide a resolution of 640 X 480 pixels on displays with 16 colors. Optional adapters, such as, extended VGA(XGA) with 1024 X 768 displays are also available.

You need additional processing capability than currently available from the CPU to develop a visual interface, which is highly interactive, has higher resolution and can also give impression of realism. The solution is to provide a dedicated graphics processor. This has two clear benefits. First, the screen can be managed faster than possible with an equivalent software algorithm executed on the CPU. Secondly, a certain amount of parallelism can be obtained by letting the main CPU assemble the next graphic command while the graphic processor is completing the current graphic command. Several manufacturers of personal computers (e.g., Commodore Amiga, IBM PS/2 with an 8514/A board) use a proprietary graphic processor. Other graphic processors coming into use include Intel 82786 and Texas Instruments 34010. The former is essentially a line drawing processor, while the latter is a high performance general purpose processor.

Personal computers provide very sophisticated graphics images (the situation has improved with the new generation of graphics adapters), they can now be used successfully for learning the principles of graphics programming and applying these to scientific and engineering problems. It can be said, without any exaggeration, that the personal computers available today are comparable in power to the mid-size mainframes that one could get in 1965, although costing less than one-hundredth as much. This will be illustrated by the following comparison:

	P.C.	**IBM 360-40**
RAM Storage (megabytes)	8-64	0.032 - 0.262
Cycle time (nanoseconds)	2-10	2500
Price (including peripherals)	$1000-3000	$300,000-600,000

ın the above paragraph, the price of the IBM 360-45 has been stated as in 1965. The current prices of comparable mainframe computers are much lower. It may be argued that this is not a fair comparison in view of the fact that the mainframe allows many users simultaneously. However, it cannot be denied that the availability of personal computers at affordable prices has led to their widespread use in scientific and engineering applications.

1.2.2 **Current Scenario**

It is pertinent to briefly review the status of processor chip technology, architecture and level of integration available on the motherboard, particularly, as selection of right processor and mother-board is important for a graphic application. A prospective buyer of a system has multiple choices of the CPU. Four companies, Intel (Pentium, Class P5 and P6), Centaur (IDT-C6, Class P5), Cyrix (6X86 Class P6) and AMD (K6 Class P6), offer P5 and P6 varieties of x86 class processors with MMX and clock speeds in the range of 200-300 MHz. Intels's 440LX chipset with support for Accelerated Graphics Port (AGP) relieves congestion on the PC's PCI bus by moving graphics traffic on a dedicated point to point channel between the graphics controller and the systems chip set. One cannot make a selection simply based on price and performance any more. The main factors to be considered for an important application are power consumption, mathematical and graphical processing capability and level of integration.

P5 and P6 class microprocessors comprise of 4.5 to 8.8 million transistors and can run 100-300 million instructions per second (MIPS). Intel has captured a major chunk of PC market share with the introduction of 100-300 MHz Pentium processors. These microprocessors will drive advanced PCs, workstations, super-servers, and promise improved graphics, better networking and video on desktop PCs.

Apple believes that the horse power of the RISC processors will be required to run system software and applications of the future and CISC hardware and software has no further potential.

RISC chips, such as a PowerPc will keep getting faster and less expensive while CISC chips such as x86, will find it difficult to keep pace. DEC, IBM, Motorola, SGI/Mips and SUN Microsystems have all gone to the RISC route. The microprocessors based on RISC technology from these companies are DEC's Alpha 21164, IBM/Motorola's PowerPc 6XX and 7 to 9XXX, Mips's T5 and SUN's JavaChip (Microjava 701 microprocessor casts "write once, run anywhere" technology in silicon) and UltraSparc RISC chips generally have smaller dies and fewer transistors as compared to CISC processors and therefore cost less to make. The fate of OS's such as Windows 95 is also closely tied to the x86 and how Java and Network Computers perform in the market. The PowerPC has an edge over Pentium in performance. Apple has so far converted all of OS code to the native code of the PowerPC and has put higher emphasis on backward compatibility, not on performance. Therefore, PowerPC desktop from Apple tend to be slower than Pentium. Apple has adopted this approach to protect investments already made by users of Mac hardware and software.

Power Macintosh's tight integration between hardware and software is complemented by its high-speed RISC processing, network connectivity, PC compatibility, and PCI slots for easy expansion. Plus, the feature set, fully loaded for multimedia, allows you to express your ideas more creatively. The Power Macintosh 233-MHz Processor Upgrade Kit designed to increase the power and speed of many older-model Power Macintosh computers or Workgroup Server systems. More specifically, The Power Macintosh 7300, 7500, 7600, 8500, 8600, 9500, and 9600 desktop computers as well as the Workgroup Server 7350 and 8550 models feature a processor card that can be replaced by the Power Macintosh 233-Mhz Processor card.

The POWER3 will be produced using IBMs advanced manufacturing process technologies - including those with copper interconnection - and achieve clock speeds of more than 500 MHz and performance exceeding 70 and 30, respectively, on the SPEC95 floating-point and integer benchmarks. The key features of Superscalar processor design are

- capability to execute eight instructions per processor cycle and high memory bandwidth, or "pipelines," to continuously feed vast amounts of instructions and data to the processor core.
- two independent, full floating-point units, three independent fixed-point units and two load/store units along with aggressive out-of-order and speculative execution and other sophisticated features.
- two high-bandwidth buses: a 16-byte PowerPC6XX architecture bus to main memory and a dedicated 32-byte bus to the L2 cache that can run at the same speed as the processor. For example, at 200 MHz, the processor has throughput of 6.4 GB (gigabytes) per second from the L2 cache, which is more than double the bandwidth of any processor available today.
- its ability for thousands of POWER3 microprocessors to be combined into a single, unified computing unit. The POWER3 processor will be at the heart of a 4096-processor RS/6000 SP (Scalable Parallel) super computer delivered to the U.S. Department of Energy at Lawrence Livermore Labs as part of the Accelerated Strategic Computing Initiative (ASCI). When the system is upgraded with POWER3 processors in 1998, the system will deliver a whopping 3.0 trillion floating-point calculations (teraFLOPS) per second, which IBM expects will make it the fastest computer in the world.

If one is planning to do any serious work on graphics-based applications using Windows, OS/2, Windows NT, or UNIX, a system based on Pentium CPU is practically a necessity. The environment of these operating systems demands fast video, as well as a large and fast hard disk drive and lots of memory. It is worth mentioning that 386/486 based systems had enough processing power for standard DOS applications but a Pentium processor is a necessity for multitasking applications. PENTIUM II features MMX technology, dual independent bus architecture (first implemented in Pentium Pro) for addressing bandwidth limitations, and dynamic execution technology which extends raw processor performance by allowing more data to be processed in parallel in a given period of time. A typical configuration which is function of the application is as under:

- 200-266 MHz Pentium II with MMX (see section 1.2.2.2 for details on MMX)
- A BIOS (stored in Flash ROM not Mask ROM and with option to boot from CD ROM) as well as Operating System that supports Plug and Play
- 16-64 MB of RAM
- 1 or 2 floppy drives
- A keyboard and a mouse
- A hard drive with capacity of 4-6 GB (Lower capacity will anyway be out of market)
- a super VGA adapter or 4-12 MB 24-bit 1280x1024 color card
- 56 Kbps modem with speaker phone features
- Audio wave table sound card
- 12-24x CD-ROM (recommended as number of vendors offer software and presentations on CD ROM only)

It is beneficial to use PnP cards, peripherals and applications that can respond to dynamic run time events although they may initially be expensive.

1.2.2.1 3D Graphics Hardware

The new high power video chips can render complex 3D scenes and will transform the average desktop PC into a sophisticated graphics workstation. One such low cost chip is Glint 300SX from 3Dlabs, San Jose, CA. It performs all the functions of a current GUI accelerator video boards and renders up to 300,000 Gouraud shaded polygons per second. With more such chips entering the market, 2D ingredients of current GUI's will be replaced by 3D objects and applications like 3D model animation, stock market visualization, games, presentations and virtual reality applications would be quite different on the PC. Vendors are waiting for Microsoft to release 3D DDI (Device Driver Interface). It will provide a set of standard 3D functions for a board to accelerate that are not specific to OpenGL.

Two of the main players in this rapidly evolving new world, are Silicon Graphics(SG), and its hot contender the PC. The PC currently requires a graphics accelerator to enable it to reach anything like the power of the SG. There are now software only solutions (e.g., RenderWare) producing quite stunning real-time 3D rendering, clipping, and transforming 3D computer models mainly aimed at the games world.

The accelerator has a low level software/hardware graphics interface, the Application Program Interface (API), SG's OpenGL 3-D Graphics appears to be the industrial graphics interface standard better than competitors that have PHIGS and PEX, whereas Microsoft

Direct3D Backgrounder and Netscape's RenderWare Datasheet appear to be the low-end (home/ business/ games) contender, supported by nearly all the new forthcoming games 3D accelerators. Microsoft is aggressively targeting the upper platforms with the acquisition of SOFTIMAGE - a previous SG only prouuct. It will now run on a PC platform.

For a serious overview of graphics cards you may visit Internet sites
http://www.cs.columbia.edu/~bm/3dcards/3d-cards1.html
http://www.cs.columbia.edu/~bm/3dcards/3d-cards1.html

You can't get to gaming nirvana without a 3D accelerator, so to review the new 3D chipsets and cards in order to find the best product for the ultimate gaming experience visit website
http://www.gamecenter.com/Hardware/Roundup/3dcards2

1.2.2.2 MMX Technology and Graphics

MMX technology enhances the audio, video and graphics applications as well as speeds data encryption and compression. The MMX engine has 8 64-bit registers named mm0 through mm7. It extends the x86 instruction set by 57 new instructions. You can get more details on MMX from Intel's website
http://developer.intel.com/drg/mmx

The MMX instruction set does not apply only to multimedia, although these were developed with the requirements of multimedia code in mind. For example, one instruction enables the processor to perform a high-speed multiply-accumulate function, which computes the sum of a series of products. This function is a central aspect of key algorithms used in digital signal processing (DSP) applications, such as telephony.

MMX uses single instruction multiple data (SIMD) architecture, which enables the CPU to perform one calculation simultaneously on two, four, or even eight data elements without any decrease in speed. MMX accomplishes this by packing multiple operands (8-, 16, or 32-bit values) into a single 64-bit register and operating on all of them in parallel. For example, a graphics program might place eight 1-byte (8-bit) color values into the register and instruct the CPU to add a value say 'x' to each of them, thus brightening their portion of the image. This operation can execute in a single clock cycle.

MMX operates on 64 bits at a time, whereas the general-purpose registers on Intel processors have only 32 bits. It does not require any new registers but uses a portion of the processor's 80-bit floating-point registers. Because of this approach, Intel recommends against mixing floating-point and MMX code; otherwise, you will limit performance.

MMX also offers a variety of features that help programmers avoid branches in code. It thus reduces the incidence of performance-sapping pipeline stalls, which occur when the processor has to fetch code from an unexpected location. For example, MMX provides saturating arithmetic, which caps the value of mathematical functions to prevent troublesome overflow conditions. MMX also lets programmers use masks, so that instructions operate on only some of the elements packed into the 64-bit register.

Most MMX instructions execute in one clock cycle. They qualify as simple instructions with regard to the Pentium's instruction-pairing logic and can thus take full advantage of the processor's superscalar capabilities. On a 200 MHz machine, MMX could theoretically composite 25 million pixels per second - the equivalent of compositing two full 1024 by 1024 screens 24 times per second. This performance is, however, difficult to achieve due to memory bandwidth bottleneck. The speed is better if the referenced memory is in the cache.

1.3 NETWORK COMPUTERS (Ncs) - a NEW COMPUTING PARADIGM

PCs have evolved in many ways, yet they have failed to provide adequate productivity improvements to keep up with their increasing cost of installation, administration, and maintenance. Oracle Systems Corp., and Sun Microsystems Inc., view the network - not the personal computer - as the cornerstone of modern computing. They are proposing that a new, simpler type of desktop computing device, called the network computer or NC for short, take over the desktop from the more complex PC, thereby becoming the entry point to the network for the majority of users.

Microsoft Corp., Wash., and Intel Corp., which now dominate desktop technology are of the view that moving away from the PC would be disastrous, not only for them but for industry and commerce as well. While they now concede that the PC could be modified to make it more manageable - a configuration they call the Network PC (Net PC) would retain the Windows/Pentium core of today's PC. The Net PC is a business PC designed specifically to enable central administration and help reduce PC support costs. As a part of Intel's Wired for Management Initiative, the Net enables enhanced management services such as:

- remote system configuration
- software installations and upgrades
- off-hours maintenance
- problem resolution
- asset management

The Net PC also features a sealed case design, which prevents modifications by end users to the hardware configuration. This means:

- no floppy disk
- no CD-ROM
- no hardware expansion slots

This design caters to task-oriented users who require no hardware expandability. Also, this saves IT managers from handling many configuration problems, thus allowing them more time for other responsibilities.

By definition, NC uses online access to define its functionality. In Oracle's view, the NC is not for business use alone, it is a device that will make computer and network technology pervasive in everyone's everyday life. But before that can happen, it seems that the NC must first be tested in the business arena, at which the first NCs to come along have been targeted and where the PC now dominates.

1.3.1 NC Reference Profile

On 20 May 1996, Oracle and four other companies - Apple, IBM, Netscape, and Sun - released the first guidelines for constructing an NC. The document was called the Network Computer Reference Profile and it stated its intention "to provide a common denominator of popular and widely used features and functions across a broad range of scalable network computing devices, *including personal computers*.

In a spirit of openness, the group emphasised that PCs could join. Indeed, it was possible for a PC to have all the attributes of an NC. But providing a bare-bones description of what an NC must have would make it difficult for a typical PC, with its large hard disks and considerable RAM, to compete with leaner, built-to-the-guidelines boxes.

NC profile comprises of :

- for output - a screen with a minimum resolution of 640 by 480 pixels
- video graphics array (VGA) or its equivalent
- audio output/input
- a pointing device such as a mouse; and text input capability.
- The display requirement would permit TV monitors to be utilised, and text input, while including keyboards, could also refer to some other means, such as handwriting or selecting text from an on-screen alphabet.

The profile also states that persistent storage, such as a disk drive, while not forbidden, is not required either.

1.3.2 NC - Protocol, Standards and File Formats

NC must support the following protocol, standards and file formats:

- the Transmission Control/Internet Protocols (TCP/IP).
- FTP/Telnet
- the simple network management protocol (SNMP),
- the network file system (NFS) and
- the user datagram protocol (UDP) used by the NFS.
- the fundamental Web standards including the hypertext transport protocol (HTTP) for transferring Web pages between a server and a browser, and the hypertext mark up protocol (HTML) which describes how a browser should display a Web pages contents.
- JPEG and GIF for images and WAV and AU for sound
- the Java virtual machine with its runtime environment and class libraries.
- e-mail, which would need support for three protocols: the simple mail transfer protocol (SMTP), the Internet message access protocol version 4 (IMAP4) and the Post Office protocol version 3 (POP3).
- APIs for security as well as, optionally SmartCard (ISO 786) standards and the Europa, MasterCard and Visa specification for secure financial transactions.

Again in keeping with the network centric view, the NC must be designed to boot up on the network. Just as a PC has its basic I/O system (BIOS) which tells it to load its main operating system from a hard disk drive the NC has a boot program that tells it how to connect to the network and identify itself. The guideline offers one of two boot configuration options: the dynamic host configuration program (DHCP) or the bootstrapping protocol (Bootp). While there are differences between the two protocols (Bootp) requires that information in a server database be manually pre-configured while DHCP allows for dynamic configuration.. What's important is they allow an NC to discover its own IP address, the address of a server and the name of a file to be loaded into its memory and executed.

The NC has no hard disk and hence can not locally store the full applications that Microsoft refers to when discussing application flexibility for the hard-disked Net PC. But the types of applications that NC supporters see in its future are all thin clients based on Java and therefore do not require the Net PCs hard disk. The Net PC is tied to one platform architecture - Intel's and Microsoft's while the NC opens the door to other processors and operating systems.

1.3.3 NC Applications

NCs provide access to UNIX, PC, and Java applications through a variety of remote windowing technologies, which are similar to the X Windows system. Methods of implementing this access through remote windowing protocols vary and are offered by several companies. In particular, the combination of GraphOn's GO-Joe with RapidX , Insignia's NTRIGUE with Keoke, and Citrix Systems' WinFrame. Thin-Client/Server Software with ICA provide a complete solution for remote windowing on the JavaStation NC. GO-Joe provides access to any Solaris application, Keoke Client provides access to Microsoft Windows applications within the intranet, and ICA is recommended for access to Microsoft Windows applications over low-bandwidth, modem-based and ISDN connections. As a group they deliver today's required access to applications and network resources while companies transition to the Java Computing Environment.

13.4 NC - First Vendors

Although number of vendors will keep on increasing with the popularity of the NCs, following list includes the main vendors in the year 1996/97:

- HDS Network Systems Inc. King of Prussia Pa, introduced its @ workstation on June 11, 1996.
- On Sept. 5, 1996 IBM Corp. led the way for the reference-document partners unveiling the IBM Network Station. The box jointly manufactured by IBM and the X-terminal manufacturer Network Computing Devices (NCD) Inc., was built around a 32 bit PowerPC RISC chip.
- Network Computing Devices is also offering the HMX series of NCs which are based on 64-bit MIPS R4000 RISC processors and have greater memory capacity. None of the systems has a hard-disk drive, but a floppy drive is an option.

- Boundless Technologies, Austin Texas is offering the XL and XLC series of NCs which are based on Intel's RISC processor the i960.
- Wyse Technology Inc. San Jose Calif has chosen to base its Wintern 4000 series NCs on the blazingly fast (200 Mhz) StrongArm 110 - a processor designed by Digital Equipment Corp. using the ARM architecture it licensed from that company.
- On Oct. 29, 1996 SUN introduced its own version of the NC the Javastation. Its CPU is a mircoSparc II 100-MHz RISC processor equipped with both Citrix software to run Windows applications and Sun's JavaOS to run Java application.

1.4 OPERATING SYSTEMS

Hardware is made up of chips, wires and boards. Software is made up of instructions, flow charts and modules. The programs that make the product function according to specific requirements are termed "application" programs and those which help the applications are termed "system programs." A collection of system programs when bundled into one program is called an "Operating System."

On the earliest digital computers, a job had exclusive control of the computer for its complete duration. The user had to provide necessary protocol for handling of I/O devices and other resources without any assistance. When the program execution was completed, an operator manually halted the machine and prepared it for the next job. The idea of batch processing came into being in mid 1950s and early operating systems (OSs) did little more than loading programs and managing I/O devices. The concept of more generalized operating systems emerged in the late 1960s and included not only batch processing but also modes for time-sharing and some real-time processing.

OS such as Digital Research's CP/M and Microsoft's MS-DOS are in fact little more than program loaders that also support a local disk drive. Today, OSs include facilities, such as, distributed access, graphics, time-sharing, multi-processing, security, networking, multi-threads and multi-processor capability. Based on the computers on which an operating system runs, it can vary in size, complexity and functionality to fulfill users' requirements. The new 32-bit OSs offer features that harness the true power of Intel's highly evolved processors. The 32-bit OSs manage memory in a simple and effective way than DOS. Memory is accessed using a flat model - a single unified 4-GB address space. Thus, there are no headaches in managing upper, high, extended, and/or expanded memory.

In the following subsection, a brief description of operating systems currently used on microcomputers is given.

1.4.1 MS-DOS

It was the most widely used operating system for personnel computers till 1995. The salient features of MS-DOS Version 6.x are described below:

- It can run MS-DOS in the high memory area if the host system has expanded memory. This makes more conventional memory available to a user program.
- It has device drivers and programs that can be run in the upper memory area on an 80386 or higher systems. This feature improves the speed and performance of MS-DOS programs when run with Microsoft Windows version 3.x.

- It has an improved graphical interface in form of MS-DOS shell. The shell allows one to manage programs and switch between them, view the directory structure of any disk, view the contents of several directories and navigate through files and directories quickly.
- It has two new commands, Informed and Entailed that provide added data security. Microsoft diagnostics and Interlink programs easily transfer files between two computers are useful.
- Version 6.x allows creation of disk partitions of up to 2 GB.
- The Doskey program enables recalling, editing, and executing commands that one has already used. It can also be used to create macros to perform a series of tasks frequently.
- It has QBasic - an improved basic program and environment that include extensive on-line help, graphical user environment and a built-in graphical library.
- It supports 2.88-MB floppy disks.
- Antivirus, a program that can identify and remove number of viruses.

1.4.2 MS-Windows

Microsoft Windows 3.x is more than just a front-end for DOS. It has released today's powerful PCs from the constraints of DOS, and led to the development of a completely new level of powerful applications on a PC. Since it appeared in May 1990, Windows has now become an operating environment of choice for the IBM compatible computers.

The success of Windows 3.x can be attributed to a variety of factors: easy-to-use GUI, multitasking, capability to access a large amount of memory, integrated application environment, networking, extensive hardware support, device independence, and DOS compatibility. These factors are significant for users and for developers. Windows GUI provides a standard approach to computer operations such as starting an application, copying and removing files and so on. Windows requires Microsoft MS-DOS version 3.1 or later. It can operate in one of the following two modes:

- 386 enhanced mode: a personal computer with 80386 processor or higher and 640 KB of memory plus 1024 KB of extended memory, 8 MB of free disk space and at least one floppy disk drive.
- Standard mode: a personal computer with 80286 processor or higher and 640 KB of conventional memory plus 340 KB of extended memory, 6 MB of free disk space, and at least one floppy disk drive. In this mode the hard disk is used as virtual memory up to 64 MB and multiple DOS sessions can be run, each in its own window.

The salient differences with respect to program execution between DOS and windows are as follows:

DOS	Windows
Programs are run sequentially	Programs are event-driven.

Static link	Dynamic link library (DLL)
EXE Files carry all run-time libraries inside the program DLL.	EXE files will load the required DLLs at run time. DLLs are re-entrant., i.e., only single copy need be loaded.

Windows version 3.1 provides true-type fonts, such as fonts consisting of full set of characters with enough variety to meet virtually any printing needs. These are scalable, i.e., one can use the same fonts at 12 points for the main text of a report and 16 points for topic head. The desired page will appear quickly and will be seen clearly on the screen.

The other features include object linking and embedding, a new file manager, drag and drop features, and multimedia features. Multimedia features enable applications to use multimedia devices so that different kinds of media including sound, graphics, animation and video can be edited to files and documents. Support for many popular sound devices, such as, sound cards and devices with MIDI) is also included. It allows playing MIDI (Musical Instrument Digital Interface) information on a MIDI synthesizer. The following sound features are included with Windows:

- Media Player to control the playing of various kinds of media files on hardware, such as, sound cards, CD-ROM drives, and video disc players. It can play animation, sound, and MIDI sequencer files.
- Sound recorders to play, record, and edit sound files that have the .WAV format. The sound recorder window graphically displays the sound wave as if it were being displayed on an oscilloscope.

Windows NT looks like Windows 3.1 but internally, Windows NT is as similar to Windows 3.1 as CPM is to VAX/VMS. It is a true preemptive multitasking OS and runs on 32-bit CPUs (80386 or higher) with a recommended configuration of 8 MB of RAM and 100 MB or more of disc space. The design of NT is completely object-based. Virtually everything in the operating system is an object, an important component of NT - called the object manager - is dedicated solely to foreseeing the creation, usage, and destruction of the objects. NT is not a true object oriented OS as most of it is written in C, not C++. Thus, some advantages of C++, e.g., inheritance and polymorphism were not used. NT represents files, threads, RAM sections, drivers, and devices all as objects. Daytona, the second generation of Windows NT for Alpha, is a multi-threaded 32- bit OS with strength in the areas such as performance, Windows emulation and network connectivity.

Microsoft's new version of Windows is called Windows 95 (or Chicago). It will run any application or device driver that DOS or Windows 3.x can run. Windows 3.x display drivers are monolithic whereas Chicago offers layered minidrivers on DIB (Device Independent Bit Map) engine. Microsoft has incorporated OpenGL in Windows NT and Windows 95. The salient features of Windows 95 are:

- Stability: Like NT, Windows 95 separates Win32 applications into private address spaces. It runs each DOS and Win16 application on its own thread and keeps records of resources such as memory, file handles, and graphical device interface on a per thread basis. If a DOS application crashes the reclamation of resources occurs immediately.

However, in case of crashing of a Win16 application clean up operation is taken up only when all running WIN16 applications quit. Windows 3.x lacks memory protection and an application can grab resources of other applications. Multiple DOS boxes in Windows 3.x share the VM (Virtual Machine) that runs the DOS code. In case memory of a VM gets corrupted both Windows and all DOS VMs meet with catastrophe. Win16 and Win32 applications remain stable as long as one does not use real mode drivers in Windows 95. DOS applications can be safeguarded by using write-protect memory in DOS virtual machines. To enhance stability in Windows 95 its debug version of the kernel will validate parameters passed to the VxDs (Virtual Device Drivers). This will help in identifying crisis before VxDs reach the field. Thus a developer can be allowed to write new VxD's as well as fix the bugs in them.

• Multitasking:

Windows 3.x does multitasking poorly as it runs tasks on cooperative basis. Windows 95 schedules Win32 applications preemptively and users are advised to avoid running applications with interrupts disabled.

• Management:

Windows 3.x is hard to manage. Windows 95 fully describes system in terms of buses and devices in the system registry. RPC (Remote Procedure Call) enabled editor will facilitate remote monitoring of Windows 95 systems. It will also be feasible to export registry data to SNMP or DMI (Desktop Management Interface) to help in management.

• Networking:

Windows 3.x works poorly with NetWare as well as on WANs. To improve performance, Windows 95 includes a 32-bit NetWare redirector, Novell's IPX/SPX as default transport, UNC (Universal Naming Convention) for NetWare, and 32-bit TCP/IP. It is a DHCP (Dynamic Host Configuration Protocol) client and WINS (Windows Internet Naming Service) Client. DHCP facilitates automatic assignment of IP addresses on the fly and WINS maps between network names and IP addresses.

1.4.2.1 **Memphis: Windows 98**

Its salient improvements over Windows 95 are

- One can directly log off from the machine instead of going through the shutdown - close all programs and log on as a different user.
- It can drive multiple monitors - up to 4 eventually 9 if you have enough slots for the extra video cards. This is an old capability of Mac and Unix work stations.
- Integration of the Internet Explorer interface on to the operating system.
- Under accessories options, multimedia options, ISDN Tools, and Kodak Imaging for Windows.
- System tools include WBEM security, FAT 32 (a new file system) converter, System Information Utility, Sys file checker, and Windows tune-up Wizard.

- By using existing television signals, this software bypasses the current bandwidth limitations of the Internet and provides users with a richer multimedia experience on their PC.
- Active Desktop enables dynamic content, e.g., HTML pages, pictures - BMPs, and Internet shortcuts on the desktop.
- Emergency boot disk including CDROM driver, Registry Editor, ScanDisk, Sys, Format, Fdisk and more. It also allows even uninstalling Windows 98 from the hard disk.

1.4.2.2 **Windows CE 2.0**

Windows CE 2.0 - The new operating system - designed to empower a variety of computing appliances from set-top boxes and DVD players to Handheld PCs and smart phones--includes support for 32-bit color displays, international character sets, LAN connectivity, printers, ActiveX, Java, and more. Windows CE includes Toolkits for Visual Basic 5.0, Visual C++ 5.0, Visual J++ 1.1 and the Embedded Toolkit for Visual C++ 5.0.

1.4.2.3 **Windows/NT**

Windows NT version 4.0 includes a number of new security components, application programming interfaces, and many other enhancements and other features to enhance your productivity.

Windows NT Server, Enterprise Edition (NTS/E) 4.0 improves on the scalability and availability of the regular version of NT Server. Its key features are

- NTS/E supports up to 8 CPUs in one Intel-based machine. Vendors such as Axil Computer, Digital Equipment, NCR, Advanced Logic Research, and Unisys have already committed to delivering 6-way and 8-way symmetric multiprocessing (SMP) servers for NTS/E.
- NTS/E adds a RAM tuning feature called 4GB RAM Tuning (4GT). It increases the potential RAM allocated to applications from 2GB to 3GB, by reducing the RAM allocated to the NT kernel from 2GB to 1GB. This feature will work only on Intel 32-bit processors.
- NTS/E introduces Microsoft Cluster Server (MCS-formerly, Wolfpack). Because NTS/E lets you connect two NT Servers in a cluster, it can automatically recover from server or application failures Adding cluster support can significantly increase the availability of NT Server, which is important when it's running business critical applications. MCS is part of an overall availability suite that includes Microsoft Transaction Server (MTS) and Microsoft Message Queue Server (MSMQ). MTS and MSMQ let developers use transactions and messages to create highly available applications. Now, MTS and MSMQ will ship with every version of NT Server 5.0, creating a huge market opportunity for NT developers.

LOOX Software's LOOXWin, an interactive graphical editor for NT, lets you create animated vector drawings. The product is a compilation of the LOOXMaker editor and the LOOXLib object-based programming library. LOOXWin provides pre-built objects that you can integrate with other standard tools. With LOOXWin, you can create graphics, import images, create and customise dynamic objects, and configure object animation for WYSIWYG results.

1.4.3 **IBM's OS/2**

The OS/2 operating system exploits complete capability of Intel 386 and Intel 486 technology. It is a true 32-bit, multi-threaded, multi-tasking operating system suitable for desktop as well as server applications. Support for existing DOS and Microsoft Windows 3.x applications is built right into the OS. It features a complete GUI for all applications including wordprocessing, printing and playing a game. In fact, one works with objects that graphically represent an activity to be performed. It allows features such as managing, copying, moving, printing, deleting, opening objects through pull-down menus and/or mouse interactions. For smooth running OS/2 needs 8 MB of RAM on the computer. However, it can work with 6 MB also. Running OS/2 with 4 MB is painful as the system will be accessing the hard disk a lot.

It allows OS/2 program, DOS program and windows program to run in both window session and full screen session. These programs can run successfully in both the foreground and the background. However, under certain conditions, DOS applications that use the graphical display mode may become suspended in the background session.

OS/2 2.x provides DOS support as virtual DOS machines. The default DOS box uses a DOS Kernel that OS/2 supplies. The second method is to boot a specific version of DOS (say, DOS 6.x) from a floppy disk or a boot image built with OS/2s VMDISK command. Using default DOS box has advantage as it provides user defined settings to invoke features such as EMS, DPMI (DOS Protected Mode Interface), UMB (Upper Memory Block), video memory settings, and many other. DOS programs run easily under OS/2. The memory management is invisible and virtual memory up to 32 MB per program is available.

OS/2 supports Windows also in two modes: full screen and "seamless" - to open the folder called windows program. In the full screen mode, Windows applications multi-task on a normal window desktop under the control of the program manager; in the seamless mode they occupy PM windows and obey the WPS (Work Place Shell). Programs such as PageMaker 4, Word for Windows, Excel, and Turbo Pascal for Windows run under OS/2 both in full screen and seamless modes. However, the virtual DOS machine overheads affect the performance of Windows under 2.x. Facilities of windows, such as wall-paper, are not supported.

The strength of OS/2 2.x comes from features like DOS support, multi-tasking support for Windows 3.x software, a 32-bit memory model, demand paged virtual memory, and threaded multi-tasking. Since, OS/2 is fully written in the *C* language, it is easily portable to other platforms. It has weaknesses in the areas of performance, stability, and ease of use.

IBM announced the OS/2 Warp in October 1994. It displays screen objects, specially drive objects, faster than previous versions of OS/2. With this, it is easier than ever to avoid command line sessions and run programs in low memory situations where earlier versions of OS/2 failed. Device support is one of the weak points of OS/2. Therefore, one has to be careful when adding a video adapter, sound card or any other adapter to a computer.

Warp displays configurable `"Launch Bar" to start programs. The Launch Bar shows text icons horizontally or vertically on the screen. The primarily used icons can be put either on the launch bar or in the drawers which you can open and close. Warp provides additional drag and drop features to object oriented interface of its predecessors. It offers Window fast load option to enable you to run Windows programme. A Warp tool diagnoses hardware problems caused due to IRQ assignments, extended memory used, SCSI addresses and other system level data. It has drivers for more video adapters, printers, SCSI cards and CD ROM drives.

Warp runs on at least a 386 XS machine equipped with 6 MB RAM, mouse, VGA or some other video adapter, 35-55 MB hard disk space plus up to 35 MB for the Bonus Pak components.

Windows support requires use of Windows 3.1, and Windows for Work Group distribution disks. Even with only 4 MB of RAM, one can run two, and sometime three DOS sessions, along with a small OS/2 program. However, on a system with 6 MB or more memory Warp runs with speed. Windows 3.x programs under Warp run as fast as they would run under Windows. The management of expanded/extended memory is good. Game software runs well in OS/2. Multimedia Presentation Manager/2 is IBM's sound and video utility that has been bundled in previous versions of OS/2 for seeing and displaying GIF, PCX and TIFF images. A comparison of OS/2 Warp and Windows 95 is given below :

OS2/Warp	Windows 95
Runs in 4 MB although 6 MB is better	Needs more than 4 MB to run
Multitasks16-bit Windows applications in separate Windows session	Runs such programs cooperatively, not preemptively.
DOS programs are not allowed to share the interrupt tables in the memory.	Cannot protect multiple DOS programs from crashing because it lets them share the same interrupt tables in the memory.
Plug and Play support is limited to hot plugging of PCMCIA cards. IBM plans to provide full PnP support in its next version of OS/2.	Claims to have full PnP support.

OS/2 Warp 4 has support for Java applications; Voice Recognition technology - IBM VoiceType: a completely speech aware Desktop, speech enabling of OS/2 applications and a fast and very accurate dictation system; and appealing graphical user interface, TCP/IP connectivity, DB2 universal database, Lotus SmartSuite, Netscape Navigator. It takes you from the client server to network centric era of computing. You can run Java applications in OS/2 without using your browser and benefit from integrity, reliability and security of the operating system.

1.4.4 **APPLE's OS**

The operating system on Mac is almost 11 years old, however, features such as 32 bit addressing and colour matching are only now appearing in Windows. Windows 95 and Windows NT and even OS/2 are ahead of the Mac OS in some critical areas: preemptive multi tasking, multi threading, memory protection, multiprocess security and portability. The last three features are provided only by NT and Windows 95. Macs have robust cooperative multi tasking and crash recovery on system.

Componentware, another approach pursued by Apple, enables you to build your customized solutions by linking together software modules optimized for specific tasks. Microsoft's OLE is a similar technology but Microsoft is protecting it's large applications like Excel and Word by offering them as components.

Apple wants Mac to become part of a common PowerPC platform started by IBM and other PowerPC system vendors. IBM is selling PowerPC workstations but not PCs. IBM does not have software for IBM's PReP (PowerPC Reference Platform), Windows NT and OS/2 for PowerPC.

Apple is working on new technologies such as OpenDoc and the Taligent OS through open affiliation with IBM and HP. Taligent is an offshoot of Apple's next generation OS formerly known as Pink. This will use object oriented design and will be capable of multi-processing and distributed computing. This OS would run application designed for the Macintosh OS, DOS, Windows, and UNIX. TalAE (Taligent Application Environment) is based on the object oriented framework. It contains 1730 objects classes and 53,000 methods as compared to 1500 in Windows. The code of Taligent is also very compact. It is only 6,00,000 lines of code as compared to about 4 millions lines in Windows NT and an estimated 16 million in Cairo, an object oriented version of NT.

Component Integration Laboratories (Sunnyval, CA) controls development of OpenDoc. It has support of Adobe, Apple, Borland, IBM, Lotus, Novell, Oracle, Sun and Xerox. OpenDoc will have following advantages over OLE:

- Wide cross platform support - Mac, Windows and OS/2;
- Easier development - it's API code size is said to be one third in size of OLE's; and
- It handles the multitasking and event messaging that OLE leaves to the user.

After failed initiatives with Taligent, Pink and Copland Apple has come up with the new version Mac OS 8 which is a major upgrade since 1984 and has following salient features:

- New multitasking Finder lets you copy large files while you launch applications or open documents. The new Finder also features Pop-up windows that keep files handy.
- The Internet Setup Assistant helps you get online in minutes, allowing you to connect to, explore, and publish on the web, using your choice of popular browsers.
- Publish a personal web site in just a few easy steps.
- View, open, and edit Windows files within the Mac OS.
- Enjoy the magic of multimedia, including virtual reality scenes, 3-D graphics, full-screen video, digital music, and more.
- Install your favorite photo or graphic as your desktop picture.
- The new installer and Mac OS Setup Assistant install and configure Mac OS 8 quickly and easily.
- Run Java software directly from your desktop rather than through a web browser

1.4.5 UNIX

The UNIX Operating System has evolved from its modest beginning as a simple, small, portable, powerful, time-sharing operating system to one with commercial strength. It is still the most portable and configurable of all operating systems. UNIX has adopted to the new hardware architecture and application requirements by incorporating new functionalities like distributed file system, X-11 based GUIs, multi-threading, distributability etc.

In 1969, Bell Laboratories had just ended its participation in a joint development for a new operating system called Multics. One of the researchers Ken Thompson developed an interactive operating environment as a private research project on a PDP-7 machine. The new operating system was called UNIX. To help in migrating to this new environment Thompson began to develop a FORTRAN compiler but ended up developing an interpreter language called *B*. Dennis Ritchie, later refined the *B* language and developed a compiler for the modified language, which was christened *C*.

In 1973, the operating system was rewritten in *C*. This step had a profound implication in the years to come. Initially running only on the PDP-7 and later on PDP-11 systems, UNIX became quite popular within Bell Labs. A significant role in the development of UNIX came from the University of California at Berkeley. In 1988, an effort was initiated by AT&T and Sun Microsystems to form UNIX International, a governing committee for UNIX releases. Almost at the same time another consortium promoted by IBM, DEC and HP called the Open Software Foundation(OSF) was formed to pilot the development of a UNIX like operating system.

A number of standardization efforts are centered around the UNIX operating system. The POSIX.x standards, X/Open standards and SVID 3 standards are some of the standards that were defined based on a UNIX environment. In fact, UNIX and C have become defacto standard on workstation platform as operating system and programming language respectively.

Computer Graphics Interface (CGI) is a device independent interface to graphics devices. It allows a computer to control several graphics devices simultaneously without regard for their individual characteristics. It supports graphics functions (e.g. Polylines, Polymarkers, text, circle, arc) with control over primitive attributes, viz., colour, fill style and line style. It can take positional character string, selection from menus, single value etc. as graphics input. It also supports features, such as, mouse driven pop-up menus, icons, flexible and higher quality text, and definable clipping regions. It also has status inquiry functions to get state of the screen, attribute settings, active devices and device/system capabilities. The mechanism called computer graphics metafiles (CGM) provides for the exchange of pictures between applications. It supports bitmap facility for the creation and manipulation of graphics images. UNIX provides graphics support in one or more of the following forms:

- through graphics tools, e.g. AIX has functions like graph, spline and tplot;
- computer graphics interface(CGI) drivers which provide the execution support for hard copy devices and screen output. This is available with UNIX version such as SCO UNIX and AIX.
- PostScript (trade mark of Adobe Systems Incorporated) printer support.

Although *C* does not provide general portability across different graphical user interface(GUIs), there is one arena in which, with a modicum of effort, graphically oriented programs can be portable. With the advent of MIT's X window system and the OSF/Motif user interface, the UNIX world has achieved a high degree of portability.

With care to avoid Berkeley/System X and hardware dependencies, a programmer can write an interactive, graphically oriented program that will run on a range of UNIX Systems from virtually every hardware vendor in such a way as to require only recompilation. Unfortunately, this portability does not extend to the most popular platform: an interactive graphical program written for X11 is not likely to transfer to Windows or the Macintosh without substantial effort.

Unix OS available from different vendors are: Interactive Unix Version 4.0 from SunSoft with X11, Motif and VPix DOS emulator; OpenLinux Standard 1.1 from Caldera Inc.; Internet Server 3.0 from Berkeley Software Design; Novell Unix, Version 1.1 from Novell with strength in networking; SCO Open Server 5.04 from Santa Cruz Operation, Windows, high end desktop and mission critical server applications; UnixWare Personal Edition and Application Server with support for DOS and Windows from UNIVEL; and Solaris from x86, Version 2.6 for Intranets, also for SunSoft with Open Network Computing Plus, OpenWindows, GUI alongwith canned productivity tools. A features chart comparing some key parameters of some Unixes is given below.

Features Chart

Features	Berkeley Software Design Internet Server 3.0	Caldera OpenLinux Standard 1.1	The S C O OpenServer 5.0.4	Sun Solaris Server for Intranets 2.6
CPU	At least 386	386, 486, Pentium	386, 486, Pentium	SPARC, UltraSF, 486, Pentium/Pro PowerPC
Memory	4MB	8MB	16MB minimum 2GB maximum	16MB; 32MB recommended
Maximum RAM	256MB	128MB	2,048MB	64GB
Maximum Disc	Unlimited	2 terabytes	1 terabyte file System unlimited	20+ terabyte
Maximum Processors	1	16	30	64
Bus Architecture	PCI, EISA ISA	ISA, EISA, PCI, VL-Bus	MCA, PCI EISA, ISA	MCA, PCI, EISA, SBUS
X Window	X11R6	XFREE86 3.2	X11R5	CDE
OpenLook	No	No	No	Yes
Web server	Apache, Netscape Fast Track	Netscape Fast Track Server	Netscape Fast Track Server	Sun WebServer
Web client	Netscape Navigator Gold	Netscape Navigator	Netscape Navigator Gold	Java VM/HotJava
Development Tools	C, C++, Perl 4/5	JDK, Perl 5.0	Open Server Development System	Solaris Development System
TCP/IP, PPP, HTTP, FTP, POP3, Telnet	Yes	Yes	Yes	Yes
NNTP	Yes	Yes	No	No
IMAP4	Yes	Yes	No	Yes
SNMP/MIB Support	Yes	Yes	Yes	Yes
Web Browser based Management	Yes	Yes	No	Yes
Internet Site	www.bsdi.com	www.caldera.com	www.sco.com	www.sun.com

1.4.5.1 **Why and how select Unix**

Why Unix? One key reason is that for the beginners, it includes Internet/intranet networking, already offering the very things IBM, Microsoft, and Novell are striving to add to their products. Most Unix servers come equipped with a full complement of TCP/IP services, including ftp (File Transfer Protocol), telnet, World Wide Web, DNS, E-mail, newsgroup, and Network File System (NFS) servers. Unix also has a long legacy of well-documented and tested security measures.

Novell Inc. is in the process of rapidly ridding IntranetWare of its IPX/SPX and NCP (NetWare Core Protocol) legacy in favour of a new TCP/IP matrix. Microsoft Corp. still struggles under the weight of NetBEUI and a lack of high-performance TCP/IPservices such as Domain Naming Service (DNS). And IBM is busy trying to reinvent OS/2 as an open system capable of running enterprise distributed services such as the Distributed Computing Environment (DCE).

Unix-on-Intel vendors are building an OS capable of coexisting with other networking environments. Common to most, for example, is support for IPX/SPX, NetBEUI, and even AppleTalk protocols. Sun Microsystems Inc. feels that Solaris will become a viable replacement for IntranetWare by providing native Novell clients with identical file and print services. Unix servers continue to support central IS through SNMP and are becoming more manageable within LAN workgroup, internet and intranet, Web, and departmental database server environments. This has been accomplished through development of improved management tools and simplified installation and configuration routines.

Stability and robustness is given for the Intel-based Unix whereas same is still improving for the products from Novell and Microsoft. Unix vendors are delivering clustering solutions that work today. The Santa Cruz Operation Inc., for example, just released ReliantHA, a software product supporting four-way clustering that promises to provide both reliability and performance enhancements through load balancing.

With such features, Unix obviously makes sense for an Internet and intranet environment. In fact, The Standish Group International Inc. found recently that more than 48 percent of survey respondents would choose Unix for a Web server, while only 33 percent would choose Microsoft Windows NT.

But choosing the correct product among the many Unix offerings is not an easy decision to make. Selection of Unix server would, however, depend on

- the type of work, e.g., Web services, E-mail, news, general-purpose collaboration, and/or mission-critical application platform.

- a product with a strong management tool set that is GUI-based so that there is no need to remember the cryptic commands.
- the level of integration your server must provide within your existing network. Most Intel-based Unix servers come with multiprotocol support, but it's often based on different perspectives.
- need to act as a connecting point between Novell clients and the Internet and/or to serve as a workstation that can access NetWare as a client.

1.5 PROGRAMMING LANGUAGES

In the early days of the development of computers, most of the programs were written in machine language. Therefore, the programmer had to learn not only the proper algorithm for solving the problem under consideration but also the characteristics of the particular computer. Furthermore, since the hardware was very expensive, more emphasis was placed on utilizing it fully. Hence, it was expected of the programmer to spend a lot of time in developing a program which required the minimum amount of time for running. As a result, there was little incentive for the development of high level programming languages. In addition, it was generally believed that programs written in high level languages could not be as efficient as those written in machine or assembly language.

The situation began to change as hardware became less expensive and the cost of programming increased. It was soon observed that not only did programming in machine language require more effort and time but it was also necessary to spend a lot of time in testing and debugging the programs. Hence, a large portion of available computer time was spent only on program development. This led to the realization that a high level programming language, which would make this task simpler, would be very useful.

The first high level programming language was proposed in 1953-54 by John Backups of IBM. It came to be known as FORTRAN, which is the acronym for FORmula TRANslation. As the name implies, the objective was to be able to write the algorithm in a form close to the mathematical expression and then have it translated into machine code by a translator or compiler. The language was designed to make programs as efficient as possible. It was felt that although it was much simpler to program in FORTRAN, the community of programmers, accustomed to machine language, could be persuaded to learn FORTRAN only if the execution time for programs written in it would be of the same order as for the programs written in machine language. The result was that major emphasis was placed on the design of the translator rather than on the design of the language itself. The main objectives in the development of FORTRAN, therefore, was to make programming on the IBM 704 computer faster, cheaper and more reliable. Although initially FORTRAN was used only on the computers made by the IBM, soon other computer manufacturers started providing FORTRAN compilers for their machines. Attempts were then made to develop a standard version of the language. Soon it gained widespread use and acceptance by scientists and engineers in North America and, to a lesser extent, in Europe.

It was later found that FORTRAN had many shortcomings. The early versions of the language did not provide for debugging since it was assumed that there will be no need for this. It was also realized that FORTRAN was difficult to learn and cumbersome to use in business applications. The lack of suitable control structures was the worst aspect of FORTRAN and resulted in the programmer resorting to the undisciplined use of the "go to" statement. This had the effect of making such a program difficult to understand, debug or modify. Many scientific programs tend to be long and complicated, in addition to being based on many different ideas. However, each line of a FORTRAN program typically draws on several of these ideas at once. This makes reading and documentation of the program very difficult. Additional problems are caused due to the great pressure for optimization of the programs in order to minimize the running costs. Both the writing and the optimization of such programs are highly error-prone processes.

Thus, there was a need for a programming language that would be easy to learn and could be executed in an interactive or conversational manner. This led to the development of BASIC (Beginners' All-purpose Symbolic Instruction Code) at Dartmouth College in the early 1960s. It was intended for use by people who had little or no previous experience with computers and were not necessarily adept at mathematics. The original syntax of the language contained only those functions that would be needed by a beginner. The main advantage of BASIC is its interactive nature so that one does not have to wait until compilation to find the errors in syntax. Since BASIC requires a relatively small amount of memory, it has been especially popular with personal computers. However, it suffers from some of the disadvantages mentioned earlier in connection with FORTRAN, in addition to being much slower due to its interpretive nature. The most serious problem with both of these languages is their lack of readability caused by the indiscriminate use of the "go to" statement. A long and complex program written in these languages has been compared to the "rat's nest" of wires that one found in early television sets and radio receivers, making them difficult to repair.

The FORTRAN language provided a linkage between portability and its use. FORTRAN statements were machine independent and could easily be translated in an assembly language on any machine. FORTRAN was designed to facilitate numerical calculations leading to the identification of high level abstractions in FORTRAN with a focus being at algebraic formula.

The programming language Pascal was developed in the early 1970's. It was created by Professor Niklaus Wirth of Switzerland as a vehicle for teaching good programming techniques. Since then, it has become popular outside academia as well. As mentioned in section 1.3.1.5, the need for higher level abstraction that would facilitate the writing of operating systems drove the development of *C*. One can, therefore, conclude that *C* represents the higher level abstraction of assembly language programming. The various advantages of Pascal and *C* will be discussed in the next section.

1.6 ADVANTAGES OF PASCAL and *C* OVER OTHER PROGRAMMING LANGUAGES

Pascal and *C* are structured languages, rich in expressive power and applicable to a wide variety of uses while being unusually simple as well as consistent in its syntax and semantics. An important feature of Pascal as well *C* is their modular structure. The blocks forming the various modules can be read like the paragraphs of a book, since each block is designed to contain just the right amount of information required for the reader to understand its purpose. To continue the analogy of electronic hardware mentioned in the previous section, a well-designed Pascal or *C* program is very much like a modern television receiver built with plug-in printed-circuit boards (or modules). Hence, in the event of malfunction, it is much easier to replace or modify the bad module. Furthermore, it is much easier to test each module separately. Similarly, well-written Pascal and *C* programs (not using too many manipulations of pointers) are easier to understand, maintain and modify. These advantages gain more importance as a program grows in size and complexity. A good strategy for solving a complex problem is to first decompose it into smaller and simpler subproblems. Each of these subproblems is then solved separately. Finally these are combined together to obtain the solution to the original problem. This is called "top-down design" and can also be applied to computer programming. A large program is often written by a team of programmers working separately, each writing and testing a different module. Pascal and *C* go even further by imposing requirements that make it awkward or difficult to avoid good structure. Hence, the programming process lends itself to the same orderly and systematic approach underlying the design and development of any other product.

Because of these features, Pascal as well as *C* are used by most computer science departments as the main language for teaching programming methodology and is regarded as the primary tool for software engineering. It is worth noting that the programming language ADA, developed under contract with the U.S. Department of Defense, can be considered as an enhancement of Pascal. Unfortunately, it has not yet been implemented on personal computers. Furthermore, attempts have been made to imitate the structured nature of Pascal in some versions of BASIC and FORTRAN.

As mentioned earlier, in the first version of FORTRAN, developed for the IBM 704, no special provision was made for debugging, as it was naïvely assumed that this would not be needed. Even later versions of this language can give rise to problems which a compiler will fail to detect. In their book Pascal for FORTRAN programmers, R.H. Perrot and D.C.S. Allison give an interesting example. The first American probe to the planet Venus was aborted after it went off course. The reason was traced to a statement in the FORTRAN program which was syntactically correct. The statement was of the form

DO 6 I = 1, 25

where the comma had been punched as a period by mistake. This caused the FORTRAN compiler to create a new variable called DO6I and to give it the value of 1.25. This error, due to the confusion between a comma and a period, went undetected during the reading, testing and debugging of the program. An error of this type would have been detected by a Pascal or *C* compiler in the very first attempt at compilation. Since Pascal and *C* compilers subject a program to a series of rigorous compile-time and optional run-time checks, which are applied to both the program and data structures, this has the effect of substantially reducing the chance of programmer errors by requiring a little more discipline in programming.

As a result, *C* has become a powerful tool for system application development. There are many good reasons for popularity of *C* language. The *C* code is small, fast, portable and flexible. *C* has become a language of choice for today's professionals and developers. *C* exhibits striking machine independence, even with respect to different operating system and file architecture.

C programs by no means are perfectly portable, e.g., the standard libraries are different with compilers, the default size of integer variables differs across CPUs, and the peculiar structure of Intel processor complicates the issue under MS-DOS. In addition, *C* does not provide support for GUI's except through tool kits which are not standardised across platform.

In view of the above features of Pascal and *C*, we shall utilize Pascal for describing algorithms and *C* as the primary programming language throughout this book. It is felt that not only will this make the programs more transparent to the reader, but will also allow to understand develop a better understanding of the design techniques used in structured programming and stepwise refinements.

1.7 PASCAL and *C* FOR PERSONAL COMPUTERS

Several Pascal compilers have been developed for use on personal computers. The most notable among these are UCSD Pascal, Microsoft Pascal and Turbo Pascal. Historically, UCSD Pascal was the first Pascal compiler developed for small computers. It also supported Turtle-Graphics, developed at M.I.T. by Seymour Peppert to make the concepts of graphics more intelligible by replacing Cartesian coordinates with easier-to-understand polar coordinates. Microsoft Pascal compiles the program into code which is almost identical to the native code of the micro-processor. Hence, it runs much faster but takes an even longer time to compile. Turbo Pascal and *C* compiler of Borland have the advantage of very fast compilation, in addition to the fact that the compiler and the editor require less than 40 kilobytes of memory. For IBM Personal Computers and clones, it also supports some basic graphics routines. This makes it possible to develop good graphics programs with much less effort. In view of these, it is proposed to use Turbo Pascal throughout this book. It may be noted that it will require very little effort to change these to any other version of Pascal or C. A brief description of Pascal and *C* compilers from Borland is given to give readers an appreciation of the graphics support available in the software presently available in the market. Compilers from other vendors also have more or less similar facilities.

1.7.1 Features of PASCAL Compilers

Borland Pascal with Objects 7.0 is an object oriented programming system and comes with Borland's object oriented Application Frameworks: Turbo Vision for DOS and ObjectWindows for Windows. It has an event driven architecture as well as library of time saving reusable objects. Your applications inherit a multi-window mouse based user interface with Windows, menus, dialogs, editors, scroll bars etc. It provides integrated development environments (IDEs) for working both in Windows and DOS. IDE for DOS runs in protected mode so that large programs can be compiled. It breaks the DOS's 640K barrier and allows you to create large DOS protected mode (DPMI) applications without overlays. You can also create DOS Dynamic Link Libraries (DLLs) that can be loaded at runtime and can be distributed separately from .EXEs and can be shared with many other DOS as well as Windows applications. It can compile more than 85,000 lines per minute and is source code compatible with Turbo Pascal 5.x and later.

Turbo Pascal for Windows 1.5 and Turbo Pascal 7.0 are Windows and DOS versions respectively. Turbo Pascal for Windows 1.5 utilises full support for Windows 3.x including Object Linking and Embedding (OLE), multi-media, drag and drop and true type fonts. You can create visually dialogs, menus, bitmaps, icons, and other resources using Resource Workshop. Turbo Pascal 7.0 is an object oriented programming system and provides two IDEs:

- TPX.EXE - runs in DOS protected mode, i.e., very large applications will have the memory necessary to compile.
- TURBO.EXE - runs on any 80x86 system.

It supports graphics through a graph unit - a complete library of more than 50 graphics functions including several fill, line styles and fonts that may be magnified, justified and oriented horizontally and vertically. IDE in version 7.0 provides features, such as, object browsers, syntax highlighting, undo and redo, tools menu, message window, multiple user installable help file support, facility to save single information across sessions and compilations. Although, this version is not a windows version but it can run under Windows 3.x.

1.7.2 Features of *C* Compilers

Turbo *C++* is for *C++* and *C* programmers, a fast and efficient compiler and offers full implementation of AT&T *C++* version 2.0. It is also compatible with American National Standard Institute (ANSI) *C* standard and fully supports the Kernighan and Ritichie definition. It includes *C++* class libraries, mouse support, multiple overlapping windows, multi file editor, hypertext help, far objects and error analysis.

It runs on IBM PC family and all true IBM compatibles. It requires DOS 2.0 or higher and atleast 640 KB of memory. Turbo C++ comes with a complete set of graphics functions to facilitate preparation of charts and diagrams. It supports the same graphics adapters as Turbo Pascal. The graphic library consists of over 70 graphics functions ranging from high level support like facility to set view port, draw 3 - dimensional bar charts, draw polygons to bit-oriented functions like get image and put image. The graphics library supports numerous objects, line styles and provides several text fonts to enable one to size, justify and orient text, horizontally and vertically. It may be noted that graphics functions use far pointers and graphics is not supported in the tiny memory model. There is only one library for all memory models, i.e., tiny, small, large and very large. The graphics functions support activities, such as, graphic system control, drawing and filling, manipulating screen and view ports, text output, color control, error handling and state queries.

Borland C++ 4.5 and Database Tools comprise of C++ compiler and programming tools with the Borland Database Engine and SQL links, a profiler, and OWL (Object Windows Library) enhanced with OLE. In fact, it is a Win32 application that runs under Windows 3.1. A new 32-bit back end makes compilation very fast. Borland *C++* has advantage in the area of using the power of *C++* in DLLs. OWL itself can be placed in DLL and shared by several applications. Other compilers have advantage in the area of debugging or optimisation. While MFC (Microsoft Foundation Class) is based directly on the suucture of the existing Windows API, OWL provides building blocks such as built-in file and editor windows with automatic scrolling. In brief, OWL is deep in some areas and Microsoft foundation classes are broad.

Borland C++ 3.1 supported object oriented development environment, Windows 3.1 Application Programming Interface (API) facilitating one to produce windows applications in contrast to Microsoft *C/C++* 7.0, Borland *C++* 3.1 is intended to comply with the AT&T *C* front 3.0 de facto standard. Borland C++ 4.5 provides a visual development environment for application development on DOS, Windows 3.x, Win 32s, Windows NT, and Windows 95. It comprises of AppExpert to create foundation of your Windows application; ClassExpert to modify and review these applications, Resource Workshop to visually design and create bitmaps, icons, cursors, fonts and other components of the user interface; an Integrated Debugger to step through code and a Turbo Profiler to view/analyze performance of code.

Microsoft *C, C++* version 7.0 was first *C++* compiler with more than 60 *C++* classes (called Microsoft Foundation Classes) that abstract the functionality of the Windows API and provided advanced *C++* design, features new compiler optimization techniques, and an application framework for objects under Windows. It also included Microsoft Quick *C* compiler. Quick *C* provides an integrated programming environment including program editor, compiler, debugger, an integrated program and library maintenance facilities. Microsoft *C, C++*7.0 made full use of all the machine resources available including the flat 32-bit space of the 386 or the higher processors. A common run-time library for MS-DOS and Xenix installation enables to transport program easily from Xenix development environment to MS-DOS machine or vice-versa.

Microsoft Visual C++ 2.0 adds ANSI C++ language features and 32-bit OLE support to applications. Use of AppWizard and MFC library automatically incorporates OLE. Its Custom Control Developer's Kit facilitates you in creating OLE controls quickly on 16- and 32- bit platforms. Its main strength is portability across platforms. It runs on Personal Computer using a 386 or higher processor running Windows NTTM Workstation OS Version 3.5 or later. Minimum installation when used with a CDROM drive is 10MB and typical installation takes 100MB. The system should have more than 16MB of memory. For DOS applications, the 16-bit compiler, Microsoft Visual C++ 1.5 is a completely separate tool which runs with MSDOS OS Version 5.0 or later and Windows 3.x. It takes 80MB of disk space and runs well on systems with 8MB memory. Both version 1.5 and 2.0 support VGA or higher resolution monitors.

A number of C and C++ programming environments such as Borland C++ 4.5 and Database Tools, Borland C++ for OS/2 2.x, Meta Ware High C/C++ on DOS, Windows 3.x & NT 3.x and OS/2 3.x, Microsoft Visual C++ 2.0, IBM C Set++ Version 3.x, Symantee C++ Version 7.0 and Watcom C/C++ 10.0 are available. The emphasis in all the packages is toward GUI based integrated development environment.

A comparison of Borland C++ 4.5 and Microsoft Visual C++ 2.0 is given below.-

Features	Borland C++ 4.5	Microsoft Visual C++ 2.0
Emphasis	Developing a highly modular set of OLE tools.	Cross platform coverage - 32-bit thread-safe MFC library is source-code portable across Intel, Mips RISC 4000, DEC Alpha, and Apple Macintosh platforms.
Custom Control	OLE custom controls (OCXs) are not supported, but both 16-bit and 32-bit VBX's are.	OLE Custom Control Development Kit for creating OLE controls quickly leads developers through a set of choices and generates extensive skeleton codes. A programmer need only incorporate the application specific code.
Code generator	AppExpert in OCF tool set is a source-code generator. It can auto-matically update pre-viously generated code with OLE support.	AppWizard source-code generator is a single-pass utility that establishes for all time the class of library support built into the application templates it creates.
Portability Layer	Adds a 32-bit portability layer allowing Windows applications to use 16-bit VBX's (Visual Basic Custom Controls) under Windows 95 and NT.	This support is not yet available.
International Language support	Through VBX one can map its property list to alias tables that translate the property names to various languages allowing VBX to the language dynamically.	Separate DLL is required for each language.
Component Framework	Enables one to write OLE-activated applications that plug cleanly into OWL, MFC, C++, and ordinary C programs for Windows. Thus old code can have OLE features.	No direct support.
Improvements	IDE tools and OWL class libraries	IDE Expanded Class Library

The latest versions of *C* development systems from Borland and Microsoft are reviewed in the following sections.

1.7.2.1 **Borland's C++Builder**

It is the long-awaited C++ version of Delphi. Thus, as Delphi positioned Turbo Pascal in the RAD arena, C++Builder serves to move Borland C++ into the same marketplace. The RAD arena covers the category of tools that support visual programming targeted primarily at enterprise applications. So why should you consider C++Builder over the myriad other products (such as Microsoft's Visual Basic, Powersoft's PowerBuilder and IBM's Visual Age) available? Keep in mind another advantage that a RAD interface to C++ provides. For those programmers who are still catching up speed on C++ from other languages such as COBOL or Visual Basic, C++Builder helps provide a relatively seamless transition for a learn-as-you go experience.

C++Builder is Borland C++, just as Delphi provides a visual interface to Object Pascal. rogramming with C++Builder feels like using a slower version of Delphi. Turbo Pascal (and Delphi) has always been one of the fastest compilers available, comparing favorably to the speed of the interpreted Visual Basic. Further, Object Pascal was optimized for Turbo Pascal and Delphi, whereas Borland didn't have that option for C++Builder. Similarities of C++Builder to Delphi and other key features are as under:

- The programming environment of C++Builder, as with Delphi, is a delight to use.
- Series of tabbed pages lets you choose components ranging from standard, to data access, to Internet, to ActiveX. As with Delphi, Visual Basic, and other tools oriented toward visual programming, you design a form on a second window, the form window, and drop components selected from the tabbed pages on it.
- As you select, components, a third window, the Object Inspector lets you modify the properties of the selected component.
- Finally, if you wish to work directly with the generated C++ code, an edit window gives you access to it.
- Changes in the visual design are reflected in the source code, and changes to the source code are reflected in the visual design.
- You can also compile the Object Pascal visual component library source code from within C++Builder.
- Both Borland's object windows library (OWL) and Microsoft's MFC, most likely you'll eventually have to learn the innards of the visual component library.
- Borland C++Builder is built on Borland's proven C++ compiler technology and shares Delphi's award-winning Visual Component Library, giving you great interoperability with both Borland C++ and Delphi.

If you want to work with MFC, however, you'll find two shortcomings relative to the visual component library. First, C++Builder does not provide MFC headers or source code, thus you're required to obtain the needed files from another compiler. Second, the two-way form-to-source and source-to-form interaction that makes using C++ so effective is not available when using MFC.

Programming with C++Builder will not let you generate C++ code which can port to directly port to other platforms. Although C++Builder is a visual front end to Borland C++, and code written with Borland C++ can be ported to other platforms, the nonstandard C++ constructs to support the component architecture that Borland inserts in the generated C++ code will ensure that extensive rewriting would be required to move the code to, say, a UNIX environment. Given such requirement, it would be simpler to use the C++Builder application as a prototype for the version to run on UNIX.

C++Builder is available in three versions: standard, professional, and client/server. The standard edition, consists of the IDE, compiler, debugger, and libraries, provides the tools to write simple applications. It supports building OLE automation servers and controllers, and through that mechanism you can integrate programs written in C++Builder into the larger world.

The professional version takes all of C++Builder's standard features and adds several features for developing corporate applications. Chief among the productivity-oriented features is the data dictionary, which lets you store attribute sets for field components. Attribute sets for fields include such parameters as field type (int, string) and default values. Extended field attributes are used to control how the field is formatted and displayed.

The professional version also provides increased support for database programmers. Take advantage of complete ODBC connectivity and fast, native SQL links to Oracle, Sybase, MS SQL Server, Informix, DB2, and InterBase Build on what you know and have C++Builder recompiles all your existing ANSI C++ code, and lets you use C++ to build fast, productive front ends for your Borland C++ applications.

The client/server version of C++Builder includes all the features of the professional version. The local InterBase engine is upgraded to a four-user licensed Windows NT version, and a SQL monitor is supplied to help you test, debug, and tune your applications. To help the programming team with configuration management, the client/ server version of C++Builder includes an integrated version of Intersolv's PVCS. Databases supported include, in addition to Borland's own InterBase, native drivers for Oracle, Sybase, Informix, DB2, and SQL Server. With ODBC, users can work with data in Access, dBase, Paradox, and FoxPro. Borland's strategy lets you build applications that work equally well with Microsoft-centric environments where DCOM, ISAPI, ActiveX, and ODBC rule, as well as with Internet environments built around CORBA, DCE, Java, JavaScript, and JDBC.

Borland customers who use Entera application server technology can use any client tool, any server tool, and access any relational database on any platform. Entera provides platform support and connectivity for IBM's 3270 terminals and Open Edition MVS. It also supports several flavors of UNIX, including Digital's OSF/1, Hewlett Packard's HP-UX, Unisys's SVR4, Sun's Solaris, and IBM's AIX/6000. On the desktop, Entera supports the Apple Macintosh, IBM's OS/2, and Microsoft's Windows 95 and Windows NT.

A recent, nonexclusive licensing deal between Borland and Oracle, that gives Oracle the right to incorporate Borland's C++ and Java development technology into Oracle products, may answer whether Borland will be around for the long haul. The biggest factor, of course, will hinge on how well Borland does compete against Microsoft's suite of development tools.

1.7.2.2 Microsoft's Visual C++ 5.0

Microsoft Visual C++ development system version 5.0 has been extended to include native support for Component Object Model (COM) programming, primarily on the client side. The major new feature is the ability to directly read type libraries, translating the contents into C++ source that is included in the compilation source. In addition, there are language extensions for COM support. The key features are

- Visual C++ Technology Preview enables you to start on developing for Internet Explorer 4.0 by accessing the power and flexibility of Dynamic HTML and the new Common Controls.
- Internet Explorer 4.0 support allows you to integrate the Web directly into your MFC applications. Please note that the Technology Preview will be integrated into the next major release of Visual C++, but some features may change.
- By using the new CHtmlView class in MFC you can create a view in your MFC application that hosts Dynamic HTML. This view has all the power and browsing capabilities of Internet Explorer.
- You can build browser-based front ends to leverage all your existing work. With Dynamic HTML support ActiveX controls can use Dynamic HTML to interact "on the fly" with data you have downloaded to the browser and enables you to reduce server round trips by manipulating data and performing calculations right on the Web page, without going back up to the server.
- These new controls include the Internet Explorer -style toolbars, the IP Address control, the Date Picker and Month Calendar controls, and the Extended Combo Box control.
- In addition, the Visual C++ Technology Preview makes it easy to use the enhancements to the Slider, Toolbar, Tab, Status Bar, Image List, Hot Key, Progress Bar. and Tool Tip controls.
- It will support writing ActiveX document containers including support for printing, saving, and loading. You get seamless support to get all the functionality of programs like Excel or in your MFC applications with DocObject Containment. Easily put full-featured charts, graphs, or even Web browsers right in your MFC applications, with full menu merge.
- OLE DB provides high performance access to any data source - relational and non-relational, email and file systems, text and graphics, custom business objects, and more.

1.8 JAVA

In 1963 when ALGOL was announced, it appeared to have potential to become the Universal Common Language, i.e. the same code could run on heterogeneous platforms. But ALGOL could not succeed. Then Pascal arrived. Pascal got a huge following as PL/I was too big, messy, and unruly (much like C/C++ today). It didn't solve the Universal Common Language problem any more than ALGOL. Then Ada came into being. It was supposed to be a better Pascal, but the Ada command economy also failed. Then C++ was introduced.

Java was first unveiled publicly on May 23, 1995. Perhaps a revolution spawned by the platform - independent, easy-to-use, object - oriented Java language is its key role in the new Network Computer (NC), also called a "thin client." Java is a Universal Common Language that allows all kinds of systems to talk to each other and share applications. That's because Java is platform independent. It allows the same applications to run on every kind of device: PC, Mac, UNIX machine, set - top box, PDA, cellular phone, even smart appliances.

Java's developers realised that if all computers can be described in terms of general functions, then programs that are written using only general functions could run on all computers. Turning the general functions into the specific tasks would be a simple job for the computer on which the program ran.

For a computer to run a Java program, it needs only an interpreter to translate the Java code into instructions it can execute directly. Unlike current Windows applications, Java programs do not care what the computer's underlying operating system or processor is. By freeing people from a particular type of system software, Java was Sun's declaration of war on proprietary system software in general and Microsoft's Windows in particular.

Elegant minimalism is one of the goals of Java. It is a simple language, just as Pascal was simple language. Java is also incomplete as a general purpose language: e.g., it lacks I/O, intrinsic functions. Most of Java features include :

- diluted C++,
- retrofitting of Pascal's features, such as strong typing, keywords, packages - from the UCSD P-code version - and portable byte code
- APIs to an OS
- many of Pascal's minimalist attributes (byte codes, strong typing, restricted pointers, and meaningful keywords instead of cryptic symbols).
- 10 object modifiers: Public, Private, Protected, Static, Final, Native, Synchronized, Abstract, Thread-safe, and Transient.

The Public modifier completely breaks down encapsulation in Java. Static, Final, and Public are contradictory and confusing. Native is unforgivable in a language that claims platform independence.

1.8.1 **Java's Strengths**

Main strengths of Java are:

- Its threads are vast improvement over UNIX tasking, but they are certainly nothing new.
- Applets and servlets are truly new, but there is no real-world requirement that they have to be written in Java. Applets are Java programs which run on the client side inside your browser, such as, Internet Explorer or Netscape and servlets run on the server.
- Its error-handling capability, single inheritance, and interface specification constructs are good.
- Its wisely borrowed features from pre-C/C++ languages.
- Its idea of an HTML-tagged applet.
- Its many security features such as strong memory protection, encryption and signatures, rules enforcement and run - time verification.
- Its support for encryption technology to verify that an applet came from an authorized source and has not been modified.
- Its run - time verification system that ensures that all applets downloaded to the client will not violate the integrity of the environment.

Java's platform independence means software developers can create one version of an application and deploy it on a wide array of systems. This "write once/run anywhere" ability saves companies the difficulty and time of mastering many different programming environments and tools, and it frees them from having to port software to multiple platforms.

In addition, since Java devices get all of their programs and data over the network, they can be configured without local removable storage. In some situation, this is desirable in order to keep data within the network, or keep viruses out of the network. In essence, the network - centric nature of Java greatly simplifies security solutions. Which is easier: guarding a single server or guarding a network of individual clients ?

As an object - oriented language, Java promotes reuse of code, saving time and also enhancing application reliability. Java also encourages good software engineering practices with clear separation of interfaces and implementations, as well as easy exception handling. In addition, Java's automatic memory management and lack of pointers removes some of the leading causes of programming errors.

1.8.2 Java's Drawbacks

Main drawbacks of Java include :

- Java still retains too many of the error-prone features of C/C++.
- In C tradition, Java arrays start from zero, instead of one. This will continue to bother programmers who may spend hours locating off-by-one errors.
- Scope, range and synchronisation constructs are overly complex, sometimes contradictory, and mostly poorly thought-out.
- Like Pascal, Java eschews I/O. Both Pascal and Java off-load I/O to ill-defined, incomplete libraries. As a consequence, I/O libraries are already starting to flourish, creating a variety of Java dialects.

On the positive side, Java does enforce strong typing, restrictions on pointers, and single inheritance. On the negative side, Java is subject to C/C++ syntax problems; non-standardized APIs; the fragile base class problem, whereby interface changes to abstract classes destroy entire class hierarchies; and the fragile interface problem, whereby one change in an interface specification can propagate to all points in a large program that use the interface, to name just a few. Java takes only a small step toward early defect removal.

1.8.3 Java Programming Tools

Java is a relatively new programming language that, until recently, has suffered from a lack of good programming tools. Visual J++ (VJ++) is Microsoft's new Java development tool, positioned to compete with products such as Symantec's Café and Borland's Latte. VJ++ is fast, easy to use, fits neatly into its own ActiveX technology.

VJ++ uses the same Developer Studio environment that comes with Microsoft's Visual C++ 4.0. Microsoft has incorporated its existing tools into VJ++. For example, to create dialog boxes for your Java applets, you use the same dialog box editor found in VC++ 4.0's Developer Studio.

VJ++'s Java Applet Wizard helps in creating Java applets. After you respond to the Wizard's few simple questions, it creates a commented Java source-code skeleton and an HTML file to host the applet. The Applet Wizard has an especially handy feature that lets you specify the HTML applet parameters in a tabular form. By default, VJ++ uses Microsoft Internet Explorer 3.0/4.0 rather than an applet viewer to run and test its Java applets. VJ++ offers a stable and productive environment that should help speed up applet development.

Java Workshop 2.0 from SUN provides far better ease in creating a platform-neutral gridbag layout, than any competing Java development environment. The gridbag layout-based visual designer takes some getting used to, but it is well worth the effort. The difficulty in learning this tool isn't as much the fault of Java Workshop as it is a consequence of moving from a traditional WYSIWYG design environment to one where platform neutrality reigns supreme. Once you've mastered the approach, design is a breeze. You can drop components and size them across grid cells very easily. You manipulate gridbag constraints settings such as weights and fill-factors by clicking on sections outside the grid.

The visual programming features of Java Workshop 2.0 are very rudimentary. For example, you can specify a list of operations that will take place when you click a button. But unless the operation is something very basic (such as "hide the listbox"), you have to write the code yourself. The template code generated by Java Workshop is very heavily commented, which proves very useful. Java Workshop has one of the leanest default palettes of visual components. You get everything you need for most applications, but precious little more.

Java developers have had very few tools to help them link their Java applications to corporate databases. Symantec aims to change that situation with Visual Café Pro, a complete package for developing database-enabled applets and applications in Java.

Visual Café Pro is based on Visual Café, Symantec's Java graphical development environment. Symantec's dbAnywhere is the key, implementing Sun's Java Database Connectivity (JDBC) API to connect your applets and applications to database systems such as Oracle, Microsoft Access, and the included SQL Anywhere.

1.8.4 Java Applications

And as the expected flood of Java applications are available, the options for the user will increase. For example, Java - based word processing, spreadsheet and presentation applications are under development by atleast three major vendors and are expected soon. Many major vendors are revamping their enterprise applications using Java, such as Oracle, SAP, PeopleSoft, Baan, Dun & Bradstreet and others. The next wave will be a migration of Java Computing beyond the corporate IT world, into games, cellular phones, beepers, set-top boxes and other devices. Already, Corel has announced plans to develop a Java-based hand-held organizer with Internet functions that could appear by early 1998.

1.9 TRENDS

The next IT revolution is for three dimensional displays on desk top PC. Accelerated 3D is continuing its race to the mass market. It is estimated that presently over 50% of new computers are being shipped with 3D rasterization acceleration.

Apple is betting its future on the success of PowerPC, the Mac OS and the Componentware. The days of ISA and EISA bus are also numbered as a 32 bit OS would also need a 32-bit bus on the computer. The first P6 processor from Intel ran at 133-MHz and delivered 200 SPECmarks (a measure of integer performance) compared to a 100-MHz Pentium which gives only 100 SPECmarks. The POWER3 from IBM would achieve clock speeds of more than 500 MHz and performance exceeding 70 and 30, respectively, on the SPEC95 floating-point and integer benchmarks

Intel's product roadmap calls for new high-end chips to supplant existing models so quickly that by the next year, a 200/233/266 MHz Pentium with MMX will be considered low-end technology and sell in PCs priced as low as $1,200. Intel is planning a new 300MHz Pentium II processor, code-named Deschutes, to top its product line for desktops, servers. Mobile versions of Deschutes offering speeds of 233 Mhz and 266 Mhz will be available next year. A chip for mobile systems, code-named Tillamook, a Pentium chip with MMX, is also in the offing.

NCs are much more secure than PCs because they don't persistently store information. Companies store most of their information on centralised computers. NCs are just a lower cost alternative to get some jobs done mainly due to savings in administration and maintenance and would, therefore, not replace PCs. For applications where a PC is too complicated and expensive to operate, Java Computing devices deliver a powerful new option. Sun estimates based on extensive study by its CIO reveal that Java devices cost only $2,500 per seat per year, vs. $11,900 for conventional fat clients such as PCs. The savings stem from a variety of sources, including the lower acquisition cost of hardware, the lower cost of developing and deploying software and the decreased system administration burden.

The DOS era has reached its end. This includes DOS which bootstraps 16-bit Windows. A number of 32-bit OS custom-designed for 32-bit Intel processors are ready to take over. New operating systems from Microsoft and IBM are catching up with, and even surpassing the Mac OS in key areas of technology, while PCs are now acquiring some long standing hardware advantages of the Macintosh, such as Plug and Play. It appears that in near future there will be three main streams i.e. MS-DOS losing to Windows 95/98 and NT, OS/2 and Apple's Mac OS 8 and the third stream consisting of UNIX like operating system.

Microsoft has emerged as the leading desktop OS vendor and now seeks to dominate the OS market, including LAN servers and high-end workstations. It's Windows NT OS is key to that strategy and as per Windows roadmap all Windows products will merge in NT only by year 2000. NT is desisigned to offer companies the power of UNIX and simplictty of Windows.

Object-oriented technology is the most important advance in the last thirty years and it represents a total shift in the approach to building computer applications. Object-oriented programming (OOP) remains the key adjective for programming technology. Although, object oriented languages fail to solve all programming problems, they facilitate a good programmer design modular, and reusable software. C++ has become the most favored object oriented language for many key applications, mainly, because it is a superset of the familiar *C* language. Two key features, viz., templates and exception handling will soon be fully implemented in *C++* to enable programmers (i) to write one parameterized description of list, which can be specialized to provide type-safe lists of strings, icons etc., and (ii) mechanisms to match error conditions with error handlers at run time, rather than compile time, thus, providing user robust error recovery and better information. The evolution of language technology would lead to development of more powerful compilers, better GUI tools, and stronger frameworks.

Java is doomed to gain over C//C++ as object oriented language and become language of choice by the developers due to its features, such as, platform independence, "write once/run anywhere" ability and freedom to port software to multiple platforms without any effort and rapid improvement in the quality of tools. Companies are putting lot of effort to improve performance of Java tools and have already developed Java Computing applications that run up to a two-and-a-half-time faster compared to those developed with conventional programming using languages like C and C++.

1.10 SCOPE OF THE BOOK

This book is intended for a use as a one-semester sophomore level course in science and engineering, but can also be used for self-study. The emphasis is on graphics techniques for personal computers. The Personal Computer has been considered as the basic machine for this purpose. Turbo Pascal and *C* programs have been included throughout the book, particularly, as C programs often become cryptic and difficult to understand. Programs are available in source form both in Pascal and *C* languages and will make it possible to use these methods on all compatibles.

Throughout the book, a large number of worked examples are included in order to fully explain the theory and methods that have been developed. In particular, Chapter 8 contains examples from several engineering disciplines, including the listings of programs. Special attention has been given to the topic of interactive graphics and Chapter 5 has been devoted to it. This should be valuable for students interested in computer-aided design. Chapters 9 and 10 present an introduction to virtual reality and multimedia, and review core hardware systems, software tools and applications to get going.

This book has been written without any conscious bias towards any particular branch of science or engineering. It is expected that the reader has some background in programming in Pascal and/or *C* language.

1.11 REFERENCES

1. David Price, *Pascal, a considerate approach*, Prentice-Hall, 1981.
2. R.H. Perrot and D.C.S. Allison, *Pascal for FORTRAN Programmers*, Computer Science Press, Rockville, Maryland, 1984.
3. Ted G. Lewis, *Pascal for the IBM Personal Computer*, Addison-Wesley, 1983.
4. Hansen Augie, *Proficient C*, Microsoft Press, Washington, 1986.
5. Kernighan Brian W., and Dennis M. Ritchie, *The C Programming Language*, Prentice-Hall, Inc, Englewood Cliffs, 1987(Fourth print).
6. Kernighan Brian W., and Rob Pike, *The UNIX Programming Environment*, Prentice-Hall, Inc, Englewood Cliffs, 1984.
7. Plum Thomas, *Learning to Program in C*, Plum Hall, Inc., Cardiff, New Jersey, 1983.
8. Schildt Herbert, *C Made Easy*, Osborne McGraw Hill, Berkeley, California, 1985.
9. Schulman Andrew, *Unauthorized Windows 95: A Developer's Guide to Exploring the foundations of Windows "Chicago"*, IDG books Worldwide, 1995.
10. Barkakati Nabajyoti, *Borland C++ 4 Developer's Guide*, Sams Publishing, 1994.

CHAPTER 2

RASTER AND RANDOM SCAN GRAPHICS

2.1 INTRODUCTION

The basic hardware for graphics displays is some type of a cathode ray tube where the picture is produced by a beam of electrons striking a phosphor-coated screen. This beam is caused by an electron gun and focussed at various points on the screen by applied voltages. By pointing the beam at different spots on the screen, we can create a picture. When the beam strikes at a certain point on the phosphor coating, the screen lights up at that spot for a fraction of a second. The same device is used in television receivers. In order that we may be able to see the picture on the screen, we need a method for keeping the spot lighted for a longer period. There are two basic techniques for doing this.

One method for keeping the picture lighted for a longer time is to scan the tube repeatedly over the various points on the screen at a rate that is sufficiently fast to give the impression of a continuous picture. It has been found that if the repetition rate is at least 30 times per second, the human eye will perceive a steady picture, without any flicker. Typically, the scanning rate is kept between 30 and 60 times per second. This type of display is called a "refresh" cathode ray tube, since the entire picture is refreshed during each scan.

Another method for maintaining the picture is to store the pattern of lighted spots in the picture and keep them lighted unless some change is required for another picture. This type of display requires a storage type cathode ray tube having an additional electron gun (called the flood gun) and a special wire screen (called the collector grid) for storing the electrical charge pattern that produces a certain picture. The flood gun emits a continuous flow of electrons that activate the phosphor screen according to the charge pattern on the collector grid. This keeps the phosphor glowing continuously at those locations on the screen which form the picture. A cathode ray tube of this type is called a "direct-view storage" tube. Because the picture is maintained on the screen by a flood of electrons instead of repetitive retracing of the electron beam, the image on the screen is stable and free from flicker. The hardware in this case, however, is much more expensive. Therefore, most microcomputer systems are presently based on refresh type displays. Notebook PCs and wall mounted high definition TVs' use flat screen displays.

In this chapter we will discuss the various methods of scanning as employed in typical refresh type microcomputer display systems. Application to the display of text and natural images will also be described.

2.2 DIFFERENCE BETWEEN RASTER AND RANDOM SCAN

Scanning in refresh type video displays can be done in two different ways. These are called "raster" and "random" scans. In a raster scan, the electron beam follows a fixed path, as shown in Figure 2.1. The beam starts at the upper left corner of the screen and moves horizontally to the right. This defines a scan line. During the scan, the intensity of the beam is modulated according to the pattern of the desired image alo ̦ ıne line. At the right edge of the screen, the beam is blanked and moved to the left edge, positioned one unit below the previous starting point. This is shown as a dotted line. This pattern of scanning is continued until the bottom corner on the right hand is reached. At this point, one scan is completed, and the beam is then repositioned at the upper left corner of the screen for starting another scan.

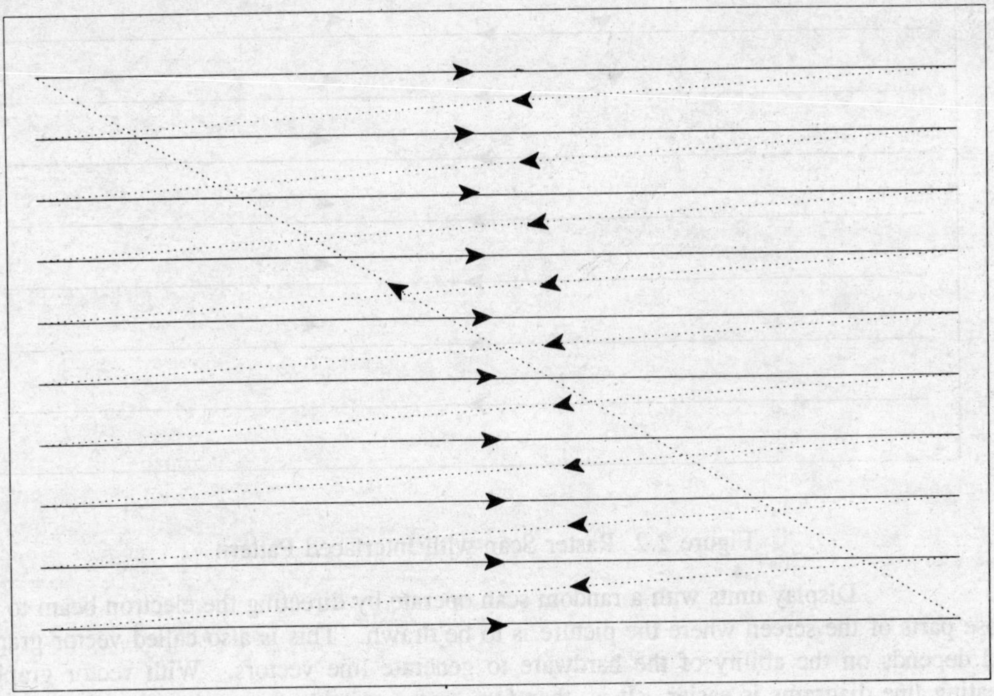

Figure 2.1 Raster Scan Pattern

Television systems in North America operate at 525 scan lines. Usually, the refresh cycle is arranged such that the electron beam sweeps across every other line on one pass from top to bottom, and then returns to sweep across the remaining lines in the next pass. This interlaced scanning pattern helps to reduce flicker in the image, since the entire screen is essentially scanned in half the time that would have been required for sweeping across all the lines from the top to the bottom. A raster scan of this type is shown in Fig. 2.2. For most computers, the number of scan lines varies between 100 and 1000. The CGA and VGA card on an IBM Personal Computer support 200 and 480 scan lines, respectively, for raster graphics.

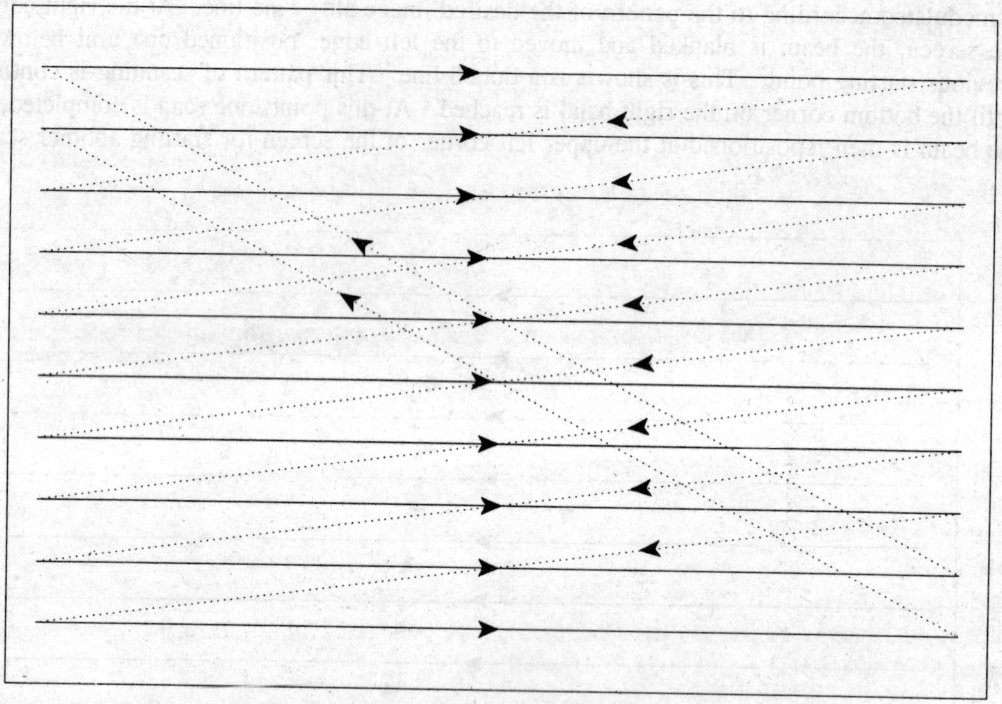

Figure 2.2 Raster Scan with Interlaced Pattern

Display units with a random scan operate by directing the electron beam to only those parts of the screen where the picture is to be drawn. This is also called vector graphics and depends on the ability of the hardware to generate line vectors. With vector graphics, creating line diagrams is easier. It is, therefore, more suitable for engineering and scientific drawings. On the other hand, raster graphics can be used to provide animation, where, necessary.

The essential difference in the hardware is the requirement that the random scan display must have a vector generator. Using software for drawing vectors in raster scan systems is possible as well. All pen plotters and direct-view storage devices use random scan, whereas all television-type cathode ray tube devices use raster scan. Due to the higher cost of hardware for random-scan displays, most microcomputers, including the IBM Personal Computer, use raster scans, although they require more memory for storing information about the image. This has been possible mainly due to the sharp decline in the cost of memory. Therefore, we will discuss raster scan in more detail in section 2.5. In the following section we shall briefly describe the types of display technologies used with personal computers.

2.3 DISPLAY TECHNOLOGIES

Two types of display technologies are commonly used with personal computers. The conventional cathode ray tube, which has been around for a long time, is mostly used with desk-top computers. On the other hand, lap-tops and portables require a more compact display of the flat screen type. Both of these can be either of the monochrome or colour types.

2.3.1 Cathode Ray Tube Displays

In a cathode ray tube, a beam of electrons, emitted from an electrode (called the cathode), passes through a focussing and deflection system and strikes a phosphor-coated screen. The number of electrons is determined by the voltage applied to the anode (electron gun). Focussing and deflection of the beam is also controlled by voltages. These produce electric and magnetic fields to focus the beam to a particular spot on the screen, which lights up when the beam strikes it. The intensity of a light spot is determined by the number and velocity of electrons striking it. A picture is produced by directing the beam to different points on the screen. Since the light emitted by the phosphor coating lasts on the screen for only a small fraction of a second, the picture is maintained on the screen by repeatedly passing the electron beam over the same points on the screen, This is called scanning the picture, and is further discussed in sections 2.4 and 2.5.

Colour is produced by using more than one type of phosphor coating on the screen since different types of phosphors emit lights of different colours. A range of colours can be produced by combining lights from two or more phosphors.

2.3.2 Flat Screen Displays

Flat screen display technologies are of two types - the colour active matrix LCDs (called AMLCDs) and passive matrix colour LCD. Most monochrome notebook computers use simpler passive LCDs, like the super twisted nematic (STN) units. The display signal in both active and passive displays is applied to the columns of pixels in parallel while rows in such a display are addressed sequentially. The method of time division of voltage is also referred to as multiplexing. The portion of the entire display cycle during which an address signal is applied to a pixel to turn it 'ON' is called the pixel duty cycle. Thus, for a 240-row display the maximum duty cycle will be 1/240 of the frame period (usually 1/60 second). A display with a small duty cycle will have poor contrast ratio, a narrow viewing angle and fewer grey levels. To show smooth cursor movements a pixel on-time should be roughly 125 milliseconds and for the video applications the pixel on-time of 50 milliseconds is required. A designer, therefore, compromises between the number of rows of pixels in the display against the length of time during a frame that the display circuitry needs to apply voltage to a turned 'ON' pixel.

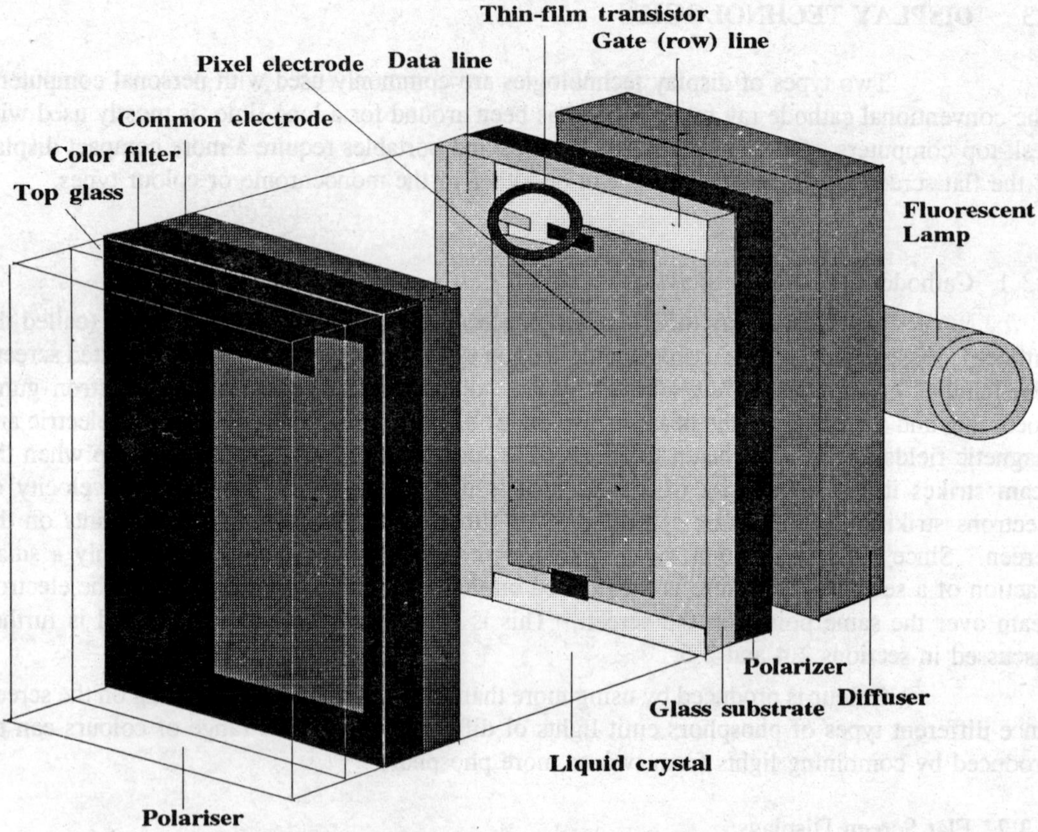

Figure 2.3 Active matrix LCD display based on thin film transistor technology

Since voltage to column pixels is applied in parallel, pixel intensities in a column containing both 'ON' and 'OFF' pixels may vary from the desired levels. This phenomenon is called crosstalk and is a major problem for the passive displays. The level of crosstalk varies from display to display. Although LCD material with characteristics such as high viscosity and slow response helps in reducing flicker, it reduces the response time - restricting the display's capability to show fast changing graphics like cursor movement.

AMLCDs (see figure 2.3) were developed to overcome the above limitations of passive displays. Researchers at Westinghouse Corporation, Pittsburgh, discovered in 1970 that placing a switch at each pixel location was one way of solving the crosstalk problem. However, to make a 640-by-480 full colour pixels, with each pixel having a red, a green, and a blue subpixel required 920,000 transistors to be deposited on say, a 10-inch substrate. This approach enables the pixels to operate at 100 percent duty cycle as active device can maintain voltage across each pixel continuously. This improves contrast, compared with a display in which voltage is applied to pixels in short pulses. However, investment for setting up production facilities for AMLCDs is very high. This led others to think of alternate technologies.

In 1992, Focus Systems developed a new method of driving passive LCDs that had most of the benefits of AMLCDs - like use of faster liquid crystal material, bright flicker free display, and small ghosting effects. This was achieved by using complex row functions to distribute selection intervals over the frame period and by combining row functions with complex computed column functions. This approach necessitates the use of complex electronics to calculate a column voltage whose value is function of every pixel in the column. It offers an alternative to the display manufacturers to take out the transistor for each pixel for AMLCDs off the display glass and implement the electronics in a less expensive conventional way. The display glass in this way becomes similar to any passive display with more responsive liquid crystal material and thinner cells. The manufacturing process is also identical to that of making passive displays.

Passive colour displays are more expensive than monochrome because every colour pixel must have three colour subpixels with a red, green, and a blue filter. The advantage of passive displays over AMLCDs is that they do not need thin-film transistor switches at every subpixel. This reduces investment in manufacturing equipment for passive LCDs by a factor of seven as compared with that for AMLCDs. For battery powered applications, a display's power consumption is an issue. For laptop monochrome displays, typical luminance power values are 65 cd/m^2 at 2W. Some manufacturers run their LCD displays in reflective mode, doing away with the back light. However, as AMLCDs become more affordable in next 2-to-3 years, they will take away the laptop notebook market of passive displays.

2.4 RASTER CO-ORDINATE SYSTEM

The raster display system consists of three main components, the frame buffer, the display controller and the display monitor. The frame buffer is simply a block of digital memory for storing the image as a matrix of the values of the intensity at different points on the screen. The colour graphics monitor adapter for the IBM Personal Computer provides a memory of 16 kilobytes for this purpose. The display controller is the interface that passes the contents of the frame buffer to the monitor. This must be done at least 30 times per second to avoid flicker and maintain a steady image on the screen. A monitor is just like that for a home television receiver without the tuner. It can be either monochrome or colour. The basic structure of a raster display system is shown in Fig. 2.3.

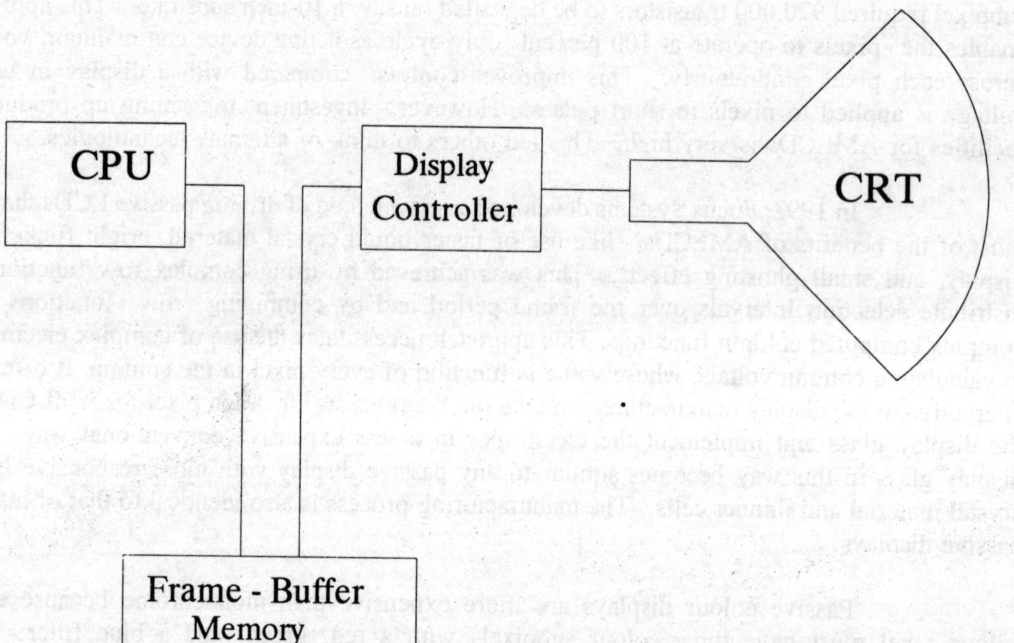

Figure 2.3 A Raster Display System

The image is stored inside the frame buffer as a pattern of binary numbers. Each of these represents a rectangular array of picture elements, called pixels. In the black-and-white high resolution mode, the IBM Personal Computer supports 640 pixels in the horizontal direction and 200 pixels in the vertical direction. Therefore, as shown in figure 2.4, we can visualize the screen of the display monitor as a rectangular grid of 640 vertical and 200 horizontal lines for a CGA card. The points at the intersection of these lines on the grid denote the location of the pixels. A small rectangle at any of these points can represent a picture element. If a particular pixel is to be lighted then the number 1 is stored in the buffer for that point, otherwise zero is stored. In this way, we get a binary digit indicating the status of each pixel along a scan line. So, with the storage requirement of one binary digit for each pixel, we need a total buffer memory of 640×200 bits (or 16000 bytes) to represent a picture on the screen. This large requirement of memory could not have been met economically until quite recently and is possible only due to the sharp decline in the price of memory chips. For a VGA card supporting 256 colours, the memory requirement is $640 \times 480 \times 8$ bits.

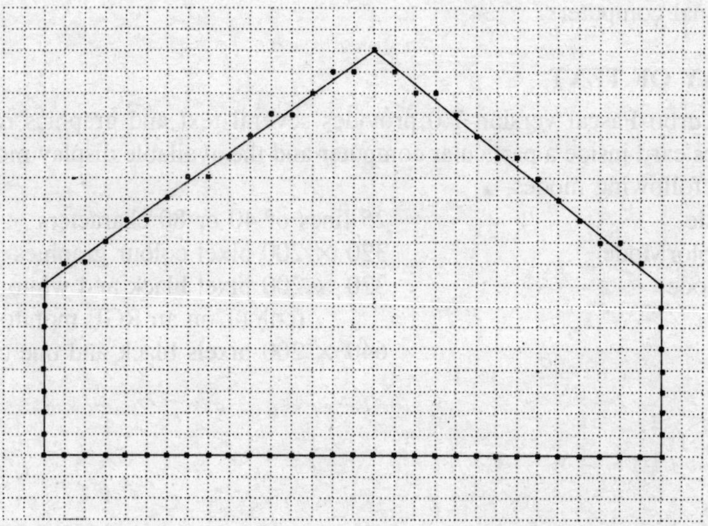

Figure 2.4 Displaying a House with Raster Scan

The outline of a house in raster scan display is shown in figure 2.4. It may be noted that the lines are replaced by a series of rectangular dots. This will not be quite noticeable if the dots are sufficiently close to each other. Thus, increasing the number of pixels in each direction will improve the quality of the picture at the cost of increasing the memory requirement.

In the colour (or medium resolution) mode, the IBM Personal Computer allows the display of three colours anytime. Therefore, we must store a two-bit number for each pixel, corresponding to the three colours and the "off" or unlighted option. For a CGA card, since the buffer memory is fixed at 16000 bytes, the resolution is reduced to 320 × 200 pixels.

2.5 DISPLAY OF LINE ON RASTER/RANDOM SCAN

A basic problem with raster images arises due to the use of a discrete array of samples to represent a picture. As a result, although lines that are horizontal or vertical look all right, others have a pronounced jagged appearance. This is commonly called "rastering" or "stair casing." It is caused by the fact that each lighted pixel appears on the screen as a small rectangle with horizontal and vertical sides, instead of a mathematical point at the intersection of the grid lines only. A typical display of such lines, on a screen with a raster scan, is shown in figure 2.5. It will be seen that the inclined line AB looks ragged because of the "coarseness" of the grid. This is avoided with lines CD and EF because they pass through the intersections of the grid lines.

On the other hand, a straight line on a random scan display system does not suffer from this difficulty. This is due to vector graphics, which causes an almost perfect straight line to be drawn between two points. Due to the higher cost of such displays, they are not currently used with personal computers.

2.6 DISPLAY OF TEXT

Turbo Pascal version 7.0 provides several text and graphics modes compatible with the graphics card inside a particular computer and the available display monitor. The CGA card allows the following modes.

TextMode	25 lines of 40 or 80 characters
GraphColorMode	320 × 200 pixel colour graphics
GraphMode	320 × 200 pixel black and white graphics (colour on an RGB monitor)
HiRes	640 × 200 pixels black and one colour graphics

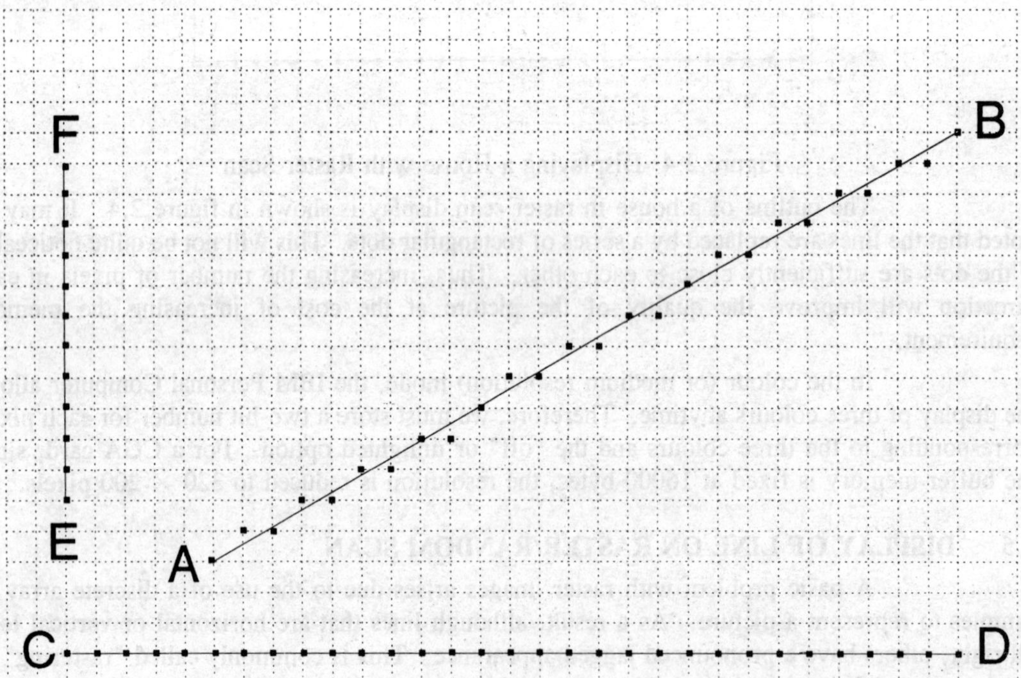

Figure 2.5 Display of Lines with Raster Scan

In the text mode, displaying 25 lines of either 40 or 80 characters is possible. The command for selection of a specific mode is

TextMode (Mode: WORD);

where the following constants are defined:

```
CONST  {CRT modes}
  BW40 = 0;           {40×25 B/W on color graphics adapter}
  BW80 = 2;           {80×25 B/W on color graphics adapter}
  Mono = 7;           {80×25 B/W on monochrome adapter}
  CO40 = 1;           {40×25 color on color graphics adapter}
  CO80 = 3;           {80×25 color on color graphics adapter}
  Font8×8 = 256;      {For EGA/VGA 43 and 50 line}
```

Any other value causes TextMode to give the CO80 mode.

When TextMode is called, the current window is reset to the entire screen, and the current video is stored in LastMode. (Note: These terms will be described in detail in chapter 3.)

2.7 DISPLAY OF NATURAL MODES

With the color graphics adapter, in the high resolution mode the IBM Personal Computer allows 640 pixels in the horizontal direction and 200 pixels in the vertical direction but the pixels can only be black or white. The image produced on the screen can be made natural by adjusting the grey level of each individual pixel. In this section, we will discuss an ordered dither algorithm that can be used for converting a continuous-tone image to a bi-level representation by comparing the image value, I_{xy}, to a position dependent set of thresholds contained in the new dither matrix D^n. The following rules are used for generating this bi-level representation:

(i) An element, d_{ij}, of the matrix, D^n is selected from the C. ordinates of the point (x,y) through the relationships

i = x modulo n

j = y modulo n

(ii) The decision rule for representing a cell (x,y) as white is

If $I_{xy} > d_{ij}$ then pixel value is 1 (or white)

Else pixel value is 0 (or black).

This matrix selection rule causes the dither matrix to be repeated in checkerboard fashion over the entire source image.

For example, consider the case when the input image has grey levels in the range 0 to 3. These can be represented by two binary digits. We may define a dither matrix

$$D^2 = \begin{bmatrix} 0 & 2 \\ 3 & 1 \end{bmatrix}$$

Thus, levels 0, 1, 2 and 3 can be represented by the following 2×2 matrices:

$$\text{level 0: } \begin{bmatrix} 0 & 0 \\ 0 & 0 \end{bmatrix}$$

$$\text{level 1: } \begin{bmatrix} 0 & 0 \\ 0 & 1 \end{bmatrix}$$

$$\text{level 2: } \begin{bmatrix} 0 & 1 \\ 0 & 1 \end{bmatrix}$$

$$\text{level 3: } \begin{bmatrix} 0 & 1 \\ 1 & 1 \end{bmatrix}$$

Consider now the following 4×4 picture matrix, where each pixel has grey level in the range 0 to 3. The corresponding binary image matrix is given below:

$$\begin{bmatrix} 0 & 0 & 1 & 1 \\ 0 & 0 & 1 & 1 \\ 2 & 2 & 3 & 3 \\ 2 & 2 & 3 & 3 \end{bmatrix}$$

$$\begin{bmatrix} 0 & 0 & 0 & 0 & 0 & 0 & 0 & 0 \\ 0 & 0 & 0 & 0 & 0 & 1 & 0 & 1 \\ 0 & 0 & 0 & 0 & 0 & 0 & 0 & 0 \\ 0 & 0 & 0 & 0 & 0 & 1 & 0 & 1 \\ 0 & 1 & 0 & 1 & 0 & 1 & 0 & 1 \\ 0 & 1 & 0 & 1 & 1 & 1 & 1 & 1 \\ 0 & 1 & 0 & 1 & 0 & 1 & 0 & 1 \\ 0 & 1 & 0 & 1 & 1 & 1 & 1 & 1 \end{bmatrix}$$

It will be seen that each grey level is replaced by its 2×2 representation and the resultant matrix is 8×8. In a similar manner it is possible to generate a 4×4 dither matrix for representing grey levels in the range of 0 to 15 from a 2×2 matrix using a recursive procedure. This is described below.

Let us define

$$V^n = \begin{bmatrix} 1 & 1 & \cdots & 1 \\ 1 & 1 & \cdots & 1 \\ \vdots & \vdots & \cdots & \vdots \\ 1 & 1 & \cdots & 1 \end{bmatrix}.$$

Then

$$D^4 = \begin{bmatrix} 4D^{\frac{n}{2}} + d_{00}^2 V^{\frac{n}{2}} & 4D^{\frac{n}{2}} + d_{01}^2 V^{\frac{n}{2}} \\ 4D^{\frac{n}{2}} + d_{10}^2 V^{\frac{n}{2}} & 4D^{\frac{n}{2}} + d_{11}^2 V^{\frac{n}{2}} \end{bmatrix}$$

where dij^2 is the element in the ith row and j^{th} column of the 2×2 matrix D. Using this relationship, we obtain the 4×4 dither matrix

$$D^4 = \begin{bmatrix} 0 & 8 & 2 & 10 \\ 12 & 4 & 14 & 6 \\ 13 & 11 & 1 & 9 \\ 13 & 7 & 13 & 15 \end{bmatrix}$$

2.8 SUMMARY

In this chapter, we have discussed the basic principles for displaying images on a video monitor. The most popular and economical approach with microcomputers is to use raster scan graphics. The quality of the image depends on the fineness of the grid into which the screen is divided in the scan process. This is usually described in terms of pixels (or picture elements). The IBM Colour Graphics Adapter (CGA) card provides a resolution of 640 pixels in the horizontal direction and 200 pixels in the vertical direction in black and white. In the colour mode, the resolution is reduced to 320 pixels in the horizontal direction and 200 in the vertical direction. Better resolution is provided by the Extended Graphics Adapter (EGA) card and the Video Graphics Array (VGA) card. The resolution for various graphics cards is described in chapter 3, along with the graphics procedures and functions available with Turbo Pascal. The result of the limited resolution in raster graphics is that straight lines (if they are not vertical or horizontal), may look ragged with the "staircase" effect. This can be improved by increasing the resolution at the cost of increasing the display buffer memory. The display of text and natural images was also discussed. By having several levels of grey in a picture, images can be made more natural. A method for achieving this by using a dither matrix was presented.

2.9 PROBLEMS

1. Determine the buffer memory requirement for a computer that must display an image in eight possible colours with a resolution of 800x600 pixels.

2. The video graphics adapter (VGA) of the IBM PC provides a resolution of 640x480 pixels in the colour mode. Determine the buffer memory requirement for this card.

3. Given a dither matrix D^3 to represent grey levels between zero and seven, determine the dither matrix D^6 using the method described in section 2.6.

$$D^3 = \begin{bmatrix} 7 & 2 & 6 \\ 3 & 0 & 1 \\ 5 & 4 & 8 \end{bmatrix}$$

2.10 REFERENCES

1. Charles White (editor), "Computer Graphics," Infotech State of the Art Report (Infotech Limited, 1980)
2. J.F. Jarvis, C.N. Judice and W.H. Ninke, "A Summary of Techniques for the Display of Continuous-Tone pictures in Bi-Level Displays," Computer Graphics and Image Processing, vol. 5, 1976, pp.13-14.
3. Werner Kenneth I., "The Flat Pannel's Future," IEEE Spectrum, vol. 30, no. 11, Nov. 1993, pp. 18-26.

CHAPTER 3
GRAPHICS PROGRAMMING IN WINDOWS AND DOS

3.1 INTRODUCTION

The Windows operating system provides a multitasking graphical environment that runs multiple applications simultaneously. Each application displays all output in a rectangular area of the computer screen called a window. If an application decides to write on the screen, it calls a function contained in API (Application Programming Interface) within Windows. Internally Windows decides the function calls and translates it to the hardware commands. If Windows was installed specifying VGA video system, VGA hardware commands are sent out. DOS does disk file access best, therefore, Windows designers used DOS disk file commands in Windows. Windows is also a DOS program so DOS is already running before Windows is run. All the disk support functions are available to Windows as they are available to DOS. A comparison of Windows and DOS programs is given in table 3.1.

Table 3.1- Comparison of Windows and DOS Programs

Feature	Windows	DOS
Resource Sharing	Each application shares the resources of the system through the API.	A DOS program captures all the resources of the system.
Graphical User Interface (GUI)	It has a GUI which is intuitive in nature. Each application is given access to the graphical display through a window.	A DOS application typically has a character oriented user interface.
Standardization	Every program has the same look and feel due to the use of menus, dialog boxes, push buttons, combo boxes, etc.	Programs can be different and a user may take lot of time to get used to their environments.
Input facilities	An application is structured to accept input whenever it is produced by the user.	Input is demanded from the user when needed by the application.
Device Independent Graphics	An application is not allowed to interact directly with hardware. The same program can produce graphics on display as well as printer or any other Windows supported device.	An application interacts directly with the hardware. Therefore, it becomes device dependent.
Memory management	Memory blocks are dynamic, and can pre-load or load on call. They can be fixed, moveable, discardable, or non-discardable.	Memory blocks are static.

The integrated Windows environment provided by C and Pascal compilers from Microsoft, Borland and many other vendors enables a programmer to carry out individual steps in compilation and linking (see figure 3.1) automatically through the use of development tools. Windows programs have separate resource file that contain static data such as menu and bitmaps. Resource data is supplied by a separate compiler called resource compiler.

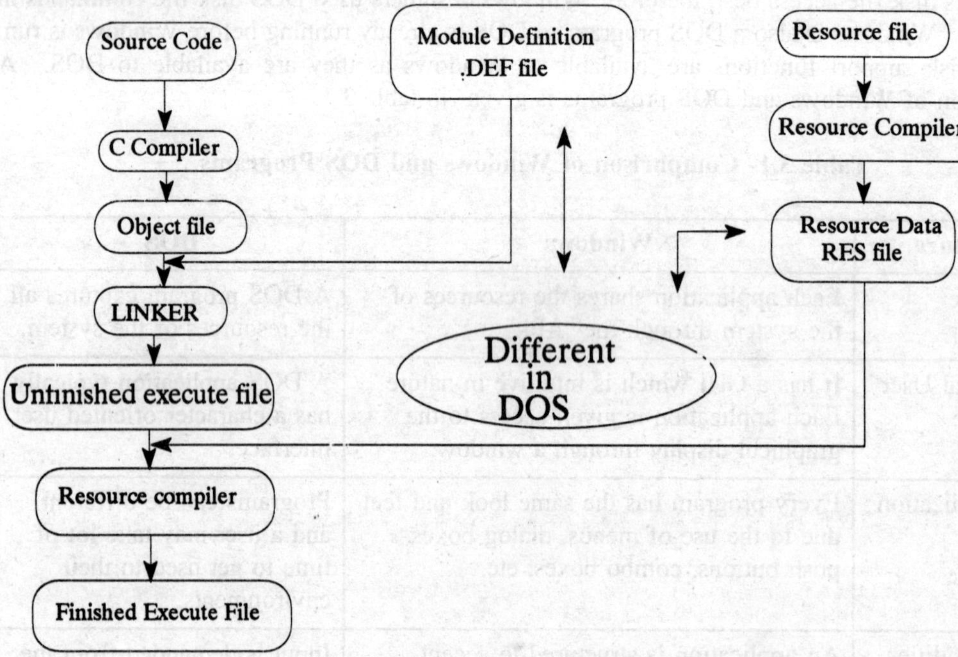

Figure 3.1 Windows program compilation and linking procedure

Section 3.3 in this chapter describes graphics programming under DOS. This section will be useful to those users who still prefer to operate under DOS.

3.2 WINDOWS GRAPHICS PROGRAMMING

Functions from the Windows Graphics Device Interface (GDI) are used for displaying graphics in an application's window. These can be accessed through the *TGdiBase* class hierarchy in *OWL in* Borland *C*.

We briefly review some of the important concepts applicable to programming in Windows. Many uppercase identifiers are used. Several of these identifiers contain a two-letter or three-letter prefix followed by an underscore, e.g., *WM_PAINT, DT_SINGLELINE, CS_VREDRAW, IDC_ARROW* etc. These are simply numeric constants and indicate a general category to which the constant belongs, as indicated in table 3.2. Handles are used quite frequently in Windows. A handle is a 16-bit number that refers to an object. The handles for icon, cursor, and brush are called *HICON, HCURSOR*, and *HBRUSH, respectively*. The actual value of the handle is unimportant to a program, since the Windows module that gives the program the handle knows how to use it to reference the object. One also encounters uppercase identifiers for various types of handles, such as *HANDLE, HWND*, and *HDC* for general handle, handle to a window and handle to a device context, respectively.

Table 3.2 Prefix and category

Prefix	Category
CS	Class style
IDI	ID for an icon
IDC	ID for a cursor
WS	Window style
CW	Create Window
WM	Window message
DT	Draw text

We will use the ObjectWindows application framework for graphics programming. ObjectWindows supports the following classes of Window:

- Windows
  TWindow is the base class for all windows. It represents the functionality of all windows e.g. dialog boxes, controls, Multiple Document Interface (*MDI*) windows and so on.
- Frame windows
  TFrameWindow is derived from *Window* class. Frame windows manage application-wide tasks,like menus and tool bar,and support a client window which can be specialized to do a single task. Changes (i.e. adding tool or status bars) introduced in a frame window do not affect client windows.

- *MDI* windows
  MDI manages multiple documents or windows in a single application.
- Decorated windows
  Several classes, such as *TLayoutWindow* and *TLayoutMetrics* provide support for decoration controls like tool bars, status bars, and message bars.
- Dialog Box Classes
  TDialog is a derived class of *TWindow*. It is used to create dialog boxes that handle a variety of user interactions, such as choosing files, fonts, colors, and printing options as well as searching and replacing text, inputting text, and aborting printing jobs.
- Control Classes
  TControl is a class derived from *TWindow* for supporting behaviour common to all controls. *ObjectWindows* supports standard controls from Windows, such as widgets, gadgets and decorations.
- Graphics Classes
  Windows supports a graphics library called Graphics Device Interface (GDI). *ObjectWindows* encapsulates GDI to make it easier to use device context (DC) classes (*TDC*) and GDI objects (*TGDIObject*).
- Printing classes
  TPrinter and *TPrintout* encapsulate the communications with printer devices and the task of printing a document respectively.
- Module and Application Classes
  TApplication is responsible for initializing the windows and directing the messages received from Windows to the proper window. Application objects are used for deriving an application object from the *TApplication* class, creating an application object, overriding base class function to customize the application behavior, using Borland custom control and Microsoft control 3D libraries. To create and use *TApplication* object one must include the correct header files, create an application object, and call the application's call function. The following example shows a small program representing an application of *ObjectWindows*.

Program 3.1

```
// p3_1.cpp - An application creating a main window with the caption "trial". It can
//resize, move, minmize, maximize, and close the generated window.

#include <owl\applicat.h>  // This header file has definition of Tapplication which is
                           //derived from TModule and includes owl\module.h.

int OwlMain(int /*argc*/, char* /*argv*/ [])

        return    TApplication("trial").Run();
```

It is necessary to derive a new class from *TApplication* to introduce more functionality in the application. Initializing an *ObjectWindows* application requires the following steps:

i. Constructing the application object
Member functions are *InitApplication, InitInstance*, and *InitMainWindow*. One can override any of these members to customize initialization of one's application. The constructor for the *TrialApp* class derived from *TApplication* shown in the following example takes application name as only argument. The default value is zero indicating no name. The application name is referenced by a char far* member of the *TModule* base class called Name.

Program 3.2

```
// p3_2.cpp -  Creates and shows a window entitled, " Trial".

#include  <owl\applicat.h>

class TrialApp: public Tapplication
{
public:
TrialApp(const char far* name = 0): TApplication(name) {}
};

int
OwlMain(int /*argc*/, char* /*argv*/ [])
{
        return TrialApp("trial").Run();
}
```

ii. Initializing the application
There are three initialization functions - *InitApplication* initializes the first instance of the application; *InitInstance* initializes the each instance of the application; and *InitMainWindow* initializes the application's main window.

iii. Initializing each new instance
One can run multiple instances (copies) of an application simultaneously.

iv. Initializing the main window
Tapplication::InitMainWindow creates a frame window with the same name as the application object. This window is not very useful as it can't receive or process any user input. It is therefore essential to override *InitMainWindow* to create a window object that does process user input. The following example creates a *TFrameWindow* object and makes it the main window:

Program 3.3

```
// p3_3.cpp - Creates and shows a maximized window entitled, "First Main
// Window".
#include <owl\applicat.h>
#include <owl\framewin.h>

class TrialApp: public TApplication
{
public:
   TrialApp(char far *name): TApplication() {}
   void InitMainWindow();
};
// override InitMainWindow
void TrialApp::InitMainWindow()
{
//SetMainWindow takes a pointer to the TframeWindow object and returns a
//pointer to the old main window. The return value is zero for a new application
//that has not set a main window as yet.
SetMainWindow(new TFrameWindow(0, "First Main Window"));
// value of nCmdShow controls the parameters of the window, e.g. when set to
//SW_SHOWMAXIMIZED will show a maximized window whenever you run
//this application.
nCmdShow = SW_SHOWMAXIMIZED;
}
int OwlMain(int /*argc*/, char* /*argv*/ [])
{
        return TrialApp("trial").Run();
//The application name given in the TApplication constructor is used only if you
//do not provide a main window. As this program has used SetMainWindow
//function -- the caption bar is titled "First Main Window" and not "trial".
}
```

- Doc/View Classes
  In Doc/View model data is contained in and accessed through a document object and displayed and manipulated through a view object. It comprises of *TDocManager, TDocument* and *TView* classes.

- Miscellaneous Classes
  ObjectWindows miscellaneous classes include menus and clipboard classes.

Once an application is initialized, the application object's *MessageLoop* starts running. All incoming messages from Windows are processed by the *MessageLoop*. One can override the default message handling functions and introduce additional message processing capability in the application. *TAppliaction* includes functions, such as *MessageLoop*, *IdleAction*, *PreProcessMenu,* and *ProcessAppMsg* which provide message handling functionality for any *ObjectWindows* application. *TAppliaction* also includes functions that enable one to load the Borland Custom Control Library (*BWCC.DLL* for 16- and 32- bit applications) and Microsoft 3-D Control Library (*CTL3DV2.DLL* and *CTL3D32.DLL* for16- and 32- bit applications, respectively. Function *TApplication::EnableBWCC* is used to open and close the Borland Custom Control Library. When one passes *True* to *EnableBWCC*, the function loads the *DLL* if it is not already loaded. Similarly, if one passes *False* to *EnableBWCC* it unloads the *DLL*. *EnableCTL3D* function works in the same way as *EnableBWCC* for loading and unloading Microsoft 3-D Control Library.

Response tables are used to handle all events in an ObjectWindows application. These tables are used in the following way:

- Define the response table
  ObjectWindows provides DEFINE_RESPONSE_TABLEX macro to help a user to define response tables.

```
DEFINE_RESPONSE_TABLE1( TrialFrame, TframeWindow)

        EV_WM_LBUTTONDOWN,
        EV_WM_LBUTTONUP,
        EV_WM_MOUSEMOVE,
        EV_WM_RBUTTONDOWN,

END_RESPONSE_TABLE;
```

- Define the response table entries
  When a window or control receives a message, it checks the response table to see if there is an entry for that message. If an entry is found, it is passed to the corresponding function else the message is passed to its parent. If parent is the main window, message is passed to the application object. If application object also does not have a response entry , the message is processed by the ObjectWindows default processing mechanism.

- Declare and define the response member functions
  ObjectWindows provides a large number of macros, called *command message macros,* that let a user assign command messages to any function. The different types of command message macros and the corresponding function are given Table 3.3.

Table 3.3 Command Message Macros

Macro	Description
EV_COMMAND (CMD, UserName)	Calls function *UserName* when the CMD message is received.
EV_COMMAND_AND-ID (CMD, UserName)	Calls function *UserName* when the CMD message is received. Passes the command's ID(WPARAM parameter) to *UserName*.
EV_COMMAND_ENABLE(CMD, UserName)	Used to automatically enable and disable command controls such as menu items, tool bar buttons and so on.
EV_MESSAGE(MSG, UserName)	Calls *UserName* when the user- defined message MSG is received, MSG is passed to *UserName* without modification.
EV_REGISTERED(MSG, UserName)	Calls *UserName* when the registered message MSG is received. MSG is passed to *UserName* without modifications.

Program 3.4

It illustrates the use of a response table to capture events such as pressing of the left and right buttons of the mouse. A message box with the caption "Message Sent" and message "Left mouse button pressed" appears when the left button of the mouse is pressed. Similar message will appear when the right button of the mouse is pressed. The program also shows how to override the CanClose member function of *TWindow* to ensure that everything has been cleaned up before saving.

```
//------------------------------------------------------------------------
// p3_4.cpp
//------------------------------------------------------------------------
#include <owl/framewin.h>
#include <owl/owlpch.h>
#include <owl/applicat.h>
class TrialWindow : public TWindow
{
  public:
    TrialWindow(TWindow* parent = 0);
  protected:
    // Override member function of TWindow - provide user an opportunity to ensure that
    // everything has been cleaned up before saving.
    bool CanClose();
```

```
    // Message response functions
    void EvLButtonDown(uint, TPoint&);
    void EvRButtonDown(uint, TPoint&);
  DECLARE_RESPONSE_TABLE(TrialWindow);
//must be the last macro in its class
};
DEFINE_RESPONSE_TABLE1(TrialWindow, TWindow)
  EV_WM_LBUTTONDOWN,
  EV_WM_RBUTTONDOWN,
END_RESPONSE_TABLE;
TrialWindow::TrialWindow(TWindow* parent)
{
  Init(parent, 0, 0);
}
bool TrialWindow::CanClose()
{
// A message box is popped to get user feedback
        switch(MessageBox("Do you want to save?", "Not Implemented",
                                        MB_YESNOCANCEL | MB_ICONQUESTION))

 // one can add desired functionality here like saving data on a file.

 return true;
 }
void TrialWindow::EvLButtonDown(uint, TPoint&)
{// whenever one presses left button of the mouse, a message box with caption "Message Sent"
// and message "Left mouse button pressed" appears. Attribute MB_OK will put an "OK" button.
  MessageBox(" Left mouse button pressed", "Message Sent", MB_OK);
}
void TrialWindow::EvRButtonDown(uint, TPoint&)
{
  MessageBox(" Right mouse button pressed", "Message Dispatched", MB_OK);
}
class TrialApp : public TApplication
{
 public:
  TrialApp() : TApplication() {}
   void InitMainWindow()
   {
     SetMainWindow(new TFrameWindow(0, " Trial program", new TrialWindow));
   }
```

```
int OwlMain(int /*argc*/, char* /*argv*/ [])
{
 return TrialApp().Run();
}
```

3.2.1 Graphics Device Interface

It refers to the graphics output function of Windows and isolates a Windows program from the physical output device such as display or printer. In addition to producing output on the physical devices it also supports output on two pseudo devices bitmaps and metafiles. Bitmaps refer to a rectangular array of pixels and metafiles. Most of the PC output devices like video display adapters, dot-matrix printers, and laser printers are raster devices and represent images as a pattern of dots, i.e., bitmaps. The important *GDI* functions can be grouped in following categories:

- Vector drawing functions to draw graphical objects such as lines, circles and rectangles;
- bitmap manipulation functions;
- text output functions; and
- palette management functions to display colors supported by a display adapter.

Palette management in systems with super VGA and other enhanced graphics adapters, supporting more than 16 colors, is useful.

3.2.2 Device Context (DC)

DC can be considered as a generalized model of a graphics output device and is key to the *GDI*'s support for device independent graphics in Windows. To perforn any sort of graphical operation in Windows, one needs a DC for the window or the area one wants to work with. DC, in fact, is a data structure which includes drawing objects , such as brush, pen and bitmap and graphics attributes, such as background color, text color, fill style, and fonts which control the appearance of the graphics and text. To generate graphics output using DC, one must call an appropriate *GDI* graphics function to access the DC, use this DC to draw and then release the DC. Windows permits only upto 5 DCs to be open at any given time for the entire Windows system.

The handle to the DC (*HDC*) is a protected member variable of the *TDC* class. TDC is the root class for encapasulation of *ObjectWindows GDI* device contexts and is used for drawing in a variety of devices and screen areas, including the *TClientDC* for drawing in the client area of a window, *TmemoryDC* for drawing on to an in-memory bitmap, and *TPrintDC* for output to a printer. All GDI functions are member functions of the *TDC* class. The names of the member functions are the same as the GDI functions but the member functions do not need *HDC* as an argument. Table 3.2 gives an example below of the call pattern of functions to draw a line from **(xleft, ytop)** to **(xright, ybottom)** using *GDI* functions, *OWL* classes and *TDC* Class in *OWL* 2.0 with *TPoint* objects as argument, respectively.

3.2.3 Contents of a DC

A DC has the following graphics objects:

- A pen which controls the appearance of lines and borders of rectangles, ellipses, and polygons. Drawing mode specifies how to combine pen's color with the color that already exists on the drawing surface.
- A brush which defines a fill pattern.
- Font specifies the shape and size of textual output.
- Palette is an array of colors. Palette facilitates to pick the current selection of available colors out of the millions of colors that can be shown on the display.
- Bitmap is used to draw images.
- Region is defined by a combination of rectangles, ellipses and polygons used for drawing or for clipping.

Table 3.4 Call Pattern of Functions

GDI Functions	**ObjectWindows Library (OWL) Classes**	**TDC class with TPoint objects (represents a point in the x-y plane) as arguments**

HDC hdc;
// Assume that handle to DC is // properly set up
	TclientDC dc(HWindow);
	// Assume that TclientDC
	// is a member of the //
	TWindow class
		TclientDC dc(HWindow);
		TPoint start, end;
		// Assume that the
		//TPoint objects are
		//initialized

MoveTo(hdc, xleft, ytop); **LineTo(hdc, xright, ybottom);**	**dc.MoveTo(xleft, ytop);** **dc.LineTo(xright,ybottom);**	**dc.MoveTo(start);** **dc.LineTo(end);**

3.2.4 Acquiring a DC

In order to draw on a graphics output device, it is necessory to first obtain a handle to a DC. Windows provides several methods for acquiring a DC handle. A DC can be acquired in response to the *WM_PAINT* message because this event causes redrawing of an application's window. Using *OWL* classes and deriving application's main window from the TWindow class, one can generate all graphics output in a member function named Paint. The prototype of the Paint function is

```
void Paint(  TDC&    dc,      //  Device context for the display
             Bool    erase,   //  TRUE = erase the background
             Trect&  rect);   //  Rectangle to be redrawn - defines area
```

The Paint function is called by OWL whenever Windows sends a message to the window. To avoid waiting for the *WM_PAINT* message to update the window, one can either call the *updateWindow* function or create an instance of the *TClientDC* class to get a *DC*. When the *TClientDC* is destroyed, the DC is automatically released.

Changes made the attributes from the handle to a DC are lost when the DC is released. One may also create a private DC for a window so that changes carried out in the attributes of the DC persist until the window is destroyed. The following example shows the procedure to create a persistent DC:

- a window class TrialWindow is derived from the OWL class *TWindow*
- override the *GetWindowClass* function
- add the CS_OWNDC flag to the class style as given below:

```
//      TrialWindow:            public TWindow
void TrialWindow :: GetWindowClass(WNDCLASS&  wclass);
{
        TWindow::GetWindowClass(wclass);
        wclass.style    |= CS_OWNDC;
}
```

Now each window created using the window class will have its own private DC that exists until the window is destroyed. While using the *CS_OWNDC* style, the DC attributes need initialization only once and continue to be valid until they are changed. The *CS_OWNDC* style affects only the DC retrieved from *GetDC* and BeginPaint and not the DC obtained from other functions, such as *GetWindowDC*. One needs 800 bytes of storage for the DC for each window with the *CS_OWNDC* style. Thus, the window associated with each instance of TrialWindow class has its own private DC. One must still release the DC before exiting from the window function. *SaveDC* and *RestoreDC* functions let a user save the current DC, make temporary changes in the attributes and revert back to the original attributes.

3.2.5 Graphics output using a DC

A typical procedure to generate graphics output using DC is given below:

- Create the TDC object. For example, to draw in the client area of the window, one needs to create a *TClientDC* object.
- Define the graphics attributes.
- Invoke appropriate GDI drawing functions.
- If the new operator is used to create the *TDC* object, it must be destroyed by invoking the delete operator.

DC can also be used to determine the capabilities of a device, such as number of color planes in a graphics display by calling the GetDeviceCaps function.

Program 3.5

This program makes it possible to create a freehand line drawing while keeping the left button of the mouse pressed. One can release the left button and move the mouse to a new position. Pressing the left button would let one draw freehand from the new position of the mouse. Pressing the right button of the mouse clears the entire client area of the window.

```
//---------------------------------------------------------------------------------------------
// p3_5.cpp: draws freehand line drawing
//---------------------------------------------------------------------------------------------
#include <owl/owlpch.h>
#include <owl/applicat.h>
#include <owl/framewin.h>
#include <owl/dc.h>
// Definition of the TrialWindow class -- data member CommonDC, a pointer to the TClientDC
// object, is not destroyed automatically when TrialWindow object is destroyed. It is necessory
// to add a destructor to TrialWindow to ensure proper cleanup.
class TrialWindow : public TWindow
{
 public:
   TrialWindow(TWindow* parent = 0);
  ~ TrialWindow()  // Delete CommonDC
   {
    delete CommonDC;
   }
 protected:
       // provides a valid device context across functions EvLButtonDown,
       // EvMouseMove, and EvLButtonUp.
       TDC* CommonDC;
   // Override member function of TWindow
   bool CanClose();
   // Message response functions
       void EvLButtonDown(uint, TPoint&);
       void EvRButtonDown(uint, TPoint&);
       void EvMouseMove(uint, TPoint&);
       void EvLButtonUp(uint, TPoint&);
  DECLARE_RESPONSE_TABLE( TrialWindow);
};
DEFINE_RESPONSE_TABLE1( TrialWindow, TWindow)
  EV_WM_LBUTTONDOWN,
  EV_WM_RBUTTONDOWN,
  EV_WM_MOUSEMOVE,
  EV_WM_LBUTTONUP,
END_RESPONSE_TABLE;
 TrialWindow:: TrialWindow(TWindow* parent)
{
  Init(parent, 0, 0);    // Initialize TrialWindow base class
```

```
  CommonDC = 0;       //Initialize CommonDC-- a pointer to the TClientDC--to zero.
}
bool  TrialWindow::CanClose()
{
  return MessageBox("Do you want to save?", " Not Implemented",
                    MB_YESNO | MB_ICONQUESTION) == IDNO;
}
void  TrialWindow::EvLButtonDown(uint, TPoint& point)
{
  if (!CommonDC)
  {
        SetCapture();
        CommonDC = new TClientDC(*this);
        CommonDC->MoveTo(point);
  }
}
void  TrialWindow::EvRButtonDown(uint, TPoint&)
{
  Invalidate();                   // clears the entire client area of the window
}
void  TrialWindow::EvMouseMove(uint, TPoint& point)
{
  if (CommonDC)
        CommonDC->LineTo(point);
}
void  TrialWindow::EvLButtonUp(uint, TPoint&)
{
  if ( CommonDC)
  {
   ReleaseCapture();
        delete CommonDC;
        CommonDC = 0;
  }
}
class TDrawApp : public Tapplication
{
 public:
   TDrawApp() : TApplication() {}
   void InitMainWindow()
   {
            SetMainWindow(new TFrameWindow(0, "Freehand Draw", new TrialWindow));
   }
```

```
};
int  OwlMain(int /*argc*/, char* /*argv*/ [])
{
  return TDrawApp().Run();
}
```

3.2.6 GDI Coordinate System

The GDI supports two coordinate systems referred to as physical(or device) and logical coordinates. The physical coordinate system is fixed for a device, e.g., for a window on the screen the origin is at the upper left corner of a window's client area, the positive x-axis extends to the right, and the positve y-axis extends downwards. In all device coordinate systems, units are in terms of pixels. Windows supports several logical coordinates systems and maps each one of them to the physical systems before displaying any graphics output.

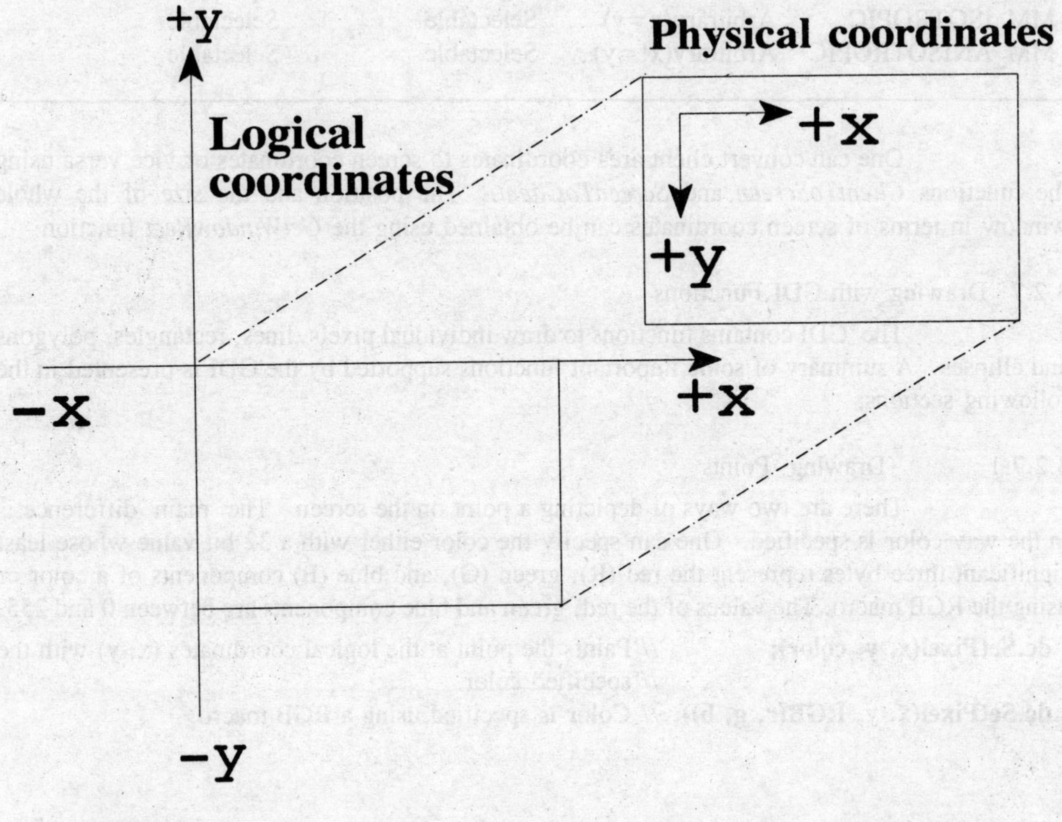

Figure 3.2 Mapping of logical coordinate system to physical coordinate system

Windows supports eight mapping mode identifiers specifying logical units as 0.001 inch, 0.01 inch, 0.01 millimeter, or 0.1 millimeter and the positive y-axis extending downward or upwards. One can use the *SetMapMode* function to set a mapping mode, such as *MM_ANISOTROPIC* so that logical units along x- and y- axes can be set independently, or MM_TEXT in which logical coordinate is the same as the physical one. The *GetMapMode* function is available to determine the current mapping mode. The mapping modes are listed in table 3.5.

Table 3.5 Mapping Modes

Mapping Mode	Logical Unit	X-axis	Y-axis
MM_TEXT	Pixel	Right	Down
MM_LOMETRIC	0.1 mm	Right	Up
MM_HIMETRIC	0.01 mm	Right	Up
MM_LOENGLISH	0.01 in.	Right	Up
MM_HIENGLISH	0.001 in.	Right	Up
MM_TWIPS	1/1440 in.	Right	Up
MM_ISOTROPIC	Arbitrary(x=y)	Selectable	Selectable
MM_ANISOTROPIC	Arbitrary(x!=y)	Selectable	Selectable

One can convert client area coordinates to screen coordinates or vice versa using the functions *ClientToScreen* and *ScreenToClient*. The position and the size of the whole window in terms of screen coordinates can be obtained using the *GetWindowRect* function

3.2.7 Drawing with GDI Functions

The GDI contains functions to draw individual pixels, lines, rectangles, polygons and ellipses. A summary of some important functions supported by the GDI is presented in the following sections.

3.2.7.1 Drawing Points

There are two ways of depicting a point on the screen. The main difference is in the way color is specified. One can specify the color either with a 32 bit value whose least significant three bytes represent the red (R), green (G), and blue (B) components of a color or using the RGB macro. The values of the red, green and blue components are between 0 and 255.

```
dc.SetPixel(x, y, color);          // Paints the point at the logical coordinates (x, y) with the
                                   // specified color.
dc.SetPixel(x, y, RGB(r, g, b));   // Color is specified using a RGB macro.
```

3.2.7.2 Drawing Lines

The following functions are used for drawing a line from the point (x1, y1) to the point (x2, y2):

```
dc.MoveTo(x1, y1);     // moves the pen to the point (x1, y1) without drawing
dc.LineTo(x2, y2);     // draws a line from current position to point (x2, y2)
```

The style, width and color of the line are determined by the selection of the pen. This can be done in two ways: i) calling the *SelectObject* function to select a predefined pen into the device context or ii) calling *CreatePen* to create a new pen with the desired properties. The pen must be selected into the DC and after use returned by calling *RestorePen* function.

A Polyline function is included in GDI to draw multple lines between a given number of points. For example, one needs to write following statements to connect the points (x1, y1), (x2, y2), (x3, y3) and (x4, y4) with the line segments:

```
POINT points[4] ={TPoint(x1, y1), TPoint(x2, y2), TPoint(x3, y3), TPoint(x4, y4)};
dc.Polyline(points, 4);
```

To draw a closed figure using Polyline function, one has to ensure that the coordinates of the first and the last point in the array are the same.

3.2.7.3 Drawing Arcs

The Arc function draws a curved line which is part of an ellipse and has two forms. The first form requires the coordinates of four points as its arguments. The first two define the upper left and the lower right corners of the bounding box, while the third and the fourth give the start and the end point of the arc. A prototype of the function is given below:

```
BOOL Arc(
    Short x1, Short y1,
    Short x2, Short y2,
    Short xStart, Short yStart,
    Short xEnd, Short yEnd;
```

The second form of the Arc function uses TRect and TPoint as its arguments:

```
BOOL Arc(
    Const Trect& r,        // defines upper left and lower right corners of the bounding
                           // rectangle
    Const TPoint& start,
    Const TPoint& end);
```

3.2.7.4 Drawing Closed Figures

The member functions included in the *TDC* class to draw closed figures are given in Table 3.6.

Table 3.6 Functions to Draw Closed Figures

Function	Figure
Rectangle(int xleft, int ytop, int xright, int ybottom);	Draws a rectangle whose upper left corner is **(xleft, ytop)** and lower right corner is **(xright, ybottom)**.
RoundRect(int xleft, int ytop, int xright, int ybottom, int x_ellipse, int y_ellipse);	Draws a rectangle with rounded corner. Each corner is rounded by a small ellipse whose width and height are **x_ellipse and y_ellipse**.
Ellipse(int xleft, int ytop, int xright, int ybottom);	Draws an ellipse bounded by rectangle whose opposite corners are given by two points.
Pie(int xleft, int ytop, int xright, int ybottom, int xbegin, int ybegin, int xend, int yend);	Draws a pie shaped wedge. The bounding rectangle is defined by the point **(xleft, ytop)** and point **(xright, ybottom)**. The two straight edges of the pie are defined by the line joining the center of the ellipse and the points **(xbegin, ybegin)**, and **(xend, yend)**.
Chord(int xleft, int ytop, int xright, int ybottom, int xbegin, int ybegin, int xend, int yend);	Draws a segment of ellipse similar to the Pie but unlike Pie, joins the end points by a straight line.
Polygon(TPoint* pt, int numpt);	Draws a polygon by joining the points in the array **pt** by straight lines. The first and last points in the array **pt** are joined by a line segment to give a closed figure.

GDI provides a number of function to manipulate rectangles. OWL provides the RECT structure of Windows API, which is defined in the header file <windows.h) as follows:

```
typedef     struct  tagRECT
{
        int     left;   //      upper left corner of the rectangle
        int     top;
        int     right;  //      lower left corner of the rectangle
        int     bottom;
}       RECT;
```

The functions included in GDI that manipulate rectangles are

CopyRect Copyrect(&dest_rect, &src_rect); copy one rectangle structure to another

EqualRect EqualRect(&rect1, &rect2); returns TRUE if two rectangle structures are

		equal
Fill Rect	dc.FillRect(rect, hbrush);	fills the rectangle with the specified brush
FrameRect	dc.FrameRect(rect, brush);	uses the brush to draw a rectangular frame
InvertRect	dc.InvertRect(rect);	inverts all the pixels in the rectangles
OffsetRect	OffsetRect(&rect, x, y);	move a rectangle a number of units along the x- and y-axes
InflateRect	InflateRect(dx,dy);	increase or decrease the size of a rectangle
SetRect	SetRect(&rect, left, right, top, bottom);	sets the fields of a RECT structure
IntersectRect	IntersectRect(&destrect, &srcrect1, &srcrect2);	Obtains the intersection of two rectangles,
UnionRect	Un ionRect(&result_rect, &rect1, &rect2);	Sets the fields of a RECT structure to be union of two other rectangles
SetRectEmpty	SetRectEmpty(&rect);	Sets the fields of a RECT structure to empty
PtInRect	PtInRect(&rect, point);	Returns TRUE if a point is in a rectangle

3.2.7.5 Creating and Painting Regions

A region is a description of an area of the display that is a combination of rectangles, polygons, and ellipses. Regions are GDI objects like pens brushes and bitmaps. Regions are also useful in clipping by selecting the region in the device context. When one creates a region, Windows returns a handle to the region of type HRGN. Two ways of creating rectangular regions are given below:

hRgn = CreateRectRgn (xleft, ytop, xright, ybottom);

or

hRgn = CreateRectRgnIndirect(&rect);

One can use the *TRegion* class to define a region in the device context and perform a number of operations, such as painting, filling, inverting and so on. Table 3.7 describes the GDI functions available for manipulating regions.

Table 3.7 GDI functions that manipulate regions

FUNCTION	DESCRIPTION
CreateRectRgn (xleft, ytop, xright, ybottom);	Creates a rectangular region using specified coordinates for the opposite corners of the rectangle.
CreateRectRgnIndirect (&rect);	Creates a rectangular region using the fields of a *RECT* structure.
CreateRoundRectRgn	Creates a rectangular region wih rounded corners - similar to *RoundRect* function.

CreateEllipticRgn (xleft, ytop, xright, ybottom);	Creates an elliptic region.
CreateEllipticRgnIndirect (& rect)	Creates an elliptic region using the fields in a RECT structure
CreatePolygonRgn (points, npoints, fill_mode);	Creates a polygon region. Parameter fill mode is *ALTERNATE* to *WINDING*
CreatePolyPolygonRgn	Creates a region out of multiple polygons.
CombineRgn(hresult_rgn, hrgn1, hrgn2, combine_flag);	Combines two regions into one according to a speicifed combining mode.
EqualRgn (hrgn1, hrgn2);	Returns *TRUE* if two regions are equal.
dc.FillRgn (rgn, brush);	It belongs to the *TDC* class that fills a region with the specified brush.
FrameRgn (rgn, brush, pt); //pt is a TPoint with width and height of the frame	It belongs to the *TDC* class and draws a frame around a region with the specified brush.
rgn.GetRgnBox (rect);	It belongs to the *TRegion* class that returns the bounding box of the region.
InvalidateRgn (hrgn, erase_flag);	It belongs to the *TWindow* class that marks the specified region for repainting.
dc.InvertRgn (rgn);	A member function of the TDC class that inverts the pixels in a region.
OffsetRgn (hrgn, x, y);	Moves a region by a specified x-and y-offset
dc.PaintRgn (rgn);	Fills the region with the current brush:
PtInRegion(hrgn, x, y);	Returns *TRUE* if the specified point is in the given region.
RectInRegion(hrgn, & rectangle);	Returns *TRUE* if any part of the specified rectangle is in the region.
rgn.SetRectRgn (rect);	It belongs to the *TRegion* class that changes the region to a rectangular shape specified by the TRect argument.
ValidateRgn (hrgn);	A member function of the *TWindow* class that removes the region from the area to be repained:

3.2.8 Drawing Mode

GDI consists of number of line modes which can be used for combining the pen color with the existing color and draw lines and filled figures. The mode name starts with R2_ prefix. The default mode is R2_COPYPEN which overwrites whatever exists on the drawing surface. The drawing mode is also referred to as raster operation (ROP).

The following statement can be used to set a new drawing mode and to save the previous mode:

```
int old_ROP = dc.setROP2 (R2_BLACK);
```

Table 3.8 lists the drawing modes supported in GDI.

Table 3.8 Drawing modes in Windows GDI

Mode Name	Boolean Operation	Comments
R2_BLACK	all bits zero	Draws in black irrespective of pen color and existing color
R2_COPYPEN	pen	Draws with the pen color
R2_MASKNOTPEN	(NOT pen) AND dest	Inverts the bits in the pen color and performs a bitwise-*AND* with existing color
R2_MASKPEN	pen AND dest	Performs bitwise-*AND* of pen color and exisitng color
R2_MASKPENNOT	pen AND (NOT dest)	Inverts existing color and does bitwise-*AND* with pen color
R2_MERGENOTPEN	(NOT pen) OR dest	Inverts pen color and does bitwise-*OR* with existing color
R2_MERGEPEN	pen OR dest	Performs bitwise-*OR* of pen color and existing color
R2_MERGEPENNOT	pen OR (NOT dest)	Inverts existing color and does bitwise-*OR* with pen color
R2_NOP	dest	Leaves existing color unchanged (hence the name *NOP* for "no operation")
R2_NOT	NOT dest	Inverts existing color
R2_NOTCOPYPEN	NOT pen	Draws with inverted pen color

R2_NOTMASKPEN	NOT (pen AND dest)	Performs bitwise-*AND* of pen and existing color and inverts the result
R2_NOTMERGEPEN	NOT (pen OR dest)	Does bitwise-*OR* of pen and existing color and inverts the result
R2_NOTXORPEN	NOT (pen XOR dest)	Performs bitwise exclusive-*OR* of pen and existing color and inverts the result
R2_WHITE	all bits 1	Draws in white color
R2_XORPEN	pen XOR dest	Does bitwise exclusive-*OR* of pen color and existing color

3.2.9 Colors, Palettes and Bitmaps

3.2.9.1 Colors

Windows *API* defines a 32- bit integer called *COLORREF*. The low order bytes contain the intensities of the red, green and blue colors (see figure 3.3) and the most significant byte contains the type which indicates whether to interpret the value as a color or a palette entry.

31 — 24	23 — 16	15 — 8	7 — 0
Type	Blue(B)	Green(G)	Red(R)

Figure 3.3: Contents of 32-bit *COLORREF* value. Parameter **'Type'** has three values: 0,1 and 2 representing explicit RGB color, logical palette index and RGB from pallete respectively.

The *RGB* macro represents the *RGB* color, e.g. RGB(0, 0, 255) denotes a full intensity blue color. Each color is represented by 8-bits, i.e. by intensities between 0 to 255. *TColor* class in *OWL* 2.0 maintains color as *COLORREF* value. Windows uses dithering (described in chapter 2) only when filling areas to display neighbouring pixels in different colors to create unique shades. It cannot use dithering when drawing points lines and text.

3.2.9.2 Palettes

The number of colors that can be displayed at a time is determined by the number of bits of storage allocated for each pixel. In a standard VGA, there is 4-bits of storage torepresent each color pixel, therefore, this adapter can display only 2^4, i.e., 16 simultaneous

A super VGA card can have memory to support upto 8-bits per pixel and hence can display 2^8 (or 256) simultaneous colors. A display adapter represents each color by the RGB intensities. Given below is the number of distinct colors supported and number of simultaneous colors shown by a display adapter:

Adapter	Bits/pixel Components	Intensities R	G	B	Distinct Colors available	Bits/Pixel Supported	Simultaneous Colours
VGA	6	2^6	2^6	2^6	$2^6 \times 2^6 \times 2^6 = 262{,}144$	4	$2^4 = 16$
SVGA	8	2^8	2^8	2^8	$2^8 \times 2^8 \times 2^8 = 16{,}777{,}216$	8	$2^8 = 256$

The display adapter converts each pixel's contents into a color by interpreting the pixel's value as an index into a table called color palette. The entries in this table are the RGB values. Windows defines a system palette which has 16 predefined colors for EGA and VGA. System palette has 20 predefined colors for display adapters which support more than 256 colors.

The concept of logical palette in Windows enables a user to take advantage of the large number of colors available in the system. Windows supports an extended system palette that is the mirror image of the hardware palette. Windows assigns 20 values corresponding to the default colors in the extended pallete. Windows maps each color in the logical palette to the extended system palette as follows:

- If color in logical palette already exists in the system palette, that color is mapped to the matching color index in the system palette.
- If color in logical palette does not exist in the system palette, it is added in the system palette if there is space.
- In case the system palette is full, a color in the logical palette is mapped to the closest matching color in the system palette.

Windows supports only 20 default colors in the system palette. One needs to use a logical palette to develop applications with all 256 colors in the Super VGA mode. Table 3.9 gives a brief description of the Windows functions to manipulate palette.

Table 3.9 Functions to manipulate palettes

Function	Description
pal.AnimatePalette (start_indx, count, pal_entries);	Belongs to the *TPalette* class - changes entries in a logical palette resulting in instant changes to colors on the display.
CreatePalette	Creates a logical palette and returns a handle (that can be used to create a *TPalette*) to the palette
pal.GetNearestPaletteIndex (color);	Belongs to the *TPalette* class - returns the index of the palette entry that most closely matches a specified TColor
pal.GetPaletteEntries (start_indx, count, pal_entries);	Belongs to the *TPalette* class - retrieves the color values for a specified number of entries in a logical palette
dc.GetSystemPaletteEntries (start, num, pal_entries);	Belongs to the *TDC* class - retrieves the color values for a specified number of entries in the system palette
GetSystemPaletteUse ();	Belongs to the *TDC* class - returns a flag indicating whether an application can change the system palette
dc.RealizePalette ();	Belongs to the *TDC* class - maps the entries of the currently selected logical palette into the system palette
dc.ResizePalette();	Belongs to the *TPalette* class - enlarges or reduces the size of a logical palette after it has been created
pal.SetPaletteEntries (start, count, pal_entries);	Belong to the *TPalette* class - changes the color values of a specified number of entries in the logical palette
SetSysColors	Sets one or more colors in the system palette, identified by constants such as *COLOR_ACTIVEBORDER*, *COLOR_MENU* and *COLOR_WINDOW*
dc.SetSystemPaletteUse (flag);	Belongs to the TDC class - allows the active application to change the entries in the system palette and flag is one of *SYSPAL_NOSTATIC* or *SYSPAL_STATIC*
dc.UpdateColors ();	Belongs to the class - updates the color of the pixels in the client area of a window to reflect the current entries in the system palette

In case an application uses a logical palette, it should handle the following three palette specific Windows messages:

- Whenever the application's window becomes active, Windows sends a *WM_QUERYNEWPALETTE* message. This is the time when one can load the desired set of colors using RealizePalette function which maps logical palette to the system palette.
- Windows sends a *WM_PALETTECHANGING* message to the top level windows of all applications when the system palette is about to change.
- *WM_PALETTECHANGED* message is sent to the top level windows of all applications when the system palette has changed.

3.2.9.3 Bitmaps

Bitmap is a digital representation of the picture. Each pixel in the picture represents one or more bits in the bitmap. Monochrome bitmaps require only one bit per pixel but color bitmaps require additional number of bits to indicate the color of each pixel.

Device Independent Bitmap (*DIB*) format is called device indepedent because it consists of the color table. The color table gives the pixel values corresponding to the *RGB* color values. The *DIB* format is an extension of bitmap format of *OS/2* presentation manager. The *WINDOWS.H* header file contains a few structures that support *OS/2* bitmaps. The *GDI* bitmap objects are called device dependent bitmap (*DDB*) objects because they must be compatible with a specific graphics output device. The *DIB* is represented by the *TDib* class and has no *GDI* handle like a regular bitmap as it is not a *GDI* object. The *DIB* is, therefore, kept outside *GDI* either as files or in the memory. One can convert a *DIB* into a *GDI* object but in such case the device independent color information in the *DIB* is lost.

The *DIB* format is useful for storing images in a file. One can create a *DIB* using Microsoft Image Editor, Paintbrush, or Borland Resource Workshop. The files, thus, created have extension *.BMP* or in some cases extension *.DIB*. The internal representation of data, i.e., number of bits per pixel is : i) 1 for monochrome bitmaps; ii) 4 for 16- color bitmaps; iii) 16 for 256- color bitmaps and iv) 24 for 16,777,216 - color bitmaps. Given below is a constructor for creating a *TDib* object:

Tdib(int width, int height, int ncolors, uint 16 mode=DIB_RGB_COLORS);

'width' and 'height' parameters give the width and the height of the *DIB* in pixels; ncolors and mode refer to number of colors and RGB or PAL palette respectively.

Program 3.6

```
//--------------------------------------------------------------------------------------------------------
// p3_6.cpp
// This program shows how to
//a) create a menu and use of SetMainWindow and GetMainWindow functions to activate the
//    menu "COMMANDS" to set Pen Width & color;
//b) declare and define response table;
//c) process events caused by pressing and releasing of mouse buttons;
```

```
//d) create a freehand line drawing while keeping the left button of the mouse pressed;
//   The left button can be released to move the mouse to a new position. Pressing the left
//   button would allow freehand drawing from the new position.)
//e  clear the entire client area of the window when the cleanup option is selected from the setup
//   menu;
//f) output text (in the chosen color) on the window;
//g) show current mouse position by pressing the right button of the mouse;
//h) terminate a running program through use of menu Exit/Close option;
//i) select color  using TChooseColorDialog;
//j) take value of a parameter using TInputDialog;
//k) use message box (MessageBox).
//-----------------------------------------------------------------------------------------------------------
#include <owl/owlpch.h>
#include <owl/applicat.h>
#include <owl/framewin.h>
#include <owl/dc.h>
#include <owl/inputdia.h>
#include <stdlib.h>
#include <string.h>
#include "p3_6.rc"

// Definition of the TrialWindow class -- data member CommonDC, a pointer to the TClientDC
// object, is not destroyed automatically when  TrialWindow object is destroyed.  It is necessory
// to add  a destructor to TrialWindow to ensure proper cleanup.

class  TrialWindow : public TWindow
{
 public:
   TrialWindow(TWindow* parent = 0);
   ~ TrialWindow()  // Delete CommonDC
     {
            delete CommonDC;
            delete Pen;
     }

      void GetPenSize();
      void SetPenSize(int newSize);
      void SetPen(TColor& newColor, int penSize = 0);

 protected:
      // provides a valid device context across functions  EvLButtonDown,
      // EvMouseMove, and EvLButtonUp.
      TDC* CommonDC;
      TPen*  Pen;
```

```
        int PenSize;
        TColor Color;

        // Override member function of TWindow
        bool CanClose();

        // Message response functions
        void EvLButtonDown(uint, TPoint&);
        void EvRButtonDown(uint, TPoint&);
        void EvMouseMove(uint, TPoint&);
        void EvLButtonUp(uint, TPoint&);
        //Menu processing functions
    void CmPenSize();
        void CmPenColor();
        void CmAbout();
        void CmClearWindow();
        void CmClose();

  DECLARE_RESPONSE_TABLE( TrialWindow);
};

DEFINE_RESPONSE_TABLE1( TrialWindow, TWindow)
  EV_WM_LBUTTONDOWN,  //Mouse left button down
  EV_WM_RBUTTONDOWN,  //Mouse right button down
  EV_WM_MOUSEMOVE,
  EV_WM_LBUTTONUP,    //Mouse left button up
  EV_COMMAND(CM_PENSIZE, CmPenSize),
  EV_COMMAND(CM_PENCOLOR, CmPenColor),
  EV_COMMAND(CM_ABOUT, CmAbout),
  EV_COMMAND(CM_CLEARWINDOW, CmClearWindow ),
  EV_COMMAND(CM_CLOSE,CmClose ),
END_RESPONSE_TABLE;

 TrialWindow:: TrialWindow(TWindow* parent)
 {
  Init(parent, 0, 0);           // Initialize TrialWindow base class
  CommonDC = 0;                 // Initialize CommonDC-- a pointer to the TClientDC--to zero.
  PenSize  = 1;                 // Initialize pen size
  Color = TColor::Black;        // Initialize color
  Pen = new TPen(Color, PenSize);           //TColor::Black defined in owl\color.h
 }

 void  TrialWindow::SetPen(TColor& newColor, int penSize)
 {
```

```
  // If penSize isn't the default (0), set PenSize to the new size.
  if (penSize)
        PenSize = penSize;
  Color = newColor;
  delete Pen;
  Pen = new TPen( Color, PenSize);          // pickup a pen of new color
}

bool  TrialWindow::CanClose()      // file save feature not implemented
{
  return MessageBox("Do you want to save?", "Not implemented",
                                   MB_YESNO | MB_ICONQUESTION) == IDNO;
  // insert logic for saving the file
}

void  TrialWindow::EvLButtonDown(uint, TPoint& point)
{

  if (!CommonDC)
  {
        SetCapture();
        CommonDC = new TClientDC(*this); //'this' is a local variable avialable
                                                                   // in the
body of a nonstatic function

        CommonDC->SelectObject(*Pen); //select pen in device context
        CommonDC->MoveTo(point);
  }
}

// Let us learn to output text on the window.  Output mouse position when right button of mouse
// is pressed.
void  TrialWindow::EvRButtonDown(uint, TPoint& point)
{
char str[40];
  short posx = point.x;
  short posy = point.y;
  TClientDC  CommonDC(*this);
  wsprintf(str, "Mouse Position (%d,%d)          ", posx, posy);
  CommonDC.SetTextColor(RGB(255,0,0));          // set text color to red
  CommonDC.SetTextAlign(TA_BOTTOM | TA_LEFT);          //Text Alignment
  CommonDC.TextOut(20, 20, str, strlen(str));
}
```

```
void  TrialWindow::EvMouseMove(uint, TPoint& point)
{
  if (CommonDC)
  CommonDC->LineTo(point);
}

void  TrialWindow::EvLButtonUp(uint, TPoint&)
{
  if ( CommonDC)
  {
        ReleaseCapture();
        delete CommonDC;
        CommonDC = 0;
  }
}

void TrialWindow::CmPenSize() //Processes menu command Pen Size
{
  GetPenSize();
}

void TrialWindow::CmPenColor()
{
  TChooseColorDialog::TData colors;  //Processes menu command Pen Color
  static TColor custColors[16] =
  {
    0x010101L, 0x101010L, 0x202020L, 0x303030L,
    0x404040L, 0x505050L, 0x606060L, 0x707070L,
    0x808080L, 0x909090L, 0xA0A0A0L, 0xB0B0B0L,
    0xC0C0C0L, 0xD0D0D0L, 0xE0E0E0L, 0xF0F0F0L
  };

  colors.Flags = CC_RGBINIT;
  colors.Color = TColor::Black;
  colors.CustColors = custColors;
  if (TChooseColorDialog(this, colors).Execute() == IDOK)
        SetPen(colors.Color);
}

void TrialWindow::GetPenSize()
{
 char inputText[6];

  wsprintf(inputText, "%d", PenSize);
```

```
 if ((TInputDialog(this, "Line Thickness",
                                   "Input a new`thickness:",
                                   inputText,
                                   sizeof(inputText))).Execute() == IDOK)
{
        int newPenSize = atoi(inputText);

        if (newPenSize < 0)
        newPenSize=1;
        SetPenSize(newPenSize);
  }
}

void TrialWindow::SetPenSize(int newSize)
{
  delete Pen;
  PenSize = newSize;
  Pen     = new TPen(Color, PenSize);
}

void TrialWindow::CmClearWindow()
{
  Invalidate(); // clears the entire client area of the window
}

void TrialWindow::CmAbout()
{
  TDialog(this, IDD_ABOUT).Execute();
}

void TrialWindow::CmClose()        // terminate the program
{
        EvClose();     // shuts down the main window and ends the application
}

class TDrawApp : public TApplication
{
  public:
    TDrawApp() : TApplication() {}

    void InitMainWindow();
};

void TDrawApp::InitMainWindow()
```

```
{
  SetMainWindow(new TFrameWindow(0, "Freehand Drawing", new TrialWindow));
  GetMainWindow()->AssignMenu("COMMANDS");
}

int
OwlMain(int /*argc*/, char* /*argv*/ [])
{
  return TDrawApp().Run();
}
```

Resource file for p3_6.cpp

```
//------------------------------------------------------------------------
  //p3_6.rc
//------------------------------------------------------------------------
#include <owl/inputdia.rc>
#include <owl/except.rc>

#define CM_ABOUT       205
#define CM_PENSIZE     206
#define CM_PENCOLOR   207
#define CM_CLEARWINDOW 208
#define IDD_ABOUT      211
#define CM_CLOSE      212
#ifdef RC_INVOKED
#ifndef WORKSHOP_INVOKED
# include <windows.h>
#endif

COMMANDS MENU
{
 POPUP "&Setup"
 {
  MENUITEM "Pen &Size",   CM_PENSIZE
  MENUITEM "Pen &Color", CM_PENCOLOR
  MENUITEM "&CleanUp",    CM_CLEARWINDOW
 }
 POPUP "&Help"
 {
  MENUITEM "&About",      CM_ABOUT
 }
  POPUP "&Exit"
  {
```

```
  MENUITEM "&Close",      CM_CLOSE
  }
}

STRINGTABLE
{
 CM_PENSIZE,            "Change the pen width"
 CM_PENCOLOR,           "Change the pen color"
 CM_ABOUT,              "show an information dialog box"
 CM_CLEARWINDOW, "Clear window"
 CM_CLOSE,                          "Terminate the Program"
}

IDD_ABOUT DIALOG 37, 25, 170, 95
STYLE DS_MODALFRAME ¦ WS_POPUP ¦ WS_VISIBLE ¦ WS_CAPTION ¦ WS_SYSMENU
CAPTION "About Freehand Drawing"
FONT 8, "MS Sans Serif"
{
 DEFPUSHBUTTON "Ok", IDOK, 60, 70, 50, 14
 CTEXT "ObjectWindows 2.5 Program", -1, 23, 46, 127, 10
 CTEXT "Freehand Drawing", -1, 23, 24, 126, 8
}
#endif  // RC_INVOKED
```

3.2.10 Tool Bar and Status Bar

A tool bar generally appears at the top of main window of an application and consists of collection of push buttons. It enables the user to quickly initiate action as compared to the pull down menu. For example, in Word Perfect, the tool bar comprises of buttons, such as New Blank Document, Open, Save, Print, Cut, Copy, Paste, Undo, Redo, Bold, Italic, Underline, and Quick Format. Most packages provide buttons for special functions, like File open and Edit dialog box.

A status bar is another common decoration that is included in many Windows applications. This is an area at the bottom of the main window where an application displays help messages as well as the status of some keys (Caps lock, Num lock and Insert).

To insert status and control bars one has to change the main window from a *TFrameWindow* to a *TDecoratedFrame* and modify the function InitMainWindow() as follows:

```
// Create the decorated frame window
TDecoratedFrame* frame = new TDecoratedFrame(Name, "Caption of window", new
                                                    TdrawWindow, true);
//Create a status bar
TStatusBar* sb = new TStatusBar(frame, Tgadget::Recessed,
                                       TstatusBar::CapsLock¦
                                       TstatusBar::NumLock¦
```

```
                                    TStatusBar::OverType);
// Create a control bar
TControlBar* cb = new TcontrolBar(frame);
// Insert button gadgets into the TControlBar. Each button gadget has an associated bitmap
// resource ID and a control ID that tie together a message response function to that button.
cb->Insert(*new TButtonGadget(CM_FILENEW, CM_FILENEW, TButtonGadget::Command));
cb->Insert(*new TButtonGadget(CM_FILEOPEN, CM_FILEOPEN,
TButtonGadget::Command));
cb->Insert(*new TButtonGadget(CM_FILESAVE, CM_FILESAVE,
TButtonGadget::Command));
cb->Insert(*new TButtonGadget(CM_FILESAVEAS, CM_FILESAVEAS,
TbuttonGadget::Command));

// Insert the status bar and control bar into the frame
frame->Insert(*sb, TDecoratedFrame::Bottom);
frame->Insert(*cb, TDecoratedFrame::Top);
```

3.2.11 Programming in *Windows 3.1 SDK* (Software Development Kit)

For readers interested in Windows 3.1 SDK programming in *C* language only, we are giving below a well-documented program in *C*. This program creates a main window, and two dialog boxes. It illustrates how one can draw graphics in main window as well as dialog boxes selectively.

Program3.7

```
//p3_7.c --  A Windows 3.1 SDK program written in conventional environment.
// windows.h contains declaration of the windows functions, the Windows structures, the new
// data type and numeric constants.
#include <windows.h>
#include "p3_7.h"
HMENU      hMenu;
HINSTANCE hInst;
HWND          hwnd ;
// Forward declaration of WdnProc, Windows2DlgProc, and Windows3DlgProc
LRESULT FAR PASCAL _export WndProc( HWND, UINT , WPARAM, LPARAM );
BOOL FAR PASCAL _export Window2DlgProc( HWND , UINT , WPARAM , LPARAM );
BOOL FAR PASCAL _export Window3DlgProc( HWND , UINT , WPARAM , LPARAM );
// Entry point of Windows - function WinMain uses the PASCAL calling sequence
int PASCAL WinMain (HINSTANCE hInstance, HINSTANCE hPrevInstance,
                                            LPSTR lpszCmd, int nCmdShow)

     MSG          msg;
     WNDCLASS     wndclass;   //WNDCLASS structure is defined in windows.h
     static char szAppName[] = " Trial" ;
```

```
if (!hPrevInstance)
{       //Define 10 fields of the WNDCLASS structure
// CS_HREDRAW and CS_VREDRAW identifiers with a bitwise operator ensure
// that all windows created are to be completely repainted whenever horizontal or vertical
// window size changes
        wndclass.style              = CS_HREDRAW | CS_VREDRAW ;
        wndclass.lpfnWndProc        = (WNDPROC)WndProc ;
        wndclass.cbClsExtra         = 0 ;  // reserves extra space
        wndclass.cbWndExtra         = 0 ;
        wndclass.hInstance          = hInstance ; // instance handle of the program
        wndclass.hIcon              = LoadIcon(hInstance, szAppName);
        wndclass.hCursor            = LoadCursor (NULL,IDC_ARROW) ;
        //hbr prefix stands for handle to brush-returns handle to a white brush
        //The background of the client area of the window will be solid white
        wndclass.hbrBackground      = GetStockObject(WHITE_BRUSH);
        wndclass.lpszMenuName       = NULL;
        wndclass.lpszClassName      = szAppName ; // defines name of the class

        RegisterClass (&wndclass) ;     // register the window class
}
hMenu = LoadMenu(hInstance,MAKEINTRESOURCE( MENU_1));
hwnd = CreateWindow (szAppName, // window class name
        "Simple Program",    // window caption
        WS_OVERLAPPEDWINDOW, // window style-a normal overlapped window
        CW_USEDEFAULT,       // Initial x position of the upper left corner
        CW_USEDEFAULT,       // Initial y position
        CW_USEDEFAULT,       // Initial x size - width
        CW_USEDEFAULT,       // Initial y size - height
        NULL,  // parent window handle-NULL as window has no parent window
        hMenu,               // window menu handle
        hInstance,           // program instance handle
        NULL                 // creation parameters
        );
hInst = hInstance;
    // CreateWindow call creats the window internally. To show the window on the screen,
    // we need to invoke ShowWindow and UpdateWindow function.
    // If nCmdShow = SH_SHOWNORMAL (=1) then window is displayed normally
    //            = SH_MINNOACTIVE (=7) then window is initially displayed as icon
    ShowWindow (hwnd, nCmdShow) ;
    UpdateWindow (hwnd) ;   // causes the client area to be painted
    // window is now fully visible - prepare to receive keyboard and mouse input
    // message loop
    while (GetMessage (&msg, NULL, 0, 0))
    {
        TranslateMessage (&msg) ;
```

```
        DispatchMessage  (&msg). ;
    }
    return msg.wParam ;
}
void PaintWindow(HWND hwnd,short nColor,short nFigure)
{
    static DWORD  dwColor[3] = {RGB(255,0,0),RGB(200,255,0),RGB(0,255,200)};
    HDC hdc;
    HBRUSH hBrush;
    RECT rect;
    hdc = GetDC(hwnd);
    //  retrieve the co-ordinates of the client area in rect.left ,rect.top,
    //  rect.right,rect.bottom
    GetClientRect(hwnd,&rect);
    hBrush = CreateSolidBrush( dwColor[nColor -1]);
    hBrush = SelectObject(hdc,hBrush);
    if(nFigure == 1)
            Ellipse(hdc,rect.left ,rect.top,rect.right,rect.bottom);
    else
            Rectangle(hdc,rect.left ,rect.top,rect.right,rect.bottom);
            DeleteObject(SelectObject(hdc,hBrush));
            ReleaseDC(hwnd,hdc);
    }
 void PaintTheBlock(HWND hCtrl,short nColor,short nFigure)
    {
    //  adds a rectangle to the window's update region
    InvalidateRect(hCtrl,NULL,TRUE);
    //  updates the client area of the desired window by sendind a WM_PAINT message
    UpdateWindow(hCtrl);
    PaintWindow(hCtrl, nColor, nFigure) ;
    }
//  window procedure - hwnd : handle to the window receiving the message
//  - message : is a 16 bit unsigned integer that identifies the message
//  and the last two parameters provide more information regarding the message
LRESULT FAR PASCAL _export WndProc (HWND hwnd, UINT message,
                                    WPARAM wParam, LPARAM lParam)
{
 DLGPROC w2DlgProc;
 HDC hdc;
 PAINTSTRUCT ps;
 RECT rect;
   switch (message)
   {
```

```
  // WM_PAINT message is most important in Windows programming as it informs program
  //  when part or all of window's client area is invalid
  case WM_PAINT:
      hdc = BeginPaint(hwnd,&ps);
      PaintWindow(hwnd, 2,1);
      EndPaint(hwnd,&ps);
      return 0;
 case WM_COMMAND:
      switch (wParam)
      {
      case IDM_NEXTWINDOW:
              w2DlgProc = (DLGPROC)
              MakeProcInstance((FARPROC)Window2DlgProc,hInst);
              // create a modal dialog box from a dialog box template resource
              DialogBox( hInst, MAKEINTRESOURCE(DIALOG_1), hwnd,w2DlgProc);
              FreeProcInstance((FARPROC)w2DlgProc);
              return 0;
      case CM_EXIT :
              DestroyWindow( hwnd );
              return 0;
      }
      break;
      //WM_DESTROY indicates that Windows is in the process of destroying a window based
      //on a command from the user
      case WM_DESTROY:
              PostQuitMessage (0) ;
              return 0 ;
 }
 return DefWindowProc (hwnd, message, wParam, lParam) ;
}

BOOL FAR PASCAL _export Window2DlgProc ( HWND hDlg, UINT message, WPARAM
wParam, LPARAM lParam)
{
 DLGPROC w3DlgProc;
 static HWND hCtrlBlock;
 static short nColor,nFigure;
  switch (message)
  {
    case WM_INITDIALOG :
      nColor  = 1 ;
      nFigure = 1 ;
      //  retrieve the title/text associated with a control in a dioalog box
```

```
        hCtrlBlock = GetDlgItem( hDlg,IDD_PAINT);
            // Set input focus to a given window. All keyboard input will now come to the
            selected // window.
        SetFocus(GetDlgItem( hDlg,IDD_PAINT));
        return TRUE;
      case WM_COMMAND:
       switch ( wParam)
       {
        case IDOK:
            w3DlgProc=(DLGPROC) MakeProcInstance((FARPROC)Window3DlgProc,hInst);
          DialogBox( hInst, MAKEINTRESOURCE(DIALOG_2), hwnd,w3DlgProc);
          FreeProcInstance((FARPROC)w3DlgProc);
          EndDialog(hDlg,0);
          return TRUE;
          }
        break;
        case WM_PAINT:
          PaintTheBlock(hCtrlBlock, nColor,nFigure);
          break;
        case WM_CLOSE:
          EndDialog(hDlg,TRUE); // hides a modal dialog
          return (TRUE);
    }
   return FALSE;


 ƆOL FAR PASCAL _export Window3DlgProc ( HWND hDlg, UINT message,
                                        WPARAM wParam, LPARAM lParam)
{
   static HWND hCtrlBlock;
   static short nColor,nFigure;
   switch (message)
   {
       case WM_INITDIALOG :
          nColor  = 3 ;
          nFigure = 2 ;
          hCtrlBlock = GetDlgItem( hDlg,IDD_PAINT1);
          SetFocus(GetDlgItem( hDlg,IDD_PAINT1));
          return TRUE;
       case WM_COMMAND:
       switch ( wParam)
       {
```

```
            case IDOK:
               EndDialog(hDlg,0);
               return TRUE;
            }
         break;
         case WM_PAINT:
            PaintTheBlock(hCtrlBlock, nColor, nFigure);
            break;
         case WM_CLOSE:
            EndDialog(hDlg,TRUE);  // hides a modal dialog
            return (TRUE);
   }
   return FALSE;
}
```

P3_7.rc - Resource File

```
*****************************/*****************************************************
p3_7.rc
Developed using Borland Resource Workshop
**********************************************************************************/

#include " p3_7.h"
MENU_1 MENU
{
 MENUITEM "Next Window", IDM_NEXTWINDOW
 MENUITEM "Exit", CM_EXIT
}
DIALOG_1 DIALOG 6, 14, 207, 111
STYLE DS_MODALFRAME | WS_POPUP | WS_VISIBLE | WS_CAPTION | WS_SYSMENU
CAPTION "WINDOW 2"
FONT 8, "MS Sans Serif"
{
 DEFPUSHBUTTON "OK", IDOK, 130, 66, 60, 14
 LTEXT "Window No 2", -1, 146, 31, 60, 8
 EDITTEXT IDD_PAINT, 15, 16, 113, 88
}
DIALOG_2 DIALOG 6, 15, 207, 111
STYLE DS_MODALFRAME | WS_POPUP | WS_VISIBLE | WS_CAPTION | WS_SYSMENU
CAPTION "WINDOW  3"
FONT 8, "MS Sans Serif"
{
 DEFPUSHBUTTON "OK", IDOK, 144, 81, 50, 14, BS_DEFPUSHBUTTON | WS_GROUP |
```

```
WS_TABSTOP
 LTEXT "Window 3 !!!", -1, 137, 35, 60, 8
 EDITTEXT IDD_PAINT1, 11, 24, 117, 80
}

/***************************************************************************
      p3_7.h
***************************************************************************/

#define DIALOG_2   2
#define IDD_PAINT1          101
#define MENU_1    1
#define IDM_NEXTWINDOW          101
#define CM_EXIT    102
#define DIALOG_1   1
#define IDD_PAINT 101
//---------------------------------------------------------------------------
```

3.3 DOS GRAPHICS PROGRAMMING

Turbo Pascal and C compilers from Borland as well as from many other vendors support a large number of basic graphics functions on the IBM PC and clones. All Pascal and C compilers support all popular graphics adapters. Futhermore, it is possible to write a graphics program in Turbo Pascal and C in such a manner that it identifies the adapter installed in the system. This is possible because of the availability of graphics drivers for each of the popular cards, containing code and data. A list of graphic functions available in Tubo Pascal, C, and Borland C is given in Appendix I. Compilers from other vendors also have similar graphic support. Graphic functions and their prototypes in case of Pascal and C are in 'Graph Unit' and 'graphics.h' respectively. At run-time, the 'InitGraph'(or 'initgraph' in C) procedure (this will be described in the sequel) identifies the graphics hardware, loads and initializes the appropriate graphics driver, puts the system into the graphics mode, and then returns control to the calling routine.

For display of graphics one may use either a monochrome or a color (or RGB) monitor. The various graphics adapters support either of these, but the resolution is generally lower with color.

3.3.1 PROCEDURES AND FUNCTIONS IN THE GRAPH UNIT

The procedures and functions that are contained in the Graph unit of Turbo Pascal can be divided into ten different groups, as listed below:

- Routines for high level error handling,
- Routines for detection, initialization and changing the CRT mode,

- Routines for controlling the screen and the viewport,
- Point-oriented routines,
- Line-oriented routines,
- Procedures for drawing and filling polygons and similar figures,
- Procedures related to drawing circles, arcs and other curves,
- Routines related to colors and palettes,
- Routines related to bit-images,
- Routines for displaying text in the graphics mode.

The Graph unit also declares a set of constants and variables which are used through out the unit. These will be described in section 3.3. We shall now describe the various functions and units since it is necessary to understand them thoroughly in order to utilize them in graphics programs. Short examples of the use of these procedures and functions will be included in order to help in understanding their usage.

3.3.2 Functions for high level error handling

In writing computer programs one often encounters error messages while compiling or running the program. In the Graph unit, two functions are available for high level error handling. The main objective is to display an error message that is easily understood by the user, instead of just returning a cryptic message like "error code 3".

(i) Function GraphResult

This function returns an error code, in the form of an integer (between -15 and 0), that results from the last graphics operation. It is used in several routines, including DetectGraph, InitGraph, SetViewPort, ImageSize, SetFillStyle, SetTextStyle and SetGraphMode. It may be noted that GraphResult is set to zero after it has been called. Hence, the user should store its value into another variable and then test it.

(ii) Function GraphErrorMsg

This function, used in conjunction with the above, displays an error message string in accordance with the error code returned. Table 3.10 lists the error codes and the corresponding messages.

Table 3.10 Error codes and corresponding messages

Error Code	Graphics Error Constant	Corresponding Error Message String
0	grOk	No error
-1	grNoInitGraph	(BGI) graphics not installed (use InitGraph)
-2	grNotDetected	Graphics hardware not detected
-3	grFileNotFound	Device driver file not found
-4	grInvalidDriver	Invalid device driver file
-5	grNoLoadMem	Not enough memory to load driver
-6	grNoScanMem	Out of memory in scan fill
-7	grNoFloodMem	Out of memory in flood fill
-8	grFontNotFound	Font file not found
-9	grNoFontMem	Not enough memory to load font
-10	grInvalidMode	Invalid mode for selected driver
-11	grError	Graphics error
-12	grIOerror	Graphics I/O error
-13	grInvalidFont	Invalid font file
-14	grInvalidFontNum	Invalid font number

Program 3.8 illustrates the use of both of these functions.

Program 3.8

```
PROGRAM ShowGraphResult;
Uses Graph;
VAR GraphDriver, GraphMode, ErrorCode : INTEGER;
BEGIN
    GraphDriver := Detect;
    InitGraph (GraphDriver, GraphMode, ' ');
    ErrorCode := GraphResult;
    IF ErrorCode <> grOk THEN { If the error code is not zero }
        BEGIN
            WRITELN ('GraphicsError: ', GraphErrorMsg (ErrorCode));
            WRITELN ('Program aborted...');
            Halt(1) { Show the error message and halt }
        END;
    Rectangle (0, 0, GetMaxX, GetMaxY); {Draw a rectangular border}
    READLN;
    CloseGraph      { Exit graph mode }
END.
```

The program first checks the graphics hardware. If a nonzero error code is returned then it displays the appropriate error message, as listed in the table 3.9 and halts. Otherwise a rectangular border is drawn. The display returns to text mode after the return key is pressed.

3.3.3 Routines for detection, initialization and changing the CRT mode

These procedures and functions are required for detecting the type of graphics hardware, initializing the graphics screen and for changing from the text mode to the graphics mode and vice versa. The graph unit contains 15 functions and procedures in this group. These are described below.

(i) Procedure InitGraph

This procedure initializes the Graphics system and puts the hardware in the graphics mode. It is declared as follows.

```
InitGraph (VAR GraphDriver : INTEGER; VAR GraphMode : INTEGER;
           DriverPath : STRING);
```

Note that both GraphDriver and GraphMode are variable parameters. The various possible values of GraphDriver are given below:

Value	Definition	Value	Defnition	Value	Definition
0	Detect	1	CGA	2	MCGA
3	EGA	4	EGA64	5	EGAMono
6	Reserved	7	HercMono	8	ATT400
9	VGA	10	PC3270		

If the value of GraphDriver is equal to 0 (or Detect), the procedure DetectGraph is called, the appropriate graphics driver is initialized and a graphics mode is selected. If GraphDriver is not equal to 0, the value of GraphDriver is assumed to be a drive number. In this case, that driver is selected and the system is put into the mode specified by GraphMode. Note that although in this way it is possible to override autodetection, the user must supply a valid GraphMode parameter for the driver requested. For most graph drivers several graphics modes are possible. These are shown below for a few graphic adapters:

Mode	Value	Description
CGAC0	0	320×200 palette 0: LightGreen, LightRed, Yellow; 1 page
CGAC1	1	320×200 pallete 1: LightCyan, LightMagenta, White; 1 page
CGAC2	2	320×200 palette 2: Green, Red, Brown; 1 page
CGAC3	3	320×200 palette 3: Cyan, Magenta, LightGray;1 page
CGAHi	4	640×200; 1 page
EGALo	0	640×200; 16 color; 4 pages
EGAHi	1	640×350; 16 color; 2 pages
EGA64Lo	0	640×200; 16 color; 1 page
EGA64Hi	1	640×350; 4 color; 1 page
EGAMonoHi	3	640×350; 64K on card, 2 pages; 256K on card, 1 page
HercMonoHi	0	720×348; 2 page
VGALo	0	640×200; 16 color; 4 pages
VGAMed	1	640×350; 16 color; 2 pages
VGAHi	2	640×480; 16 color; 1 page
PC3270Hi	0	720×350; 1 page
IBM 8514HI	1	1024x768, 256 color
IBM 8514LO	0	640 x480, 256 color

DriverPath specifies the directory where the graphics drivers can be found. If DriverPath is null, the driver files must be in the current directory.

(ii) Procedure DetectGraph

This procedure checks the hardware and determines which graphics mode and driver are to be used. It requires the following declaration.

DetectGraph (VAR GraphDriver, GraphMode : INTEGER);

It returns the detected driver and mode value that can be passed to InitGraph, which will then load the correct driver. In no hardware was detected, the GraphDriver parameter and GraphResult will return a value of -2 (i.e. grNotDetected).

Unless instructed otherwise, InitGraph calls DetectGraph, finds and loads the correct driver, and initializes the graphics system. The only reason to call DetectGraph directly is to override the driver recommended by DetectGraph. The following example shows such a program. If the graphics driver is identified as a 64K or 256K EGA, the program instructs the loading of the CGA driver. It should be noted that in such cases the user must also pass in a valid GraphMode for the driver requested.

Program 3.9

(a) Pascal version

```
PROGRAM UseCGA;
Uses Graph;
VAR   GraphDriver, GraphMode : INTEGER;
      BEGIN
            DetectGraph (GraphDriver, GraphMode);
```

```
        IF GraphDriver IN [EGA, EGA64] THEN
           BEGIN
              GraphDriver := CGA;
              GraphMode := CGAHi
           END;
        InitGraph (GraphDriver, GraphMode, ' ');
        IF GraphResult <> grOk THEN
              Halt(1);
        Rectangle (0, 0, GetMaxX, GetMaxY);
        READLN;
        CloseGraph
     END.
```

(b) *C* version

```
     UseCGA()
     {
      int GraphDriver,GraphMode;
            detectgraph(&GraphDriver, &GraphMode);
            if(GraphDriver == EGA || GraphDriver == EGA64){
                GraphDriver = CGA;
                GraphMode = CGAHI;
            }
            initgraph(&GraphDriver, &GraphMode,"");
            if(graphresult() != grOk) exit(0);
            rectangle(0,0,getmaxx(),getmaxy());
     getch();
     closegraph();
     }
```

(iii) Procedure SetGraphBufSize

This procedure allows the user to change the size of the buffer used for scan and flood fills. It is declared as

SetGraphBufSize (BufSize : WORD);

The internal buffer size is set to BufSize and a buffer is allocated on the heap when a call is made to InitGraph. Note that this procedure must be called before InitGraph, otherwise it is ignored.

The default value of Bufsize is 4K, which is sufficiently large to fill a polygon with about 650 vertices. Hence, increasing the size of the buffer will be necessary only in rare cases. Such cases will be indicated by a buffer overflow.

(iv) Procedure SetGraphMode

This procedure clears the graphics screen and sets the system to the graphics mode. It is declared as

SetGraphMode (Mode : INTEGER);

The integer mode must be a valid mode for the current device driver, as listed under the procedure InitGraph. A call to this procedure is necessary only when the desired graphics mode is different from the default mode set by InitGraph. This procedure also resets all graphics settings (current pointer, palette, color, viewport, etc.) for the desired graph mode. If an attempt is made to select an invalid graph mode for the current device driver, GraphResult will return a value of -10 (i.e., grInvalidMode).

(v) Procedure GetModeRange

This procedure returns the lowest and the highest valid graphics modes for a given driver. It is declared as

```
GetModeRange (GraphDriver : INTEGER;
        VAR   LoMode, HiMode : INTEGER);
```

For example, consider the following program for a CGA driver.

Program 3.10

(a) Pascal Program

```
PROGRAM GetCGAModeRange;

Uses Graph;
VAR  Lowest, Highest : INTEGER;

     BEGIN
      GetModeRange (CGA, Lowest, Highest);
      WRITE ('Lowest = ', Lowest);
      WRITELN (' and Highest = ', Highest)
     END.
```

(b) *C* Program

```
GetCGAModeRange()
{
int Lowest,Highest;
getmoderange(CGA, &Lowest, &Highest);
printf("Lowest = %d  and Highest = %d", Lowest,Highest);
}
```

The output of this program will be

Lowest = 0 and Highest = 4.

If an invalid value of GraphDriver is used, the parameters that are returned will be set to -1.

(vi) Function GetGraphMode

This function returns an integer representing the current graph mode. This will have a value between 0 and 5, depending upon the graph driver being used currently. The possible values of the mode constant are shown in the description for InitGraph, as well as in section 3.3.

(vii) Procedure GraphDefaults

This procedure resets the graphics system to the default values. This includes homing the current pointer and setting the viewport, the palette, drawing and background colors, line style and line pattern, fill style, fill color and fill pattern, active font, text style, text justification, and user character size.

(viii) Procedure RestoreCrtMode

This procedure restores the screen mode to the state that existed before graphics was initialized. It can be used with SetGraphMode to switch between graphics and text modes. The following program illustrates how this can be done.

Program 3.11

(a) Pascal Program

```
PROGRAM SwitchModes;
Uses Graph;
VAR GraphDriver, GraphMode, ErrorCode : INTEGER;
 BEGIN
   GraphDriver := Detect;
   InitGraph (GraphDriver, GraphMode, ' ');
   ErrorCode := GraphResult;
   IF ErrorCode <> grOk THEN { If the error code is not zero }
    BEGIN
      WRITELN ('GraphicsError: ', GraphErrorMsg (ErrorCode));
      WRITELN ('Program aborted...');
      Halt(1) { Show the error message and halt }
    END;
   OutText ('Press <RETURN> to leave graphics: ');
   READLN;
   RestoreCrtMode;
   WRITELN ('Now in text mode');
   WRITE ('Press <RETURN> to enter graphics mode: ');
   READLN;
   SetGraphMode (GetGraphMode);
```

```
    OutTextXY (0, 0, 'Back in graphics mode');
    OutTextXY (0, 2×TextHeight('B'), 'Press <RETURN> to quit: ');
    READLN;
    CloseGraph      { Exit graph mode }
  END.
```

(b) *C* Program

```
SwitchModes()
{
int GraphDriver, GraphMode, ErrorCode;

      GraphDriver = DETECT;
      initgraph( &GraphDriver, &GraphMode,"");
      ErrorCode = graphresult();
      if(ErrorCode != grOk)
      { /* If the error code is not zero */
            printf("\nGraphics Error: %s", grapherrormsg(ErrorCode));
            printf("\nProgram aborted...");
            exit(0); /* Show the message and quit */
      }
      outtext("Press <RETURN> to leave graphics :");
      getch();
      restorecrtmode();
      printf("\nNow in text mode");
      printf("\nPress <RETURN> to enter the graphics mode :");
      getch();
      setgraphmode(getgraphmode());
      outtextxy(0, 0, "Back in graphics mode");
      outtextxy(0, 2 * textheight("B"), "Press <RETURN> to quit: ");
      getch();
      closegraph();
}
```

(ix) Procedure CloseGraph

This procedure restores the screen mode that existed before the graphics mode was initialized. It also frees the memory allocated on the heap for the graphics scan buffer and deallocates driver and font memory buffers if they were allocated by calls to GraphGetMem and GraphFreeMem.

(x) Function RegisterBGIdriver

The purpose of this function is to register a user-loaded or linked-in BGI driver with the graphics system. It is declared as

```
RegisterBGIdriver (driver:pointer): INTEGER;
```

If an error occurs, a negative value is returned, otherwise the function returns the graph driver number. With this routine, a user can load a driver file and "register" the driver by passing its memory location to RegisterBGIdriver. When that driver is used by InitGraph, the registered driver will be used, instead of being loaded from disk by the Graph unit. A user-registered driver can be loaded from disk onto the heap, or converted to an OBJ file (using BINOBJ.EXE) and linked into the .EXE file.

The following program loads the HercMono driver onto the heap and calls InitGraph after registering the driver with the graphics system.

Program 3.12

```
PROGRAM LoadHercDriver;
Uses Graph;
VAR  GraphDriver, GraphMode : INTEGER;
     DriverFile : FILE;
     DriverPointer : POINTER;
BEGIN
  (* Open driver file, read into memory and register it *)
  Assign (DriverFile, 'CGA.BGI');
  Reset (DriverFile, 1);
  GetMem (DriverPointer, FileSize(DriverFile));
  BlockRead (DriverFile, DriverPointer^, FileSize(DriverFile));
  IF RegisterBGIdriver(DriverPointer) < 0 THEN
    BEGIN
      WRITELN ('Error registering driver: ',
                        GraphErrorMsg(GraphResult));
      Halt(1)
    END;
  (* Intialize graphics *)
  GraphDriver := HercMono;
  GraphMode := HercMonoHi;
  InitGraph (GraphDriver, GraphMode, ' ');
  IF GraphResult < 0 THEN
    Halt (1);
  MoveTo (20, 40);
  SetTextStyle (TriplexFont, HorizDir, 4);
  OutText ('Hercules driver loaded by user program');
  READLN;
  CloseGraph
END.
```

(xi) Function RegisterBGIfont

It registers a user-loaded or linked-in BGI font with the graphics system. It is declared as

RegisterBGIfont (font:pointer):INTEGER;

The value returned is negative if an error occurs, otherwise the internal font number is returned. This routine enables a user to load a font file and "register" the font by passing its memory location to RegisterBGIfont. When that font is selected with a call to SetTextStyle, the registered font will be used (instead of being loaded from disk by the Graph unit). A user-registered font can be loaded from disk onto the heap, or converted to an .OBJ file (by using the BINOBJ.EXE file and linked into an .EXE file.

The following program loads the SansSerif font onto the heap, registers it with the graphics system and then alternates between using triplex and triplex font (the latter is loaded from dis by the Graph unit).

Program 3.13

```
PROGRAM LoadFont;
Uses Graph;
VAR GraphDriver, GraphMode : INTEGER;
    FontFile : FILE;
    FontPointer : POINTER;
BEGIN
  (* Open font file, read into memory and register it  *)
  Assign (FontFile, 'Sans.CHR');
  RESET (FontFile, 1);
  GetMem (FontPointer, FileSize(FontFile));
  BlockRead (FontFile, FontPointer^, FileSize(FontFile));
  IF RegisterBGIfont(FontPointer) < 0 THEN
  BEGIN
    WRITELN ('Error registering font; ',
             GraphErrorMsg(GraphResult));
    Halt(1)
  END;
  (* Initialize graphics *)
  GraphDriver := Detect;
  InitGraph (GraphDriver, GraphMode, '');
  IF GraphResult < 0 THEN Halt(1);
  (* Select registered font *)
  SetTextStyle (SansSerifFont, HorizDir, 5);
  OutText ('SansSerif loaded by user program ');
  MoveTo (0, TextHeight('a'));
  READLN;
  (* Select font that must be loaded from disk *)
  SetTextStyle (TriplexFont, HorizDir, 4);
  OutText ('Triplex loaded from disk ');
  MoveTo (0, GetY + TextHeight('a'));
```

```
READLN;
(* Re-select registered font (already in memory)  *)
SetTextStyle (SansSerifFont, HorizDir, 8);
OutText ('Back to SansSerif ');
READLN;
CloseGraph
END.
```

(xii) Function GetX

This function returns an integer value correponding to the X coordinate of the current position (CP). It works only in the graphics mode and is relative to the viewport. For example, if we call the function GetX following the command

SetViewPort (10, 20, 200, 200, TRUE);

it will return the value 0, not 10, although the absolute value of the CP is (10, 20).

(xiii) Function GetY

This function returns an integer value correponding to the Y coordinate of the current position (CP). It works only in the graphics mode and is relative to the viewport. For example, if we call the function GetY following the command

SetViewPort (10, 20, 200, 200, TRUE);

it will return the value 0, not 20, although the absolute value of the CP is (10, 20).

(xiv) Function GetMaxX

This function returns an integer value corresponding to the right-most column (x resolution) of the current graphics driver and mode. For example, with the EGA card in the EGAHi mode (resolution 640×350), GetMaxX will return a value of 639 (the left-most position is 0).

(xv) Function GetMaxY

This function returns an integer value corresponding to the bottom-most row (y resolution) of the current graphics driver and mode. For example, with the EGA card in the EGAHi mode (resolution 640×350), GetMaxX will return a value of 349 (the top-most position is 0).

3.3.4 Procedures for setting screen, viewport and page

The Graph unit contains six procedures which can be used for controlling the screen, viewport (or windows) and the graphics pages. Only EGA (256K), VGA and the Hercules graphics cards support multiple pages. With multiple graphics pages, a program can direct graphics output to an off-screen page, then quickly display the off-screen image by changing the visual page. This technique is especially useful for animation.

(i) Procedure ClearDevice

This procedure clears the screen, moves the current pointer to (0, 0) in the viewport and prepares for output.

(ii) Procedure SetViewPort

It sets the current output viewport or window for graphics output. The declaration is given below.

```
SetViewPort (x1, y1, x2, y2 : INTEGER; Clip : BOOLEAN);
```

where (xleft, y1) defines the upper left corner of the window and (x2, y2) defines the lower right corner. Evidently, we must have 0<xleft<x2 and 0<y1<y2. If invalid input is passed on to SetViewPort, GraphResult will return the error code 11 (grError). The boolean variable Clip determines whether drawings will be clipped at the boundaries of the current viewport. The following constants are defined:

```
CONST  ClipOn  = TRUE;
       ClipOff = FALSE;
```

After the viewport is set up, the coordinates of the upper left corner are set at (0, 0) and all graphics commands (e.g., GetX, GetY, OutText, MoveTo) are viewport relative.

(iii) Procedure ClearViewPort

This procedure clears the current viewport. It also sets the fill color to the background color and moves the current pointer to (0, 0).

(iv) Procedure GetViewSettings

It returns the current viewport and clipping settings, as set by the procedure SetViewPort. It is declared as

```
GetViewSettings (VAR ViewPort : ViewPortType);
```

It may be noted that ViewPortType is a predeclared record variable, as follows:

```
TYPE
  ViewPortType =  RECORD
                    x1, y1, x2, y2 : INTEGER;
                    Clip : BOOLEAN;
                  END;
```

The points (xleft, y1) and (x2, y2) are the upper left and the lower right corners of the viewport, respectively, and are given in the absolute screen coordinates.

(v) Procedure SetVisualPage

The purpose of this procedure is to set the visual graphics page number. It is declared as

```
SetVisualPage (Page : WORD);
```

which makes the integer page the visual graphics page.

(vi) Procedure SetActivePage

This procedure is used for setting the active page for graphics output. It is declared as

SetActivePage (Page : WORD);

and makes the integer page the active graphics page. All graphics output will now be directed to page.

As stated earlier, multiple pages are supported only by EGA(256K), VGA and Hercules cards. These are useful for animation, where a program can direct graphics output to an off-screen page and then quickly display the off-screen image by changing the visual page. Such a program is given below.

Program 3.14

(a) Pascal version

```
PROGRAM Animation;
Uses Crt, Graph;
VAR GraphDriver, Graphmode,x1, y1 : INTEGER;
BEGIN
  GraphDriver := Detect;
  InitGraph (GraphDriver, GraphMode, ' ');
  IF GraphResult <> grOK THEN Halt(1);
  IF GraphDriver IN [HercMono, EGA, EGA64, VGA] THEN
    BEGIN
     x1 := 0;
     y1 := 0;
     SetActivePage (0);                    {Active page is 0}
     REPEAT
       IF GetMaxColor > 7 THEN
         SetColor (LightRed);
       Rectangle (x1, y1,x1+10, y1+10);    {Draw a rectangle}
       SetActivePage(1);                   {Active page is 1}
       IF GetMaxColor > 7 THEN
         SetColor (LightGreen);
        Circle (x1, y1, 12);               {Draw a circle}
       SetActivePage (0);                  {Active page is 0}
       x1 := x1 + 20;
       y1 := y1 + 20
     UNTIL (y1 > GetMaxY);
     WHILE NOT KeyPressed DO
       BEGIN
         SetVisualPage (0);                {Display page 0}
         SetVisualPage (1)                 {Display page 1}
       END;
```

```
    END
  ELSE  WRITELN ('No paging supported. ');
  CloseGraph
 END.
```

(b) *C* version

```
animation()
{
int GraphDriver, GraphMode, x1, y1;

GraphDriver = DETECT;
  initgraph(&GraphDriver, &GraphMode, "");
  if(graphresult() != grOk) exit(0);
  if( GraphDriver == HERCMONO || GraphDriver == EGA ||
      GraphDriver == CGA ||   GraphDriver == VGA ){
        x1 = 0;
        y1 = 0;
        setactivepage(0);                          /* Active page is 0 */
        do{
                if(getmaxcolor() > 7) setcolor(LIGHTRED);
                rectangle(x1, y1, x1 + 10, y1 + 10);   /* Draw a rectangle */
                setactivepage(1);                  /* Active page is 1 */
                if(getmaxcolor() > 7) setcolor(LIGHTGREEN);
                circle(x1, y1, 12);                /* Draw a circle */
                setactivepage(0);                  /* Active page is 0 */
                x1 += 20;
                y1 += 20;
                }while( y1 <= getmaxy());
        while( !kbhit()){
                setvisualpage(0);                  /* Display page is 0 */
                setvisualpage(1);                  /* Display page is 1 */
        }
  }

  else printf("\n No  page supported. ");
  closegraph();
}
```

3.3.5 Point-oriented routines

There are two point-oriented routines in the Graph unit. These are described below.

(i) Procedure PutPixel

It is used for plotting a point in the desired color at a given location. It is declared as

PutPixel (x, y : INTEGER; Color: WORD)

The coordinates of the point are given by (x, y), which must be valid integers within the current viewport. Color must be a valid integer, as in the list of constants given in section 3.3.

(ii) Function GetPixel

It is declared as

GetPixel (x, y : INTEGER) : WORD;

and is used for determining the color of the pixel at the point (x, y).

3.3.6 Line-oriented routines

There are seven procedures that are related to drawing lines. These are described below.

(i) Procedure Line

It draws a line between two given points, (x1, y1) and (x2, y2), and is declared as

Line (x1,y1, x2,y2 : INTEGER)

It should be kept in mind that the location of the current pointer is not affected by this procedure.

(ii) Procedure LineTo

This procedure draws a line from the current pointer (CP) to the point (x, y) and is declared as

LineTO (x, y : INTEGER)

The CP is moved to (x, y).

(iii) Procedure LineRel

It draws a line from the current pointer (CP) to a point at a specified relative distance from the CP and is declared as

LineRel (Dx, Dy : INTEGER)

If the CP is at (x1, y1), then the above command will draw a line from this point to (x1+Dx, y1+Dy). The CP is moved to (x1+Dx, y1+Dx).

(iv) Procedure MoveTo

It moves the current pointer to the point (x, y), and is declared as

MoveTo (x, y : INTEGER)

If a viewport is active, the x and y values are added to the values of the upper left corner of the viewport.

(v) Procedure MoveRel

It moves the current pointer a given relative distance from its present location. It is declared as

```
MoveRel (Dx, Dy : INTEGER)
```

If the current pointer is at (x1, y1), then the above command will move it to the point (x1+Dx, y1+Dy).

(vi) Procedure SetLineStyle

The Graph unit allows the user to select from many available patterns, thicknesses and styles of lines using this procedure. It is declared as

```
SetLineStyle (LineStyle : WORD; Pattern : WORD;
              Thickness : WORD)
```

The following constants are defined.

```
Linestyles      SolidLn = 0;
                DottedLn   = 1;
                CenterLn   = 2;
                DashedLn   = 3;
                UserBitLn  = 4;

Thickness       NormWidth  = 1;
                ThickWidth = 3;
```

Pattern is ignored unless LineSytle = UserBitLn. In this case, the line is output using the 16-bit pattern defined by the parameter pattern.

(vii) Procedure GetLineSettings

This procedure returns information about the current line style, line pattern and line thickness as set by a previous call to SetLineStyle. It is declared as

```
GetLineSettings (VAR LineInfo : LineSettingsType);
```

where LineSettingTypes is a record variable, defined as below.

```
TYPE LineSettings     Type =  RECORD
                                  LineStyle : WORD;
                                  Pattern   : WORD;
                                  Thickness : WORD;
                              END;
```

The various constants for LineStyle and Thickness are as described with Procedure SetLineStyle.

3.3.7 Procedures for drawing and filling polygons and similar figures

The Graph unit contains ten very useful built-in routines for drawing and filling polygons and related figures. These are described below.

(i) Procedure Rectangle

It draws a rectangle, with lines parallel to the x- and y-axes. The coordinates of the upper left corner of the rectangle are (x1, y1) while those of the lower right corner are (x2, y2). It is declared as

```
Rectangle (x1, y1, x2, y2 : INTEGER)
```

The rectangle is drawn using the current line style and color, as set by SetLineStyle and SetColor.

(ii) Procedure DrawPoly

It draws the outline of a polygon, using the current line style and color. It is declared as

```
DrawPoly (NumPoints : WORD; VAR PolyPoints : PointType)
```

In order to draw a closed figure with N vertices, NumPoints must be set equal to (N+1) and the coordinates of (N+1) points be specified. Also the coordinates of the first and the last point must be identical. PointType is a record variable, predeclared in the Graph unit as below.

```
PointType = RECORD
  x, y : INTEGER;
END;
```

The following program illustrates how a triangle can be drawn using this procedure.

Program 3.15

```
PROGRAM DrawTriangle;
Uses Graph;
CONST
   Triangle : ARRAY [1..4] OF PointType = (( x:80; y:240),
                                           ( x:280; y:40),
                                           ( x:480; y:240),
                                           ( x:80;  y:240) );
VAR GraphDriver, GraphMode, ErrorCode : INTEGER;
BEGIN
  GraphDriver := Detect;
  InitGraph (GraphDriver, GraphMode, 'C:\DRIVERS');
  ErrorCode := GraphResult;
  IF ErrorCode < > grOk THEN
  BEGIN
    WriteLn ('Graphics error: ', GraphErrorMsg(ErrorCode));
    Halt(1)
  END;
  SetLineStyle (UserBitLn, $BBBB, ThickWidth);
  Rectangle (0, 0, GetMaxX, GetMaxY);
  SetLineStyle (SolidLn, 0, NormWidth);
  DrawPoly (4, Triangle);
```

```
   READLN;
   CloseGraph;
  END.
```

(iii) Procedure Bar

This procedure draws a filled-in rectangle using the current color and fill style. It is used mainly for bar charts. It is declared as

Bar (x1, y1, x2, y2 : INTEGER);

where, as before, (x1, y1) are the coordinates of the upper left corner and (x2, y2) are the coordinates of the lower right corner.

The following example shows how bars can be drawn with different types of filling styles.

Program 3.16

```
PROGRAM DrawBars;
Uses Graph;
VAR GraphDriver, GraphMode : INTEGER;
    i, width : INTEGER;
    color, filling : WORD;
BEGIN
  GraphDriver := Detect;
  InitGraph (GraphDriver, GraphMode, '');
  IF GraphResult <>GrOk THEN Halt(1);
  width := 30;
  color := white;
  filling := 1;
  FOR i := 1 TO 5 DO
    BEGIN
      SetFillStyle (filling + i, color);
      BAR (150+i×width, i×10, 150+Succ(i)×width, 200);
    END;
  READLN;
  CloseGraph
END.
```

(iv) Procedure Bar3D

This procedure draws a 3-dimensional bar using the current fill style and color. It is declared as

Bar3D (x1, y1, x2, y2 : INTEGER; Depth : word; Top : BOOLEAN)

The outline of the bar is drawn in the current line style and color. Depth defines the depth of the 3D-outline of the bar, and is measure in the number of pixels used. If Top is True, a 3-D top is put on the bar. If Top is False, it is possible to stack several bars on top of each other. The Graph unit defines the following constants.

```
CONST       TopOn  = TRUE;
            TopOff = FALSE;
```

A suitable value of depth is about 25 % of the width of the bar. It is possible to obtain an outlined two-dimensional bar by drawing a 3-D bar with zero depth. A typical program for drawing 3-dimensional bars is given in the following example.

Program 3.17

```
PROGRAM Draw3DBars:
Uses Graph;
VAR  GraphDriver, GraphMode : INTEGER;
BEGIN
  GraphDriver := Detect;
  InitGraph (GraphDriver, GraphMode, '');
  IF GraphResult <>GrOk THEN Halt(1);
  SetColor (white);
  SetFillStyle (SlashFill, brown);
  Bar3D (50, 10, 130, 180, 20, TopOff);  (* bar with top off *)
  SetFillStyle (BkSlashFill, yellow);
  Bar3D (200, 20, 280, 180, 20, TopOn);   (* bar with top on *)
  Bar3D (350, 20, 430, 180, 0, TopOff);  (* outlined bar *)
  READLN;
  CloseGraph
END.
```

(v) Procedure SetFillStyle

This procedure is used for setting the style and color of the fill. It is declared as

```
SetFillStyle (Pattern : WORD; color : WORD);
```

Several fill patterns are available. The following constants are pre-declared in the Graph unit.

```
CONST       EmptyFill      = 0;  (Fills area in background color)
            SolidFill      = 1;  (Fills area in solid fill color)
            LineFill       = 2;
            LtSlashFill    = 3;
            SlashFill      = 4;
            BkSlashFill    = 5;
            LtBkSlashFill  = 6;
            HatchFill      = 7;  (Fills area with light hatch)
            XHatchFill     = 8;  (Fills area with heavy hatch)
            InetrleaveFill = 9;
            WideDotFill    = 10;
            CloseDotFill   = 11;
```

The choice of color depends upon the graphics card used. The available colors are described in the list of constant declarations given in section 3.3.

(vi) Procedure GetFillSettings

This procedure returns the last fill pattern and color set by a previous call to the procedures SetFillStyle or SetFillPattern. It is declared as

GetFillSettings (VAR FillInfo : FillSettingsType)

FillSettingsType is a predeclared record variable in the Graph unit, defined as

```
TYPE  FillSettings Type  =   RECORD
                                 Pattern : WORD;
                                 Color   : WORD;
                             END;
```

(vii) Procedure SetFillPattern

This procedure selects a user-defined fill pattern and thus provides the user with the opportunity to create patterns that are different from those provided by procedure SetFill Style. It is declared as

SetFillPattern (Pattern : FillPatternType; Color : WORD)

FillPatternType is predefined as

```
TYPE
FillPatternType = ARRAY [1..8] OF BYTE;
```

The fill pattern is based on the underlying byte values contained in the pattern array, which is 8 bytes long with each byte corresponding to 8 pixels in the pattern. Whenever a bit in a pattern is valued at 1, a pixel is plotted. An example of a fillpattern will be shown with the procedure FillPoly in this subsection.

(viii) Procedure GetFillPattern

It returns the last fill pattern that was set by a previous call to the procedure SetFillPattern. It is declared as

GetFillPattern (VAR FillPattern : FillPatternType)

As stated earlier, the fill pattern is an eight-byte long array, with each byte corresponding to 8 pixels in the pattern. If no call has been made to SetFillPattern then this procedure will return an array filled with $FF.

(ix) Procedure FillPoly

It draws and fills a polygon using the scan converter. Unlike the procedure DrawPoly, in this case it does not require an extra vertex in order to draw a closed figure. It is declared as

FillPoly (NumPoints : WORD; VAR PolyPoints : PointType)

NumPoints specifies the number of points (or vertices) in the polygon and PolyPoints contain the coordinates of each of the vertices. An example of the use of FillPoly, along with SetFillPattern, is shown in the following program.

Program 3.18

```
PROGRAM DrawFilledTriangle;
Uses Graph;
CONST
    Triangle : ARRAY [1..3] OF PointType = (( x:80; y:240),
                                            ( x:280; y:40),
                                            ( x:480; y:240));
    Gray50:FillPatternType = ($AA, $11, $AA, $11,
                              $AA, $11, $AA, $11);
VAR GraphDriver, GraphMode, ErrorCode : INTEGER;
BEGIN
  GraphDriver := Detect;
  InitGraph (GraphDriver, GraphMode, 'C:\DRIVERS');
  ErrorCode := GraphResult;
  IF ErrorCode < > grOk THEN
  BEGIN
    WriteLn ('Graphics error: ', GraphErrorMsg(ErrorCode));
    WriteLn ('Program aborted....');
    Halt(1)
  END;
  SetLineStyle (UserBitLn, $BBBB, ThickWidth);
  Rectangle (0, 0, GetMaxX, GetMaxY);
  SetLineStyle (SolidLn, 0, NormWidth);
  SetColor (white);
  SetFillPattern (Gray50, white);
  FillPoly (3, Triangle);
  READLN;
  CloseGraph;
END.
```

(x) Procedure FloodFill

This procedure fills a bounded region using the current fill pattern and fill color. It is declared as

FloodFill (x, y : INTEGER; Border : WORD)

The current fill pattern, as defined by SetFillStyle or SetFillPattern, is used to flood the area bounded by the color defined by border. If the point (x, y) is inside the area bounded by a closed curve (or polygon) then the interior of the area is flooded. On the other hand, if (x, y) lies outside the closed curve, then the exterior of the area is flooded.

3.3.8 Procedures related to arcs, circles and other curves

The Graph unit contains six procedures which are related to the drawing of arcs, circles and other curves. These are described below.

(i) Procedure Circle

It draws a circle with centre at a specified point and a given radius and is declared as

Circle (x, y : INTEGER; Radius : WORD)

The circle is drawn with centre at (x, y), in the current color, as set by the procedure SetColor. The Graph unit determines the aspect ratio for each graphics driver and utilises this information to get a proper circle.

(ii) Procedure Arc

It draws a circular arc with centre at a specified location from a given start angle to end angle. It is declared as

Arc (x, y : INTEGER; StartAngle, EndAngle, Radius : WORD)

Following the usual convention, all angles are measured in degrees in the counter-clockwise direction, with zero in the direction of the positive x-axis. The full circle will be drawn with start angle 0 and end angle 360.

(iii) Procedure GetArcCoords

It allows the user to obtain the coordinates of the last arc command and is declared as

GetArcCoordinates (VAR ArcCoords : ArcCoordsType)

where ArcCoords is a predelcared record variable, defined as

```
TYPE  ArcCoords = RECORD
        x, y,
        xStart, yStart, xEnd, yEnd : INTEGER;
        END;
```

The coordinates of the centre of the arc are given by (x, y), whereas the coordinates of the start and end points are given by (xStart, yStart) and (xEnd, yEnd), respectively. These values are often useful, e.g., when it is desired to draw a straight line through the start and end points.

The following program illustrates the use of this procedure to draw a straight line joining the start and end points of an arc.

Program 3.19

```
PROGRAM DrawArcSegment;
Uses Graph;
VAR  GraphDriver, GraphMode, ErrorCode : INTEGER;
     ArcCoords : ArcCoordsType;
BEGIN
  GraphDriver := Detect;
  InitGraph (GraphDriver, GraphMode, 'C:\DRIVERS');
  ErrorCode := GraphResult;
  IF ErrorCode < > grOk THEN
  BEGIN
```

```
    WriteLn ('Graphics error: ', GraphErrorMsg(ErrorCode));
    Halt(1)
  END;
  SetLineStyle (SolidLn, 0, NormWidth);
  SetColor (white);
  SetFillStyle (WideDotFill, GetMaxColor);
  Arc (320, 240, 0, 90, 200);
  GetArcCoords (ArcCoords);
  With ArcCoords DO
    Line (xStart, yStart, xEnd, yEnd);
  FloodFill (510, 230, GetMaxcolor);
  READLN;
  CloseGraph;
END.
```

(iv) Procedure Ellipse

It can be used for drawing an elliptical arc and is declared as

Ellipse ((x, y: INTEGER; StartAngle, EndAngle: WORD;
xRadius, yRadius: WORD);

The arc is drawn from start angle to end angle, using (x, y) as the centre and xRadius and yRadius as the horizontal and vertical axes. The complete ellipse will be drawn with start angle 0 and end angle 360. According to the usual convention, angles are measured in the counter-clockwise direction from the positive x-axis

(v) Procedure GetAspectRatio

Each graphics driver and graph mode has an aspect ratio associated with it (maximum y resolution divided by the maximum x resolution). This ratio is needed in order to makes circles round. This procedure determines the effective resolution of the graphics screen from which the aspect ratio can be calculated. The declaration is

GetAspectRatio (VAR xAsp, yAsp : WORD)

The following program illustrates the use of GetAspectRatio together with the procedure Rectangle to draw a square on the screen.

Program 3.20

```
PROGRAM DrawSquare;
Uses Graph;
VAR GraphDriver, GraphMode, ErrorCode : INTEGER;
    xAsp, yAsp : WORD;
    xSideLength, ySideLength : INTEGER;
    AspectRatio : REAL;
BEGIN
  GraphDriver := Detect;
```

```
InitGraph (GraphDriver, GraphMode, 'C:\DRIVERS');
ErrorCode := GraphResult;
IF ErrorCode <> grOk THEN
BEGIN
  WriteLn ('Graphics error: ', GraphErrorMsg(ErrorCode));
  WriteLn ('Program aborted....');
  Halt(1)
END;
SetLineStyle (UserBitLn, $BBBB, ThickWidth);
Rectangle (0, 0, GetMaxX, GetMaxY);
SetLineStyle (SolidLn, 0, NormWidth);
SetColor (white);
SetFillStyle (LtSlashFill, GetMaxColor);
GetAspectRatio (xAsp, yAsp);
AspectRatio := xAsp/yAsp;
xSideLength := 300;
ySideLength := Round (xSideLength×AspectRatio);
Rectangle (60, 80, xSidelength, ySideLength);
FloodFill (200, 130, GetMaxcolor);
READLN;
CloseGraph;
WRITELN ('Aspect Ratio is ', AspectRatio:6:3)
END.
```

(vi) Procedure PieSlice

It draws and fills a pie slice, with (x, y) as the centre and given start and end angles. It is declared as

PieSlice (x, y : INTEGER; VAR StartAngle,
EndAngle, radius : INTEGER)

The pie slice is outlined using the current color and filled using the pattern and color defined by SetFillStyle or SetFillPattern.

3.3.9 Routines related to colors and palettes

The Graph unit contains eight routines related to colors and palettes. These are described below.

(i) Procedure SetColor

This procedure sets the current drawing color using the palette. It is declared as

SetColor (Color : WORD)

Drawing colors may range between 0 and 15, depending upon the graphics driver and graph mode used. The predefined constant declarations for the available colors are given in section 3.4.

(ii) Function GetColor

It returns the color value entered by the previous successful call to SetColor. The result is a variable of type "word", i.e., an integer between 0 and 65535.

(iii) Procedure SetBkColor

It sets the current background color using the palette. As in the case of SetColor, a choice of up to 16 background colors may be available. It is declared as

```
SetBkColor (Color : WORD)
```

SetBkColor(N) makes the Nth color from the palette the color of the background. The only exception is SetBkColor(0), which makes the background color black.

(iv) Function GetBkColor

This function returns a variable of type "word", corresponding to the index of the current background color in the palette.

(v) Function GetMaxColor

It returns the highest value of color that can be used in the procedure SetColor. The value returned will depend upon the graphics card and graph mode used. For example, with a 256K EGA card, the value returned by the function GetMaxColor will be 15. On the other hand, with a CGA card in the high resolution mode, the value will be 1, since only the colors 0 and 1 are supported in this case.

(vi) Procedure SetPalette

This procedure changes one palette color as specified by ColorNum and Color. It is declared as

```
SetPalette(ColorNum: WORD; Color : SHORTINT)
```

The value of the entry ColorNum is changed to color. For example, SetPalette (0,LightCyan) makes the first color in the palette light cyan. Depending upon the current graphics driver and graph mode, ColorNum may range between 0 and 15. Changes made to the palette are seen immediately on the screen.

(vii) Procedure GetPalette

It returns the current palette and its size in a predeclared variable of type PaletteType. It is declared as

```
GetPalette (VAR Palette : PaletteType);
```

where PaletteType is defined as

```
CONST    MaxColor = 15;
 TYPE
   PaletteType  =  RECORD
                   Size : BYTE;
                   Colors : ARRAy [0..MaxColors] OF SHORTINT;
```

The field "size" reports the number of colors in the palette for the current driver in the current graph mode. The field "colors" contains the actual colors ranging between 0 and Size-1.

(viii) Procedure SetAllPalette

This procedure changes all palette colors as specified. It is declared as

SetAllPalette (VAR Palette);

where Palette is an untyped parameter. The first byte is the length of the palette. The next n bytes will replace the current palette colors. Each color may range from -1 to 15. A value of -1 will not change the value of the previous entry.

As with the procedure SetPalette, changes made to the palette are seen immediately on the screen.

3.3.10 Routines related to bit images

The Graph unit has three routines related to bit images. These can be used for either saving a bit image of the specified region of the screen into a buffer or for putting a bit image onto the screen.

(i) Function ImageSize

This function returns the number of bytes that will be required to store a rectangular region of the screen. It is declared as

ImageSize (x1, y1, x2, y2 : INTEGER);

where x1, y1, x2 and y2 define a rectangular region on the screen. The output is of the type "word". The image size includes space for two word variables that store the width and height of the region. The maximum value of image size is limited to 64 K bytes, otherwise a value of 0 is returned, along with GraphResult of -11 (grError).

(ii) Procedure GetImage

It saves a bit image of the specified rectangular region of the screen into a buffer. It is declared as

GetImage(x1, y1, x2, y2 : INTEGER; VAR BitMap);

where x1, y1, x2 and y2 define a rectangular region on the screen. BitMap is an untyped parameter that must be greater than or equal to 4 plus the amount of area defined by the region. The first two words of BitMap are reserved for the width and the height of the region. The remaining part of BitMap is used to save the bit image itself. The main restriction is that the memory required to save the image must not exceed 64 K bytes.

(iii) Procedure PutImage

It puts a bit image onto the screen and is declared as

PutImage(x, y : INTEGER; VAR BitMap; BitBlt : WORD)

where (x,y) is the upper left corner of a rectangular region on the screen. BitMap is an untyped parameter that contains the height and width of the region, and the bit image that will be put on the screen. BitBlt specifies which binary operator will be used for putting the image on the screen. The following constants are predefined:

```
CONST
    NormalPut   =   0;   { MOV }
    XORPut      =   1;   { XOR }
    OrPut       =   2;   { OR }
    AndPut      =   3;   { AND }
    NotPut      =   4;   { NOT }
```

Each constant corresponds to a special binary operation. For example, PutImage(x,y,BitMap,NormalPut) puts the image stored in BitMap at (x,y) using the assembly language MOV instruction for each byte in the image.

Similarly, PutImage(x,y,BitMap,XORPut) puts the image stored in BitMap at (x,y) using the assembly language XOR instruction for each byte of the image. This technique is often used for animation and results in "dragging" an image around the screen.

PutImage(x,y,BitMap,NotPut) inverts the bits in BitMap and then puts the image stored in BitMap at (x,y) using the assembly language MOV for each byte in the image. Thus, the image appears in inverse video of the original BitMap.

It should be noted that PutImage is never clipped to the boundary of the viewport. Moreover, with one exception, it is not actually clipped at the edge of the screen either. Instead, if any part of the image would go off the screen then no image is output.

An example program, that utilizes GetImage and PutImage, is given below.

Program 3.21

```
PROGRAM Images;
Uses Graph;
VAR  GraphDriver, GraphMode : INTEGER;
     P : POINTER;
     Size : WORD;
BEGIN
  GraphDriver := Detect;
  InitGraph (GraphDriver, GraphMode, '');
  IF GraphResult <> grOk THEN Halt(1);
  SetColor (white);
  SetBkColor (black);
  SetFillStyle (SlashFill, brown);
  Bar3D (20, 20, 100, 300, 0, TopOff);
  Size := ImageSize (10, 20, 30, 40);
  GetMem (P, Size);   { Allocate memory on heap }
  GetImage (20, 20, 100, 300, P^);
  READLN;
```

```
ClearDevice;
PutImage (100, 50, P^, NormalPut);
PutImage (400, 50, P^, XORPut);
READLN;
CloseGraph;
END.
```

3.3.11 Routines for displaying text in the graphics mode

The Graph unit contains eight routines related to the display of text in the graphics mode. These are described below.

(i) Procedure OutText

It sends a string of characters to the output device, starting at the current pointer. It is declared as

OutText (TextString : STRING)

TextString is truncated if it is too long to fit in the viewport. If one of the stroked fonts is active, TextString is truncated at the boundary of the screen. If a default font is active then no text is displayed if the string is too long to fit the screen.

Outtext uses the font set by SetTextStyle. It also uses the output options set by SetTextJustify. The current pointer is updated only if the direction of the text is horizontal and the justification is left.

(ii) Procedure OutTextXY

It sends a string of characters to the output device, starting at the point (x,y). It is declared as

OutTextXY (x, y : INTEGER; TextString : STRING)

If TextString is too long, it is truncated as in the procedure OutText. However, the current pointer is not updated by this procedure.

(iii) Procedure SetTextJustify

It sets text justification values used by the procedures OutText and OutTextXY. It is declared as

SetTextJusitfy (Horiz, Vert : WORD)

The text output after SetTextJustify will be justified around the current pointer as specified in the command. In the horizontal direction, the text can be left justified, right justified or centered around the current pointer. In the vertical direction, the text may be justified at the bottom, the top or the centre of the current pointer. The following constants are predeclared in the Graph unit.

```
CONST     { Horizontal justification }
```

```
LeftText    = 0;
CenterText  = 1;
RightText   = 2;
{ Vertical justification }
BottomText  = 0;
CenterText  = 1;
TopText     = 2;
```

It should be noted that CenterText for horizontal justification is different from CenterText for vertical justification. For example, the command SetTextJustify (CenterText, CenterText), will justify the centre of the text both horizontally and vertically with respect to the position of the current pointer.

(iv) Procedure SetTextStyle

It sets the current text font, style and character magnification factor and is declared as

```
SetTextStyle (Font: WORD; Direction: WORD; CharSize: WORD)
```

All text output using either OutText or OutTextXY is affected. The Graph unit supports five fonts, which are declared as below.

```
CONST    DefaultFont    = 0; { 8×8 bit mapped font }
         TriplexFont    = 1;
         SmallFont      = 2;
         SansSerifFont  = 3;
         GothicFont     = 4;
```

The last four are called "stroked" fonts and will be clipped at the screen edge.

The direction of the text can be either horizontal or vertical. The following constants are predeclared.

```
CONST    HorizDir = 0;   { Left to right }
         VertDir  = 1;   { Bottom to top }
```

The size of each character can be magnified by the choice of the factor CharSize. A value of 1 for CharSize will display the 8×8 bit-mapped font in an 8×8 pixel rectangle on the screen, whereas a value of 2 will display the 8×8 bit-mapped font in a 16×16 pixel rectangle. Hence, the resolution of text in this font deteriorates as the CharSize is increased. On the other hand, the resolution of the stroked fonts is not affected by the value of CharSize, although the characters are magnified.

(v) Procedure SetUserCharSize

This procedure allows the user to vary the character width and height for stroked fonts. It is declared as

```
SetUserCharSize (MultX, DivX, MultY, DivY : BYTE)
```

The normal width of a character is multiplied by the ratio MultX/DivX for the active font. Similarly, the normal height is multiplied by the ratio MultY/DivY. For example, in order to make a character twice as wide, one may set MultX to 2 and DivX to 1.

The following program shows an example of the use of this procedure to change the height and width of text. It should be noted that the command SetUserCharSize is followed immediately by SetTextStyle.

Program 3.22

```
PROGRAM CharacterSize;
{ It shows the use of SetUserCharSize }
Uses Graph;
VAR GraphDriver, GraphMode, GraphError : INTEGER;
BEGIN
  GraphDriver := Detect;
  InitGraph (GraphDriver, GraphMode, '');
  GraphError := GraphResult;
  IF GraphError < 0 THEN
    BEGIN
      WRITELN ('Graphics error: ', GraphErrorMsg(GraphError));
      Halt(1)
    END;
  SetTextStyle (TriplexFont, HorizDir, 4);
  OutTextXY (320, 20, 'Normal    ');
  SetUserCharSize (1, 1, 1, 2);
  SetTextStyle (TriplexFont, HorizDir, UserCharSize);
  OutTextXY (330, 90, 'Short     ');
  SetUserCharSize (7, 2, 4, 1);
  SetTextStyle (TriplexFont, HorizDir, UserCharSize);
  OutTextXY (1, 150, 'Tall and Wide');
  READLN;
  CloseGraph
END.
```

(vi) Procedure GetTextSettings

It returns the current text font, direction, size of characters, and justification as set by SetTextStyle and SetTextJustify. It is declared as

GetTextSettings (VAR TextInfo: TextSettingsType);

where the record variable TextSettingsType is defined as below.

```
TYPE  TextSettingsType = RECORD
                Font : WORD;
                Direction : WORD;
                CharSize : WORD;
                Horiz : WORD;
                Vert : WORD;
              END;
```

The various constants for font, direction and justification are as defined for the procedure SetTextStyle.

(vii) Function TextHeight

It returns the height of a text string in pixels and is declared as

TextHeight(TextString : STRING)

The output of the function is a variable of type "word". It is useful for adjusting the spacing between lines. Although it is possible to compute the spacing manually for any given font and character size, the use of this function makes it unnecessary to alter the spacing if a font of different size is selected.

(viii) Function TextWidth

It returns the width of a text string in pixels and is declared as

TextWidth(TextString : STRING)

The output of the function is a variable of type "word". It is useful for applications like determining the width of a viewport so that a title may fit on a graph, or in a box.

3.4 Constants and Variables declared in the Graph unit

A large number of constants and variables are declared in the Graph unit. Although some of these have been described with various procedures and functions in section 3.3, they will all be given in this section for completeness.

```
CONST
{ GraphResult error return codes }
grOk                 =  0;   { No error }
grNoInitGrap         = -1;   { (BGI) graphics not installed }
                                 (use InitGraph)
grNotDetecte         = -2;   { Graphics hardware not detected }
grFileNotFound       = -3;   { Device driver file not found }
grInvalidDriver      = -4;   { Invalid device driver file }
grNoLoadMem          = -5;   { Not enough memory to load driver }
grNoScanMem          = -6;   { Out of memory in scan fill }
grNoFloodMem         = -7;   { Out of memory in flood fill }
grFontNotFound       = -8;   { Font file not found }
grNoFontMem          = -9;   { Not enough memory to load font }
grInvalidMode        = -10;  { Invalid mode for selected driver }
grError              = -11;  { Graphics error }
grIOerror            = -12;  { Graphics I/O error }
grInvalidFont        = -13;  { Invalid font file }
grInvalidFontNum     = -14;  { Invalid font number }
grInvalidDeviceNum   = -15;  { Invalid device number }
```

```
{ Graphic Drivers }
Detect      = 0;      { Requests autodetection }
CGA         = 1;
MCGA        = 2;
EGA         = 3;
EGA64       = 4;
EGAMono     = 5;
Reserved    = 6;
HercMono    = 7;
ATT400      = 8;
VGA         = 9;
PC3270      = 10;
{ Graphics modes for each driver }
CGA         = 0;   {320×200 palette 0: LightGreen, LightRed, Yellow; 1 page }
CGAC1       = 1;   {320×200 pallete 1: LightCyan, LightMagenta, White; 1 page
}
CGAC        = 2;   {320×200 palette 2: Green, Red, Brown; 1 page }
CGAC        = 3;   {320×200 palette 3: Cyan, Magenta, LigthGray;1 page }
CGAHi       = 4;   {640×200;  1 page }
MCGAC0      = 0;   {320×200 palette 0: LightGreen, LightRed,    Yellow; 1 page
}
MCGAC1      = 1;   {320×200 pallete 1: LightCyan, LightMagenta,White; 1 page
}
MCGAC2      = 2;   {320×200 palette 2: Green, Red, Brown; 1 page }
MCGAC3      = 3;   {320×200 palette 3: Cyan, Magenta, LigthGray; 1 page }
MCGAMed     = 4;   {640×200;  1 page }
MCGAHi      = 5;   {640×480;  1 page }
EGALo       = 0;   {640×200;  16 color; 4 page }
EGAHi       = 1;   {640×350;  16 color; 2 page }
EGA64Lo     = 0;   {640×200;  16 color; 1 page }
EGA64Hi     = 1;   {640×350;  4 color; 1 page }
EGAMonoHi   = 3;   {640×350;  64K on card, 2 page; 256K on card, 1 page }
HercMonoHi  = 0;   {720×348;  2 page }
ATT400C0    = 0;   {320×200 palette 0: LightGreen, LightRed,    Yellow; 1 page
}
ATT400C1    = 1;   {320×200 pallete 1: LightCyan, LightMagenta,White; 1 page
}
ATT400C2    = 2;   {320×200 palette 2: Green, Red, Brown; 1 page }
ATT400C3    = 3;   {320×200 palette 3: Cyan, Magenta, LigthGray;1 page }
ATT400Med   = 4;   {640×200;  1 page }
ATT400Hi    = 5;   {640×480;  1 page }
VGALo       = 0;   {640×200;  16 color; 4 page }
VGAMed      = 1;   {640×350;  16 color; 2 page }
```

```
    VGAHi          = 2;   {640×480;        16 color; 1 page }
    PC3270Hi       = 0;   {720×350;  1 page }
  { Colors for SetPalette and SetAllPalette }
    Black          = 0;
    Blue           = 1;
    Green          = 2;
    Cyan           = 3;
    Red            = 4;
    Magenta        = 5;
    Brown          = 6;
    LightGray      = 7;
    DarkGay        = 8;
    LightBlue      = 9;
    LightGreen     = 10;
    LightCyan      = 11;
    LightRed       = 12;
    LightMagenta       = 13;
    Yellow         = 14;
    White          = 15;
  .Line styles and widths for GetLineStyle and SetLineStyle }
    SolidLn              = 0;
    DottedLn             = 1;
    CenterLn             = 2;
    DashedLn             = 3;
    UserBitLn            = 4;
    NormWidth            = 0;
    ThickWidth           = 3;
  { Constants for SetTextStyle and GetTextStyle }
    DefaultFont          = 0;      { 8×8 bit-mapped font }
    TriplexFont          = 1;      { "Stroked" fonts }
    SmallFont            = 2;
    SansSerifFont                = 3;
    GothicFont                   = 4;
    HorizDir             = 0;      { Left to right }
    VertDir              = 1;      { Bottom to top }
    UserCharSize         = 0;
  { Clipping constants }
    ClipOn         = TRUE;
    ClipOff        = FALSE;
  { Bar3D constants }
    TopOn          = TRUE;
```

```
    TopOff          = FALSE;
{ Fill patterns for SetFillStyle and GetFillStyle }
    EmptyFill      =  0;
    SolidFIll      =  1;
    LineFill       =  2;
    LtSlashFill    =  3;
    SlashFill      =  4;
    BkSlashFill    =  5;
    LtBkSlashFill  =  6;
    HatchFill      =  7;
    XHatchFill     =  8;
    InterleaveFill =  9;
    WideDotFill    = 10;
    CloseDotFill   = 11;
    UserFill       = 12;

{ BitBlt operators for PutImage }
    NormalPut      = 0;
    XORPut         = 1;
    OrPut          = 2;
    AndPut         = 3;
    NotPut         = 4;
{ Horizontal justification of text for SetTextJustify }
    LeftText       = 0;
    CenterText     = 1;
    RightText      = 2;
{ Vertical justification of text for SetTextJustify }
    BottomText     = 0;
    CenterText     = 1;
    TopText        = 2;
{ Maximum number of possible colors }
    MaxColors      = 15;
{ Predefined record variables }
TYPE
  PaletteType      = RECORD
                          Size   : BYTE;
                          Colors : ARRAY [0..MaxColors] OF ShortInt;
                          END;

  LineSettingsType = RECORD
                          LineStyle : WORD;
```

```
                    Pattern   : WORD;
                    Thickness : WORD;
                END;
TextSettingsType = RECORD
                    Font      : WORD;
                    Direction : WORD;
                    CharSize  : WORD;
                    Horiz     : WORD;
                    Vert      : WORD;
                END;
FillSettingsType = RECORD
                    Pattern : WORD;
                    Color   : WORD;
                END;
FillPatternType  = ARRAY [1..8] OF BYTE;
                PointType = RECORD
                    x, y : INTEGER;

ViewPortType = RECORD
                    x1, y1, x2, y2 : INTEGER;
                    Clip           : BOOLEAN;
                    END;
ArcCoordType = RECORD
                    x, y           : INTEGER;
                    xStart, yStart : INTEGER;
                    xEnd, yEnd     : INTEGER;
                    End;
VAR     GraphGetMemPtr  : POINTER;   { Used for heap allocation }
        GraphFreeMemPtr : POINTER;   { Used for heap deallocation }
```

3.5 A PROGRAM FOR PLOTTING GRAPHS

As an example of the use of the various built-in routines, we shall describe a program for plotting the graph of a given function. The graph allows the axes to be scaled to fit the specified minimum and maximum values of x and y, but also allows the user to interactively change these limits. The program has been written in such a way that it will work for any of the common graphics adapters. Provision has also been made to label the axes and to make the y-axis of the graph increase while moving upwards on the screen although the screen coordinates have their origin at the upper left corner of the screen, making the downwards direction positive. The program is listed below.

Program 3.23

```
{$N+}      {Compiler directive for using double precision arithmetic}
{$IFDEF CPU87 }
{$E-}
{$ELSE}
{$E+}
{$ENDIF}  { Compiler directive for utilizing the coprocessor if available }
PROGRAM PlotGraph;
Uses Crt, Graph;
CONST
  number = 500;  { Number of points for plotting graph }
 VAR
  xMin, yMin, xMax, yMax, Xscale, Yscale : REAL;
  deltaX, deltaY, xOffset, x1, yOffset, y1 : INTEGER;
  response : CHAR;
FUNCTION F( x : REAL ) : REAL;  (* Function to be plotted *)
BEGIN
  F := 1.0 - exp(-x)×(cos(3×x) + sin(3×x)/3.0)
END;
PROCEDURE Greeting;
BEGIN
  ClrScr;
  GoToXY(7,6);
  WRITELN('Welcome to the graph plotting program');
  WRITELN;
  WRITELN('It can be used for obtaining the graph of a function y = f(x).');
  WRITELN('The user must supply the function as well as the lower and',
          ' upper limits');
  WRITELN('of  x  and  y.');
  WRITELN;
  WRITELN('The graph can be redrawn for different limits.');
  WRITELN;
  WRITELN ('Press <RETURN> to continue...');
  READLN;
  ClrScr
End;
PROCEDURE GetLimits;
BEGIN
  WRITE('Enter the minimum value of x:  ');
  READLN (xMin);
  WRITE('Enter the maximum value of x: ');
  READLN (xMax);
  WRITE('Enter the minimum value of y:  ');
```

```
  READLN (yMin);
  WRITE('Enter the maximum value of y: ');
  READLN (yMax)
END;
PROCEDURE Initialize;
VAR
  Driver, ErrorCode, Mode : INTEGER;
BEGIN
  Driver := Detect;
  InitGraph (Driver,Mode,'');
  ErrorCode := GraphResult;
  IF ErrorCode <> grOk THEN
    BEGIN
      WRITE ('Graphics error: ');
      WRITELN (GraphErrorMsg(ErrorCode));
      Halt(1)
    END;
  SetBkColor(0)
END;
PROCEDURE Scale;
BEGIN
  xOffset := GetMaxX DIV 10;            { Minimum x on graph }
  x1 := GetMaxX - xOffset;              { Maximum x on graph }
  yOffset := GetMaxY DIV 10;            { Minimum y on graph - from top }     y1 :=
GetMaxY - yOffset;           { Maximum y on graph - from top }        deltaX := (x1 - xOffset)
DIV 10;    { Distance between ver. grid lines }
  deltaY := (y1 - yOffset) DIV 10;      { Distance between hor. grid lines }
  x1 := xOffset + 10×deltaX;            { Max x on graph }
  y1 := yOffset + 10×deltaY;            { Max y on graph - from top }
  Xscale := (x1 - xOffset)/(xMax - xMin);
  Yscale := (y1 - yOffset)/(yMax - yMin)
END;
PROCEDURE DrawAxes;
VAR
  x, y : INTEGER;
  i : BYTE;
BEGIN
    IF (GetMaxColor > 7) THEN
    SetColor (LightRed)
  ELSE SetColor(GetMaxColor);
  Line (xOffset,y1, x1,y1);             { Draw x-axis }
  Line (xOffset,yOffset, xOffset,y1);   { Draw y-axis }
  IF (GetMaxColor > 7) THEN
```

```
    SetColor (LightBlue);
  FOR i := 1  TO  10  DO
    BEGIN
      x := xOffset + i×deltaX;
      y := y1 - i×deltaY;
      Line (x,yOffset, x,y1);           { Draw vertical grid line }
      Line (xOffset,y, x1,y)            { Draw horizontal grid line }
    END
END;
FUNCTION RealToString( x : REAL ): String;
{ Convert a real number to a string for output }
VAR
  s : String;
BEGIN
  Str(x:3:1,s);
  RealToString := s
END;
PROCEDURE LabelAxes;
VAR  xLabel, yLabel : STRING[20];
BEGIN
  IF (GetMaxColor > 1) THEN
    SetColor (Yellow)
  ELSE  SetColor(GetMaxColor);
  SetTextStyle(0,HorizDir,1);
  SetTextJustify(CenterText,CenterText);
  xLabel := 'x';
  yLabel := '1 - exp(-x)×(cos(3×x) + sin(3×x)/3)';
  OutTextXY(xOffset,y1 + 10,RealToString(xMiN));
  OutTextXY(x1,y1 + 10,RealToString(xMax));
  OutTextXY(xOffset - 25,y1,RealToString(yMin));
  OutTextXY(xOffset - 25,yOffset,RealToString(yMax));
  OutTextXY(xOffset - 25,y1 - 5×deltaY,RealToString((yMin + yMax)/2.0));
  OutTextXY(xOffset + 5×deltaX,y1 + 10,RealToString((xMin + xMax)/2.0));
  SetTextStyle(TriplexFont, HorizDir, 1);
  OutTextXY(xOffSet + 5×deltaX,GetMaxY - 9, xLabel);
  SetTextStyle(TriplexFont, VertDir, 1);
  OutTextXy(22,y1 - 5×deltaY, yLabel)
END;
PROCEDURE DrawGraph;
VAR
  xb, yb : INTEGER;
  x, delta, p : REAL;
  i : WORD;
```

```
BEGIN
  delta := (xMax - xMin)/number;
  IF (GetMaxColor> 7) THEN
    SetColor (LightGreen)
  ELSE SetColor (GetMaxColor);
  yb := y1 - Round ((F(xMin) - yMin)×Yscale);
  MoveTo (xOffset, yb);
  FOR i := 1 TO number DO
    BEGIN
      p := i×delta;
      xb := Round(p×Xscale) + xOffset;
      yb := y1 - Round((F(xMin + p) - yMin)×Yscale);
      LineTo (xb, yb)
    END
END;

BEGIN (* Main program *)
  Greeting;
  REPEAT
    GetLimits;
    Initialize;
    Scale;
    DrawAxes;
    LabelAxes;
    DrawGraph;
    READLN;
    CloseGraph;
    WRITE('Do you want the graph redrawn with another scale?   (Y or N)   ');   READ
      (response)
  UNTIL NOT (UpCase(response) = 'Y')
END.
```

A more advanced and user-friendly program for plotting the graph of a function will be described in chapter 8. One important feature of that program is that the computer first calculates the function to be plotted for the given range of the independent variable (x-axis) and then determines the optimum scale for the graph. Another useful feature is that it allows the function to be input from the keyboard, so that the user does not have to recompile the program every time a new function is to be plotted.

3.6 SUMMARY

In this chapter, we have described the following:

- functions from the Windows Graphics Device Interface (GDI) for displaying graphics in the application's window. These can be accessed through the *TGdiBase* class hierarchy in *OWL in* Borland *C*. We have also given an example program in Windows 3.1 SDK.

the built-in graphics routines which are available in the Graph unit of Turbo Pascal. A very useful feature of this unit is that one can write a program which will work with all currently available graphics drivers for personal computers that are compatible with the IBM PC. Several short programs in the text illustrate the use of some of these routines. Finally, in section 3.5, a program for plotting the graph of a function has been given. It has been written in such a way that it can be used for plotting the graph of a given function, independently of the type of graphics card on a given computer. It also allows the user to interactively change the graph after a plot has been displayed.

The reader is advised to try writing some short Windows programs using OWL, and SDK and DOS programs in order to fully exploit the valuable features of the GUI. Some of the problems given in the next section would be very helpful.

The Windows 3.1 graphics programming as described in this chapter will be useful even for Windows 95 as most of the improved graphics architecture of Windows 95 is already available as API's for Windows 3.1. The DIBEngine would enable users to bypass the GDI and blast DIB directly to the screen, thus games under Windows 95 would run as fast as under DOS.

3.7 PROBLEMS

1. Write a program that will draw on the screen as large a circle as possible, and also draw the vertical and horizontal axes through the centre of the circle. This should be followed by inscribing the largest possible regular hexagon within the circle (see program 3.7).

2. Write a computer program that will draw as large an equilateral triangle on the screen that is possible.

3. Write a computer program that will first draw a circle with diameter 100 units and centre at the point (125, 80). This should be followed by drawing an ellipse that has the same centre point, having major axis of 100 and minor axis 50. Finally, fill the ellipse with widely spaced dots.

4. Write a program for displaying a histogram of the prices of three objects over a five-yer period, as detailed below, utilizing the routines for drawing bars (including 3-d bars if you wish).

Item	1983	1984	1985	1986	1987
A	5000	4200	3500	3000	2500
B	3000	3500	4000	4500	3800
C	2000	4000	3500	3800	3000

It would look nicer if the bars representing prices of different objects are shaded differently.

5. Write a program for displaying the pie-chart representing the budget allocations of a country. The four main items in the budget are (i) defence (30%), (ii) education (40%), (iii) health (20%) and (iv) welfare (10%). The various slices of the pie should be labelled appropriately. Use the procedure PieSlice and suitable fill patterns.

6. A cardioid can be described through the following equation,

$$(x^2 + y^2)^2 = a^2(x^2 - y^2)$$

Write a computer program which will plot the cardioid for specified values of a. Use the function GetAspectRatio to make certain that the shape of the curve is not changed.

7. Repeat for the case when the equation of a cardioid is given in the polar form,

$$r^2 = a^2 \sin 2\Theta.$$

8. Write a program to draw the side view of a wheel. Use GetImage and PutImage to produce the impression that the wheel is rolling in the horizontal plane.

9. Repeat the previous problem using the procedures SetActivePage and SetVisualPage to produce animation.

10. The program for plotting the graph of a function, given in section 3.5, uses the formula of the function to calculate points on the graph and plots a segment while calculating the next point. Write another program which would first calculate and store the coordinates of 500 data points before plotting them. The program should also give the user the option of reading the points from a disk file; this may be specially suitable for plotting data obtained experimentally, as well as for optimising the scales of the graph.

11. Modify the program written for the previous problem by using the procedures SetActivePage and SetVisualPage, so that the user may see the graph being plotted at a higher speed.

12. Modify program 3.4 such that it puts small circle at the location of the mouse cursor on the screen when left button of the mouse is pressed and puts a a small rectangle at the cursor spot when right button of mouse is pressed. Note that program 3.4 pops a message box indicating that left or right button of mouse is pressed.

13. Write a program using ObjectWindows Library to emulate all the functions of program 3.7.

14. Introduce status and control bars in program 3.6. The functions given in the menu should be available as buttonson the control bar. Also incorporate file save feature in the CanClose function.

3.8 REFERENCES

1. Jim Conger, *Windows Programming Primer Plus*, The Waite Group, 1994.
2. N. Barkakati, *Borland C++ 4 Developer's Guide*, Sams Publishing, 1994.
3. Borland International : Reference Manual for Turbo Pascal version 7.0
4. Borland International : Reference Manual for Turbo *C/C++*
5. Borland International : Reference Manual for Borland *C++*
6. Borland International: *Borland ObjectWindows - Programmer's Guide*, version 2.5, 1994.
7. Borland International: *Borland ObjectWindows - Tutorial*, 1994.
8. Borland International: *Resource Workshop* - User's Guide.

CHAPTER 4

DATA STRUCTURES FOR COMPUTER GRAPHICS

4.1 INTRODUCTION

The collection and processing of graphical data requires the data to be stored in the computer memory. The function of an interactive computer program is to analyze and manipulate this data efficiently to incorporate the changes desired and present the results quickly in graphical form. The data can be stored in memory by: (i) declaring it in the program, (ii) reading it into the program (from disk, tape, graphics tablet/digitizer, or other input devices), or (iii) creating it while the program is run.

The question now arises as to how to store this data? Should it be scattered throughout the memory or collected in a single file? Efficient arrangement of data will optimize the storage needs, access time and execution speeds. An organization of data in the computer memory is called a data structure. Some primitive data structures available as a standard feature in programming languages are types of data like integer, real, Boolean, character and arrays.

There is no standard nomenclature for the parts of data structure and a variety of names (e.g., elements, components, members, nodes, items) are used in the literature. Data structure not shoule not only describe the organization of the data but also include the natural inter-relationship between its elements. For example, to analyze an electrical circuit, it is not sufficient to know the number and types of components and their respective values. One must also necessary to know how these components are inter-connected.

The data structure for a graphical application should describe a picture in terms of primitives (e.g., points, lines, curves, the position of text strings) and inter-relationships between them. It should be sufficiently flexible to allow the following operations:

(i) reference to any graphical element in the picture,

(ii) modification of the picture by deleting or adding one or more elements,

(iii) scaling, translation and/or rotation of a part or whole of the picture (these operations are defined in chapter 6 and 7).

An application program may perform one or more of these operations and will create a new display file or update the existing display file.

Borland C++ comes with large number of container classes, known as Borland International Data Structures (BIDS), that provide objects such as linked lists and dynamic arrays. The BIDS container classes offer two level of abstraction, (i) Fundamental Data Structures (FDS) such as vectors and linked lists, and (ii) Abstract Data Type (ADT) such as stacks and queues. An ADT can be implemented using any FDS. The class templates include in FDS are: Vectors (<classlib\vectimp.h>), singly-linked lists (<classlib\listimp.h>), doubly-linked lists (<classlib\listimp.h>), hash tables (<classlib/hashimp.h>), and binary trees (<classlib\binimp.h>). The ADT container classes are: arrays (<classlib\arrays.h>), associations (<classlib\assoc.h>), bag (<classlib\bags.h>), queue (<classlib\ queues.h>), deque (<classlib\deques.h>), dictionary (<classlib\ dict.h>), sets (<classlib\ sets.h>) and stacks (<classlib\ stacks.h>). For description of the classes, the reader can refer to the documentation which comes with the C++ compiler.

In the following sections, we shall discuss the various data and picture structures, that are suitable for graphics and illustrate their use through some programming examples in Pascal, C, and C++ including container classes..

4.2 TYPES OF DATA STRUCTURES

Many different types of data structures are used. We shall start with some basic definitions.

Data: It consists of numerical values, names, codes or an attribute. Each of these can be separately called a data element or an item.

Record: It is a collection of data elements.

Block: The elements of a record are stored in continuous memory locations called blocks.

File: It is a collection of records.

Pointers: A pointer is used as a means for linking one piece of data to another. In the simplest case, it is a word which contains an address.

4.2.1 Linear List

A linear list is a one-dimensional structure that associates a collection of identical data types as its members. The block of data is identified by a simple name. We can represent a list by a set of nodes L(1), L(2), . . . , L(N), where N > 0. The first node is L(1) and the last node is L(N). For 1 < n < N, the nth node L(n) is preceded by node L(n-1) and is followed by node L(n+1).

In Pascal, a list can be constructed by declaring an ARRAY. It has the following form

name : ARRAY [1 . . . dimension] OF type.

Any Pascal data type, such as INTEGER, REAL of STRING can appear after the reserve word OF. It defines the nature of each element of the array.

Computer memory is one-dimensional in access and the addresses are assigned serially. Therefore, the list can be easily mapped from its conceptual representation into internal form by assigning contiguous memory locations to its elements. The address of node can be computed from the following expression.

$$\text{Address } [L(n+1)] = \text{Address } [L(n)] + C$$

where C is the number of words per node. Usually $C = 1$, but when $C > 1$, it is convenient to split a single list into C parallel lists. In general,

$$\text{Address } [L(n)] = A_1 + (n-1)*C$$

where A_1 is the address of the first node and $(n-1)*C$ is the displacement of the nth node from the first node.

With linear list organization, the data in the nodes can be retrieved quickly, but inserting a new node or deleting an existing node is a difficult and time-consuming process since the whole list must be updated each time a change occurs. However, linear lists, in which insertion of a node, deletion of a node, or access to a node occur from the first or the last node, are often encountered. The next subsection will describe three structures of this type. These are called the stack, the queue and the deque.

4.2.1.1 Stack

In this structure, all insertions, deletions and usually all accesses are made at one end of the list. A pointer is maintained which always points to the top element in the stack. This avoids the need to physically push or pop the elements from the stack. Figure 4.1 shows a typical stack. In the stack, the data entered last is available on the top of the stack. Therefore, stack organization is also called "last in first out" (LIFO).

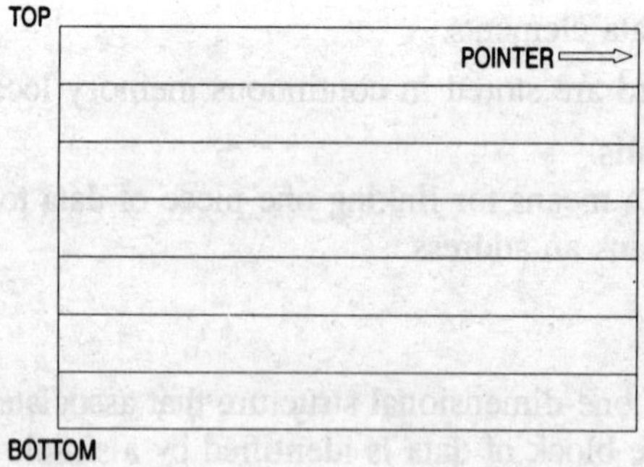

Figure 4.1 A Stack

The Pascal procedures PUSH (insert) and POP (delete) are given below:

```
PROCEDURE Push (VAR pointer : INTEGER; data : REAL);
BEGIN
        pointer := pointer + 1;
        IF pointer > 1 THEN Overflow;
        L [pointer] := data
END;

PROCEDURE Pop (VAR pointer : INTEGER; data : REAL);
BEGIN
        IF pointer = 0 THEN Underflow;
        data := L [pointer];
        pointer := pointer - 1
END;
```

The *C* version of these procedures is listed below:

```
push( pointer, data)
```

```
int pointer;
float data;
{
    pointer += 1;
    if( pointer > 1) Overflow();
    L[pointer] = data;
}
pop( pointer, data)
int pointer;
float data;
{
   if( pointer == 0) Underflow();
   data = L[pointer];
   pointer -= 1;
}
```

The *C++* version of the above procedures is listed below:

```
// Implementation of an integer stack
#include   <studio.h>
#include   <string.h>
class stack{
  private:
      int *top;
         int *bottom
  public:
      stack()
      {
        top = bottom = new int ( 100);
      }
      void push ( int i)
      {
        if (( top - bottom ) < 100 )
                *top++ = i;
      }
      void pop () {
        if ( --top >= bottom )
                return *top;
      }
      ~stack()
      {
        delete bottom;
      }
};
```

Table 4.1 gives the class templates for implementation of stacks included in Borland C++. The term managed class refers to the class templates that accept a storage allocator as an argument for the template. In the table this argument is denoted by the *Alloc* in the template names. Public members function are add, detach, find, flush, ForEach, ItemsInContainer and IsEmpty. Stack container functions manage ordered chain of objects of type *T*. Objects are placed on to the chain and can be added or removed only from the first (top) position in the chain. This family includes the container classes given in the table.

Table 4. 1 Abstract Data Type (ADT) container classes for Stacks in Borland C++ 4.5 (declared in <classlib\stacks.h>)

Class Template	**Description**
TMStackAsVector<T, Alloc>	A managed stack of objects
TMStackAsVectorIterator<T, Alloc>	An iterator for TMStack as Vector classes
TStackAsVector<T>	An unmanaged stack of objects
TStackAsVectorIterator <T>	An iterator for TStack as Vector classes
TMIStackAsVector <T, Alloc>	A managed stack of pointers to objects
TMIStackAsVectorIterator <T, Alloc>	An iterator for TMIStack as vector classes
TIStackAsVector <T>	Unmanaged stack of pointers to objects of type T
TIStackAsVector Iterator <T>	Iterator for TIStack as Vector classes
TMStackAsList <T, Alloc>	A managed stack of objects
TMStackAsListIterator <T, Alloc>	An iterator for TMStack as List classes
TStackAsList <T>	An unmanaged stack of objects
TStackAsListIterator <T>	An iterator for TStack as List classes
TMIStackAsList<T, Alloc>	A managed list of pointers to objects
TMIStackAsListIterator <T, Alloc>	An iterator for TMIStack as List classes
TIStackAsList <T>	An unmanaged list of pointers to objects
TIStackAsListIterator <T>	An iterator for TIStack as List classes
TStack <T>	Same as TStack as Vector <T>
TStackIterator <T>	Same as TStack as Vector Iterator <T>

4.2.1.2 Queue

In a queue all insertions are made at one end of the list, deletions and accesses are made at the other end, as shown in figure 4.2. One end of the queue can be referred to as the front and the other as the rear. Two pointers called FRONT and REAR, are maintained to indicate the corresponding positions in the queue. The maximum number of permissible nodes in the queue can be denoted by the symbol N.

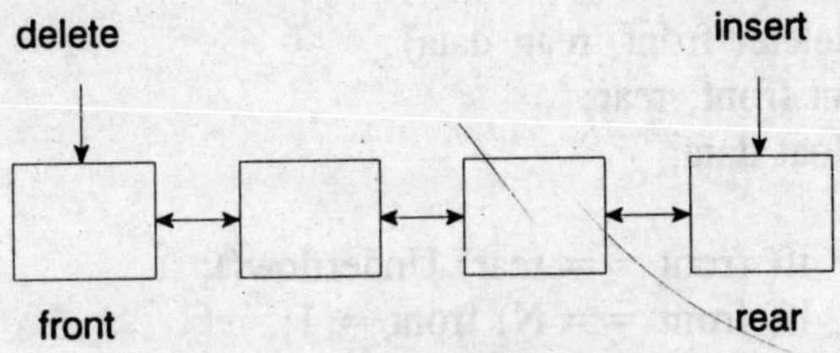

Figure 4.2 A Queue

For an empty queue the pointers FRONT and REAR will both be equal to 1. The procedures for the operations INSERT and DELETE are given below:

(a) Pascal version

```
PROCEDURE Insert (VAR front, rear : INTEGER; data : REAL);
BEGIN
    IF rear = N THEN
        rear := 1
    ELSE
        rear := rear + 1;
    IF rear = front THEN  Overflow;
    L [rear] := data
END;

PROCEDURE Delete (VAR front, rear : INTEGER; data : REAL);
BEGIN
    IF front = rear THEN Underflow;
    IF front = N THEN
        front := 1
    ELSE
        front := front + 1;
    data := L [front]
END;
```

(b) *C* version

```
insert( front, rear, data)
int front, rear;
```

```
float data;
{
   if (rear == N) rear = 1;
   else rear += 1;
   if (rear == front) Overflow();
   L[rear] = data;
}
delete( front, rear, data)
int front, rear;
float data;
{
   if( front == rear) Underflow();
   if( front == N) front = 1;
   else front += 1;
   data = L[front];
}
```

The overflow and underflow errors indicate that a program is attempting to operate on areas beyond the specified list boundary. A program can use this condition to decide the next course of action.

4.2.1.3 Deque

It is a double-ended queue. All operations, such as insertion, deletion and access can be performed from both ends of the list as shown in figure 4.3. Hence, a deque can grow or shrink in both directions.

Deques can be effectively employed in applications where a computer program

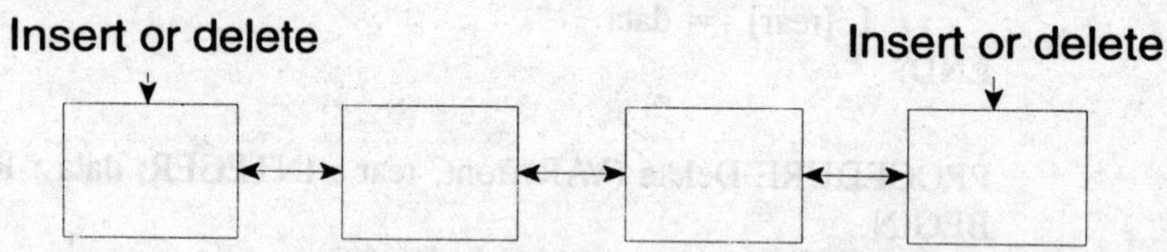

Figure 4.3 A Deque

may need to add or delete items at both ends of a queue. Situations of this type may occur in a time-sharing system where users may be served in a round-robin fashion (i.e., a user being served from one end of the deque is returned to the other end after completion of service request). Also, some users needing immediate service can be added to the serving end of the deque rather than the receiving end.

4.2.2 Linked list

Instead of keeping a linear list in sequential memory locations, a much more flexible scheme is to include in each node a link to the next node of the list. Figure 4.4 shows the cases of sequential and linked allocations.

Sequential		Linked		
A1:	DATA 1	A1:	DATA 1	A2
A1 + C:	DATA 2	A2:	DATA 2	A3
A1 + 2C:	DATA 3	A3:	DATA 3	A4
A1 + 3C:	DATA 4	A4:	DATA 4	NIL

Figure 4.4 Sequential and Linked Allocation

In sequential allocation, the program uses a variable or constant the value of which indicates the number of data items in the list. The index can be used to derive the address of the node. Each node in the linked list has two fields: the first field contains data and the second field is a pointer to the next list element. The program in this case uses a variable the value of which points to the first node of the list, say A1. From A1, all the data items of the list can be found. The last item in the linked list has NIL link. The linked allocation takes additional memory space for the storage of links. In cases where data items do not occupy the whole word, the link information can be packed in the same word. Another way to save memory is to combine several data items in one node and use only one link.

In linked allocation, it is very easy to delete one item. For example, to delete item "DATA 2" in Fig. 4.4, only the link associated with the item "DATA 1" need be changed to "A3". The modified list is shown in Figure 4.5.

A1:	DATA 1	A3
A2:	DATA 2	A3
A3:	DATA 3	A4
A4:	DATA 4	NIL

Figure 4.5 Deleting an item from a linked list

Similarly, an item can be easily inserted into the middle of a linked list. For example, to insert an item between "DATA 2" and "DATA 3", we need only change two links, as shown in figure 4.6. The main drawback of this scheme is in access to a random node of the list. To locate the desired node, one has to start from the top of the list and march down to the right place. On the other hand, operations such as merging two lists into a single list, or splitting a given list into two separate list can be easily accomplished. The linked scheme frees the programmer from constraints imposed by the sequential nature of computer memory.

A1:	DATA 1	A2
A2:	DATA 2	A5
A3:	DATA 3	A4
A4:	DATA 4	NIL
A5:	DATA 5	A3

Figure 4.6 Inserting an Item into a Linked List

It can be seen that nodes deleted from a linked list create unused spaces in the memory. This will not cause any problems in programs that use small memory space, but we cannot afford to waste the empty pockets created by these deletions when we need large memory space. In such cases, there is a need to keep track of empty memory space. One common method is to maintain a special list of all available memory space. This list has links to all nodes not currently in use. The link pointer (P) refers to the top of the available memory list. To extract a node for future use, the following steps are taken:

```
N := P;
P := Link [P];
```

where N is the address of the node extracted and Link [P] gives the address of the next node in the available memory pool.

Similarly, to add a node (with address N) to the available memory pool, we set

```
LINK [N] := P;
P := N;
```

We must also consider how to set up an available memory list at the beginning of a program. First we need to decide the amount of linked memory available for storing node data. The nodes are linked to form an available memory list. The last node is made the NIL link. The highest memory location is assigned a variable name, say MAX memory. The user program checks that it does not use space beyond MAX memory, else an overflow error is generated. However, in this case, when a link equal to NIL is encountered, it indicates an overflow condition.

Example 4.1

Figure 4.7 shows a list of five nodes, with addresses 10, 20, 30, 40 and 50, linked to form available memory list. The top of the list is indicated by pointer P. When we reserve a node for use then,

```
N := P;
P := LINK [P]
```

The result is that the pointer P points to location 20 which is the next free node. The node with address 10 is reserved for future use.

Address	Data	Link
10		20
20		30
30		40
40		50
50		NIL

Figure 4.7 Available memory list

Similarly, if we want to return a node with address 100 to the available memory list then,

```
LINK [100] := 20;
P := 100;
```

4.2.2.1 Creating a Linked List

We shall now describe the method for creating a linked list. First, a way of referencing the list is to be established. This can be done by defining a pointer to the first element of the list, also referred to as the list head.

To create a linked list with three nodes, as shown in figure 4.8, the following steps are required:

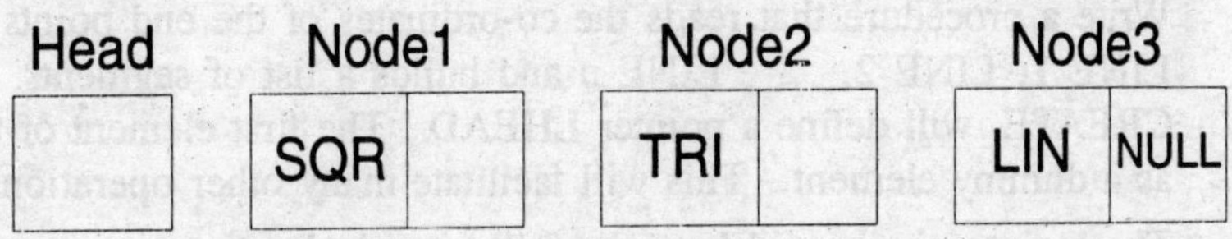

Figure 4.8 Linked List

Step 1: To represent a linked list in the memory, a record type with at least one field of type pointer must be declared. The new pointer type (l-pointer) points to the elements (records) of type l-node.

```
TYPE
    Symbols = PACKED ARRAY [1..3] OF CHAR;
    lPointer = ↑lNode;
    lNode=    RECORD
                      Data : Symbols;
                      Link : lPointer;
              END; (* lNode *)
```

Step 2: Declare three pointers, HEAD, I and J, to nodes 1, 2 and 3, respectively.

VAR HEAD, I, J : lPointer;

Step 3: Define data fields of a new list element (Node 1) referenced by pointer HEAD.

NEW (HEAD);
HEAD↑ DATA := 'SQR';

Step 4: Define link field of the Node 1 which should point to Node 2.

NEW (I);
HEAD↑.LINK := I;

The effect of the above statement is to create a new element that is pointed by I. The value of I is entered into the link field of Node 1.

Step 5: Enter data into Node 2 and create Node 3. The pointer J to the Node 3 is entered in the Link field of Node 2.

I↑.DATA := 'TRI';
I↑.LINK := J;

Step 6: 'LIN is written in the data field of Node 3. Since Node 3 is the last node, we write NIL (even a 0 can be used) in the link field.

J↑.DATA := 'LIN';
J↑.LINK := NIL;

Example 4.10

Write a procedure that reads the co-ordinates of the end points of line segments LINE 1, LINE 2, ... , LINE n and builds a list of segments. This procedure, CREATE, will define a pointer LHEAD. The first element of the list is defined as a dummy element. This will facilitate many other operations.

The main program will have the following declarations:

```
TYPE
      Symbol = PACKED ARRAY [1..5] OF CHAR;
      Segment =    RECORD
                       Name : Symbol;
                       xCordI : INTEGER;
                       yCordI : INTEGER;
                       xCordF : INTEGER;
                       yCordF : INTEGER
                   END;
      sPointer = ^ sNode;
      sNode =      RECORD
                       Data : Segment;
                       Link : sPointer
                   END;
```

The procedure, Create, is listed below;

```
PROCEDURE Create (VAR Lhead : sPointer);
VAR          Last, Next : sPointer;
PROCEDURE        CreateNode (VAR Next : sPointer);
VAR k : INTEGER;
BEGIN
        New (Next);
        With Next^.Data DO
                BEGIN
                        For k := 1 to 5 DO
                                READ (Name [k]);
                        READ (xCordI, yCordI, xCordF, yCordF);
                        READLN;
                        Link := NIL
                END,
END;
BEGIN (* Create *)
        New (Lhead);
        WITH Lhead^.Data DO
                BEGIN
                        Name := 'Dummy';
                          (* The first element is defined as dummy *)
                        xCordI := 0;
                        xCordY := 0;
                        xCordF := 0;
                        yCOrdF := 0;
                        Link := NIL
                END;
                (*  Read each line segment data with node :Next"  *)
        Last := Lhead;
        WHILE NOT EOF (DataFile) DO
                BEGIN
                        CreateNode (Next);
                        Last^.Link := Next;
                        Last := Next
                END;
END;  (* Create *)
```

A *C* version of this program is listed below:

```
typedef char Symbol[5];
typedef struct{
        Symbol Name;
        int xCordI;
        int xCordY;
```

```
        int xCordF;
        int yCordF;
        }Segment;
typedef struct{
        Segment Data;
        struct sNode *Link;
        }sNode;
typedef sNode *sPointer;
Create(Lhead)
ssPointer *Lhead;

{
        ssPointer Last, Next;
  (*Lhead) = (sNode *)malloc(sizeof(sNode));
  strcpy((*Lhead) -> Data.Name ,"Dummy");
  (*Lhead) -> Data.xCordI = 0;
  (*Lhead) -> Data.xCordY = 0;
  (*Lhead) -> Data.xCordF = 0;
  (*Lhead) -> Data.yCordF = 0;
  (*Lhead) -> Link = NULL;
  Last  = (*Lhead);
  while(!feof(DataFile)){
        CreateNode(&Next);
        Last -> Link = Next;
        Last = Next;
  }
}
CreateNode(Next)
        ssPointer *Next;
{
int k;
(*Next) = (sNode *)malloc(sizeof(sNode));
for(k = 1; k <= 5; k++)
        fscanf(DataFile,"%c",(*Next)-> Data.Name[k]);
        fscanf(DataFile,"%d %d %d %d\n", &(*Next) -> Data.xCordI, &(*Next) ->
        Data.yCordF,
        &(*Next) -> Data.xCordF, &(*Next) -> Data.yCordF);
        (*Next) -> Link = NULL;
```

4.2.2.2 Traversing the List

To access the data contained in the nodes of the list, we take the pointer to the first node of the list and then use this pointer in the link field of the first node to locate the second node. This procedure is repeated until we encounter the last node which has the entry NIL in its link field. The process of looking at Node 1 Node 2, etc., of the list is called traversing the list. The procedure "traverse" displays the data field of each node.

```
PROCEDURE Traverse (Head : sPointer);
 (* Head initially points to the first node of the list *)
BEGIN
        WHILE Head < > NIL DO
                BEGIN
                        WRITELN (Head^.data);
                        Head := Head^.Link
                END;
END;
```

4.2.2.3 Deleting a Node

The procedure for deleting a node will be illustrated by deleting Node 2 from the list shown in figure 4.8. Two pointers, LAST and NEXT, are used. NEXT points to the node

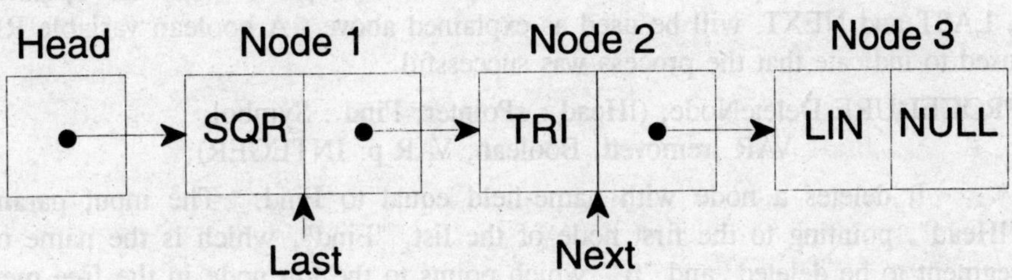

Figure 4.9 Pointers for delete operation

being deleted and LAST points to the node preceding it, as shown in figure 4.9.

If we set

$$LAST\uparrow.LINK := NEXT\uparrow.LINK$$

the data structure is modified as shown in figure 4.10. In effect, the link field pointed by LAST, i.e., Node 1 now points to Node 3 and not to Node 2. Thus, Node 2 is deleted from the linked list.

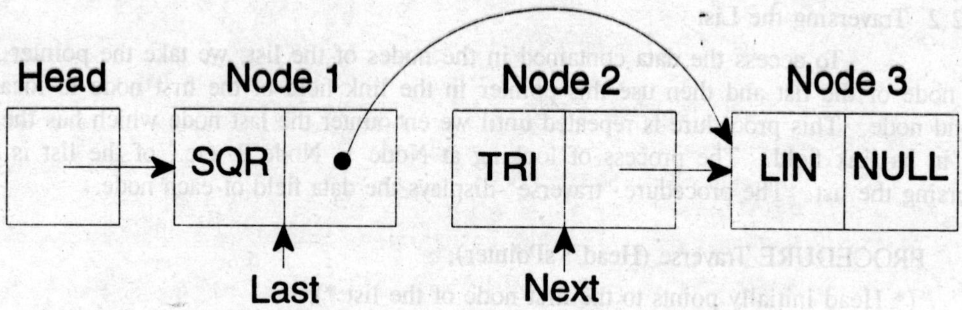

Figure 4.10 Linked list after delete operation

As described in section 4.2.2, the Node 2 can now be returned to the available memory list, so that it can be reused later. If P is the pointer to the top of the available memory list, then the following steps will add this node to the free memory pool:

```
NEXT↑.LINK := P;
P := NEXT;
```

Example 4.3

We shall now give a procedure to delete a specified line segment from the segment list, with the name of the segment being an input parameter.

Here, we should traverse the list to locate the node to be deleted. In section 4.2.3, the procedure traverse uses a pointer to the list head as an input to start the operation. Two pointers, LAST and NEXT, will be used as explained above. A boolean variable REMOVED will be used to indicate that the process was successful.

```
PROCEDURE DeleteNode; (lHead : sPointer; Find : Symbol;
                  VAR removed: Boolean; VAR p: INTEGER);
(*      It deletes a node with name-field equal to Find. The input parameters are
"lHead", pointing to the first node of the list, "Find", which is the name of the line
segment to be deleted, and "p", which points to the top node in the free memory list.
The output parameter "removed" is a Boolean variable which has the value 1 if
deletion is successful and 0 otherwise. *)
VAR           last, next      :      sPointer;
BEGIN
  next := lHead;
  WHILE (next^.data.Name < > Find) AND (next^.Link < > NIL) DO
    BEGIN
        last := next;
        next := next^.Link
    END;
        IF next^.data.Name = Find THEN
          (* The desired node has been found. Delete it. *)
```

```
        BEGIN
            last^.Link := next^.Link;
                    (*     Add desired node to the free memory list   *)
            next^.Link := p;
            p := next;
            removed := TRUE
        END
      ELSE
        removed := FALSE
  END;  (* DeleteNode *)
```

4.2.2.4 Inserting a Node

Insertion of a node in the midst of a list is quite simple in the linked allocation scheme. Two pointers, J and K, are used. These point to the nodes that immediately precede and follow the new node to be inserted. The following statements modify the data structure and insert a new node, as shown in figure 4.11.

```
NEW (J.Link);
J.Link := K;
```

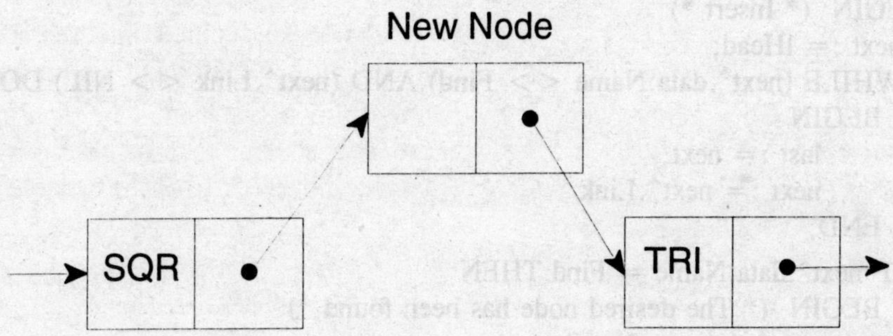

Figure 4.11 Insertion of a new node in the list

Example 4.4

We shall now write a procedure for inserting a new node in the line segment list created in example 4.2. The data for the new node, i.e., Name, and the co-ordinates of the initial and final points of the line segment, along with a pointer to the first node of the list is to be given as input parameters. Furthermore, the name of a line segment (say LINE 1, LINE 2, ...) is to be given to locate the position of the node after which a new node is to be added. As in the case of the procedure DeleteNode, two pointers LAST and NEXT will be useful to traverse the list of line segments to locate the desired segment. The address of the new node is taken from the free memory list.

```
PROCEDURE Insert (lHead: sPointer; Find: Symbol;
                        Newsegment: Segment; VAR p: INTEGER);
```

```
(*      Insert a new line segment in the line segment list.  The input parameters are
"lHead", pointing to the first node of the list, "Find", for locating the position of the
node after which the new segment is to be inserted,        "NewSegment" is the segment
to be inserted and "p", which points to the top of the free memory list.  *)

VAR  last, next : sPointer;

PROCEDURE InsertNode (NewSegment : Segment; VAR  j, k : sPointer);
(*      Insert a new node between the nodes pointed by j and k *)
BEGIN
        NEW (j^.Link);
        WITH j^.Link DO
                BEGIN
                        data := NewSegment;
                        link := k
                END;
END;  (* InsertNode *)

(* Search segment list to locate the position of the nodes between which the new node
is to be located *)

BEGIN  (* Insert *)
  next := lHead;
  WHILE (next^.data.Name <> Find) AND (next^.Link <> NIL) DO
    BEGIN
        last := next;
        next := next^.Link
    END;
  IF next^.data.Name = Find THEN
    BEGIN  (* The desired node has been found *)
        next^.data := NewSegment;
        InsertNode (NewSegment, last, next)
    END;
END;  (* Insert *)
```

4.2.3 Circular (Ring) List

This list has the property that the last node links to the first node (see figure 4.12). Thus, it does not have a NIL link. The advantage of this structure is that the list can be accessed starting at any given node. There is no first or last node. The node structure is similar to list and hence it is very easy to update the ring. Insertion of a new node at a desired place can be done by rearranging the links to include the new node in the ring. Deletion of a node is performed by adjusting the links as in the case of ordinary linked list.

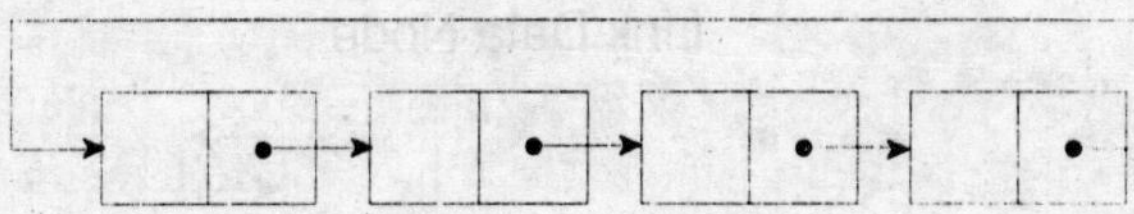

Figure 4.12 Circular List

Since there is no first or last node, the problem of locating the head of the list must be solved. The following solutions are possible:

i) while moving through the list from one node to the next, we may stop when we return to the node from where we started,

or ii) include a special recognizable node into each circular list as a convenient stopping place. This special node is often called the list head, as shown in figure 4.13.

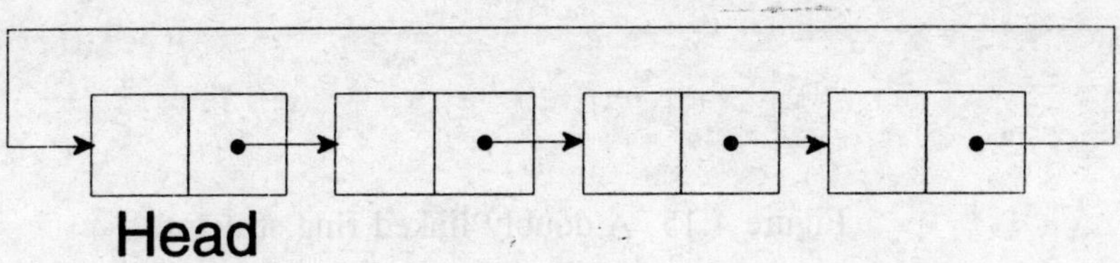

Figure 4.13 Circular list with special node

4.2.4 Multi-Lists

A more general list structure is one in which data elements belong to several lists. This type of structure is called a multi-list. The nodes of such lists have more than one link. For example, we can include two links in each node, pointing to the items on both sides of the node. This structure is called a doubly-linked (two-way) list.

As shown in figure 4.14, each node has three fields; two link fields: one each for forward and backward links and the data field. The following Pascal statements will declare the list in its general form:

```
TYPE
        Link = ^DoubleNode;
        DoubleNode = Record
        •
        •    data fields
        •
             Forward : Link;
             Backward : Link;
        END;
```

Figure 4.14 Doubly linked list

It can be seen that both the left and the right nodes of the list have NIL links. A doubly linked ring structure with link head (described in section 4.2.3) is shown in Fig. 4.15.

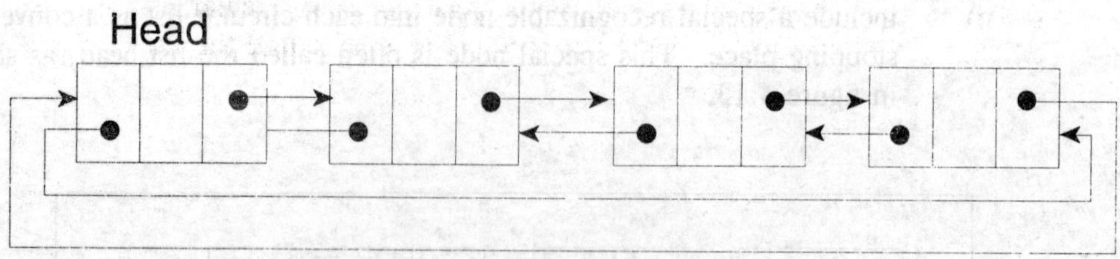

Figure 4.15 A doubly linked ring structure

The cost of the double link structure is the need for extra memory to keep the second link.

Deletion of a node X from a doubly linked list is shown in figure 4.16.

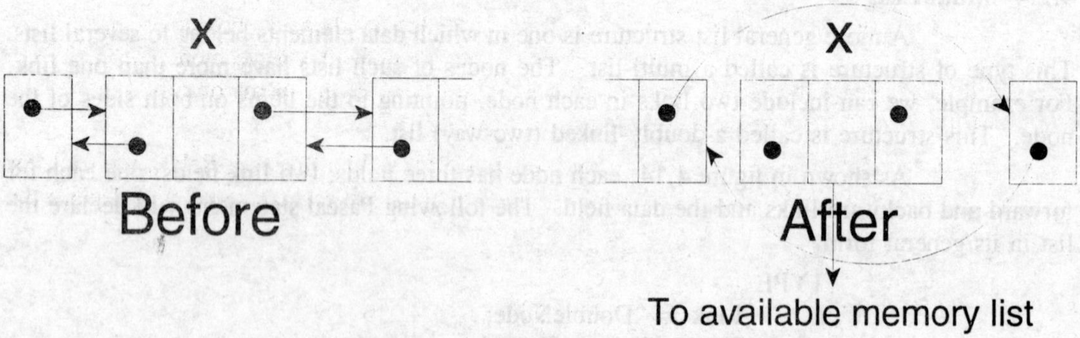

Figure 4.16 Deletion of node X

In a list with one-way link, we cannot delete a node unless we know which node precedes it. The steps for deletion in this case are shown below:

Step 1:

ForwardLink [BackwardLink [X]] := ForwardLink [X];
BackwardLink [ForwardLink [X]] := BackwardLink [X];

Step 2:

The node x is returned to the free memory pool.

Link [X] := P;
P := X;

The steps for inserting a node adjacent to node X are shown below:

Step 1:

Get a node from the free memory pool.

N := P;
P := Link [P];

Step 2:

BackwardLink [N] := X;
ForwardLink [N] := BackwardLink [X];
BackwardLink [ForwardLink [X]] := N;
ForwardLink [X] := N;

This operation affects the setting of five links (including the link from the free memory pool), as compared with three changes required for the case of a one-way linked list. Thus insertion is slower for a doubly linked list.

Updating a multi-list, which may have more than two links, is also quite easy. For instance, to delete a node from one-way linked lists, all lists containing this node are to be properly arranged. This necessitates searching the whole list structure to locate the node before deletion can be carried out. This procedure is quite time-consuming for large structures. In lists which have two-way multi-link structures, each node has pointers to the lists in which it occurs. Thus, only those lists, which have the node to be deleted need be processed. This saves processing time at the cost of some memory for storing all links.

Example 4.5 Figure 4.17 shows a line drawing of triangles PQS and PQR and a square APQB. The line PQ is common to three figures, as shown. A possible data structure for representing the diagram is shown in figure 4.18(a). Each figure is represented by separate ring. The node of each ring represents a line segment. The node representing the line PQ is common to all the three rings. In case we wish to delete line segment PQ, we will have to delete this from all the ring structures and pointers must be rearranged. Figure 4.18(b) shows the data structure after deletion of segment PQ.

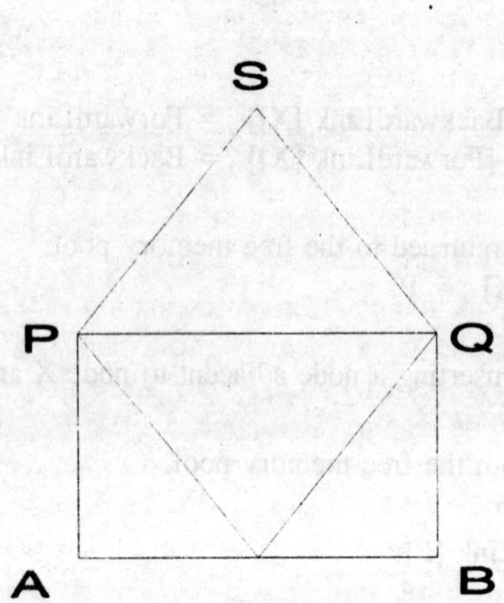

Figure 4.17 A line drawing

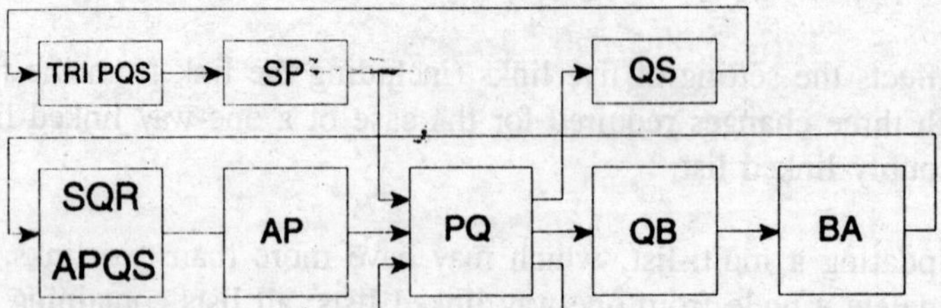

(a) Original list structure

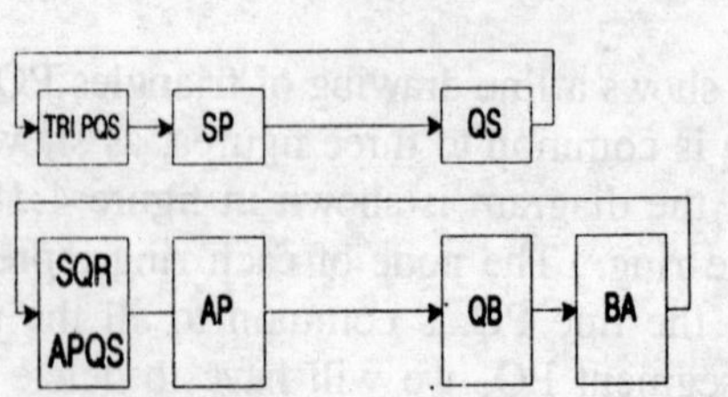

(b) List after deletion of line segment PQ

Figure 4.18 delete operation to multi-list structure

4.2.5 Arrays

One of the simplest generalizations of a linear list is a two-dimensional or higher dimensional array of information. The values in the array must all be of one type, which is called the 'base type' of the array. The number of dimensions and the size of each dimension cannot change the execution of the program.

Arrays are used in graphics for representation of black and white (binary) or colored pictures. For a black and white picture, an element takes a value '0' or '1'. For representing a gray scale, values between '0' and '63', are commonly used. For representing a single frame of black and white picture (as it appears on a TV screen), we need an array of 512*512 elements where each element would have a value between 0 and 63. Similarly, to represent a full colour picture three arrays of size 512*512 will be required to represent the three basic colors: red, green and blue.

The following Pascal declarations describe general digital pictures which may have grey levels between 0 and 63 or have limited colors; say green, blue, violet and orange.

```
CONST    PictureSize = 80; Black = 63; Black = 0;
TYPE
    Colour = [green, blue, violet, orange];
    Pixel = white..black;
    PixelType = [colored, BlackWhite];
    PixelRange = 1..PictureSize;
    SimplePixel = PACKED ARRAY [PixelRange, PixelRange] OF Pixel;
    ColorPixel = ARRAY [Colour] OF SimplePixel;
    Picture = RECORD
                        Name : STRING[80];
                        CASE Pixel Type OF Colored : (C : ColorPixel);
                                           BlackWhite : (S : SimplePixel);
                        END;   (* Case *)
                END;  (* Record *)
```

For pictures of size 100*100, with grey scale from 0 to 31, we need to change the constant values PictureSize to 100 and Black to 31.

4.2.5.1 Organization of Array

Let us take an array Picture [J,K], where J and K represent the maximum dimensions of the rows and columns of the array. Each node of the array, Picture [J,K] belongs to two linear lists:

```
Row j:        list Picture [j,0], ..., Picture [j,K-1]
Column k:     list Picture [0,k], ..., Picture [J-1,k]
```

The orthogonal row and column lists essentially account for the two-dimensional structure of the matrix.

The array is stored in sequential memory locations given by the following formula:

$$\text{LOCATION (Picture[j,k])} = a_0 + a_1\, j + a_2\, k$$

where a_0, a_1 and a_2 are constants. In this case a_0 is the address of the first element of the array or the base address, a_1 is equal to K and a_2 is equal to 1. Hence,

$$\text{LOCATION (Picture[j,k])} = a_0 + K*j + k.$$

4.2.6 Hash Coding

This is a random method of storage assignment. The record name is used for the address calculation, by treating it as a number. The result of the calculation is used as an address to store this record. An example is shown in figure 4.19. The name 'TRI' is stored in character form in the computer. The digits 0, 1, ..., 9 are represented by character values 0, 1, ..., 9 and the alphabets A, B, ..., Z by values 10, 11, ..., 35, respectively. The name 'TRI' will, therefore, be represented by values 29, 27 and 18. To calculate the address of the record 'TRI' we add the three character values to obtain 74. The value of the third character, 'I', is used by shifting it two places to the left and the address is obtained as 1800 + 74 = 1874. The record 'TRI' is then stored at the memory location 1874. With this technique, it is possible that two or more names may hash to the same address. This situation is called collision or conflict.

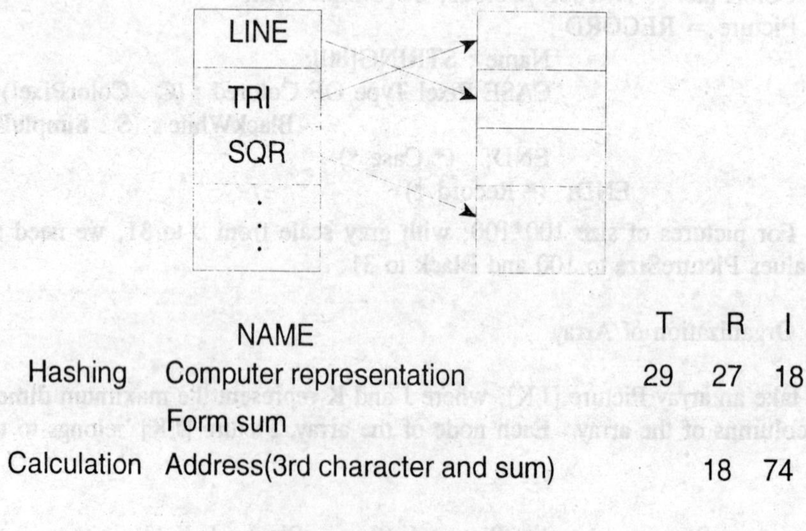

Figure 4.19 Hash coding

One way to avoid it is to form a list of all names and the corresponding data which hash to the same address. We first perform the hash operation followed by list search to locate the desired record. Data structures in graphic applications use this technique together with list structures to avoid conflicts. Other methods may also be used [25].

Table 4.2 lists the container classes for Hash Tables included in Borland C++. The iterator classes provide the capability to access the contents of a container. The public member functions of *TMHashTableImp* class are add, detach, find, flush, ForEach, GetItemsInContainer and IsEmpty. The protected member functions are EqualTo, LessThan and DeleteNode. Hash table containers define hash table data structure which manages data of type *T*. All container classes in this family use hash function to assign unique key to data placed in table. Hash table classes family includes four container classes, together with their corresponding iterator classes. Storage allocation is managed by the class *Alloc* or by the class *TStandard* Allocator. A brief description of this is given in Table 4.2.

Table 4.2: Fundamental Data Structure (FDS) Container Classes in Borland C++ 4.5 for Hash Tables

Class Template	**Description**
TMHashTableImp<T, Alloc>	A hash table of objects of type 'T'.
TMHashTableIteratorImp <T, Alloc>	An iterator for a hash table of objects
THashTableImp<T>	A hash table of objects . Storage allocation is managed by the class *TStandard* Allocator.
THashTableIteratorImp <T>	A hash table of objects of type 'T'. Storage allocation is managed by the class *TStandard* Allocator.
TMIHashTableImp<T, Alloc>	A hash table of pointers to objects.
TMIHashTableIterator Imp<T, Alloc>	An iterator for a hash table of pointers to objects.
TIHashTable Imp <T>	A hash table of pointers to objects . Storage allocation is managed by the class *TStandard* Allocator.
TIHashTableIterato Imp<T>	An iterator for a hash table of pointers to objects. Storage allocation is managed by the class *TStandard* Allocator.

4.2.7 Trees

A tree is a special type of multi-linked list with no closed rings. An identification node is put at the top of the tree, with pointers to the second level nodes, which in turn have pointers to the next level of nodes. This process is repeated until we reach the terminal node or leaf. A non-terminal node is called a branch and the level 1 node is called a root. A general tree structure is shown in figure 4.20.

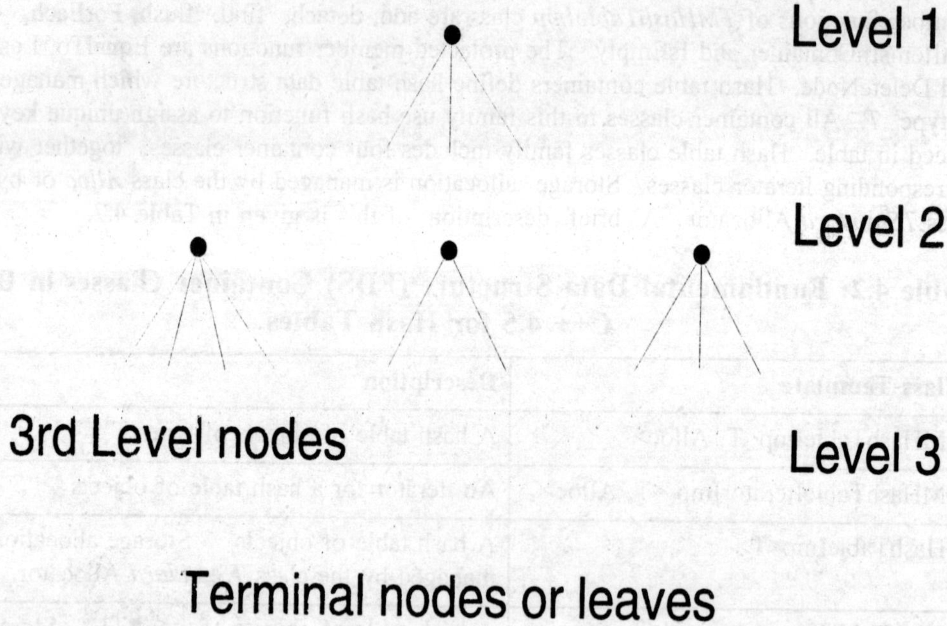

Figure 4.20 A general tree structure

Example 4.6

A clamp is made of four parts. These are a plate, brackets, nuts and bolts, as shown in figure 4.21(a). Figures 4.21(b) and 4.21(c) illustrate the geometry of parts and their representation in the form of a tree. Each part is defined and stored as a separate data segment. To assemble the clamp, we need a bracket to be used at two instances. Since the data segment for the clamp already exists, we use this segment and perform the necessary translation and rotation to position the part at the right of the assembly. This procedure is repeated for the nut and the bolt. This is done by creating suitable identification blocks with parameters for new conditions and maintaining pointers to the existing data segment. The structure of the clamp is shown in figure 4.21(d).

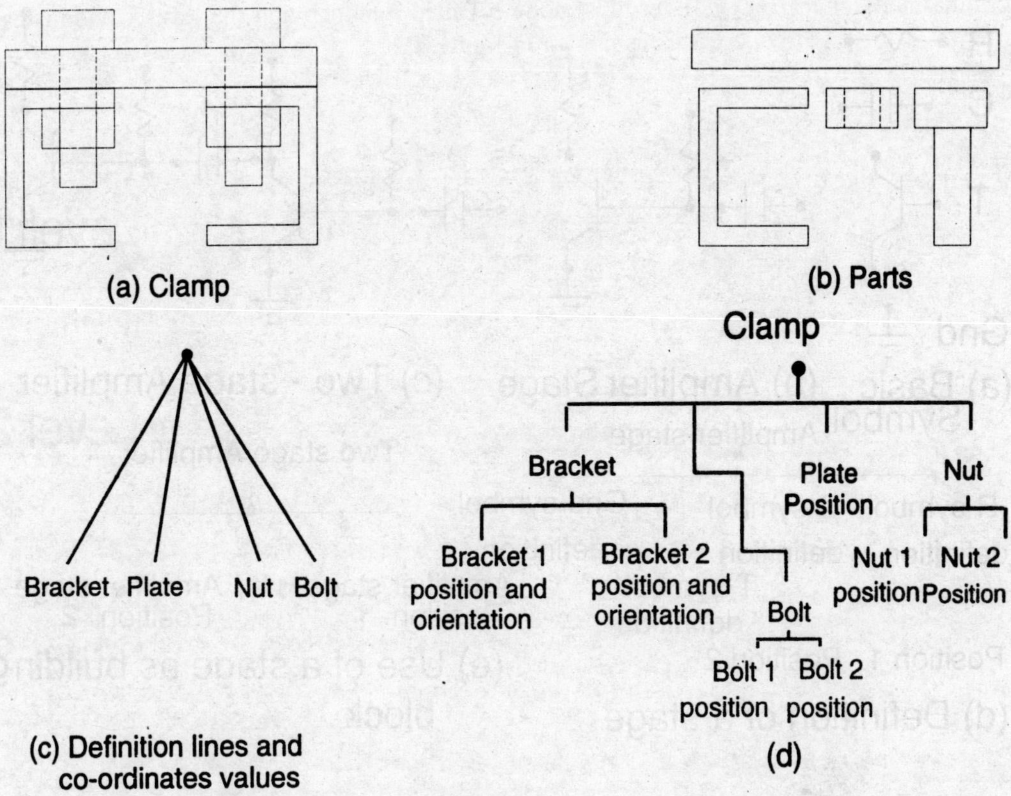

Figure 4.21 Application of tree structure to the assembly of clamp

Example 4.7

This example illustrates the use of the tree structure for the display of an electronic circuit (see figure 4.22). Four basic symbols, R, C, T and Gnd are used as building blocks for storage of one stage of the amplifier circuit. This is used two times, in two different positions, to display a two-stage amplifier. This procedure is more efficient in storage than defining one stage of the amplifier two times. An n-stage amplifier can also be displayed using the same technique.

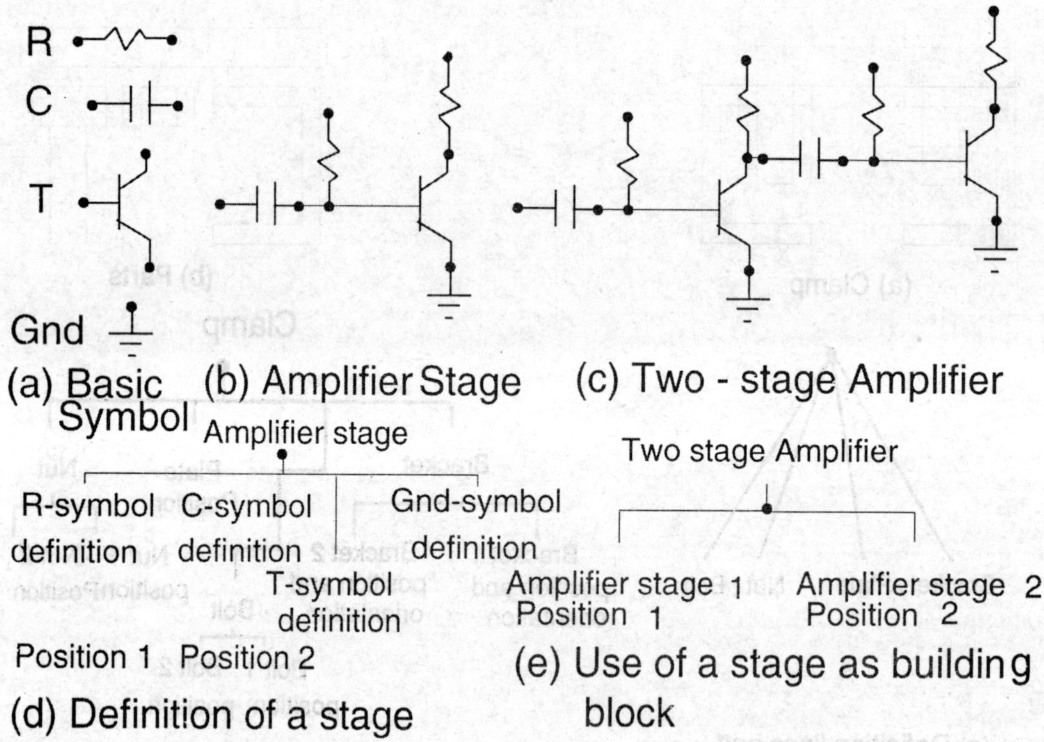

Figure 4-22 An electronic amplifier circuit and its tree structure

4.2.7.1 Binary Tree

In this data structure each node (except the leaf node) has two branches called the left and the right branch. In graphics, the binary tree is used for describing a string of numbers which represent regions of different colour, say on a map. For simplicity, we will describe the procedure for one row. A row length of power of 2, say $n = 2^i$ is generally used. The leaves of the tree represent runs of lengths 2^0, 2^1, 2^2, ..., depending on the level of the node.

The root node of the tree represents the entire row. If the entire row has one value, the root node is labeled with this value. The tree in this case has just one node. Otherwise, we add two descendent to the node. Each descendent represents half of the elements of the row. If any of the halves has just one value, we do not provide any descendants to the node representing that half of the row, i.e., it becomes a leaf node. This procedure is repeated until we reach the single element (pixel) level. At level i, the nodes are leaf nodes and correspond to a single pixel. These nodes are labeled with their pixel value.

Table 4.3 gives class templates included in Borland C++ for binary search trees. 'BT' denotes an object.

Table 4.3: Fundamental Data Structure (FDS) container classes for Binary Search Trees.

Class Template	Description
TBinarySearchTreeImp<T>	A binary search tree of objects of type 'T'.
TBinarySearchTreeIteratorImp <T>	An iterator for binary search trees. It stores objects of type 'T'.
TIBinarySearchTreeImp <T>	A binary search tree of pointers to objects of type 'T'.
TIBinarySearchTreeIteratorImp <T>	An iterator for binary search trees that stores pointers to objects of type 'T'.

A sample program using binary tree class templates is given below:

```
//-----------------------------------------------------------------------------------------------
// Program : illustrates the use of binary tree class.
//-----------------------------------------------------------------------------------------------
//ObjectWindows Library
#include <owl/owlpch.h>
#include <owl/applicat.h>
#include <owl/framewin.h>
#include <owl/dc.h>
//Class Library
#include <classlib\binimp.h>
#include <iostream.h>
typedef TBinarySearchTreeImp<int> IntegerBinaryTree;
typedef TbinarySearchTreeIteratorImp<int> IntegerBinaryTreeIterator;
class TrialWindow : public TWindow
{
  public:
        TrialWindow(TWindow* parent = 0);
     ~ TrialWindow()  // Delete CommonDC
        {
              delete CommonDC;
        }
```

```
 protected:
       TDC* CommonDC;
       // Message response functions
       void EvPaint();
       DECLARE_RESPONSE_TABLE( TrialWindow);
};
DEFINE_RESPONSE_TABLE1( TrialWindow, TWindow)
  EV_WM_PAINT,
END_RESPONSE_TABLE;
TrialWindow:: TrialWindow(TWindow* parent)
{
  Init(parent, 0, 0);     // Initialize TrialWindow base class
  CommonDC = 0;           //Initialize CommonDC-- a pointer to the TClientDC--to zero.
}
void TrialWindow::EvPaint()
{
if (!CommonDC)
  {
          char str[30];
          IntegerBinaryTree bintree;
          SetCapture();
          CommonDC = new TClientDC(*this);
          // Add some elements
         bintree.Add(13);
         bintree.Add(7);
         bintree.Add(6);
         bintree.Add(9);
         bintree.Add(1);
         short numnodes = bintree.GetItemsInContainer();
         short posy = 40;
         wsprintf(str, "items in tree %d          ", numnodes );
         CommonDC->TextOut(10, posy, str, strlen(str));
        // Traverse through tree and display the elements
         IntegerBinaryTreeIterator traverse(bintree);
         while(traverse)
         {
                 numnodes = traverse++ ;
                 posy = posy + 20;
                 wsprintf(str, " node value  %d          ",  numnodes );
                 CommonDC->TextOut(10,  posy, str, strlen(str));

         }
  }
              ReleaseCapture();
              delete CommonDC;
```

```
        CommonDC = 0;
}

class TDrawApp : public TApplication {

 public:
    TDrawApp() : TApplication() {}
    void InitMainWindow()
    {
        SetMainWindow(new TFrameWindow(0, " Binary Tree", new  TrialWindow));
    }
};

int  OwlMain(int /*argc*/, char* /*argv*/ [])
{
  return TDrawApp().Run();
}
```

This program will produce the following output:

```
items in tree  5
node value     13
node value     7
node value     9
node value     6
node value     1
```

Example 4.8

A row of numbers having values between 0 and 7 and of length 2^5 is represented by a binary tree (see figure 4.23). It can be seen that the tree has a total of 39 nodes, of which 20 are leaf nodes. The memory required to store a trace is proportional to the number of nodes. If the row of numbers consists of only a few runs, the tree will have relatively fewer nodes.

7006 0550 4444 4444 0100 1022 2222 0330

(a) String of length 2 to the power 5

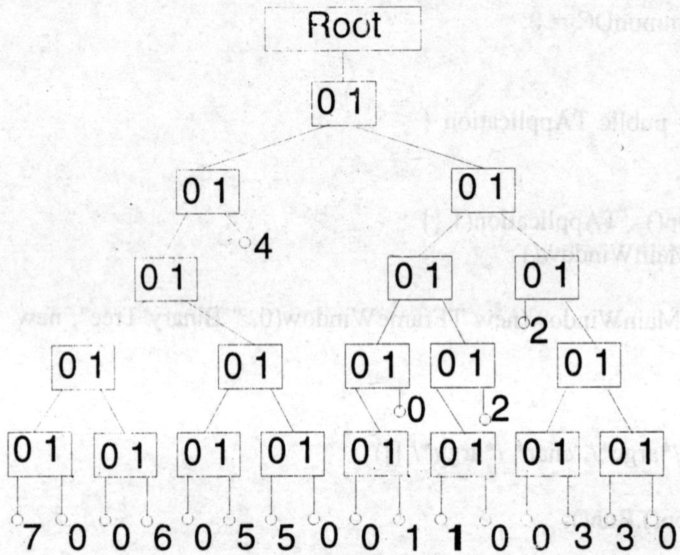

(b) Tree: solid and open circles represent leaf nodes

Figure 4.23 Binary tree representation of string of numbers

Example 4.9

For representing a few colour pictures (see figure 4.24 a) tree structures are quite efficient. Let us consider an example where colors are represented by integers 0, 1, ..., 7, each number corresponding to a unique colour. The digital representation of the picture is shown as an 8*8 matrix (figure 4.24b).

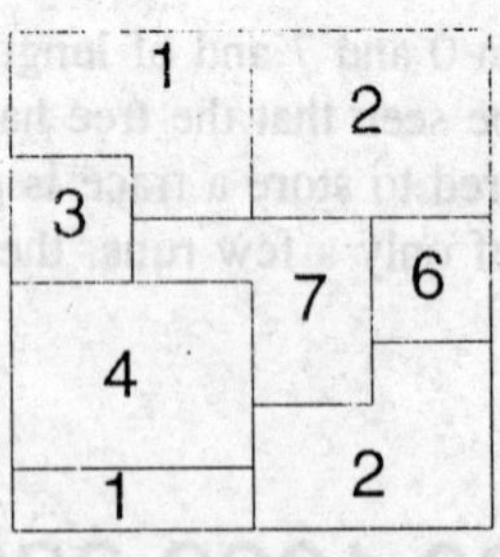

(a) Shows a colour picture (Numbers in the blocks represent the colour in the block)

$$\begin{bmatrix} 1&1&1&1&2&2&2&2 \\ 1&1&1&1&2&2&2&2 \\ 3&3&1&1&2&2&2&2 \\ 3&3&7&7&7&7&6&6 \\ 4&4&4&4&7&7&6&6 \\ 4&4&4&4&7&7&2&2 \\ 4&4&4&4&2&2&2&2 \\ 1&1&1&1&2&2&2&2 \end{bmatrix}$$

(b) Digital picture obtained from (a) is represented by an 8 by 8 matrix

Figure 4.24 Representation of a colour picture

The storage requirements can be reduced considerably if the picture has large homogeneous (same colour) areas. Figure 4.25 illustrates the division scheme of the matrix into blocks. This can be done on the basis of whether the level index is odd or even.

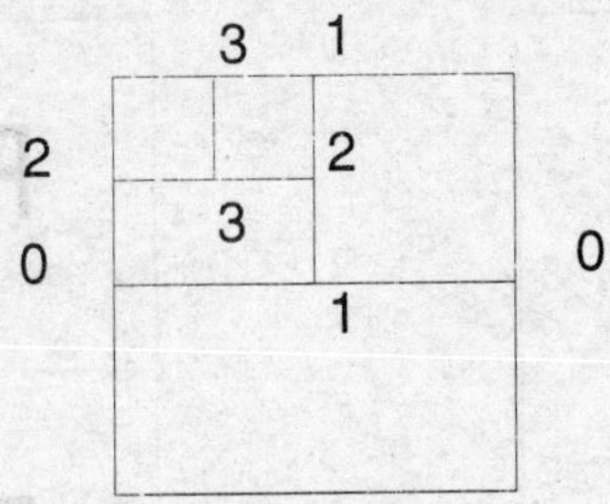

Figure 4.25 Subdividing the image until the limit ofresolution is reached. The order of division is shown by the lines 00, 11, 22, and 33.

The division is carried out if the region represented by the block is heterogeneous (all pixels are not of the same colour). It can be seen that the tree has 35 nodes. Eighteen of these are leaf nodes.

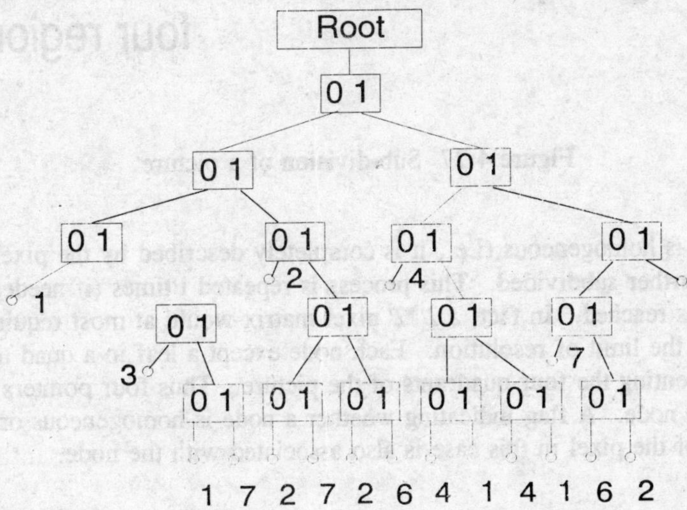

Figure 4.26 Binary tree for the picture

4.2.7.2 Quad Trees

A quad tree is a popular data structure for graphical representation of two-dimensional digital pictures. As in the case of binary trees, this technique is suitable when the picture is a square matrix with dimension 2^i, where i is a positive integer. Then the picture P can be subdivided into four square matrices (or regions) P0, P1, P2 and P3, as shown in figure

4.27. The dimension of each submatrix is half of that of P.

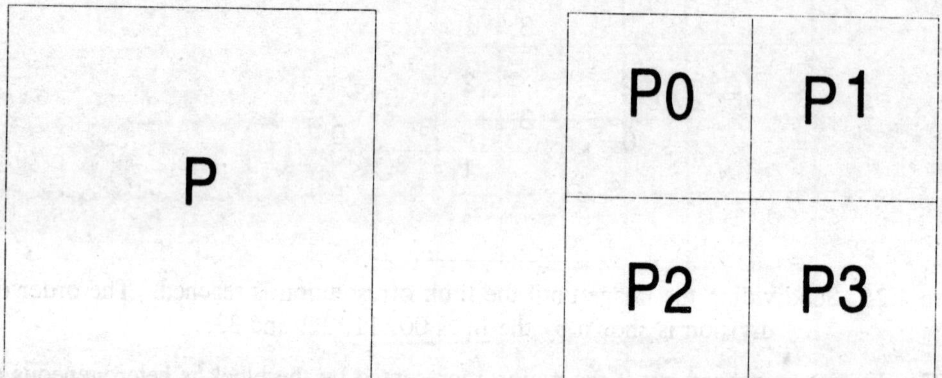

(a) The original picture (b) Sub division into four regions

Figure 4.27 Sub-division of a picture

If a region is homogeneous (i.e., it is completely described by the pixel value that fills it), it is not further subdivided. This process is repeated i times (if needed), until the single pixel level is reached. In fact, a 2^i*2^i pixel matrix would at most require an i-level quad tree to reach the limit of resolution. Each node except a leaf in a quad tree has four descendants representing the four quadrants of the picture. Thus four pointers needed be maintained at each node. A flag indicating whether a node is homogeneous or not is also used. The value of the pixel in this case is also associated with the node.

The root node of the quad tree describes the picture entirely. Each node has a unique address. To reach a desired node, we have to traverse the tree starting from the root node. A sequence of pointers is to be followed from the root node until the desired node is located. Figure 4.28 shows that the high-lighted node is reached from the root node by following the pointer sequence [2,1,1]. This corresponds to (x,y) binary picture address of (011, 100).

The node address is used for linking the implicit geometry found in the quad tree structure with the (x,y) position of pixels in the picture matrix. The disadvantage of the quad tree is that it is shift-variant. Two pictures which vary only by a translation give rise to different quad trees. The memory space required to store a quad tree is proportional to the number of nodes.

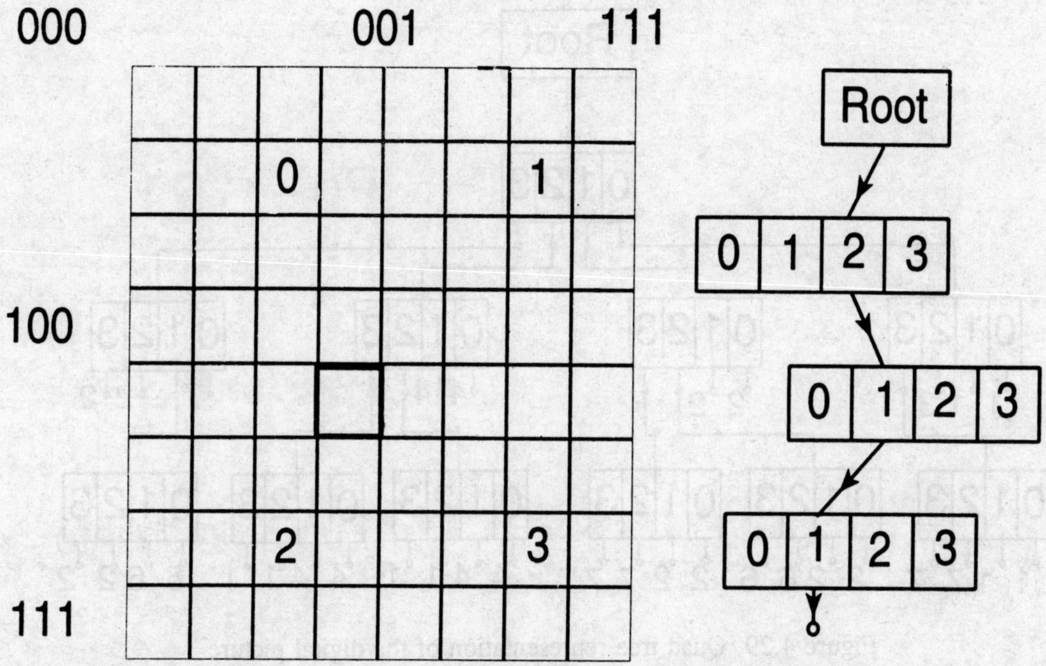

(a) An 8 by 8 picture with binary addresses for its elements (b) Pointer Sequences

Figure 4.28 A quad tree

Example 4.11

Figure 4.29 shows a quad tree for the picture given in figure 4.24.

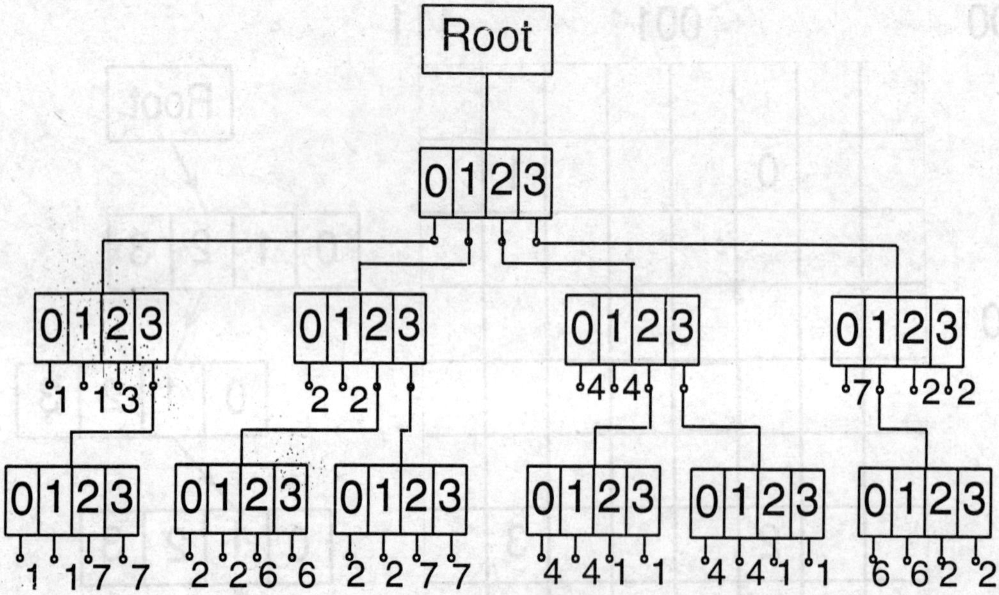

Figure 4.29 Quad tree representation of the digital picture

4.2.7.3 Oct-tree

The oct-tree refers to a data structure which is an alternative representation for a three-dimensional matrix and is an extension of two-dimensional quad tree structures. Since the oct-tree permits grouping of adjacent array elements containing the same data, it is possible to achieve substantial saving in the storage area otherwise required.

In graphics, oct-trees are used for representing regions of space. We may recall that the quad tree represents area. A common method involves cubical regions of space and their decomposition into octants. A unit cube corresponds to volume elements called 'voxels'. A region of space is homogeneous if all voxels have the same value. A heterogeneous region is decomposed along the three primary axes to produce octants of the original region. A node of an oct-tree, therefore, has eight pointers corresponding to each of the octants.

Let us consider a solid object made of different materials. The boundary between two types of materials would be the inside surfaces of the regions. This boundary does not allow the adjacent voxels to combine and form larger cubes. Thus, we can conclude that the oct-tree representation is a function of surface area and not the volume. Hence, if we take an object which has low surface area/volume ratio and represent it by an oct-tree, a saving in memory space for storing the object will be achieved.

Figure 4.30 shows the node structure and the corresponding octants in the regions of space.

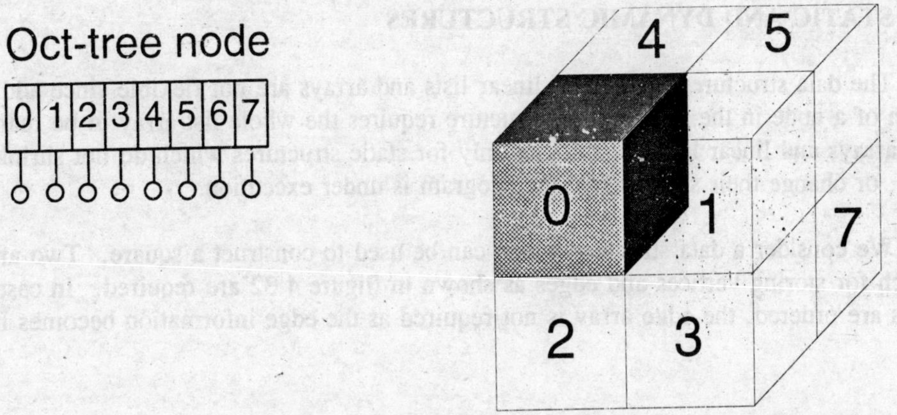

Figure 4.30 Depicts a block and its representation into octants

(The octants are numbered 0, 1, ..., 7. The pointers 0, 1, ..., 7 in the node correspond to the respective octants.)

Example 4.12

An oct-tree structure for the object shown in figure 4.31(a) is given in figure 4.31(b). The black leaves correponding to the material portion of the object are shown by the darkened circle. The empty portion (regions of space) is shown by a blank circle in the oct-tree.

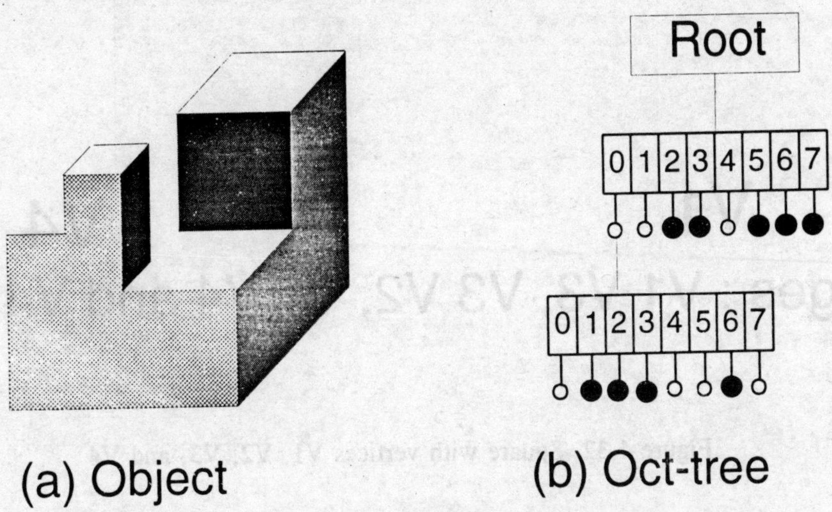

Figure 4.31 A simple object and its oct-tree

4.3 STATIC AND DYNAMIC STRUCTURES

The data structures defined by linear lists and arrays are not flexible since addition or deletion of a node in the midst of the structure requires the whole list/array to be rearranged. Hence arrays and linear lists are suitable only for static structures which do not shrink, expand, or change their shape while the program is under execution.

We consider a data structure which can be used to construct a square. Two arrays: one each for storing vertices and edges as shown in fiigure 4.32 are required. In case, vertices are ordered, the edge array is not required as the edge information becomes implicit.

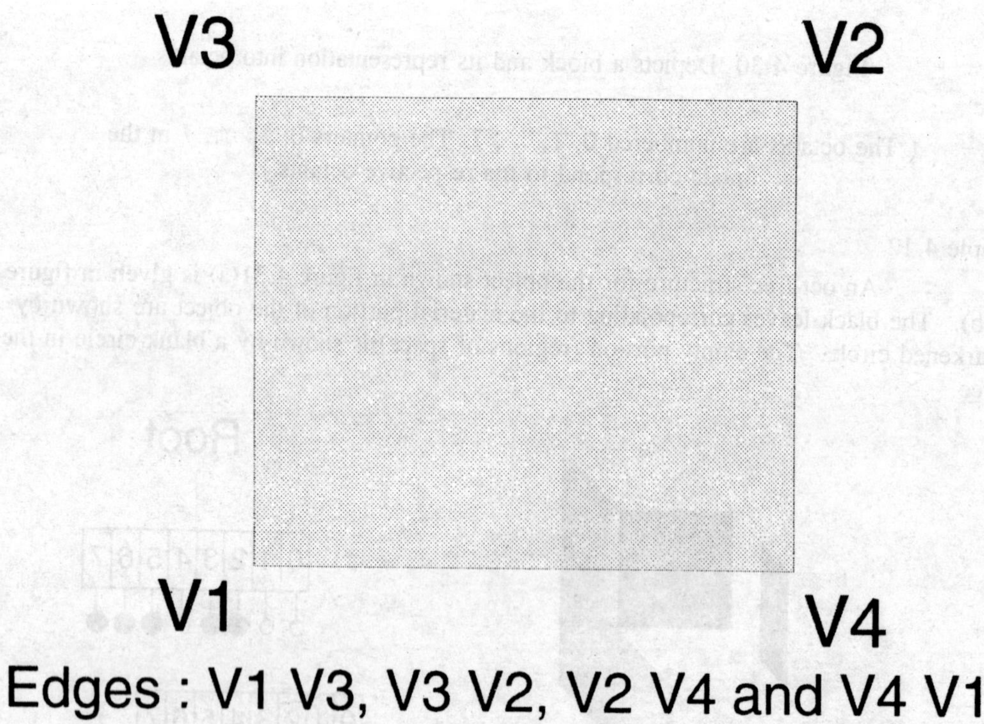

Figure 4.32 Square with vertices V1, V2, V3, and V4

Similarly, we can represent a cube by using three arrays: one each for vertices, faces and edges, as shown in Table 4.4. A cube described by static data structure (in the table) is shown in figure 4.33.

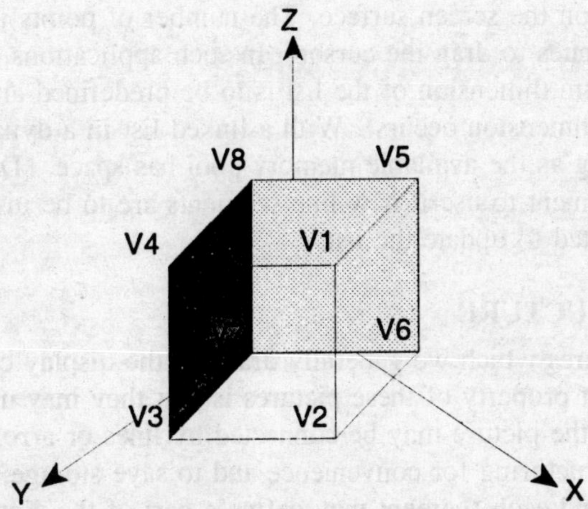

Figure 4.33 A cube described by data structure given in Table 4.1.

Table 4.4: Cube represented by using three arrays: one each for vertices, faces and edges

	Vertices		Faces		Edges
	V1	F1:	V1, V5, V8, V4	E1:	V1 V4
E7:	V7 V8				
	V2	F2:	V5, V6, V7, V8	E2:	V4 V3
E8:	V8 V5 V3				
E9:	V5 V1				
	V4	F4:	V1, V4, V3, V2	E4:	V2 V1
E10:	V8 V4				
	V5	F5:	V8, V7, V3, V4	E5:	V5 V6
E11:	V6 V2 V6	F6:	V6, V5, V1, V2	E6:	V6 V7
E12:	V7 V3 V7 V8				

Dynamic data structures grow or shrink as the program executes. A linear list or an array that contains space for a fixed number of elements (nodes) are not suitable for dynamic structure as memory requirement changes dynamically while the program is under execution. Hence, linked list or tree structures along with a mechanism for maintaining available memory pool are suitable for this purpose.

Dynamic data structures are used in an interactive environment, where graphical data is to be manipulated and new data accommodated in a continuously changing situation. An example would be plotting the path of a cursor (by small line segments) dragged by a light pen on the screen surface. The number of points in the data structure grows as the user continues to drag the cursor. In such applications, if we use a linear list (1-D array) the maximum dimension of the list is to be predefined and the program may be aborted if overflow in dimension occurs. With a linked list in a dynamic structure, however, the list can grow as long as the available memory pool has space. Dynamic structures are very flexible and convenient to use if new line segments are to be inserted or existing line segments are to be deleted to update the list.

4.4 PICTURE STRUCTURE

The pictures which we generally draw on the display consist of lines, symbols, labels, etc. An inherent property of these pictures is that they may use the same symbol repeatedly and parts of the picture may be connected by lines or arrows. The programmer also introduces some structuring for convenience and to save storage. The display file is divided into segments and each segment may define a part of the picture. The display file itself can be used for defining a picture structure but for complex pictures a separate display file is used. In example 4.6, to assemble a clamp, two instances of brackets were used, although bracket was defined only once. The second instance of bracket was generated by the application of a suitable transformation to the original definition in such a fashion that data of the original bracket remains intact. To construct an efficient data structure which can be easily manipulated, the following approach can be used:

i) define the building blocks (graphic elements),

ii) create instances of building blocks with transformation (such as scaling, translation and rotation),

iii) group building blocks into larger entities to represent parts of a picture,

and iv) add relationships among the constituents of the picture.

In this section, we shall utilize various types of data structures described in section 4.2. The types of data structures that are used most commonly to represent a picture are tree, relational and hierarchical. These will be described in the following subsections.

4.4.1 Tree Picture Structure

This aspect is covered in section 4.2. A simple example of tree structure is given in example 4.6. The parts (nut, bolt, plate and bracket are first defined and then assembled in different positions to describe the picture of a clamp. This is more efficient than describing each part separately in different orientations. Moreover, these parts can also be used to assemble another object. As another example, to draw the picture of a tree, it is sufficient to draw a single picture of a leaf which can then be used to make, say, 1000 more leaves.

4.4.2 Relational Picture Structure

A relational structure employs simple tabular structures and provides easy access to elements. It can represent many-to-many and one-to-many correspondence, a feature which is also present in hierarchical data structures. A relation is represented conveniently as a table in which each row is an n-tuple (i.e., has n elements) and each column is a domain. An example is shown in Table 4.5. The name of the key attribute by which tuples can be uniquely identified is shown underlined. The structured definition of tuples can be expressed as under:

ASSEMBLY (Part name, Position, Transformation, definition, material*, colour*, ...)

Definition (x, y, Mode*, Type*)

Table 4.5: Assembly

Part Name	Position	Transformation	Definition	Material*	Colour*
Plate	x1, y1	T1	def.1		
Bracket	x2, y2	T2	def.2		
Nut	x3, y3	T3	def.3		
Bolt	x4, y4	T4	def.4		
.	.	.	.	.	.

(The domains marked by an * are optional)

Definition 1

Table 4.6: An example relation and its structure

x	y	Mode	Type
0	0	Move	.
200	0	Draw	.
200	100	Draw	.
.	.	.	.
.	.	.	.
.	.	.	.

The definition of a part is simply a relation of (x,y) co-ordinates that define each line and its attributes as given in Table 4.6. The tuples in this relation are ordered as each line is drawn from the current position (of turtle) to the next, only one end point of each line is stored in each tuple. If the tuples are not ordered, then both the end points are to be stored in a tuple. This uses extra memory space but simplifies processing because the addition or deletion of a line then simply becomes a matter of the addition or deletion of a tuple. The tuple MODE indicates whether a line is visible or invisible (DRAW or MOVE). The tuple 'Type' can be used to indicate a solid, dotted or dashed line.

In relation 'Assembly' the tuples 'Part_name', 'Position', 'Transformation' and 'Definition' give the name of the part, its relative position in the assembly, the transformation parameters and part definition, respectively. The optional tuples 'material' and 'colour' can be used to describe the material of parts and their colour.

The table can be constructed using a simple or linked structure to suit the application. Linked structure would provide greater flexibility and ease in manipulation in operations such as addition or deletion of information.

Table 4.2 contains variety of data. To create a display it is necessary to know which domains contain graphical data. An interpreter program can, then, be used to trace through the relation (from a given starting point) and extract the information for display.

4.4.3 Hierarchical Picture Structure

A hierarchical structure is similar to tree structure and has levels of hierarchy, but it is constructed from rings [1]. From the initial ring, there may be branches off from a node to logically related nodes. These related nodes are connected in a ring structure. It is very easy to update such structures as no data movement is required in storage, only pointers have to be suitably adjusted. The processing for delete operation of a node is a bit involved as one has to make sure that all pointer chains are re-established. This method also has overhead of extra memory to store all pointer chains.

Example 4.12

The hierarchical structure for the assembly of clamp (see example 4.6) is shown in figure 4.34. While using definition of bracket 1 to generate bracket 2, care has to be taken in the program that parameters of bracket 1 are not affected.

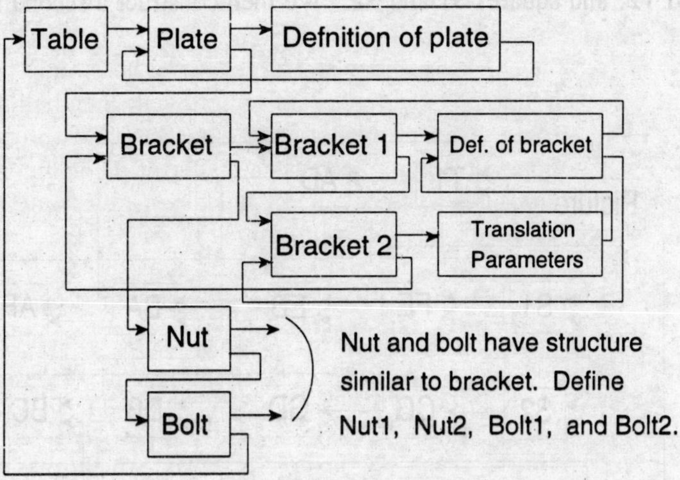

Figure 4.34 Hierarchical picture structure

Example 4.13

Figure 4.35 shows the picture of two triangles ABD and BEC and two squares ABEF and DBCG.

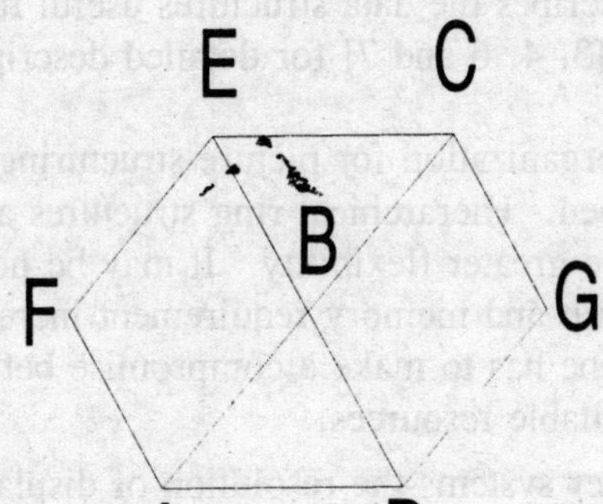

Figure 4.35 Picture comprising of two triangles and two squares

Figure 4.36 shows a possible hierarchical structure for the picture. It can be seen that the structure uses rings for its construction. The initial ring describes a picture consisting of triangles T1 and T2, and squares S1 and S2. We then construct a second ring describing T1 and and so on.

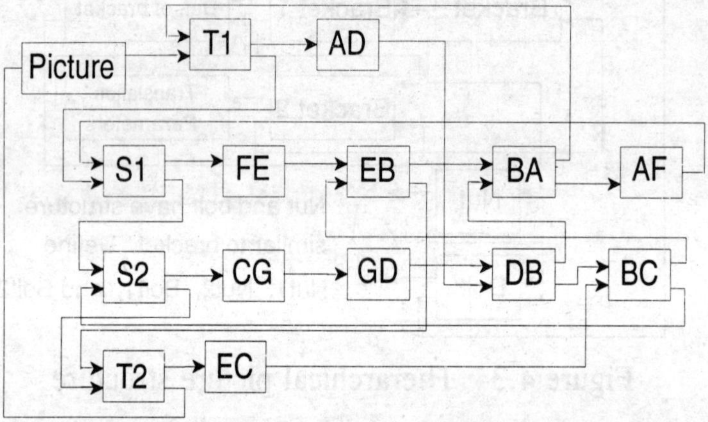

Figure 4.36 Hierarchical picture structure for figure 4.35

4.5 SUMMARY

This chapter describes the data structures useful for storage and manipulation of pictures. You can refer to [3, 4, 6 and 7] for detailed description of data structures and their use in graphics.

Three types of organization for picture structuring, tree, relational and hierarchical, have been described. Hierarchical ring structures are generally used in large graphic systems as they provide greater flexibility. It may be noted, however, that implementation becomes difficult and memory requirement increases as more pointer chains must be established. Hence, one has to make a compromise between what is desired and what can be achieved with available resources.

In small computer systems the resolution of display and the available memory are the limiting factors and force the use of simpler data structures. The concepts discussed are useful for developing a graphic processing system.

4.6 REFERENCES

[1] Dodd, G.G., "Elements of Data Management Systems", Computer Surveys, 1, 2, June 1969, pp. 115-135.

[2] Feldman, J.A. and P.D. Rovner, "An ALGOL based Associative Language", Comm. ACM, 12, 8, August 1969, pp. 439-449.

[3] Klinger, A., K.S. Fu and T.L. Kunii, "Data Structures, Computer Graphics and Pattern Recognition", Academic Press, Inc., New York, 1977.

[4] Knuth, D.E., "Fundamental Algorithms: The Art of Computer Programming (Volume 1), Addison-Wesley Publishing House, Massachusetts, 1973.

[5] Morris, R., "Scatter Storage Techniques", Com. ACM. 11, 1, January 1968, pp. 38-64.

[6] Pavlidis, T., "Algorithm for Graphics and Image Processing", Computer Science Press, Rockville, MD, 1982.

[7] Williams, R., "A survey of data structures for computer graphics systems", Computing Surveys, 3, 1, March 1971, pp. 1-27.

4.7 PROBLEMS

1. A deque is described in section 4.2.1.3. Explain the insert and delete operations for a deque.

2. In section 4.2.2.2, a Pascal program to traverse a linked list and display the data fields is given. Assume that each node of the list contains in the data field the co-ordinates of the end points of a line segment. Modify the TRAVERSE program to display the line segments as the list is traversed.

3. Write a program in *C* corresponding to the Pascal program described in the previous problem.

4. Develop a linked list structure for stack, queue and deque. Define insert and delete peration for each case.

5. The public member functions of *TMHashTableImp* class are add, detach, find, flush, ForEach, GetItemsInContainer and IsEmpty. Write a program to add upto 10 words in a hash table. Perform operations, such as find a item, find number of entries in the table, delete all entries using the member functions.

6. Write a program in Pascal to draw a two-stage amplifier circuit using the structure shown in example 4.7. Modify the program to accept component values from the keyboard and calculate the gain of the amplifier. Display component values and gain of the resulting amplifier.

7. Repeat tje previous problem using *C* instead of Pascal.

8. Write a program in Pascal for creating a quad-tree to represent a picture of size 2^n*2^n where $n \le 5$. What type of node structure will you use?

9. Repeat the previous problem using *C* instead of Pascal.

10. **Draw an oct-tree for the object shown below.**

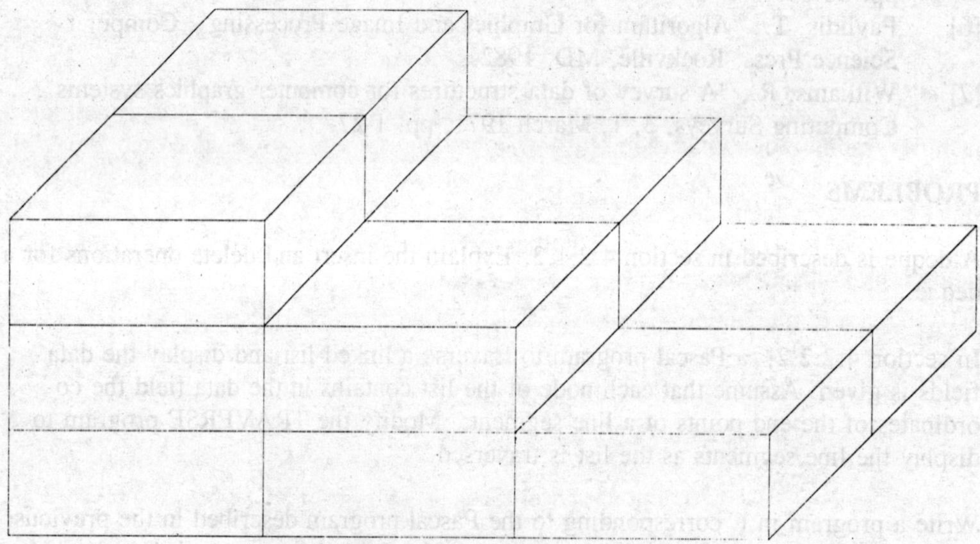

CHAPTER 5

INTERACTIVE GRAPHICS

5.1 INTRODUCTION

The term "interactive graphics" refers to devices and systems that facilitate the man-machine graphic communication, in a way which is more convenient than the writing conventions on which we otherwise largely rely. For example, to draw a straight line between two points, one has to input the coordinates of the two end points, but with a graphical input technique, only the two end points need be indicated on the display. While designing such a system emphasis is placed on

i) ease of interaction, i.e., how conveniently one can communicate with the system, and

ii) speed of interaction, i.e., how fast one can modify a displayed image.

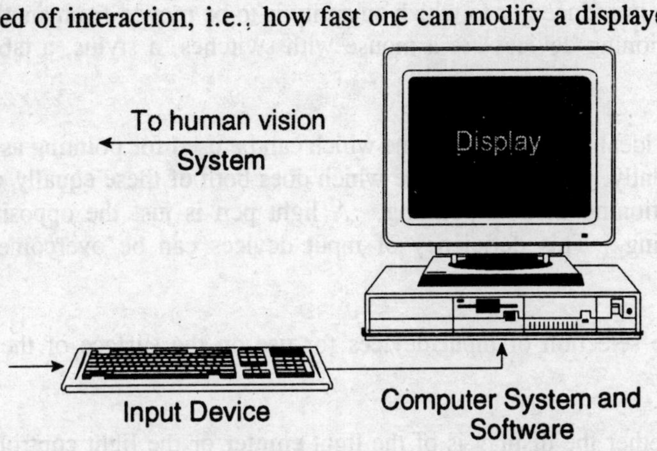

Figure 5.1 Components of an interactive graphics system

The hardware components required to generate interactive graphics are the input device, the output device (usually a display) and the computer system as shown in figure 5.1. The human operator is also an integral part of the interactive system. The text and graphics displayed act as an input to the human vision system and, therefore, the reaction of the human being will depend on how quickly one can see and appreciate the graphics present on the display.

Input devices are equally important as they are used by the human operator to give commands to the graphic system to make the desired changes. Therefore, it follows that the particular ways in which the user may interact with the system are important and the part of the system intended for the man-computer interface must be designed with care. System designers have exercised considerable freedom in adapting a man-computer interface to its intended user and this has led to the development of different types of graphical input devices. The level of interaction will depend on how well the driving software is integrated with the input devices, display device and the user's thoughts and reactions.

5.2 INPUT DEVICES

A user can react to the whole or part of the graphics present on the screen and communicate with the computer through an appropriate input device of his or her choice for creating, manipulating and designing graphic objects on the display by pointing, positioning, touching, keyboard input (in the form of a number or a string of characters), or even by giving a verbal command. Typical examples are

i) addition of a symbol at a desired location,
ii) deletion of a symbol from a given location,
(iii) moving a symbol from one location to another
and iv) drawing a straight line to connect two points.

Pointing is used for the selection of a displayed entity. The principal example of a pointing device is the light pen, although other devices, like a mouse with a pick switch can also be used. Positioning is used for indicating the position or location on the screen where a new entity is to be introduced or to which an entity is to be moved from another location. Some examples of positioning devices are a mouse with switches, a stylus, a tablet, a joystick or a touch panel.

An ideal input device is one which can be used for pointing as well as positioning operations. Currently, there is no device which does both of these equally well. Most devices are better at positioning than at pointing. A light pen is just the opposite since it is more effective at pointing. This deficiency of input devices can be overcome by using suitable software.

The selection of input devices for use on the surface of the screen depends to some extent on

i) whether the display is of the light emitter or the light controller type
and ii) the mode of writing, which may be random, sequential (as on the television screen), or of matrix format (as for flat panel displays).

Input devices which cannot be used on the surface of the screen are also very useful. For example, a light pen cannot be used on a storage tube display since the picture is constantly visible on the screen, from the instant of its creation to the time when it is deleted. Hence, one has to use devices like joysticks, tracker balls, potentiometers and tablets which control the cursor on the screen. These devices can also be used with refresh type displays.

Devices can be classified on the basis of their capabilities for the operations of pointing and positioning, direct use on the surface of the screen or to provide a two/three dimensional input. The following sections describe input devices based on their capabilities for providing efficient interaction. Table 5-1 summarizes the characteristics of interactive devices.

Table 5-1 Characteristics of Interactive Devices

Relation	Device	Result (Output)
Time	Light pen\cursor	Count/time
Convention	Keyboard	Code
Predefined	Function key	Code
Association	Speech oriented devices	Code
Spatial position	Monitored devices	x-y coordinates
	tracker ball	
	joystick	
	Mouse	
	Potentiometer	
	Touch wire	
	Graphic tablets	
	Rand	
	Piezo-electric	
	Magnetostrictive	
	Sonic	
	Optical	
	Analog voltage	
	Eye monitors	

5.2.1 Interaction related to Time

Many input devices take advantage of the fact that certain displays build up in time and form a sequence of light spots on the screen. By determining the time of occurrence of a spot on the display screen, the device can locate the part of the graphics being drawn at that instant.

5.2.1.1 Light Pen

The light pen consists basically of a photoelectric cell which is packaged in a slender tube having the dimensions of a pen (see figure 5.2). It can detect light incident upon the display, when held perpendicularly against the tube. An optical system focuses on to the photo-cell any light in the field of view of the pen. The output of the photo-cell is then amplified and carried over a shielded cable to the light pen interface.

A 'detect' by the light pen can either be used to cause an immediate interrupt to the computer through an interface or to set a flip flop which is cleared when read by the computer.

The time of 'detect' by the light pen determines the part of the memory that is being accessed at the moment by the computer or refresh controller. Thus, the system can identify the part of the graphics (e.g., line or symbol) to which the pen is pointing. In displays where x and y registers are maintained and are continuously updated as the spot moves across the screen, the light pen can be used to determine the x and y coordinates. In fact, x and y registers are sampled by momentarily stopping the display controller after the light pen sees the spot on the display.

In the case of a point-plotting display, one can test the light pen flip flop after displaying each point. Thus the exact location of the spot to which the light pen is pointing can be detected.

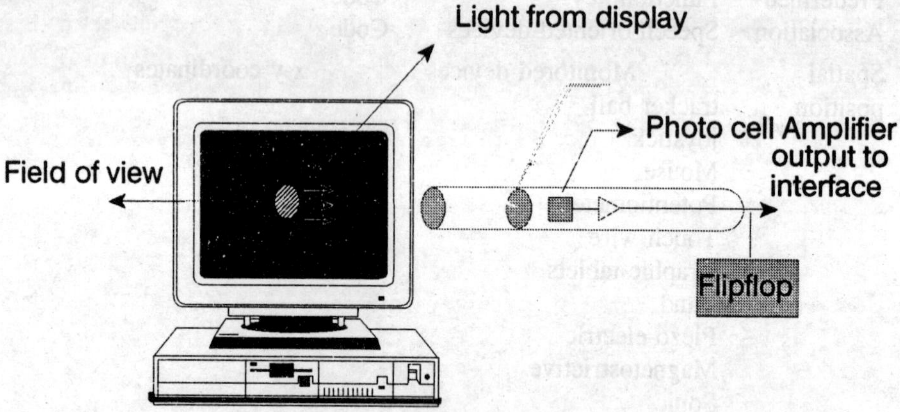

Figure 5.2 Basic design of a light pen

A light pen is a pointing device. For using a light pen for positioning, a tracking program is run on a computer. In the case of other positioning devices, there exist tracking hardware for monitoring the position of the stylus and the x and y buffers are continuously updated. The computer reads these buffers at fairly regular intervals.

To facilitate the operation of the light pen, a finger operated switch or shutter is provided to control the light reaching the photo-cell. This avoids spurious inputs to the light pen. The display processor also has the capability to disable the light pen during the refresh cycle. This ensures that the inputs not desired by the operator are ignored.

The response time of the light pen is also important. For slow displays, one can use a light pen consisting of transistor type photo-cells such as photo-diodes, which are small and inexpensive. Such a device is suitable for hand-held operation. The response time of such a device is of the order of one microsecond. For a high speed display system, where display instructions are to be executed in less than one microsecond, the light pen should have a photo-cell of the type of a photo-multiplier tube. This is quite bulky. In such cases, the light is focussed on the tube using a fibre-optic cable, which allows the light pen to be handy.

An improved type of light pen ensures tracking of a spot on the display without losing it, even if the light pen is moved very quickly. This pen consists of a matrix of fibre optic sensors (as shown in figure 5.3), to detect the position of the electronic beam which is to be portrayed as a single point. The fibre detecting the spot activates the spot-positioning controller, which moves the spot to the centre position '5'. The position detected by the light pen remains unchanged, even it is rotated by a small angle.

The light pen is particularly suitable for CRT displays using free vector or television format for generating graphics, but it can also be used when the graphics output is built up in time. Matrix addressed displays, which fall in the flat panel category, are all refreshed in a sequential manner. A light pen can be used effectively for interaction in these cases since the time for refresh is very important.

A matrix of light-emitting diodes is addressed by x and y drivers and the response of the light pen can locate the information of interest. The plasma panel consisting of a honeycomb of neon cells which are also energized by x and y lines above and below the plane of the cell are only amenable to light pen interaction if they are energized in a sequential manner. Liquid crystal displays are also amenable to light pen interaction if sequential refreshing is performed. This may not be viable due to the inherent slow response time of the liquid crystal technology.

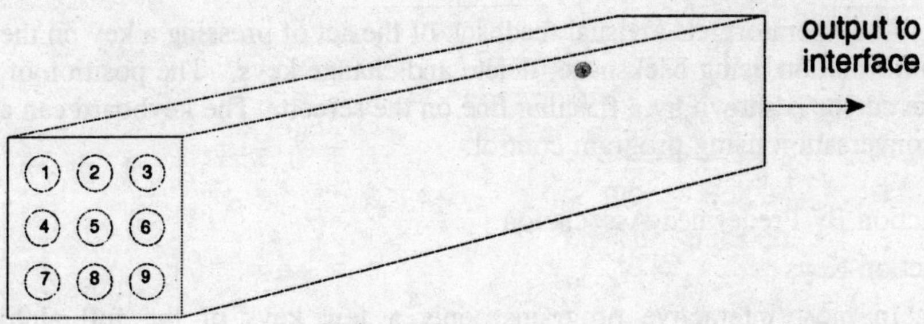

Figure 5.3 A modified type of light pen

5.2.1.2 The Cursor

The time related cursor is another device for pointing to the part of the graphics on the display. The position of the cursor corresponding to the memory is displayed by flashing or brightening the symbol that is being drawn using the contents of the memory location. A set of keys can be used to change the location of the cursor through the display memory to select any portion of the display. The use of a cursor is similar to the light pen except that the technique is quite slow.

5.2.2 Interaction by Convention

5.2.2.1 Keyboard

The main device for interaction with the display according to a convention is the keyboard. Every key on the keyboard (see figure 5.4) produces a unique code when pressed. The codes are associated with the alpha-numeric character and are transparent to the user. The keyboard is used as a standard device for the input of alpha-numeric data to the computer.

Figure 5.4 The keyboard of an IBM Personal Computer

The operator gets a visual feedback of the act of pressing a key on the screen and can edit the information using backspace, delete and change keys. The position of the current location of the cursor is shown by a flashing line on the screen. The keyboard can also be used for graphic conversation using program control.

5.2.3 Interaction By Predefined Association

5.2.3.1 Function Keys

In most interactive programs, only a few keys of the full alpha-numerical keyboard are used for performing functions or assembling a command. The alternative is, therefore, to use very specific keyboards (function keys) to enable quick interaction. Such special keys (see figure 5.5) are often incorporated on an alphanumeric keyboard.

Function keys either have fixed overlays peculiar to a system or the functions of the keys can be varied under program control (as in the case of the IBM Personal Computer) and associated overlays can be placed on the function keyboard. This mode of operation is often referred to as interaction by predefined association.

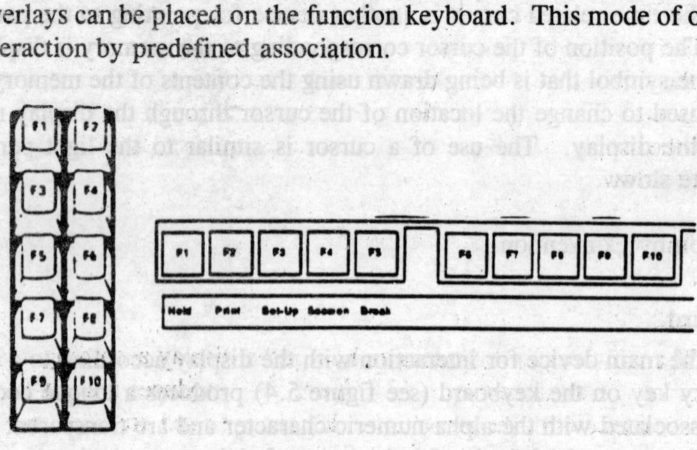

Figure 5.5 Function keys on the IBM Personal Computer

Overlays with codings, which can be read by the sensors and, thus, enable the system to identify the overlays are used in certain advanced systems. This avoids the need for the input of the overlay information to the system when the overlay is changed.

5.2.3.2 Speech Oriented Devices

Speech is one of the best ways of communication between humans. We feel most comfortable when conveying a command orally. Although, graphics applications are mainly visible, interaction by speech has been used to advantage as a man-machine interface in several systems for the following reasons:

i) In a graphic application, hands and eyes of the operator are busy. Speech input gives some relief to the operator and may increase the productivity of the operator.

ii) It can be used to replace/complement inputs from conventional devices, such as keyboard function keys and/or tablets.

(iii) It can improve the response of the operator and the accuracy of the input information.

Speech input is fed to a Voice Recognition Module (VRM) which generates a unique code for every voice input. The system software recognizes the input from the VRM [13] in a manner similar to the case when the input had come from a keyboard or a function key. A schematic diagram of a voice recognition system is shown in figure 5.6

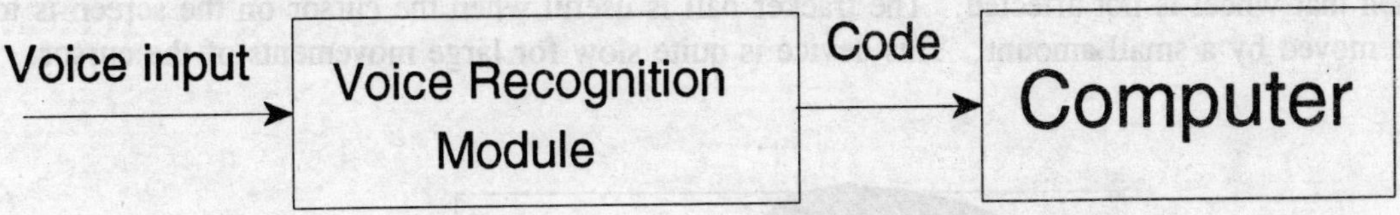

Figure 5.6 Voice recognition system

Voice inputs are effective, provided that the capability of the voice recognition equipment is properly matched with the application. The key factors are the size and type of vocabulary available and the use of isolated words versus continuous utterances. The voice input can be in the form of a command or alpha-numeric data.

One of state-of-the-art product, the Phonetic Engine 400 from Sound Systems Inc. is a speech recognition system for developing speech based DOS and Windows applications. The system can convert speaker independent continuous speech input into text input and comes with a 40,000-word vocabulary that users can augment.

The use of voice input technology in CAD/CAM or other commercial systems will depend upon the price/productivity ratio as compared with the alternative options for increasing productivity.

5.2.4 Interaction by Spatial Position

The effectiveness of this technique is based on the visual feedback available on the screen in the form of a cursor. The movement of the cursor is controlled by the x and y registers of the input device. These registers are updated as the device is moved by the user and the computer reads the device periodically.

The cursor is superimposed on the image and is in the form of a cross or a spot of light. The user can observe the movement of the cursor with respect to the movement of the device and can compensate for the nonlinear behaviour of the device.

5.2.4.1 Monitored Devices

These devices are monitored by the computer at regular intervals to find the current x and y coordinates of the cursor. The action to be taken on the input parameters is decided by the application program.

5.2.4.2 The Track Ball

Two orthogonal wheels controlling the potentiometers are driven by the tracker ball (figure 5.7). If the ball is moved at right angles to the direction of one of the wheels then that wheel is not affected. The tracker ball is useful when the cursor on the screen is to be moved by a small amount. This device is quite slow for large movements of the cursor.

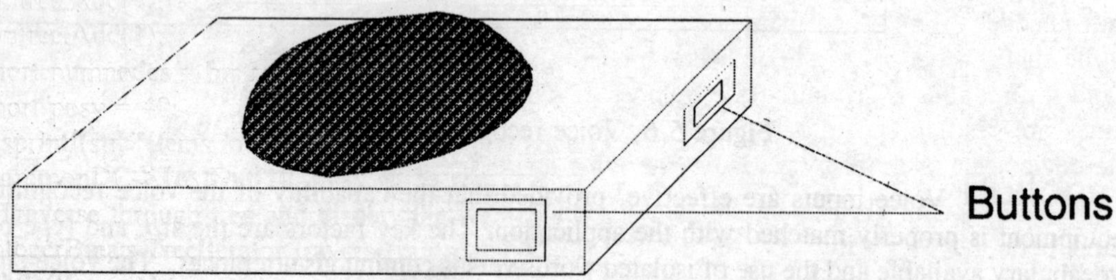

Figure 5.7 A track ball

5.2.4.1.2 The Joystick

This device (figure 5.8) is similar to the tracker ball except that the movement is limited. The potentiometers are mounted in such a manner that they are moved when the joystick is moved in their direction, but not when the joystick is moved at right angles.

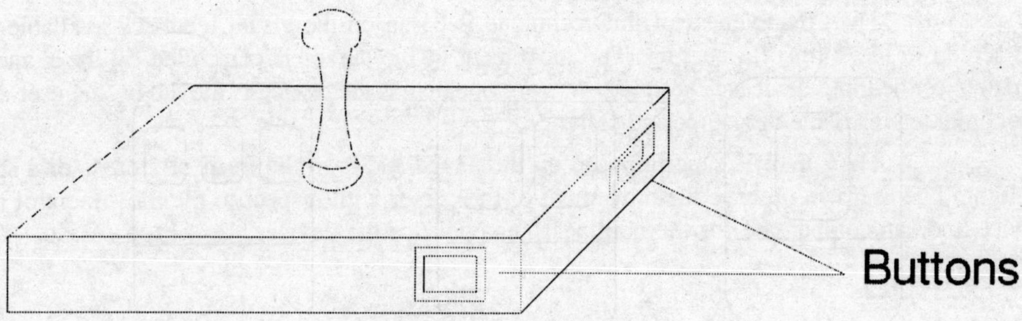

Figure 5.8 Joystick

The limited movement of the joystick is sufficient for moving the cursor from one edge of the screen to the other. This results in lack of fine control as compared with the tracker ball but the cursor can be moved very quickly from one corner of the screen to the other. However, software techniques can be used very effectively to provide a variety (fast or slow) of cursor control modes to the user. It can even be used as a precision device in CAD work.

5.2.4.1.3 The Mouse

It is a small device that was developed at the Stanford Research Institute [7,4]. It has two wheels at right angles to each other. Each of these wheels is connected to the shaft encoder. For every incremental rotation of the wheel, an electrical signal is produced by the shaft encoder. As the device is moved on a flat surface, the movement is coded in the x and y directions by counting the number of pulses received from the shaft encoder. These values are held in separate registers and the computer can sample them at a suitable rate. The device can, therefore, be used for moving a cursor around the display screen.

In an experiment conducted at the Xerox Palo Alto Centre [10], the mouse was found better for selecting text on a CRT screen than a joystick or normal cursor control keys, or text keys (e.g., para, line, etc.).

Some properties of the mouse are described below:

i) The user need not pick up the device in order to use it.

ii) If the device is picked up from a location and put down at some other location the x and y values will not change (i.e., the cursor will not move).and

iii) The x and y coordinates generated by the mouse wrap around when overflow occurs. This feature can be used to advantage by the software.

The mouse cannot be used for tracing drawings from paper since a small amount of rotation or a loss of contact results in cumulative errors. Figure 5.9 shows a one, two and three button mouse.

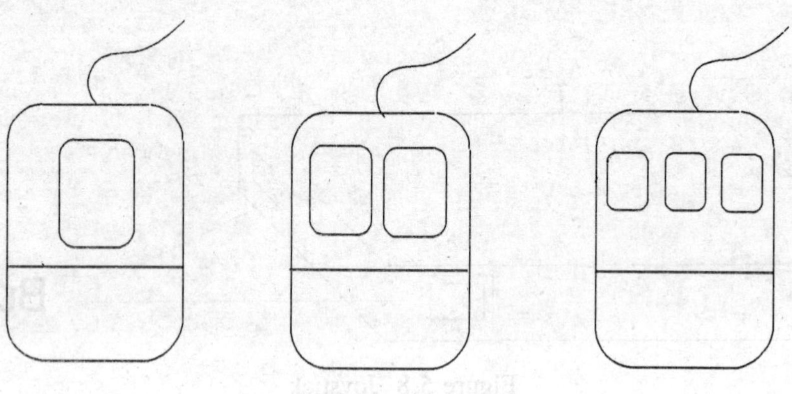

(a) (b) (c)

Figure 5.9(a-c) Shows one, two and three button mouse

5.2.4.1.4 Potentiometers

A potentiometer is used for the input of numerical data. The total range of the potentiometer (say 0 to 5 volts) can be used for representing one dimension of the screen by numerical values between 0 to 255 or any other convenient range. A linear potentiometer has resolution up to 1/1000. It cannot, therefore, be used for ranges beyond 0 to 1023.

The value obtained can be used directly by the program or can be scaled (say logarithmic, square, exponential, etc.) to a desired form by the user. This device is particularly useful for exercising a continuous control over the part of the graphics on the display, e.g., controlling the speed of a car in a video game or 'zooming' on an object on the display.

5.2.4.1.5 Touch Wire Technique

Two techniques are commonly used for detecting the location of the wires being touched by a finger. These are based either on the principle of the change of capacitance of the wire, or on the change of resistance between two wires separated by a resistive layer when touched by a finger.

Two touch wires are embedded in a transparent overlay which is mounted on the top of the display screen. The interaction, therefore, is directly on the display device. The location of wires touched by the user can be detected. A suitable code is generated which a computer interprets for determining the location of the area of interest on the display.

It is also possible to sense the pressure of the finger on the display when touched by the operator. This parameter can be used for denoting the z-coordinate of an object on the screen. This system is good for applications which need low resolution. The interaction is quite natural as the operator can point to the object of interest on the screen.

5.2.4.2 Graphic Tablets

These are used along with the display device to input/update graphical data directly to the computer system, e.g., for free-hand sketching, tracing a map, engineering drawing, electrical circuits, etc. The tablet is a flat surface on which the user draws with a cursor or stylus. Thus, one can interact with the device as if writing with a pen on paper.

The feedback of one's actions is available on the display by the cross hairs or a square whose movement is locked with the motion of the stylus, when pressed on the tablet. The resolution of such a device can be as high as 0.1%, corresponding to a digital accuracy of 10 binary digits.

A number of mechanisms have been developed for translating the position and direction of cursor movement on the tablet into a signal which can be used by the computer. Some of the popular techniques are described in the following sections.

5.2.4.2.1 Rand Tablet

It was developed in the early 1960's at the Rand Corporation [5] and provides a flat drawing area of 10 inches square. The flat surface has 1024 wires parallel to the X-axis and 1024 wires parallel to the Y-axis. Each wire carries a sequence of pulses corresponding to the position of that wire in the tablet. A stylus placed at the junction of the wires picks up a sequence of pulses for the X-wire followed by a sequence from the Y-wire. The X and Y sequences are fed to the decoding logic which determines the integer values of the X and Y coordinates.

The sequence of pulses is in grey code. This ensures that there is no more than one transition in moving the stylus to an adjacent position and thus avoids the accumulation of gross errors due to small misalignments.

5.2.4.2.2 Piezo-electric Tablet

It is made of a glass plate with an optional overlay on it. Piezoelectric transducers are mounted on the edge of the tablet. These transducers generate a high frequency surface wave. When the stylus is in contact with the tablet, it reflects the wave back to the source. The time elapsed between sending the incident wave and receiving the reflected wave is proportional to the distance of the stylus from the edge.

5.2.4.2.3 Magnetostrictive Tablet

It is used in low-price systems. The tablet is a sheet of magnetostrictive material which acts as row of delay lines. The stylus has a small magnetic sensor on its tip. Electric pulses are generated simultaneously in a number of parallel conductors in the X-direction. The stylus is used for detecting the time delay between the issue and detection of a pulse, which is measured by a digital counter. The above procedure is repeated using parallel conductors in the Y-direction and the time delay is stored in a separate counter. The position of the stylus can be located from these time delays.

5.2.4.2.4 Sonic Tablet

It can be used in any environment as no physical surface is needed for the transmission of sound. The tablet [2,15] has ribbon microphones installed on the two edges, as shown in figure 5.10. The stylus can generate a small spark on its tip at regular intervals. The delay between the generation of the spark and reception by the X and Y microphones is used for obtaining the position of the stylus.

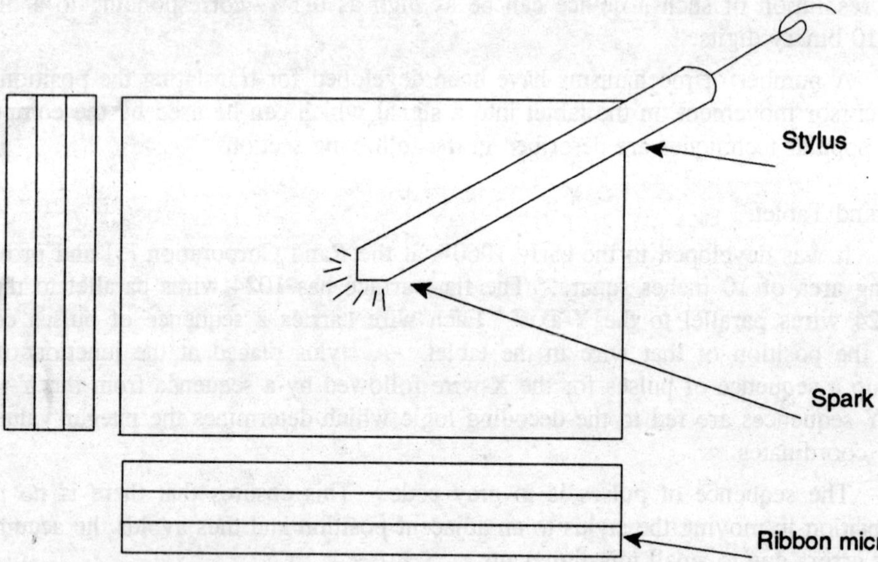

Figure 5.10 Sonic tablet

5.2.4.2.5 Optical Tablet

In this case, a set of parallel light beams is generated along one edge of the tablet at discrete locations. These beams are detected by photo detectors mounted on the other edge, as shown in figure 5.10. When a stylus or a finger is located on the tablet, the corresponding light beams in the X and Y direction are blocked. Detection and decoding the address of the beam enables the computer to obtain the X and Y coordinates of the location.

The resolution of the system is determined by the spacing of the light beams. In some systems. the frame containing the hardware for generation and detection of beams is mounted on the top of the display. The interaction in this case is quite realistic as operators can point directly to the area of interest on the display by a finger. This technique can be used on all types of displays (e.g.,refreshed, storage and flat panel).

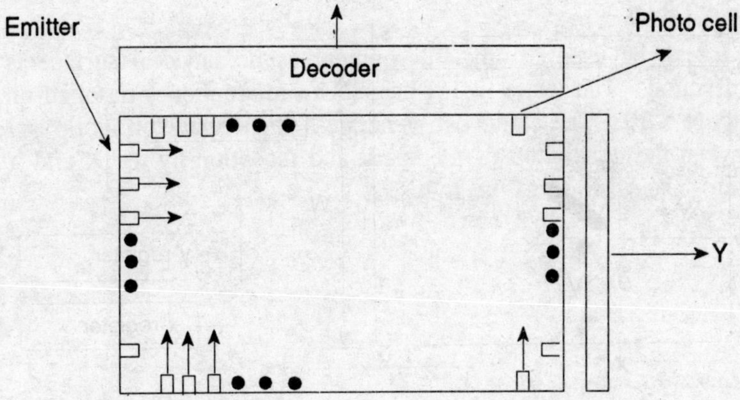

Figure 5.11 Use of optical method in tablet

5.2.4.2.6 Eye Monitoring Technique

Some devices developed by researchers work on the principle of identifying a part of the graphics on the display by determining the direction of the eyes of the user looking at the object of interest. In a system developed at Massachusetts Institute of Technology [10], two reflections are obtained -- one from the cornea and the other from the retina of the user's eye. These can be focussed to give a spot within a circle of light. The relative position of the spot with respect to the circle is an indication of the viewing angle. An accuracy of within half a degree can be obtained.

5.2.4.2.7 Analog Voltage Sheet

In a straightforward approach to determine the *X* and *Y* coordinates of the location of the stylus, voltage gradients across a sheet made of partially resistive material are created alternatively in *X* (0 to V_x) and *Y* (0 to V_y) directions, as shown in figure 5.12. Given a sheet of length *L* and width *W*, one can determine the x-coordinate of a point *P* as

$$x = \frac{V_x L}{VX}$$

Similarly, the *y*-coordinate of *P* is given by

$$y = \frac{V_y W}{VY}$$

The analog voltage sensed by the stylus, when in contact with the tablet, can be converted into the digital form by an analog-to-digital converter. The values that correspond to the X and Y coordinates are stored into two separate X and Y registers which are accessible to the computer.

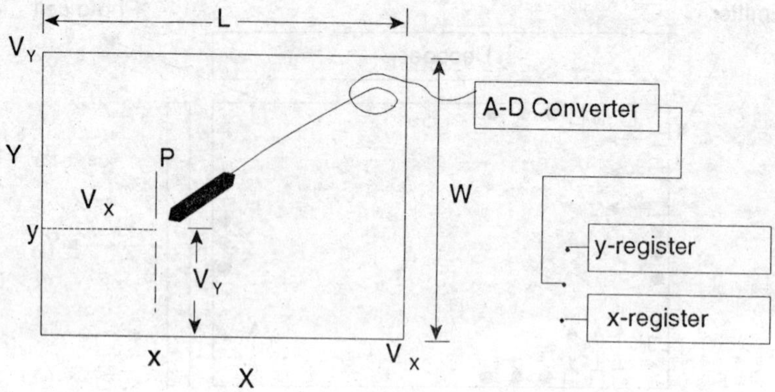

Figure 5.12 Analog voltage sheet

A similar tablet has been developed [18] in which the resistive sheet is a layer of stannous oxide fused into a glass plate and covered with another glass plate. This system uses high frequency alternating current so that the phase detected by the stylus varies for different positions on the tablet. It gives good resolution on the tablet because of the use of the high frequency alternating current.

5.3 DEVICE INDEPENDENCE

A system designer can select from a variety of input devices available to produce human interface suitable for a particular application. Unfortunately, this diversity also creates problems for software designers. Therefor, the modern trend in graphic programming is to develop device-independent software. This approach has led to the classification of input devices based on their function. The CORE definition subgroup of ACM/SIGGRAPH had recommended the following definitions for 'virtual' input devices, which are similar to those suggested by Foley and Wallace [8]:

- PICK: for a pointing device;
- LOCATOR: for a positioning device;
- VALUATOR: for a numerical data input device;
- TEXT: for a character data input device; and
- CHOICE: for a device used for input of commands.

The application programmer can use only these virtual devices and then utilize standard routines for accomplishing functions of pick, locator, valuator, text and choice. There is no need to worry whether the pick operation is performed using a light pen or a cursor, whether location is carried out by tracking through a pen or a tracker ball/joystick, the choice is through a physical key or a virtual key on the display. This necessitates the use of a software interface between the handlers for virtual and physical devices. Such interface programs can be built in as integral parts of the programming system and can be made transparent to the user.

The graphical input routines are constructed in such a way that on one side they are compatible with the standard input statements of the programming language, while on the other side they also fit the graphical output concept. For example, in standard Pascal, there is a procedure 'READ' which is used as input mechanism for the type of variable, with which it is called. A typical set of input procedures could be:

i) PROCEDURE ReadPosition (digitizer, x, y);
{Input of coordinates could also be from a light pen}

ii) PROCEDURE ReadMap (digitizer, P);
{Any device which can pick a point from the drawing plane can be used}

iii) PROCEDURE ReadData (keyboard, x);
{Input a real number from any valuator}

iv) PROCEDURE ReadCh (keyboard, ch) {Input of character}

On invoking any of the above procedures, the program will pause (as with the READ operation in Pascal) until input is received from the physical device associated with the procedure. If the input is not of the expected form, an error will be generated and the program will be terminated. Input devices can also be connected to output devices by providing the following procedure:

PROCEDURE Connect (device, screen);

With the above graphical input facilities, the user can write interactive programs for an arbitrary computer system in a high level language.

This approach facilitates standardizing software and enables applications to be made relatively independent of their hardware environment. The application programmer can select and use any of the characteristics of any physical device. Reassignment of devices may need a small amount of reprogramming, as long as they are of similar type. For dissimilar devices different user interface will be necessary.

5.4 ELEMENTS OF GRAPHICAL INPUT DEVICES

Any graphical input device may be described [1] by using combinations of the following elements:

i)state, ii) event, and iii) action.

5.4.1 State

The state of a device can be described by the contents of data variables of any type, structure, or complexity associated with it. The transparent component of the state of a device can be freely examined at any time by other devices. The remaining components are referred to as hidden.

A device may also have information about the transparent component of the state of other devices. This may be called the external component of the state of this device. In case the device releases this information to its own users, the external state is transparent, otherwise it is hidden. Figure 5.13 shows the various components of the state of a virtual device.

A few examples illustrating the objective meaning of the state of a device are the position of a tracker ball, joystick, or a switch (on or off), and the status of the light on a function key.

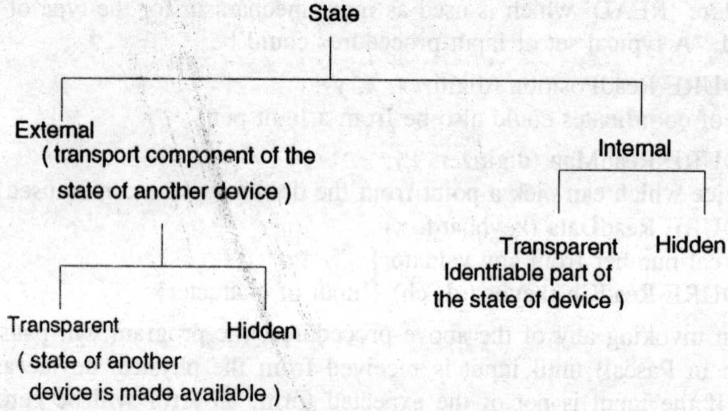

Figure 5.13 Components of a state of a device

5.4.2 Event

An event is caused by an action and may also trigger an action in one or more devices. The parameters of the action may be provided by the event. Some examples of an event are pointing a light pen to an object on the display, pressing a key on the keyboard, or touching a touch wire.

5.4.3 Action

Actions occur in response to events. An action may alter the internal state of a device, signal an event and then may terminate within a short span of time.

A device which has an internal state needs initialization by invoking an action. The external state of a device cannot be changed by invoking any action in it. A device can influence the state of other devices by initiating action in them. Thus, each device has control of its own structure.

Some examples of action in a device are turning on or off the light of a function key or adding a character to the string being composed through a keyboard.

A set of examples are given below which illustrate a few interactive devices.

Example 5.1: To illustrate the elements of an input device, we shall describe a general purpose interactive function key [1]. It has two states: up or down. Pressing the key (an event), or releasing the key (another event) changes its state from up to down or vice-versa. The key, therefore, has two actions, each of these changes a one-bit state. In general, a key may also have one or more of the following features:

i) Software may query the location of the key;
ii) When pressed, an interrupt is generated;
iii) When released, an interrupt is generated;
iv) A light is available which can be turned on or off under software control (to give feedback to the status of the key to the user); and
v) A unique value is passed with each interrupt.

The key may be described through the following Pascal program.

```
PROCEDURE FnKey (ID : INTEGER);   (* Device *)
VAR  name : 0..9;
     lighted, down : BOOLEAN;  (* state *)
     keypress : BOOLEAN;
PROCEDURE Initialize;
VAR i : INTEGER;
BEGIN
  FOR i := 0 TO 9 DO
    BEGIN
      lighted := FALSE;   (* The light is initially off *)
      down := FALSE       (* The key is initially up *)
    END
END;
BEGIN  (* FnKey *)
  Initialize;
  READ (Keyboard, ID);
  IF ID IN name THEN
        keypress := TRUE
  ELSE keypress := FALSE;
  IF keypress THEN
        BEGIN
          name := ID;
          down := TRUE;
          lighted := TRUE
        END
END;
```

Example 5.2: An input device valuator can be described by a transparent state which is a real value. Typically, this value lies between zero and one. This may correspond to the angular position (external state) of some device, such as a knob. The description of the device is given below.

```
PROCEDURE Valuator (value : REAL);   (* Device *)
VAR    KnobAngle : INTEGER;    (* external state *)
BEGIN
  value := KnobAngle/360
END;
```

Such a description can be used to develop modules for an interactive system. It is easy to use and can be adapted easily to changes in the input hardware.

5.5 INPUT TECHNIQUES

Input methods for graphical interaction use the basic principle of visual feedback. The system displays certain information on the screen and the user responds by providing suitable inputs through the input devices. An immediate response of the user's interaction is shown on the display. Some of the most effective and useful techniques are described in the following sections. The user can select a suitable technique for a given application by controlling a sequence of actions in order to achieve a certain goal quickly and with minimal effort.

5.5.1 Positioning

This operation is used for locating or introducing a symbol at a desired location on the display, for defining end points of a straight line, and/or for generating polygons, circular arcs or other geometric figures. In general, a special symbol of one of the forms shown in figure 5.14 is used. This is generally called a cursor or tracking-cross.

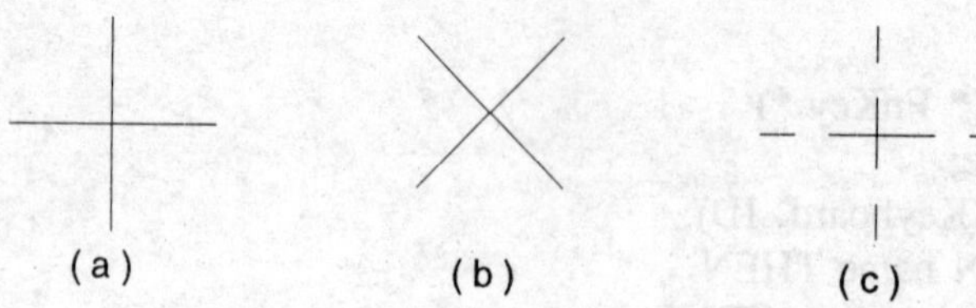

Figure 5.14 Types of tracking patterns

The following steps are used for positioning:

- move cursor to the desired position on the screen; and
- inform the computer by either pressing the button available on the input device, or by pressing a key on the keyboard.

The operation performed is decided by the application program which is written to match the characteristics of the input devices.

5.5.1.1 Use of Light Pen

A light pen can be used only indirectly for positioning since primarily it is a pointing device. One method is to enable the light pen by pressing the switch and pointing it onto the desired position on the display, and simultaneously displaying a grid of bright spots on the screen. The light pen can pick up one or more points falling in the field of view of the pen. The accuracy of the position obtained is limited by the spacing of the grid.

The second method uses a cursor on the screen. The cursor is picked by the light pen (by pressing the switch) and is moved to the desired position. The switch is then released. The cursor is, thus, detached from the light pen. The centre of the cursor indicates the point the user wanted to locate. This procedure can be repeated many times. The main problem in moving the cursor is of losing the light pen. The user has to adjust the movement of the light pen across the screen with the velocity of the movement of the cursor. If the program controlling this process is too slow, or if it does not move the cursor in the same direction as the pen, it will not be possible for the pen to move the cursor.

There is a trend to stray away from the light pen for the following reasons:

i) it is a .ward to draw at 90 degrees to the horizontal;

ii) when user are faced with a baffling problem, they tend to tap the light pen on a hard surface, sometimes rather strongly;

iii) it is easy to pull a light pen loose from its moorings accidentally by dropping and stepping on it, or having it wedged between a printer and a plotter;

iv) it is rather fragile.

Example 5.3: Consider the example of positioning a square symbol (already stored in computer memory) to a position defined by the coordinates (X,Y) on the display. A program to control a cursor under light pen control is available and the symbol can be placed at any desired position by using the switch on the light pen.

To solve this problem,

i) the user has to locate the point (X,Y) on the screen accurately,

ii) to align the symbol with respect to the cursor. One way is to align the centre of the symbol with the centre of the cursor. Alternatively, one of the vertices of the square can be aligned with the centre of the cursor.

The existing program should be modified to incorporate the following features:

i) A low intensity grid of suitable resolution is generated when the switch of the light pen is pressed. The grid remains on the screen until the cursor is moved to the desired location. and

ii) when the operator releases the light pen switch, the grid is deleted and the symbol is placed with the desired alignment.

The procedure is illustrated in figure 5.15.

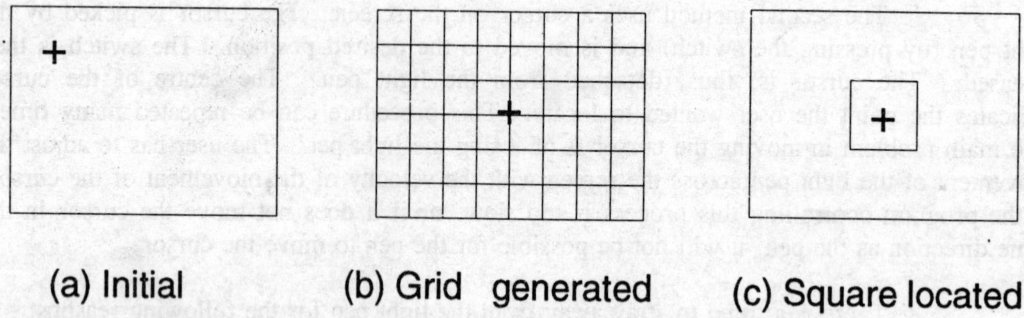

Figure 5.15 Use of light pen or any other pointing device

5.5.1.2 Keyboard

The user can give graphic commands to the system by using alphanumeric, control or function keys. The inputs can be used to control the movement of a cursor. The following program can be used to draw a sketch by incremental movement in the four basic direction: left, right, upwards and downward. The four arrow keys (see figure 5.16) available on the keyboard are used for these operations. However, any other four keys could also be used. Pressing the character 'E' on the keyboard will abort the program. The trace of the cursor is available on the screen in the form of dots since at each position of the cursor, a dot is put on the screen by the system.

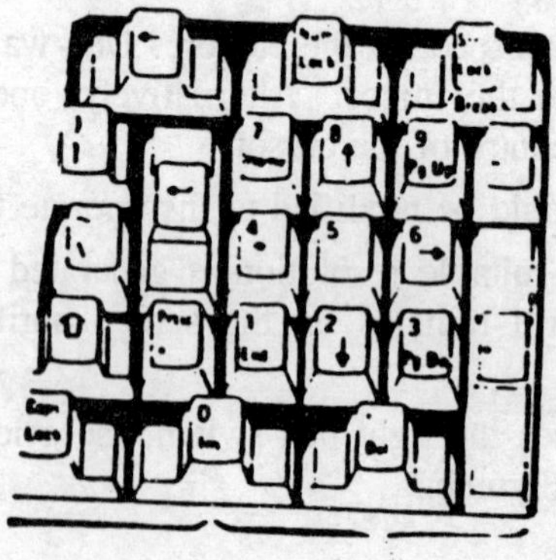

Figure 5.16 Cursor control keys

```
PROGRAM Position;
Uses Graph;
VAR  ch : CHAR; delay, GraphDriver, GraphMode, ErrorCode : INTEGER;
BEGIN
    GraphDriver := Detect;
    InitGraph (GraphDriver, GraphMode, 'C:\DRIVERS');
    ErrorCode := GraphResult;
    IF ErrorCode <> grOk THEN
    BEGIN
      WriteLn ('Graphics error: ', GraphErrorMsg(ErrorCode));
      Halt(1)
    END;
  REPEAT
    REPEAT
       Forward (1);
      FOR delay := 1 to 50 DO
         READ (ch)
      UNTIL keypress;
        CASE ch OF
        '↑' : SetHeading (0);
        '→' : SetHeading (90);
        '↓' : SetHeading (180);
        '←' : SetHeading (270)
        END
   UNTIL ch = 'E';
   READLN;
     CloseGraph;
  END;
```

5.5.1.3 Other Devices

There are several positioning devices such as joysticks, tracker balls and tablets. They can be used for controlling the movement of a cursor on the screen. The two values available from these devices are interpreted by the program as the coordinates of the cursor. The switches available on these devices (to signal an event) are used in the same way as on the light pen. A program for drawing sketches using paddles is given below:

```
PROGRAM Sketch;
Uses Graph;
VAR   i, j, delay : INTEGER;
GraphDriver, GraphMode, ErrorCode : INTEGER;
 BEGIN
    GraphDriver := Detect;
    InitGraph (GraphDriver, GraphMode, 'C:\DRIVERS');
    ErrorCode := GraphResult;
    IF ErrorCode <> grOk THEN
```

```
BEGIN
  WriteLn ('Graphics error: ', GraphErrorMsg(ErrorCode));
  Halt(1)
  END;
REPEAT
   i := paddle (0);
   (* Paddle is a function embedded in the programming language
           and is similar to ReadData (valuator, i) *)
   FOR delay := 1 TO 5 DO
   j := paddle (1);
   SetPosition (i,j)
UNTIL button (0);  (* choice of the type of device *)
READLN;
CloseGraph
END;
```

5.5.1.4 Rubber band

In this technique a straight line is drawn between an initial point and successive positions of the tracking pattern. This is carried out be retaining the initial position of the pattern in the display list and by joining it by a straight line to the current position of the pattern. A button on the input device of a key on the keyboard is used to 'fix' the line on the screen by specifying the end points by the position of the tracking pattern. Each of the end points becomes the initial point for the next operation. A number of straight lines can be drawn by the repeated use of this operation. A typical procedure for the user's action for rubber-band operation using an input device (say, a mouse) is given below:

Step 1: Press the button on the input device to bring it in the track mode.

Step 2: Move the tracking pattern to the initial point of the line.

Step 3: Press the button on the device to fix the initial point.

Step 4: Move the tracking pattern towards the end point of the line. On the display, a line dynamically connects the initial point and the successive positions of the pattern.

Step 5: When the end point is reached, press the button on the device to fix the end point and stop tracking. On the display, a line connecting the initial and the end point is drawn.

As would be evident, this technique puts a heavy load on the computing resources. To avoid strain on the user's eyes and to have a smooth movement (without flicker) of the cursor along the line on the display, the line must be drawn at least 5 to 6 times per second. On terminals with local intelligence to handle display files and the capability to draw lines, this technique can be effectively implemented to advantage for applications where lines must be drawn to pass through or near points of interest.

Example 5.4: The rubber-band technique is very effective for connecting a set of data points by straight line segments. Figure 5.17 (a) shows such a situation where points

1, 2, 3, 4 and 5 are to be connected by segments 12, 23, 34 and 45. Using the rubber band technique, first we fix point 1 by moving the cursor on this point and then join points 1 and 2. The point 2 is then taken as the initial point and segment 23 is drawn. The procedure is repeated until all points are connected. Figure 5.17 (b) shows the final graph.

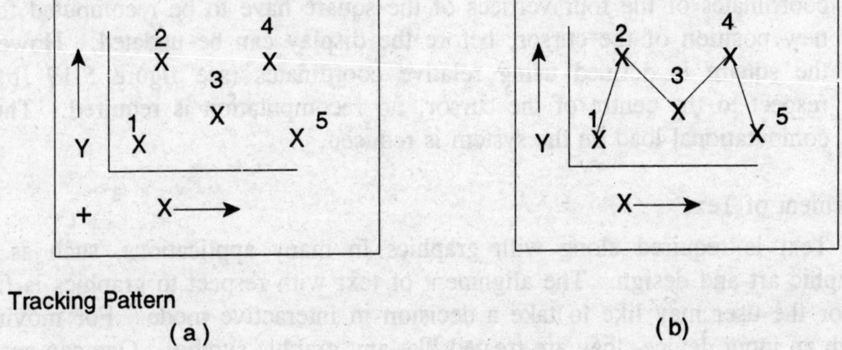

Figure 5.17 Application of the rubber-band technique

5.5.1.5 Drag

Moving the cursor under the control of the input device on the screen is useful in the positioning operation. If instead of moving a cursor, one can also attach a symbol which can be dragged along with the cursor by the user, the alignment of the symbol to a position is greatly facilitated (see figure 5.18).

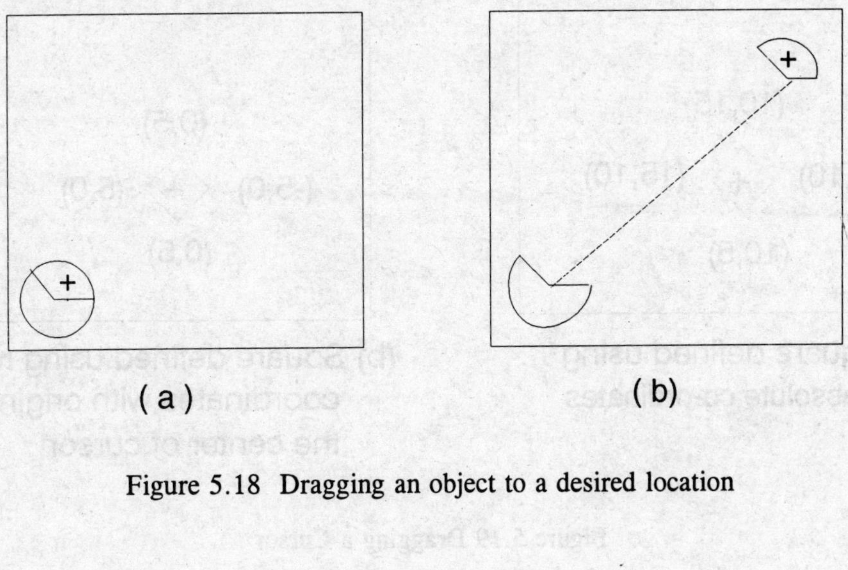

Figure 5.18 Dragging an object to a desired location

This technique also needs local computation. The position of the object must be updated many times in order to produce a continuous movement in the display. This is necessary to avoid unpleasant flicker on the picture.

Example 5.5: Let us consider a situation where the cursor is at location (10, 10) and a square defined by the coordinates of its vertices (as shown in figure 5.19 (a), is attached to the cursor. As the cursor is dragged to new positions, the coordinates of the four vertices of the square have to be recomputed for each new position of the cursor, before the display can be updated. However, if the square is defined using relative coordinates (see figure 5.19 (b)) with respect to the centre of the cursor, no recomputation is required. Thus, the computational load on the system is reduced.

5.5.4.6 Placement of Text

Text is required along with graphics in many applications, such as mimic diagrams, graphic art and design. The alignment of text with respect to graphics is fixed in the program or the user may like to take a decision in interactive mode. For moving text strings through an input device, they are treated like any graphic symbol. One can perform a drag operation to move a text string from one position to the other and align it using the lower left corner of the first character, the lower right corner of the last character, or the centre point of the string as a reference. Cursor movement can be slowed down under program control to facilitate fine alignment.

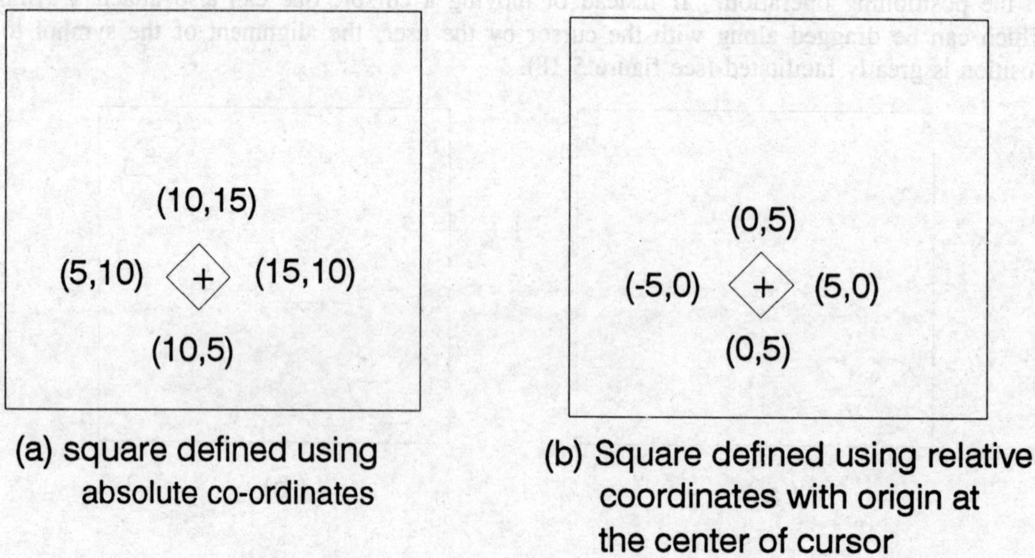

Figure 5.19 Dragging a Cursor

Example 5.6: Align the string 'TEXT' using the lower left corner of the first character as a reference, with the centre of the circle as shown in figure 5.20 (a).

To perform this operation, dragging is quite suitable. A cursor is attached at the reference point and the string is dragged to the position as shown in figure 5.20 (b). The velocity of cursor movement is adjusted to get precise positioning.

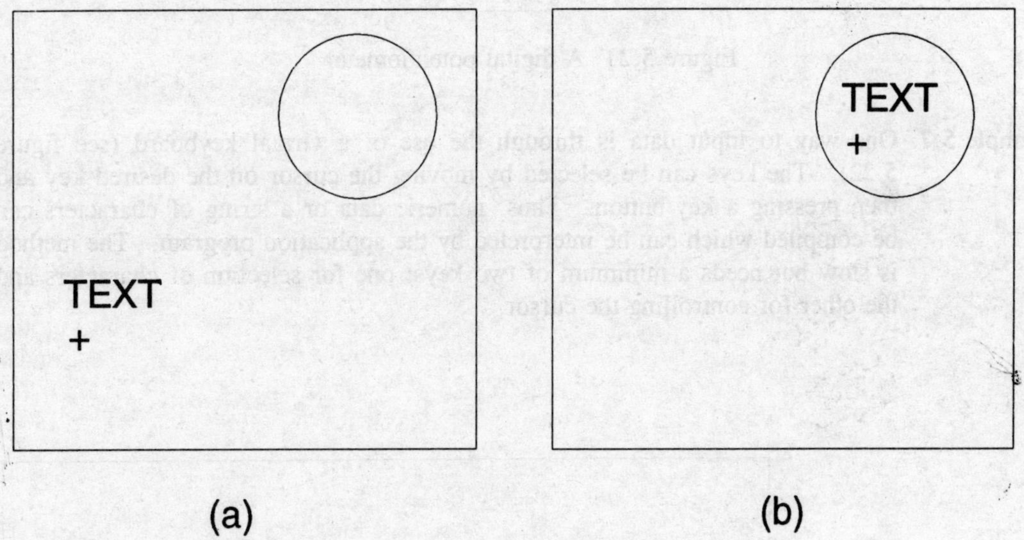

Figure 5.20 Positioning of text by dragging

5.5.1.7 Input of data

There is no direct method for the input of data using graphical input devices. However, some help may be obtained through these devices by use of special techniques. One simple approach [11] is to associate one digit of an integer with every position of the cursor (see figure 5.21) and provide feedback to the user by displaying this along with the current position of the cursor. This technique is, in fact, simulating a digital potentiometer. Another possibility is to program a counter which can be started or stopped at a desired value by pressing a key/button. Separate controls can be used for counting by ones or tens (and so on). This is similar to simulating a set of thumb wheel switches. The input of data through the keyboard is much more convenient than input through a light pen, joystick or tablet.

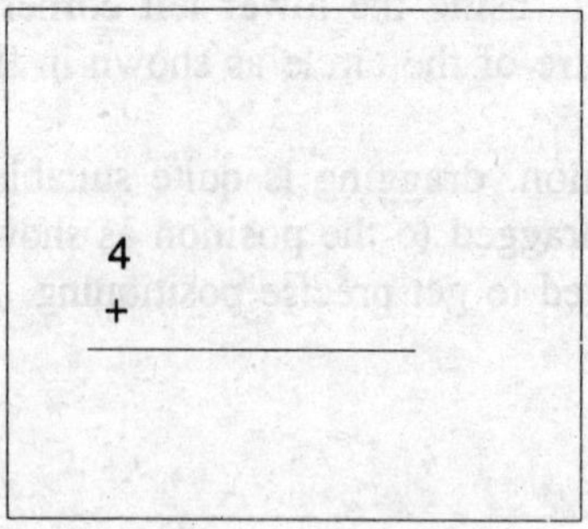

Figure 5.21 A digital potentiometer

Example 5.7: One way to input data is through the use of a virtual keyboard (see figure 5.22). The keys can be selected by moving the cursor on the desired key and then pressing a key/button. Thus, numeric data or a string of characters can be compiled which can be interpreted by the application program. The method is slow but needs a minimum of two keys: one for selection of characters and the other for controlling the cursor.

Figure 5.22 A virtual keyboard

Example 5.8: One can adopt the following approach for drawing a rectangle of length 20 units and width 10 units with the point (10,10) at the lower left corner:

Step 1: Program a graphical cursor so that its current position in terms of its X and Y coordinates is displayed as shown in figure 5.23 (a). As the cursor is moved, the coordinates of its previous position are deleted.

Step 2: Move the cursor to the point (10,10) and fix the starting point (figure 5.23 (b)) by pressing a button or key.

Step 3: Switch to the rubber-band mode and fix a line (see figure 5.23 (c)) between points (10,10) and (30, 10).

Step 4: Repeat step 3 to fix the other three sides of the rectangle.

The completed rectangle is shown in figure 5.23 (d).

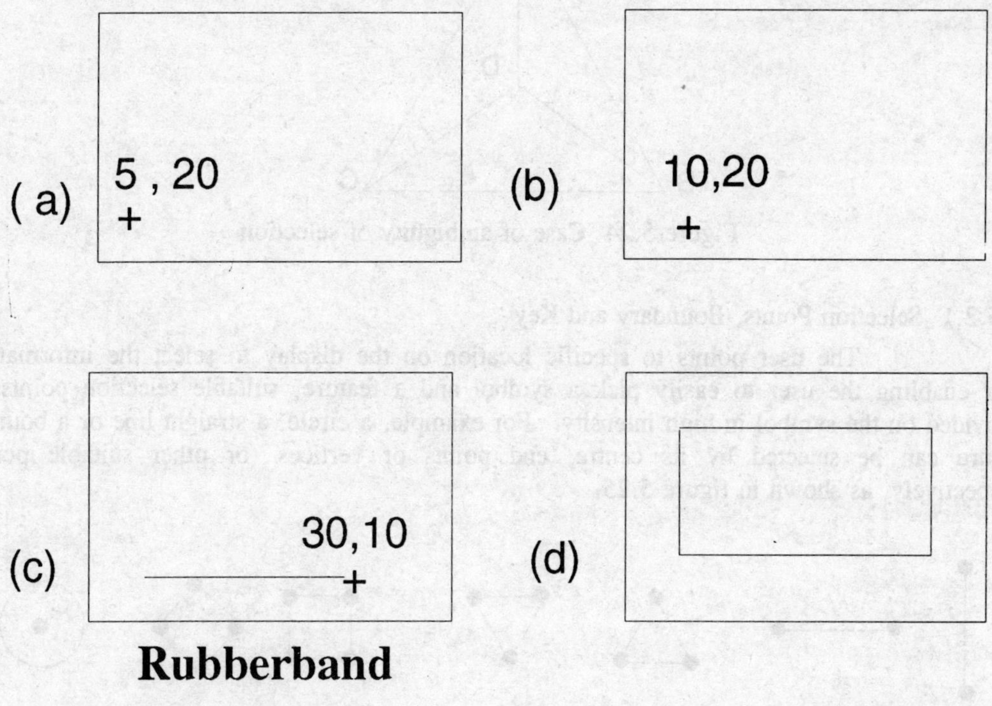

Figure 5.23 Steps for drawing a rectangle using a graphic cursor

5.5.2 Pointing

This method is used for selecting information or objects from the data or graphics already displayed on the screen by pointing to the area of interest. The action to be taken is decided by the user program. Two main problems are encountered:

i) Object identification or selection of data; and

ii) Definition of the selected zone, i.e., how much of the area is to be selected.

For example, refer to the picture shown in figure 5.24 where three lines meet at each of the points A, B, C or D. If the user points in the vicinity of any of these, it will be difficult to select any of these lines. In the same way, it is difficult to define the selected zone during a pointing operation. One method which is commonly used to avoid ambiguity is to provide feedback to the user by modulation of intensity or by blinking the selected symbol or points. Some useful selection techniques are described in the following section.

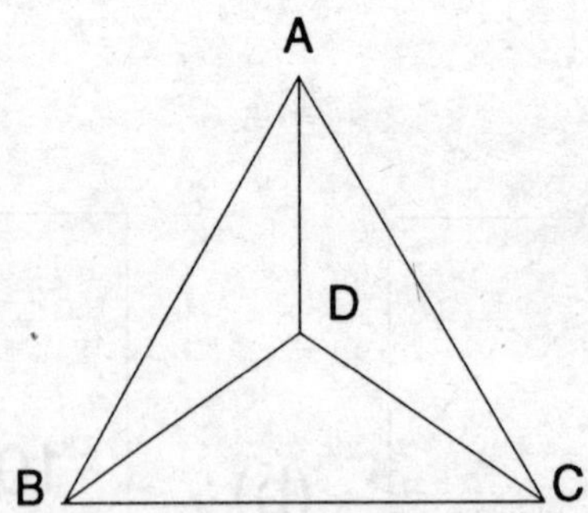

Figure 5.24 Case of ambiguity of selection

5.5.2.1 Selection Points, Boundary and Key

The user points to specific location on the display to select the information. For enabling the user to easily pick a symbol and a feature, suitable selection points are provided on the symbol in high intensity. For example, a circle, a straight line or a bounded figure can be selected by its centre, end points or vertices (or other suitable points) respectively, as shown in figure 5.25.

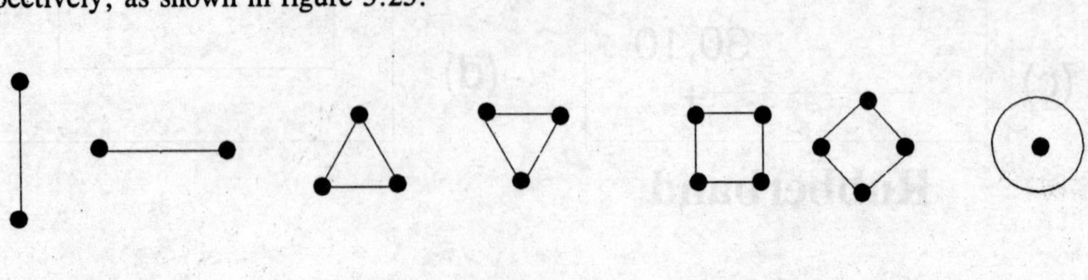

Figure 5.25 Selection points are shown using high intensity on graphic objects

A closed boundary can also be defined to activate the selection zone. This zone can be rectangular or circular (see figure 5.26) and may or may not be displayed. A user can select any symbol or text inside the zone by directing a pointing device to any of the points or features inside this zone.

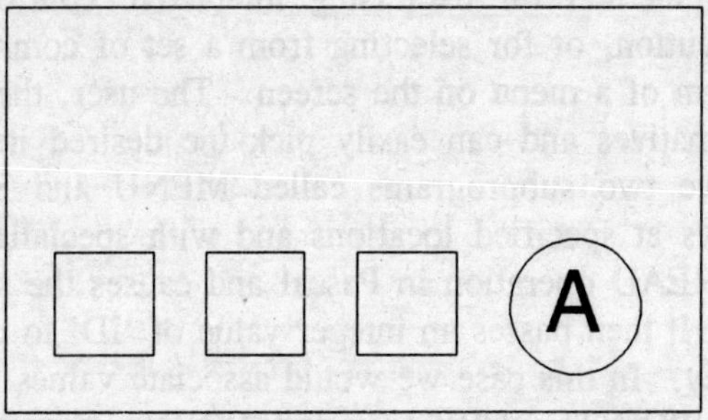

Figure 5.26 Rectangular or circular selection zone

The number of keys/buttons available on the input device can be programmed to select only a particular type of feature. If a device has red, green and black buttons, each of these can be associated to enable selection of features such as a line, a character or a symbol (see figure 5.27). Thus, ambiguity in selection can be avoided to some extent.

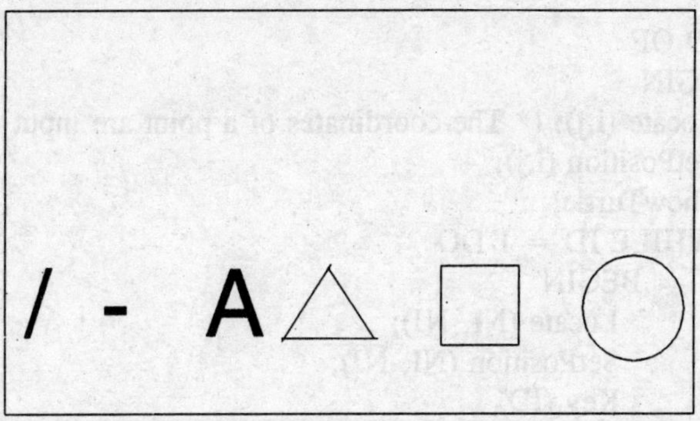

Figure 5.27 Selection of line, character, and symbol through use of button

5.5.2.2 Modes

Instead of using multiple keys for selecting different features, a user can set a number of modes in the program. In one mode the program allows the selection of only one feature. For selecting another feature, the mode of operation has to be changed.

5.5.2.3 Cyclic Presentation

In case a user wishes to select a feature in a zone where number of features are clustered the system highlights the features one by one, i.e., each time you press mouse button, a different feature is highlighted. This is done in a cyclic order. Thus, this method enables a user to select any feature even in a complex drawing.

5.5.3 Menu

A very popular method for exercising interactive control for changing the mode of a program under execution, or for selecting from a set of commands is to display the available options in the form of a menu on the screen. The user, therefore, has no need to remember the various alternatives and can easily pick the desired item from the menu. We shall assume that we have two subprograms called MENU and KEY. The program MENU displays four light keys at specified locations and with specialized identifers. The program KEY is similar to a READ operation in Pascal and causes the system to wait for a key to be pressed by the user. It then passes an integer value of 'ID' to the calling program, which identifies the selected key. In this case we would associate values '1', '2', '3' and '4' with the light keys 'LINE', 'POINT', 'CIRCLE' and 'END', respectively. A skeleton Pascal program is given below.

```
PROCEDURE MENU (- - - ); (* Display the menu *)
(* Arguments may be the number of characters in each light key, array of integers
representing the ID of the keys, character vector containing message for each key,
location of each key *)
        BEGIN
          key (ID);
          CASE ID OF
          1 :   BEGIN
                  Locate (i,j); (* The coordinates of a point are input *)
                  SetPosition (i,j);
                  ShowTurtle;
                  WHILE ID = 1 DO
                        BEGIN
                          Locate (NI, NJ);
                          SetPosition (NI, NJ);
                          Key (ID)
                        END
                END;
          2 :   BEGIN

                END;

        END;
```

5.5.4 Dialogue

It is a common method for establishing an exchange between users and a computer through a character string (using the keyboard and virtual display), depression of a function key, or selection of graphical components from a displayed image. State diagrams can be used very efficiently to describe a dialogue system [6]. Figure 5.28 shows a simple dialogue system using keyboard and display. The user can interact with the system to draw a triangle or a square on the display.

A dialogue generated using the specifications of Figure 5.28 is given below.

? Display Triangle
    Get coordinates of the vertices
    Join vertices by lines
    Stop
? Display
    Triangle or square
? Square
    Get coordinates of the vertices
    Join vertices by lines
    Stop
? Exit
    Bye

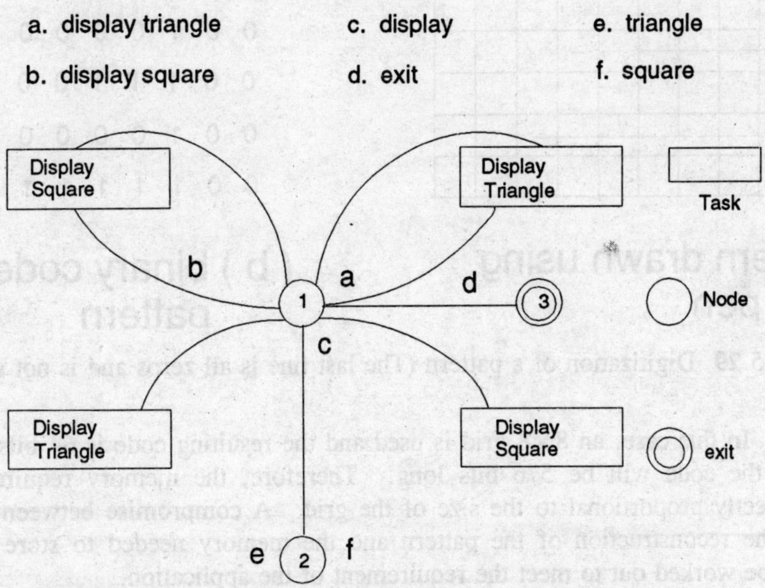

Figure 5.28 State diagram representing a dialogue system

5.5.5 Applications

The following examples will show two simple applications.

Example 5.10: In an application, it is desired to input handwritten characters to a computer. The characters are to be stored in the memory for future reference, The input can be given either by a light pen or a tablet.

A grid is displayed in low intensity. In figure 5.29 an 8*8 grid is shown. The spacing between the lines and number of lines on the grid is decided by the nature of the application. One can draw a character directly on the screen with a pointing device. It is advisable to draw the alphabet such that it covers the entire grid to ensure that all features of the character are visible. In converting the information into a binary code the following method is used:

i) if the character stroke passes through a square of the grid a '1' is written;

ii) else a '0' is written.

Figure 5.29 (b) shows the binary code generated internally by the system for the character 'E'.

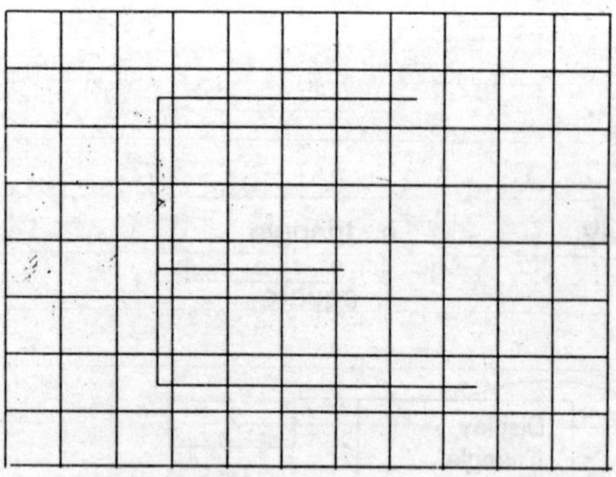

a) pattern drawn using light pen

0 0 0 0 0 0 0 0

0 0 1 1 1 1 0 0

0 0 1 0 0 0 0 0

0 0 1 0 0 0 0 0

0 0 1 1 1 0 0 0

0 0 1 0 0 0 0 0

0 0 1 1 1 1 1 0

(b) binary code for the pattern

Figure 5.29 Digitization of a pattern (The last line is all zeros and is not shown.)

In this case, an 8×8 grid is used and the resulting code is 64 bits long. For a 24×24 grid the code will be 576 bits long. Therefore, the memory required to store a pattern is directly proportional to the size of the grid. A compromise between the accuracy desired for the reconstruction of the pattern and the memory needed to store the digitized pattern is to be worked out to meet the requirement of the application.

Example 5.11

Two-dimensional models of a process can be created on the display in an interactive mode, in order to better understand the behaviour of various stages of the process. A graphical database is created to store the symbols along with their selection points. These symbols are used to represent the blocks of the process. Figure 5.30 shows a simple graphic database. A user can pick a symbol using the selection point through a light pen and position it at the desired location. A simulation diagram can be developed by picking symbols one by one from the database to depict various stages of the process.

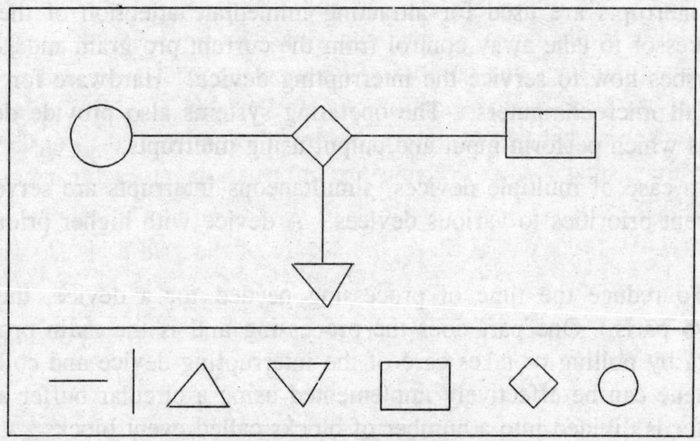

Figure 5.30 A simulation model

5.6 EVENT HANDLING

In a situation where only one input device is used in program, the instructions may be of the following type:

IF LeftMouseButtonPressed THEN <PROGRAM1> ELSE <PROGRAM2>.

LeftMouseButtonPressed is a Boolean variable, associated with the left mouse button and can take the value FALSE or TRUE. The flow of the program is controlled by the button position.

It is often required to use more than one input device with the system. With an instruction of the type READ (see section 5.3) to get the input from a device (say, the keyboard), the program waits until a key is pressed. However, if the user has a change of mind and wishes to use another device, there is no way to inform the system.

One can resolve this problem by periodically checking the status of each device in a predefined order. This process is called 'polling'. Input devices usually have separate registers to indicate their status and to store data. For a light pen, the status may only be a one bit information and the data may be the X and Y coordinates. Similarly, a knob may have a one bit status and provide a value proportional to an angle. In most cases, the status bit is set by the device and is cleared by the system. The status of each device is checked periodically to ascertain if there is an input ready to be fetched. The program then decides the next course of action.

Polling enables the use of more than one input device. However, there is a possibility that data may be lost. For example, if the user moves the light pen on the display, the polling program will look for light pen input only when it is checking the status of the light pen. The intermediate positions of the light pen are lost. If the number of input devices is large, or if the processing of a device takes longer time, the turn of a particular device will be delayed.

Interrupts are used for attracting immediate attention of the processor. This enables the processor to take away control from the current pro-gram and jump to a new program that describes how to service the interrupting device. Hardware for interrupt handling is available in all microcomputers. The operating systems also provide device handlers for standard devices which perform input and output using interrupts.

In case of multiple devices, simultaneous interrupts are served on the basis of assigning different priorities to various devices. A device with higher priority will be served first.

To reduce the time of processing needed for a device, the program can be divided into two parts. One part does the processing and is the main program. The other part fetches data by polling or takes care of the interrupting device and collects this data in a queue. The queue can be effectively implemented using a circular buffer as shown in figure 5.31. The buffer is divided into a number of blocks called event blocks.

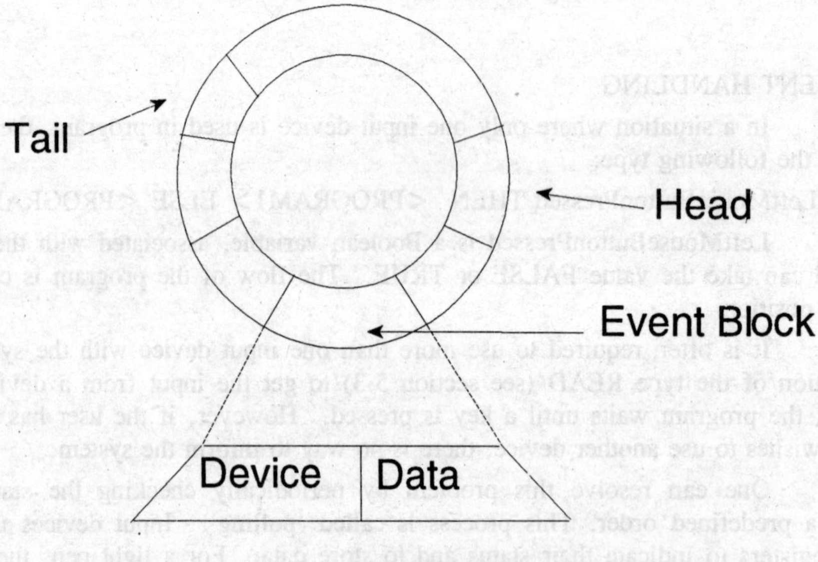

Figure 5.31 A queue implemented using circular buffer

A block contains the name of the device and the data pertaining to an event. The main program fetches an entry from the head of the queue and activates the appropriate program pertaining to the device. A new event is entered in the block pointed by the tail of the queue. The positions of the head and tail pointers are dynamically adjusted. The queue is full when the position of the head and tail pointers are the same. The number of events which can be stored depends on the size of the buffer. An overflow condition will occur if the rate of generation of events is higher than the speed of the program for handling events. Instead of using a circular buffer, one can also use a set of contiguous blocks in the memory which can be linked together to form a queue.

5.7 GRAPHICAL USER INTERFACE

Designing the user interface for a computer application can be considered equivalent to designing a house. Just as an architect works with a set of building blocks when designing a house, a user works with number of graphical elements and use techniques described in this chapter to design the way a user will interact with the application. The main task of the designer of the user interface is to decide which of the existing procedures to use in the application and how best to present them to enable a user of an application to run it with least effort. An ideal GUI environment should allow user to input parameters through mouse and keyboard based graphical forms including menus, buttons, meters, and slides or similar other tools to create an animated representation of the system and graphs and charts of the key variables. Figure 5.32 shows a view of the MS-Windows GUI.

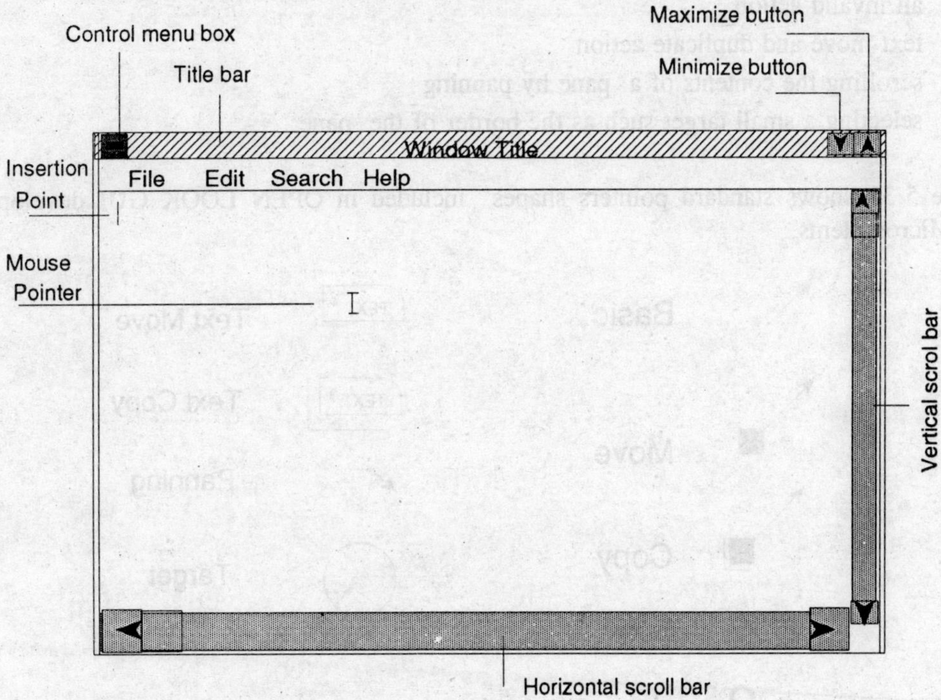

Figure 5.32 A view of MS-Windows GUI

5.7.1 THE WORKSPACE

The workspace has its own menu to enable users to start up applications, access utilities, customize settings, or exit the GUI. The location of various control buttons, mouse location and text pointers, scroll bars to keep desired text, graphics, line drawing, and images in the user area is marked in figure 5.32. Workspace menu also provides necessary controls to customize the environment.

5.7.2 THE POINTER

It is one of the smallest but most important element on the work space. When a user moves the mouse or any other pointer control device, the pointer moves on the screen (work space). When a button is pressed on a mouse or any pointing device, standard visual feedback shows that an action has been initiated or a selection has been made. In case, no action is taken and the button on the device is released, the feedback is cleared and the action is not completed. Standard pointers available with the graphic user interfaces include :

- basic operation
- move and duplicate operations
- busy feedback
- an invalid action
- text move and duplicate action
- scrolling the contents of a pane by panning
- selecting a small target such as the border of the pane

Figure 5.33 shows standard pointers shapes included in OPEN LOOK GUI developed by Sun Microsystems.

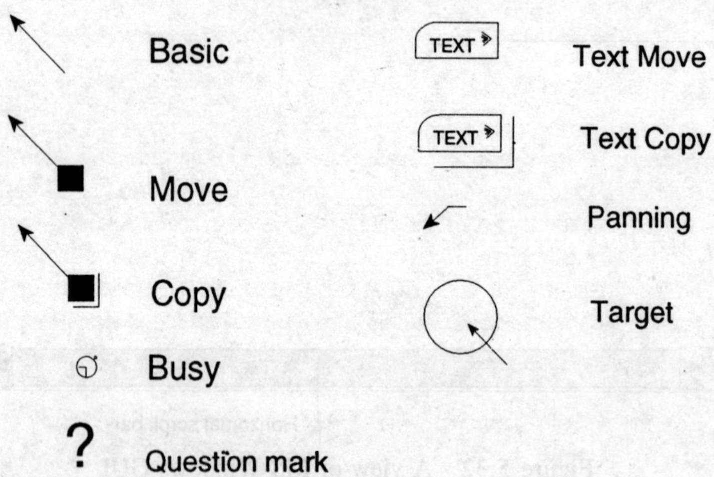

Figure 5.33 Pointer shapes

In general, the pointer changes its shape when a button is pressed on a mouse or an equivalent input is given through any other device like keyboard. The pointer returns to its previous appearance when the button is released. The busy pointer is the only pointer controlled by application behaviour and not by user manipulation.

5.7.3 MENU PROPERTIES

GUIs provide a user certain properties to view and choose from menus. However, properties available to the user depend on the level of complexity of the tool kit.

5.7.3.1 COLOUR

Colour controls permit user to set default colour for the workspace, for windows, and for the selection. It enables a user to alter the default settings and customize settings for individual applications.

5.7.3.2 BUTTON

Buttons are used for single commands. The name of the command is generally the title on the button, e.g., to open a project or a file, the button may have label "OPEN". In certain tool kits and window applications when a button has three dots after its label, choosing it causes a window to be displayed. Such buttons are called window buttons. Figure 5.34 shows examples of a command and the window button.

Figure 5.34 Shows command and window buttons

Menu buttons have menu mark (a triangle) after the label. The triangle marks the location where menu will be displayed. When the button is pressed, it highlights to provide visual feedback. Figure 5.35 depicts a menu button 'DRAW' before and after activation when it is highlighted and a menu appears.

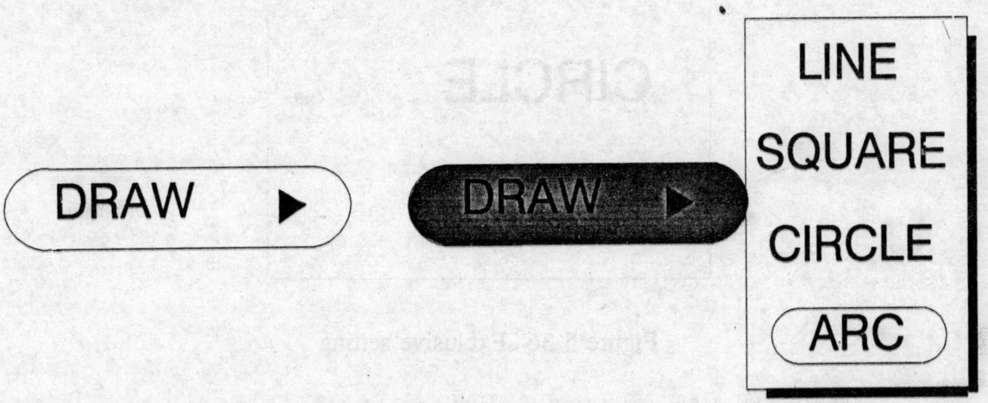

Figure 5.35 Menu button before and after being pressed

5.7.4 MENUS

Menus are used to allow the user to select actions as the program is running. Menus can be divided into following categories:

- Button menus - display when a user chooses a menu button
- pop-up menus - which pop-up at the pointer location

Figure 5.35 also illustrates use of a button to pop-up a menu. Menu items are used on menus and have the same functionality as buttons. The only difference between item and button is by their looks. Figure 5.34 shows menu 'DRAW' with items, viz., LINE , SQUARE, CIRCLE, and ARC. The item ARC is selected on the menu. When there is not enough space to create all menu buttons in one or two menu bars for all the commands one may need - pop-up menu (also referred to as "pull down", or "drop down") are used. This allows a user to exercise many more options from which to choose.

5.7.5 EXCLUSIVE and NONEXCLUSIVE SETTINGS

Given an object which has several states, a user can select only one of the available states of the object in case of exclusive settings, e.g., in a graphic application, the draw menu may have items such as line, polygon, circle etc. A user will, however, be able to select only one item at a time. Figure 5.36 depicts an example of exclusive setting.

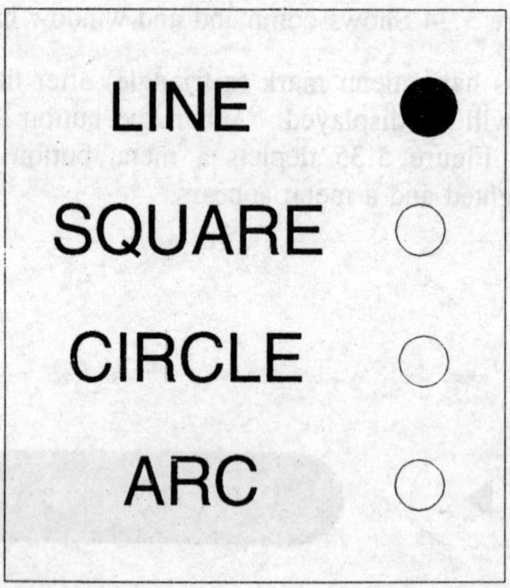

Figure 5.36 Exclusive setting

The facility of non-exclusive settings enables a user to set as many values for one particular object, e.g., in a word-processing application text attributes bold, italic, underline can all be set for the same word. Figure 5.37 shows an example of non-exclusive setting.

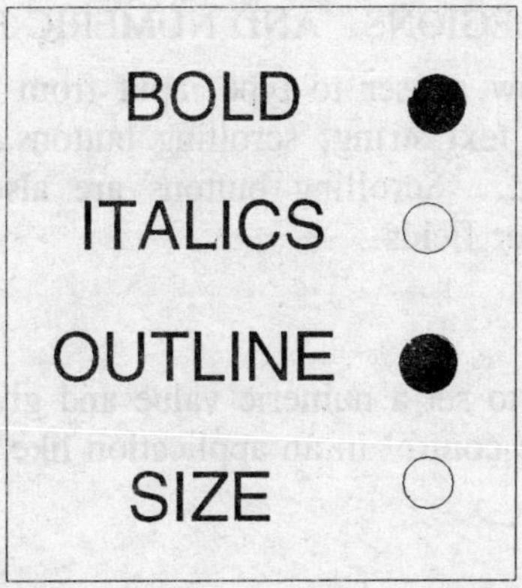

Figure 5.37 An example of non-exclusive setting

5.7.6 CHECK BOXES

Check boxes are used to set a binary choice, e.g., Yes/No or On/Off choice. A user can select all some or none of the options by toggling the check box. Figure 5.38 gives an example of check box.

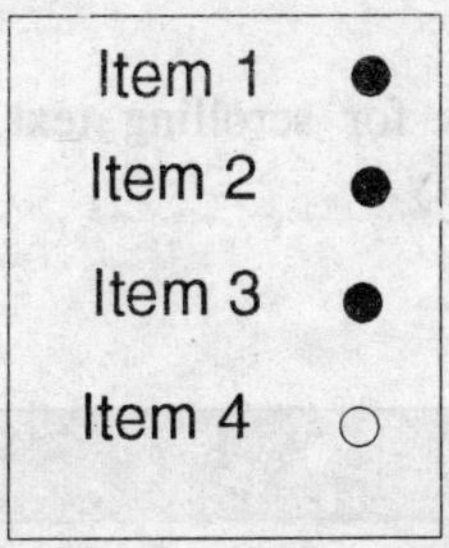

Figure 5.38 Check box in which Item1, Item2 and Item3 are selected

5.7.7 ABBREVIATED BUTTONS

These are similar to normal button but take less space. Abbreviated buttons are normal buttons but no text level inside them. They can have a glyph inside the button. Figure 5.39 shows an abbreviated button. Up and down arrows inside the button signify the purpose of the buttons which is maximizing and minimizing the size of the active window.

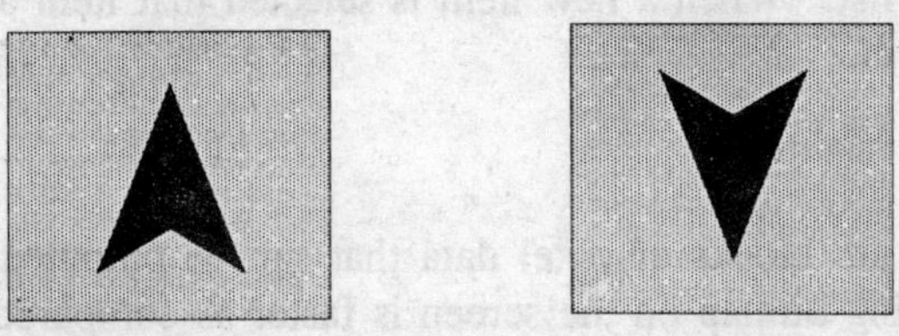

Figure 5.39 These button are located on top right corner and are used in MS-Windows for minimizing or maximizing a window

5.7.8 TEXT FIELD, TEXT REGIONS, AND NUMERIC FIELDS

These fields allow a user to type input from the keyboard. In case a given field cannot display the entire text string, scrolling buttons are displayed to enable user to scroll the content of the field. Scrolling buttons are also used to increment/decrement numbers displayed in the number fields.

5.7.9 SLIDERS

Sliders are used to set a numeric value and give a visual indication of setting. These can be used to adjust the control in an application like adjusting the volume of a beep(see figure 5.40).

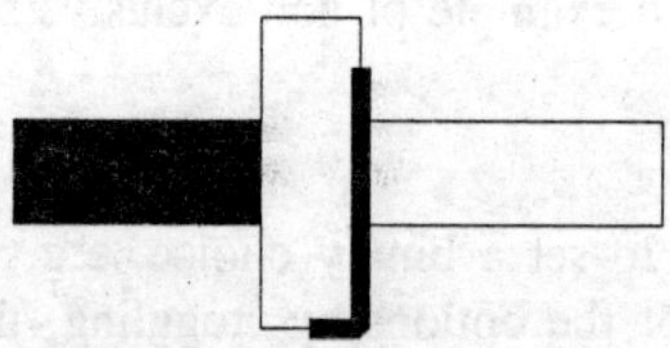

Figure 5.40 Slider

Figure 5.41 shows the scroll bar controls for scrolling text, line drawing, graphics and images in user area horizontally and vertically.

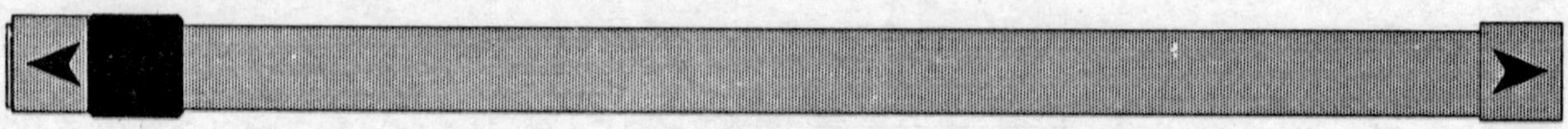

Figure 5.41 Horizontal scroll bar for a window

5.7.10 SCROLLING LIST

Scrolling list presents an unbounded list of items in a small well defined region. These are similar to settings. An exclusive scrolling list permits a user to choose only one item from the list. When a new item is selected that item automatically supersedes a previously selected item.

5.7.11 BIT MAPS :

Bit maps are blocks of pixel data that can be output directly to a device, such as video display. Painting bitmap on the screen is faster as compared to use of functions like rectangle, line etc. The drawback of bit maps is that it takes a lot of memory. Bit maps can be created in device independent format called a "device independent map (DIP) as well as device dependent bit map (DDP).

5.7.12 ICONS

Icons are small bit maps (generally images of 32x32 or 32x16 pixels) and are used as place-holders for applications. Icons are used in window based GUIs at a suitable location of the screen (usually the bottom left corner of the screen) when applications are minimised. These provide a convenient way to user to memorise and invoke the application they represent by double clicking by mouse on them. Icons can be created in MS-Windows using Paint Editor. Figure 5.42 shows icon of Word Perfect program.

Figure 5.42 Shows Word Perfect Icon

5.7.13 GRAB HANDLES

The small squares that are displayed at the corners and mid points of the region that defines a selected graphic object are called grab handles (see figure 5.43). These provide a way of selecting an object from a group of objects and performing operations, such as, moving, copying, scaling, rotating etc.

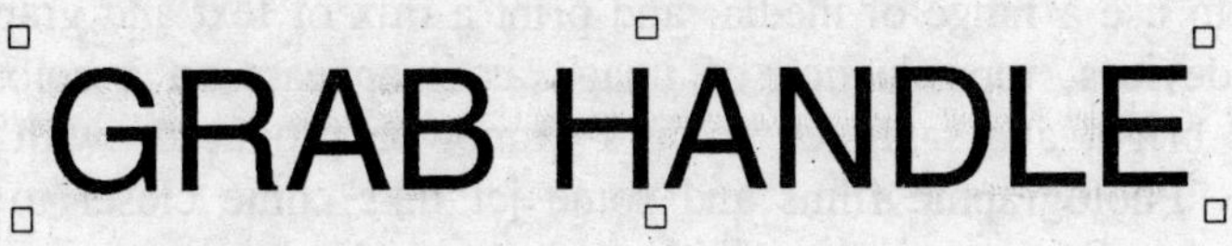

Figure 5.43 Grab handles shown as small squares shown around text

In a window environment, it becomes often necessary to size a window. Grab handles used for sizing a window in MS-Windows is are shown in figure 5.44.

Figure 5.44 Grab handles for a window to adjust its size

5.7.14 GAUGES or METERS

These are used to give a visual indication of how full or empty an object is. It can also be used to show percentage completion of a job.

5.8 HARD COPY DEVICES

Hard copy output in text or graphical form in black and white or a number of colours is required for off-line analysis. The hard copy devices required for micro-computer based systems for office and other commercial applications require better print quality than required in data processing and scientific applications. With the development of a strong market for personal computers, manufacturers have come out with printers which are less expensive and have many modes of operations, e.g., data processing quality at high speed, word processing quality at lower speed, and/or graphic capability to provide hard copy of graphics developed on the CRT. In addition, increased use of colour terminals has resulted in a greater demand for colour hard copy devices since such systems provide better clarity, and enable a user to highlight important data results for quick perception. Until recently, colour hard copy devices were quite expensive and attempts are being made by manufacturers to develop new low cost techniques to bring down prices to a level that will enable use of these devices with micro-computers.

We shall discuss seven basic technologies [2,22,23] which are available for obtaining hard copy of text and graphics. Table 5-2 shows a comparison of these technologies. It can be seen that no single technology meets all the requirements. The user has to consider relative merits of each technology (cost, speed, cost of supplies, flexibility, reliability, quality of image, and availability of software) to meet the requirements of a particular application for selection of a suitable hard copy device and speed. Flexibility is the capability of a device to use a range of media, and print a mix of text and graphics. In case of colour hard copy devices, reproduction of image as it appears on a colour terminal is important. However, bright and saturated colours cannot be produced with pigments and dyes on white paper. Photographic films and some jet inks come closer to matching the quality of terminal output. Some typical applications are given below:

i) for creating working copies or print required for verification of results/data should be available quickly & should also be easy to interpret,

ii) for generating limited distribution reports high print quality is required. It may be preferable to use a mix of monochrome text and colour graphics on plain paper,

iii) for presentations requiring transparencies for overhead projection the print and/or slides quality with high colour saturation is required, and

iv) for reports which are to be archived the colour quality should be such that it shall not fade.

5.8.1 Impact Printers

A dot matrix printer creates alpha-numeric characters and graphics output with a matrix of small dots. The printhead has number of pins called hammers arranged in a column. The hammers can be selectively activated by a command to transfer dot of ink from an inked ribbon on to paper. The number of pins in the printhead usually varies from 9 to

24, enabling printer to produce as many dots at the same instant. Printers with more pins can produce better formed characters in the same pass. A 9 - pin head is commonly used in dot matrix character printers and figure 5.45 shows a few standard characters formed using a 7×9 matrix.

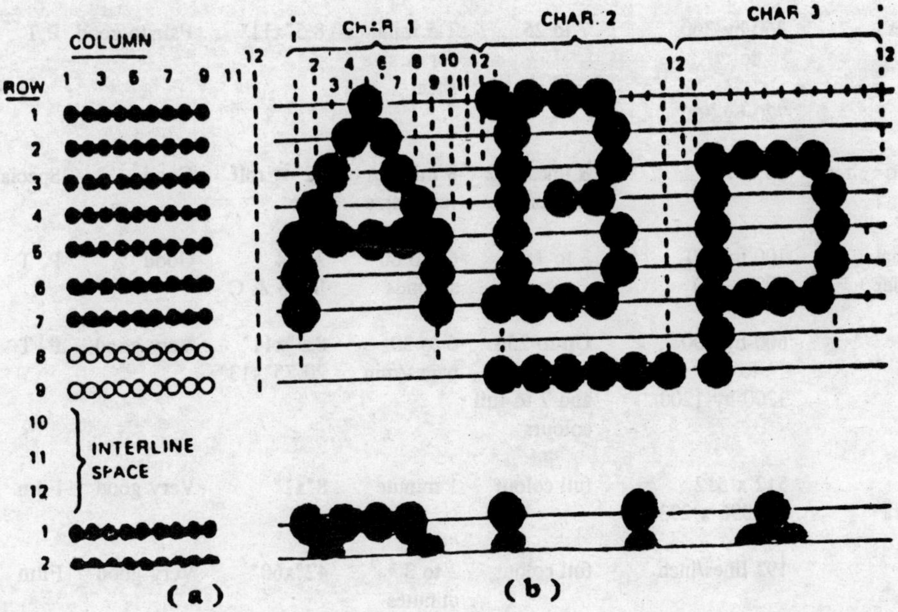

Figure 5.45 (a) A 7x9 matrix and interline space

One simple way to convert an ordinary dot matrix printer into a colour printer using minimal additional hardware is to add a mechanism for positioning the ribbon to a different colour band. The ribbon used has several colour bands across the width. Different colours are obtained by moving the ribbon carrier up & down to position the desired colour band in front of the print head.

TABLE 5.2 Comparison of Colour Hard Copy Technology

Technology	Resolution dots/inch (dpi) and/or x×x bitmap graphics	Colour	Speed	Size	Image Quality	Medium Plain Paper (P) Transparency (T)
Impact Printer	100 to 720 dpi	3 to 128	40 to 300 ch/s	8.5"x11" 11"x13.2"	Fair	P
Pen Plotter	0.001 inch (typical)	1 to 8	up to 24" per sec	8.5"x11" to E-size	Fine line	P
Ink-Jet	360-by-360 to 720-by-360	7 to 25	1-5 minutes for A size sheet	8.5"x11"	Fair to good	P,T
Electro-static	up to 200	8 lines/512 shades	8 minutes for E-size	42"× roll sixe	Good	Special
Thermal Transfer	100 to 400 300 x 300	3 to 7	60 to 80 seconds	A/A4 B/A3 & C	Good	P, T
Laser Printe	600-by-600 to 1200-by-1200	Up to 256 grey levels and 7 to full colours	6 to 30 pages/min	8.5"x11" 20.75"x13"	Very good	P, T
Film Camera	512 x 512 to 4096 x 2732	full colour	1 minute	8"x1"	Very good	Film
Film Plotter	192 lines/inch	full colour	2 to 3 minutes	42"x60"	Very good	Film
Imagesetters (Capstan type) (separate film for each colour)	600 to 3600	Mono-chrome	5" to 57.6"	12" to 25.6"	Excellent	Film Bromide paper

Another approach is to arrange the different colour bands across the length of the ribbon instead of width. This approach is suitable for impact line printers which print all the data across the paper in one print cycle. To obtain several colour output the ribbon is moved to one colour in one cycle and print cycle is executed. The ribbon is then moved to the next colour band and without advancing the paper, dots in another colour are printed. This process is repeated for each desired colour. In one such unit, instead of line, one full page is printed in one colour. Then paper is repositioned and the second colour is printed. Thus, life of ribbon is extended but the printer mechanism gets complicated.

The first seven rows are used for characters. Row number eight is used for lower case descender only and ninth row is used for underline and lower case descender.

A third approach, uses separate print head & ribbon for each colour. The cost of such printer is very high though life of ribbon is extended. These printers are limited in colour choice (say, three colours), resolution, and image size. These printers are suitable for applications needing low resolution colour plots.

A French inventor has announced the world's first double-sided printer. It is called "Recto Verso Printer" and can print on the both sides of a paper simultaneously. The printer has two printing mechanisms, two homing systems and two print heads. A special printer driver has been developed which can fit into modern software and utilize features of this printer. In applications where the text printing is the primary requirement, and colour graphics is secondary, impact printer will continue to dominate the scene.

5.8.2 Pen Plotters :

Pen plotters are of drum type and flat bed type using roll of paper (with fixed width & long length), and sheet of paper (maximum size of paper is equal to the size of the bed) respectively. On a flatbed plotter the paper is secured to a flat surface(also called Platen) and the pen is held in a carriage. The pen is moved parallel to two axes to draw lines. Figure 5.46 shows a typical multi-pen plotter. In a drum plotter paper is moved back and forth parallel to one axis while pen moves along the other axes.

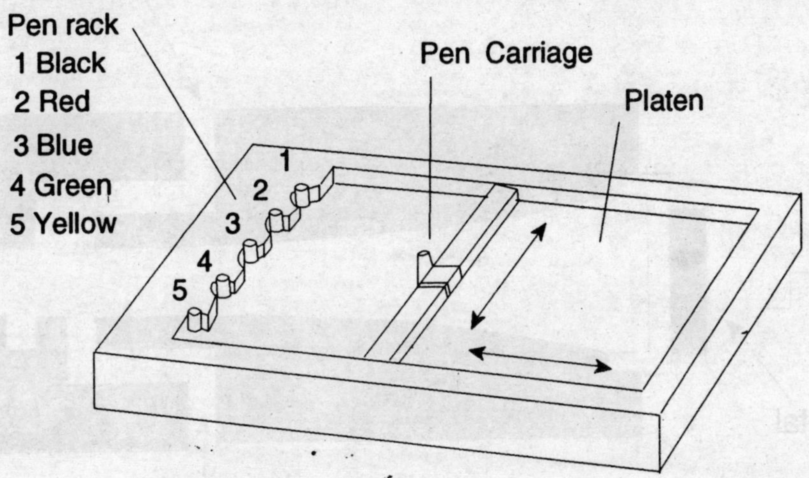

Figure 5.46 Multi pen flat bed plotter

These are traditional hard copy devices for colour graphics. A single pen plotter can be used for producing multi-colour charts by changing pens of different colours under software control. Multi-colour plotters hold number of pens in a rack and can select a pen through a command received from the computer. This device can accept paper, vellum, and transparent as well as frosted plastic films in wide range of sizes.

Pen Plotters provide accurate & fine line quality. Only pen plotters can produce smooth edged diagonal lines. Improvement of pens used for plotting has greatly reduced the problem of pen clog and skips. Simple line drawings are produced in reasonable time but in applications where shaded areas or complex plots are to be generated, these plotters can be prohibitively slow and are not suitable. Plotters are widely used for large format applications requiring very high addressability and good colour to colour registration, such as integrated circuit layout, cartographic applications, computer-aided-design and drafting, but their slow speed and inability to produce complex plots makes them vulnerable to faster nonimpact technologies. However, for personal computers small format plotters are quite popular because of acceptable quality of output and low cost.

5.8.3 Ink-Jet-Printer/Plotter :

In these systems, a matrix approach is used, with droplets of ink shot onto paper to form the desired character or graphics. - The two most common types of ink jets are continuous stream and drop on demand (see figure 5.47). The continuous flow systems can be messy and drop on demand systems have problems of clogging. Some systems use the hybrid technique to avoid clogging and flush the system at regular intervals. Some printers use a removable cartridge containing fluid in which the nozzle rests when not in use.

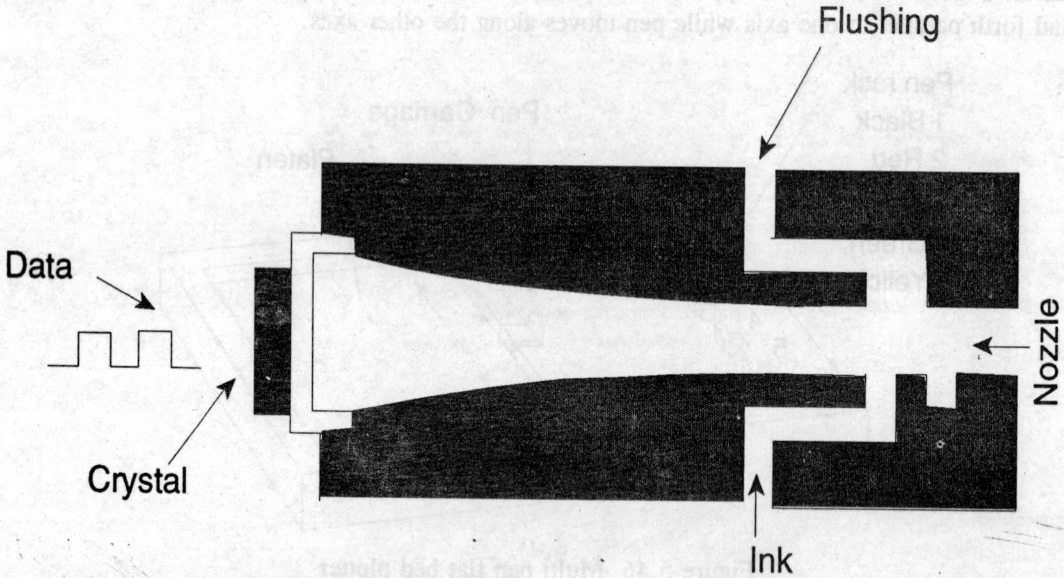

Figure 5.47 Drop-on-demand nozzle for ink jet printer
(Flushing is done at regular intervals to avoid clogging)

The printing mechanism producing drop on demand to avoid clogging consists of Piezo-electric crystal and an ink chamber in its close contact. When a electric pulse corresponding to the data to be printed is applied on the crystal it constricts, causing a pressure wave through the ink chamber. - This forces ink to come out of the nozzle at a speed of several meters per second towards the direction of the paper. However, rate of generation of drop using this technique is low. To avoid this problem the nozzles are combined in groups to increase rate at which drops can be generated.

For monochrome printing only one jet is sufficient but for colour printing multiple jets are used. One colour system uses 12 nozzles in a drop-on-demand ink-jet print head. The 12 nozzles are separated into three groups of four each to print in ink of three separate colours.

Solid inkjet printers provide freedom from the problem of clogging and create prints of quality that rivals the 'embossed' look of lithography. The mechanism in these printers heats the solid ink pellets which melt down into a heated chamber. The melted ink is moved into a compression chamber. The print signal from the host activates the Piezo- electric drop-on-demand transducer to force the ink droplet through the nozzle onto a paper or transparency. The solid ink does not have aqueous base. Therefore, there is no evaporation and clogging of the nozzle or wicking of the paper. In fact, solid ink freezes as compared to water based inks which evaporate on the paper.

In other approaches, only one colour can be printed at a time & paper is to be accurately reregistered causing inaccuracy. But inkjet deposits all the colour in one pass. Therefore, for applications where major need is colour graphics as compared to text data this printer is suitable for adding splashes of colour to borders, logos and clip art. Further, it is a quiet, high speed device capable of producing output on a plain paper and transparent film. Mid range and high end colour ink jet printers can produce full colour output with quality quite comparably to that obtained by offset printing. Further advances in ink technology may enable these printers to print directly on textiles/ wall paper/ carpets and to produce full colour print comparable to photographs.

Very high quality ink-jet engines are under development to print at a rate of 4 ppm which is good for proofing, for colour printing. Mitsubishi Heavy Industries has developed a new 72 ppm new colour press in Japan. Ink jet machines provide speed and cost efficiencies at the high end of the market, especially in throughput and customization.

5.8.4 Electrostatic Plotters:

This type of printer/plotter requires a specially treated paper with one side having coating of insulating material which is its major limitation. An electrostatic plotter manufactured by M/s Versatec can provide eight line colours, 256 predefined area colours, and 256 user defined colours.

In electrostatic plotters, programmed voltage is applied to an array of densely spaced nibs embedded in a stationery print head. The selection of nibs is done under digital control. The selected nibs create minute electrostatic dots on the paper passing over the print head. The paper is then exposed to the liquid toner and permanent image is retained on the paper. For producing a plot in one colour the paper is passed through one toner station. However, for generating a n-colour plot the paper is passed through n-toner stations where every station is meant for one colour as shown in figure 5.48.

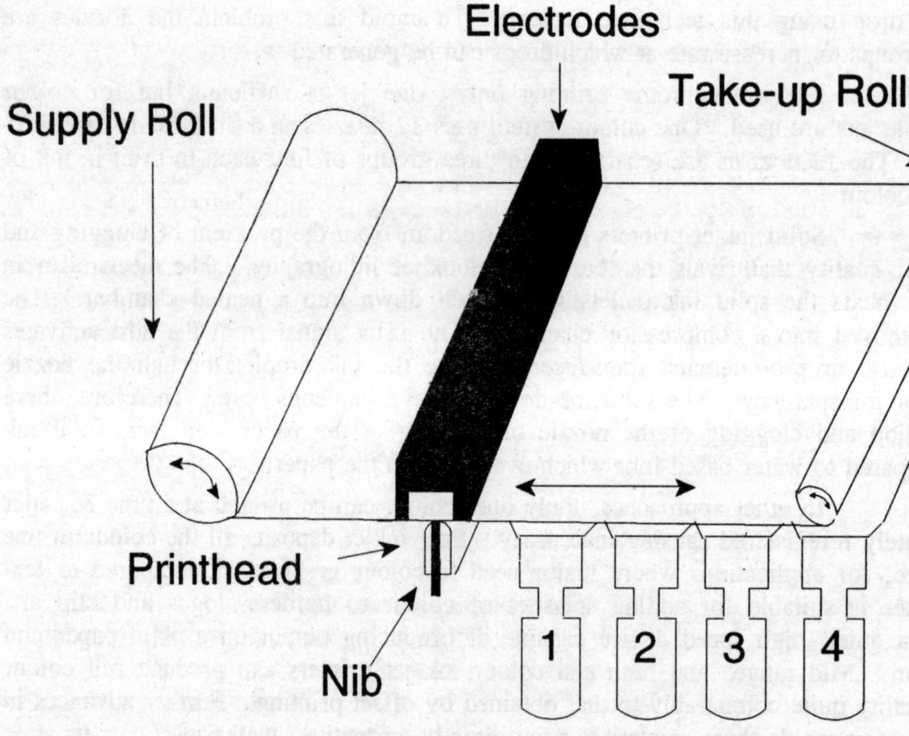

Figure 5.48 Block diagram of colour electro-static printer

The starting and end of pass positions on the paper are marked. This enables to accurately position the paper by rewinding automatically to the starting positions.

This type of plotter can provide large output format, high resolution, good colour to colour registration, and high throughput and is, therefore, suitable for applications such as integrated circuit drawings, maps, solid modelling, etc.

5.8.5 Thermal Transfer Colour Printer :

In the older direct thermal printers the characters and graphics was created by burning a special chemically impregnated heat sensitive paper with heated pins. Thermal transfer technology [2] employs a donor film(see figure 5.49) that is coated with a wax based ink and a printhead consisting of resistors. To print, a set of selected resistors in the print head become active and colour on the donor film under these resistors melts and is transferred to the paper (see figure 5.50) . In colour printing, the film is coated in page size blocks of primary colours viz. cyan, magenta, yellow, and in some cases true black. A page is printed in one colour & then repositioned to print other colours. Secondary colours viz. green, orange, & purple can be produced by overprinting. The quality of final image depends on precise paper handling to achieve true colour registration, or precise overlap of different colour dots.

Figure 5.49 Colour scheme on the donor film

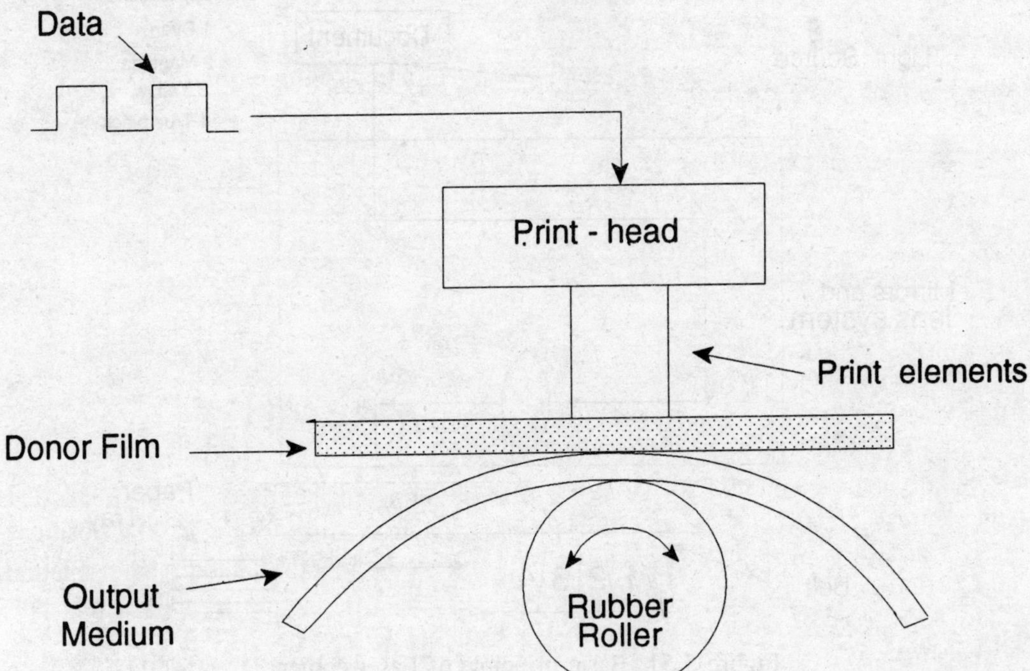

Figure 5.50 Depicts the thermal transfer technique

Colour thermal printers are raster devices and accept data in bit map format. To avoid rasterization some manufacturers are providing a video interface. WAX based inks used in this printer produce less vivid luminance in the imprints on the transparencies as compared to white paper but the ink is more durable as compared to inks used in ink jet printers. The colours generated are less saturated as compared to ink jet or photographic devices, but this printer is less messy when compared to ink jet, electrostatic and photographic printers. The operational cost is high as the film can be used only once. Thermal printer have advantages in publishing, business graphics, and applications where only a few proof copies are required.

5.8.6 Laser Copier/Printer :

Laser Copier is based on effective combination of laser and Xerographic technology [22]. A light source is used to scan the document to be copied. An optical system consisting of lens & mirrors is used to translate an image to a photo sensitive belt/drum which in turn picks up the toner and transfers the image to the paper. A line diagram illustrating this concept is given in Fig. 5.51. The major limitation of this device is its high cost and small format. A few vendors have announced systems with limited colour capability but their reliability is not established as yet.

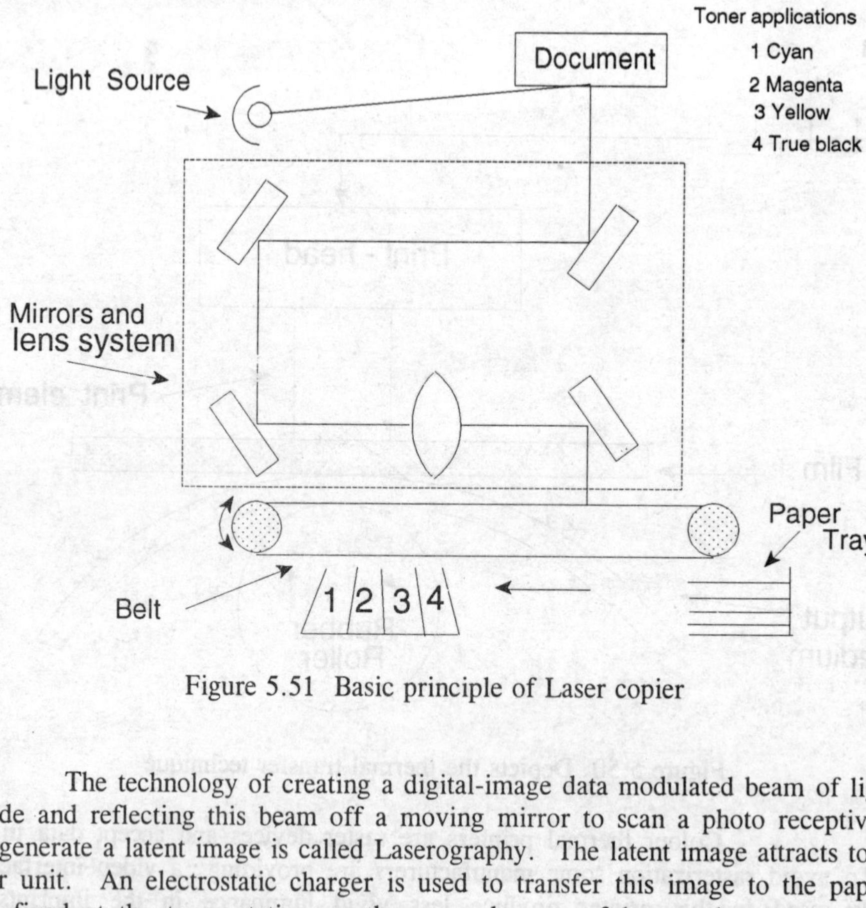

Figure 5.51 Basic principle of Laser copier

The technology of creating a digital-image data modulated beam of light using laser diode and reflecting this beam off a moving mirror to scan a photo receptive belt or drum to generate a latent image is called Laserography. The latent image attracts toner from developer unit. An electrostatic charger is used to transfer this image to the paper. The image is fixed at the toner station on the paper by use of heat and pressure to make it permanent. A block diagram based on this principle of laser printer is shown in figure 5.52.

Laserography can be used to generate colour output by developing the latent image with coloured dry toner and transferring it to the paper. This process is repeated for each primary colour (i.e., data from red colour is received and a latent image of red colour is created and transferred on paper using cyan coloured toner, then images of green and blue colour are put on the paper using magenta and yellow toners respectively) and image is fixed on the paper. However, a reliable colour laser printer is still unavailable.

Laser printers can broadly be divided into following three categories as given below:

a) Low cost printers are intended as replacement of daisy wheel and dot matrix printers, mainly used with personal computers. These machines have typical speeds of 6 to 10 pages per minute and can print up to 600 dots per inch with at least 4 MB of RAM. Such printers are suitable for stand-alone use and for small work-groups. These units print text and graphics of highly acceptable quality and some printers also accept files in PostScript Level 1 and 2.

b) Mid range printers have speeds of 10 to 20 pages per minute & can print up to 1200 dots per inch, support PCL 5 / standard (or optional) PostScript and output near-typeset-quality text, and

c) high end printers with speeds of over 20 pages per minute.

Electro-mechanical black boxes, called Laser Engines, responsible for putting image on the paper are available from several vendors, e.g., Canon, Ricoh, Mita, Xerox and many others. Selection of an engine determines the factors such as print quality, dot density and printing speed. Factors external to the engine are font availability (ROM based and down-loadable fonts), programmability, and the size of the image the printer can handle. These factors vary from company to company depending on selection of microprocessor, on board memory, capacity to work with application software and graphic word processors.

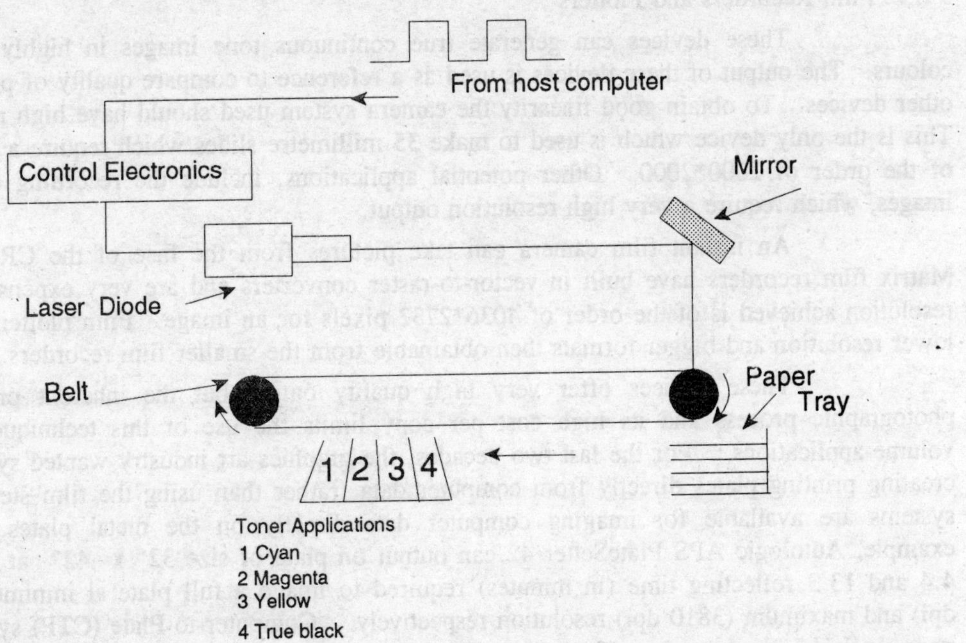

Figure 5.52 Basic principle of Laser printer

The printer speed is also a function of complexity of data on the pages. For this reason, to evaluate laser printer performance it is necessary to use software to generate a large document & print it on the printers to be benchmarked. However, the following specifications of a printer are important for evaluation :

Speed and Price
Maximum resolution horizontal/vertical dpi
Pages per minute monochrome/colour
Interfaces -- RS 232C/ RS422A, SCSI and Ethernet/Localtalk/Token Ring
Average Printing Area
Paper Sizes Supported
Emulation completeness e.g. PDLS -- HPGL and Level 1 / 2
(with respect to standard printers viz. HP, NEC, and Diablo, etc.)
Availability of manual paper input slot
Number of font cartridges available
Print quality

These systems can produce fine line quality and solid area coverage. Half tone technique can be used to generate images which look like continuous tone images. Typical systems can plot in 7/256 colours/shades on 8×11 inch to 24×34 inch paper with resolution of 300 to 600 dots per inch. Advances in laser printing technology will affect the future of the non-impact printer market.

5.8.7 Film Recorders and Plotters :

These devices can generate true continuous tone images in highly saturated colours. The output of these devices is used as a reference to compare quality of prints from other devices. To obtain good linearity the camera system used should have high resolution. This is the only device which is used to make 35 millimetre slides which require a resolution of the order of 2000*2000. Other potential applications, include the recording of landsat images, which require a very high resolution output.

An instant film camera can take pictures from the face of the CRT screen. Matrix film recorders have built in vector-to-raster converters and are very expensive. The resolution achieved is of the order of 4036*2732 pixels for an image. Film plotters produce lower resolution and bigger formats then obtainable from the smaller film recorders.

These devices offer very high quality output but the inherent problem in photographic process and its high cost per copy limits the use of this technique in high volume applications. For the last two decades, the graphics art industry wanted systems for creating printing plates directly from computer data, rather than using the film step. Now, systems are available for imaging computer data directly on the metal plates. As an example, Autologic APS PlateSetter 42 can output on plate of size 32" x 42" at speeds of 4.4 and 13.3 reflecting time (in minutes) required to image a full plate at minimum (1270 dpi) and maximum (3810 dpi) resolution respectively. Computer-to-Plate (CTP) systems are now available from number of vendors and would eliminate use of imagesetters and film processors commonly used to generate computer data output on film in the printing industry.

5.9 SUMMARY

This chapter describes the principles of design of input devices and interactive techniques for establishing meaningful man-machine communication. Three-dimensional input devices are not described. The interested reader can see references [3, 9, 12, 14, 16, 17]. Input devices have been divided into five classes (namely, pick, locator, valuator, text and choice), so that application programmers can standardize the device handling software. Most modern systems will use a digitizer tablet with a menu and pre-sketching area as the main interactive graphics device tool in engineering and drafting practice.

The basis of effective interaction is the feedback available to the user on the graphical display. To enable immediate reaction on the display to an action by the user, the modern trend is to use displays with built-in dedicated processors capable of performing graphical manipulations.

Interactive graphics provides very powerful tools to an application designer and facilitates in enhancing a user's capability and creativity. The variety of input and output devices and techniques described in this chapter are used in many applications. Some examples are the development of realistic models of physical systems, computer aided design (CAD), computer-aided instruction (CAI) and virtual reality(VR) applications described in chapter 8 and 9.

5.10 REFERENCES

1. Anson Ed, "The Semantics of Graphical Input", Computer Graphics, vol. 13, No. 2, August 1979, pp. 113-120.
2. Barrel Jerry, "Thermal Printing heats up colour hard copy market", Mini-Micro Systems, Jan. 1986, Reed Publishing, U.S.A., pp. 102-108.
3. Bremer A.E. and P. de Bruyne, "A Sonic Pen: A Digital Stylus System", IEEE Electronic Computers, vol. 19, No. 6, June 11970, p. 546.
4. Burton R.P. and I.E. Sutherland, "Twinkle Box: A 3-D Computer Input Device", NCC 1974, pp. 513-520.
5. Card S.K., W.K. English and B. Burr, "Evaluation of Mouse, Rate-Controlled Isometric Joystick, Step keys and Text keys for TEXT Selection on a CRT", Xerox Palo Alto Research Centre, SS-77-1, April 1977.
6. Davis M.R. and T.O. Ellis, "The Rand Tablet: A Man-Machine Graphical Communication Device", FJCC 1964, Sparton Books, Baltimore, Md., p. 325.
7. Edmonds, E.A., "Adaptive Man-Computer Interfaces", in Computer Skills and User Interfaces, edited by M.J. Coombs and J.L. Alty, Academic Press, New York, 1981, pp. 389-426.
8. English W.K., D.C. Engelbart and M.L. Breman, "Display Selection Techniques", IEEE Trans. HFE, vol. 8, No. 1, 1967, p. 5.
9. Foley J.D. and V.L. Wallace, "The Art of Natural Graphic Man-Machine Conversation", Proc. IEEE, vol. 62, April 1974, pp. 462-471.
10. Fuchs H.J., J. Duran and B. Johnson, "A System for Acquisition of 3-D Data", NCC 1977, pp. 49-53.

11. Infotech Ltd., "Computer Graphics: Analysis", No. 5, Series 8, Maidenhead, Berkshire, England, 1980, (ISBN 8553-9660-1).
12. Newman W.M., "A Graphical Technique for Numerical Input", Computer J., vol. 11, May 1968, pp. 63-64.
13. Newman W.M. and R.F. Sproll, "Principles of Interactive Computer Graphics", McGraw-Hill Inc., New York, 1979.
14. Rabin Richard et al, "Speech Recognition as a Computer Graphics Input Technique", Computer Graphics, vol. 16, No. 3, July 1982, pp.179-180.
15. Roberts, L.G., "The Lincoln Wand", FJCC 1966, Sparton Books, Washington, D.C., p. 223.
16. Science Accessories Corporation, "Graf/Pen Sonic Digitizer", Southport, Conn., 1970.
17. Sutherland I.E., "A Head Mounted 3-D display", FJCC 1968, Thompson Books, Washington, D.C., p. 757.
18. Sutherland I.E., "3-D Data Input by Tablet", Proc. IEEE, vol. 62, No.4, April 1974, p. 64.
19. Scheifler and James Gettys, X- windows System, Prentice Hall of India, New Delhi, 1991.
20. Sun Microsystem Inc., OPEN LOOK - Graphical user Interface Application Style - Guidelines, Addison - Wesley, Reading, Massachusetts, 1990.
21. Teixeira J.F. and R.P. Sallen, "The Sylvania Tablet: A New Approach to Graphic Data Input", SJCC 1968, Thompson Books, Washington, D.C., p. 315.
22. Warren C., "Laser printers draw from copier technology" Mini-Micro Systems, October 1987, Reed Publishing, U.S.A., pp, 87-99.
23. Watkins H.S. and J.S. Moore, "A Survey of Colour Graphics Printing", IEEE Spectrum. vol. 21, No, 7, July 1984, pp. 26-37.

5.11 PROBLEMS

5.1 Draw a flow chart that will show the steps necessary to use (i) a tablet, or (ii) a joystick to simulate the following virtual devices, (a) Pick, (b) Locator, (c) Valuator, and (d) Choice.

5.2 Modify the procedure described for the valuator device in example 5.2 to incorporate an error signal called 'ERROR'. The variable 'ERROR' is Boolean and is defined as follows:

ERROR = 0 if the value of the variable 'VALUE' lies between zero and one,
= 1 otherwise.

5.3 Write a subroutine for displaying an item at a specified location on the display and then drag/track it using an input device available on your system. The arguments of the procedure are given below:

ItemName	:	Cursor, Square, or Triangle
Mode	:=	0 show path of item being dragged,
	:=	1 do not show the path.

X and Y are used to initially generate the item with this point as the centre. At the termination of the procedure this point gives the co-ordinates of the centre of the final position of the item.

Tracking is initiated when the device button is pressed and is stopped when the button is released. Move the device at various speeds. Sometimes the device may fail to track the item. Suggest refinements in the tracking procedure which will lead to more reliable and effective tracking.

5.4 Write a program to implement the procedure given in Example 5.3. The program written for problem 5.3 can be used for tracking.

5.5 Write a general purpose procedure for implementing the rubber band technique. The arguments of the procedure are

(x1, y1) : Co-ordinates of the starting point of the vector. They can be specified by moving the cursor to this point and then pressing a 'FIX' button on the input device.

(x2, y2) : Co-ordinates of the end point of the vector. The position of this point is interactively changed using the input device. The position is fixed by using a 'FIX' button on the input device.

MODE : It is the input parameter and its value decides the function of the program.

MODE = 0 A line connects the starting point and the point denoted by the current position of the cursor.

MODE = 1 The line connecting the starting and the end point is constrained to be parallel to one of the axes. This directional constraint is useful for applications requiring only vertical and horizontal lines.

MODE = 2 To draw a rubber band arc of a circle with the starting point as the centre, allowing the user to interactively change the angle subtended by the arc.

5.6 Implement the procedure MENU to display the menu shown in figure 5.28. The arguments of the program are

i) NCH: Number of characters in each light key (assume equal for all keys)

ii) ID: Identifiers for the light keys (array of integers)

iii) TEXT: Character vector of the light keys (padded by blanks to equal length), and

iv) Location: Vector indicating the size and position of each key and the first character of each key. (The keys are equally spaced.)

5.7 Write program segments to perform the following actions.

i) draw a tic-tac-toe diagram in the centre of the display,

ii) control the movement of a cursor through the joystick, and

iii) position the symbol 'X' at the current cursor location when the button 0 is pressed and the symbol '0' when the button '1' is pressed.

Combine the above segments into a complete program for playing the tic-tac-toe game. It should also display a prompt message indicating the turn of player 1 and 2, and the result of the game.

5.8 A special keyboard (see the figure 5.53) is used to control two cursors, *A* and *B*. Cursor *A* is used for selecting a character from a virtual keyboard (see figure 5.22) available at the lower half ot the display, The upper half is used for assembling text messages. The position of the messages is controlled by the cursor *B*. The 'change cursor' key makes other cursor active. A character is selected by moving cursor *A* on the desired character of the virtual keyboard using the arrow keys and pressing the 'select character' key. This character is then displayed at the position of cursor *B*, which is now advanced to the next character position.

Write a program to implement the above scheme. Use any six keys on the normal keyboard to simulate the special keyboard.

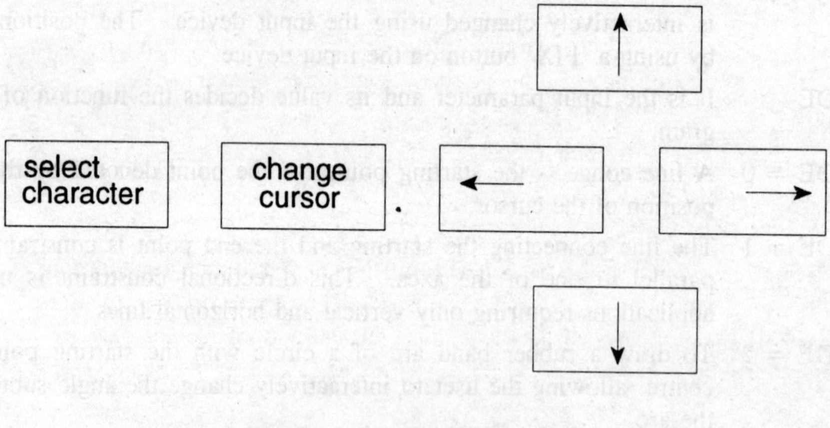

Figure 5.53 Special keyboard

5.9 Write a procedure to implement a dialogue system according to the specifications given in figure 5.28. Add a 'DELETE' command and draw the modified state diagram.

5.10 Write a program to fetch input from the keyboard and any other input device using polling, as shown in the flow chart in figure 5.54. Disable device and input keys from keyboard. Then enable device and move the cursor on the display and simultaneously press keys. Explain the behaviour of the program in both cases.

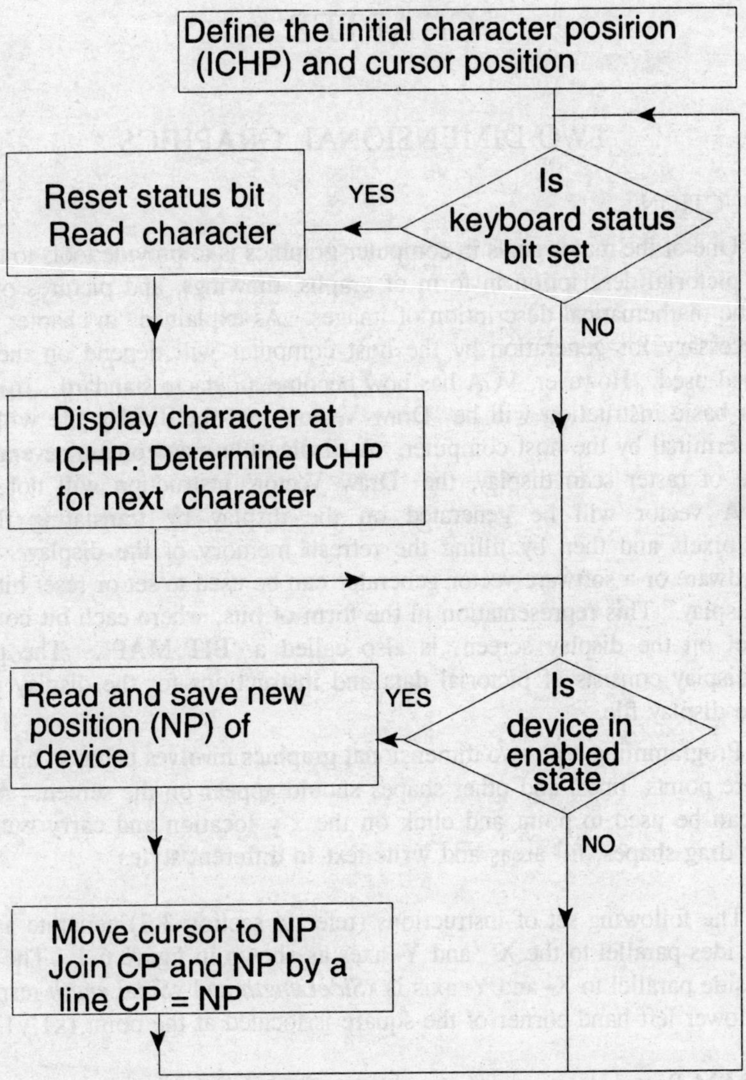

Figure 5.54 Flow chart for problem 5.10

CHAPTER 6

TWO DIMENSIONAL GRAPHICS

6.1 INTRODUCTION

One of the major goals in computer graphics is to provide tools to the programmer for creating a pictorial description in form of graphs, drawings, and pictures on the computer display from the mathematical description of images. As explained in chapter 2, the pictorial description necessary for generation by the host computer will depend on the type of video display terminal used. However, VGA has now become a defacto standard. In case of random scan display, a basic instruction will be 'Draw Vector' and the display file will be transferred to the display terminal by the host computer. A display file may contain several basic instructions. In case of raster scan display, the 'Draw Vector' instruction will not be a primitive instruction. A vector will be generated on the display by translating the vector into corresponding pixels and then by filling the refresh memory of the display. Therefore, the output of a hardware or a software vector generator can be used to set or reset bits in the refresh buffer of the display. This representation in the form of bits, where each bit corresponds to an individual pixel on the display screen, is also called a 'BIT MAP'. The program which generates the display consists of pictorial data and instructions for the display processor. It is often called the display file.

Programming with two dimensional graphics involves using x- and y- coordinates to specify where points, lines, and other shapes should appear on the screen. An input device like a mouse can be used to point and click on the x-y location and carry out functions like scale, rotate or drag shapes, fill areas and write text in different styles.

Example 6.1: The following set of instructions (refer to section 3.3) generate a rectangle with sides parallel to the X- and Y- axes as shown in figure 6.1. The length of each side parallel to X- and Y- axis is *xSideLength* and *ySideLength* respectivley. The lower left-hand corner of the square is located at the point (x1,y1).

```
PROGRAM Rectangle;
Uses Graph;
VAR   GraphDriver, GraphMode, ErrorCode : INTEGER;
      xAsp, yAsp : WORD;
x1, y1, xSideLength, ySideLength : INTEGER;
AspectRatio : REAL;
BEGIN
  WRITE ('Enter the x - y co-ordinates of the upper left corner: ');
  READLN (x1, y1);
  WRITE ('What should be the length of the sides of the rectangle?   ');
  READLN (xSideLength, ySideLength);
  GraphDriver := Detect;
```

```
  InitGraph (GraphDriver, GraphMode, '');
  ErrorCode := GraphResult;
  IF ErrorCode <> grOk THEN
 BEGIN
  WriteLn ('Graphics error: ',
  GraphErrorMsg(ErrorCode));
  WriteLn ('Program aborted....');
  Halt(1)
 END;
 SetBkColor (0);     {Background color is set to black}
 SetColor (1);       {Color for drawing lines}
 SetLineStyle (SolidLn, 0, NormWidth);
 GetAspectRatio (xAsp, yAsp);
 AspectRatio := xAsp/yAsp;
 ySideLength := Round (ySideLength*AspectRatio);
 MoveTo (x1, y1);
 LineTo (x1 + xSideLength, y1);
 LineTo (x1 + xSideLength, y1 + ySideLength);
 LineTo (x1, y1 + ySideLength);
 LineTo (x1, y1);
 READLN;
 CloseGraph;
END.
```

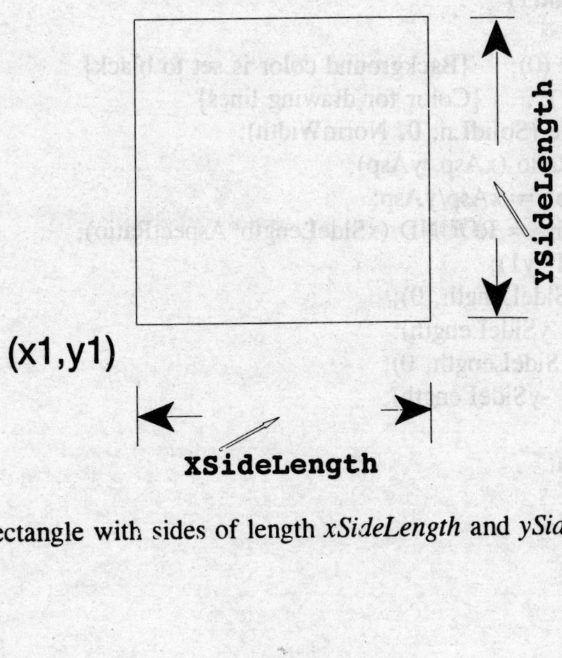

Figure 6.1 A rectangle with sides of length *xSideLength* and *ySideLength*

Example 6.2: Instead of using the procedure *LineTo* to draw the sides of the rectangle, you could use the procedure *LineRel*. This method will, particularly, be useful to perform operations, such as translation and rotation. The following program illustrates use of *LineRel* function.

```
PROGRAM Rectangle2;
Uses Graph;
VAR  GraphDriver, GraphMode, ErrorCode : INTEGER;
     xAsp, yAsp : WORD;
     x1, y1, xSideLength, ySideLength : INTEGER;
     AspectRatio : REAL;
BEGIN
     WRITE ('Enter the x - y co-ordinates of the upper left
               corner: ');
     READLN (x1, y1);
     WRITE ('What should be the length of the side of the
               square?  ');
     READLN (xSideLength);
     GraphDriver := Detect;
     InitGraph (GraphDriver, GraphMode, 'C:\DRIVERS');
     ErrorCode := GraphResult;
     IF ErrorCode <> grOk THEN
     BEGIN
       WriteLn ('Graphics error: ', GraphErrorMsg(ErrorCode));
       WriteLn ('Program aborted....');
            Halt(1)
     END;
     SetBkColor (0);     {Background color is set to black}
     SetColor (1);       {Color for drawing lines}
     SetLineStyle (SolidLn, 0, NormWidth);
     GetAspectRatio (xAsp, yAsp);
     AspectRatio := xAsp/yAsp;
     ySideLength := ROUND (xSideLength*AspectRatio);
     MoveTo (x1, y1);
     LineRel (xSideLength, 0);
     LineRel (0, ySideLength);
     LineRel (-xSideLength, 0);
     LineRel (0, -ySideLength);
     READLN;
     CloseGraph;
END.
```

In examples (6.1) and (6.2), the instruction *READLN* is used to keep the graphics on the display until you press the return key. The instruction *CloseGraph* switches the system back to the text mode. To delete the rectangle thus drawn the above programs can be modified for drawing the rectangle using the command *SetColor(0)* instead of *SetColor(1)*.

The above examples give simple illustrations of the methods for generating or deleting two-dimensional objects on the display. The scope of this chapter is to describe methods useful for the display and handling of two-dimensional objects only.

6.2 MATHEMATICS OF 2-D GRAPHICS

The principles and procedures of mathematics and analytical geometry must be clearly understood and they are often applied in interactive computer graphics. For example, a designer should be able to magnify, reduce, translate, and/or rotate a figure or a picture to suit his/her needs. As an another example, one may also be interested in applying some known constraints on the location of points and slopes, and specifying other points and slopes, and then may wish to see the resulting curves and surfaces. The following sections describe some of the mathematical steps necessary to accomplish these goals.

6.2.1 2-D Transformations

Three geometrical operations are of great interest in two-dimensional graphics. These are translation, rotation, and scaling. By definition, these transformations are bijective mapping from the co-ordinate space onto itself. The picture structure as defined previously is not altered and the given incidence relations between the points of the picture (e.g., two points of a picture may be connected by a relation like line, arc, etc.) are preserved. Therefore, these transformations are strictly performed on the data points and the program to generate the display remains the same.

6.2.1.1 Translation

Translation signifies moving a point (x,y) to a new location (x', y'). This is achieved by adding a positive or negative constant to each co-ordinate of the point, i.e.,

$$x' = x + X_T \tag{6.1}$$

$$y' = y + Y_T \tag{6.2}$$

where X_T and Y_T are translation parameters in the X and Y directions, respectively.

Example 6.3: The rectangle in example (6.1) can be translated to a new location (x', y') by replacing ($x1$, $y1$) with (x', y') in the MoveTo command in the program. Figure 6.2 shows the effect of translation.

6.2.1.2 Rotation

Consider the rotation of the X-Y co-ordinate system in the cartesian plane with the origin as the pivotal point. The geometric relations between any point (x,y) in the X-Y system

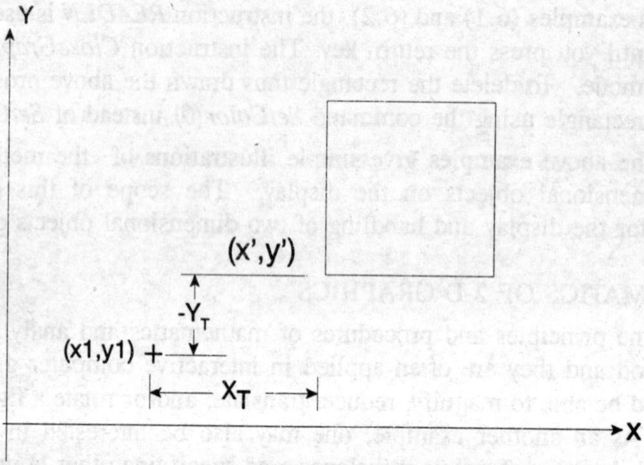

Figure 6.2: Translation of a rectangle

and the new point in the $X' - Y'$ system obtained after rotation through a clockwise ϕ angle around the origin is given by,

$$x' = x \cos(\phi) + y \sin(\phi) \tag{6.3}$$
$$y' = -x \sin(\phi) + y \cos(\phi) \tag{6.4}$$

Figure 6.3 shows the effect of rotation through the angle ϕ. This can be done quite easily by replacing the coordinates of the points in the various 'LineTo' commands in example 6.1 by values calculated using equations (6.3) and (6.4). Alternatively, in example 6.2 the arguments used in the 'LineRel' commands may be modified as below:

```
LineRel (ROUND(xSideLength*cos(φ)), ROUND(ySideLength*sin(φ)));
LineRel (-ROUND(xSideLength*sin(φ)), ROUND(ySideLength*cos(φ)));
LineRel (-ROUND(xSideLength*cos(φ)), -ROUND(ySideLength*sin(φ)));
LineRel (ROUND(xSideLength*sin(φ)), -ROUND(ySideLength*cos(φ)));
```

A computer program for rotating the square by a specified angle is shown below. The rotated square in shown in figure 6.3.

```
PROGRAM RotateSquare;
Uses Graph, Crt;
VAR GraphDriver, GraphMode, ErrorCode : INTEGER;
    xAsp, yAsp : WORD;
    x1, y1, xSideLength : INTEGER;
    AspectRatio, phi, theta, ySideLength : REAL;
    xa, xb, ya, yb : INTEGER;
```

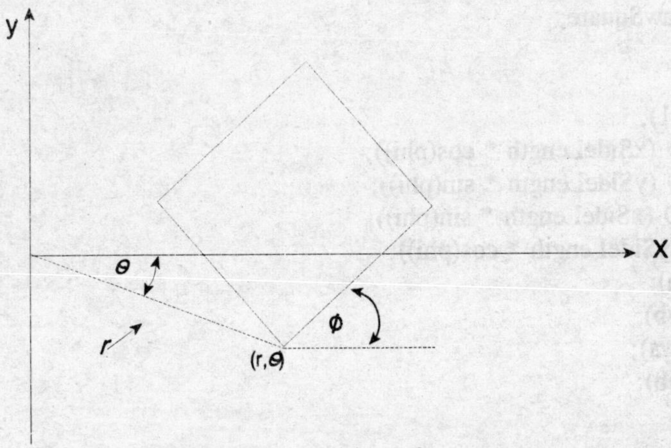

Figure 6.3 Rotation of a square

```
    answer : CHAR;
PROCEDURE Initialize;
BEGIN
  GraphDriver := Detect;
  InitGraph (GraphDriver, GraphMode, ' ');
  ErrorCode := GraphResult;
  IF ErrorCode <> grOk THEN
    BEGIN
      WRITELN ('Graphics error: ', GraphErrorMsg(ErrorCode));
      WRITELN ('Program aborted .... ');
      Halt(1)
    END;
  SetBkColor (0);  {Background color is set to black}
  SetColor (1);    {Color for drawing lines}
  SetLineStyle (SolidLn, 0, Normwidth);
  GetAspectRatio (xAsp, yAsp);
  AspectRatio := xAsp/yAsp;
  ySideLength := xSideLength*AspectRatio;
END;
PROCEDURE GetData;
BEGIN
  ClrScr;
  WRITE ('Enter the x - y co-ordinates of the upper left corner: ');
  READLN (x1, y1);
  WRITE ('What should be the length of the side of the square?  ');
  READLN (xSideLength)
END;
```

```
PROCEDURE DrawSquare;
BEGIN
   Initialize;
   MoveTo (x1, y1);
   xa := ROUND (xSideLength * cos(phi));
   ya := ROUND (ySideLength * sin(phi));
   xb := ROUND (xSideLength * sin(phi));
   yb := Round (ySideLength * cos(phi));
   LineRel (xa, ya);
   LineRel (-xb, yb);
   LineRel (-xa, -ya);
   LineRel (xb, -yb);
   READLN;
   CloseGraph
END;
BEGIN (* Main program *)
  GetData;
  phi := 0.0;
  DrawSquare;
  REPEAT
   WRITE ('Do you want to rotate the square? (Y or N): ');
   READ (answer);
   IF UpCase (answer) = 'Y' THEN
     BEGIN
       WRITE ('Enter the angle of rotation in degrees: ');
       READLN (theta);
       phi := phi + theta*pi/180;
       DrawSquare
     END
  UNTIL UpCase(answer) = 'N';
END.
```

6.2.1.3 Scaling

Scaling is performed by multiplying the X- and Y- co-ordinates of the point by a scaling factor. Thus, the new co-ordinates are given by,

$$x' = X_S\, x \tag{6.5}$$

$$y' = Y_S\, y \tag{6.6}$$

where $X_{S\,s}$ and $Y_{S\,s}$ are the scaling factors in the X- and Y- directions, respectively.

Example 6.4: If the rectangle with corners at points (40,40), (80,40), (80,70), (40,70) is to be reduced to half its original size, the value of the scaling factor X_S and Y_S will be

0.5. The scaled rectangle will have corners at points (20,20), (40,20), (40,35), and (20,35). Figure 6.4 displays the effect of the scaling operation.

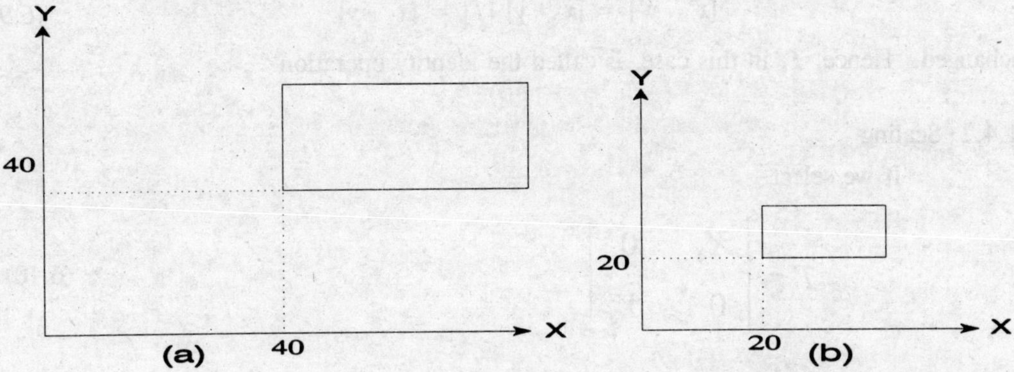

Figure 6-4 Scaling operation on a rectangle

6.2.1.4 Matrix Representation of Transformations :

Transformations of a point in a two-dimensional plane can also be represented as the product of the row vector [x,y], representing its co-ordinates with a 2×2 transformation matrix *T* defined as,

$$T = \begin{bmatrix} T_{11} & T_{12} \\ T_{13} & T_{14} \end{bmatrix} \tag{6.7}$$

Hence, the transformed co-ordinates (x',y') can be computed by the product

$$[x' \quad y'] = [x \quad y][T] \tag{6.8}$$

It is apparent that the selection of the values of the elements T_{11}, T_{12}, T_{13}, T_{14} of the *T* matrix will define the transformation.

6.2.1.4.1. Identity

If we select

$$T = \begin{bmatrix} 1 & 0 \\ 0 & 1 \end{bmatrix}$$

which is the identity matrix, we get the identity transformation. The new point (x',y') computed by the equation

$$[x' \quad y'] = [x \quad y]\,[T] = [x \quad y] \tag{6.9}$$

is unchanged. Hence, T, in this case, is called the identity operation.

6.2.1.4.2 Scaling

If we select

$$T = \begin{bmatrix} X_s & 0 \\ 0 & Y_s \end{bmatrix} \tag{6.10}$$

where X_S and Y_S are the scaling factors in the directions of the X and Y axis respectively, then the new point (x', y') can be computed by the following equation,

$$[x' \quad y'] = [x \quad y][T] = [xX_s \quad yY_s] \tag{6.11}$$

6.2.1.4.3 Reflection

If we select

$$T = \begin{bmatrix} -1 & 0 \\ 0 & 1 \end{bmatrix} \text{ or } \begin{bmatrix} 1 & 0 \\ 0 & -1 \end{bmatrix}$$

then the new point (x',y') will be reflection through the X or Y axis.

Reflection through the Y-axis is defined below

$$[x' \quad y'] = [x \quad y]\begin{bmatrix} -1 & 0 \\ 0 & 1 \end{bmatrix} = [-x \quad y] \tag{6.12}$$

Similarly, reflection through X-axis is given by

$$[x' \quad y'] = [x \quad y]\begin{bmatrix} 1 & 0 \\ 0 & -1 \end{bmatrix} = [x \quad -y] \tag{6.13}$$

Example 6.5: Find the reflection of rectangle defined by points (40,40), (80,40), (80,70), and (40,70) through the Y-axis. We apply the transformation and the resultant rectangle is defined by the points (-40, 40), (-80, 40), (-80, 70), (-40,70). Figure 6.5 shows the result of reflection operation.

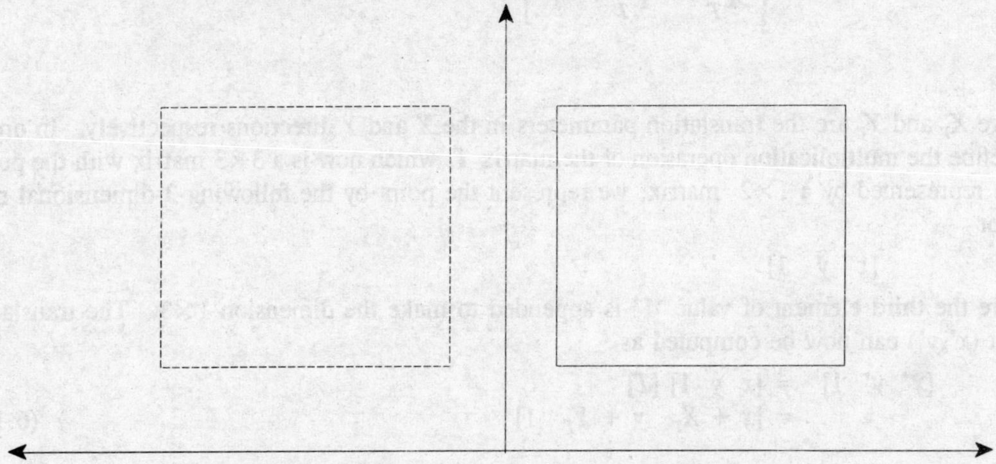

Figure 6.5 Reflection of a rectangle through the Y-axis

6.2.1.4.4 Rotation

If we select

$$T = \begin{bmatrix} \cos\phi & -\sin\phi \\ \sin\phi & \cos\phi \end{bmatrix} \tag{6.14}$$

then the new point (x', y') can be computed as follows.

$$\begin{aligned}[x' \quad y'] &= [x \quad y]\,[T] \\ &= [x\cos\phi + y\sin\phi \quad -x\sin\phi + y\cos\phi]\end{aligned} \tag{6.15}$$

which is identical to the expression derived in section 6.2.1.2 denoting the rotation of the point (x, y) through the angle ϕ about the co-ordinate system in the clockwise direction.

6.2.1.4.5 Translation

We add a third column and a third row to the 2×2 transformation matrix to express translation in the matrix form. The new matrix $\boldsymbol{T}$ is, therefore, a 3×3 matrix with the first two elements of the third column equal to 'O' and third element equal to '1', as given below

$$T = \begin{bmatrix} 1 & 0 & 0 \\ 0 & 1 & 0 \\ X_T & Y_T & 1 \end{bmatrix} \tag{6.16}$$

where X_T and Y_T are the translation parameters in the X and Y directions respectively. In order to define the multiplication operation of the matrix T, which now is a 3×3 matrix with the point (x,y) represented by a 1×2 matrix, we represent the point by the following 3-dimensional row vector

$$[x \quad y \quad 1]$$

where the third element of value '1' is appended to make the dimension 1×3. The translated point (x', y') can now be computed as

$$\begin{aligned} [x' \quad y' \quad 1] &= [x \quad y \quad 1]\,[T] \\ &= [x + X_T \quad y + Y_T \quad 1] \end{aligned} \tag{6.17}$$

6.2.1.4.5 Combined Transformations

It is possible to combine rotation and translation into a single matrix **T** where

$$T = \begin{bmatrix} \cos\phi & -\sin\phi & X_t \\ \sin\phi & \cos\phi & Y_T \\ 0 & 0 & 1 \end{bmatrix} \tag{6.18}$$

defines a translation operation followed by rotation.

6.2.2 Homogeneous Co-ordinates:

In defining the translation operation a point was denoted by the 3-dimensional row vector $[x \quad y \quad 1]$. This can also be interpreted as if a point (x,y) in two dimensions is represented by a vector of three numbers: $[a \quad b \quad c]$. In order to transform a point (x,y) into a homogeneous representation, we choose a nonzero number 'h' and form a vector :

$$[hx \quad hy \quad h]$$

The number 'h' is called the scale factor or the homogeneous co-ordinate parameter.

Example 6.6: If we take a point (2, 3) in the two-dimensional space, its representation in homogeneous co-ordinates will be [2 3 1] for h = 1, [4 6 2] for h = 2, or [-4 -6 -2] for h = -2.

The above example illustrates that the homogeneous representation of a point in 2-D space is not unique. Furthermore, it is possible to keep the values of the homogeneous co-ordinates within desirable limits by selecting a proper value of the parameter 'h'. This characteristic can be utilised for avoiding the underflow and overflow condition generated during computations or to keep a point within the viewing zone.

6.2.2.1 Points and Lines

Points are 3-element row vectors:

$$P = [x \quad y \quad w] \tag{6.19}$$

Lines are 3-element column vectors:

$$L = \begin{bmatrix} a \\ b \\ c \end{bmatrix} \tag{6.20}$$

The matrix or dot product of the row and column vector is a scalar:

$$P{\cdot}L = ax + by + cw \tag{6.21}$$

If the value is zero, the point lies on the line.

To find the line containing two given points, one has to compute their 3-D cross product and view the result as a column vector:

$$P_1 \times P_2 = (x_1,\ y_1,\ w_1) \times (x_2,\ y_2,\ w_2) = \begin{bmatrix} y_1 w_2 - y_2 w_1 \\ x_2 w_1 - x_1 w_2 \\ x_1 y_2 - x_2 y_1 \end{bmatrix} \tag{6.22}$$

To find out the intersection point of two lines, one has to take their 3-D cross product and view the result as row vector:

$$L_1 \times L_2 = \begin{bmatrix} a_1 \\ b_1 \\ c_1 \end{bmatrix} \times \begin{bmatrix} a_2 \\ b_2 \\ c_2 \end{bmatrix} \tag{6.23}$$

$$= [\, b_1 c_2 - b_2 c_1, a_2 c_1 - a_1 c_2, a_1 b_2 - a_2 b_1]$$

6.2.2.2 Transformations

Points are transformed by multiplication on the right by a 3x3 transformation matrix

$$P' = PT$$

Line is transformed by multiplication on the left by the adjoint of the matrix T, referred by T':

$$L' = T'L$$

In fact, the adjoint is same as the inverse except for a scale factor.

The homogeneous co-ordinate system is a very useful tool for the description of projective transformations. This aspect will be discussed in detail in chapter 7.

6.3 DISPLAY OF 2-D FIGURES

A figure may be composed of a number of dots (pixels), lines, or arc segments. Moreover, the line or arc segment may also be drawn by a number of pixels. The pictorial data can thus be viewed as a sequence of pixels that can be represented by points denoted by their X- and Y- coordinates. However, this method of representation of figures by pixels is not efficient. It is better to have a display with a built-in processor with the capability to execute high level display commands, e.g., drawing lines, polygons, circles, arcs, etc. The display processor then fills up the corresponding pixels in the refresh memory. In cases where display is not equipped with such a processor, the programmer has to generate the primitive two-dimensional figures.

6.3.1 Lines

A line segment is a basic entity in creating computer graphics. It is used extensively in the creation of drawings such as electrical circuits, chemical structures, histograms, graphs, engineering drawings, block diagrams, etc., to cite only a few examples. A line segment PQ is defined by the co-ordinates of its two end points, P and Q as shown in figure 6.6.

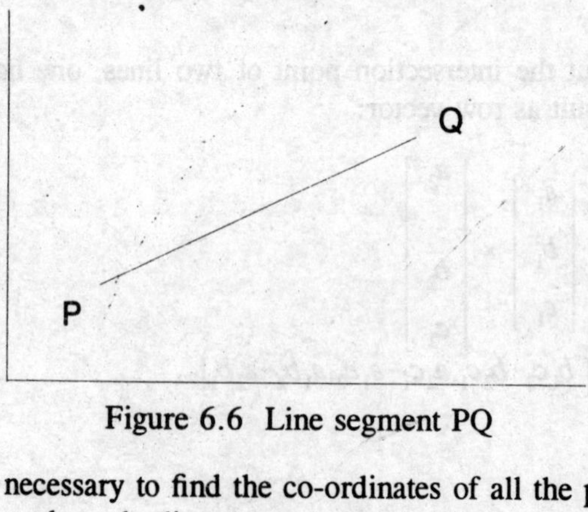

Figure 6.6 Line segment PQ

It will be necessary to find the co-ordinates of all the points on the display grid between points P and Q to draw the line segment on the display, such that these points satisfy the equation of the line joining the points P and Q as closely as possible (see figure 6.7).

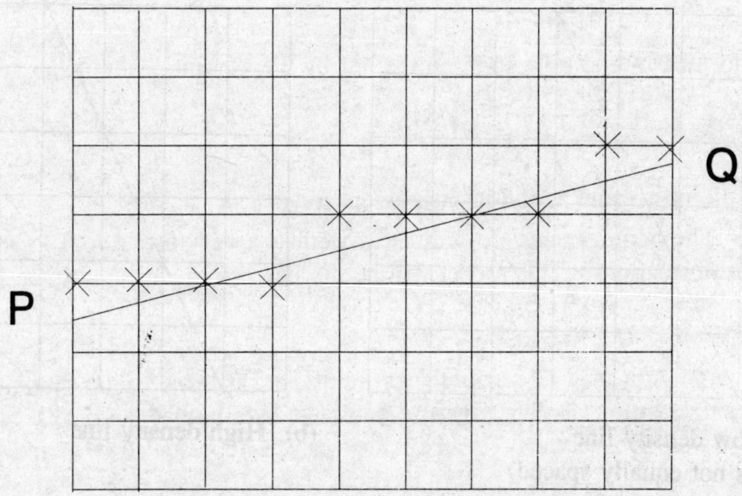

Figure 6.7 Line segment PQ on the display grid

A common equation of a straight line with slope m and intercept c is

$$Y = mX + c \tag{6.24}$$

This form is inconvenient when describing lines parallel to the Y-axis. Hence, the following general form is often used.

$$aX + bY + c = 0 \tag{6.25}$$

It can represent a line parallel to the Y-axis by setting $b = 0$.

To generate intermediate points on a line segment the following criteria should be met :

i) Straightness: The lines which are parallel to or inclined at 45° to the X and Y axes, can be represented accurately on the display grid. The selection of the point for lines with other inclinations is not that simple. However, the selection should be such that the line drawn on the display screen should appear straight.

ii) Termination: Similarly, lines which are in the second category may also pose a problem in the computation of the precise point of termination. These lines should terminate at the proper end points, otherwise, undesirable gaps are created on the display at points where two line segments meet.

iii) Density: The number of pixels used to generate a line segment should be equally spaced. The density of a line is defined by the ratio of the number of pixels displayed to the length of the line. The line density should not vary with the slope and the length of the line. Figure 6.8 shows line segments with low, high, and varying densities.

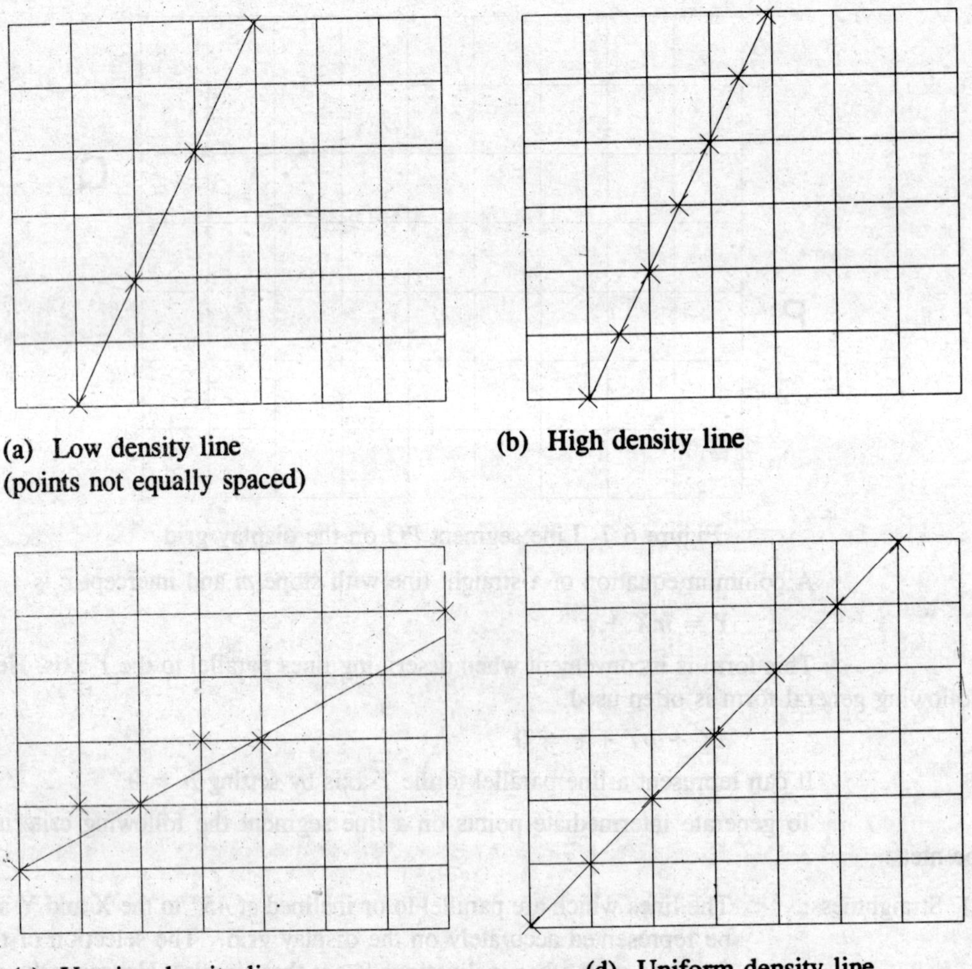

(a) Low density line (points not equally spaced)

(b) High density line

(c) Varying density line

(d) Uniform density line

Figure 6.8 Line segments

iv) Symmetry: A line is said to satisfy the property of symmetry if the points selected to represent the line segment are the same irrespective of the direction of generation. Figure 6.9 shows the non-symmetric situation where the points on the line segment PQ are generated by first taking the point P and then taking the point Q as the starting location. The points generated in the forward and backward directions are shown by the symbols '×' and '•' respectively.

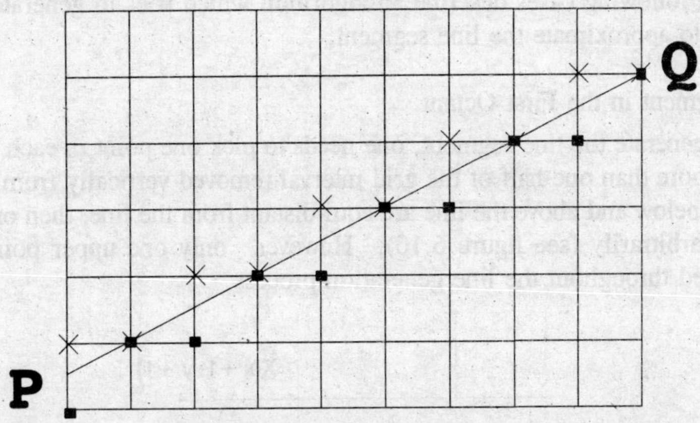

Figure 6.9 Non symmetric point generation of segment PQ

In the interactive mode of operation a user frequently needs to add or delete points on a line segment. The symmetric technique of line segment generation allows a user to back-track and delete the undesired points from the memory.

v) Speed: For interactive applications it is desirable that line segments be drawn quickly. This necessitates that the amount of computation be minimal. In expensive displays line segments are generated by custom-designed hardware.

The above factors are also related to the resolution of the display. Incremental techniques are very effective in generating co-ordinates of the points to draw a line segment PQ by starting at the point P and moving towards the point Q or vice-versa and by selection of unit increments in X or Y or both directions to locate points closest to the line segment.

Such algorithms need only simple arithmetic operations and are executed very fast on a micro-computer or specially designed hardware to suit custom applications. Computation of the intermediate points on a line segment using equation (6.24) or (6.25) is not suitable as it increases the number of arithmetic operations, and thus, requires more processing time.

6.3.1.1 A Non-symmetric Digital Line Segment Generation Algorithm

This linear algorithm was developed by Bresenham [2] and Horn [3] for digital generation of points on a grid as close as possible to the line segment. The algorithm needs only additions for computing the points. Consider a line segment defined by the points (Xinit, Yinit) and (Xfinal, Yfinal), which are the initial and the final points on the segment. We also assume that the starting point of the segment is the origin of the co-ordinate system used, a restriction which we will later remove. The equation of the line passing through these points is given by

$$bX = aN \qquad (6.26)$$

where
$$a = Xfinal - Xinit$$
$$b = Yfinal - Yinit$$

The following cases describe an algorithm which tries to generate a set of contiguous grid points to approximate the line segment.

Case I: Line Segment in the First Octant

To generate the line segment, one needs to pick one point in each vertical column such that it is no more than one-half of the grid interval removed vertically from the line. If the nearest points just below and above the line are equi-distant from the line, then only one of these points is selected arbitrarily (see figure 6.10). However, only one upper point 'X' or lower point 'Y' is selected throughout the line generation process.

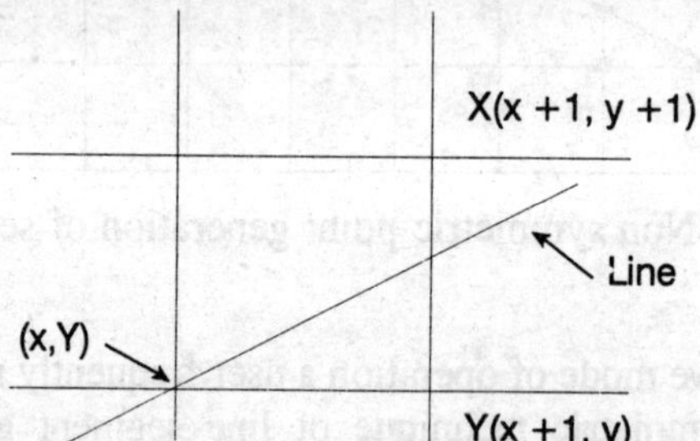

Figure 6.10 Points X and Y are equidistant from the line

The points so defined lie on or above the line

$$bX = a(y + 0.5) \tag{6.27}$$

and below the line

$$bX = a(y - 0.5) \tag{6.28}$$

Only one point in the vertical column lies within these limits. Movement from one column to the next column is achieved by incrementing the x co-ordinate. Hence, if the point (x,y) has been selected, we have choice of either the point (x+1, y) or the point (x+1, y+1). If the line passes through or is below the point (x+1, y+0.5) then the point (x+1,y), is selected otherwise the point (x+1, y+1) is selected. A test function F(x,y) can be defined as follows:

$$F(x,y) = a(y + 0.5) - b(x + 1) \tag{6.29}$$

IF $F(x,y) < 0$ THEN point (x+1, y+1) is selected..
ELSE point (x+1, y) is selected.

If we start generating points on the line from the point (x,y), which lies on the line, the test function can be computed recursively from the following relation :

$F_N(x,y) = a(y + 0.5) - b(x + 1)$
$= 0.5\,a$ (since the point (x,y) lies on the line and error is computed in the y-direction corresponding to (x+1))

The next test function is computed by using the next point (x(n), y(n)) on the grid as follows:

$$F_{n+1}(x,y) = a[y(n)+0.5] - b[x(n)+1]$$

$$= a[y(n-1)+0.5] - b[x(n-1)+1] - b + \left| \begin{array}{l} 0 \text{ if } F_N(x,y) \geq 0 \\ a \text{ if } F_N(x,y) < 0 \end{array} \right.$$

$$F_{n+1}(x,y) = F_N(x,y) - b + \left| \begin{array}{l} 0 \text{ if } F_N(x,y) \geq 0 \\ a \text{ if } F_N(x,y) < 0 \end{array} \right. \tag{6.30}$$

The above recursive equation can be used to generate points on the grid to approximate a line a segment.

Example 6.6:

To illustrate the use of this algorithm, we generate the line segment joining points (0,0) and (6,3) from the point (0,0) onwards. The initial value of the function

$$F_0(x,y) = 0.5\ a$$

and the values of a and b are 6 and 3 respectively. Using the relationship given by equation (6.25), we find

$$F_1(x,y) = 0.5\times 6 - 3 + \left| \begin{array}{l} 0 \text{ if } F_0(x,y) \leq 0 \\ 6 \text{ if } F_0(x,y) > 0 \end{array} \right. \qquad \text{Horizontal step point (1,0)}$$

$$F_2(x,y) = 0 - 3 + 0 = -3 \qquad \text{Diagonal step point (2,1)}$$

$$F_3(x,y) = -3 - 3 + 6 = 0 \qquad \text{Horizontal step point (3,1)}$$

and similarly, we can generate the other points which are (4,2), (5,2) and (6,3) as shown in figure 6.11. It can easily be shown that if we generate the line segment starting at the point (6,3) and towards the point (0,0), the points generated will be (6,3), (5,3), (4,2), (3,2), (2,1), (1,1) and (0,0). Figure 6.11(a) shows the plot of the points generated during the forward and backward process by symbols '+' and '-' respectively. It is observed that the points in the two directions are different because of the non-symmetric algorithm used for generation.

Case 2: Line segment in the second and other Octants :

By swapping the x and y values, a line segment in the second octant can be generated. Changing the sign of x or y or both will take care of the other octants.

Example 6.7: In example (6.6), a line segment from (0,0) to (6,3) was generated. The points obtained in the forward direction were (0,0), (1,0), (2,1),(3,1), (4,2), (5,2) and (6,3). It is noticed that the line segment is in the first octant.

To map this segment in the second octant, we can swap the x and y co-ordinates of the points. The new points will be (0,0), (0,1), (1,2), (1,3), (2,4), (2,5) and (3,6). A plot of the line segment in the first and the second octant is shown in figure 6.11(b).

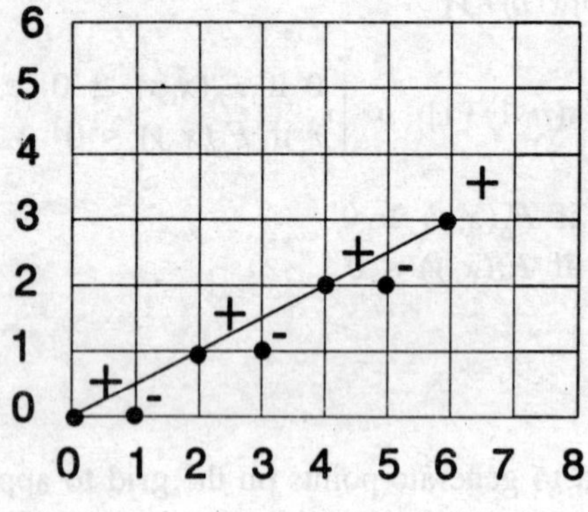

Figure 6.11(a) Digital plot of line segment (0,0) and (6,3).

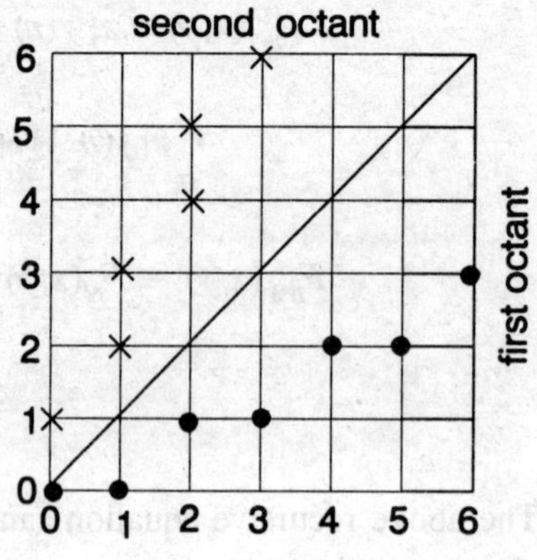

Figure 6.11(b) Plot of line segment in the first(.) and the second(X) octant

3 Line Segment Starting at an Arbitrary Grid Point:

Adding offsets allows a line segment to start at any suitable points.

6.3.1.2 A Symmetric Algorithm

A symmetric linear algorithm was proposed for digital generation of a line segment by Thong [3]. This algorithm incorporates a simple modification to the Bresenham algorithm which fails to meet the symmetry condition when

$$F(x,y) = 0$$

This condition occurs in equation (6.24) if

i) '*a*' is even, and

ii) '*b*' common divisor (*a*,*b*) is odd and is different from 1.

It can be observed from example 6.6 and figure 6.11 that for all those points when $F_N(x,y)$ is zero, different points were selected during the forward (octant 1) and backward (octant 5) generation of the points of the line segment. To resolve this situation, Thong proposed that instead of the test function *F*(*x*,*y*), a new test function *F*'(*x*,*y*), defined below, should be used:

$$F'(x,y) = F(x,y) + \left| \begin{array}{l} 0 \text{ if } (\text{Yfinal} - \text{Yinit}) \geq 0 \\ -1 \text{ if } (\text{Yfinal} - \text{Yinit}) < 0 \end{array} \right.$$

A Pascal program of the symmetric digital line segment algorithm is given below. It uses some initial right shift operations followed by only addition operations.

Example 6.8: Listing of the Pascal program for generating a symmetrical digital line segment

```
PROGRAM Vector;
USES Graph;
VAR  x_init, y_init, x_final, y_final, delta_x, delta_y,
     i, x, y, check, dx_sign, dy_sign, GraphDriver,
     GraphMode, ErrorCode : INTEGER;
PROCEDURE Plot_dot (x, y : INTEGER);
```

```
PROCEDURE Plot_dot (x, y : INTEGER);
BEGIN
 PutPixel (x, y, 1);
END;
PROCEDURE Value (VAR d_abs, d_sign, init, final : INTEGER);
  {Procedure to compute the absolute value and sign of the
     difference between initial and final values of x or y}
BEGIN
 IF final >= init THEN
   BEGIN
    d_abs := final - init;
    d_sign := 1;
   END
  ELSE BEGIN
       d_abs := init - final;
       d_sign := -1;
     END;
END;
BEGIN  {Main program}
  WRITE ('Enter the x-y co-ordinates of the initial point:  ');
  READLN (x_init, y_init);
  WRITE ('Enter the x-y co-ordinates of the final point:  ');
  READLN (x_final, y_final) ;
  GraphDriver := Detect;
  InitGraph (GraphDriver, GraphMode, 'C:\DRIVERS');
  ErrorCode := GraphResult;
  IF ErrorCode <> grOk THEN
    BEGIN
      WRITELN ('Graphics error: ', GraphErrorMsg(ErrorCode));
      Halt(1)
    END;
  SetBkColor (0);
  SetColor (1);
  x := x_init;
  y := y_init;
  VALUE (delta_x, dx_sign, x_init, x_final);
  VALUE (delta_y, dy_sign, y_init, y_final);
  check := (dy_sign - 1) DIV 2;
  IF delta_x >= delta_y THEN
    {Case 1: Vector is closer to the x-axis}
    BEGIN
      check := (delta_x + check) DIV 2;
      FOR i := 1 TO delta_x DO
        BEGIN
```

```
          check := check - delta_y;
          x := x + dx_sign;
          IF  check < 0 THEN
            BEGIN
              y := y + dy_sign;
              check := check + delta_x;
            END;
          Plot_dot (x, y);
        END;
      END
    ELSE
      {Case 2: Vector is closer to the y-axis}
      BEGIN
        check := (delta_y + check) DIV 2;
        FOR i := 1 to delta_y DO
          BEGIN
            check := check - delta_x;
            y := y + dy_sign;
            IF check < 0 THEN
              BEGIN
                x := x + dx_sign;
                check := check + delta_y;
              END;
            Plot_dot (x, y);
          END;
      END;
    READLN;
    CloseGraph;
  END.
```

6.3.2 Polygons

Polygons are composed of straight line segments and are closed two- dimensional well-defined shapes. The minimum number of vertices necessary to make a polygon is three, describing a triangle. As the number of vertices is increased we get figures called rectangle, pentagon, hexagon, etc. A polygon is called regular if it has all sides of equal length and all internal angles equal. If the process of increasing the number of sides is continued and the length of the side of a regular polygon is reduced, the figure generated looks very similar to a circle. A Pascal program to generate a regular polygon (using the property that the sum of internal angles of a polygon is $(n-2)\pi$ radians where 'n' is the number of sides) is given below.

Example 6.9 : Program for generating a regular polygon.

```
PROGRAM RegularPolygon;
  USES Graph;
```

```
    GraphDriver, GraphMode, ErrorCode : INTEGER;

PROCEDURE Polygon;
VAR angle, sum : REAL;
    i, x, y     : INTEGER;
    xAsp, yAsp : WORD;
BEGIN
  sum := pi*( NumberOfSides - 2);
  angle := sum/NumberOfSides; (* angle in radians *)
  MoveTo (x1, y1);
  LineRel (side, 0);
  GetAspectRatio (xAsp, yAsp);
  FOR i := 1 to (NumberOfSides - 1) DO
    BEGIN
      x := ROUND (side*cos((pi-angle)*i));
      y := ROUND (side*sin((pi-angle)*i)*xAsp/yAsp);
      LineRel (x, y)
    END;
END;

BEGIN  (* Main program *)
    WRITE ('Enter the x-y co-ordinates of the bottom left corner: ');
    READLN (x1, y1);
    WRITE ('Enter the number of sides of the regular polygon:  ');
    READLN (NumberOfSides);
    WRITE ('What should be the side of the polygon?  ');
    READLN (side);
    GraphDriver := Detect;
    InitGraph (GraphDriver, GraphMode, 'C:\DRIVERS');
    ErrorCode := GraphResult;
    IF ErrorCode <> grOk THEN
      BEGIN
        WriteLn ('Graphics error: ', GraphErrorMsg(ErrorCode));
        Halt(1)
      END;
    SetBkColor(0);
    SetColor (1);
    MoveTo (x1, y1);
    Polygon;
    READLN;
    CloseGraph;
END.
```

6.3.3 Circles

Most display devices have hardware line generators but do not have circle generators. Circles and circular arcs are used as basic building blocks for displaying objects, in the design of mechanical parts and also as standard symbols in many other applications. Hence, it is important to be able to draw them on the display.

The simplest way to draw a circle using the Graph unit of TurboPascal is to use the built-in procedure 'Circle'. The command used is of the form

Circle (x, y, r);

where the integers x and y are the corresponding coordinates of the centre of the circle and the integer r is its radius. The Graph unit determines the aspect ratio of each graph driver and utilizes this information to draw a proper circle. A program for drawing a circle is given in example 6.10.

Example 6.10 The Pascal program for drawing a circle is given below.

```
PROGRAM DrawCircle;
Uses Graph;
VAR GraphDriver, GraphMode, ErrorCode : INTEGER;
    x, y : INTEGER;
    radius : WORD;
BEGIN
  WRITE ('Enter the x - y co-ordinates of the centre: ');
  READLN (x, y);
  WRITE ('What should be the radius of the circle?  ');
  READLN (radius);
  GraphDriver := Detect;
  InitGraph (GraphDriver, GraphMode, '');
  ErrorCode := GraphResult;
  IF ErrorCode <> grOk THEN
     Halt(1);
  Circle (x, y, radius);
  READLN;
  CloseGraph;
END.
```

The reader is advised to key in this short program and note the time required to draw circles of different radii.

6.3.4 Curves

Curves are used in graphics to meet the following objectives :

(i) to model two-dimensional complex shapes, and

(ii) to obtain a precise fit to a given set of data points to reduce the storage requirements.

Curves can be divided into two categories : Closed and Open curves. A closed curve is a general curve that is generated by interpolating the location of pixels around four or more specified locations (see figure 6.12). It has a bounded shape like a circle and a ellipse.

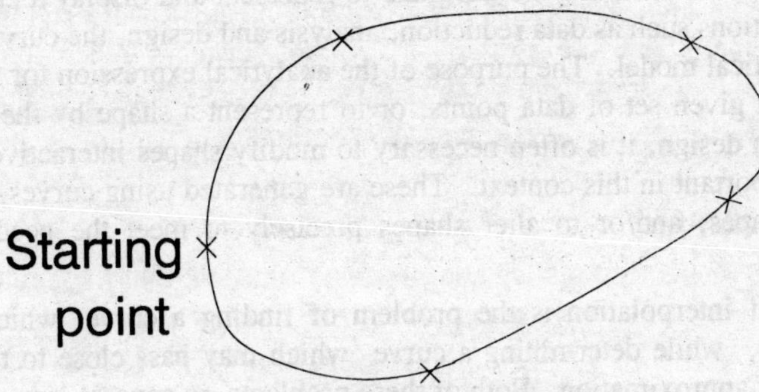

Figure 6.12 A bounded closed curve

An open curve is also a general curve that is obtained by interpolating the location of pixels around several specified locations. The end points of an open curve are not supposed to meet. Figure 6.13 shows a typical open curve drawn using the four points (x1,y1), (x2,y2), (x3,y3), and (x4,y4). The points (x1,y1) and (x4,y4) are called the start point and the end point, respectively.

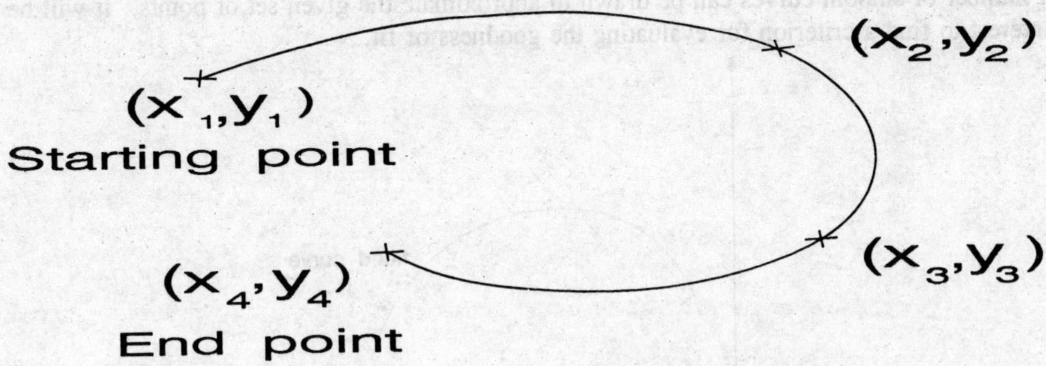

Figure 6.13 Unbounded open curve

An arc of a circle is also an open curve and can be specified by the centre of the circle, the starting angle, and the end angle. The Graph unit in TurboPascal has a simple built-in command for drawing an arc. It is given as

```
Arc (x, y, StartAngle, EndAngle, Radius);
```

where x, y are the corresponding coordinates of the centre, the start and end angles are in degrees (measured in the usual counterclockwise direction, with zero along the positive x-axis). All of these values must be integers.

6.4 INTERPOLATION AND APPROXIMATION OF CURVES

In certain applications, it may be adequate to represent and display a curve by a set of pixels. But for applications such as data reduction, analysis and design, the curve, should be represented by a mathematical model. The purpose of the analytical expression for the curve is to obtain a precise fit to a given set of data points, or to represent a shape by the minimal number of measurements. In design, it is often necessary to modify shapes interactively. The synthetic use of shapes is important in this context. These are generated using curves, with the capability to define new shapes, and/or to alter shapes precisely to meet the needs of the designer.

The process of interpolation is the problem of finding a curve, which passes through a set of given points, while determining a curve which may pass close to the set of given points is the problem of approximation. Both of these problems, in general, are expressed by the single term "curve fitting". In the following section we shall describe some common techniques of curve fitting.

6.4.1 A Measure of Goodness of Fit

Suppose that we are given a set of.points (X_0, Y_0), (X_1, Y_1)...., (X_N, Y_N), displayed on a computer terminal. The objective is to connect these points by a smooth curve (say, using a mouse). This may be done as shown in figure 6.14 and is subject to judgement. In fact, a number of smooth curves can be drawn to approximate the given set of points. It will be of interest to find a criterion for evaluating the goodness of fit.

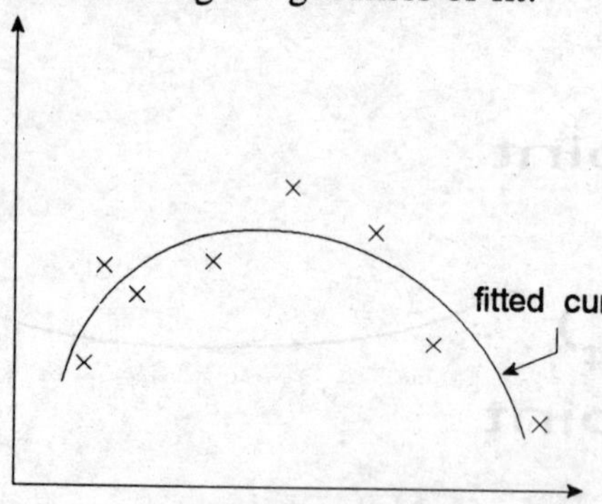

Figure 6.14 A curve fitted to a set of given points by an operator

First of all, we determine the value of the Y co-ordinate on the fitted curve for a given X. Let these values be (X_0, Y_0), (X_1, Y_1),..... One measure of goodness of fit is :

$$R^2 = 1 - \frac{\sum_{I=1}^{N} (Y_I - Y'_I)^2}{\sum_{I=1}^{N} (Y_I - Y_{mean})^2} \tag{6.31}$$

R^2 is often called the correlation co-efficient and Y_{mean} is the mean of the values of Y's. One can observe that if the curve passes through all the points, that is, $Y_I' = Y_I$ for I = 0, 1, ..., n, then the numerator of the fraction in equation (6.31) becomes zero and the value of R becomes one. This denotes a case of best fit, although the curve may oscillate between the points. If the value Y_I' is equal to the mean value Y_{mean} then the numerator becomes equal to the denominator. This case illustrates a situation when Y' does not improve the fit. The value of R in this case is equal to zero, and this represents the worst fit.

The value of R^2, thus, gives an indication of the goodness of a fit. The closer it is to unity the better the fit. In other words, the value of R^2 is an indication of the closeness of the predicted value Y' to the actual value Y (for a given X co-ordinate).

So far we have considered the following :

i) a method to measure the goodness of a fit, which is independent of the curve fitting technique, and

ii) the capability to edit the data to remove undesirable spurious points or add new points to improve the fit. This is done by selecting such points which bring the value of R closer to unity.

6.4.2 The Two-Dimensional Least Squares Method:

For the computer representation of a given set of points, it is necessary to find a mathematical model of a smooth curve. A standard technique to find the equation of the curve is to use the least squares technique. This is done by minimizing the sum of the squares of the deviations between values of Y co-ordinates of the given points and the corresponding values of the fitted Y' co-ordinates.

One obvious method to obtain the least squares fit for a given set of points is by trial and error, i.e., compute the sum of squared deviations and change the co-efficients of the equation that results in the minimum sum of squared variations. In the case when polynomials are used to obtain the least squares fit, the co-efficients can be computed directly.

To obtain the best linear fit to a set of data, we have to compute the coefficients C_0 and C_1 such that the values of Y' computed from the equation and minimize the sum of squared deviations between the computed value of Y' from equation (6.32) and the actual value of Y for a given value of X.

$$Y' = C_0 + C_1X \tag{6.32}$$

We shall not go into details since these can be found in any book on Statistics. The following equations can be used for computing the values of the coefficients C0 and C1 for the least squares fit:

$$C_0\sum I + C_1\sum X_I = Y_I$$
$$C_0\sum X_I + C_1\sum X_I^2 = Y_I\sum X_i \tag{6.33}$$

where the symbol Σ shows the summation over n points. In case, we use the second degree polynomial,

$$Y' = C_0 + C_1X + C_2X^2 \tag{6.33}$$

The coefficients C_0, C_1 and C_2 are to be computed to obtain the least square fit. The following equations can be used to achieve this goal :

$$\begin{aligned} C_0\sum I + C_1\sum X_I + C_2\sum X_i^2 &= \sum Y_I \\ C_0\sum X_I + C_1\sum X_I^2 + C_2\sum X_I^3 &= \sum X_I Y_I \\ C_0\sum X_I^2 + C_1\sum X_I^3 + C_2\sum X_I^4 &= \sum X_I^2 Y_I \end{aligned} \tag{6.34}$$

The above set of equations can be extended for a polynomial of any degree and the co-efficients C_0, C_1, C_2,..., can be computed to obtain the best fit in the least squares sense.

It can be observed that a straight line passes through two points. If we take a third point, the straight line may not pass through it. Similarly, if we take a second degree polynomial, it will pass through three given points. In general we can find an n-1 degree polynomial which will pass through a given set of n points. Thus if we fit a polynomial of degree D to a given set of n points, the resultant curve will pass through all the points if D = n-1. The degree of freedom in this case is zero. In general, for a polynomial fit of degree D to a set of n points, the degree of freedom, F, is given by

$$F = n - D - 1$$

To obtain a proper fit, a polynomial of a suitable degree is desired. It is possible to fit a variety of polynomials to a given set of data points in an interactive mode, and to select the most suitable one. In case it is desired that the computer should take a decision, the closeness of R, the correlation co-efficient, to unity can be used as a criterion.

The value of R gives an indication of closeness of the fit to a given set of points. However, it does not provide the quality of fit with respect to each point. A typical case arises when a fitted curve may pass through all the points, resulting in R = 1 but the curve is of oscillatory nature. Figure 6.15 shows such a fit. Clearly, this is not an acceptable solution. In such situations, interactive graphics is very effective as it combines the use of human judgement as well as computer power of trying out various alternatives quickly.

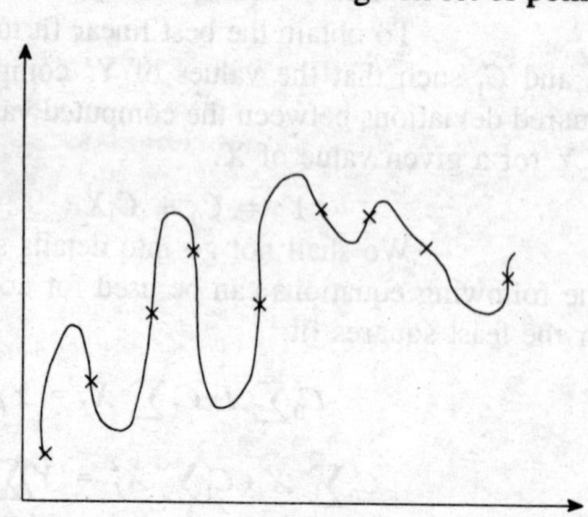

Figure 6.15: A curve passing through all points but oscillatory in nature

A general Pascal program for calculating the coefficients of the polynomial of a given degree for the least squares fit is given below:

calculating the coefficients of the polynomial of a given degree for the least squares fit is given below:

Example 6.11: Program for determining the co-efficients of a polynomial of given degree for least squares fit to a set of N points.

```
PROGRAM CurveFit;
{Program to determine the coefficients of a polynomial of degree m,
 given by a[0] + a[1] x + ... + a[m] xm, for least-squares fit
 to a set of N points with co-ordinates (x[i], y[i]) }
CONST MaxN = 50; MaxM = 20;
TYPE VectorM      = ARRAY [1..MaxM] OF REAL;
   VectorN        = ARRAY [1..MaxN] OF REAL;
   RowVector      = ARRAY [1..MaxM] OF REAL;
   ColumnVector   = ARRAY [1..MaxM] OF REAL;
   Matrix         = ARRAY [0..MaxM, 0..MaxM] OF REAL;
VAR A,B,C         : VectorM;
   x,y            : VectorN;
   MA             : Matrix;
   i,j,k,m,n      : INTEGER;
   rows, columns  : INTEGER;
FUNCTION Power (C : REAL; D : INTEGER) : REAL;
VAR i : INTEGER;    {calculation of CD, where D is an integer}
 BEGIN
   IF D > 0 THEN
      Power := Power (C,D-1) * C
   ELSE Power := 1;
 END;
 PROCEDURE GetData;
 BEGIN
   WRITE ('Enter the number of data points: ');
   READLN (n) ;
   WRITE ('Enter the degree of power series: ');
   READLN (m);
   FOR i := 1 TO n DO
     BEGIN
       WRITE ('Enter the value of x[ ', i, '] : ');
       READLN ( x[i] );
       WRITE ('Enter the value of y[ ', i, ' ] : ');
       READLN ( y [i] );
     END;
 END;
PROCEDURE GetElements;
{Calculate the elements of the Hankel matrix from the given X[I]}
```

```
VAR
    i, j, k : INTEGER;
    P       : REAL;
BEGIN
    rows := m + 1;
    columns := m +2;
    FOR i := 1 TO (m + m + 1) DO
    BEGIN
      j := 1;
      P := Power (x[j], i-1);
      FOR K := 1 TO n-1 DO
      BEGIN
      j  := j+1;
      P := P + Power (x[j], i-1) ;
    END;
    B [i] := P;
   END;
END;
PROCEDURE SetMatrix;
{Set-up an (M+1)*(M+2) matrix to solve for the coefficients}
  VAR I, J, K : INTEGER;
    P      : REAL;
  BEGIN
    FOR I := 1 TO (M+1) DO
    BEGIN
      FOR J := 1 TO (M + 1) DO
        MA[I,J] := B[I + J - 1];
    END;
    FOR I := 1 TO rows DO
    BEGIN
      J := 1;
      P := Power (X[J], I-1) * Y[J];
      FOR K := 1 TO (N - 1) DO
      BEGIN
        J := J + 1;
        P := P + Power (X[J], I-1) * Y[J];
      END;
      MA[I, M + 2]  := P;
    END;
END;
PROCEDURE Solve;
{Solve the set of simultaneous equations by transformation}
{of matrix MA to the Hermite normal form}
CONST
```

```
    Field        =     10;
    Decimal      =      3;
    epsilon      = 1.0E-07;
VAR
    B                    : RowVector; {Row vector}
    C                    : ColumnVector;  {Column vector}
    I,J,K,L,P            : INTEGER;
    BIG, AB,pivot, tolerance : REAL;
    CH                   : CHAR;
    FOUND                : BOOLEAN;
FUNCTION Max (A,B: REAL) : REAL;
BEGIN
    IF A < B THEN Max := B
    ELSE Max := A
END;
PROCEDURE Norm; {Test for zero number, tolerance}
VAR
    I,J  : INTEGER;
BEGIN
    tolerance := 0;
    FOR I := 1 TO rows DO
      BEGIN
        FOR J := 1 TO columns DO
            tolerance := Max (tolerance, ABS (MA[I,J]))
      END;
    tolerance := tolerance * epsilon
END;
{Procedure for searching for the pivot in the Pth row and Lth column}
PROCEDURE Search;
VAR
  J : INTEGER;
BEGIN
  BIG  := tolerance;
  WHILE (L <= columns) AND (BIG <= tolerance) DO
    BEGIN
      FOR J:= K TO rows DO
        BEGIN
          AB := ABS (MA[J,L]);
          IF BIG < AB THEN
             BEGIN
               BIG := AB;
               P := J
             END;
        END;
```

```
      IF BIG <= tolerance THEN
       BEGIN
        FOR J := K TO rows DO
           MA[J,L] := 0;
        L := L + 1
       END
      END;
    IF BIG > tolerance THEN FOUND := TRUE
    ELSE FOUND := FALSE;
END;
{Copy row with pivot and interchange rows K and P}
PROCEDURE Interchange;
VAR
    J : INTEGER;
  BEGIN
    FOR J := 1 TO columns DO
      BEGIN
        B[J] := MA[P,J]; {Row with pivot}
        MA[P,J]  := MA[K,J];
        MA[K,J]  := B[J]
      END
    END;
{Obtain column for outer product}
PROCEDURE Column;
VAR
    I  :  INTEGER;
BEGIN
    FOR I  :=  1 TO rows DO
      C[I] := MA[I,L];
    C[K] := C[K] - 1
END;
{Add outer product to transform the Lth column}
PROCEDURE AddOuterProduct;
VAR
    I,J  :  INTEGER;
BEGIN
    pivot  :=  MA[K,L];
    FOR I  :=  1 TO rows DO
      BEGIN
        FOR J := L TO columns DO
           IF (C[I] <> 0) AND (B[J] <> 0) THEN
              BEGIN
                 MA[I,J] := MA[I,J]- (C[I]* B[J])/pivot;
                 IF ABS (MA[I,J]) <= tolerance THEN
```

```
                    MA[I,J] := 0
              END
        END
    END;
    {Transform the MA-matrix by adding the outer product for each pivot.}
       BEGIN  {Solve}
         Norm;
         L := 1;
         K := 1;
         WHILE (K <= rows) AND (L <= columns) DO
           BEGIN
             Search;
             IF FOUND THEN
                BEGIN
                     Interchange;
                     Column;
                     AddOuterProduct;
                     L := L + 1;
                     K := K + 1;
                END;
           END;
       END;
    BEGIN {Main Program}
       GetData;
       SetMatrix;
       Solve;
       WRITELN;
       FOR I := 0 TO M DO
         WRITELN ('a[', I, '] = ', MA[I+1, columns] : 8 : 4);
    END.
```

Example 6.11: Consider a set of four points with co-ordinates (2,-2), (2,0), (0,2) and (-2,0). We shall fit curves of different degrees.

Case 1 - Linear Fit

$$Y = C_0 + C_1 X$$

The values of coefficients C_0 and C_1 are computed using equation (6.33). The least squares solution is

$$Y' = \frac{2}{11} - \frac{4}{11} X$$

Case 2 - Quadratic Fit

$$Y = C_0 + C_1 X + C_2 X^2$$

The value of coefficients is computed using equation (6.34). The least squares solution is given by

$$Y' = 2 - \frac{1}{4}X - \frac{5}{8}X^2$$

The plots of linear and quadratic least squares fits are shown in figure 6.16.

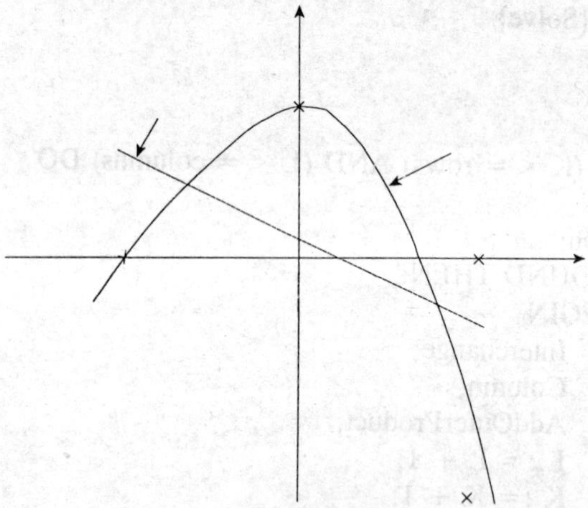

Figure 6.16 Linear and quadratic least square fits

6.4.3 Spline functions [11]

In many applications, it is necessary to generate a smooth curve which passes through all the points. Further, certain parts of the curve may be modified without affecting other parts of the curve. For example, it may be necessary to join the points obtained by digitizing a map by a smooth curve passing through all the points and also to edit the points occasionally and modify the resulting curve. If we fit only one curve to a set of points, a change in the location of even one point will necessitate the recomputation of the complete curve. One solution to avoid this problem is to use piecewise linear polynomial functions, i.e., we divide the number of points in a set into subsets and fit a polynomial to points in each subset. This method is similar to the French curve or spline technique used by draftsmen for joining a set of data points; by matching the French curve on small intervals to find the best fit and repeating this process till the pieces of curves cover all the points.

A mathematical cubic spline is a piecewise polynomial function defined by following general expression :

$$Y_I = C_{0I} + C_{1I} X_I + C_{2I} X_I^2 + C_{3I} X_I^3 \qquad (6.35)$$

such that $X_I < X < X_{I+1}$ for $I = 1,2,\ldots, n-1$ for the Ith segment of n given points. Therefore, we shall need four input conditions to calculate the coefficient C_{01}, C_{11}, C_{21} and C_{31} for each segment. Thsee can be obtained in several ways, as follows,

i) use co-ordinates of points (X_I, Y_I), (X_{I+1}, Y_{I+1}) and estimated slopes of the curve at these points.

ii) introduce dummy point (X,Y) between (X_I, Y_I) and (X_{I+1}, Y_{I+1}) and use the slope of the curve at any of these points, or

iii) use first four points (X_1,Y_1), (X_2,Y_2), (X_3,Y_3) and (X_4,Y_4), to derive a cubic through them. The slopes at say point (X_1, Y_1) and (X_2, Y_2) can be derived from this cubic.

Using this data one can generate a cubic between the first and the second point. The idea is to generate four equations necessary to calculate the co-efficients of the cubic. This provides the designer with a certain amount of flexibility in exercising control on the shape of the curve. Cubic splines have attracted considerable attention in the field of computer graphics because of the following properties:

i) they provide a continuous curve with continuous first and second derivatives, and

ii) discontinuities occur only in the third derivative, with the result that the curves look quite smooth to the human eye.

6.4.4 Bezier Curves [5, 7, 8, 10 and 11]

Bezier curves, $P(U)$, are defined in terms of the location of $n+1$ control points (P_0 through P_N), with co-ordinates (X_0, Y_0), (X_1, Y_1)..., (X_N, Y_N), by the following equation

$$P(U) = \sum_{I=0}^{N-I} P_I \frac{N!}{N!(N-I)!} U^I(I-U)^{N-I} \tag{6.36}$$

which can also be written in the following compact form

$$P(U) = \sum_{I=0}^{N-I} P_I B_{IN}(U) \tag{6.37}$$

$$B_{IN}(U) = C(N,I)\, U^I(I-U)^{N-I} \tag{6.38}$$

$$C(N,I) = \frac{N!}{I!(N-I)!} \tag{6.39}$$

The term $B_{I,N}(U)$ is called the interpolating or blending function and $C(N,I)$ is the Binomial co-efficient which denotes the number of combinations of N objects taken I at a time. Equation (6.33) is a vector equation. We can write a single equation for each variable x and y as follows:

$$\begin{aligned} x(U) &= \sum_{I=0}^{N} x_I B_{IN}(U) \\ y(U) &= \sum_{I=0}^{N} y_I B_{IN}(U) \end{aligned} \tag{6.40}$$

The Binomial co-efficient $C(N,I)$ can be computed efficiently using the following recursive equation.

$$C(N,I) = C(N\text{-}1,I) + C(N\text{-}1,I\text{-}1) \qquad (6.41)$$

The behaviour of the Bezier curve is governed by the interpolating functions $B_{I,N}(U)$.

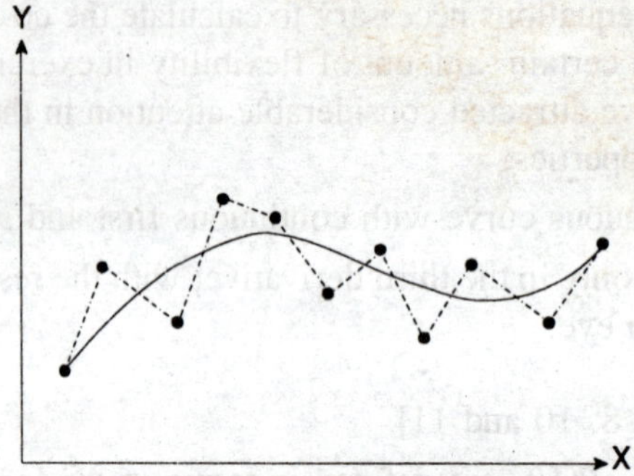

Figure 6.17 A smooth Bezier curve drawn in interacive mode using ten control points

Bezier polynomials can be used effectively in the interactive mode by allowing the user to edit the control points to obtain a desired shape. Figure 6.17 shows a Bezier curve drawn using ten control points. A smooth curve is obtained by interactively adjusting the locations of the control points. To obtain the desired shape quickly, the user needs some experience since the change in the location of one point affects the overall shape of the curve.

Example 6.12: Given a set of four points (0,1), (2,5), (5,5) and (8,0) as shown in figure 6.18 we can write the following Bezier equations (see Eq. 6.36) for the x and y parameters:

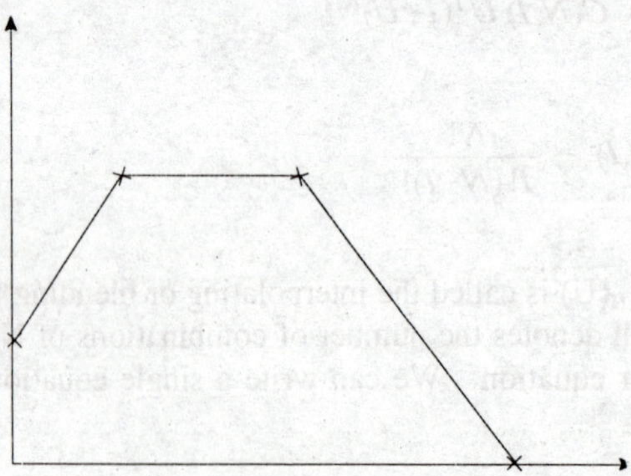

Figure 6.18 Location of four control points for computation of Bezier curve

$$x(U) = (I\text{-}U)^3\ x_0 + 3U\,(1\text{-}U)^2\,x_1 + 3U^2\,(1\text{-}U)\,x_2 + U^3\,x_3$$

$$y(U) = (I\text{-}U)^3\ y_0 + 3U\,(1\text{-}U)^2\,y_1 + 3U^2\,(1\text{-}U)\,y_2 + U^3\,y_3$$

where (x0, y0), (x1, y1), (x2, y2) and (x3, y3) are the co-ordinates of the four control points. Starting with U = 0 and increasing to 1 in steps of 0.1, we can compute the co-ordinates of the point (x[U], y[U]) on the curve. The following table gives the values:

U	x[U]	y[U]
0	0	1
0.1	0.63	2.08
0.2	1.31	2.91
0.3	2.04	3.5
0.4	2.82	3.82
0.5	3.62	3.87
0.6	4.46	3.66
0.7	5.33	3.18
0.8	6.21	2.41
0.9	7.1	1.35
1.0	8.0	0

The resultant Bezier Curve is shown in figure 6.19.

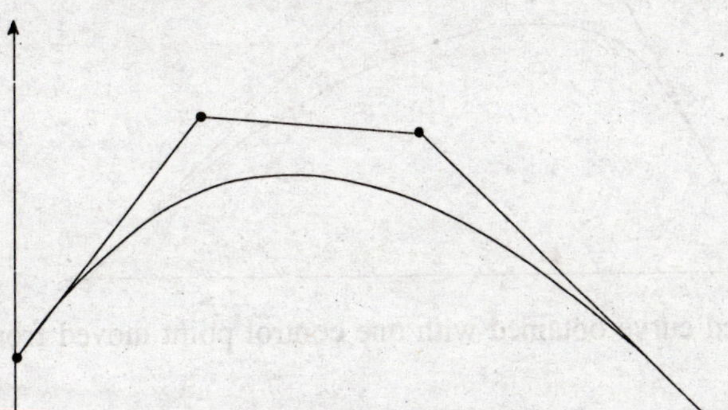

Figure 6.19 Bezier curve for four control points

Example 6.13: If we change the location of one control point say, from (2,5) to (2,7) and recompute the co-ordinates, x[U] and y[U], of the curve we get,

U	x[U]	y[U]
0	0	1
0.1	0.63	2.56
0.2	1.31	3.68
0.3	2.04	4.37
0.4	2.82	4.68
0.5	3.62	4.62
0.6	4.46	4.24
0.7	5.33	3.55
0.8	6.21	2.6
0.9	7.1	1.4
1.0	8.0	0

The resultant curve is shown in figure 6.20. It can be observed that changing the Y-co-ordinate of one control point has changed the values of the y[U] co-ordinates only. Further, the Bezier curves do not pass through the given set of points. The curve generated using the Bezier method does not oscillate away from the control points as it always remains within the convex hull of the control points. For representing a complex shape, one approach could be to increase the number of control points.

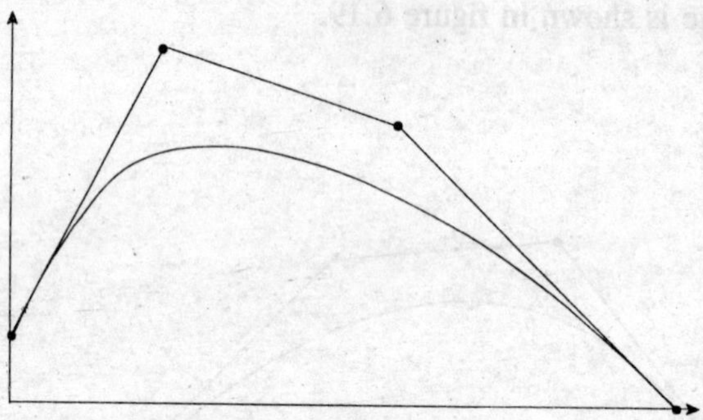

Figure 6.20 Stretched curve obtained with one control point moved from (2,5) to (2,7)

However, the degree of the polynomial increases with the increase in the number of the control points and the local control on the shape of the curve is reduced. The other approach for obtaining complex shapes is to group a number of Bezier curves together in such a way that the joints of the curves should meet. For obtaining zero-order continuity, the edges of the two curves should meet. This can be accomplished by causing the end control points of the two curves to coincide. Figure 6.21a depicts this case. The last point P_3 on the first curve and first point Q_1 on the second curve are the same. For first-order continuity, the last two control points of the first curve (point P_N and P_{N-1}) and the first two points of the second curve (Q_1 and Q_2) should be made collinear (see figure 6.21b).

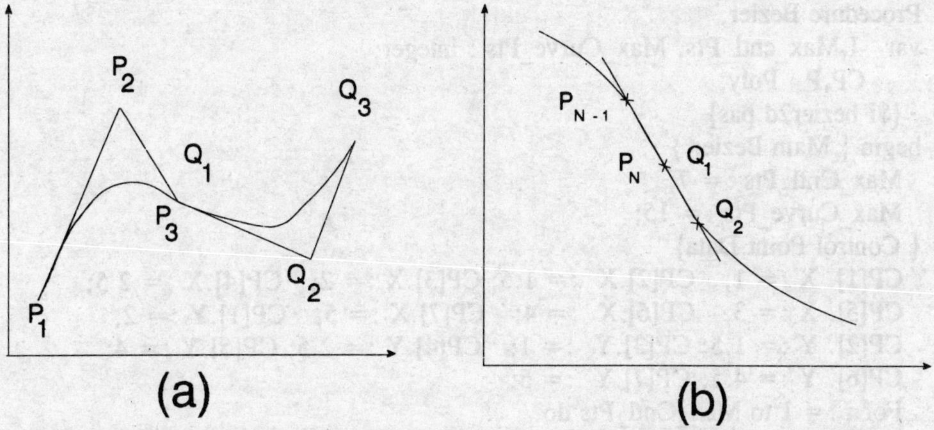

Figure 6-21 (a) zero order connectivity (b) First order connectivity

The degree of the Bezier curve is decided by the number of the control points. Thus, once we divide the set of points into subsets, the number of points in a subset automatically decides the degree of the polynomial to be fitted in that span in case a piecewise fit is attempted.

These curves are quite suitable for interactive graphics and are used in the automobile and aviation industries for modeling of surfaces. A program for generating a two-dimensional Bezier Curve is given below:

```
PROGRAM Graphics_2D;
{ World_Range    range of X_ and Y_ co-ordinates      }
{ Viewport_size  size of viewport                     }
{ Screen_Size    size of screen reserved for wire-frame }
Uses   Crt,dos,Graph;
Const
   Viewport_Size  =  340;
   World_Range    =    6;
   Screen_Size    =  350;
   LineStyles : array[0..4] of string[9] =
  ('SolidLn', 'DottedLn', 'CenterLn', 'DashedLn', 'UserBitLn');
Type
  RPointType= Record
  X: Real; Y: Real; End;
  Poly = array[1..25] of RPointType;
  IPoly = array[1..25] of PointType;
Var      ch : char;
    Screen : IPOLY;
{$I initial.pas}
{$I viewport.pas}
```

```
Procedure Bezier;
var   I,Max_cntl_Pts, Max_Curve_Pts : integer;
      CP,P : Poly;
  {$I bezier2d.pas}
begin { Main Bezier }
  Max_Cntl_Pts := 7;
  Max_Curve_Pts := 15;
{ Control Point Data}
  CP[1]. X := 1;   CP[2].X  := 1.5; CP[3].X := 2;   CP[4].X := 2.5;
  CP[5]. X := 3;   CP[6].X  := 4;   CP[7].X := 5;   CP[1].Y := 2;
  CP[2]. Y := 1.5; CP[3].Y  := 1;   CP[4].Y := 2.5; CP[5].Y := 4;
  CP[6]. Y := 4.5; CP[7].Y  := 5;
  For i := 1 to Max_Cntl_Pts do
  World_Screen(CP[i].X,CP[i].Y,Screen[i].X,Screen[i].Y);
  SetLineStyle(DottedLn, 0, NormWidth);
  DrawPoly(Max_Cntl_Pts,Screen);
  Bezier_curve;
  For i := 1 to Max_Curve_Pts do
  World_Screen(P[i].X,P[i].Y,Screen[i].X,Screen[i].Y);
  SetLineStyle(SolidLn, 0, ThickWidth);
  DrawPoly(Max_Curve_Pts,Screen);
end; { Bezier }
Begin { Main Program }
 ClrScr;
 Initialize;
 Line (20,150,300,150);
 Line (20,150,20,30);
 OutTextXY(10,4,'Bezier Curve : Solid Thick Line');
 OutTextXY(10,14,'Control Point Polygon : Dotted line');
 OutTextXY(10,180,'Change control points in Program to');
 OutTextXY(10,190,'    draw another Bezier Curve');
 OutTextXY(10,170,'    Press any key twice to EXIT');
 bezier;
 ch :=  readkey;
 while (not keypressed) do;
 CloseGraph;
End.
```

This program refers to three include files, Bezier2D.Pas, Initial.Pas and Viewport.Pas. These are listed below:

```
Procedure Bezier_Curve;   {Bezier2D.Pas}
const   Max_control_pts = 25;
type    C_Array = array[0..Max_Control_Pts] of real;
var   N, I, U_Inc : integer;
```

```
    U, XU, YU, Prod, DeltaU, Quot : real;
    C : C_Array;
Procedure binocoeff;
Var j : Integer;
begin
 for j := 0 to Max_Cntl_Pts - 2 do
 C[j + 1] := C[j] * (Max_Cntl_Pts - j) / (j + 1);
end;  { computes binomial coeff. of C[j,I]}
begin
  Max_Cntl_Pts := Max_Cntl_Pts - 1;
  DeltaU := 1.0 / (Max_Curve_Pts - 1);
  C[0] := 1;
  C[Max_Cntl_Pts] := 1;
  binocoeff;   { Extracts the binomial coefficients of C[N,I]}
for U_Inc := 1 to Max_Curve_Pts do
  begin
    U := (U_Inc - 1) * DeltaU;
    if U <= 0.5 then
      begin
        Prod := 1.0 - U;
        Quot := Prod;
        for N := 1 to Max_Cntl_Pts - 1 do
          Prod := Prod * Quot;
        Quot := U / Quot;
        XU := CP[(Max_Cntl_Pts + 1)].X;
        YU := CP[(Max_Cntl_Pts + 1)].Y;
        for N := Max_Cntl_Pts downto 1 do
        begin
          XU := C[N - 1] * CP[N].X + Quot * XU;
          YU := C[N - 1] * CP[N].Y + Quot * YU;
        end;
      end
    else
      begin
        Prod := U;
        Quot := Prod;
        for N := 1 to Max_Cntl_Pts - 1 do
          Prod := Prod * Quot;
        Quot := (1 - U) / Quot;
        XU := CP[1].X;
        YU := CP[1].Y;
        for N := 1 to Max_Cntl_Pts do
        begin
          XU := C[N] * CP[N + 1].X + Quot * XU;
```

```
        YU := C[N] * CP[N + 1].Y + Quot * YU;
      end;
    end;
   P[U_Inc].X := XU * Prod;
   P[U_Inc].Y := YU * Prod;
  end;
end; { Bezier_curve }
Procedure Initialize;      {Initial.Pas}
Const
  { The names of the various device drivers supported }
  DriverNames : array[0..10] of string[8] =
  ('Detect', 'CGA', 'MCGA', 'EGA', 'EGA64', 'EGAMono',
   'RESERVED', 'HercMono', 'ATT400', 'VGA', 'PC3270');
var
 GraphDriver                    : integer;  { The Graphics device driver }
 GraphMode                      : integer;  { The Graphics mode value }
 ErrorCode                      : integer;  { Reports any graphics errors }
{ Initialize graphics and report any errors that may occur }
begin
  { when using Crt and graphics, turn off Crt's memory-mapped writes }
  DetectGraph(GraphDriver, GraphMode);     { Test for RESERVED driver }
  if GraphDriver = RESERVED then
    begin
      GraphDriver := CGA;                 { Force RESERVED driver to }
      GraphMode := CGAHi;                  { CGA driver and mode!     }
    end
  else
  GraphDriver := Detect;               { use autodetection }
  InitGraph(GraphDriver, GraphMode, ''); { activate graphics }
  ErrorCode := GraphResult;            { error? }
  if ErrorCode <> grOk then
    begin
      Writeln('Graphics error: ', GraphErrorMsg(ErrorCode));
      Halt(1);
    end;
end; { Initialize }
{Viewport.Pas}
Procedure World_Viewport(X,Y :Real; Var Screen_X,Screen_Y : Integer);
 { Aspect ratio is taken as  0.667 }
 { World_Range defines the range of X and Y in the object space}
 {  Global : Const World_Range and Screen_Size  }
 Begin
 Screen_X := round(0.667*((Viewport_Size*X/(2*World_Range))
               + Viewport_Size/2 ));
```

```
Screen_Y := Viewport_Size - round(((Viewport_Size*Y/(2*World_Range))
            + Viewport_Size/2 ));
End;{ World_Viewport}
Procedure World_Screen(X,Y :Real; Var Screen_X,Screen_Y : Integer);
{ Aspect ratio is taken as  0.667 }
{ World_range defines the range of X and Y in the object space}
{ Const   Global : World_range and Screen_Size}
Begin
  Screen_X := round(0.667*((Screen_Size*X/(2*World_range))+Screen_Size/2 ));
  Screen_Y:= Screen_Size - round(((Screen_Size*Y/(2*World_range))
      + Screen_Size/2 ));
End;{ World_Screen}
```

6.4.5 B-SPLINE CURVES [5,7,8,11]

The curve created by using the vertices of a defining polygon is dependent on some interpolation or approximation scheme which establishes the relationship between the curve and the polygon. This scheme is provided by choice of the basis function. The bezier curves are generated using Bernstein basis. These curves, however, limit the flexibility of the resulting Bezier curves due to number of specified polygon vertices fixes the order of curves, e.g., a cubic needs to be defined by polygon with 4 vertices and 3 spans. Thus, the degree of curves can be reduced or increased only by controlling the number of vertices, i.e. we cannot fit a Bezier cubic curve through say, n points without the use of multiple curve segments; and due to the global nature of the Bernstein basis, the value of the blending function $B_{I,N}$ in the equation 6.33 is non-zero for all parameters values over the entire curve. This property reduces the local control within a curve as any point on Bezier curve is result of blending the values of all defining vertices, i.e., a change in one vertex has some effect on the entire curve.

B-spline (short form of Basis-spline) is a special case of Bernstein basis. B-splines exhibit non-global behaviour due to the fact that each vertex is associated with a unique basis function. This allows each vertex to affect the shape of a curve only over a range of parameter values where its associated basis function is non-zero. In case of B-spline, degree of resulting curve can be changed without changing the number of defining polygon vertices.

Given an input set of N+1 control points P_I and I varying from 0 to N, points on B-spline curve are defined as follows

$$P(U) = \sum_{I=1}^{N} P_I B_{IK}(U), \quad U_{\min} \le U \le U_{\max} \text{ and } I \le K < N-1 \tag{6.42}$$

where the function $B_{I,K}$ is a polynomial of degree K-1 or order K. Representation of the blending function in the polynomial form helps to define them recursively over various sub-intervals of the range for parameter U. We need to fix number of control points N and select range of K as well as the range of parameter U which varies from 0 to N-K+2 instead of 0 to 1, as was also the case for the Bezier curves. For N+K intervals, we define the blending functions recursively as

$$B_{I,1} = \begin{cases} 1 & \text{if } U_1 < U < U_{I+1} \\ 0, & \text{otherwise} \end{cases}$$

$$B_{I,K} = \frac{U-U_I}{U_{I+K-1}-U_1} B_{I,K-1} + \frac{U_{I+K}-U}{U_{I+K}-U_{I+1}} B_{I+1,K-1} \tag{6.43}$$

In cases where denominator of equation 6.41 becomes 0, any term computed as 0/0 is assigned value 0.

The positions of sub-intervals of U, say U_J where J varies from 0 to N+K, is referred to as *break points* and points corresponding to breakpoints on the B- spline as *knots*. The break points can either be equi-distant, i.e., U_J = J or can be defined by an equation as follows:

$$U_J = \begin{cases} 0 & \text{if} \quad J < K \\ J-K+1 & \text{if} \quad K < J < N \\ N+K+2 & \text{if} \quad J > N \end{cases} \tag{6.44}$$

The maximum order of the curve is equal to the number of defining polygon vertices. B-spline curve exhibits the variation diminishing property. The curve, therefore, does not oscillate about any straight line more than its defining polygon. The curve remains within the convex hull of its defining polygon. The convex hull property of B-spline curves is stronger than that of Bezier curves. For example, if all the vertices of the defining polygons are colinear, then the resulting B-spline curve is straight line for all orders K. Figure 6.22 shows the convex hull property for colinear curve segments within the defining vertices of the polgon.

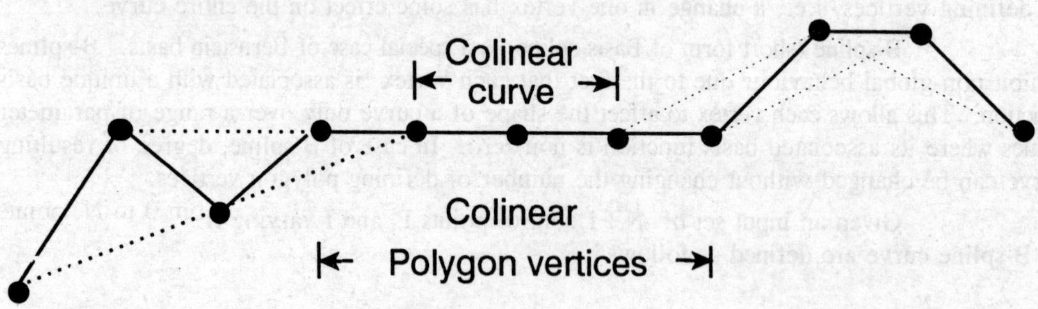

Figure 6.22 Collinear curve segments within the defining vertices

Similarly, closed B-splines curves can be generated by specifying the first and the last control points at the same position. Figure 6.23 illustrates this property of B-splines. It can be noted that control point C_0 and C_5 are co-located.

Figure 6.24 shows the local control property of the B- splines as a designer can specify any number of control points without increasing the degree of the curve. Notation C_{21}, C_{22} and C_{23} in figure 6.24 (a) - (c) shows one, two, and three control points respectively near one location to obtain curves of different shapes.

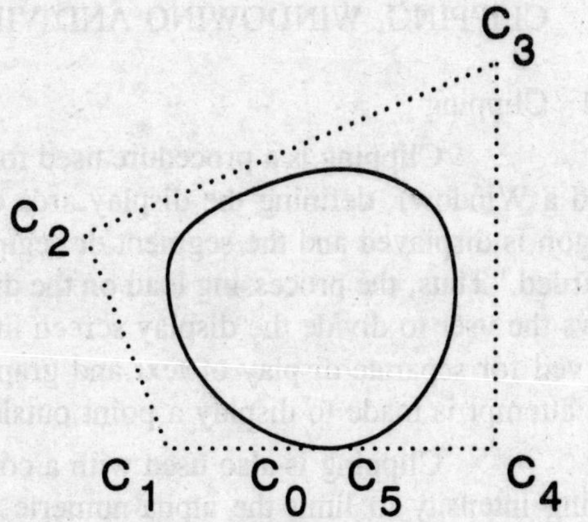

Figure 6.23: B-Spline closed curve generated with first and second control points C_0 and C_5 co-located

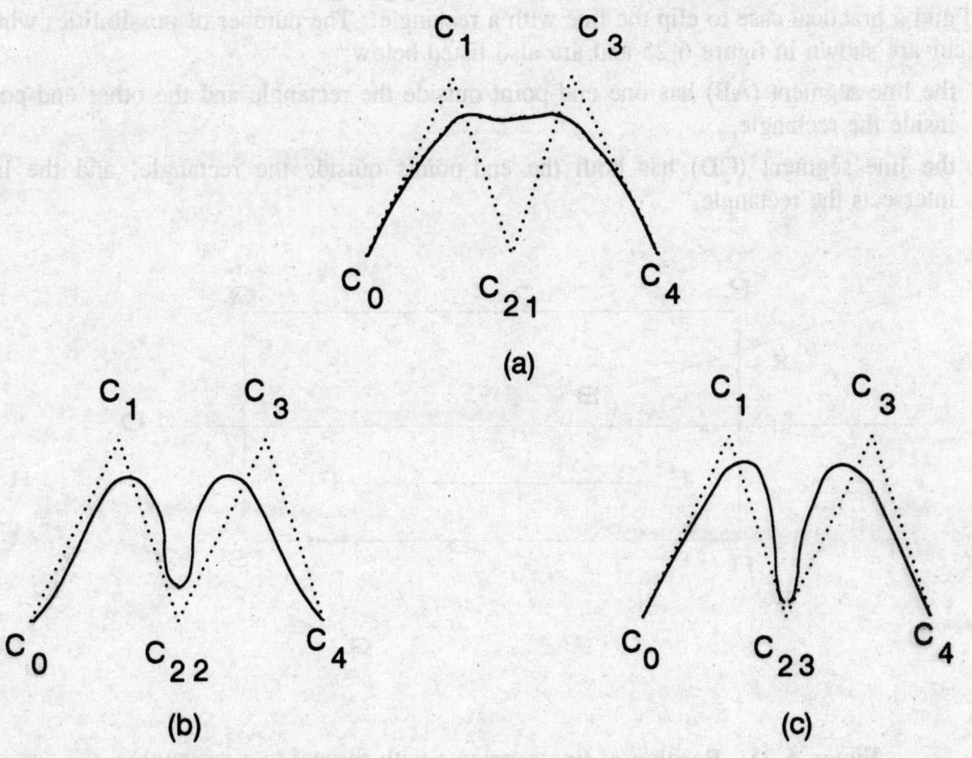

Figure 6.24: Behaviour of curve when (a) one control point, (b) two control points and (c) three control points are co-located at C_2

6.5 CLIPPING, WINDOWING AND VIEWPORTS

6.5.1 Clipping

Clipping is a procedure used for finding whether a line intersects a polygon (often called a Window), defining the display area on the screen. The segment of the line inside the polygon is displayed and the segment or segments (as the case may be) outside the polygon are discarded. Thus, the processing load on the display hardware is considerably reduced. Clipping allows the user to divide the display screen into a number of partitions. These partitions can be reserved for separate display of text and graphics. The problem of wrap-around which occurs if an attempt is made to display a point outside the display area is also avoided.

Clipping is also used with a continuous tone picture defined by a set of points of varying intensity to limit the alpha-numeric data within a rectangular window on the display screen.

6.5.1.1 A Line Segment Clipping Algorithm

A general algorithm will clip a line by a polygon. Here, we shall consider a special and a practical case to clip the line with a rectangle. The number of possibilities which can occur are shown in figure 6.25 and are also listed below:

i) the line segment (AB) has one end-point outside the rectangle and the other end-point inside the rectangle,

ii) the line segment (CD) has both the end-points outside the rectangle, and the line intersects the rectangle,

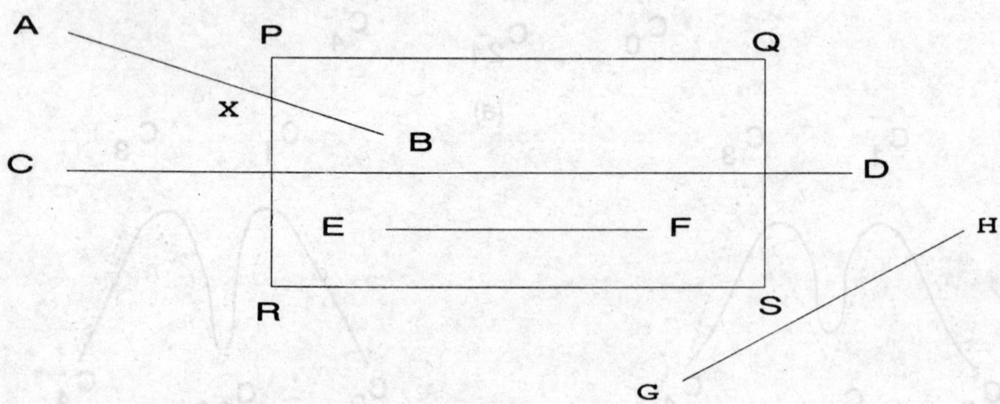

Figure 6.25: Position of line segments with respect to a rectangle

iii) the line segment (EF) has both the end-points within the rectangle,

iv) the line segment (GH) has both the end-points outside the rectangle, and it does not intersect the rectangle.

It can be noticed that clipping will generate only one visible line segment in each of the above cases (except case iv) and will reject a line segment if it falls outside the boundary of the rectangle. The zone adjacent to the display rectangle is divided into eight regions by extending the edges of the rectangle as shown in figure 6.26. The region E represents the display area.

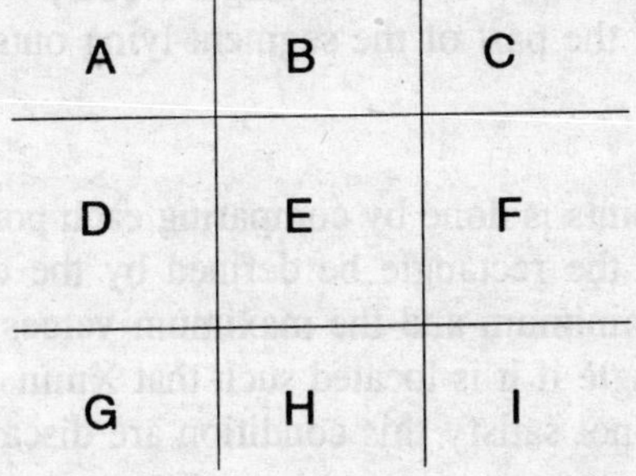

Figure 6.26 Region adjacent to the display region 'E'

A four-bit code is assigned to each of these regions. The least significant bit or bit 1 is '1' if one of the end-points of the line is to the left of the left edge of the rectangle (zone A.D. or G). The second, third, and fourth bits are assigned the value '1' if the end-point of the line segment is to the right, below the bottom, or above the top edge of the rectangle, respectively. The codes, thus, generated for the nine regions, are given below:

Region	Code
A	1001
B	1000
C	1010
D	0001
E	0000
F	0010
G	0101
H	0100
I	0110

It can be observed that if both end-points of a line segment fall in regions (A,B,C), (A,D,G), (G,H,I) or (C,F,I) then the segment is not visible. If we take the logical intersection of the codes of two end-points of such a line, we get a non-zero result. This result is significant as this can be computed very fast and the line segment under consideration is rejected if a non-zero result is obtained.

If both end-points generate a zero code then the line segment is completely in the region E(the display region) and is visible.

For clipping a line segment in other cases, it has to be subdivided. The point of intersection of the line segment with the edge of the rectangle can be found and used for deciding which part of the line segment is in the visible area. Line segment 'AB' intersects the edge of the rectangle at a point 'X' (see figure 6.25). The line segment AX is discarded being outside the display area. It may, however, be noted that we are finding the intersection of two line segments (vectors) AB and PR. Note that vectors PQ and AB do not intersect. For the line segment CD which intersects two edges of the rectangle PQRS, we repeat the same procedure for the other portion and discard the part of the segment lying outside the display region.

6.5.1.2 Clipping of Points

Clipping of the points is done by comparing each point with the boundary of the rectangle. Let the boundary of the rectangle be defined by the co- ordinates Xmin, Xmax, Ymin, and Ymax denoting the minimum and the maximum values of X and Y co-ordinates. A point (x,y) is within the rectangle if it is located such that Xmin $<$ x $<$ Xmax and Ymin $<$ y $<$ Ymax. The points that do not satisfy this condition are discarded.

6.5.1.3 Clipping of Text

It is easy to completely clip a character which is partially in the visible zone. Since characters are displayed in standard formats (commonly in the form of 5×7 or 7×9 matrices) and therefore to clip a character information on only the starting point is required. The problem then becomes a simple matter of clipping points. If any of the points defining the boundary of the character fall outside the visible zone, the character is clipped. For displaying partial characters, the matrix representation of the character is needed and clipping is performed by considering the location of each point with respect to the viewing zone.

6.5.2 Windowing and Viewports:

Windows are areas on the screen where graphical information can be displayed. Viewports refer to rectangular areas inside the window that display graphical data. Viewports can, therefore, be of different sizes but are always smaller than the size of the window. For practical applications, we need a transformation to translate and scale the window to any size by moving it to a specified rectangular area on the screen. This area is commonly called the viewport. The choice of the window decides what we want to see on the display and the choice of the viewport decides where we want to see it on the display screen. This concept enables a user to divide the screen into virtual partitions. For example, see figure 6.27 where the same screen is used for simultaneous display of text, graphics, and menu in different viewports P_1, P_2, and P_3 respectively. Most graphics libraries have a function or a set of functions to define areas on the screen as viewports. As an example, Borland's BGI function *SetViewport*( ) can define any region of the screen as a viewport.

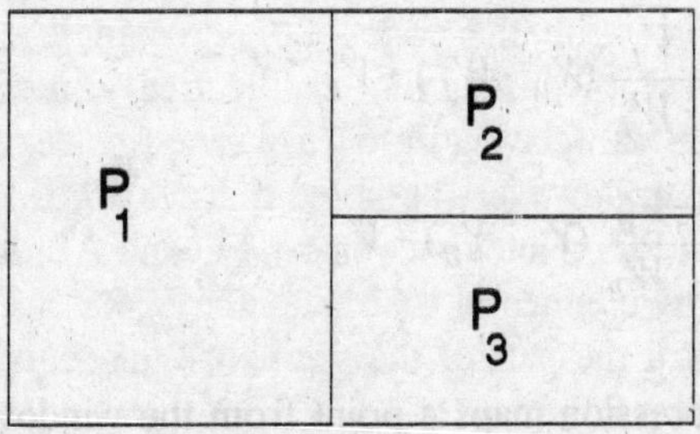

Figure 6.27 Virtual partitioning of the display screen

The display hardware divides the screen into a number of pixels arranged in a grid. With each pixel are associated its X- and Y- coordinates. The top left corner of the screen is called the origin of the co-ordinate system. The value of the X- co-ordinate increases from the left to the right and the value of the Y co-ordinate from the top towards the bottom. These co-ordinates are referred to as device/screen co-ordinates. For the VGA graphics card, the size of the display grid is 640×480 (see figure 6.28)

Similarly, a suitable co-ordinate system can be selected for objects in the space. The co-ordinates so defined are called world co-ordinates. It may sometimes be desirable to select a part of the object or a drawing for display, in order to obtain sufficient detail of the object on the display. The part of interest is enclosed in a rectangular boundary called a window. For displaying, one has to convert the world co-ordinates into the screen co-ordinates. This transformation is called viewing transform. In general, the viewing transform consists of operations such as scaling, translation and rotation.

Given a window with corner points (W_L, W_B), (W_R, W_B), (W_L, W_T), and (W_R, W_T) in world co-ordinates and a viewport with corner points (V_L, V_B), (V_R, V_B), (V_L, V_T), and (V_R, V_T) in screen co-ordinates (see figure 6.29a and b), the following expression can be used to transform a point (X_W, Y_W) in the window to a point (X_S, Y_S) in the view port:

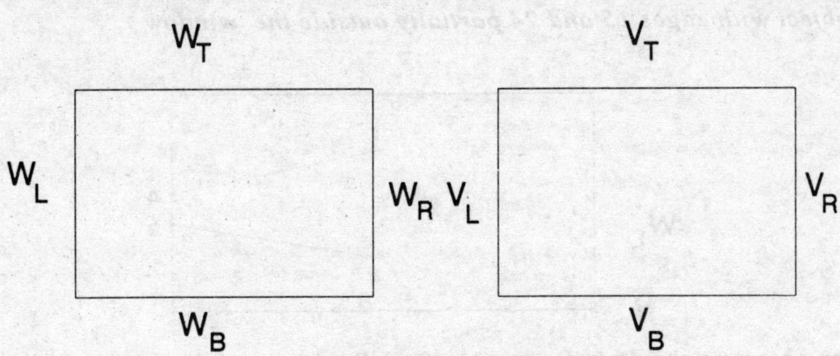

(a) a window (b) a viewport

Figure 6.29 Window and viewport

$$X_S = \frac{V_R - V_L}{W_R - W_L}(X_W - W_L) + V_L$$

$$Y_S = \frac{V_T - V_B}{W_T - W_B}(Y_W - Y_B) + V_B \tag{6.45}$$

The above expression maps a point from the window to the corresponding point in the viewport. For a picture to be transformed from the window to the viewport, we have to translate each edge point from the window to the viewport and then join the mapped edge points by line segment using the linkage information. In cases where a part of the picture is outside the window, we first perform the clipping and then map the resultant edge points to the viewport. **This operation saves the computation time as it avoids the transformation of edge points which are outside the window boundary. Figure 6.30 shows an object which has five edge points. Only four operations are required if we clip first and then transform.**

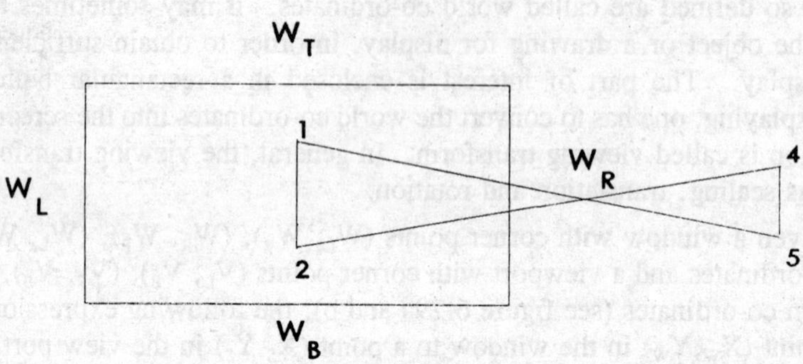

(a) an object with edges 15 and 24 partially outside the window

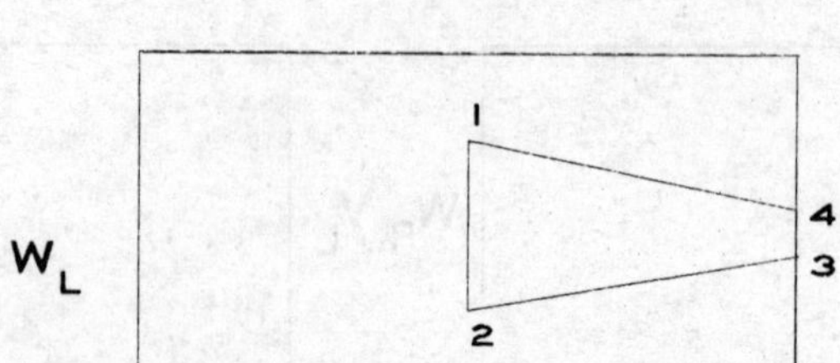

(b) same object as shown in figure (a) after clipping operation

Figure 6.30 Clipping Operation

6.6 CONTOUR FILLING

Many two-dimensional pictures with regions of uniform intensity can be described by the contour points of the regional boundaries. The contour points, along with linkage information, can then be stored instead of the complete picture. This provides an efficient method for storing pictorial information, provided there is a method available to reconstruct the picture from the contour points, and to fill up the regions of the picture. Figure 6.31a depicts an object which is defined by two closed polygons: outer polygon P, and inner polygon Q. These polygons can be represented by one of the following methods:

i) an ordered list of vertices P_1, P_2,.....,P_{11} and Q_1, Q_2,....., Q_5 represent polygon P and Q respectively. The ordering is done such that adjacent vertices in the list represent edges, or

ii) by the list of edges, e.g., P_1, P_2,.....,P_{11} for the polygon P.

To reconstruct this picture its interior is to be filled as shown in the figure 6.31b. The interior of this picture is found by considering equation of all the edges (defined by straight line) and then locating all the pixels that lie inside the polygonal boundaries. Such techniques are said to be polygon based and are also used for scan conversion. In case we map contour information on a discrete grid, the method used for filling is called pixel based.

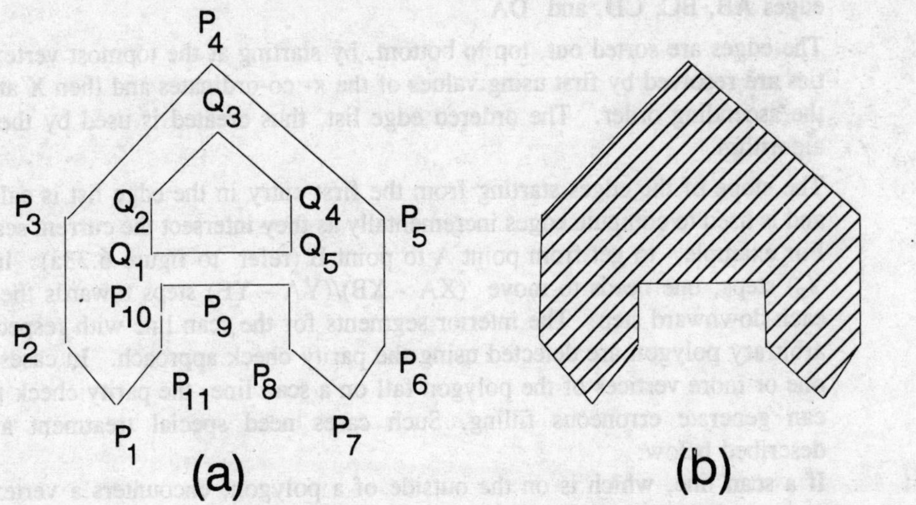

Figure 6.31: (a) Skelton of character 'A' represented by polygon 'P' and 'Q'
(b) picture of 'A' after filling both polygon 'P' and 'Q'

6.6.1 Polygon Based Technique

The basis of filling algorithm is to find whether a point is in the interior of the polygon. One simple technique commonly used is called 'Parity Check'. If we take a point 'A' (see figure 6.32) located in the interior of the polygon ABCDE and draw a imaginary horizontal line (pq) to the right of the point 'P', it intersects the polygon boundary at point '2', '3', and '4'. Similarly, a line (pr) drawn to the left of the point 'p' intersects the polygon at the point

'1'. Therfore, the conclusion is that a horizontal line drawn from a interior point intersects the polygonal boundary an odd number of times.

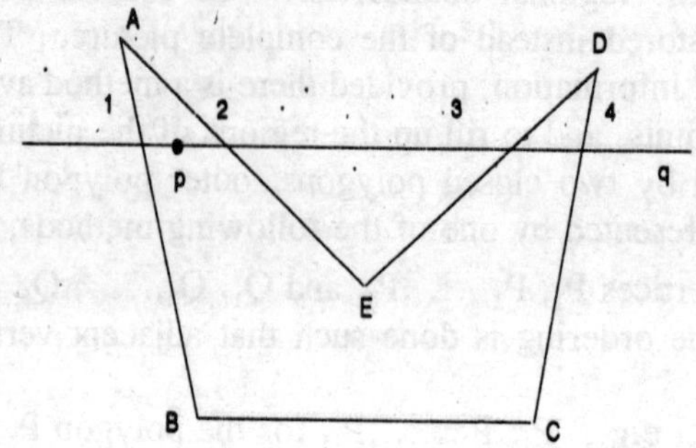

Figure 6.32 Application of parity check principle to find the interior point

A general polygon fill algorithm using the above principle is described below :

Step 1: The polygon is divided into edges, e.g., polygon shown in figure 6.33a had edges AB, BC, CD, and DA.

Step 2: The edges are sorted out, top to bottom, by starting at the topmost vertex. The ties are resolved by first using values of the x- co-ordinates and then X and Y in the ascending order. The ordered edge list, thus created is used by the filling algorithm.

Step 3: The slope of the edges starting from the first entry in the edge list is calculated and is used to compute edges incrementally as they intersect the current scan line. For example, to get from point A to point B (refer to figure 6.33a) in (Y_A - Y_B) steps, one needs to move (XA - XB)/(YA - YB) steps towards the left in each downward step. The interior segments for the scan line with respect to an arbitrary polygon are detected using the parity check approach. In cases where one or more vertices of the polygon fall on a scan line, the parity check method can generate erroneous filling. Such cases need special treatment and are described below:

Case 1: If a scan line, which is on the outside of a polygon, encounters a vertex point (where two edges meet), it remains on the outside of the polygon. For this intersection either only a vector one pixel long is generated (see figure 6.33b), or the intersection is ignored. Similarly, a scan line which is on the inside of the polygon before encountering a vertex point remains inside. In these cases, both the edges are either below, or above the scan line.

Case 2: A vetex point lying on a scan line may have one edge above the line and the other edge below the line. In other words, the scan line passes through edges, but whether it is inside or outside of the polygon changes (see figure 6.33c) needs to be resolved.

To resolve case 1 and 2, one can observe scan lines just above and below the one currently being used for the parity check. If one of the lines intersects the contour, it implies that the current scan line used for parity check is tangent to the contour. In case 2, both the scan lines (i.e., above and below the current scan line) will intersect the contour.

Another possible solution to distinguish case 1 and 2, is to truncate one of the edges in case 2 at the time of preparing the edge list. Thus, only one edge will appear at the intersection point.

Case 3: Horizontal edges (see figure 6.33d) do not intersect the scan lines and require special treatment during the fill process. If horizontal edges are ignored, it may result into complete filling of the area. Figure 6.33e depicts such a case. For obtaining a correct fill either edge CB or edge DE is to be shortened. The selection of the edge will depend on the ordering of the vertices. Failing to do this would result in three intersections on the scan line, and half of the horizontal line will not be filled in.

Step 4: Repeat step 3 for each line, sorting edges from left to the right and filling the scan line segments using parity check and taking special cases into consideration, till all edges in the edge list are processed and bottom-most vertex is reached.

The speed of the fill will depend on the algorithm used for the top-to-bottom sort of the edge list, and the number of edges in the polygon.

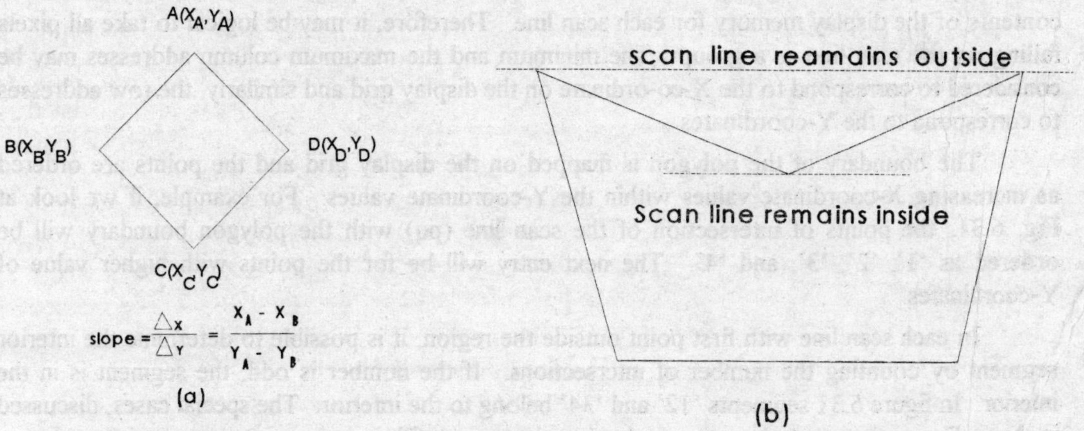

Figure 6.33 Special cases when vertices of the polygon fall on the scan line (continued on the following page)

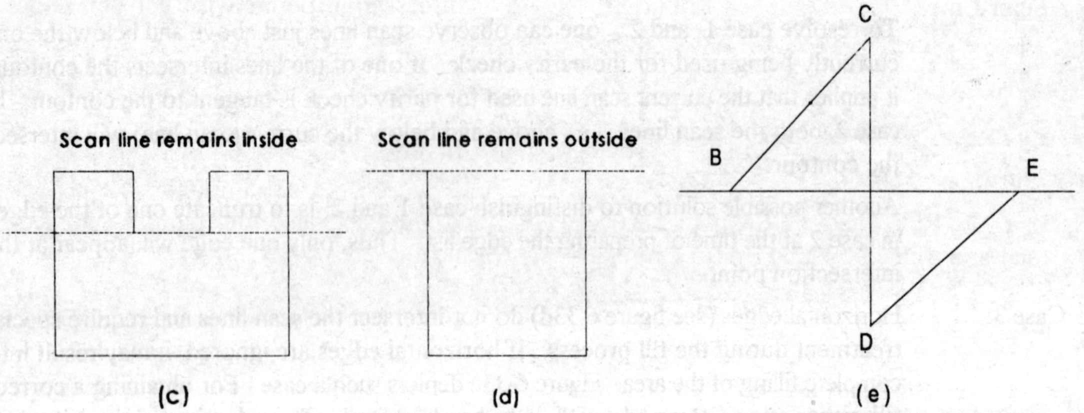

Figure 6.33 Special cases when vertices of the polygon fall on the scan line

6.6.2 Pixel Based Technique

Instead of using one pixel to test whether it is on the inside or the outside of a polygon boundary, one can use a group of pixels. For a raster scan display device, it is easy to test the contents of the display memory for each scan line. Therefore, it may be logical to take all pixels falling on the scan line as a group. The minimum and the maximum column addresses may be considered to correspond to the X-co-ordinate on the display grid and similarly, the row addresses to correspond to the Y-coordinates.

The boundary of the polygon is mapped on the display grid and the points are ordered as increasing X-coordinate values within the Y-coordinate values. For example, if we look at Fig. 6.31, the points of intersection of the scan line (pq) with the polygon boundary will be ordered as '1', '2', '3', and '4'. The next entry will be for the points with higher value of Y-coordinates.

In each scan line with first point outside the region, it is possible to determine the interior segment by counting the number of intersections. If the number is odd, the segment is in the interior. In figure 6.31 segments '12' and '34' belong to the interior. The special cases, discussed in the earlier section are to be processed to get the correct fill.

Example 6.14: Consider a polygon ABCD defined by vertices A(1,0), B(1,4), C(5,4) and D(5,0). The area of the polygon is 16 units. Fill the polygon by activating the pixels inside it.

The following scan-lines are considered to fill or scan convert the polygon ABCD:

Scan Line	Equation	Intersection points with polygon edges
1	Y = 0	
2	Y = 1	
3	Y = 2	X = 0 and X = 5
4	Y = 3	
5	Y = 4	

Thus, all the pixels between X=1 and 5 are activated for scan line 1 to 5. The total area filled is equivalent to 25 units as shown in figure 6.33.

Example 6.15:

Modify the filling technique so that the area of filled polygon does not change. To ensure that filled polygon is of same size as original polygon, half-scan line convention is used. The half scan lines are considered to pass through the centre of the raw of pixels. A pixel (x,y) is defined by the coordinates of Centre (x + 1//2, y + 1/2). To activate a pixel on a scan line y +1/2, the centre of pixel must not fall to the right of interval defined by x1 & x2, i.e.,

$$x1 < x+\frac{1}{2} < x2$$

where x1 & x2 are intersection of scan line y + 1/2 with the polygonal edges. The result using above convention is tabulated below :

Scan Line	Equation	Intersection Points	Pixels to be activated
1	Y = 0.5	(1,0.5), (5, 0.5)	(1,0), (2,0), (3,0) & (4,0)
2	Y= 1.5	(1,1.5), (5, 1.5)	(1,1), (2,1), (3,1) & (4,1)
3	Y = 2.5	(1,2.5), (5, 2.5)	(1,2), (2,2), (3,2) & (4,2)
4	Y = 3.5	(1,3), (5,3)	(1,3), (2,3), (3,3) & (4,3)

The filled polygon is shown in figure 6.33 (b). The area of filled polygon is 16 units.

6.7 SUMMARY

In this chapter, the basic concepts useful in two-dimensional graphics have been described. The treatment of lines and circles has been given using discrete geometry. This enables a user to describe shapes and figures in the pixel form. The pixel representation is useful for creating graphics on microcomputers with simple display devices.

The techniques for generation and approximation of curves are introduced. For simple graph-plotting and drawing of shapes one need use single-valued and multi-valued curves respectively. In the case of a single-valued curve, it is useful to construct some interpolating function y = f(x). Cubic splines can be used very effectively in such situations. The Bezier curves are quite flexible but it is sometimes awkward to work with control points off the curve. An alternative approach allowing the designer to work with points on the actual curve and yet retain the local control of the shape is described in [5]. For a detailed treatment of this subject the reader can refer to [6-12]. One important aspect of the curves, which has not been explored here, is the relationship of the curves and surfaces. This will be discussed in the next chapter.

Contour filling is useful in situations where the same contour is to be used several times. For raster scan displays the pixel based algorithms [8] are very efficient and are commonly used.

6.8 PROBLEMS

6.1 Write a program to draw the following figure on the display using the scaling operation. Now, delete the figure in stages starting from the inner-most rectangle.

6.2 In section 6.2.1.4.6 a transformation matrix for a translation operation followed by rotation was given. Write the transformation matrix T for the rotation operation followed by translation.

6.3 Generate a square defined by the points (50,50), (70,50), (70,70) and (50,70). Use the digital straight line program to draw the edges. Rotate the square by a fixed angle first around the point (50,50) and then point (60,60) which are the corner and the centre point of the square. Compare the two outputs.

6.4 Modify the digital circle program to generate circular arcs defined by,

i) radius

ii) centre of the arc ,

iii) the angle subtended at the centre.

6.5 Given three points P_1 (x_1, y_1) P_2 (x_2, y_2) P_3 (x_3, y_3) and the slope (P_2), find the equation of the cubic spline which fits the points.

6.6 Write an interactive program to generate a Bezier curve passing close to a set of n points. You should be able to change the number and location of the control points to adjust the shape of the curve.

6.7 Suppose that graphical objects are shown on a display in the range [0:640]×[0:480]. Write a procedure for the clipping of a line

PROCEDURE CLIP(IX1,IX2,IY1,IY2,XI,XF,YI,YF)

The window boundary is specified by the parameters IX1, IX2, IY1, and IY2 (which are four equation : IX1 = C, IX2 = C, IY1 = C, and IY2 = C, where C is a constant). The procedure clip changes the end points (X_I, Y_I) and (X_F, Y_F) of the input straight line and returns the end points of the clipped line as (X_I, Y_I) and (X_F, Y_F).

6.8 Write a program to implement the general filling algorithm described in the section 6.6.1. Select a suitable sorting algorithm for handling the edge list.

6.9 REFERENCES

1. Bezier, P., *Numerical Control*, John Wiley, New York, 1972
2. Bresenham, J.E, "Algorithm for computer control of a digital plotter", IBM Systems J.4(1), 25-30, Jan.1975.
3. Horn, B.K.P., "Circle Generators for the Display Devices", Computer Graphics and Image Processing, 5, 280-288, Jan. 1978.
4. Kulpa, J., A note on the paper by B.K.P. HORN, "Circle Generators for display devices", Comput. Graphics and Image Processing, 9, 102 -103, 1979.
5. Brewer J.A. and Anderson, D.C., "Visual Interaction with Overhauser Curves and Surfaces", Computer Graphics, 11, 2, 132- 137, 1977.
6. Farin Gerald, *Curves and Surfaces for Computer Aided Design,* Academic Press, Boston, 1988.
7. Law, A.G. and Sahney, B.N., *Theory of Approximation with Application,* New York : Academic Press, 1976.
8. Mortenson M.E., *An Introduction to the Mathematics and Geometry, Computer Graphics*, Industrial Press Inc., New York, 1989.
9. Pavlidis, P., *Algorithms for Graphics and Image Processing*, Computer Science Press, 1982.
10. Rogers, David F. and Adams, J, Alan, *Mathematical Elements for Computer Graphics*, Second Edition, McGraw Hill Publishing Co., New York, 1989.
11. Spath, H., *Spline Algorithm for Curves and Surfaces,* Winnipeg : Unita Mathematica publ., 1974..
12. Sylvan, H. Chasen, *Geometric Principles and Procedures for Computer Graphics Applications*, Prentice Hall, Inc. New Jersey, 1978.

CHAPTER 7

THREE-DIMENSIONAL GRAPHICS

7.1 INTRODUCTION

Most real life objects which we would like to model and display are three-dimensional. Since, computer displays are two-dimensional, we must solve the problem of creating a two-dimensional representation for a three- dimensional object that shows the depth (the third dimension) on the display as well as on the other graphics output device. In the pre 1990 days, PC graphics was mostly restricted to the two dimensions, however, due to increased speed, improved interface design, and advanced programming techniques a PC screen can produce three dimensional worlds which look realistic. In fact, a 16-color palette is not quite sufficient when rendering complex 3-D objects with light sources - even 256 colors are bare minimum. One needs to create all the colors that the eye can see. Now that true color graphic cards are affordable, one can use sophisticated photorealistic rendering techniques.

In generating such a view of an object or a collection of objects (scene), three-dimensional transformations are required to produce the effect of different viewing positions. Moreover, for creating a realistic display of three dimensional objects the visibility problem must be solved, i.e., the hidden lines or hidden surfaces are to be removed. The following sections describe the techniques used for achieving these goals.

7.2 MATHEMATICS OF THREE-DIMENSIONAL GRAPHICS :

Some special mathematical tools are required for developing methods for solving geometric problems, positional transformations and projections. Homogeneous co-ordinates are particularly useful as they allow many geometric transformations to be represented uniformly and elegantly. In section 7.2.1, we shall define homogeneous co-ordinates and in section 7.2.2, develop three dimensional transformations based on a unified 4×4 matrix.

7.2.1 Homogeneous Co-ordinates

Homogeneous co-ordinates were described in section 6.2.2 for the case of two-dimensional operations. A point (x,y,z) in a three-dimensional system is represented by the four-dimensional vector

$$[hx \quad hy \quad hz \quad h]$$

where h (a non zero number) is referred to as the homogeneous co-ordinate or a scale factor.

The four components of the vector represent co-ordinates in a 4-dimensional space. The relationship between 3-dimensional space and the homogeneous 4-dimensional space is given by the transformations

$$[x \quad y \quad z] \rightarrow [hx \quad hy \quad hz \quad h]$$

and

$$\begin{bmatrix} x & y & z & h_1 \end{bmatrix} \rightarrow \begin{bmatrix} \frac{x}{h_1} & \frac{y}{h_1} & \frac{z}{h_1} \end{bmatrix}$$

The points at infinity and certain transformations (viz., translation and perspective projections) cannot be represented by 3-dimensional scheme. For simple transformations, such as, scaling and rotation we can use a 3×3 matrix but to generalize, so as to include other transformations as well, a 4×4 matrix as defined below is used.

$$T = \begin{bmatrix} t_{11} & t_{12} & t_{13} & t_{14} \\ t_{21} & t_{22} & t_{23} & t_{24} \\ t_{31} & t_{32} & t_{33} & t_{34} \\ t_{41} & t_{42} & t_{43} & t_{44} \end{bmatrix}$$

7.2.1.1 Points, Lines and Planes

It may be noted that a line in 2-D (see section 6.2.2.1) becomes a plane in 3-D. Points are 4-element row vectors:

$$P = [\, x \ y \ z \ w \,]$$

Planes (denoted by E) are 4-element column vectors:

$$E = \begin{bmatrix} a \\ b \\ c \\ d \end{bmatrix}$$

A conic section in 2-D is a family of 3-D surfaces comprising of cones, cylinder, ellipsoids and the like.

To find a plane passing through three given points, one must compute the cross product of P_1 and P_2. It is given by:

$$P_1 \times P_2 = (x_1, y_1, w_1) \times (x_2, y_2, w_2) = \begin{bmatrix} y_1w_2 - y_2w_1 \\ x_2w_1 - x_1w_2 \\ x_1y_2 - x_2y_1 \end{bmatrix} = \begin{bmatrix} a \\ b \\ c \end{bmatrix}$$

where

$$a = \det \begin{bmatrix} y_1 & w_1 \\ y_2 & w_2 \end{bmatrix}$$

We can write similar deteminants for b and c also. By analogy, the 4-D cross product of P_1, P_2 and P_3 is a column vector with:

$$a = \det \begin{bmatrix} y_1 & z_1 & w_1 \\ y_2 & z_2 & w_2 \\ y_3 & z_3 & w_3 \end{bmatrix}$$

The expression for b, c and d can be written similarly.

A 3-D homogeneous line [6] can be represented by an asymmetric matrix with six elements p, q, r, s, t and u. The matrix is given by

$$L = \begin{bmatrix} 0 & p & -q & r \\ -p & 0 & s & -t \\ q & -s & 0 & u \\ -r & t & u & 0 \end{bmatrix}$$

Given two points P_1 and P_2, we can find

$$p = \det \begin{bmatrix} z_1 & w_1 \\ z_2 & w_2 \end{bmatrix}, \quad q = \det \begin{bmatrix} y_1 & w_1 \\ y_2 & w_2 \end{bmatrix}, \quad r = \det \begin{bmatrix} x_1 & w_1 \\ x_2 & w_2 \end{bmatrix}$$

$$s = \det \begin{bmatrix} x_1 & w_1 \\ x_2 & w_2 \end{bmatrix}, \quad t = \det \begin{bmatrix} x_1 & z_1 \\ x_2 & z_2 \end{bmatrix}, \quad u = \det \begin{bmatrix} x_1 & y_1 \\ x_2 & y_2 \end{bmatrix}$$

If there are two planes E_1 and E_2, the equation of the line formed by their intersection can be calculated by using similar expressions. A given point $[x,y,z,w]$ lies on the line L, if the following vector/matrix product results in four zeros.

$$[x \;\; y \;\; z \;\; w]\, L = [0,\, 0,\, 0,\, 0]$$

7.2.2 Three-dimensional transformations

The cartesian co-ordinate system is generally used for representing transformations in three dimensions. As in the case of two dimensional transformations (section 6.2.1), we can express tranformations by a single entity, the transformation matrix. A complex transformation is obtained either by performing a sequence of primitive operations or by concatenating these operations in a single transformation matrix.

7.2.2.1 Scaling :

This transformation scales a point (x,y,z) to (x',y',z') as shown by the following equation,

$$[x' \quad y' \quad z' \quad 1] = [x \quad y \quad z \quad 1]\, T_s \tag{7.1}$$

where the matrix T_s is given by

$$T_s = \begin{bmatrix} T_{sx} & 0 & 0 & 0 \\ 0 & T_{sy} & 0 & 0 \\ 0 & 0 & T_{sz} & 0 \\ 0 & 0 & 0 & 1 \end{bmatrix}$$

The diagonal terms T_{sx}, T_{sy} and T_{sz} define the local scaling factors in the x, y and z directions, respectively. For getting uniform overall scaling we set, $T_{sx} = T_{sy} = T_{sz}$. Figure 7.1 shows the effect of scaling.

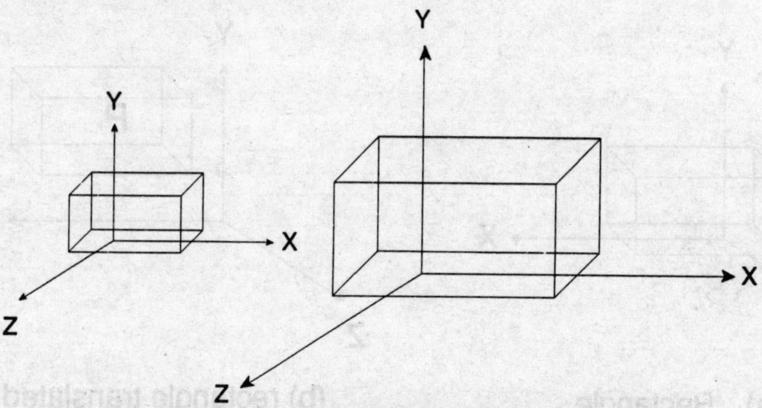

(a) Rectangle (b) Rectangle scaled by a factor of two

Figure 7.1 The Scaling Operation

Tapering along a axis:

Tapering is easily developed from scaling. Select a tapering axis and differentially scale the other two components. This defines a tapering function along the selected axis. To taper along the Z-axis:

$$\begin{aligned} x' &= r\,x \\ y' &= r\,y \\ z' &= z \end{aligned} \tag{7.2}$$

where $r = f(z)$ is a linear or non-linear tapering function.

7.2.2.2 Translation

A point (x,y,z) is translated to a position (x',y',z') through the following transformation,

$$[x' \quad y' \quad z' \quad 1] = [x \quad y \quad z \quad 1]\,T_T \tag{7.3}$$

where

$$T_T = \begin{bmatrix} 1 & 0 & 0 & 0 \\ 0 & 1 & 0 & 0 \\ 1 & 0 & 0 & 0 \\ T_{T_x} & T_{T_y} & T_{T_z} & 1 \end{bmatrix}$$

The terms T_{Tx}, T_{Ty} and T_{Tz} are the components of translation in the x, y, and z directions, respectively. Figure 7.2 shows the effect of translation.

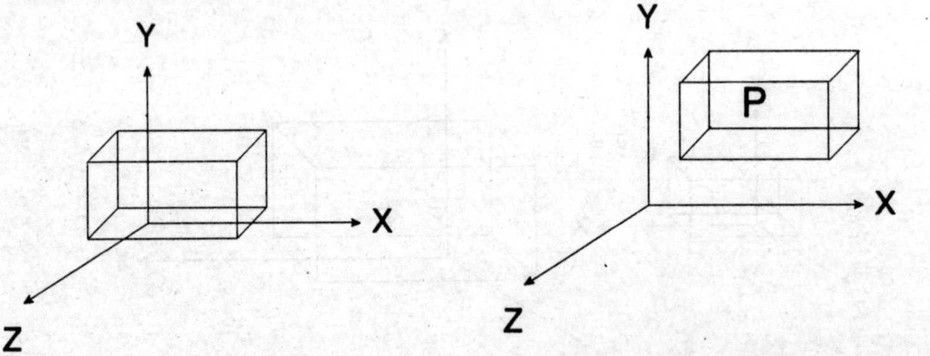

(a) Rectangle (b) rectangle translated to a new point (x' , y' , z')

Figure 7.2 The Translation Operation

7.2.2.3 Skewing

Skewing is a linear change of the co-ordinates of a point based on the values of certain of its other co-ordinates. A point (x, y, z) maps into another point (x', y', z') according to the following transformation

$$[x' \quad y' \quad z' \quad 1] = [x \quad y \quad z \quad 1]\, T_{SK} \tag{7.4}$$

where

$$T_{SK} = \begin{bmatrix} 1 & T_{12} & T_{13} & 0 \\ T_{21} & 1 & T_{23} & 0 \\ T_{31} & T_{32} & 1 & 0 \\ 0 & 0 & 0 & 1 \end{bmatrix}$$

The off-diagonal terms of basic 3×3 matrix (i.e., T_{12}, T_{13}, T_{21}, T_{23}, T_{31} and T_{32}) produce the skewing effect. In a simple case, skewing can transform a square into a parallelogram, as shown in figure 7.3.

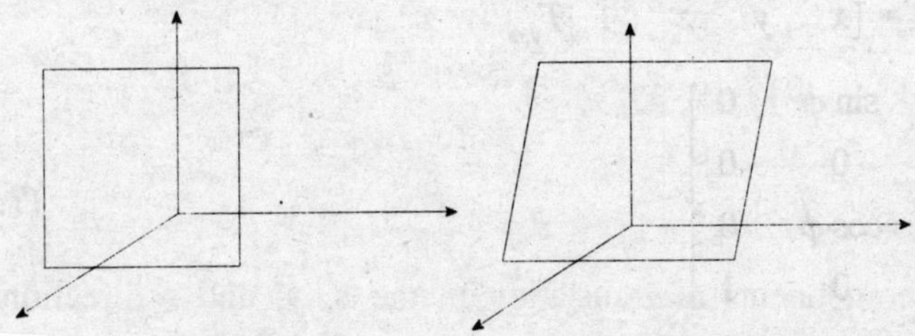

$$\begin{bmatrix} 1 & 0 & 0 & 0 \\ a & 1 & 0 & 0 \\ 0 & 0 & 1 & 0 \\ 0 & 0 & 0 & 1 \end{bmatrix}$$

(a) Original square (b) Skewed square (c) Tranformation Matrix ('a' is a constant)

Figure 7.3 Skewing Operation

7.2.2.4 Rotation :

In case of three-dimensional rotation, it is necessary to specify the axis about which to rotate. The matrices T_{RX}, T_{RY} and T_{RZ} denote rotation about axes X, Y and Z (in left handed system through an angle Θ, ϕ and ψ respectively. The angles are measured in the clock-wise directon about the origin when looking at the origin from a point on the positive side of the axis under consideration, as shown in figure 7.4.

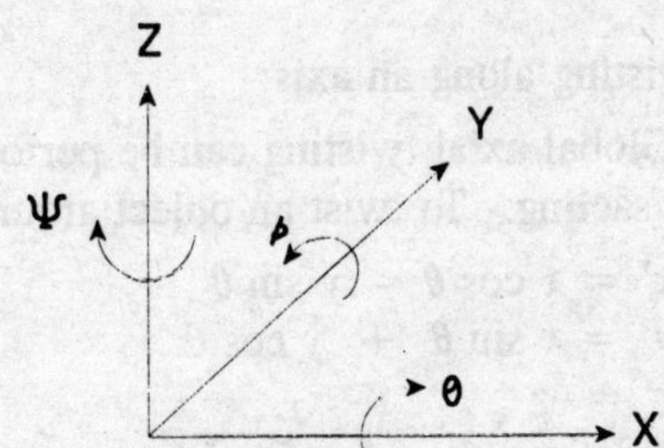

Direction of rotation is shown as seen by an observer standing on the postive side of the axis and looking at the origin

Figure 7.4 Rotation about X,Y, and Z axes in the left handed system

The various matrices for rotation are given below:

Rotation about the X axis, though the origin :

$$\begin{bmatrix} x' & y' & z' & 1 \end{bmatrix} = \begin{bmatrix} x & y & z & 1 \end{bmatrix} T_{x,\theta}$$

where
$$T_{x,\theta} = \begin{bmatrix} 1 & 0 & 0 & 0 \\ 0 & \cos\theta & \sin\theta & 0 \\ 0 & -\sin\theta & \cos\theta & 0 \\ 0 & 0 & 0 & 1 \end{bmatrix} \quad (7.5)$$

Rotation about the Y axis, through the origin :

$$[x' \quad y' \quad z' \quad 1] = [x \quad y \quad z \quad 1] T_{y,\phi}$$

where
$$T_{y,\phi} = \begin{bmatrix} \cos\phi & 0 & \sin\phi & 0 \\ 0 & 1 & 0 & 0 \\ -\sin\phi & 0 & \cos\phi & 0 \\ 0 & 0 & 0 & 1 \end{bmatrix} \quad (7.6)$$

Rotation about the Z axis through the origin:

$$[x' \quad y' \quad z' \quad 1] = [x \quad y \quad z \quad 1] T_{z,\psi}$$

where
$$T_{z,\psi} = \begin{bmatrix} \cos\psi & -\sin\psi & 0 & 0 \\ \sin\psi & \cos\psi & 0 & 0 \\ 0 & 0 & 1 & 0 \\ 0 & 0 & 0 & 1 \end{bmatrix} \quad (7.7)$$

Global axial twisting along an axis:

Global axial twisting can be performed as a differential rotation, just as tapering is a differential sacling. To twist an object around its *Z*-axis:

$$x' = x \cos\theta - y \sin\theta$$
$$y' = x \sin\theta + y \cos\theta$$
$$z' = z$$

where $\theta = f(z)$ defines the rate of twist per unit length along the *Z*-axis.

7.2.2.5 Rotation about an arbitrary point :

The following operations are needed to rotate about an arbitrary point:

i) translate the object to origin,
ii) rotate the object through the desired angle, and
iii) translate the object back to its position.

We can concatenate the above three operations to form a transformation matrix of the following form:

$$T = T_{TI} \; T_R \; T_{TF}$$

where T_{TI} = Initial translation matrix
T_R = Rotation Matrix
T_{TF} = Final translation matrix

We consider rotation about the *X*-axis followed by an equal rotation about the *Y*-axis, i.e, $\Theta = \phi$. Then

$$T_{RXY} = T_{RX}T_{RY} = \begin{bmatrix} \cos\theta & 0 & -\sin\theta & 0 \\ \sin^2\theta & \cos\theta & \cos\theta\ \sin\theta & 0 \\ \cos\theta\ \sin\theta & -\sin\theta & \cos^2\theta & 0 \\ 0 & 0 & 0 & 1 \end{bmatrix} \quad (7.8)$$

If we carry out rotation about y-axis first and about x-axis later, then

$$T_{RYX} = T_{RY}T_{RX} = \begin{bmatrix} \cos\theta & \sin^2\theta & -\cos\theta\ \sin\theta & 0 \\ 0 & \cos\theta & \sin\theta & 0 \\ \sin\theta & \cos\theta\ \sin\theta & \cos^2\theta & 0 \\ 0 & 0 & 0 & 1 \end{bmatrix} \quad (7.9)$$

We can see that $T_{RXY} \neq T_{RYX}$. The reason is that multiplication of matrices is not commutative. Therefore, changing the order of application of rotation transformation will result into different displays. Consequently, one must be very careful when concatenating a number of rotation operations.

An implementation of 3-dimensional transformations using Turbo Pascal will be discussed in section 7.8.7.

7.2.2.6 Structure deforming transformations

A global linear bend along an axis is a composite transformation. It comprises a bent region and a region outside the bent region where transformation is a rotation and a translation. Barr[2] defines a bend region along the *Y*-axis as:

$$y_{min} < y < y_{max}$$

The radius of curvature of the bend is $1/k$ and the centre of the bend is located at $y = y_0$. The bending angle is given by:

$$y' = \begin{cases} y_{\min} & \text{if} \quad y \le y_{\min} \\ y & \text{if} \quad y_{\min} < y < y_{\max} \\ y_{\max} & \text{if} \quad y \ge y_{\max} \end{cases}$$

The deformation transformation is given by:

$$x' = x$$

$$y' = \begin{cases} -\sin\theta\,(z - 1/k) + y_0 & \text{if} \quad y_{\min} \le y \le y_{\max} \\ -\sin\theta(z - 1/k) + y_0 + \cos\theta\,(y - y_{\min}) & \text{if} \quad y < y_{\min} \\ -\sin\theta\,(z - 1/k) + y_0 + \cos\theta\,(y - y_{\max}) & \text{if} \quad y > y_{\max} \end{cases} \quad (7.10)$$

$$z' = \begin{cases} \cos\theta\,(z - 1/k) + 1/k & \text{if} \quad z_{\min} \le z \le z_{\max} \\ \cos\theta\,(z - 1/k) + 1/k + \sin\theta\,(y - y_{\min}) & \text{if} \quad z < z_{\min} \\ \cos\theta\,(z - 1/k) + 1/k + \sin\theta\,(y - y_{\max}) & \text{if} \quad z > z_{\max} \end{cases}$$

7.3 Projections

Projections are used to obtain two-dimensional views of a three-dimensional object and are a very important type of transformation. Our eyes, cameras, or other imaging devices construct an image by projecting points from a three-dimensional scene onto an image plane. Figure 7.5 shows a geometry where the view point, 'V', is behind the image plane, so that the image appears right side up. If the image plane is behind the point of projection, the image will be reversed. Projections of this type are called perspective projections.

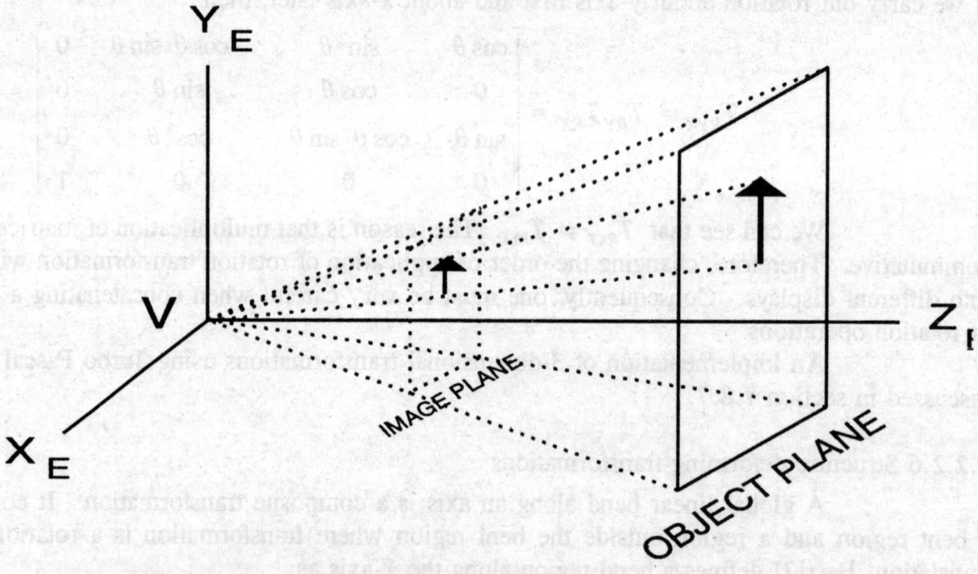

Figure 7.5 Projection of an object from object plane to image plane

To generate a perspective projection of a scene on the display we project each point of the scene on the plane of the display which in this case is the image plane. The co-ordinates of a point on the screen are represented by symbols X_s and Y_s. The distance '*F*' between the view point '*V*' and the display plane is often referred to as the *focal length* in this context. It can be observed that as the object approches the viewpoint its projection becomes larger and vice versa. This can be understood through the geometry of similar triangles *VO'R'* and *VOR* in Y_E - Z_E plane as shown in figure 7.6.

The projection height, Y_S, of the object is related to its real height, Y_E, through the equation

$$\frac{Y_s}{F} = \frac{Y_E}{Z_E} \tag{7.11}$$

Similarly, taking the relationship in the X_E - Z_E plane we can write

$$\frac{X_s}{F} = \frac{X_E}{Z_E} \tag{7.12}$$

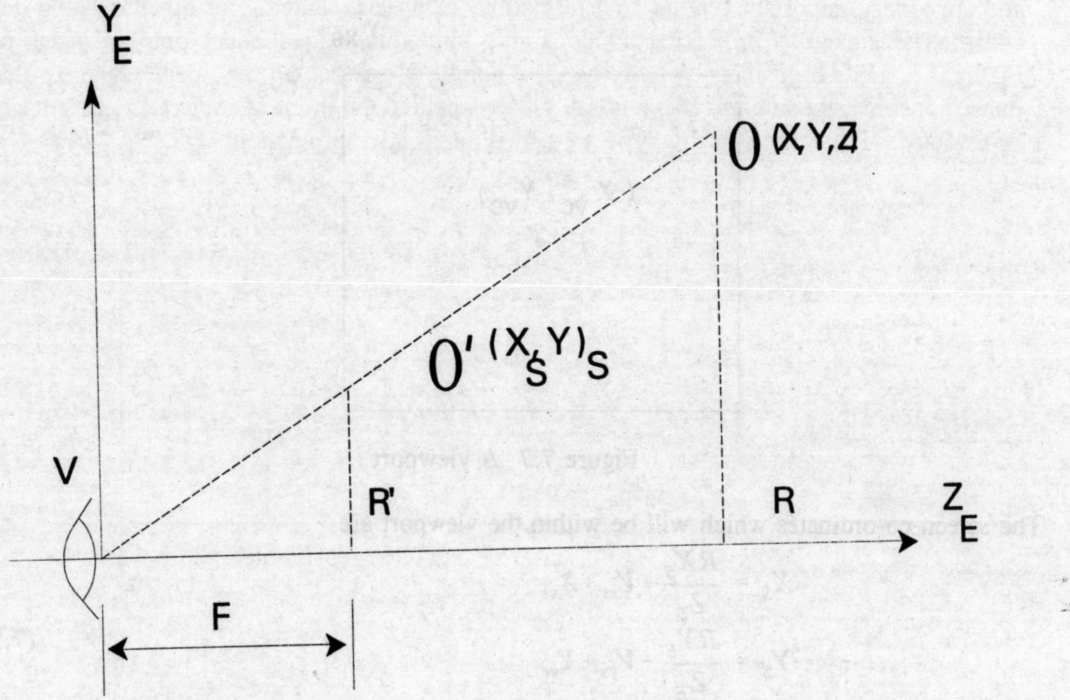

Figure 7.6 Projection of object in Y_e-Z_e plane

Thus, the screen co-ordinates X_S and Y_S of a point are given by

$$X_S = \frac{FX_E}{Z_E} \quad \text{and} \quad Y_S = \frac{FY_E}{Z_E} \tag{7.13}$$

We can convert the numbers X_S and Y_S into dimensionless quantities by dividing the values of X_S and Y_S in the above equation by the screen size, say S. If we represent ratio F/S by R then

$$X_S = \frac{RX_E}{Z_E} \quad \text{and} \quad Y_S = \frac{RY_E}{Z_E} \tag{7.14}$$

Furthermore, it may be useful to represent the image within a given viewport on the screen. The viewport can be defined having centre point at (X_{vc}, Y_{vc}), width of $2Vx_s$ units and height of $2V_{ys}$ units as shown in figure 7.7.

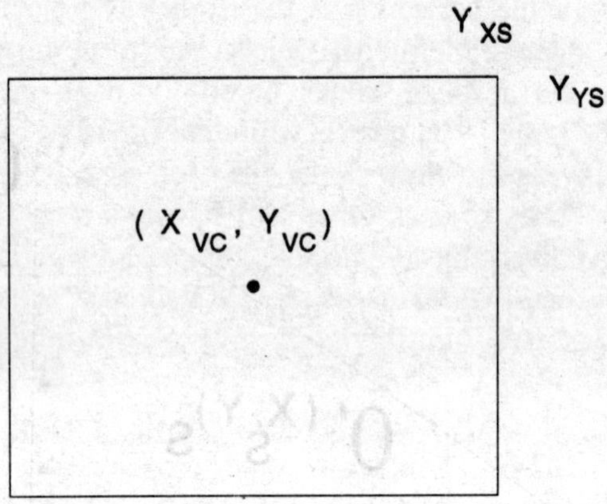

Figure 7.7 A viewport

The screen co-ordinates which will be within the viewport are

$$X_S = \frac{RX_S}{Z_E} - V_{xs} + X_{vc}$$

$$Y_S = \frac{RY_E}{Z_E} - V_{ys} + Y_{vc} \qquad (7.37)$$

Perspective projection yields orthographic (orthogonal) projection as a special case, when the viewpoint approaches infinity in the *z*-direction. This results in projection of all objects onto the image plane with no distortion of their *x* and *y* values. If the plane of projection is the *X-Y* plane, then one can simply set the *z* co-ordinate equal to zero to obtain orthographic projection. Similarly, we can set the *x* and *y* co-ordinates to zero for *Y-Z* and *X-Z* planes respectively. Figure 7.8 shows orthographic projections of an object on conventional horizontal and vertical planes.

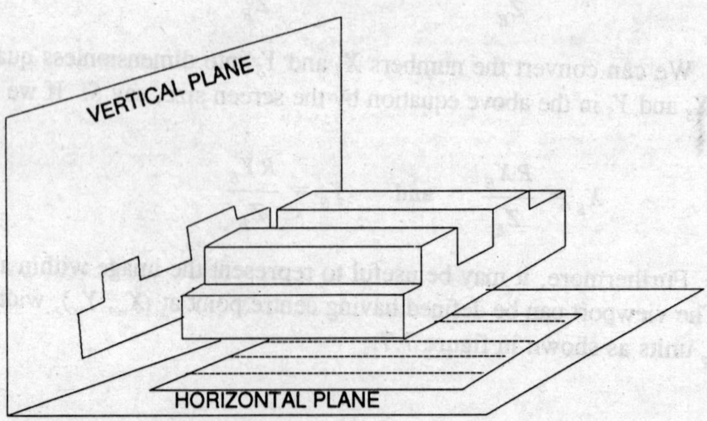

Figure 7.8 Orthographic projection of an object
on horizontal and vertical plane

Another orthographic projection is the isometric projection. Figure 7.9 is the isometric projection of the three dimensional object shown in figure 7.8. An isometric projection is obtained when the absolute values of all the components of the direction of projection specification are the same. The objects with opposite faces parallel and adjacent faces perpendicular are particularly easy to draw using the isometric projections. Other objects, having their opposite faces inclined to each other , or having a complicated shape, are not so easily drawn isometrically. Another objection to the universal adoption of 'one plane' methods of projection in industrial practice is that, unless special technique is used to prevent it, objects so depicted tend to appear distorted. Furthermore, only certain dimensions can be measured directly from such projections.

Orthographic projections are used to represent three dimensional objects on a plane surface (e.g., sheet of paper) as a standard method in engineering practice. When the projections are drawn following standard rules and conventions (types of lines, lettering, dimensioning and tolerancing , etc.) the resulted drawing is referred to as engineering drawing.

Figure 7.9 Isometric projection

All lines in the view are edges of the object, i.e., they are 'isometric lines.'

Example 7.1:

This example explains the procedure for representing three dimensional objects on a plane surface which has two dimensions only. Multiview orthographic projections (two to six two-dimensional views) are commonly used to represent three dimensional objects in engineering drawing. Figure 7.11 depicts the arrangement of six principle views as per

American Standard of the object shown in figure 7.10.

The following definitions are used in reference to figure 7.11 :

Line of sight of view:	the direction from which the object is viewed.
Adjacent views:	any two views placed side by side with common dimensions aligned.
Related views:	a view adjacent to the same view.
Parallels:	The parallel lines connecting and aligning adjacent views.

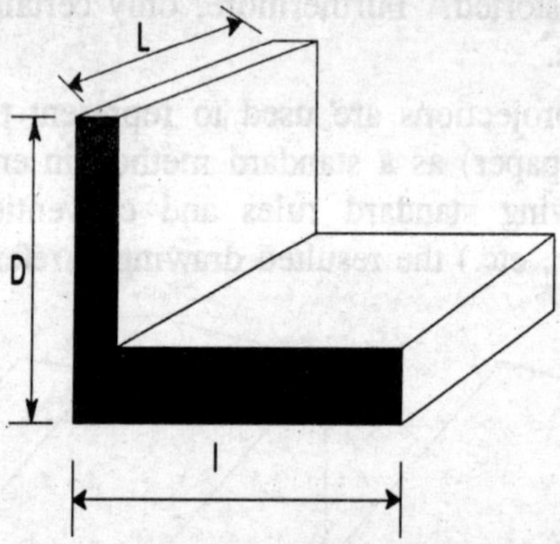

Figure 7.10 A three dimensional object

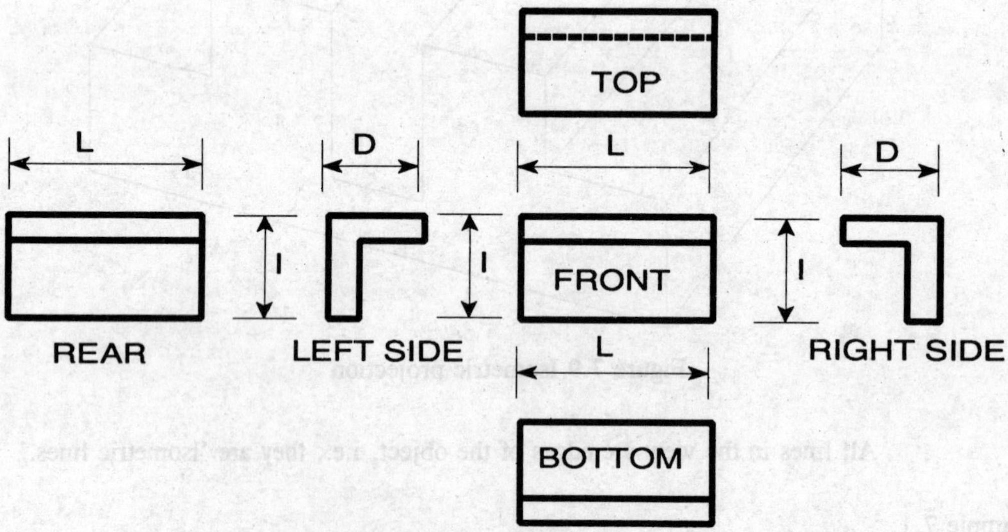

Figure 7.11 Multi-view orthographic projection of the object shown in figure 7.10

For example, the top and front views are adjacent views but the left side and top views are related views (see figure 7.11).

It is evident that each view provides information not in the other views and to understand a three-dimensional object, information from one view must be used in co-ordinated way with the other view. The hidden details are shown in a view by broken lines.

Example 7.2: Figure 7.12 shows three orthographic views (front, top and right side) of a three drawer chest.

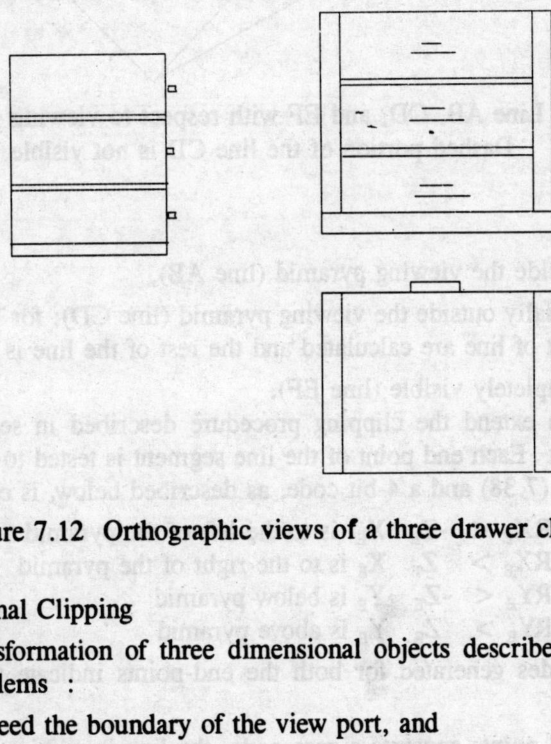

Fiogure 7.12 Orthographic views of a three drawer chest

7.4 Three Dimensional Clipping

The transformation of three dimensional objects described in section 7.2 may result in following problems :

i) Objects may exceed the boundary of the view port, and

ii) Object behind the view port may appear on the screen.

For eliminating these effects, each point in the eye co-ordinate system can be tested against a viewing pyramid, which defines the visibility zone. For a point to be within the visible zone, it must meet the following criteria:

$$-Z_E \leq RX_E \leq Z_E$$

and

$$-Z_E \leq RY_E \leq Z_E \qquad (7.16)$$

The points behind the view point have their Z_E co-ordinate value less than or equal to zero. Points satisfying these tests are mapped on the display screen by using equation (7.13).

The procedure for checking whether a line is within the viewing zone or not is not simple. Clipping technique is used to check the status of a line with respect to the viewing pyramid. The various possibilities are (see figure 7.13):

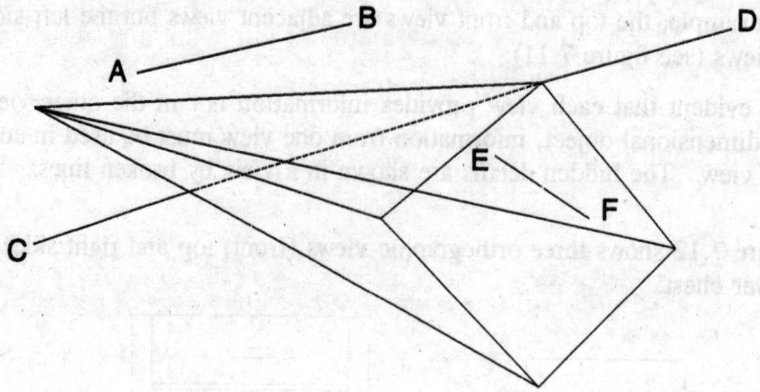

Figure 7.13 Line AB, CD, and EF with respect to viewing pyramid shown. Dashed portion of the line CD is not visible.

i) the line is outside the viewing pyramid (line AB),

ii) the line is partially outside the viewing pyramid (line CD); for such lines, end points of the visible part of line are calculated and the rest of the line is rejected,

iii) the line is completely visible (line EF).

We can extend the clipping procedure described in section 6.5 to solve three dimensional problems. Each end point of the line segment is tested to see whether it is outside the limits of equation (7.38) and a 4-bit code, as described below, is computed :

bit 1 : $RX_E < -Z_E$ X_E is to the left of the pyramid
bit 2 : $RX_E > Z_E$ X_E is to the right of the pyramid
bit 3 : $RY_E < -Z_E$ Y_E is below pyramid
bit 4 : $RY_E > Z_E$ Y_E is above pyramid

The codes generated for both the end-points indicate the status of the line as described below :

i) If both the end points generate a zero code, the line is within the viewing pyramid and is accepted,

ii) If the logical *AND* of the codes for both the end points is non-zero, the line is invisible and is rejected,

iii) else the line intersects one or more planes of the viewing pyramid. The point of intersection of line and the plane is computed and replaced by the point which is invisible.

The end points of the visible segments of the line are then mapped onto the screen and the line segment can be drawn using the procedure described in chapter 3.

A Pascal procedure for implementing the clipping algorithm is given below :

Procedure Clip_3D (VAR XI, YI; ZI, XF, YF, ZF : REAL ; visible Boolean)
{ (XI, YI, ZI) and (XF, YF, ZF) are the co-ordinates of the initial and Final points of the line segment to be clipped}

```
Type
   Segment  =  (left, right, upper, lower) ;
   End_Code =  set of Segment;
Var
   k, kI, kF  :  End-Code ;
   x, y,  z, xFI, yFI, zFI,t  :  real  ;
Procedure Code (x, y,z : real ; var k: End_Code)
begin
   k := [ ] ;
   If X < -Z  then k :=  [left]
       else  if X >  Z then  k := [right] ;
   If Y < - Z then k :=  k + [lower]
       else if y > Z then k := [upper] ;
end ; {code}
begin
 Code (XI, YI, ZI, kI) ;
 Code (XF, YF, ZF, kF) ;
 While (kI <> [ ]) or (kF <> []) do
  begin
    If (kI*kF) <> [ ]  then
      begin
        visible :=  False ;
        exit (clip)
      end;
    k := kI ;
    If k = [ ] then k := kF ;
    XFI := XF - XI;
    YFI := YF - YI;
    ZFI := ZF - ZI;
    Case k of
     left :  begin
               t := (ZI + XI)/((XI - XF) - ZFI) ;
               z := t * ZFI + ZI;
               x := -Z;
               Y := t * YFI + YI
             end;
     right : begin
               t := (ZI - XI)/(XFI - ZFI) ;
               z := t * ZFI + ZI ;
               x := z ;
```

```
            y := t * YFI + YI
          end ;
    upper : begin
            t := (ZI - YI)/ (YFI - ZFI) ;
            z := t * ZFI + ZI ;
            x := t * XFI + XI ;
            y := z
          end ;
   lower : begin
            t := (ZI + YI)/((YI - YF) - ZFI) ;
            z := t * ZFI + ZI ;
            x := t * XFI + XI ;
            y := -z
          end ;
   end; {case}
 If k = kI then
   begin
     XI : = x ; YI := y ;  ZI := z ;
     Code (x,y,z, kI)
   end
   else
     begin
        XF := x ; YF := y , ZF := z ;
        Code (X, Y, Z, kF)
     end;
 end; {while}
     {if the line segment is defined by points (XI,YI,ZI) and visible := True then
       (XF,YF,ZF) is visible}
end;  {Clip - 3D}
```

The above procedure computes the intersection of the line and the plane using following parametric equation:

$$((1-T)[XI \quad YI \quad ZI\,] + T[XF \quad YF \quad ZF\,])\begin{bmatrix} A \\ B \\ 1 \end{bmatrix} = 0 \qquad (7.17)$$

where A and B take different values to define different planes. For example, setting $A = 1$ and $B = 0$ defines the plane $x = Z$.

Example 7.3: The following examples illustrate three dimensional transformation methods.

i) Consider a solid object (see figure 7.14) which has vertex points as given in the following table.

Vertex Number	Co-ordinates		
	X	Y	Z
1	-1	1	-1
2	1	1	1
3	1	-1	-1
4	-1	-1	-1
5	-1	1	-2
6	1	1	-2
7	1	-1	-2
8	-1	-1	-2

One method of showing the edges of the object is to use the connectivity matrix. Given the vertex list and connectivity matrix, a three dimensional object is fully defined.

The connectivity matrix for the object under consideration is given in the following table.

Vertex	1	2	3	4	5	6	7	8
1	1							
2	1	1						
3	0	1	1					
4	1	0	1	1				
5	1	0	0	0	1			
6	0	1	0	0	1	1		
7	0	0	1	0	0	1	1	
8	0	0	0	1	1	0	1	1

The connectivity matrix shows how the vertices of the object depicted in figure 7.14 are connected to each other. Thus, it defines the edges. Since, the matrix is symmetrical, it is necessary to show the entries on only one side of the matrix. This also saves storage space. In this case, we can store only those subscript pairs that identify the nonzero entries of the lower triangular matrix, noting the fact that diagonal terms only give redundant information (i.e., a vertex is connected to itself). As a result, considerable saving in the memory can be obtained. The information in the connectivity matrix can then be shown as in the following table:

Connection Point	1	2	3	4	5	6	7	8	9	10	11	12
Row	2	3	4	4	5	6	6	7	7	8	8	8
Column	1	2	1	3	1	2	5	3	6	4	5	7

Figure 7.14 Shows geometry of the object

The connectivity matrix required $8 \times 8 = 64$ nodes of storage but this scheme reduces it to only 24 words. Figure 7.14 shows the interconnection of vertices of the object. The vertices define the faces of the object (see the table given below) as under:

Face Number	Vertex Number			
	1	2	3	4
1	1	5	8	4
2	5	6	7	8
3	6	2	3	7
4	1	4	3	2
5	8	7	3	4
6	6	5	1	2

The faces, in turn, are defined in terms of edges. For example, the first face, denoted by (1 5 4 8), is defined by the connectivity matrix shown in the folllowing table.

Face	1	5	4
1	1		
5	1	1	
4	1	0	1
5	0	1	1

We can generate pairs of vertices from above matrix to define edges in form of row and column. This is shown in the following table.

Connection Point	Row	Column
1	5	1
2	4	1
3	8	5
4	8	4

This information is stored in two linear lists (vectors) called ROW and COLUMN, defining the edges. As we process each face, care has to be taken that no edge is stored more than once. For example, face [6 5 1 2] has the edge (5 1), which is common with the face [1 5 4 8], and hence, is already stored in vectors ROW and COLUMN. Thus, to make a list of edges, we need efficient methods to search and insert entries. Linear linked lists and circular lists described in chapter 4 can be used to advantage.

ii) Figure 7.15 shows the perspective view of the object.

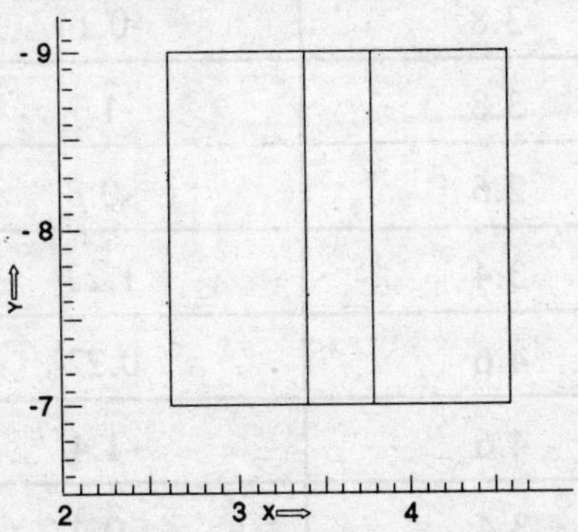

Figure 7.15 Perspective view of object before rotation

iii) The object is rotated about the origin in the direction of Y axis through 53.13 degrees and the new co-ordinates of the vertex points are computed using equation (7.20). The list of vertex point is given below:

Vertex Number	Coordinates		
	X	Y	Z
1	2.6	-7	-10.7
2	3.8	-7	-9.1
3	3.8	-9	-9.7
4	2.6	-9	-10.7
5	3.4	-7	-11.3
6	4.6	7	-9.7
7	4.6	-9	-9.7
8	3.4	-9	-11.3

iv) The object is again rotated about the origin in the direction of X-axis through an angle of -36.8°. The new vertex list, computed using equation (7.18), is given below:

Vertex Number	Coordinates		
	X	Y	Z
1	2.6	0.82	-12.7
2	3.8	-0.14	-11.4
3	3.8	-1.7	-12.7
4	2.6	-0.8	-13.9
5	3.4	1.22	-13.2
6	4.6	0.22	-11.9
7	4.6	-1.4	-13.1
8	3.4	-0.4	-14.4

The perspective view of the object after rotation first in the direction of Y and then the X axis is shown in figure 7.16.

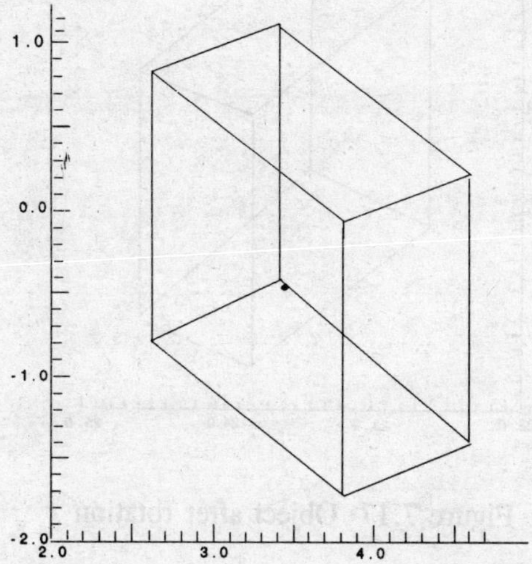

Figure 7.16 Perspective view of the object after rotation

v) The object is then translated to a point (20,0,0). The vertex points are recomputed using equation 7.20 as given below:

Vertex Number	Coordinates		
	X	Y	Z
1	22.6	0.82	-12.7
2	23.8	-0.14	-11.4
3	23.8	-1.7	-12.7
4	22.6	-0.8	-13.9
5	23.4	-1.22	-13.2
6	24.6	0.22	-11.9
7	24.6	-1.4	-13.1
8	23.4	-0.4	-11.3

Figure 7.17 shows the view of the object after translation.

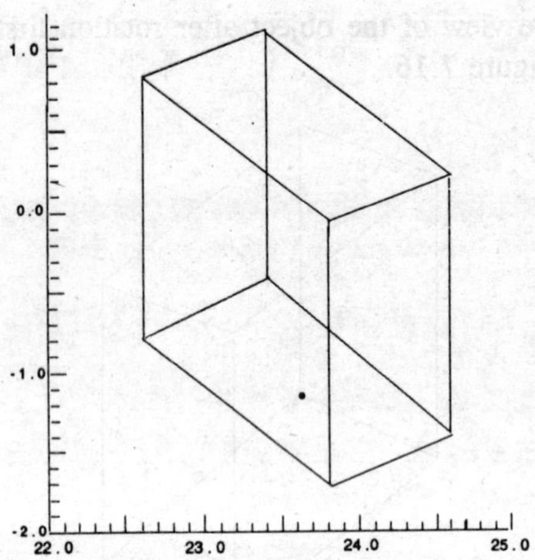

Figure 7.17 Object after rotation

7.5 Representation of depth

Perspective projection described in the earlier section produced a two- dimensional image on the screen surface. This image was described in screen co-ordinate system. In order to display a realistic image of a scene, we must consider which objects obscure others. It is necessary, therefore, to retain depth information for each point in the screen co-ordinate system.

To circumvent this problem, we define a point on the screen by three co-ordinates (X_S, Y_S, Z_S). The co-ordinate X_S and Y_S give the perspective views of a point on the screen surface. The co-ordinate Z_S is calculated to retain the information about depth. While displaying the point (X_S, Y_S, Z_S), if we ignore Z_S, the display becomes the orthographic projection of the screen co- ordinate system.

The value of Z_S should be computed such that

i) for $Z_{E1} > Z_{E2} > 0$ the value of $Z_{S1} > Z_{S2} > 0$ and

ii) a straight line in the eye co-ordinate system should map into a straight line. Also a plane must transform into a plane, i.e.,

$$AX_E + BY_E + CZ_E + D = 0 \rightarrow A'X_S + B'Y_S + C'Z_S + D' = 0$$

To satisfy above condition, Z_S should be defined in the following form :

$$Z_s = u + \frac{v}{Z_E} \tag{7.18}$$

The values of u and v should be chosen such that Z_S remains within a desirable range. To satisfy the first condition the value of 'v' should be less than zero.

The perspective transform can, therefore, be redefined as follows :

$$X_S = \frac{X_F}{h}, \qquad Y_S = \frac{Y_E}{h}$$

$$Z_S = \frac{uZ_E + v}{Rh}, \quad h = \frac{Z_E}{R} \tag{7.19}$$

The number h is directly related with depth and can be considered the fourth dimension in the eye co-ordinate system. We can now represent eq. (7.17) in the form of a 4×4 matrix.

$$[x \ y \ z \ h] \quad = \quad [X_E \ Y_E \ Z_E \ 1] \ T_P \tag{7.20}$$

where

$$T_p = \begin{bmatrix} 1 & 0 & 0 & 0 \\ 0 & 1 & 0 & 0 \\ 0 & 0 & \frac{U}{R} & \frac{1}{R} \\ 0 & 0 & \frac{V}{R} & 1 \end{bmatrix}$$

and the screen co-ordinates are given by

$$X_S = \frac{x}{h}, \quad Y_S = \frac{y}{h}, \quad Z_S = \frac{z}{h} \tag{7.21}$$

Now, we can concatenate matrix T_P with other transformations. However, we must perform clipping on the result of equation (7.19) i.e., coordinate (x,y,z), keeping the clipping limit as

$$-h \leq x \leq h \quad \text{and} \quad -h \leq y \leq h$$

to guarantee that lines will be in front of view point and within the viewing pyramid. The points obtained after clipping can be used for computing the screen co-ordinates X_S, Y_S and Z_S by equation (7.18).

Example 7.4:

This example computes the values of U and V for equation (7.17) such that the resultant value of Z_S represents the range of values of Z_E precisely and in a spepcified range. The range of values of screen co-ordinates are defined as below:

$$-1 \leq X_S \leq 1$$
$$-1 \leq Y_S \leq 1$$
$$0 \leq Z_S \leq 1$$

The above ranges permit adoption of values to suit any display size and hardware. The maximum value of depth in eye co-ordinate system is limited to a value, say M. This truncates the viewing pyramid. If we take the minimum value of Z_E equal to F (the distance of image plane from the view point), the viewing pyramid looks as shown in figure 7.18.

We can now calculate the values of U and V by using the following conditions in equation (7.17).

i) $Z_S = 0$ for $Z_E = F$ and
ii) $Z_S = 1$ for $Z_E = M$.

Hence,

$$Z_S = \frac{1}{1 - F/M}\left(1 - \frac{F}{Z_E}\right) \tag{7.22}$$

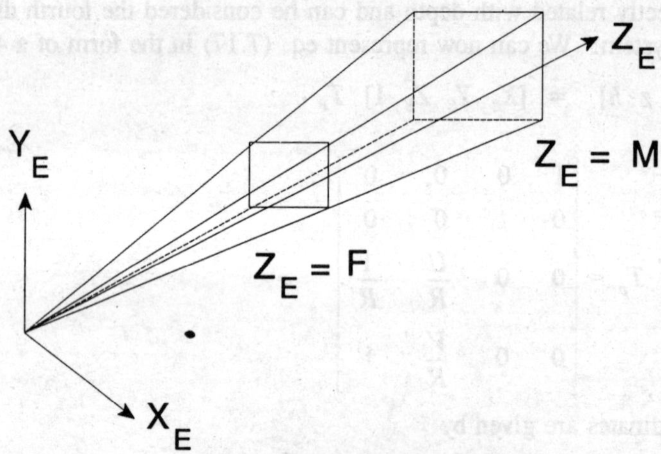

Figure 7.18 Viewbox obtained by truncation of viewing pyramid (F <= Ze <= M)

The values of U and V can be substituted in T_P, the perspective transformation matrix in equation (7.20).

7.6 Hidden Line and Surface Removal

Figure 7.19 (a) shows all the lines of a solid pyramid shaped object. Since, the object is made of opaque material, to create the impression of solid display the dashed line shown in figure 7.19(b) should be identified and removed. The invisible lines will, of course, depend on the view point. Similarly, if instead of lines, we consider the faces of the object, the problem is referred to as hidden surface removal.

In the 1960's the displays were line drawing devices and hence, the emphasis on the techniques developed in those days was on removal of hidden lines. With the use of raster scan devices for graphics, hidden surface algorthms have become popular. Micro-computers (including the IBM PC) use a raster scan display for graphics. Therefore, we shall focus our attention on hidden surface algorithms.

To display an object, Z_S can be used to represent shades of grey (or notion of depth). Thus, a 3-dimensional object in the screen co-ordinate system can be represented by a 2-dimensional matrix. The row and column number correspond to the Y_S and X_S co-ordinates respectively, and the value stored at that location corresponds to Z_S.

As large arrays of points are used to define a shaded picture, it can be reproduced by scanning it in a raster fashion. Pictures generated in this mode are called 'raster-scan' pictures.

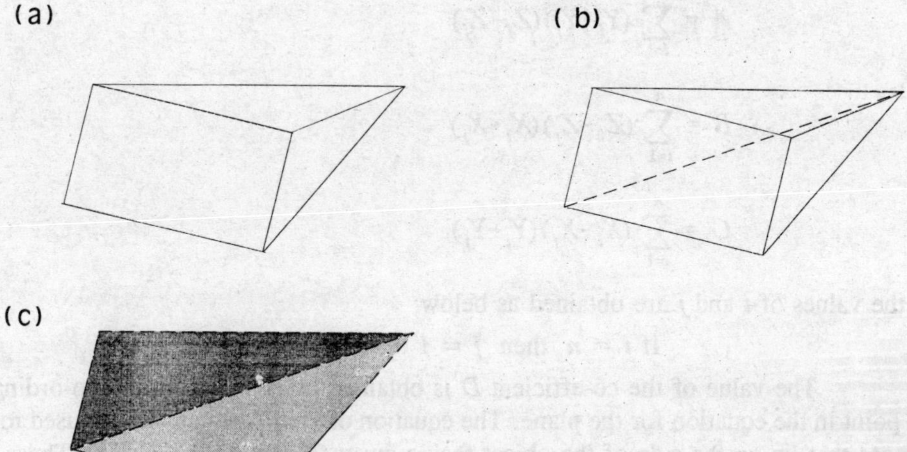

Figure 7-19 (a) A pyramid shaped object. (b) Dashed line depicts the hidden line. (c) Hatched area shows hidden surfaces.

The following steps are needed to produce a picture of an opaque object:

i) Input parameters: description of object, desired viewing point, and direction for a hypothetical observer

ii) Generate perspepctive prjection of the object, and

iii) Solve hidden surface problem for picture obtained in step (ii).

7.6.1 Equations for Planes

The equation of a plane containing a face of an object is used for computing the depth of the face at various (x, y) co-ordinates in the screen co-ordinate system. The equation of a plane representing a face is

$$AX + BY + CZ + D = 0 \tag{7.23}$$

where A, B, C and D are the co-efficients and are computed from the coordinates of the vertices or known points on the plane. Equation (7.23) may be written in the matrix form as

$$\begin{bmatrix} x & Y & Z & 1 \end{bmatrix} \begin{bmatrix} A \\ B \\ C \\ D \end{bmatrix} = 0 \tag{7.24}$$

The following procedure can be used for computing the co-efficients efficiently from a set of 'n' known points, often the vertices of the face of an object :

$$A = \sum_{i=1}^{n} (Y_i - Y_j)(Z_i + Z_j)$$

$$B = \sum_{i=1}^{n} (Z_i - Z_j)(X_i + X_j) \qquad (7.24)$$

$$C = \sum_{i=1}^{n} (X_i - X_j)(Y_i + Y_j)$$

where the values of i and j are obtained as below:

If $i = n$ then $j = 1$ else $j = j+1$.

The value of the co-efficient D is obtained by substituting the co-ordinates of a known point in the equation for the plane. The equation of the plane can also be used to identify those faces that lie on the side of the object facing away from the view point. These faces of the object are called back faces. This procedure is explained in section 7.6.5.

For convex polyhedra, removal of back faces greatly simplifies the hidden line/surface problem. In case of one object scenes (say, a cube) the removal of backfaces solves the hidden line problem.

7.6.2 Min-max Test

If two polygons do not overlap in X_S or Y_S, then possibily they also do not obscure each other (see figure 7.20(a)). This characteristic can be used to reject polygons, on the overlap basis with respect to a given polygon.

The principle is that if the maximum X_S co-ordinate of polygon is less than minimum X_S co-ordinate of another polygon, then the two polygons cannot possibly overlap each other in X_S. A similar test is carried out for the Y_S.

Thus, we enclose each polygon in a rectangular box defined by vertices, (X_{SMIN}, Y_{SMIN}), (X_{SMIN}, X_{SMAX}), (X_{SMAX}, Y_{SMAX}) and (X_{SMIN}, Y_{SMAX}). In figure 7.20(b), we see a case where boxes do overlap but the enclosed polygons do not. Hence, the minmax test fails in such situations.

In such cases, more elaborate tests have to be performed, i.e., each edge of one polygon is to be compared against each edge of the other polygon to determine intersection. Figure 7.20(c) shows a case where both polygons and boxes intersect. A min-max test in Z_S can often select the foremost of the two polygons known to overlap on X_S and Y_S.

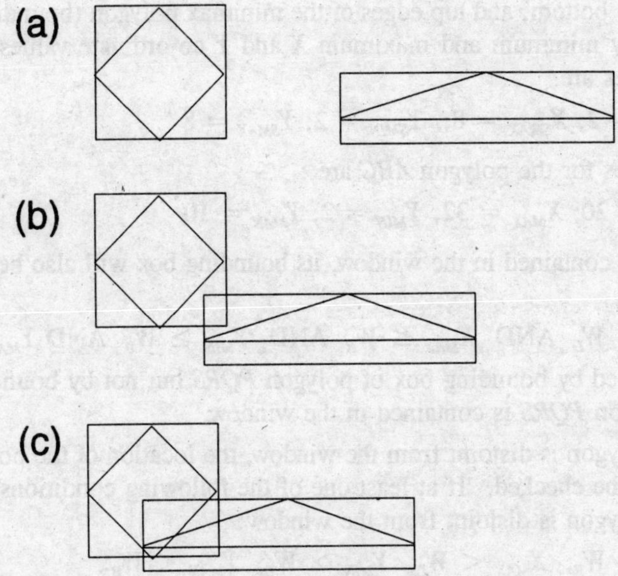

Figure 7.20 Min-max test
(a): Boxes do not overlap
(b): Boxes overlap but plygons do not overlap
(c): polygon and boxes overlap.

Example 7.5: Given a window with left, right bottom and top edges (W_L, W_R, W_B and W_T) equal to 0, 16, 0, 16 respectively, consider two polygons *PQRS* and *ABC* with vertices *P*(2,4), *Q*(4, 8), *R*(8, 4), *S*(4, 2), *A*(20, 10), *B*(32, 6) and *C*(24, 2) as shown in figure 7.21. Determine if the polygons are contained or disjoint with respect to the window.

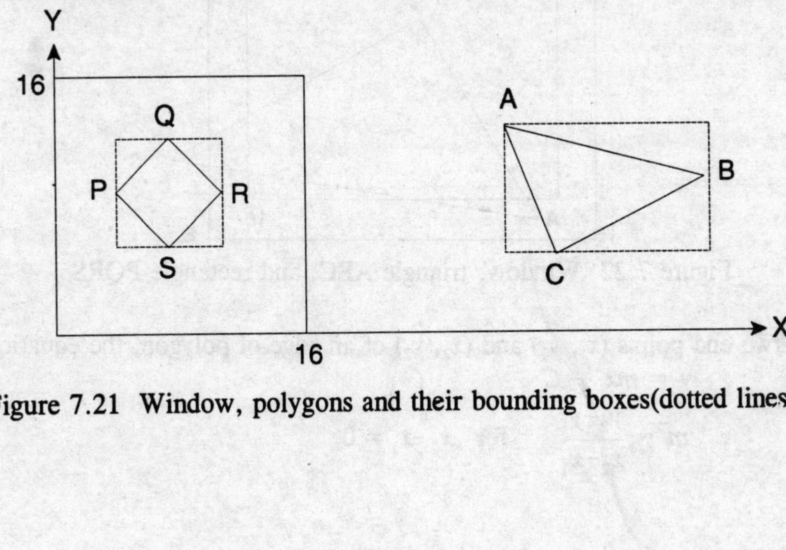

Figure 7.21 Window, polygons and their bounding boxes(dotted lines)

The left, right, bottom, and top edges of the minimax polygon (bounding box) for polygon *PQRS* are defined by minimum and maximum *X* and *Y* co-ordinate values of vertices *P*, *Q*, *R*, and *S*. These values are:

$$X_{SMIN} = 2;\ X_{SMAX} = 8;\ \ Y_{SMIN} = 2;\ Y_{SMAX} = 8$$

Similarly bounding box values for the polygon *ABC* are :

$$X_{MIN} = 20;\ X_{MAX} = 32;\ Y_{MIN} = 2;\ Y_{MAX} = 10$$

If a polygon is contained in the window, its bounding box will also be contained, i.e.,

$$X_{MIN} \geq W_L \text{ AND } X_{MAX} \leq W_R \text{ AND } Y_{MIN} \geq W_B \text{ AND } Y_{MAX} \leq W_T.$$

The above condition is satisfied by bounding box of polygon *PQRS* but not by bounding box of polygon *ABC*. Hence, polygon *PQRS* is contained in the window.

To test if a polygon is disjoint from the window, the location of the bounding box with respect to window is to be checked. If at least one of the following conditions is satisfied by the bounding box, the polygon is disjoint from the window:

$$X_{MIN} > W_R;\ X_{MAX} < W_L;\ Y_{MIN} > W_T;\ Y_{MAX} < W_B.$$

The bounding box for the polygon *ABC* satisfies the first condition. Hence, the polygon ABC is disjoint from the window.

Example 7.6: Consider a triangle *ABC* and rectangle *PQRS* with co-ordinates of vertices given by *A*(0, -1), *B*(4, 10), *C*(20, 4), *P*(-2, -2), *Q*(-2, 18), *R*(20, 18) and S(18, -2), respectively, as shown in figure 7.22. Find the location of the triangle and the rectangle with respect to the window of example 7.5.

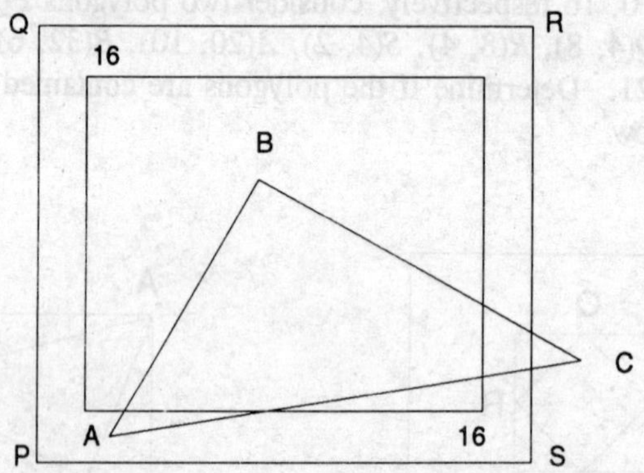

Figure 7.22 Window, triangle ABC, and rectangle PQRS

Given two end points (x_1, y_1) and (x_2, y_2) of an edge of polygon, the equation of edge is given by : $y = mx + C$

where $$m = \frac{y_2 - y_1}{x_2 - x_1} \quad \text{for } x_2 - x_1 \neq 0$$

and, $C = y_1 - mx_1$

A function F can be formed such that

$$F = y - mx - C$$

For edge AB of ABC,

$$m = \frac{10-(-1)}{4-0} = \frac{11}{4} = 2.75$$

$$C = y(0) - 2.75x(0) = -1$$

Hence, the function F for edge AB is given by

$$F = y - 2.75x + 1$$

The coordinates of each window corner are substituted in the function F and the results obtained are given below:

$$F(0, 0) = 1$$
$$F(0, 16) = 16 + 1 = 17$$
$$F(16, 16) = 16 - ((11/4)*16) + 1 = -27$$
$$F(16, 0) = 0 - ((11/4)*16) + 1 = -43$$

It is observed that value of function 'F' is positive for end points (0,0) and (0, 16) and negative for end points (16, 16) and (16, 0) of the window. Since, the sign of function F changes, the triangle intersects the window.

To find the location of rectangle $PQRS$ with respect to a window, the function F is computed for each edge. The results are tabulated below :

Edge of F polygon	Window	Value of F	Sign changes	
PQ	X + 2	0, 0	2	No
		16, 0	18	
		0, 16	2	
		16, 16	18	
S	Y - 18	0, 0	-18	No
		16, 0	-18	
		0, 16	-2	
		16, 16	-2	
RS	Y-10X+182	0, 0	182	No
		16, 0	22	
		0, 16	198	
		16, 16	38	
SP	Y + 2	0, 0	2	No
		16, 0	2	
		0, 1	1[illegible]	
		16, 16	18	

For all edges of rectangle *PQRS* the function '*F*' does not change sign for co-ordinates of window corners. Hence, rectangle *PQRS* is either disjoint or a surrounder. Figure 7.22 shows that rectangle *PQRS* is a surrounder.

7.6.3 Surrounding Polygon

Some algorithms need to test whether a point *P* is surrounded by a polygonal face *F*. For a convex polygon, if we substitute the location of point in (X_S, Y_S) into two dimensional line equation for each edge of the polygon; and the resultant signs for all edges are same, the point is inside the polygons. This test requires that signs of the co-efficients of line equations are chosen correctly.

For nonconvex polygons the following methods can be used :

i) Draw any line from a given point to infinity and count the number of times this line crosses the polygonal boundary. If this number is odd the point is inside, otherwise it is outside. Figure 7.23 shows the line and the polygon. The point '*A*' has one crossing and point '*B*' has two crossings.

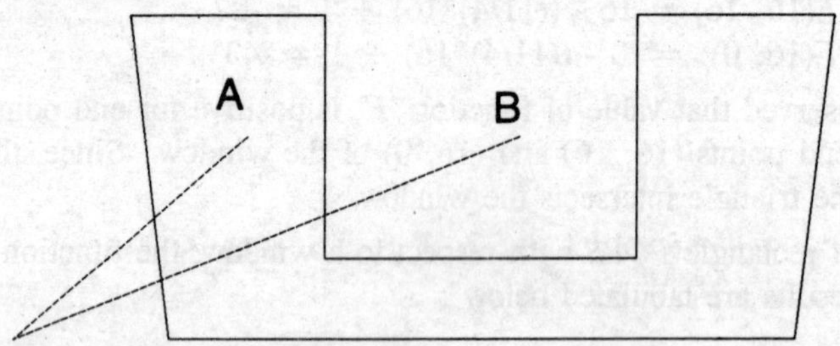

Figure 7.23 Surrounder test: point 'A' is surrounded, point 'B' is not.

The principle used is the same as for the polygon based area filling technique described in section 6.6.

ii) This test is explained by figure 7.24 *a* and *b*.

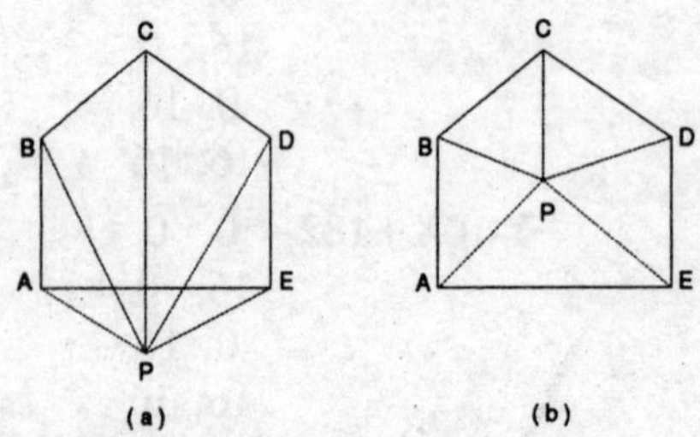

Figure 7-24 Surrounder test
(a) Point 'P' is outside (sum of angles is less than 360 degrees)
(b) Point 'P' is inside (sum of angles is equal to 360 degrees)

The sum of angles subtended by each edge as seen from the point is computed, so that,

Sum = angle [APE + ABP + BPC + CPD + DPE]

If sum = 2π then point is inside

$< 2\pi$ then point is outside.

7.6.4 Dot Product Test

This test is used to find the position of a point *P* with respect to a plane. In case the point *P* is in front of the plane it is visible, but if it is behind the plane, it is not visible.

The equation of a plane is given by

$$AX + BY + CZ + D = 0 \tag{7.26}$$

The co-efficients *A*, *B*, *C*, and *D* can be computed using equation (7.25).

Let the point *P* be given by co-ordinates $[X_p, Y_p, Z_p, 1]$.

The dot product '*DP*' is computed as follows :

$$DP = [X_p \; Y_p \; Z_p \; 1] \cdot [A \; B \; C \; D] \tag{7.27}$$

where '.' denotes the dot product.

If $DP > 0$: point *P* is in front of the plane,

< 0 : point *P* is behind the plane,

$= 0$: point *P* is on the plane.

An object is formed by a number of planes (faces). A convex solid object can be represented by a volume matrix.

$$[V] = \begin{bmatrix} A1 & A2 & \cdots & An \\ B1 & B2 & \cdots & Bn \\ C1 & C2 & \cdots & Cn \\ D1 & D2 & \cdots & Dn \end{bmatrix}$$

where each column corresponds to the co-efficients of one plane. The number of columns is equal to the number of planes forming the object.

The dot product of the co-ordinates of point *P* and co-efficients of each plane can be used to find the position of point with respect to the object as given below :

$$DP = [P] \cdot [V] \tag{7.28}$$

The following convention can be used :

If $DP \geq 0$: The point is inside the volume,

< 0 : The point is out side the volume.

To satisfy the above condition, the volume matrix is tested by considering a known point inside the volume and computing the '*DP*'. The sign of co-efficients of planes are adjusted for the planes which generate a negative value of '*DP*'. The following example illustrates the procedure.

Example 7.7: Consider a unit cube, defined by the vertices $A(1,1,1)$, $B(1,1,-1)$, $C(-1,1,-1)$, $D(-1,1,1)$, $E(1,-1,1)$, $F(1,-1,-1)$, $G(-1,-1,-1)$ and $H(-1,-1,1)$ as shown in figure 7.25.

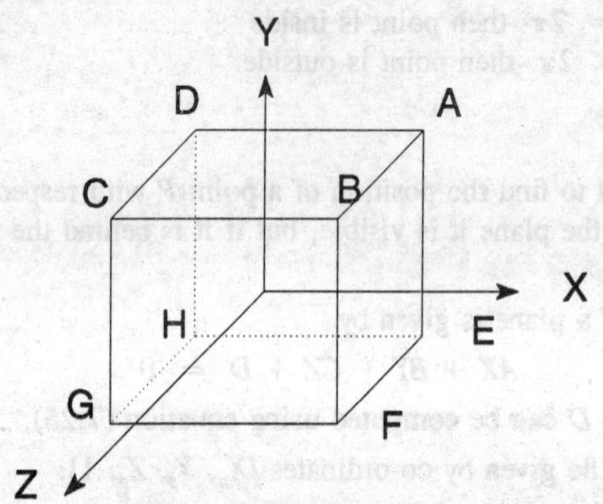

Figure 7.25 A unit cube with hidden lines.

The equations of the six faces of the cube are given in the following table.

Plane No.	**Face**	**Equation**
1	ABEF	X = 1
2	DHGC	X = -1
3	ABCD	Y = 1
4	EFGH	Y = -1
5	AEHD	Z = 1
6	BFGC	Z = -1

The volume matrix for the cube is

$$[V] = \begin{bmatrix} 1 & 1 & 0 & 0 & 0 & 0 \\ 0 & 0 & 1 & 1 & 0 & 0 \\ 0 & 0 & 0 & 0 & 1 & 1 \\ -1 & 1 & -1 & 1 & -1 & 1 \end{bmatrix}$$

To ensure that the sign of each plane equation on the volume matrix is correct, we selct a point $P = [0.5 \;\; 0.5 \;\; 0.5 \;\; 1]$ inside the cube and compute the dot product.

$$DP = [\,0.5 \;\; 0.5 \;\; 0.5 \;\; 1]\,.\,[V]$$
$$= [-0.5 \;\; 1.5 \;\; -0.5 \;\; 1.5 \;\; -0.5 \;\; 1.5]$$

The results obtained in columns 1, 3 and 5 corresponding to planes 1, 3 and 5 are negative. The columns in the volume matrix [V] are multiplied by (-1) as the point P is inside the volume. Thus, dot product *DP* will become positive for all planes. The corrected volume matrix is given below :

$$[V] = \begin{bmatrix} -1 & 1 & 0 & 0 & 0 & 0 \\ 0 & 0 & -1 & 1 & 0 & 0 \\ 0 & 0 & 0 & 0 & 1 & 1 \\ 1 & 1 & 1 & 1 & 1 & 1 \end{bmatrix}$$

7.6.5 Procedure for Removal of self hidden planes

The above example illustrates that a cube is formed by the set of six infinite planes $X = Y = Z = 1$ and $X = Y = Z = -1$. The intersections of these planes define the edges of the cube. For a point to be inside the volume the point must be towards the inside of all the planes as shown in figure 7.26, i.e., the condition $[P].[V] > 0$ must be satisfied for all planes in the volume matrix.

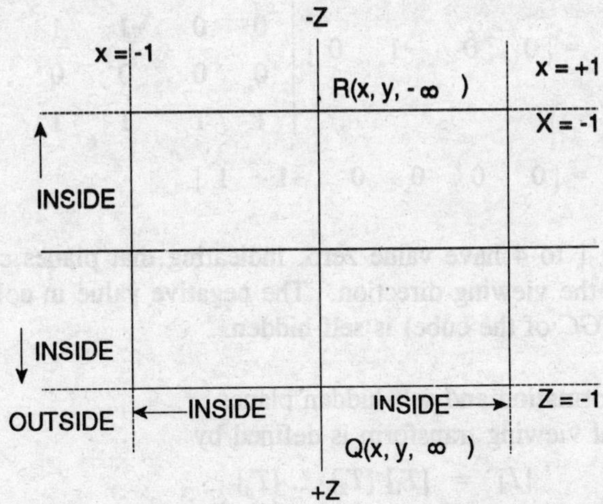

Figure 7.26 Showing Z=X=1 and Z=X= -1 infinite planes. Point P is inside the cube. Point Q and R are located in +Z and -Z planes, respectively.

A view point Q is selected anywhere on the plane on the positive side of the z-axis and we look towards the origin at any point $R(x, y, -\infty)$ on the plane at $Z = -\infty$. If the dot product of the co-ordinates of R, [0 0 -1 0], which is also the viewing direction vector and any of the planes in the [V] is negative, then the point R is outside these planes. This means that R is hidden by these planes when viewed from point Q.

Therefore, the relationship

$$[R].\ [V] < 0 \tag{7.29}$$

can be used to identify self hidden planes of a polygonal convex object. Computation of dot product is equivalent to determining the normal to each plane. The negative value of the dot product for a plane indicates that the direction of normal is away from the view point.

Such faces of the object are referred to as self-hidden planes. The intersection of two hidden faces generates a hidden line.

Example 7.8: Consider the cube of example 7.7. The view point Q is selected on plane given by $Z = +\infty$. Find the self hidden planes of the cube.

The viewing direction is from the positive side of z-axis towards the origin and is given by the vector:

$$[0 \quad 0 \quad -\infty \quad 1] \quad \text{or} \quad [0 \quad 0 \quad -1 \quad 0]$$

The above vector also represents a point on the negative z-axis of the plane described by the equation $Z = -\infty$. This is the test point. Computing the dot product using equation (7.29), we get:

$$[0 \quad 0 \quad -1 \quad 0] \cdot [V]$$

$$= [0 \quad 0 \quad -1 \quad 0] \begin{bmatrix} -1 & 1 & 0 & 0 & 0 & 0 \\ 0 & 0 & -1 & 1 & 0 & 0 \\ 0 & 0 & 0 & 0 & -1 & 1 \\ 1 & 1 & 1 & 1 & 1 & 1 \end{bmatrix}$$

$$= [0 \quad 0 \quad 0 \quad 0 \quad -1 \quad 1]$$

Columns 1 to 4 have value zero, indicating that planes corresponding to these columns are parallel to the viewing direction. The negative value in column 6 shows that the plane $Z = -1$ (face $BFGC$ of the cube) is self-hidden.

7.6.5.1 General transformation and self-hidden planes

A general viewing transform is defined by

$$[T] = [T_1]\,[T_2] \ldots [T_n] \tag{7.30}$$

where $[T_1]$, $[T_2]$ ... denote transformations (in the form of 4×4 matrices) such as translation, rotation, scaling, perspective, etc.

This transformation is applied before finding out the self hidden planes of the three dimensional objects. In case perspective transformation is used, the value of x, y and z co-ordinates are to be computed. This is important if the definition of object is in the object space and self hidden planes are to be determined. Let the co-ordinates of the vertices be given by the matrix $[M]$. The co-efficients A, B, C and D for all planes of object can be computed using equation (7.25) and volume matrix $[V]$ can be generated. The equations of planes forming the object are given by

$$[M]\,[V] = [\mathbf{0}] \tag{7.31}$$

where $[\mathbf{0}]$ is a matrix of zeros.

The vertices of the object can be transformed using the transformation $[T]$ and the new matrix $[M_1]$ is given by

$$[M_1] = [M]\,[T] \tag{7.32}$$

The co-efficients of transformed planes are contained in new volume matrix $[V_1]$.

The equation of transformed planes of the object is

$$[M_1]\,[V_1] \;=\; [\mathbf{0}] \tag{7.33}$$

Equating equation (7.31) and (7.33), we get

$$[M_1]\,[V_1] = [M]\,[V]$$

or

$$[V_1] = [T]^{-1}\,[V] \tag{7.34}$$

Therefore, equation (7.34) provides a method for computing transformed volume matrix $[V_1]$ by multiplying the inverse of transformation matrix $[T]$ with the volume matrix $[V]$.

Example 7.9: Rotate the cube of example 7.7 about X- and Y-axis by 30 and 60 degrees, respectively in clockwise direction.

The transformation matrix T_{RX} for 30 degrees rotation about the X-axis and the matrix T_{RY} for 60 degrees rotation about the Y-axis are

$$T_{RX} = \begin{bmatrix} 1 & 0 & 0 & 0 \\ 0 & \cos 30^\circ & -\sin 30^\circ & 0 \\ 0 & \sin 30^\circ & \cos 30^\circ & 1 \\ 0 & 0 & 0 & 1 \end{bmatrix}$$

$$T_{RY} = \begin{bmatrix} \cos 6o^\circ & 0 & \sin 60^\circ & 0 \\ 0 & 1 & 0 & 0 \\ -\sin 60^\circ & 0 & \cos 60^\circ & 0 \\ 0 & 0 & 0 & 1 \end{bmatrix}$$

The translation matrix $[T]$ is given by

$$[T] = [T_{RX}]\,[T_{RY}]$$

The inverse matrix $[T]^{-1}$ can either be calculated or since T_{RX} and T_{RY} are simple matrices, their inverse can be written by inspection as follows:

$$[T_{RX}]^{-1} = \begin{bmatrix} 1 & 0 & 0 & 0 \\ 0 & \frac{\sqrt{3}}{2} & \frac{1}{2} & 0 \\ 0 & -\frac{1}{2} & \frac{\sqrt{3}}{2} & 0 \\ 0 & 0 & 0 & 1 \end{bmatrix}$$

Therefore,

$$[T_{RY}]^{-1} = \begin{bmatrix} \frac{1}{2} & 0 & -\frac{\sqrt{3}}{2} & 0 \\ 0 & 1 & 0 & 0 \\ \frac{\sqrt{3}}{2} & 0 & \frac{1}{2} & 0 \\ 0 & 0 & 0 & 1 \end{bmatrix}$$

$$[T]^{-1} = [T_{RX}]^{-1}[T_{RY}]^{-1}$$

$$= \begin{bmatrix} \frac{1}{2} & \frac{\sqrt{3}}{4} & -\frac{3}{4} & 0 \\ \frac{\sqrt{3}}{4} & \frac{\sqrt{3}}{2} & \frac{1}{2} & 0 \\ \frac{3}{4} & -\frac{1}{4} & \frac{\sqrt{3}}{4} & 0 \\ 0 & 0 & 0 & 1 \end{bmatrix}$$

Using equation (7.34), [*V1*] containing the co-efficients of transformed planes of the object can be computed. The volume matrix [*V*] for the cube is given in example 7.6.

$$[V1] = [T]^{-1}[V]$$

$$= [T]^{-1} \begin{bmatrix} -1 & 1 & 0 & 0 & 0 & 0 \\ 0 & 0 & -1 & 1 & 0 & 0 \\ 0 & 0 & 0 & 0 & -1 & 1 \\ 1 & 1 & 1 & 1 & 1 & 1 \end{bmatrix}$$

$$= \begin{bmatrix} -\frac{1}{2} & \frac{1}{2} & -\frac{\sqrt{3}}{4} & \frac{\sqrt{3}}{4} & \frac{3}{4} & -\frac{3}{4} \\ -\frac{\sqrt{3}}{3} & \frac{\sqrt{3}}{4} & -\frac{3}{2} & \frac{\sqrt{3}}{2} & -\frac{1}{2} & \frac{1}{2} \\ -\frac{3}{4} & \frac{3}{4} & \frac{1}{4} & -\frac{1}{4} & -\frac{\sqrt{3}}{4} & \frac{\sqrt{3}}{4} \\ 1 & 1 & 1 & 1 & 1 & 1 \end{bmatrix}$$

Example 7.10: Find the self-hidden faces and lines when the transformed cube of example 7.9 is viewed from the point at (0, 0, -∞).

The point (0, 0, -∞) corresponds to point [0 0 -1 0] in homogeneous representation. The viewing direction corresponds to the vector

[0 0 1 0]

which is also a point on the $z = \infty$ plane.

The dot product is

[0 0 1 0] . [V1] = [-3/4 3/4 1/4 -1/4 3/4 3/4]

Hence, planes *ABFE*, *EFGH* and *AEHD* are self-hidden. The self-hidden lines are *EF*, *EH* and *EA*.

It can be seen that in example 7.9, vertex C was hidden. The viewing direction is opposite in this example, hence the opposite vertex E is hidden.

The viewing direction corresponds to vector [0 0 -1 0] which is also a point on the $z = -\infty$ plane. The dot product is computed to find the self hidden planes,

[0 0 -1 0] . [V1] = [3/4 -3/4 -1/4 1/4 3/4 -3/4]

Hence, the planes *DHGC*, *ABCD* and *BFGC* corresponding to columns 2, 3 and 6 are self hidden. The intersection of planes *DGHC* and *ABCD* is line *CD* which is also hidden. Similarly, self-hidden lines *GC* and *BC* are also identified. A sketch of the resultant cube is shown in figure 7.27.

7.7 Hidden surface algorithms [15,19, and 20]

The goal of a hidden surface algorithm is to convert a 3D scene into a 2D scene that lies on the view plane. The hidden surface procedure can be considered as a two step sorting process. The first step sorts the surface into different viewing pyramids also known as a bucket sort. The second step sorts the surface within a given viewing pyramid to determine one closest to the view point.

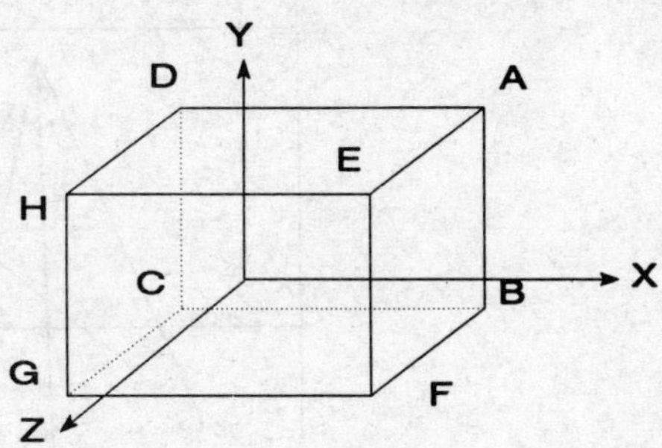

Figure 7.27 View of the cube after rotation. Self-hidden lines BC,CD and GC are shown by dashed lines.

The following approaches are of interest:

- Quadtree can be used to model the view plane even when the scene comprises of polygons of arbitrary orientation and position in the 3D space. This approach is a image-space method and is known as Warnock's algorithm.
- Weiler and Atherton devised a hidden surface algorithm which uses image-space heuristics to speed up object space methods.

7.7.1 Quad Tree Algorithm

This algorithm takes advantage of area-coherence by using the fact that a typical polygon has similar extent in both X and Y directions. The pixels which fall in these areas are coherent as they show a single surface. This algorithm does not give priority in sorting in any direction by treating both X and Y symmetrically. To capitalise on area coherence, the size of the window is changed dynamically depending on the complexity of the picture. In this algorithm [15,19] the windows of the display screen are made to correspond to the nodes of a quad-tree (described in section 4.2.7.2).

Initially the algorithm treats the whole screen as one window and tries to solve the hidden surface problem. If there are edges in the window, the window is subdivided into four sub-windows by descending the quad-tree and this procedure is repeated recursively. For a complete picture the recursion results in smaller and smaller windows till a window is found which is either solved or size of window becomes equal to a single pixel on the screen. The procedure of recursive sub-division is shown in figure 7.28. For example, the first division of the screen results in creation of windows 1, 2, 3 and 4. In figure 7.28 only window 4 is further subdivided to avoid congestion. Windows 42 and 44 have no edges and all polygons of the object (the pyramid) are disjoint to these windows. Hence, window 42 and 44 represent the background. Windows 4111, 4113, 413 etc., also do not have edges but these windows are surrounded by the polygons of the object. Such windows are called homogeneous windows. The color of these windows is decided by ordering the polygons (corresponding to face of the object) in the three directions and selecting the color of polygon which is closest to the view point. In case, window size becomes equal to size of a pixel, the color of this pixel is the color of the polygon closest to the view point.

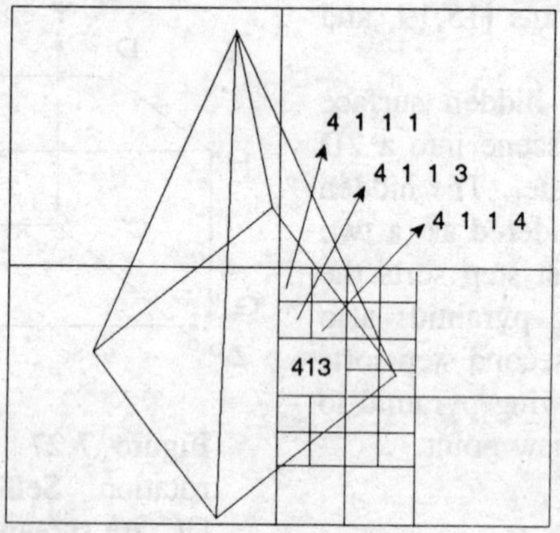

Figure 7.28 The quad tree technique for division of windows

Polygons forming the objects in the windows are analysed and assigned to one ofthe following classes as shown in figure 7.29 :

a) the polygon is disjoint from the window. (In figure 7.29 polygon 'd' falls in this class);

b) the polygon falls completely or partly inside the window (polygon 'b' and 'c'); or

c) the polygon surrounds the window (polygon 'a').

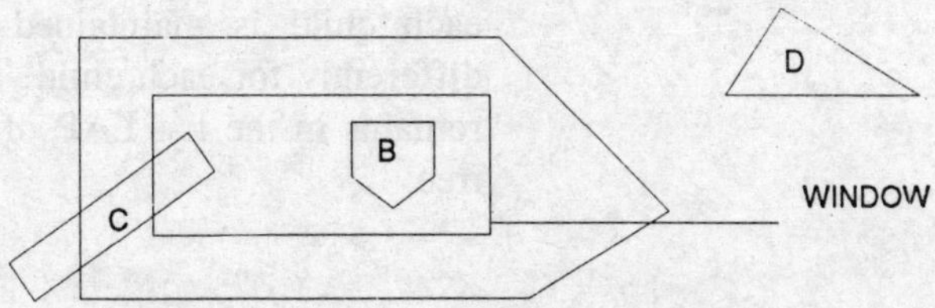

Figure 7.29 Polygons and Window

To classify the polygon into one of these classes, the procedure described in Section 7.6 can be used. The clipping procedure described in section 6.5.1.1 can also be modified. The clipping program need not compute actual intersection points of polygon edges with the edges of the window but can return to calling program as soon as it finds an intersecting side. A procedure called CLASSIFY (also see problem 7.5) can use any of the above approaches to analyze a polygon, and returns the following parameter:

VALUE = 0 : Polygon, with respect to the window, is disjoint,
= 1 : Polygon is either inside the window or intersects it,
= 2 : Polygon surrounds the window.

To implement the quad-tree algorithm the following lists are used:

List LAP : List of all polygons of the objects forming the scene.
List LSP : List of all polygons which surround the window or node.

In the beginning list LSP is empty and all relevant polygons are in list LAP. As the recursive process of subdivision of a window is carried out all polygons which are disjoint to the current window are dropped and polygons surrounding the window are transferred to the list LSP. In the end, list LAP is empty, and list LSP contains the polygons surrounding the window.

A detailed flowchart of the algorithm is shown in figure 7.30. The algorithm uses stack for efficient implementation. For each window, the algorithm calls the procedure 'CLASSIFY' for all polygons in the list LAP.

Procedure CLASSIFY returns :

i. VALUE = 0: for all polygons in the list LAP. The window is assigned color of the background.

ii. VALUE = 2: Polygon is transferred from list LAP to list LSP. If 0 and 2 are the only values returned for the polygons of a window, it implies that window is surrounded by one or more polygons. Color of the window will be that of polygon nearest to the view point.

iii. VALUE = 1: The window is subdivided, keeping in mind that polygons which were disjoint from the parent window will also be disjoint from its children (sub-windows). The children can, therefore, inherit the lists LAP and LSP. A separate copy of lists LAP and LSP for each child is maintained as the lists may need modification differently for each child. The polygon which generated value 1 remains in the list LAP of all children at that node of the quad-tree.

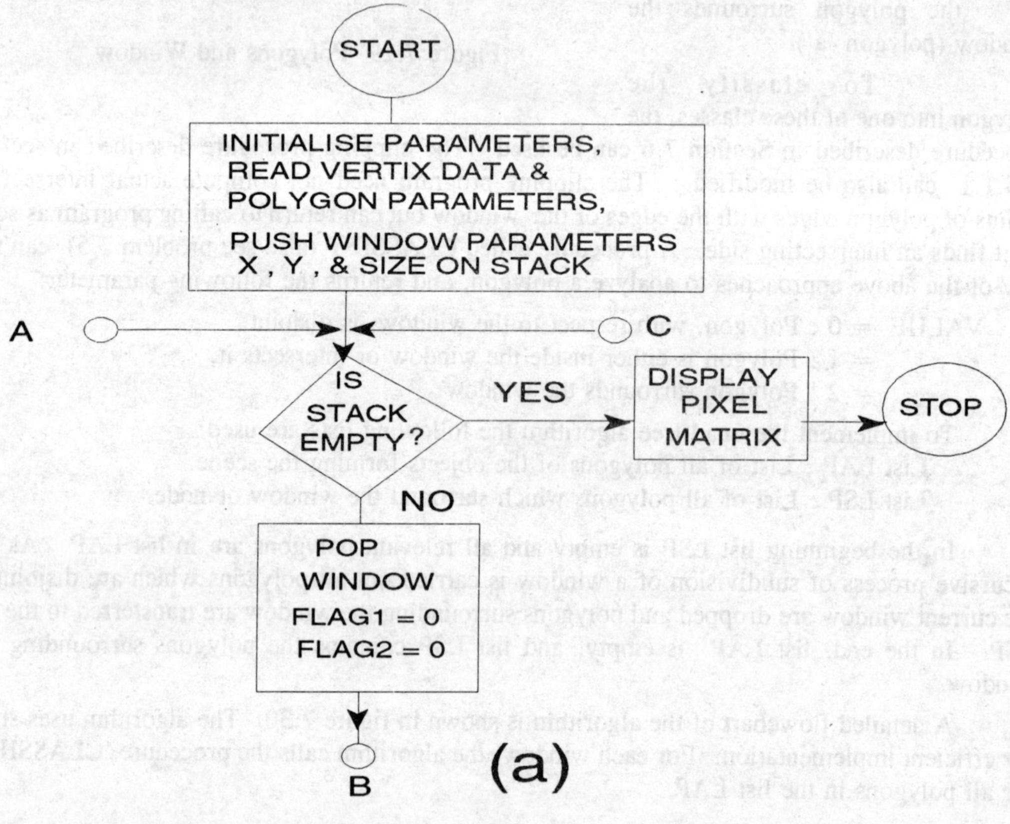

Figure 7.30 (a) Part 1 of the flow-chart of Quad-tree algorithm

The above procedure is repeated till the visibility problem is solved for all windows . If the size of a window is equal to one pixel, the color of this pixel is decided by finding out the color of polygon nearest to the view-point. This algorithm is similar to that developed by Warnock [14,16,17]. In case polygon color is non-uniform, it will be necessary to find color of polygon for each pixel of the window to determine the color of the window.

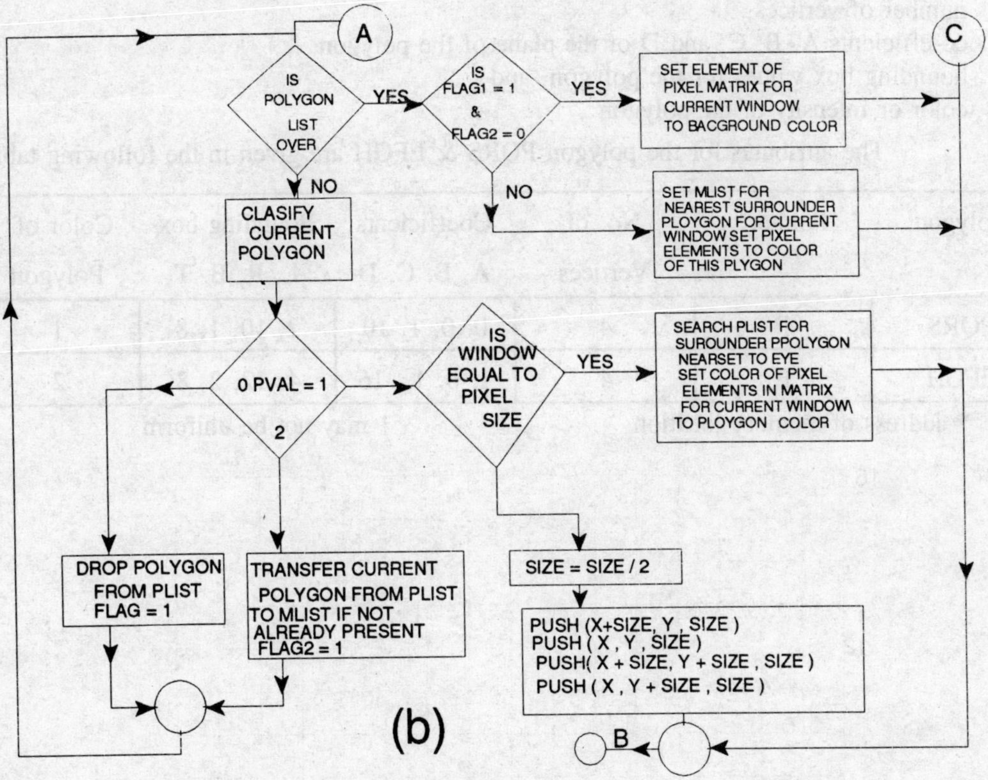

(b)Figure 7.30 Flow Chart of Quad Tree Algorithm

Example 7.11

Consider polygon P Q R S and E F G H; with vertices P (2,1,10), Q (2,8,10), R(10, 8, 10), S(10,1,10), E(4, 4, 12), F(4, 6, 12), G(12, 8, 8) and H(12, 2, 4). Draw the polygons with hidden surfaces removed. The size of display window is 0, 16, 0, 16.

Figure 7.31 shows the polygons. The pixels are aligned to the lower left corner of the window. The area of pixels falling outside the polygon boundary is ignored.

In this picture there are only two polygons but, in general, a scene consists of number of objects, each comprising of number of faces (polygons). To allow efficient processing the following attributes for each polygon are stored :

i) pointer to the array containing the co-ordinates of the vertices,

ii) number of vertices,
iii) co-efficients A, B, C, and D of the plane of the polygon
iv) bounding box values for the polygon, and
v) color or intensity of the polygon

The attributes for the polygon PQRS & EFGH are given in the following table.

Polygon	Pointer*	No. of Vertices	Coefficients A, B, C, D	Bounding box L, R, B, T	Color of+ Polygon
PQRS	P	4	0. 0. 1, 10	2, 10, 1, 8	1
EFGH	E	4	1, 0, 1, -16	4, 12, 2, 8	2

* address of memory location + may not be uniform

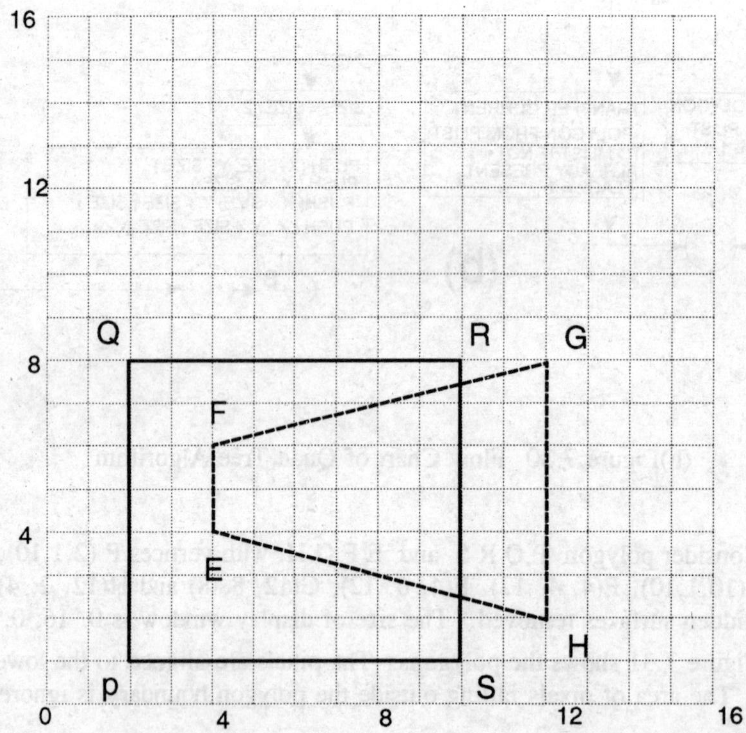

Figure 7.31 The polygon ABCD and EFGH. Window size is 0,16,0,16.

Initially the list LAP contains two polygons PQRS and EFGH. The list LSP is empty. The polygons disjoint to the window are dropped from list LAP and polygons surrounding the window are transferred to the list. The step by step result of execution of the quad tree algorithm is given in the following table:

STEP	Stack Operation Push : 0 Pop : 1	Stack (shows window #)	CALL CLASSIFY All polygons in list LP are		See note 6	
			Disjoint	Disjoint surrounder	Window #	See note 7
1	2	3	4	5	6	7
1.	0	0		0	(0,0,16)	
2.	1,0	1,2,3,4		1,2,3,4	(0,8,8), (8,8,8),	(0,0,8)
3.	1	2,3,4	DB(Note 3)	1	0	
4.	1	3,4	DB	2	0	
5.	1,0	5,6,7,8,4		5,6,7,8	(0,4,4),(4,4,4),	(0,0,4),(4,0,4)
6.	1	9,10,11,12,6,7,8,4		9,10,11,12	(0,6,2),(2,6,2),	(0,4,2),(2,4,2)
7.	1	10,11,12,6,7,8,4	DB	9	0	
8.	1	11,12,6,7,8,4	DNP(Note 4)	10	1,10	
9.	1	12,6,7,8,4	DB	11	0	
10.	1	6,7,8,4	DNP	12	1,10	
11.	1,0	13,14,15,16,7,8,4		13,14,15,16	(4,6,2),(6,6,2),	(4,4,2),(6,4,2)
12.	1,0	17,18,19,20,14,15,16,7,8,4		17,18,19,20	(4,7,1),(5,7,1),	(4,6,1),(5,6,1)
13.	1	18,19,20,14,15,16,7,8,4	DNP	17	1,10	
14.	1	19,20,14,15,16,7,8,4	DNP	18	1,10	
15.	1	20,14,15,16,7,8,4		19(Note 5)	2,12	
16.	1	14,15,16,7,8,4		20	2,11	
17.	1,0	21,22,23,24,15,16,7,8,4		21,22,23,24	(6,7,1),(7,7,1),	(6,6,1),(7,6,1)
18.	1	22,23,24,15,16,7,8,4	DNP	21	1,10	
19.	1	23,24,15,16,7,8,4	DNP	22	1,10	
20.	1	24,15,16,7,8,4		23	1,10	
21.	1	15,16,7,8,4		24	1,10	
22.	1	16,7,8,4	DNP	15	2, 12,or 11	
23.	1,0	7,8,4	DNP	16	1,10	
24.	1,0	25,26,27,28,8,4		25,26,27,28	(0,2,2),(2,2,2),	(0,0,2),(2,0,2)
25.	1	26,27,28,8,4	DB	25	0	
26.	1	27,28,8,4	DNP	26	1,10	
27.	1,0	28,8,4	DB	27	0	
28.	1,0	29,30,31,32,8,4		29,30,31,32	(2,1,1),(3,1,1),	(2,0,1),(3,0,1)
29.	1	30,31,32,8,4	DNP	29	1,10	
30.	1	31,32,8,4	DNP	30	1,10	
31.	1	32,8,4	DB	31	0	
32.	1	8,4	DB	32	0	
33.	1.0	33,34,35,36,4		33,34,35,36	(4,2,2),(6,2,2),	
34.	1,0	37,38,39,40,34,35,36,4		37,38,39,40	(4,3,1),(5,3,1), (4,2,1),(5,2,1)	
35.	1	38,39,40,34,35,36,4		37	2,12	
36.	1	39,40,34,35,36,4		38	2,11	
37.	1	40,34,35,36,4	DNP	39	1,10	
38.	1	34,35,36,4	DNP	40	1,10	
39.	1,0	41,42,43,44,35,36,4		41,42,43,44	(6,3,1),(7,3,1),	(6,2,1)(7,2,1)
40.	1	42,42,44,35,36,4		41	1,10	
41.	1	43,44,35,36,4		42	1,10	
42.	1	44,35,36,4	DNP	43	1,10	
43.	1	35,36,4	DNP	44	1,10	
44.	1,0	45,46,47,48,36,4		45,46,47,48	(4,1,1),(5,1,1),	(4,0,1),(5,0,1)
45.	1	46,47,48,36,4	DNP	45	1,10	
46.	1,0	36,4	DNP	46	1,10	
47.	1	48,36,4	DB	47	0	
48.	1,0	36,4	DB	48	0	
						(4,0,2),(6,0,2)

1	2	3	4	5	6	7
49.	1,0	49,50,51,52,4		49,50,51,52	(6,1,1),(7,1,1),	(6,0,1),(7,0,1)
50	1	50,51,52,4	DNP	49	1,10	
51.	1	51,52,4	DNP	50	1,10	
52.	1	52,4	DB	51	0	
53	1	4	DB	52	0	
54.	1,0	53,54,55,56		53,54,55,56	(8,4,4),(12,4,4), (8,0,4),(12,0,4)	
55.	1,0	57,58,59,60,54,55,56		57,58,59,60	(8,6,2),(10,6,2), (8,4,2),(10,6,2)	
56.	1,0	61,62,63,64,58,59,60,54,55,56				
57.	1,0	62,63,64,58,59,60,54,55,56		61	1,10	
58.	1,0	63,64,58,59,60,54,55,56		62	1,10	
59.	1,0	64,58,59,60,54,55,56	DNP	63	1,10	
60.	1,0	58,59,60,54,55,56	DNP	64	1,10	
61.	1,0	65,66,67,68,59,60,54,55,56		65,66,67,68	(10,7,1),(11,7,1), (10,6,1),(11,6,1)	
62.	1,0	66,,67,68,59,60,54,55,56		65	2,6	
63.	1	67,68,59,60,54,55,56		66	2,5	
64.	1	68,59,60,54,55,56	DNP	67	2,6	
65.	1	59,60,54,55,56	DNP	68	2,5	
66.	1	60,54,55,56	DNP	59	1,10	
67.	1	54,55,56	DNP	60	2,6, or 5	
68.	1	55,56	DB DNP	54	0	
69.	1,0	69,70,71,72,56		69,70,71,72	(8,2,2),(10,2,2), (8,0,2),(10,0,2)	
70.	1,0	73,74,75,76,70,71,72,56		73,74,75,76	(8,3,1),(9,3,1), (8,2,1),(9,2,1)	
71.	1	74,75,76,70,71,72,56	DNP	73	1,10	
72.	1	75,76,70,71,72,56	DNP	74	1,10	
73.	1	76,70,71,72,56		75	1,10	
74.	1	70,71,72,56		76	1,10	
75.	1,0	77,78,79,80,71,72,		77,78,79,80	(10,3,1),(11,3,1),	(10,2,1)(11,2,1)
76.	1	78,79,80,71,72,56	DNP	77	2,6	
77.	1	79,80,71,72,56	DNP	78	2,5	
78.	1	80,71,72,56		79	2,6	
79.	1	71,72,56		80	2,5	
80.	1,0	81,82,83,84,72,56		81,82,83,84	(8,1,1),(9,1,1), (8,0,1),(9,0,1)	
81.	1	82,83,84,72,56	DNP	81	1,10	
82.	1	83,84,72,56	DNP	82	1,10	
83.	1	84,72,56	DB	83	0	
84.	1	72,56	DB	84	0	
85.	1	56	DB	72	0	
86	NIL		DB	56	0	

Note 1: List LAP and LSP are also window parameters. When a parent window is divided all its children inherit list SAP and LSP. However, these lists may get modified differently for each sub-window.

Note 2: Color of background is given by number 0 for other windows color and depth are given in the form (color, depth).

Note 3: DB : Display all pixels at the window in the background color.

Note 4: DNP : Find depth for all polygon the list LSP of current window. Display color of polygon closest to the view point.

Note 5: Display color of the pixel closest to the view point for windows of minimum resolution.

Note 6: An intersector or contained polygon in list LP encountered and if window size greater than one, divide window and push on stack or solve window.

Note 7: Window parameters X, Y (see note 1) or (colour, depth) see note 2.

The display window (0,16, 0, 16) is pushed on stack which is divided into four sub-windows (1, 2, 3, 4). The process of division continues until windows are solved. The solved wndows are divided into three catagories are under :

i) DB : display window in background color
example: window 1, 2, 9, 11 .....

ii) DNP : display color of the nearest polygon to the viewpoint.

Example: Window 10 (list LSP contains polygon PQRS) window 10 is surrounded by only one polygon PQRS. Hence, color & depth of polygon corresponding to this window will be that of polygon PQRS, i.e., 1 and 10 respectively.

Example: Window 15, and 16 (list LSP for these windows contain polygon PQRS & EFGH).

Both the windows are surrounded by the polygons PQRS & EFGH. Polygon PQRS has constant depth of 10 units. The depth of polygon EFGH is not uniform. To compute depth of polygon EFGH, the equation of the plane containing the polygon is to be computed using equation (7.23). The resulting equation is

$$x + z - 16 = 0$$

The depth of plane EFGH at any point is

$$z = -(x-16).$$

The following table shows the process of selection of the color of the window and the depth of polygon EFGH for each pixel of window 15 & 16.

Window	Pixel Address	Depth of polygon		Color of window
		PQRS	EFGH	
15	4, 4	10	12	2
	4, 5	10	12	2
	5, 4	10	11	2
	5, 5	10	11	2
16	6, 4	10	10	1
	6, 5	10	10	1
	7, 4	10	9	1
	7, 5	10	9	1

The depth of the polygon varies with in the window. Hence, it is calculated for each pixel of the window. For depths greater than 10 units the color of polygon EFGH is selected as the window color.

iii) For windows with the minimum resolution, the color of pixel nearest to the view point is displayed.

The result of division of windows till each window is solved is shown in figure 7.32.

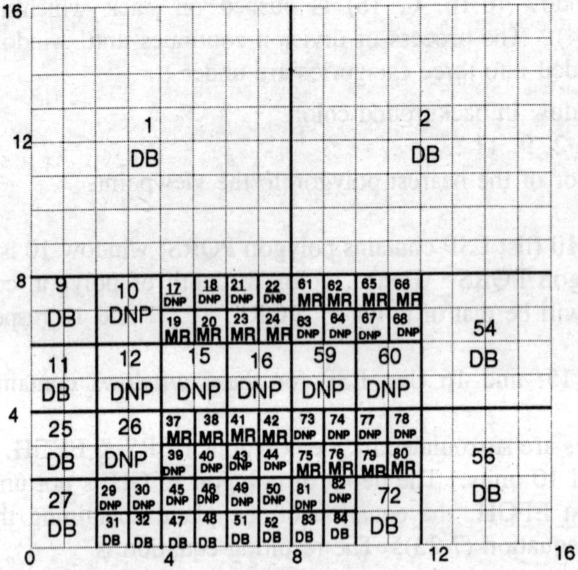

Figure 7.32 Division of windows

In case there exists a depth value in the memory corresponding to the pixels it is called a depth buffer. Figure 7.33 gives the color and depth of visible polygon in each window. The number '0' in a window represents background color.

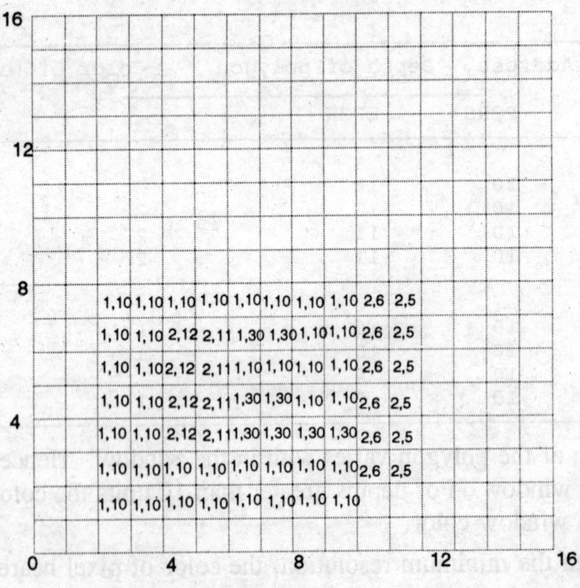

Figure 7.33 Picture with the hidden surface removed

The figure also gives the number of windows created by quad tree algorithm for solving hidden surface problem for picture given in figure 7.31. It has been assumed that pixel centre is located at the edges of the windows. Part of pixels beyond the boundary of polygons have been ignored. If the windows of figure 7.33 are displayed on the screen in the specified color, the resultant picture would represent the scene with hidden surfaces removed.

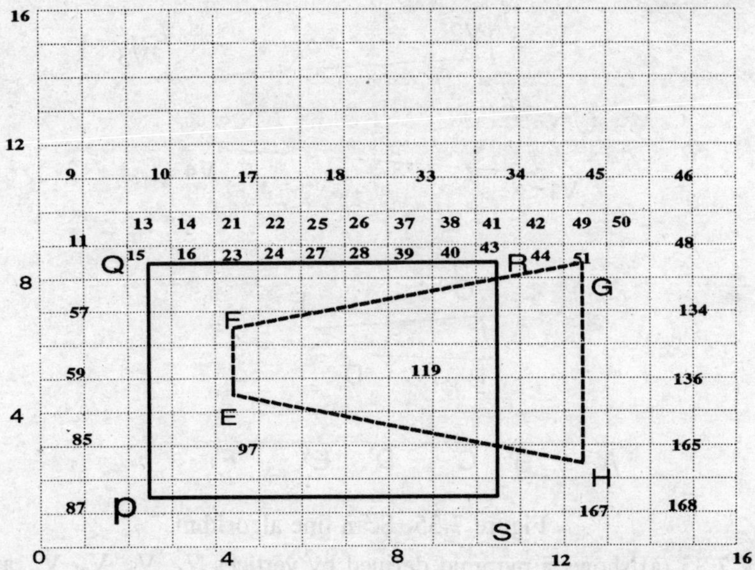

Figure 7-34 Sub-division of windows with pixels defined by the centre of the windows

The number in each pixel shows the color and depth of each pixel. The following convention is used :

0 - for background; **1** - color of polygon ABCD; **2** - color of polygon EFGH

It can be observed from figure 7.33 that the shape of polygon is distorted. To circumvent this problem, pixels are aligned to the centre of the window (x+1/2, y+1/2) where (x, y) is the lower left hand corner of the window. The resultant picture is shown in figure 7.34, with subdivision of windows with pixels defined by centre of windows, i.e., (x+1/2,y+1/2), where (x,y) is lower left corner of the window. The algorithm creates 168 solved windows in this case for the picture of figure 7.31.

7.7.2 Scan line algorithm :

This algorithm [10,14-16] solves the problem of hidden surfaces while generating display scan line by scan line. For screen co-ordinate system the view point is taken at $Z_S = -\infty$ resulting in orthogonal projection. A plane is defined by the scan line on the screen and the view point. Hence, this plane has equation Y_S = Constant. All objects in the scene are intersected by this plane. This results in a set of line segment in the X_S - Z_S plane. There may be one or more segments for each potentially visible polygon.

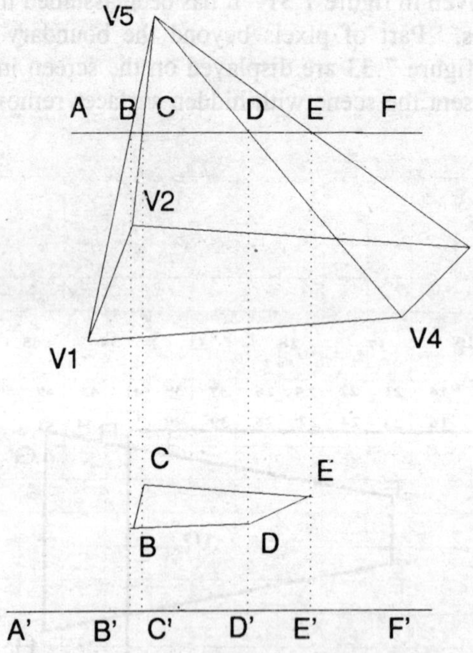

Figure 7.35 Scan line algorithm

Figure 7.35 (a) shows a pyramid defined by vertices V_1, V_2, V_3, V_4, and V_5 projected in the X_S-Y_S plane. A plane defined by Y_S = Constant (shown by line AF) intersects the pyramid edges V_1- V_5, V_2- V_5, V_4- V_5, and V_3- V_5 at points B, C, D, and E respectively The projection of the intersection in X_S-Z_S results in a polygon BCDE (see figure 7.35(b)). The points B', C', D' and E' are the projections of the vertices on line A' F'. Therefore, the visibility problem is to decide whether the algorithm will fill the internal B'D' by the color of the face V_1- V_4- V_5 or will fill the segment B'C' by color of the face V_1- V_2- V_5. Similarly, the color of each segment can be determined by processing each segment generated on the scan line, i.e., B'C', C'D', and D'E'.

A picture ray is defined by the line joining the view point and a picture point (a pixel). All segments are intersected with this ray to yield a set of points, one for each potentially visible polygon at that picture element. These points are sorted by their Z_S co-ordinate. The point with the smallest Z_S is the visible point and the intensity for this pixel is stored in a intensity array.

This process is repeated for complete scan line and then for every scan line. The resultant intensity array contains the scan with hidden surface removed. Figure 7.35 shows the scan line algorithm; the upper part of the figure shows the projection of a pyramid and the plane Y_S = *constant* plane on the X_S-Y_S plane, while the lower part shows the projection of the intersection on the X_S-Z_S plane and along a scan line.

To impement this algorithm two arrays are used:

Color := Array to store the color of the pixel to be displayed

Depth := minimum value of Z_S at each X_S of the scan line.

The following steps are performed :

i) set Color[X_S] to background level and Depth[X_S] to 1.0 for each x on the scan line.

ii) for each face of the object, find all pixels (x values) on the current scan line Y_S that lie within the polygonal boundary of the face. For each of these pixels (i.e., each x value);

a) calculate the depth z of the polygon at (x, Y_S),

b) if the z < Depth[x] , then set Color[x] equal to the color of the corresponding face and Depth[x] = z.

iii) after all faces have been processed, the color array contains the solution for the current scan line. This array can now be copied into the frame buffer.

iv) repeat step (i), (ii) and (iii) for all scan lines and prepare the frame buffer.

The frame buffer now consists of the picture which has all hidden surfaces removed. To speed up the algorithm, the highest scan lines intersected by a polygon are determined. For each polygon attributes like number of scan line covered, highest scan line, list of polygon edges, co-effecient of plane equations, color etc. are stored in a suitable data structure.

7.7.3 Weiler-Atherton's algorithm

Warnock's algorithm is an image-space hidden-surface algorithm. Weiler and Atherton[19] developed an analogous object-space hidden-surface algorithm using image-space heuristics to speed up their object-space algorithm. The object space consists of a collection of polygons. The algorithm has the following structure:

- Step 1: Order all the polygons by their smallest z value (viewer is located at a z value of minus infinity).

- Step 2: Find the closest polygon, say P, to the viewer.

- Step 3: Form two buckets of polygons. The first bucket contains those polygons (called the inner set) whose projection overlaps (partially or totally) the projection of P on viewplane. The second bucket contains those polygons (referred to as the outer set) whose projection is not entirely covered by the projection of P. If a polygon falls in both the inner and outer sets, that polygon is clipped against P and the resulting polygons are stored in the appropriate sets.

- Step 4: Remove all polygons from the inner set that do not occlude part of P.
- Step 5: If no polygons occlude P (i.e., the inner set is empty), then the hidden-surface task has now been solved for P. Proceed to solve the hidden-surface task for the outer set.

- Step 6: If there exist polygons that occlude P (i.e., the inner set is nonempty), then recursively go to step 2 and choose a "nearest" polygon from the occluding polygons in the inner set of P. Upon return, process the outer set of P.

Two preprocessing methods are proposed to reduce the number of polygons that have to be compared in step 4. The first method recursively subdivides the image space (in the x and y directions) until the number of polygons in a given region, say R, drops below a specified threshold. Within region R, the basic algorithm described above is used. Note that at step 4, only the polygons in region R need to be considered.

The second method exploits subdivision in the z direction also in addition to subdividing in the x and y directions. In particular, after subdividing in the z direction, the hidden-surface task processes the backmost volume elements first, and then this solution is used as part of the polygon list for the volume elements in the front. The last heuristic could be viewed as an octree method - for deatils see [19] the section on parallel and perspective projections.

7.8 Generation and Display of Surfaces :

The enclosing surface, or boundary, of a well-behaved three dimensional object, unambiguously specifies the objects. Different views of a solid object can be generated using the surface representation. If objects are defined by a set of points, we have to fit suitable surfaces to depict the object. In a complex object, it may be difficult to represent surfaces by a single equation, and one has to use piecewise approximations.

One solution to represent a surface is to define a set of curves and then define interpolating surface patches over these curves. Bezier curves and splines which use guiding points or planes can also be used to generate a surface patch. The ultimate requirements for generating a realistic surface using patches are continuity and smoothness.

A surface can be described by any one of the following forms:

$$Z = f(x_X, y_Y)$$

$$F(x_X, y_Y, z_Z) = 0 \qquad (7.35)$$

$$X = X(U,V), \quad Y = Y(U,V), \quad \text{and} \quad Z = Z(U,V)$$

Equations (7.35) are called explicit, algebraic, and parametric representation of surfaces. In graphics, parametric representation is very convenient to use. In the followingsections, we describe techniques for approxmating surfaces.

7.8.1 Linear Surfaces :

To represent a triangular surface, we need at least three points V_1, V_2, and V_3. Let U and V be two variables ranging from 0 to 1. The surface $P(u,v)$ of a triangle with vertices at these points is given by :

$$P(u,v) = V_1 \cdot u + V_2 \cdot v + V_3 \cdot (1-u-v) \qquad (7.36)$$

provided $u + v \leq 0$.

It can be seen that $P(1,0) = V_1$, $P(0,1) = V_2$ and $P(0,0) = V_3$. Furthermore, $P(u,0)$ is the line joining vertices V_1 and V_3. $P(0,v)$ is the line joining V_2 and V_3, and $P(u, 1-u)$ is the line joining V_1 and V_2.

7.8.2 Coons Surfaces

This is a general technique [10, 11, 18] for approximating surfaces with four sided surface patches. Coons specified the four sides of the patch with polynomials.

Let B(U, V) be a function of two variables, such that, for constant U or V, B(U,V) reduces to a parametric representation of a curve. A surface patch blends the edge curves B(U,0), B(U,1), B(0,V) and B (1, V) in the following way :

$$P(U,V) = B(U,0)\cdot(1-V)+B(U,1)\cdot V+B(0,V)\cdot(1-U)+B(1,V)\cdot U-B$$
$$-B(0,0)\cdot(1-U)\cdot(1-V)-B(0,1)\cdot(1-U)\cdot V-B(1,0)\cdot U\cdot(1-V) \tag{7.37}$$

The terms with negative sign are used to avoid counting of pairwise intersection of the four curves twice. Equation (7.35) defines a continuous surface but it may not be smooth.

In the above two sections, '.' represents simple multiplication.

7.8.3 Bezier Surfaces :

In section 6.4.4, we had described the Bezier curves. The same formulation can be extended to describe three dimensional surfaces by generating the cartesian product of two curves. We use two similar blending functions, one for each parameter:

$$P(U,V) = \sum_{I=0}^{N}\sum_{J=0}^{M} P_{I,J} B_{I,N}(U) B_{J,M}(V) \tag{7.38}$$

The surface generated will have (N+1)×(M+1) control points arranged in a mesh. The surfaces are generated by using two sets of curves. In one set we keep *U* constant and vary *V* in the range of 0 to 1. Similarly, for the other set we keep *V* constant and vary *U*. The curves of constant *U* and *V* are Bezier curves. If we set *V*=0 then equation (7.36) reduces to:

$$P(U,0) = \sum_{I=0}^{N} P_{I,0} B_{I,N}(U) \tag{7.39}$$

In case of Bezier surfaces also we can generate patches. A Bezier patch and its control points are shown in figure 7-36 where patches are created using isoparametric lines. As depicted in the figure 7-36, the 16 control points (P_{00}, P_{10},...) form the characteristic polyhedron which controls the shape of the surface in the same way as the characteristic polygon conrols the shape of the curve. It can be seen that 12 control points define the boundary edges of the surface patch and 4 conrol points define the internal shape. Only the corner vertices lie in the surface. Continuity between two patches can be achieved in the same fashion as between two curves (see figure 6.23). A point on the surface patch is given by a bi-parametric function and a set of blending or basis function are used for each parameter.

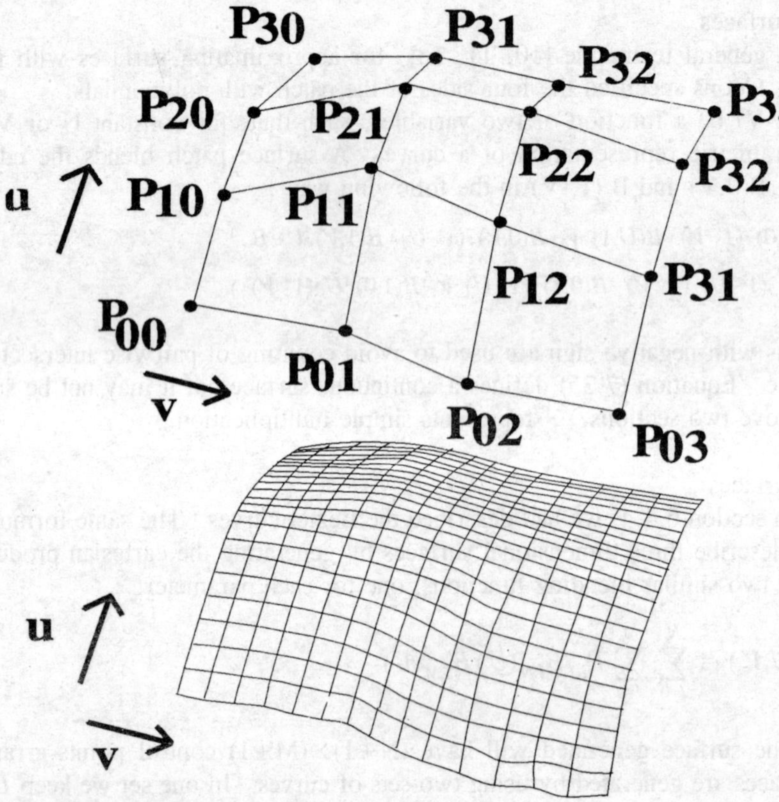

Figure 7-36 A control polyhedron and the resulting bicubic Bezier surface patch

A cubic Bezier patch is defined by changing both I and J values in equation 7.38 from 0 to 3, i.e. by 4 x 4 control points arranged in a mesh:

$$P(U,V) = \sum_{I=0}^{3} \sum_{J=0}^{3} P_{I,J} B_{I,3}(U) B_{J,3}(V) \qquad (7.39)$$

This can be represented in matrix form as follows:

$$P(u,v) = \left[u^3 \; u^2 \; u^1 \; u^0 \right] \left[BPB^T \right] \begin{bmatrix} u^3 \\ u^2 \\ u^1 \\ u^0 \end{bmatrix} \qquad (7.40)$$

where

$$B = \begin{bmatrix} -1 & 3 & -3 & 1 \\ 3 & -6 & 3 & 0 \\ -3 & 3 & 0 & 0 \\ 1 & 0 & 0 & 0 \end{bmatrix}$$

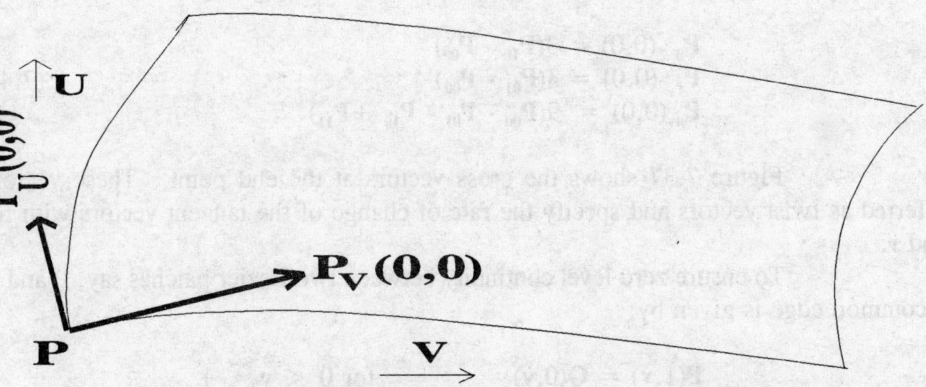

Figure 7-37 Shows tangent vectors at end point P_{00}

$$P = \begin{bmatrix} P_{00} & P_{11} & P_{12} & P_{13} \\ P_{20} & P_{21} & P_{22} & P_{23} \\ P_{30} & P_{31} & P_{32} & P_{33} \\ P_{40} & P_{41} & P_{42} & P_{43} \end{bmatrix}$$

The matrix $\mathbf{BPB^T}$ has following regions:

- end points;
- tangent vectors at each end point along the v parametric direction;
- tangent vectors at each end point along the u parametric direction; and
- cross derivatives at each point.

It can be seen that at the corner u=v=0, the relationship between the control points and the vectors or the derivatives associated with the vertex $\mathbf{P_{00}}$ is:

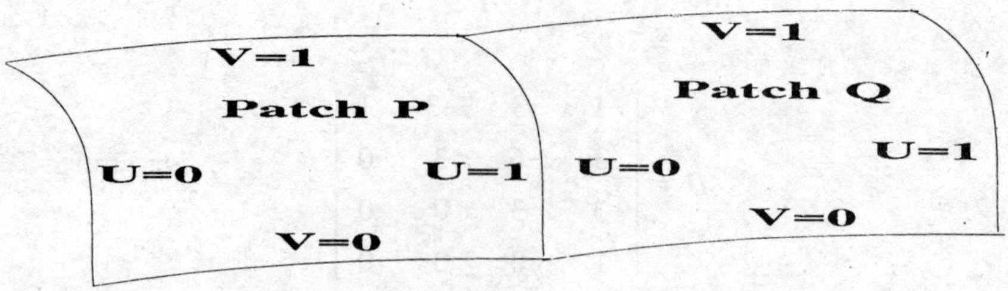

Figure 7-38 Joining two cubic Bezier patches P and Q

$$\begin{aligned} \mathbf{P}_u\ (0,0) &= 3(\mathbf{P}_{10} - \mathbf{P}_{00}) \\ \mathbf{P}_v\ (0,0) &= 3(\mathbf{P}_{01} - \mathbf{P}_{00}) \\ \mathbf{P}_{uv}(0,0) &= 9(\mathbf{P}_{00} - \mathbf{P}_{01} - \mathbf{P}_{10} + \mathbf{P}_{11}) \end{aligned} \tag{7.41}$$

Figure 7.37 shows the cross vectors at the end point. These vectors are also referred as twist vectors and specify the rate of change of the tangent vectors with respect to *u* and *v*.

To ensure zero level continuity between two Bezier patches say, P and Q, sharing a common edge is given by:

$$\mathbf{P}(1,v) = \mathbf{Q}(0,v) \qquad \text{for } 0 \le v \le 1$$

This implies that

$$\begin{aligned} \mathbf{P}_{33} &= \mathbf{Q}_{03} \\ \mathbf{P}_{32} &= \mathbf{Q}_{02} \\ \mathbf{P}_{31} &= \mathbf{Q}_{01} \\ \mathbf{P}_{30} &= \mathbf{Q}_{00} \end{aligned}$$

Further, to satisfy first order continuity the tangent vectors at $u=1$ for the patch P must match these at $u=0$ for the Q patch for all values of v. This means that each of the four pairs of polyhedron edges defining the boundary must be collinear as shown in figure 7.38. This condition is similar to the one for the Bezier curves (see Chapter6). The collinear condition is given by:

$$\mathbf{P}_{3i} - \mathbf{P}_{2i} = K\,(\mathbf{Q}_{1i} - \mathbf{Q}_{0i}) \qquad \text{For } i = 0,\ldots,3$$

It may be noted that for joining two cubic Bezier patches along a common boundary predefines 8 control points of the second Bezier patch and joining patch to the two other existing patches fixes 12 control points. This restriction imposes problems in the design of the composite surfaces. The solution to this probem is either to compromize on positional rather than gradient continuity or to use patches of higher degree than cubic.

7.8.4 Display of surfaces

The simplest method for displaying surfaces is the wire frame technique. A curve is displayed by evaluating its value for many closely spaced values of parameter U, these points are displayed and are joined by straight lines. A surface is displayed by generating a mesh of these curves holding U or V constant at a time. You can also utilize intensity modulation by using the Z-coordinate to create the notion of depth. Thus, by changing the view point you can generate different views to convey information about the shape of an object. To improve display of an object with plane surfaces a grey level or a shade is assigned to each visible surface.

7.8.5 Algorithm for Display of Bezier Surfaces

An algorithm for the display of Bezier surfaces is given below.

Input Format : The following parameters are required to describe a Bezier surface :

Pixel Buffer : It is defined as an array IMAGE [1..4, i, j] such that

$$\text{IMAGE } [1..4, i, j] = (U, V, Z, \text{ATTRIBUTE})$$

Indices i and j correspond to ij^{th} pixel on the screen. The traditional Z-buffer has only Z-value for each pixel but extended z-buffer has data fields for U and V components and an attribute word containing information about the material, color, or texture of the sample point. In the program given in the next section only traditional Z-buffer has been used.

Order : This describes the degree of the patch in U and V directions, say 'm' and 'n'. Generally the order of surface for U and V directions is taken as same.

Control Points : $(n+1)*(m+1)$ control points are required to describe a Bezier surface.

Therefore, to create a bi-cubic Bezier surface patch 16 control points are required. The patch definition consists of order in which control points are used to generate surface patches. The database contains patch definition for each patch followed by the x-, y-, and z- coordinates of control points in order.

Step 1: Initialise

Initialise all program parameters, such as viewport size, viewing matrices and pixel buffer etc. Initialise, Z components of pixel buffer to the 'Yon' clipping plane so that sample points of the object will be in front when compared with the buffer.

Step 2: First Transform Control Points

Generating sample points on the surface and transforming each sample point by viewing transform 'T' results in the same surface patch as Bezier surface patch generated by just the control points transformed by T [5,8]. This property is utilised to minimise computation as follows:

i) all control points are transformed using 'T',

ii) sample points are generated using transformed control points to create the surface.

Perspective transform is not included in the viewing transform. Thus, viewing transform remains an affine mapping. The perspective transform is applied on each of the sample points computed to create the Bezier surface.

Step 3: Clipping : It is known that all points of a Bezier surfacepatch are contained within the convex hull of the control points. This property ensures that if all the control points of the patch are within the viewing window the resulting surface patch is also within the viewing window.

If after transformation all control points of a patch go outside the viewing window, the patch is discarded. However, if after transformation some control points of a patch map outside the viewing window but on the either side of pixel buffer clipping plane then the patch is divided into four smaller sub patches. The process of sub division is applied recursively as is done in the Quad Tree Algorithm (see section 7.7.1).

It may be noted that to minimise amount of sub-division necessary for clipping, the size of pixel buffer is taken as slightly larger than the viewing window. However, in the program given in the next section, clipping based on this approach has not been implemented.

Step 4: Step size in *U* and *V* directions: The quantum of increments (or step size) in the *U* and *V* parameters is decided by the value of Num_U and Num_V parameters which correspond to number of iso-parametric lines in *U*- and *V*- directions respectively. Therefore, step size in *U*- and *V*- directions is defined by

Inc_U = 1/Num_U; Inc_V = 1/Num_V

If step size is small, surface patch created is more accurate. However, the amount of computation required to scan the surface to generate sample points on the patch is increased.

Step 5: Creation of sample points on the patch: Scanning the surface patch to create sample points amounts for the most of the computational load except in cases when the patch size is extremely small. To create sample points, parametric equation 6-38 is used to compute x, y, and *z* co-ordinates (also see example 6.15). Programs Creatsur.pas and Creatsph.pas generate cubic and quadratic Bezier curves respectively.

Step 6: Perspective Transformation : Each sample point created on the surface patch is transformed using a perspective transformation.

Step 7: Display of Wireframe: The sample points can now be displayed using suitable commands like 'move' and 'draw' supported by display hardware. A program to fill up the gaps between two sample points by a line segment can also be used. The wireframe surface display (including hidden surfaces) develops on the screen as points are computed.

Step 8: Hidden Surface Removal using Z Buffer Algorithm: The sample points created in step 6 are entered into the pixel buffer (Viewport_array in the program). As mentioned in step 1 the pixel buffer is initialised to the value defining the 'yon' clipping plane in the Z direction. The Z value of current sample point obtained after perspective transformation is compared with the existing value in the Z buffer. If current value is smaller, i.e., the point is closer to the viewer, it becomes the new value at that location in the pixel buffer.

Step 9: Scan Complete Surface Patch: Create points on current surface patch by computing all sample points for all values of $0 < U < 1$ and $0 < V < 1$ in steps of Inc_U and Inc_V. Repeat procedure from step 5 till scanning of complete patch is accomplished.

Step 10: Create other surface patches : Use control points for the next patch and repeat the procedure from step 2. After all surface patches are scanned the pixel buffer contains the intensities for the object with the hidden surfaces removed.

Step 11: Display of surface: At this stage the wireframe representation of the surface with all surfaces is shown on the sereen. The data in pixel buffer now contain the *Z* values scaled in the desired range. To display on graphic hardware, we have scaled Z in the range 0 to 31 to correspond to the intensity values. These are taken as gray levels and are displayed using half toning technique described in Chapter 2.

COMMENTS :

1. To reduce the computational requirement the effect of the perspective transform can be ignored and the perspective transorm can be included in the viewing transform. It has been observed [8] that given a curve bounded by a viewing box of size 1000 on a side and a common perspective taken at d = 2500, the worst case variation in the final picture is not more than 4%.
2. A Pascal procedure to implement this algorithm is given in the section 7.8.6.
3. The program is tested on the Teapot data on pages 12-14 of " The Origins of the Teapot" in the Displays on Display Department, IEEE Computer Graphics and Applications, Jan. 1987. Surface patches defining any object can be generated by creating data in this format.

7.8.6 Procedure to run Surface Program

The following paragraph describes the procedure for running the surface program.

Description: This is an interactive package to generate surfaces, e.g., sphere, teapot, and doughnut in the form of wireframe surfaces through use of Bezier curves.

File name: Surface.pas

Include files: initial.pas - {initialises graphic hardware}
viewport.pas - {converts world co-ordinates into screen or viewport co- ordinates}
visible.pas - {removes hidden surfaces using Z-buffer algorithm also creates a viewport array}
line.pas - {creates all points on a line from (x1, y1) to (x2,y2)
creatpnt.pas - (generates perspective view for each point and calls line procedure to generate all points on the surface}
trans3d.pas - {defines 3-dimensional transformations
ditherplot . pas - {generates gray levels based on half toning techniques described in section 2.6}
wrtimage.pas -{saves the image on the backup device}
hardcopy.pas -{generates hard copy of this screen on Epson printer}
Creatsur.pas - {creats bi-cubic surface patches}
or
Creatsph.pas - {ten control points are defined in this program to generate 2 surface patches to create a sphere}

Data files: Teapot.DTA - {contains surface patch definitions and co-ordinates of control points for teapot}
Donut.DTA - {same as above for doughnut.

source: IEEE Computer Graphics and Applications, Vol. 7, No. 4, April 87 p. 61}

Initial Settings :

1. Define viewport size, and screen size in the screen areas reserved for ditherplot and wireframe of the object respectively.
   Default values : Viewport_Size = 100, and Screen_Size = 350
2. Set value of NUM_U and NUM_V parameters to select number of iso-parametric lines in U_ & V_ directions.
3. Select object as defined in the comments given in the main program entitled 'surface'. Three objects viz. sphere, teapot, and doughnut can be selected.
4. Set Order, CP_Count, Patch_Count, Program name & data file (NAM_DTA), and World Range as given in the comment section of the surface program. Only one include file among Creatsph.pas and CreatSur.pas should be invoked at a time. Creatsph.pas file generates sphere only using Bezier curves of order two.
5. Call to procedure 'HardCopyImage' should be invoked only by uncommenting the call in the main line program if hardcopy of image on the screen is required.

Run time interaction : A typical dialogue for generating a teapot is given below :
HardCopyImage call should be commented if printer is offline.
To create a sphere, program "Creatsph.pas" should be included.
Set: Order, CP_Count, Patch_Count, Datafile, Num_U, Num_V, etc.
Select Dither :- Enter 3 - for 3×3 and 4 - for 4×4
3 <ret>
Do you Want to Transform (y/n) ?
y <Ret>
Enter "1" to Scale, "2" to Translate, Rotate Axis : "3"-X, "4"-Y, "S"-Z, 'O' to Exit
3 <Ret>
Enter three parameters for transformation in the same line
90 0 0 <Ret>
Enter "1" to Scale, "2" to Translate, Rotate Axis : "3"-X, "4"-Y, "S"-Z, 'O' to Exit
4 <Ret>
Enter three parameters for transformation in the same line
90 0 0 <Ret>
Enter "1" to Scale, "2" to Translate, Rotate Axis : "3"-X, "4"-Y, "S"-Z, 'O' to Exit
0 <Ret>

Action: 1. Transformation matrix for 90 degree rotation about the X-axis is computed. This matrix is used for concatenating the next operation i.e., 90 degree rotation about Y-axis.

2. The resulting transformation matrix is used for computing the new position of the control points of the object.

3. The program shows the wireframe of the object (as it develops) on the display in the screen area followed by gray level plot using 3 x 3 dither (see chapter 2) of the object with hidden surfaces removed in the viewport. The default viewport size is taken as 100 but the resultant display is of size 300 x 300 due to the use of the dither. Gray scale used to display the shades is also shown. You can use a VGA or a better display card and can create colour or monochrome images without the use of dither.

Wait for caption 'Ditherplot of the image' to appear on the lower left corner of the display. Press any key on keyboard twice.

A hard copy of the screen is created on the printer in case 'HardCopyImage' statement is active.

File name to save ditherplot of the object or "0" to Exit.

Filename.xxx

Action : 1. An image is created on the disk.
2. Exit to DOS.

The complete listing of the surface program, written using Turbo Pascal as well s *C* language can be obtained from the authors (see Preface).

Example 7.12: Figures 7.39 and 7.40 show pictures of 'teapot' and 'sphere' respectively with the following input parameters:

Num_U = 4; Num_V = 4.

In each case, both the dither plot and the wireframe are depicted for these input parameters.

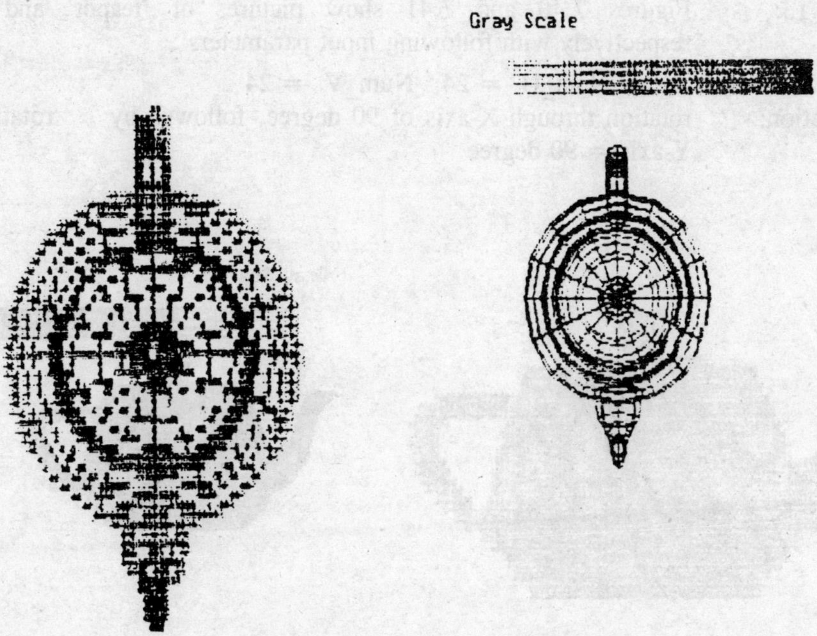

(a) Dither plot using 4*4 dither (b) Wireframe with hidden surfaces

Figure 7.39 : Dither plot and Wireframe of Teapot

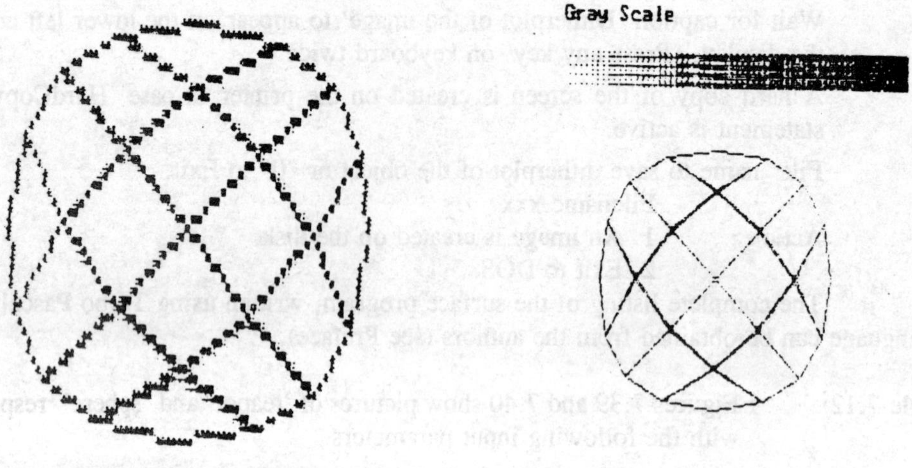

(a) Dither plot using 4*4 dither (b) Wireframe with hidden surfaces

Figure 7.40 : Dither plot and Wireframe of Sphere

Example 7.13: Figures 7.40 and 7.41 show pictures of 'teapot' and doughnut' respectively with following input parameters :

Num_U = 24; Num_V = 24

Transformation: rotation through X-axis of 90 degree, followed by rotation through Y-axis = 90 degree

(a) Dither plot using 4*4 dither (b) Wireframe with hidden surface

Figure 7.41 : Ditherplot and Wireframe of Teapot

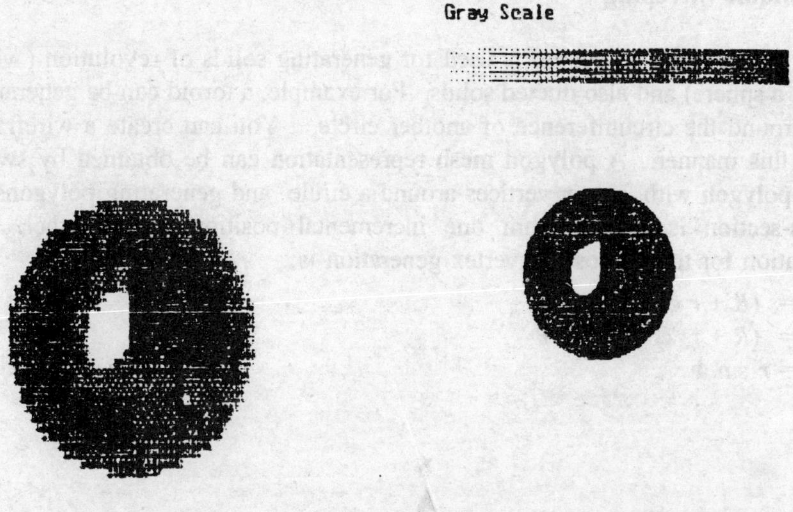

(a) Dither plot using 4*4 dither (b) Wireframe with hidden surface

Figure 7.42 : Ditherplot & Wireframe of Doughnut

Example 7.14: Set parameters for 'teapot' in the surface program, assign Num_U = 4 and Num_V = 4.

Transformation: 90 degree rotation about X-axis followed by 90 degree rotation about Y-axis.

Figure 7.43 depicts the dither plot and wireframe image of the teapot.

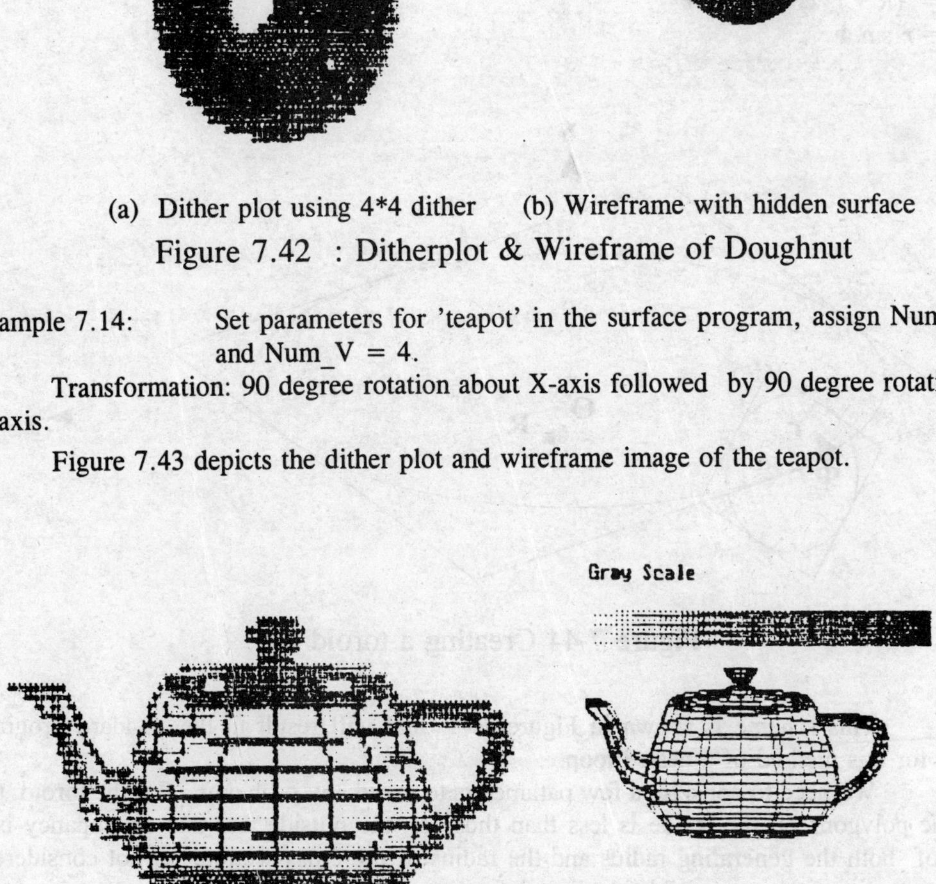

(a) Dither plot using 4*4 dither (b) Wireframe with hidden surface

Figure 7.43 : Ditherplot and wireframe of teapot

7.9 Volume Sweeping

Volume sweeping is used for generating solids of revolution (viz. a cylinder, a cone, and a sphere) and also ducted solids. For example, a toroid can be generated by sweeping a circle around the circumference of another circle. You can create a wireframe model of a toroid in this manner. A polygon mesh representation can be obtained by sweeping a cross-sectional polygon with, say, *n* vertices around a circle and generating polygons (on the fly) as the cross-section is moved from one incremental position to the other. A parametric representation for the purpose of vertex generation is:

$$x = (R + r\cos\Phi)\cos\theta$$
$$y = (R + r\cos\Phi)\sin\theta$$
$$z = r\sin\Phi$$

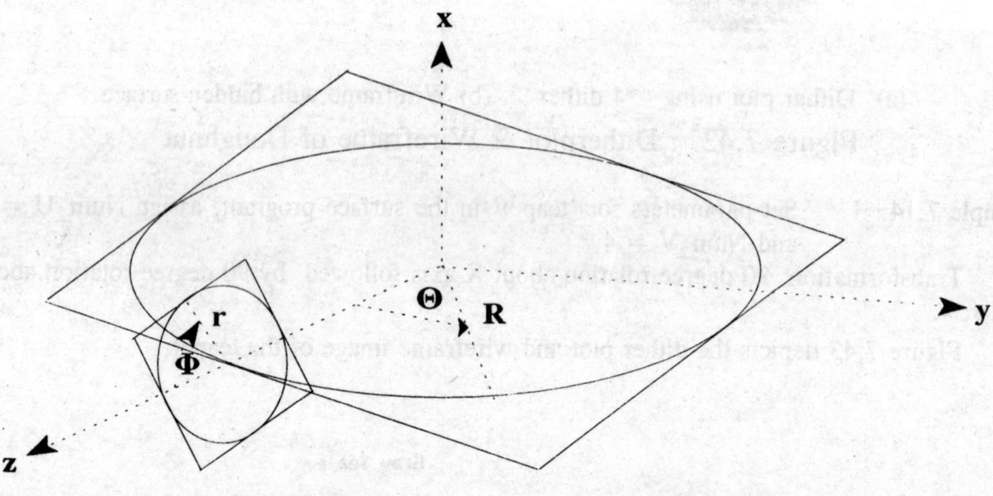

Figure 7-44 Creating a toroid

This scheme is shown in Figure 7.44 and will result in the standard program structure, for this method of a nested loop.

We need to consider a few parameters to avoid any problems. For the toroid, the size of the polygons on the inside is less than those on the outside and this discrepancy is a function of both the generating radius and the radius of the cross-section. If not considered, such discrepancies can cause visible shading defects.

Instead of a circle, one can take any object and move it around a circumference to generate other shapes. Input this shape as a cross-section to a module that derives a three dimensional polygon mesh model by rotating the cross-section around a selected circumference.

7.10 Rendering a Cylinder

A cylinder can be described by it's end points and radius. We consider a unit radius cylinder with axis along Z, stretching from Z=0 to Z=1. To make a generalized description of a cylinder, we need to develop a transformation matrix that will turn this into a cylinder stretching from (X_1,Y_1,Z_1) to (X_2,Y_2,Z_2). Following are the steps:

- Compute the length of the line from (X_1,Y_1,Z_1) to (X_2,Y_2,Z_2). It is given by:

$$D = \sqrt{(X_2 - X_1)^2 + (Y_2 - Y_1)^2 + (Z_2 - Z_1)^2}$$

- Scale the cylinder in XY by the desired radius R and in Z by length D.
- Rotate the cylinder to orient it along the line joining the points (X_1,Y_1,Z_1) and (X_2,Y_2,Z_2) and then translate it to the point (X_1,Y_1,Z_1).

In the above steps, translation and scaling operations are simple but to derive the rotation matrix, **M**, requires some work. The procedure to derive **M** is :

i. Find the unit vector along the axis of the cylinder as given below:

$$[X_a,Y_a,Z_a] = [(X_2-X_1)/D,(Y_2-Y_1)/D,(Z_2-Z_1)/D]$$

ii. The elements of the matrix **M** should be defined in such a way so as to rotate the axis of the standard cylinder, [0, 0, 1], to coincide with this axis. This requirement can be stated as follows:

$$[0,\ 0,\ 1]M = [X_a,\ Y_a,\ Z_a].$$

iii. The third row of the matrix can be written by inspection. We can exploit the following facts to determine the other rows of the matrix, **M**:

- The object under consideration is a Cylinder. We, therefore, can ignore some rotation about the cylinder's Z axis.
- Each row of the rotation matrix can be considered as a unit-length vector, and each of these vectors is perpendicular to the others. The vector perpendicular to $[X_a,Y_a,Z_a]$ will have it's dot product with $[X_a,Y_a,Z_a]$ zero. We can try following vector:

$$\left[-\frac{Y_a}{d},\ \frac{X_a}{d},\ 0\right]$$

where $d=\sqrt{X_a^2+Y_a^2}$

It satisfies the dot product condition and is, therefore, perpendicular to $[X_a, Y_a, Z_a]$. Now, we have to find the second row of the matrix **M**. The vector representing the second row has to be perpendicular to the first and the third row vectors. We can get it from the cross

$$[X_a, Y_a, Z_a] \times \left[-\frac{Y_a}{d}, \frac{X_a}{d}, 0\right]$$

$$=\left[-X_a\, Z_a/d,\; -Y_a\, Z_a/d,\; (X_a^2+Y_a^2)\right]$$

iv. Now, we can write the rotation matrix, **M**, as

$$M = \begin{bmatrix} -Y_a\,/d & X_a\,/d & 0 \\ -X_a\,Z_a\,/d & -Y_a\,Z_a\,/d & d \\ X_a & Y_a & Z_a \end{bmatrix}$$

If value of $d=0$, the cylinder axis points along Z. It may, however, point in the negative direction. We can use *X* axis, [1, 0, 0], in this case to determine the first row, and cross product of the first and the third row to compute the second row of the matrix **M**.

7.10.1 Drawing cylinder

As mentioned earlier, we use a unit standard cylinder. Further, we can use only polygons as bounding faces, so the circular base of a cylinder needs to be approximated by a regular polygon, say of *n* vertices. Now, how do we select the value of *n*? The larger the value *n*, the better is the approximation but the computation as well as storage requirement would also increase. If we select $n=4$ the solid becomes a prism and not a cylinder. To generate a cylinder a larger value of *n* is used, say 30. One can, now draw the cylinder using the following commands:

Translate	X_1,Y_1,Z_1	
Rotate	Matrix **M**	
Scale	R, R, D	R is radius and D is length of cylinder.
Draw	Cylinder	

The 'Draw Cylinder' command uses the standard unit cylinder. This command is not implemented in the package described in the earlier section. A simple approach for rendering a cylinder will be to divide it into 6 or 8 polygonal facets, i.e. $n=6$ or 8. With Gouraud shading (described in the next section) this may look acceptable but the silhouette edges and shading boundaries are only approximations. Given the eye point and lighting direction, Blinn [3] describes a technique to divide the cylinder into polygons at only *visually significant* places. This techniques helps in economizing polygons and thus speeding the rendering process. The visually significant places are of two kinds: the silhouette edges of the cylinder and break points in the intensity of the cylinder.

7.10.2 Silhouette edges

These are the points where a line from the eye is tangent to the cylinder and determine the visual extent of the cylinder on the screen. The main advantage of using coordinate system of the unit cylinder is that it becomes a 2-D problem instead of 3-D. Let us imagine an infinite cylinder centered on the Z axis and being viewed from the point $[X_E, Y_E, Z_E]$. The planes throgh the eye point and tangent to the cylinder are parallel to Z axis. Therefore, we can ignore the Z_E coordinate of the eye. Further, if the cylinder stretches from Z=0 to Z=1 then the tangent planes do not change whether Z_E is above or below the cylinder. The procedure for finding silhouette points is as follows:

- Transform the eye point by the inverse of the current viewing/modelling transformation into the coordinate system of the unit cylinder. This gives $[X_E, Y_E, Z_E]$.
- Discard Z_E.
- Find the 2D points of tangency from the point E = $[X_E, Y_E]$ to the unit circle at the origin. In a special case when eye point is on the X axis a distance E to the right (see figure 7-45). By similar triangles, dimensions of the smaller triangle (see figure 7-46) and hence, the

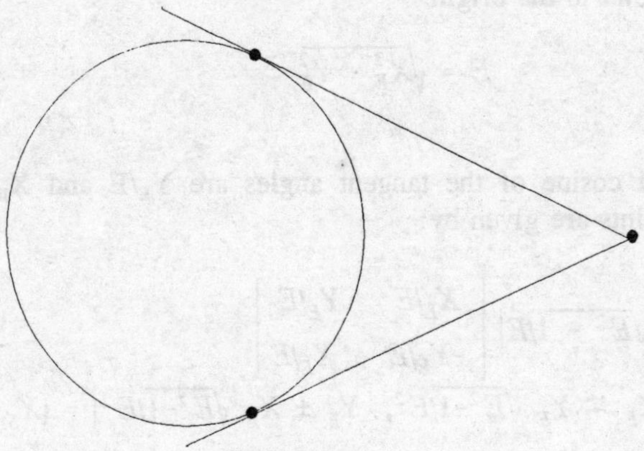

Figure 7-45 Shows silhouette points on a circle

coordinates of the tangent points are:

$$[1/E, \ \pm[\sqrt{E^2} - 1/E]$$

To compute the tangent points of a arbtrary point $[X_E, Y_E]$, just rotate as E is still

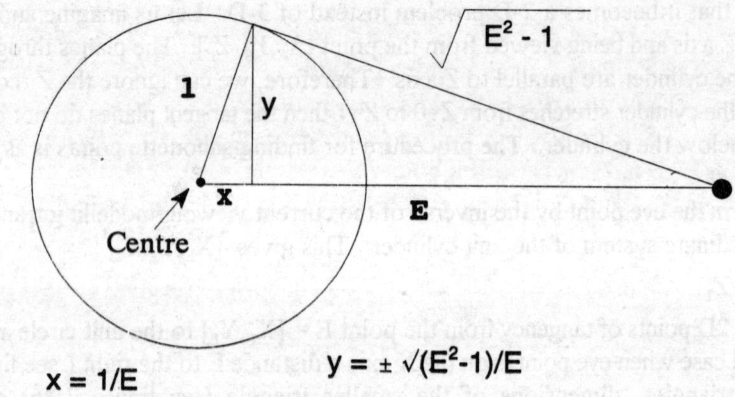

Figure 7-46 Computation of sihouette coordinates

the distance from the eye point to the origin:

$$E = \sqrt{X_E^2 + Y_E^2}$$

The sine and cosine of the tangent angles are Y_E/E and X_E/E respectively. Therefore, the silhouette points are given by:

$$\left[1/E,\ \pm\ [\sqrt{E^2 - 1}/E]\right] \begin{bmatrix} X_E/E & Y_E/E \\ -Y_E/E & X_E/E \end{bmatrix}$$
$$= \left[\ (X_E \mp Y_E \sqrt{E^2-1}/E^2,\ \ Y_E \pm X_E \sqrt{E^2-1}/E^2\right] = [X_S,\ Y_S]$$

If the eye is inside the cylinder, quantity E^2-1 may become negative.

7.10.3 Finding intensity breakpoints

We determine points where intensity might change and put edges at these points. Although, number of such points can be defined but Blinn[3] has put edges at two situations, viz. the terminator point - the boundary between day side and night side and the maximum brightness point. In case of Lambert's law shading the maximum brightness point is where the dot product of the surface normal vector and the light source direction is a maximum.

Let us take a light source L and transform it into unit cylinder coordinates to yield (X_L, Y_L, Z_L), the maximum dot product point on the circle is just uner the light source. It is given by:

$$B = \left[X_L / \sqrt{X_L^2 + Y_L^2},\ Y_L / \sqrt{X_L^2 + Y_L^2}\right]$$

The formula for the terminator points can be obtained by putting $[X_L, Y_L]$ in the formula we used for computing the the silhouette points. Thus, two terminator points are obtained but we need only which fall on the visible side of the cylinder. The light source is generally modeled as being at infinity so when we map the light source in the unit cylinder space, we encounter $[x_L, y_L, z_L, w_L]$ with $w_L = 0$. To circumvent this we need to use homogeneous formula.

7.10.4 Homogeneous formula

A homogeneous point and line are represented by a 3-element row and column vector respectively:

Point: $[x, y, w]$

Line: $\begin{bmatrix} a \\ b \\ c \end{bmatrix}$

A point on the second order curve will satisfy the equation f (x,y,w). We can also use a 3 x 3 matrix Q so that for the points on the curve:

$$f(x, y, w) = [x, y, w]\ Q\ [x, y, w]^T = 0$$

A point on the curve will have one line tangent at that point. The gradient of f will give the coordinates of that line. From the above equation, the gradient can be expressed as matrix product by differentiating f:

$$Q \begin{bmatrix} x \\ y \\ w \end{bmatrix} = \begin{bmatrix} a \\ b \\ c \end{bmatrix}$$

If we substitute a point in the equation of the curve which is not on the curve, we get another line called polar line. This line connects the two point of tangency as shown in figure 7-47. For a unit circle with centre at the origin, the matrix Q is given by:

$$\begin{bmatrix} 1 & 0 & 0 \\ 0 & 1 & 0 \\ 0 & 0 & -1 \end{bmatrix}$$

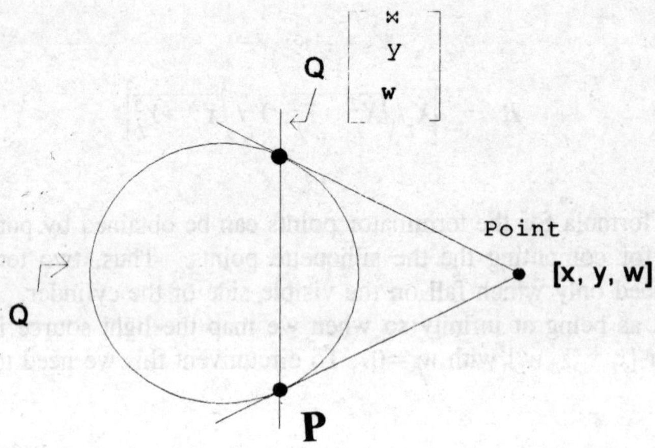

Figure 7.47 The polar line

We can easily write the equation of the polar line from the point [x, y, w] as

$$Q\begin{bmatrix} x \\ y \\ w \end{bmatrix} = \begin{bmatrix} x \\ y \\ -w \end{bmatrix}$$

To locate the two tangent points we intersect the polar line with the unit circle and write the polar line parametrically in terms of two points on it. Thus,

$$P(\alpha) = [xw, yw, x^2 + y^2] + \alpha[-y, x, 0]$$

It can be verified that both the points in the above equation lie on the polar line. The first point on the polar line is closest to the origin and the second point is the intersection of the polar line with the line at infinity. Substitute this point in PQ and solve for α. The result is

$$\alpha = (x^2 + y^2 - w^2)^{1/2}$$

If the expression inside bracket is negative, the point is inside the circle. Otherwise,

$$x_{tang} = xw \mp y\sqrt{x^2+y^2-w^2}$$

$$y_{tang} = yw \mp x\sqrt{x^2+y^2-w^2}$$

$$z_{tang} = x^2+y^2$$

This formula can be used with $[x_E, y_E, w_E]$ to get the silhouette points and with $[x_L, y_L, w_L]$ to determine the terminator points.

The use of the polar line facilitates in separating the visible part (i.e. eye point facing) of the cylinder from the not visible part. The polar line from the eye point is given by

$$Q\,E^T = \begin{bmatrix} x_E \\ y_E \\ -w_E \end{bmatrix} = V$$

We exploit the fact that the sign of the dot product of any point with a line shows on which side of the line the point is located. One can use a test point to verify this. The dot product of polar line with eye point is

$$E \,.\, V = [x_E,\, y_E,\, w_E] \begin{bmatrix} x_E \\ y_E \\ -w_E \end{bmatrix}$$

$$= x_E^2 + y_E^2 - w_E^2$$

This will be positive if the eye point is outside the circle. In other words positive sign indicates visible.

7.10.5 Algorithm for rendering

Now, we can describe the algorithm:

- Transform eye point into unit cylinder space. This gives point $[X_E, Y_E, Z_E]$. Compute silhouette point S_1 and S_2.
- Transform light source into unit cylinder space. This gives point $[X_L, Y_L, Z_L]$. Compute point T_1 and T_2.
- Calculate the sublight point B.
- Output S_1.
- If $[T_1 \,.\, V] > 0$, output T_1.
- If $[B \,.\, V] > 0$, output B.
- If $[T_2 \,.\, V] > 0$, output T_2.
- Output S_2.

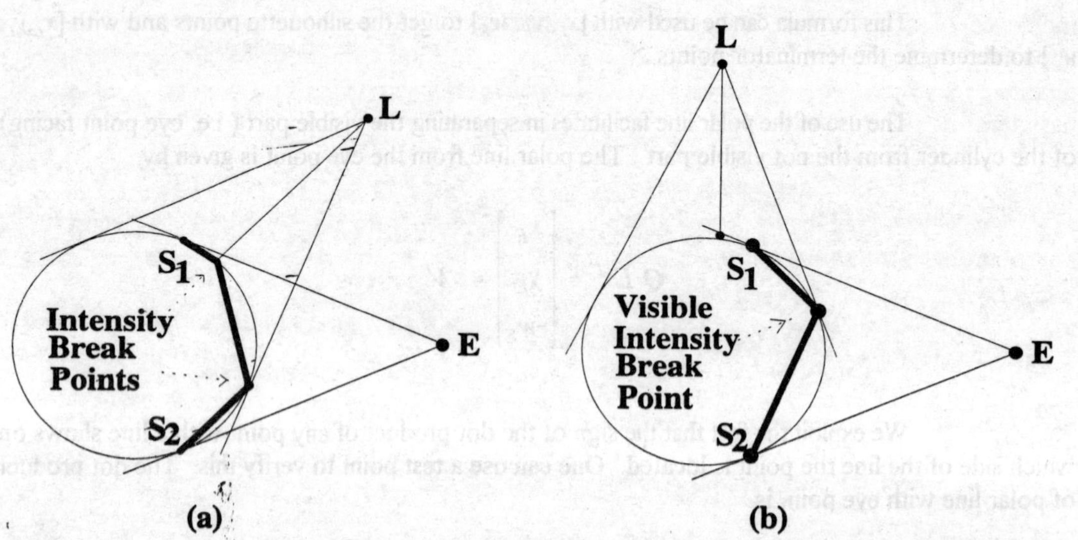

Figure 7-48 Two different sources of light and the corresponding generated polygons

The output takes only a 2-D point, say [X,Y], on the unit circle and generates a polygon edge from [X, Y, 0] to [X, Y, 1]. The normal vector along that edge to be used for shading is N = [X, Y, 0]. Join consecutive edges into polygons. Pass the edge and normal vector (using inverse of point transformation routine) to the screen.

Figure 7-48 (a) and (b) show the number of polygon edges required for light source in different location. It may be noticed that figure 7-48 (a) required two edges whereas the figure (b) was generated using only one edge because only one terminator point was in the visible zone of the circle. Blinn[2] developed this algorithm to cut down considerably the number of polygons required to model and render the Voyager space craft. This algorithm reduces the number of edges to bare minimum so as to produce acceptable images. This method is a crude approximation to real cylinder which will not hold up if we go too near it. The shading generated is good but end points of the cylinder are not sharp.

7.10 Shading

In the above section, we described a simple algorithm for rendering cylinders. A simple hidden surface elimination algorithm approximates a smooth surface as a polyhedron. Thus, the smoothness of surface is lost. The basic goal of a shading algorithm is to restore the smooth appearance and introduce considerable realism in the scene. In other words, each algorithm is an attempt to find a compromise between precision and computational cost. However, normal polyhedron shading perturbs the user as the polyhedral approximation is still visible and the edges of the object contain line segments.

A shading algorithm considers - properties of a surface, properties of the light falling on it and the interaction of light with a surface. Based on the surface properties, the light incident at it is either reflected, scattered, absorbed, or transmitted. The main properties of light are its intensity and wavelength. The main property of surface of concern are its reflectance and transparency. Reflectance determines how much of the incident light on the surface is reflected. The reflectance of a surface is function of wavelength of the incident light, and the angle of incidence. For the surface having different reflectance for the light of varying wavelengths, it appears to be coloured. The reflectance will vary with the position on a surface which has a texture or pattern on it. Transparency determines how much of light incident on a surface will pass through the surface.

A scene may comprise of

- objects which have illumination that is uniform from all directions - referred to as diffused illumination;
- light sources which cause specular reflections or highlights from the surfaces of some of the objects;
- objects whose illumination may be partially blocked due to shadows of the other objects in the scene.

7.10.1 A simple shading model

The shading model computes shading term E by taking into consideration three main components: contribution from diffused components, effect of one or more light sources, and transparency effect. These components are then added to determine the total energy coming out from a point on the object.

7.10.1.1 Contribution from diffused component

The diffused energy E_{Ad} from point A due to diffuse illumination I_d is given by:

$$E_{Ad} = R_A I_d \tag{7.42}$$

where R_A is the reflectance co-efficient at point A and it is linked to the energy emitted by point A and to that reaching it, i.e. it depends on the nature of the material and the wavelength of the incident light. The value of R_A varies between 0 to 1.

If we generate a picture using only diffused component of light, it does not look realistic because change in orientation of the surface does not change its shade. However, a surface that is a perfect diffuser, scatters light energy equally in all directions. In this case, the amount of diffused light seen by an observer does not depend on his position. Such surfaces are dull or matt. The intensity of diffuse reflected light is given by Lambert's law, which states that energy falling on a surface $E_{A\gamma}$ varies as a cosine of the angle of incidence of the light, i.e.,

$$E_{A\gamma} = (R_A \cos \alpha)\, IA\gamma, \quad 0 \leq \alpha \leq \pi/2 \tag{7.43}$$

where $I_{A\gamma}$ is the energy arriving from the light source which is reflected uniformly in all directions and α is the angle between the surface normal N_A and a ray from the light source (see figure 7-49). The surface is hidden from the light source if α is greater than 90 degrees and then $E_{A\gamma}$ is set to 0. As has been seen in the previous section, the points on the visible portion of the cylinder surface facing the light source were bright but other points though in visible zone were depicted using lower intensity. However, if we use this model the portion of the cylinder not covered by the light source, though visible will become dark. In real world, there is always some diffused light and no portion of the object becomes completely dark.

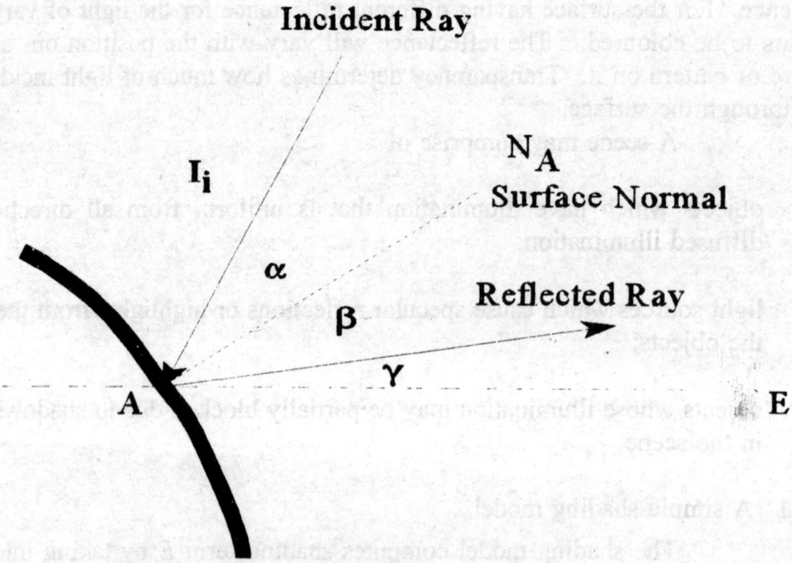

Figure 7-49 shows shading of point A

The above equation can also be written as the dot product of two vectors, by replacing cos α by $L.N_A$, as

$$E_{A\gamma} = R_A \;\; I_{A\gamma} \, (L \, . \, N_A) \tag{7.44}$$

where L is a normalized vector pointing to the light source and N_A is also a normalized vector.

7.10.1.2 Multiple light sources

The vector equation for the single light source can be generalized for multiple light sources as follows:

$$E_{A\gamma} = R_A \sum I_{A\gamma,n} (L_{a,n}, N_A) \tag{7.45}$$

where $L_{a,n}$ and $I_{A\gamma,n}$ represent the direction vector from the nth light source and the energy arriving from the nth light source respectively.

7.10.1.3 Specular reflection

To model specular reflection, we need to consider the relationship between the eye point E (position of the observer), the light source and the surface (see figure 7.48). The principal reflected ray leaves point A at an angle β which is equal to the angle of incidence α. Let us denote specular reflection coefficient by $W(\alpha)$ and the angle between the reflected ray and the observer by γ, then

$$E_A = [R_A \cos\alpha + W(\alpha)] I_{A\gamma} \cos^n \gamma \qquad (7.46)$$

where L_A is the direction vector from the light source to the point on the surface and n varies from 1 to 10 based the type of surface. The value of n is large for polished metallic surfaces as these produce very small highlight areas and it will have small value for dull surfaces. Further, specular reflection has the same colour as that of the incident light. It is due to the fact that specular reflection is not dependent on colour.

7.10.1.4 Transparency

It accounts for the energy E_{at} coming from behind at point A. Let us denote transparency coefficient at point A by T_A which varies between 0 and 1. E_{At} is then given by the following expression:

$$E_{At} = T_A\ E_{ab} \qquad (7.47)$$

where E_{Ab} is the energy arriving at A from behind as a result of modelling reflections from a surface farther away from the eye than A.

7.10.1.5 Colour

To model coloured surfaces, we need to consider the reflectance coefficient and illumination in colour coordinate system. In the red, green and blue (RGB) system, we consider only the diffuse illumination, therefore

$$\begin{aligned} E_{Ad,R} &= R_{A,R}\, I_{d,R} \\ E_{ad,G} &= R_{A,G}\, I_{d,G} \\ E_{Ad,B} &= R_{A,B}\, I_{d,B} \end{aligned} \qquad (7.48)$$

It may be noted that the specular highlights are modelled as white and is therefore common to each colour. The above equations can be combined into one equation including specular highlights and written as

$$E(R,G,B) = E_{A\gamma} + E_{AD,R} + E_{AD,G} + E_{AD,B} \qquad (7.49)$$

7.10.1.6 Total energy computation

The total energy is sum of diffuse illumination, light source illumination (from each source) and transparency, i.e.

$$E_A = E_{Ad} + \Sigma E_{As} + E_{at} \qquad (7.50)$$

We can consider E(R,G,B) instead of E_{ad} in the above equation.

7.10.1.7 Distance

Light intensity is also function of the distance of the surface from the light source. In fact, illumination from a light source reduces as the distance between the light source and point A increases. Thus, the surfaces of the same colour but at varying distances are not shown at the same intensity level. To simplify angular calculations, we assume that light sources are infinity far away from the surface and comparative distance of objects within a scene is small. Thus, the illumination of a scene from a source can be taken as constant throughout the scene.

To model the effect of distance, the total energy arriving at A given by E_A, is divided by the distance(r) from view point to the surface plus a constant say c, as follows:

$$E_A = E_A/(r+c) \tag{7.51}$$

We, however, need to use a more elaborate model to simulate haze and fading for applications like flight simulation where depth cueing is critical.

7.10.1.8 Comments on the model

This model was developed by Bui Tuong Phong [6] and is capable of producing reasonable shading effects and realism. Blinn[4] extended this model to generate more accurate highlight. The following are the main limitations of the model:

- Light sources are taken as point sources. The intensity distribution of the light source is ignored.
- The light sources are assumed to be located at infinity. The illumination of a scene from light source is taken as constant.
- Specular highlights are modelled as white regardless of material of the surface.
- The edges of the objects contain straight line segment.

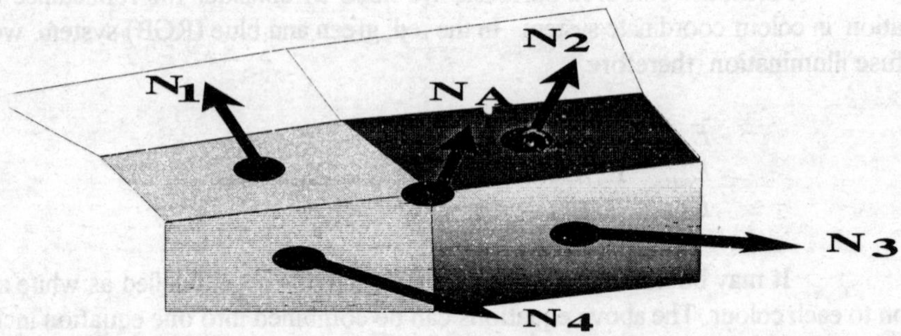

Figure 7-50 **N_1, N_2, N_3 and N_4 are the normals of the polgons that have a common vertex. The normal N_A at this vertex is average of all the four normals**

7.10.2 Gouraud shading

Gouraud shading [12] is normally restricted to the diffuse component of the reflection model developed in the previous section. The following are the steps carried out:

- We compute normal of each surface (represented by a polygon) forming an object either from a surface model or by an averaging technique using surface normals. Select a vertex, and take average of all surface normals of the surfaces meeting at this vertex. This normal is called vertex normal. In figure 7-50, vertex normal N_A is calculated as the average of the normals (N_1, N_2, N_3 and N_4) of the polygons that share a common vertex.
- Calculate the intensity at each vertex point (say, V) of each of the polygon by applying equation

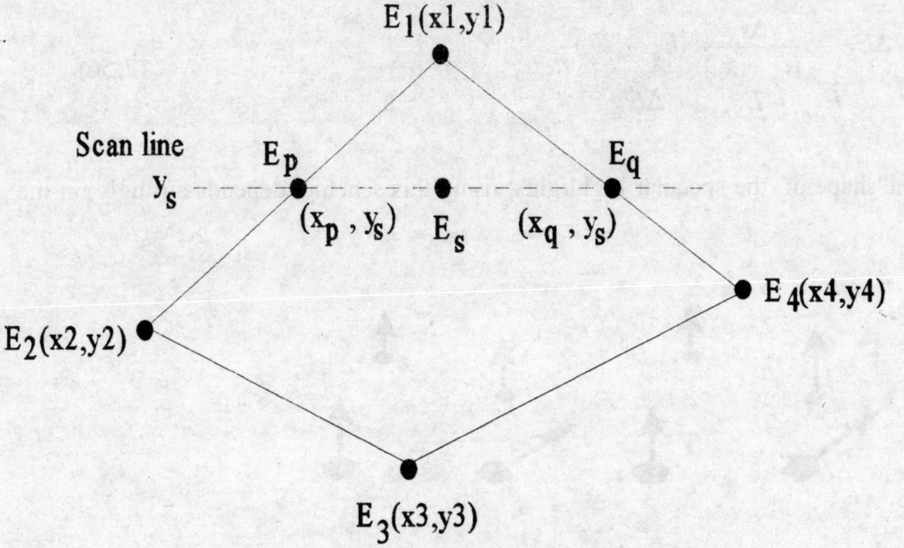

Figure 7-51 Gouraud shading of a polygon

$$E_V = R_V I_V\ (\mathbf{L} \cdot \mathbf{N}) \tag{7.52}$$

Now, we calculate intensities inside the polygon (see figure 7-52) as follows:

i. Select an edge of polygon joining points ($x1$,$y1$) and ($x2$,$y2$) with intensities at these points given by E_1 and E_2 and another edge joining points (x_3,y_3) and (x_4,y_4) with intensities at these points given by E_3 and E_4 respectively.

ii. Interpolate the intensity over a polygonal surface. Consider a scan line inter-secting two edges of the polygon at points (x_p,y_s) and (x_q,y_s). The intensity at the edge of each scan line E_p and E_q are calculated from the vertex intensities by linear interpolation as given below:

$$E_p = [E_1(y_s - y_2)\ E_2(y_1 - y_s)]/(y_1 - y_2) \tag{7.53}$$

$$E_q = [E_1(y_s - y_4)\ E_4(y_1 - y_s)]/(y_1 - y_4) \tag{7.54}$$

iii. Silmilarly, the intensity E_s on an interior point on the scan line is calculated by linear interpolation between E_p and E_q as given below:

$$E_s = [E_p(x_q - x_s) + E_q(x_s - x_p)]/(x_q - x_p) \tag{7.55}$$

The above equations are implemented as incremental calculations to achieve computational efficiency. This is particularly beneficial in the case of the third equation, which needs to be used for every pixel. If we define Δx to be the incremental distance along a scan line then ΔE_s, the change in intensity, from one pixel to the next is

$$\Delta E_S = \frac{\Delta x}{(x_q - x_p)} (E_q - E_p)$$
$$E_{S,n} = E_{S,n-1} + \Delta E_S \qquad (7.56)$$

The shape of the specular highlights, using this scheme, depends strongly on the

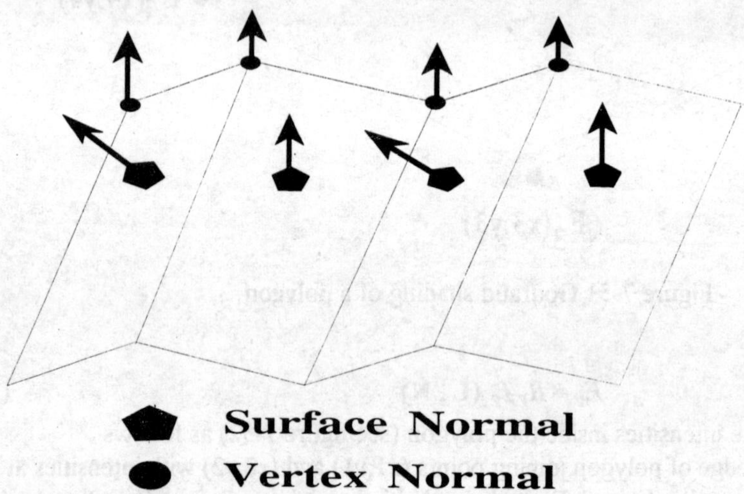

Figure 7-52 Shows vertex and surface normal

shape of the polygons used to approximate the surface rather than true surface orientation. An obvious highlight example that Gouraud shading misses altogether is the case of a highlight in the middle of a polygon. This method does not entirely eliminate the visibility of polygons. It suffers from Mach banding - where piecewise linear intensity changes across a polygon boundary trigger the human visual system into perceiving the boundary as a bright band. This is attributed to the fact that the human eye is sensitive to the second derivative of intensity to enable us to detect and enhance edges. Gouraud shading may introduce following errors in addition to Mach banding :

- This technique gives strange results if used in depicting a motion sequence because the intensity interpolation is carried out in screen coordinates whereas vertex normals are calculated in world coordinates. This is not invariant with respect to transformations such as rotation and in motion sequences frame-to-frame disturbances are possibly caused by this.

- The averaging of the surface normals to calculate the vertex normals for the intensity

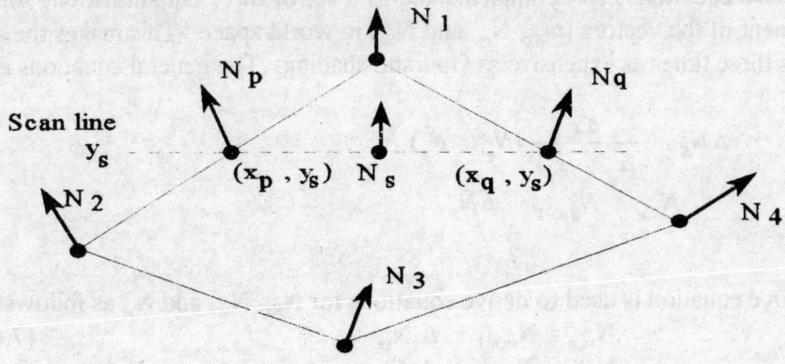

Figure 7-53 Phong shading - Surface normal $\mathbf{N_s}$ is linearly interpolated between true normals $\mathbf{N_p}$ and $\mathbf{N_q}$. Normal $\mathbf{N_p}$ is interpolated between normals $\mathbf{N_1}$ and $\mathbf{N_2}$.

calculation can cause errors which result in, for example, corrugations being smoothed out. Figure 7-52 shows a series of surfaces and associted vertex normals all pointing in the same direction. This would produce a constant shade for these surfaces because all the vertex shades are identical. Thus, we would get a visually flat surface. Although this can be a problem, it should not occur provided sufficient number of polygons are used.

7.10.3 Phong Shading

Gouraud shading algorithm was modified by Bui-Tuong Phong [6] to overcome some of the disadvantages but needs more computation. Phong's algorithm successfully models specular reflection. We can now have a specular highlight in the middle of a polygon despite the fact that each of the vertex normal angles would not produce a highlight. The algorithm is described below:

- The first step is the same as for the Gouraud method, i.e. find the vertex normals for each polygon. For each scan line in the polygon, find the normal vectors at the end of each line by linear interpolation. Figure 7-53 shows normal vectors at two vertices.
- Vector $\mathbf{N_p}$ and $\mathbf{N_q}$ are interpolated from vectors $\mathbf{N_1}$ - $\mathbf{N_2}$ and $\mathbf{N_1}$ - $\mathbf{N_4}$ respectively. We thus derive a normal vector for each point or pixel, say $\mathbf{N_S}$, on the polygon that is an approximation to the real normal on the curved surface approximated by the polygon. The following equations are used to compute normals:

$$\mathbf{N_p} = [\mathbf{N_1}(y_S - y_2) + \mathbf{N_2}(y_1 - y_S)] / (y_1 - y_2) \quad (7.57)$$

$$\mathbf{N_q} = [\mathbf{N_1}(y_S - y_4) + \mathbf{N_4}(y_1 - y_S)] / (y_1 - y_4) \quad (7.58)$$

Silmilarly, the normal $\mathbf{N_S}$ on an interior point on the scan line is calculated by linear interpolation between $\mathbf{N_p}$ and $\mathbf{N_q}$ as given below:

$$\mathbf{N_S} = [\mathbf{N_p}(x_q - x_S) + \mathbf{N_q}(x_S - x_p)] / (x_q - x_p) \quad (7.59)$$

The above equations can be implemented as a set of three equations, one for each of the component of the vectors (N_{Sx}, N_{sy}, and N_{Sz}) in world space. This makes the interpolation process three times as expensive as Gouraud shading. The general equations is

$$\Delta N_S = \frac{\Delta x}{(x_q - x_p)} (N_q - N_p)$$
$$N_{S,n} = N_{S,n-1} + \Delta N_S \tag{7.60}$$

The above equation is used to derive equations for $\mathbf{N_{Sx}}$, $\mathbf{N_{sy}}$, and $\mathbf{N_{sz}}$ as follows:

$$\mathbf{N_{sx,n} = N_{sx,n-1} + \Delta N_{sx}} \tag{7.61}$$
$$\mathbf{N_{Sy,n} = N_{sy,n-1} + \Delta N_{sy}} \tag{7.62}$$
$$\mathbf{N_{Sz,n} = N_{sz,n-1} + \Delta N_{sz}} \tag{7.63}$$

After the interpolated normal vector $\mathbf{N_s}$ is calculated for each point, the intensity equation is used to compute a shade. This feature accounts for the quality of the Phong shading. The vector interpolation in this method tends to restore the curvature of the original surface that has been approximated by a polygon mesh.

The salient features of this method are:

- Points interior to polygons can be calculated incrementally using bilinear interpolation. (This algorithm interpolates the normal vectors, rather than intensities.)
- A separate intensity is evaluated for each pixel from the interpolated normals.
- Both the light source and the viewpoint are assumed to be at infinity so that the intensity at a point is a function of only the interpolated normal.

This technique reduces the disturbing Mach bands, creates more realistic highlights, and improves frame-to-frame continuity. However, a concave polygon may result in shading anamolies like in Gouraud shading. This problem can be avoided by computing precise normal for the each point on the display.

Catmull[8] devised a scheme for shading bicubic surface patches. The basic operation is subdivision of a surface by parameter value. Each of the four corners of the surface is given by a set of numbers giving the location of the corner, the normal directions, and derivative values to subdivide the surface into four smaller surfaces and associated normal information. This process is similar to the quad- tree approach and is continued till a surface becomes smaller than a pixel. The surface is then displayed on the screen with a shade calculated from the precise normal vector that has been carried along with the subdivision. Thus, not only precise normal values but precise values of x, y, and z in the screen coordinate system are available. This algorithm together with a depth buffer is used to eliminate hidden surfaces and generate displays of smooth surfaces.

In the standard Phong algorithm, vertex normal is computed at each pixel followed by intensity. We can speed up the algorithm by using double- step interpolation with intermediate pixel calculated from simple averaging. This procedure does not result in any noticeable degradation in the quality of the image.

7.10.4 Comments on shading.

Shading models generally make a few assumtions to simplify lighting calculations. These are:

- The light has zero size and a single position in space.
- The light is infinitely far away so that light rays from it are parallel.
- The spot light has zero size, a single position in space and a cone of influence with a fixed angular spread.

Although, these assumption simlify the calculations but result in compromises with the scene's realism. The recent models remove one or more of above assumptions. One of these is radiosity model [13] which requires special coding and hence cannot readily be used with existing rendering software. The radiosity approach models light as energy whose distribution tends towards a stable algorithm or in other words it treats light as it was like heat. Gouraud shading is good for surfaces which reflect light diffusely as well as for modelling specular reflections. The degree of dependence of the shape of the specular light on the relative position of the underlying polygons is higher in Gouraud shading as compared to the Phong's algorithm.

7.11 SUMMARY

The main aim of 3-dimensional graphics is to provide capability to view and display an object or a scene from a desired point, in various sizes, rotations, or skews by projecting the view on the display. A screen coordinate system has been established which preserves the depth information as seen from a view point in the eye co-ordinate system. The values of the X_S and Y_S co-ordinates reflect the perspective view. Techniques for removal of hidden surfaces, representation of surfaces and shading of surfaces have also been described.

An interested reader can refer to [7,11, and 18] for detailed mathematical analysis of geometric projections and to [1] for a set of programs including hidden line removal in 'C' language for interacive computer graphics. Some advanced applications of hierarchical data structures such as quadtrees and octrees in computer garphics are discussed in [19]. An excellent survey of hidden surface algorithm is given in [18]. A survey of the visibility problems for nonlinear surfaces is given in [10].

7.12 PROBLEMS

7.1 Equation (7.2) describes the translation operation. Write a similar equation to perform the inverse operation, i.e., it should undo the effect of equation (7.2).

7.2 The rotation transformation in *x*, *y*, and *z* directions is given by matrices T_{RX}, T_{RY} and T_{RZ}, respectively. Write the matrix T_R, such that,

$$T_R = T_{RX}\ T_{RY}\ T_{RZ}$$

7.3 Write the steps necessary for rotation about an arbitrary axis passing through an arbitrary point. Use primitive transformations and/or their combinations. The arbitrary axis is defined by a point (*x*, *y*, *z*) on the axis and (*a*, *b*, *c*) as the direction *cosines* of the axis.

7.4 Modify the program written in problem 7.3 to incorporate the capability of producing perspective views of three dimensional objects. Draw a perspective view of three drawer chest (shown in example 7.2) from number of view points.

7.5 Draw front, top and left side orthogonal views of the figure given below

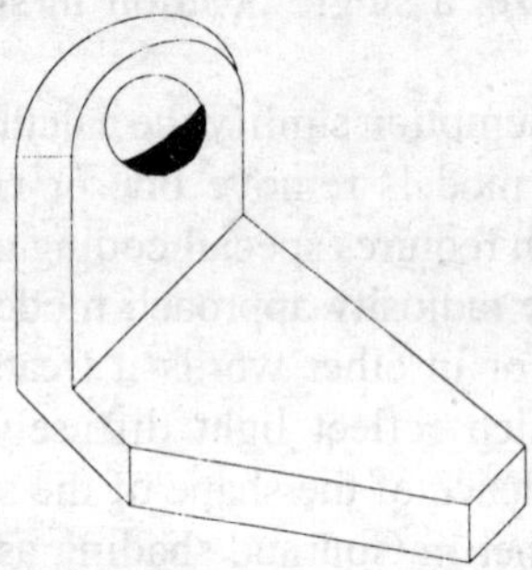

7.6 Write a program to implement the example 7.1. Also include in the program transformations for scaling and skewing.

7.7 Write a procoedure CLASSIFY (see section 7.6.1) which takes input window and face parameter and outputs a code 0, 1, or 2 to indicate whether face is disjoint, intersects or inside or surrounding the window. The clippng technique described in section 6.5.11 to clip a line segment by a regular polygon can be used with following modifications

a) actual calculation of line into sections with the window are not required,

b) return to calling program as soon as a pair of intersecting sides is found. Additional logic can be provided to generate output code 0, 1, or 2 depending on the location of face with respect to the window.

7.8 Modify the program written in problem 7.4 to determine the hidden lines.

7.9 Implement the 'Quad tree' algorithm for hidden surface removal.

7.13 REFERENCES

[1] Ammeraal Leendert, "*Interactive 3D Computer Graphics*," John Wiley and Sons, New York, 1988.

[2] Barr A.H., "Global and local deformations of solid primitives," Computer Graphics, 18(3), 1984, pp. 21-30.

[3] Blinn James F., "Optimal Tubes," IEEE Computer Graphics and Applications, vol. 9, no. 5, Sept. 1989, pp. 8-13.

[4] Blinn James F., "Models of light reflection for computer synthesized pictures," Computer Graphics, 11(2), 1977, pp. 192-198.

[5] Blinn J.F.,"Uppers and downers," IEEE Computer Graphics and Applications, vol. 12, no.2, March 1992, pp.85-90.

[6] Bui-Tuong Phong,"Illumination for computer generated pictures," CACM, 18(6), June 1975, pp. 311-317.

[7] Carlon. I., and J Paciorek, "Planner Geometric Projection and Viewing Transformations", Computing Surveys, Vol. 6 No. 1, Dec. 1978, pp. 465-502.

[8] Catmull E.E,"Computer display of curvrd surfaces," Proc. IEEE Conf. on Computer Graphics, Pattern Recognition and Data Structures, May 1975, p. 11.

[9] Coons, S. A., "Surface Patches and B-spline Curves", In Computer Aided Geometric Design, R. E. Barnhill and R. F. Risenfeld (Eds.) Academic Press, New York, 1974.

[10] Lane, J. M., L.C. Carpenter, T. Whitted, and J. F. Blinn, "Scan Line methods for Displaying parametrically defined surfaces", Comm. of ACM, Vol. 23, No. 1, Jan. 1980, pp. 23-34.

[11] Farin Gerald," Curves and Surfaces for Computer Aided Geometric Design - A Practical Guide", Academic Press Inc., Boston, 1988.

[12] Gouraud H.,"Illumination of computer generated pictures," Comm. ACM, 18(60), 1971, pp. 311-317.

[13] Greenberg D.P. and M.F. Cohen,"A radiosity solution for complex environments,"Computer Graphics (Proc. Siggraph), vol. 19, no. 3, July 1985,pp. 31-45.

[14] Newman W., and R. F Sproull, "Principles of Interactive Computer Graphics", 2nd Edition, MC Graw Hill, New York, 1979.

[15] Pavlidis T., "Algorithms for Graphics and Image Processing", "Computer Science Press", Rockville, Md., 1980.

[16] Rockwood, A.P., "Generalized Scanning Techinque for Display of Parametrically Defined Surfaces", IEEE Transactions on Computer Graphics and Applications, vol. 7, No. 8, August 1987, pp. 15-22.

[17] Rogers, D.F., Procedural Elements for Computer Graphics, McGraw-Hill, New York, N.Y., 1985.

[18] Rogers, D.F., and Adams J. Alan," Mathematical Elements for Computer Graphics", Second Edition, McGraw - Hill Publishing Company, New York, 1989.

[19] Samet Hanen and R.E. Webber,"Hierarchical Data structures and algorithm for computer graphics - Part II: Applications," IEEE Computer Graphics and Applications, vol. 8, no. 4, July 1988, pp. 59-75.

[20] Sutherland, I.E., R.F Sproull, and R. A. Schumacker, "A Characterisation of ten hidden surface algorithms", Computing Surveys, Vol. 6 No. 1 March 1979, pp. 1-55.

CHAPTER 8

APPLICATION TO SIMPLE ENGINEERING PROBLEMS

8.1 INTRODUCTION

Engineers use graphics for a wide variety of purposes. For example, one may utilize computer graphics for the presentation of reports, which are illustrated with graphs, histograms and pie-charts. Plotting, editing and labelling of these require special techniques. Other applications of computer graphics are in obtaining engineering drawings of various three-dimensional objects. Some examples are plans and elevations of buildings, bridges, and various parts of machines. Computer graphics has been used extensively in the design of very large-scale integrated (VLSI) electronic circuits, which in turn, has played a crucial role in the microcomputer revolution. Another important field that depends heavily on computer graphics is computer-aided design and manufacturing (CAD/CAM). It can be truly said that developments in computer graphics have not only freed the engineer from spending a large amount of time at the drawing board, but have also made it possible to achieve results which would not have been possible otherwise. The importance of the subject has led to the development of several software packages that engineers can use for the generation of their drawings and charts. Some of the most well-known among these are (i) Harvard Graphics, (ii) Autocad, (iii) Anvil 1000MD, (iv) Windows Draw, (v) Freelance Plus, (vi) Cadvance, (vii) DesignCAD and (viii) MicroGDS 3.2. Most of them make it possible not only to obtain suitable drawings on the computer display but also allow the user to obtain hard copies on either a printer or a plotter. As expected, these packages come with different levels of sophistication and capabilities. The most popular (and most expensive) among these is the Autocad, which has been used extensively by mechanical engineers in CAD/CAM applications. This package allows users not only to obtain views of three-dimensional objects but also to zoom and rotate them in order to provide a better understanding of the details. To use this and the other advanced software packages most effectively, it is desirable not only to have good graphics resolution but also to have a suitable pointing device like a mouse, graphic tablet, or a tracker ball.

In this chapter, we shall describe some engineering applications of computer graphics. First we shall study how to generate histograms and pie-charts on a computer using Turbo Pascal. This will be followed by a brief discussion of techniques for the plotting and editing of graphs. A general program which can be used for a plotting the graph of a function, which can be input from the keyboard, will be presented. Other applications like the drawing of the plan and elevation of a building, and image processing as well as animation will also be considered. Finally, some aspects of solid modelling will be discussed.

8.2 HISTOGRAMS

Histograms or bar charts are very useful for graphical presentation of statistical information. A histogram may be defined as a graph that conveys to the viewer the relative values of a quantity that falls into a countable number of classes. For example, consider plotting

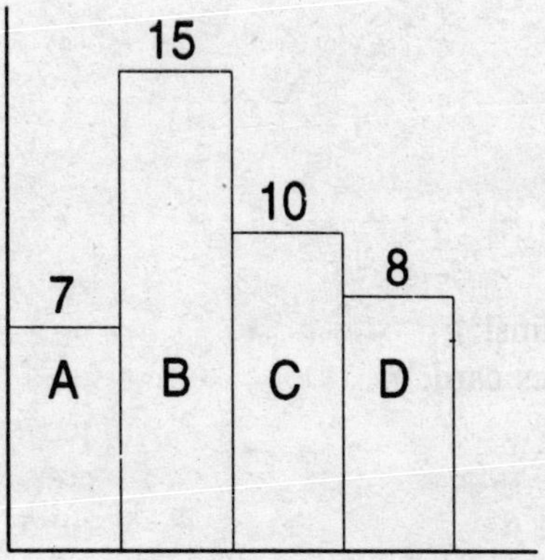

Figure 8.1(a) A Histogram - shows grades of students

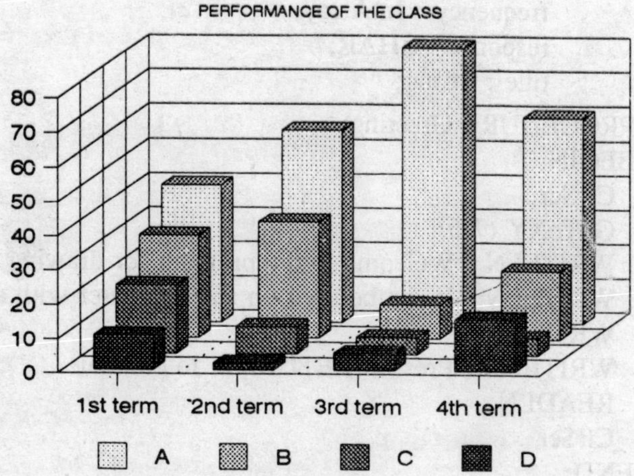

Figure 8.1(b) A 3D Histogram - shows performance of students for four terms

the histogram of the grades of the students in a certain class. Suppose that the class has 40 students: 7 of these have received the grade 'A', 15 have received the grade 'B', 10 have received the grade 'C' and 8 have received the grade 'D'. In this case, the histo-gram will consist of four rectangles of equal width, each corresponding to a particular letter grade. The height of each rectangle will represent the frequency of occurrence of that grade. Such a histogram is shown in figure 8.1(a). A 3D histogram showing performance of the class of 100 students for the four semester is given in figure 8.1(b).

We shall now present a general program for plotting the histogram on the computer from data supplied by the user. The program starts by asking the user the number of classes, n, for which the histogram is to be drawn. The number of occurrences of each class is then obtained. The histogram is scaled so that the width of each rectangle, multiplied by (n + 3) is equal to the x-axis of the display. The maximum height of the histogram is about 80 % of the y-axis. The functions GetMaxX and GetMaxY in the Graph unit of Turbo Pascal are utilized for this purpose. The bars are drawn using the procedure Bar3D from the Graph unit. This procedure with zero depth gives outlined bars. The program listing is given below;

Example 8.1 : Program for plotting a histogram

```
PROGRAM Histogram;
USES Crt, Graph;
CONST MaxNumber = 10;
TYPE IntArray = ARRAY [1..MaxNumber] OF INTEGER;
     StrArray = ARRAY [1..MaxNumber] OF STRING;
VAR  Scale : REAL;
     width, number, xOffset, yOffset, x1, y1 : INTEGER;
     name : StrArray;
```

```
      frequency : IntArray;
      response : CHAR;
      title : String;
PROCEDURE Greeting;
BEGIN
  ClrScr;
  GoToXY (7,6);
  WRITELN ('Welcome to the program for drawing histograms!');
  WRITELN ('It can be used on any computer with a graphics card.');
  WRITELN;
  WRITELN ('Press <RETURN> to continue...');
  READLN;
  ClrScr
END;
PROCEDURE GetData;
VAR  i : INTEGER;
PROCEDURE GetNumber;
BEGIN
  REPEAT
    WRITE ('Enter the number of classes: ');
    READLN (number);
    IF (number > MaxNumber) THEN
      BEGIN
        WRITE ('This program cannot have more than ');
        WRITELN (MaxNumber, ' classes!  Try again.')
      END
  UNTIL (number <= MaxNumber);
END;
BEGIN (* GetData *)
   WRITE ('Enter the title of the histogram: ');
   READLN (title);
   GetNumber;
   FOR i := 1 TO number DO
     BEGIN
       WRITE ('What is the name of class ', i, '? ');
       READLN (name[i]);
       WRITE ('Enter the number of occurrences of ', name[i], ' : ');
       READLN (frequency[i])
     END
END;
PROCEDURE Initialize;
VAR  Driver, ErrorCode, Mode : INTEGER;
BEGIN
```

```
  Driver := Detect;
  InitGraph (Driver, Mode, ' ');
  ErrorCode := GraphResult;
  IF ErrorCode <> grOK THEN Halt(1);
  SetBkColor(0)
END;
Function Max (number : INTEGER; frequency : IntArray) : INTEGER;
(* Determine the maximum value of the frequency *)
VAR  i, temp : INTEGER;
BEGIN
  temp := frequency[1];
  FOR i := 2 TO number DO
    IF (temp < frequency[i]) THEN temp := frequency [i];
  Max := temp
END;

Function Min  (number : INTEGER; frequency : IntArray) : INTEGER;
(* Determine the minimum value of the frequency *)
VAR  i, temp : INTEGER;
BEGIN
  temp := frequency[1];
  FOR i := 2 TO number DO
    IF (temp > frequency[i]) THEN temp := frequency [i];
  Min := temp
END;
PROCEDURE SetScale;
BEGIN
  xOffset := GetMaxX DIV 10;    (* Minimum x on screen *)
  x1 := GetMaxX - xOffset;      (* Maximum x on screen *)
  yOffset := GetMaxY DIV 10;    (* Minimum y on screen - from top *)
  y1 := GetMaxY - yOffset;      (* Maximum y on screen - from top *)
  width := (x1 - xOffset) DIV number;   (* width of each bar *)
  scale := (y1 - 2*yOffset)/Max (number, frequency);
END;

PROCEDURE Drawbars;
VAR  i, temp1, temp2 : INTEGER;
BEGIN
  FOR i := 1 TO number DO
    BEGIN
      SetColor(White);
      SetFillStyle (EmptyFill, Blue);
      temp1 := xOffset + (i-1)*width;
```

```
    temp2 := y1 - ROUND (scale * frequency[i]) - yOffset;
    Bar3D (temp1, y1-yOffset, temp1 + width, temp2, 0, FALSE)
  END
END;
FUNCTION RealToString (x : REAL) : String;
VAR s : String;
BEGIN
  str (x:3:1, s);
  RealToString := s
END;
PROCEDURE WriteLabels;
(* Label the histogram with the names of different items and the title *)
VAR  i, temp1, temp2, temp3 : INTEGER;
BEGIN
  SetColor(White);
  SetTextStyle (TriplexFont, HorizDir, 2);
  SetTextJustify (CenterText, CenterText);
  OutTextXY (ROUND((xOffset+x1)/2), y1, title);
  SetTextStyle (0, HorizDir, 1);
  temp3 := y1 - ROUND (Scale*Min(number, frequency)/2) - yOffset;
  FOR i := 1 TO number DO
    BEGIN
      temp1 := xOffset + ROUND((i-0.5)*width);
      temp2 := y1 - ROUND (scale * frequency[i]) - yOffset - 5;
      OutTextXY (temp1, temp2, RealToString(frequency[i]));
      OutTextXY (temp1, temp3, name[i]);
    END
END;
BEGIN (* Main Program *)
  Greeting;
  GetData;
  Initialize;
  SetScale;
  DrawBars;
  WriteLabels;
  READLN;
  CloseGraph
END.
```

As will be seen, the program includes writing labels on the histogram. The frequency of occurrence of each item in the histogram is shown at the top of the corresponding rectangle and the name of the item is shown at the level of the middle of the rectangle with the minimum height. The title of the histogram is centred at the bottom. With a view to avoiding clutter, the program allows a maximum of 10 different items in the histogram. If desired, this number can be changed by simply altering the value of the constant MaxNumber in the initial declaration. As an exercise, the reader may modify this program to create a 3D histogram as shown in figure 8.1(b).

8.3 PIE-CHARTS

A pie-chart is a graph in which the various items are represented by sectors of a circle. The angle of each sector is proportional to the magnitude of the item that it represents. Pie-charts are most useful for the visual representation of the percentages into which each entity is divided. A common example of a pie-chart is the way the tax dollar is divided in the budget presented by the government of a country. For instance, the pie-chart for the case when 25% is spent for education, 20% for defence, 30% for health and welfare, and 25 % for other items is shown in figure 8.2(a).

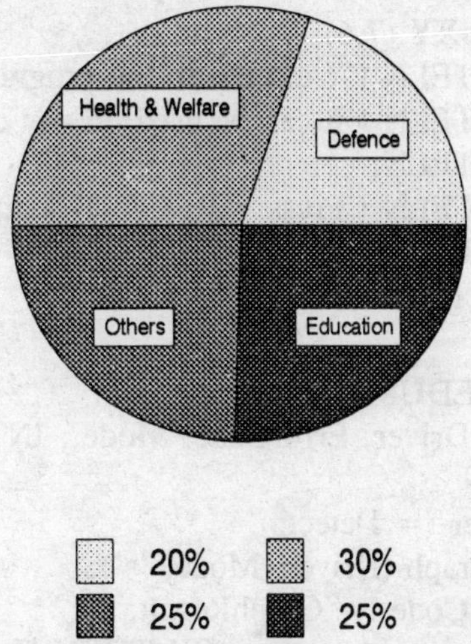

Figure 8.2(a) Pie-chart for a national budget

A program for plotting the pie-chart for this case is given below. Like the program for histograms, this program will also select the scales after detecting the type of graphics card on the computer that is being used. It has not been written for the general case, but it can be generalized in the same way as was done in the program for drawing histograms. This as well as creation of the 3-D affect along with the title of the chart as shown in figure 8.2(b) will be left as an exercise to the reader.

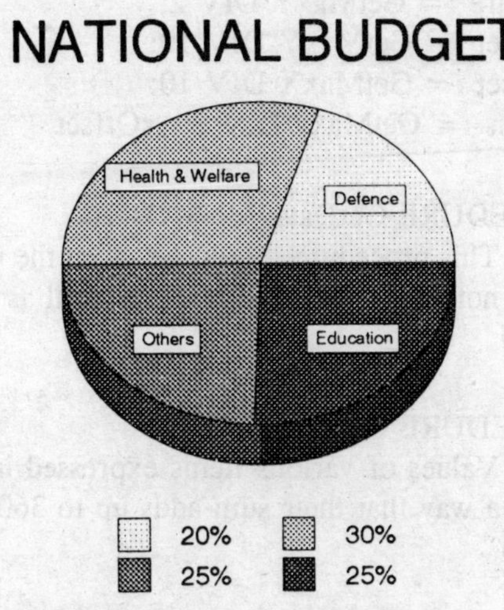

Figure 8.2(b): A 3-D Pie-chart

Example 8.2 : Program for drawing a pie-chart

```
Program PieChart;
Uses Crt, Graph;
CONST MaxNumber = 8; (* Maximum
number of items in the chart *)
TYPE       IntArray    =    ARRAY
[1..MaxNumber] OF INTEGER;
           StrArray    =    ARRAY
[1..MaxNumber] OF STRING;
VAR  Scale : REAL;
     number, xOffset, yOffset, xCentre,
yCentre, radius : INTEGER;
```

```
    name : StrArray;  (* Names of various items *)
    value, angle : IntArray;
    response : CHAR;
    title : String;  (* Title of pie-chart *)
PROCEDURE Greeting;
BEGIN
  ClrScr;
  GoToXY (7,6);
  WRITELN ('Welcome to the program for drawing piecharts!');
  WRITELN ('It can be used on any computer with a graphics card.');
  WRITELN;
  WRITELN ('Press <RETURN> to continue... ');
  READLN;
  ClrScr
END;
PROCEDURE Initialize;
VAR  Driver, ErrorCode, Mode : INTEGER;
BEGIN
  Driver := Detect;
  InitGraph (Driver, Mode, '');
  ErrorCode := GraphResult;
  IF ErrorCode <> grOK THEN Halt(1);
  SetBkColor(0)
END;
PROCEDURE GetDimensions;
BEGIN
  xCentre := GetMaxX DIV 2;
  yCentre := GetMaxY DIV 2;
  yOffset := GetMaxY DIV 10;
  xOffset := GetMaxX DIV 10;
  Radius := GetMaxy DIV 2 - xOffset
END;
PROCEDURE GetData;
(*    This procedure should get from the user the number of items for the pie-chart (this must
      not exceed MaxNumber) as well as the names and values of each of these items  *)
BEGIN
END;
PROCEDURE GetAngles;
 (*   Values of various items expressed in any unit are to be converted into  angles in such
      a way that their sum adds up to 360 degrees *)
BEGIN
END;
```

```
PROCEDURE DrawPieSlices;
(*   This has to be generalized so that the start and end angles of each pie slice can be
     obtained from the data.  Also the centres for the various pie-slices should be staggered,
     as shown.  *)
BEGIN
  SetFillStyle (EmptyFill, Blue);
  PieSlice (xCentre, yCentre, 0, 90, Radius);
  PieSlice (xCentre-5, yCentre, 90, 162, Radius);
  PieSlice (xCentre-5, yCentre+5, 162, 270, Radius);
  PieSlice (xCentre, yCentre+5, 270, 360, Radius);
END;
PROCEDURE LabelPieChart;
(* This procedure must also be generalized *)
BEGIN
  SetTextStyle(TriplexFont, HorizDir, 1);
  OutTextXY (xCentre+Radius, yCentre - Radius DIV 2 , 'Education');
  OutTextXY (xCentre-Radius*2, yCentre - Radius DIV 2, 'Defence');
  OutTextXY (xOffset , yCentre + Radius DIV 3, 'Health & Welfare');
  OutTextXY (xCentre + Radius, yCentre + Radius DIV 3, 'Others');
END;
BEGIN (* Main program *)
  Greeting;
  Initialize;
  GetDimensions;
  GetData;
  GetAngles;
  DrawPieSlices;
  LabelPieChart;
  READLN;
  CloseGraph;
END.
```

It will be seen that this program utilizes the procedure PieSlice from the graph unit in Turbo Pascal. This procedure takes advantage of the fact that the Borland graphics drivers determine the aspect ratio for the hardware being used in order to draw a real circle or circular arc.

8.4 PLOTTING GRAPHS

Graphs are often used by engineers to show how a given function varies with the independent variable. A simple program for that purpose was described in section 3.4. A more general and user-friendly program for plotting graphs should not have to be recompiled for each function to be plotted and the user should be able to input the function from the keyboard. In addition, the program should calculate the values of the function for the desired range of values of the independent variable and determine the optimal scale factors for the x- and y-axes of the graph. Such a program is given below and is included on the disk which comes with this book. It includes two units, "ReadFormulaString" and "Plotting". The former is utilized for reading a formula from the keyboard using the postfix (or reverse Polish notation), where the independent variable is t. This can then be evaluated for different values of t, as required for the graph. The latter is very much like the program described in chapter 3 and is utilized for plotting the graph from the data which may either be obtained by calculation from the formula or may have been stored in a file. The listing of the program is given below.

```
PROGRAM PlotGraph;
{$N+} (* compiler directive for using double precision *)
Uses Crt, Dos, Graph, GlobalIO, ReadFormulaString, Plotting;
CONST
  DateOfThisVersion = 'March 19, 1989';
PROCEDURE Greeting;
BEGIN
  ClrScr;
  WRITELN (' ':18,'Welcome to the graph plotting program!');
  DrawLine;
 (* A subroutine in unit "Plotting",which draws a line across the screen*)
  WRITELN (' This program can be used to draw the graph of a single function  f(t).');
  WRITELN (' The function f(t) can be supplied by a set of data points or by a formula.');
  WRITELN (' If f(t) is supplied as a formula, the user must supply the lower and');
  WRITELN (' upper limits of  t.');
  WRITELN;
  WRITELN (' The formula for f(t) may be stored in a file or entered at the keyboard.');
  WRITELN;
  WRITELN (' The graph can be redrawn for different t limits with an option to multiply');
  WRITELN (' the values of f(t) by a scale factor, provided f(t) is given as a formula.');
  WRITELN;
  WRITELN (' ':18,'Date of this version: ',DateOfThisVersion);
DrawLine;
  first := TRUE
End; (* Greeting *)
PROCEDURE GetScaleFactor;
(* This procedure multiplies the values of f(t) with a scale factor.  The default value is one *)
BEGIN
  IF  Yes('Do you want to scale the values of f(t)')  THEN
    BEGIN
      WRITE(' Enter the scale factor:  ');
      ScaleFactor := ReadReal
    END
  ELSE
    ScaleFactor := 1.0
END; (* GetScaleFactor *)
```

```
PROCEDURE GetFormula;
(* This procedure allows the input of f(t) from the keyboard. *)
VAR
  OutFile : TEXT;
  FileName : String;
BEGIN
  ClrScr;
  WRITELN('A formula for f(t) is required.') ; WRITELN ;
  DescribeFormulaEvaluator;
  DrawLine;
  WRITELN(' Enter the formula for f(t): ');
  WRITELN;
  WRITE(' f(t) = ');
  READLN(formula);
  WRITELN;
  IF  Yes('Do you want to store the formula in a file')  THEN
    BEGIN
      CreateFile(OutFile,FileName);
      WRITELN(OutFile,formula);
      CLOSE(OutFile)
    END;
  ScaleFactor := 1.0
END; (* GetFormula *)
PROCEDURE Calculate;
(* The values of f(t) are calculated for various values of t *)
VAR
  OutFile : TEXT;
  FileName : String;
  deltaT, t, fvalue : REAL;
  ok : BOOLEAN;
  k, xPos, yPos : INTEGER;
  ch : CHAR;
BEGIN
  WRITELN('Please wait as I am now calculating values of  f(t)  at');
  WRITE('    t = tmin + k*(tmax - tmin)/',number,'    for  k = ');
  xPos := WhereX ; yPos := WhereY ;
  deltaT := (xMax - xMin)/number;
  FOR  k := 0  TO  number  DO
    BEGIN
      GoToXY(xPos,yPos) ; ClrEol ; WRITE(k) ;
      t := xMin + k*deltaT;
      EvaluateFunction(t,formula,fvalue,ok);
      IF  ok  THEN
        BEGIN
```

```
      x[k] := t ; y[k] := fvalue*ScaleFactor ; z[k] := ' '
     END
    ELSE
     BEGIN
      WRITELN(' Problem in calculating values of the function at t = ',t);
      WRITELN(' Check the formula for  f(t)');
      Halt(1)
     END
  END;
 WRITELN;
 xMin := LowerBound(xMin);
 xMax := UpperBound(xMax);
 IF  ScaleFactor = 1.0  THEN
  BEGIN
   (* The data can be stored in a disk file, if desired. *)
   IF  Yes('Do you want to store the data points in a file')  THEN
    BEGIN
     CreateFile(OutFile,FileName);
     FOR  k := 0  TO  number  DO
       WRITELN(OutFile,x[k]:12,' ',y[k]:12,' ');
     CLOSE(OutFile)
    END
  END
END; (* Calculate *)
PROCEDURE GetDataSet( VAR InFile : TEXT );
(* This procedure allows the data to be read from a file. *)
BEGIN
 number := 0; DataSet := TRUE;
 WRITELN ('I am now reading the data points.  ');
 READLN (InFile,x[0],y[0],z[0]);
 GraphList[1] := z[0];
 xMax := x[0] ; xMin := xMax ; yMax := y[0] ; yMin := yMax ;
 WHILE  (NOT EOF(InFile)) AND (number < MaxPoints)  DO
  BEGIN
   number := Succ(number);
   READLN(InFile,x[number],y[number],z[number]);
   xMax := Max(xMax,x[number]) ; xMin := Min(xMin,x[number]) ;
   yMax := Max(yMax,y[number]) ; yMin := Min(yMin,y[number]) ;
  END; (* data read-in *)
 CLOSE(InFile);
 WRITELN ('There were ',Succ(number),' data points read in.');
 xMin := LowerBound(xMin) ; xMax := UpperBound(xMax) ;
 yMin := LowerBound(yMin) ; yMax := UpperBound(yMax) ;
 ScaleFactor := 1.0;
```

```
  WRITELN;
  WRITE('Enter a heading or title for the graph:  ');
  READLN(heading)
END; (* GetDataSet *)
PROCEDURE ReadFormula( x, y : INTEGER );
(* The formula can be read from a file *)
VAR
  InFile : TEXT;
BEGIN
  GoToXY(x,y) ; ClrEol ;
  WRITELN('f(t) must be entered as a formula.');
  number := 250 ; GraphList[1] := ' ' ; DataSet := FALSE ;
  IF  Yes('Is the formula stored in a file')  THEN
   BEGIN
     IF  GetFile(InFile)  THEN
       BEGIN
         ClrScr;
         READLN(InFile,formula);
         WRITELN(' f(t) = ',formula);
         DrawLine;
         CLOSE(InFile);
         ScaleFactor := 1.0
       END
     ELSE
       GetFormula
   END
  ELSE
   GetFormula;
  WRITELN;
  GetNewRange;
  Calculate
END; (* ReadFormula *)
PROCEDURE Input;
(* Procedure for input of data, either from a disk file, or in the form of  a formula.  For the
   latter case, the values of f(t) are calculated using the unit "ReadFormulaString" *)
VAR
  x, y : INTEGER;
  InFile : TEXT;
  response : CHAR;
BEGIN
  x := WhereX ; y := WhereY ; GraphNumber := 1 ; GraphStart[1] := 0 ,
  IF  Yes('Is the data to be plotted stored in a file')  THEN
   BEGIN
     IF  GetFile(InFile)  THEN
```

```
    GetDataSet(InFile)
   ELSE
    ReadFormula(x,y)
  END
 ELSE
  ReadFormula(x,y);
 PrintedOutput;
 (* It is possible to get a printed copy of the plot using a suitable screen-dump routine
     like "Pizzaz". *)
 WRITELN;
 WRITELN('After the graph completion message disappears from the screen,');
 WRITELN(' press <space> to continue.');
 WRITELN;
 WRITE(' Press <space> when ready. ') ; response := ReadKey
END; (* Input *)
PROCEDURE Redraw;
BEGIN
 continue := TRUE ;
 WRITELN ; WRITELN ;
 WRITELN('f(t) = ',formula);
 DrawLine;
 GetNewRange;
 GetScaleFactor;
 Calculate;
 GetYrange
END;
BEGIN  (* Main program *)
 Greeting;
 REPEAT
  Input;   (* Input f(t) or the data *)
  IF NOT DataSet THEN GetYrange;
  (* Get the range of y if the formula has been entered *)
  REPEAT
   IF first THEN Initialize;
  (* The procedure "Initialize", which is in the unit "Plotting", sets up the graph
     mode, corresponding to the graphics card in the computer being used. This
     is necessary only the first time the program is used. *)
   Plot;
  (* This procedure in the unit "Plotting" sets up the scales, draws and labels the
     axes, draws some grid lines and then plots the graph from the data points read
     from a file or calculated from the formula for f(t) that was either read from the
     keyboard or a text file. *)
   IF DataSet THEN continue := FALSE
```

```
ELSE
   BEGIN
     IF  Yes('Do you want to redraw the graph')  THEN  Redraw
      (*  The graph can be redrawn for different limits of t only if
          the formula, f(t), is known.  *)
     ELSE  continue := FALSE
   END
  UNTIL  NOT continue
 UNTIL  NOT Yes('Do you want to draw the graph of another function')
END.
```

To run this program, the user must have the graphics driver from Borland, that corresponds to the graphics card present on the computer. Note that the program itself is independent of the graphics card. This program when run shows up the introductory screen, which informs the user that the program can be used for plotting a graph, either from data stored in a disk file, or from the formula, *f*(*t*), of the function to be plotted. For the latter case, the formula may be either read from a file or from the keyboard and a screen describing the format of the various functions that can be used in the formula is displayed. The user is also required to input the lower and upper limits of the independent variable, *t*, for the function *f*(*t*). Values of *f*(*t*) at 250 equally spaced points within this range are calculated and the result is used for determining the optimum scales for the graph, in the same manner as in the plotting program described in chapter 3. After the curve is plotted, the user is asked if the graph is to be replotted for another range of the independent variable and the process is repeated if the answer is yes. On the other hand, if the answer is no, the user is asked if another graph is to be plotted. The program terminates only if the answer is different from yes, otherwise, a graph for another function, specified by the user is, is plotted.

Example 8.3

As an example, the graph of the function

for t in the range -20 to 20, was plotted using this routine and is shown in figure 8.3.

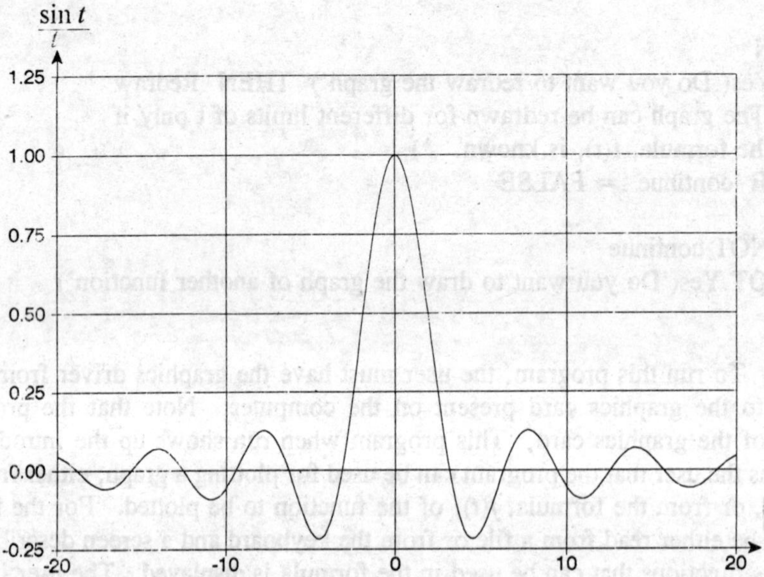

Figure 8.3 Plot of (sin *t*)/*t* against *t* for -20< *t* <20

8.5 ENGINEERING DRAWINGS

An important application of computer graphics in engineering is for obtaining line drawings of various views of different parts of machines, plans and elevation of buildings, wiring diagrams for electrical circuits, and flow charts of systems. Although it is possible to write programs for this purpose using the Graph Unit of Turbo Pascal version 5.0, it is often much easier to use commercially available program packages that have been designed especially for Computer-aided Design and Drafting (CADD). Most of these packages allow the user to draw lines using the cursor control keys (shown as up, down, left and right arrows one the keyboard), it is often more convenient to use a mouse for this purpose.

To make technical drawings of each area (e.g. mechanical, architectural, electric, and electronic), one needs specific features and custom libraries in the CAD product. One solution is to use a drafting packages meant for the specific area but this may be an expensive solution which every user may not be able to afford. Other solution is to use a generic package and customize it to tune it to meet the specific needs by adding symbol libraries and add-on software, generally available from third-party vendors.

Most popular 2-D CAD products are: Anvil 1000MD for Windows, AutoCAD 12 2.0 for Windows, Cadvance 6 for Windows - useful for architectural applications with features to place symbols in walls for automatic double line trimming and easy attribute creation but has some weakness in the area of mechanical drawing, DesignCAD 2D 7.0 for Windows, Drafix CAD Professional 3.0 for Windows 1.2, Drawbase for Windows model 4000 1.2, DynaDesigner for Windows, MicroGDS 3.2, MicroStation PC 5 and MicroStation 5 for Windows NT, Pj2 CAD System 3.1 for OS/2, TrueCAD for Windows 2.10c, TurboCAD for Windows 2.01, Ultimate CAD for Windows Base 2.1 and Vellum version 2.7 with macros and solid fill. All of these products run as native applications on Microsoft Windows, Windows NT, or IBM's OS/2. In addition, they support .DXF file import and export and include a macro language. AutoCAD is a true Windows application and other products comply to Windows standards to a varying degree. Not only can one draw the various line diagrams using these packages, but it is also possible to label them, add suitable dimension lines and give proper titles with fonts and sizes of letters selected by the user.

AutoCAD dominates this market, with over one million installations that represent over 70 percent of the market. Most users do 2-D drafting only, although 3-D use is growing. AutoCAD is probably one of the most expensive PC CAD packages. Its price is above US$3000. AutoCAD users also buy add-on software to customize the software for their specific applications. There are also products which are available for as little as $150. Such packages can also produce engineering drawings but have their own programming language, and read and write .DXF files. Two factors help one in taking a decision - availability of trained AutoCAD users and third party software.

8.5.1 Review of CAD packages

A brief review of the packages Anvil-1000MD and AutoCAD Release 12 for Windows is given below.

8.5.1.1 Anvil-1000MD, Interactive Design Consultants (DOS and Windows)

It has many built-in features for 2-D mechanical design challenges. Anvil-1000MD for Windows is simply an extension of the DOS-based version and does not use standard Windows features such as pull-down menus, dialog boxes, or toolbars. Its menu, graphics area, lists, and macro buttons are in separate windows, retaining the same interface used in the DOS- and Unix-based versions. It accesses printers and plotters directly, bypassing the Windows drivers and limiting the user only to those output devices supported by the program. The lack of support for the Windows Clipboard, DDE, and OLE simply reinforces the feeling that Anvil-1000MD is still out of place in the Windows environment.

Mnemonic hotkeys and the customizable macro window (which can have over 140 buttons) provide shortcuts to often-used functions. The macro window is configured exactly as a graphics tablet overlay, but the program doesn't actually support the use of such an overlay (although the DOS version does). A one-line hint for every interaction, awkwardly placed in the title bar of the graphics window, is the only on-line help available. There is unlimited undo/redo capability, dubbed the Chronicle, and the well-organized users' manual contains a short set of lessons and a reference section.

Modifications such as trimming, intersecting, fillets, and chamfers work with all types of geometry. Object snaps for end points, midpoints, centres, extremes, and intersections are always available from the keyboard without additional menu picks. The product's comprehensive dimension types include rarely found geometric tolerances, surface finishes, and section arrows. Default settings for the ANSI 1973, ANSI 1982, BSI, DIN, ISO, and JIS standards along with a multitude of specific modal settings provide for complete control of the appearance and positioning of dimensions and tolerances.

One needs 386 PC or better, 4MB RAM, 2MB hard disk space, math co-processor, MS Windows 3.1 or later.

8.5.1.2 AutoCAD Release 12 for Windows, Autodesk

It is the de facto standard for PC-based CAD. One can get enough third party add-ons to do *any* CAD-related job. Release 12 is the first version of AutoCAD to support Microsoft Windows and has all of the standard features, such as pull-down menus, toolbars, and dialog boxes, as well as Clipboard, DDE, and OLE support. However, some functions are still only available through the command line. The user still has the option of utilising old-style menus to retain compatibility with any customized menus. It includes context-sensitive online help and a comprehensive set of manuals.

AutoCAD supports two modes, standard or accelerated. In accelerated mode, AutoCAD maintains a display list in memory and bypasses the Windows GDI (Graphics Device Interface) for certain operations. This approach greatly speeds up the display of graphics in most cases. Another benefit provided by accelerated display mode is its Aerial view - a small window that contains an overview of the entire drawing and allows quick panning and zooming to any location. AutoCAD maintains unparalleled support for digitizser tablets, allowing them to be used both as standard Windows input devices and as command overlays that streamline and customize the AutoCAD interface.

AutoCAD Designer offers parametric, feature based design that lets users modify a design by changing dimension values. Designs are based on real world functions, e.g. a hole is defined as a hole rather than a cylindriacal Boolean substract. It also allows coordinate free sketching. This enables a user to freely draw an approximate shape and add precise dimensions later. Automated drawing generates 2D drawings from solid models and removes hidden lines.

One needs 386 PC or better, 8 MB RAM, 8 MB hard disk space, math co-processor, MS Windows 3.1 or later.

AutoCAD Release 13 will support number of platforms including Windows NT. The main improvements are mainly in the internal file structures but emphasis will be on GUI interfaces, integration with other applications through use of OLE.

Example 8.4

As an example, the plan of an apartment, drawn using Harvard Graphics, is shown in figure 8.4.

Figure 8.4 Plan of an apartment

8.6 IMAGE PROCESSING

Three areas, namely, Graphics, Pictorial Pattern Recognition, and Image Processing deal with the processing of pictorial data by computers. Graphics deals with the generation of images from non-pictorial data. In case of interactive graphics, input could be in terms of graphical entities, e.g., line, curves, etc. An example of static graphics is say production of plots while that of dynamic graphics is computer generation of games. The input in case of pictorial pattern recognition is a picture. The techniques used to process a picture either produce a description of input picture or assign the picture to one of predefined classes. For example if the input is a character from a set consisting of English alpha-numerals as its elements, (i.e., A to Z and 0 to 9) the expected output after its recognition will be its assignment to one of the elements of the set. Pattern recognition is, therefore, the inverse problem of computer graphics. It has applications in automatic mail sorting, medical diagnosis and identification of aerial photographs. In addition, it has several military applications. Image processing, may be defined as the science of modification and analysis of continuous tone pictures. Note that in this case both input and output are pictures. The following are some of the applications of image processing:

i) Image transmission : filtering for noise removal and data compaction,
ii) Over exposed, underexposed, or blurred images :contrast enhancement,
iii) Gray level image : to produce silhouettes from gray level image, and
iv) 3-D reconstruction from cross-section of human body using cross-axial tomography.

In brief, image processing is used for improvement of pictorial information for human interpretation, and processing of scene data for analysis by computers.

8.6.1 Image Formation

An image can arise from one or more of several optical or nonoptical technologies. Television-based systems convert reflected light intensities into an electrical signal. This signal is then digitized. Other systems may use radiation such as X-rays, laser-light, ultra-sound and heat. Image formation actually occurs when a sensor registers radiation due to interaction with physical objects. An image, therefore, represents an array of data samples representing some type of energy.

8.6.2 Image Quality

A standard digital image is represented by samples in an equally spaced rectangular grid quantized at equal interval of gray levels. The spatial co-ordinate elements represent brightness and colour and are referred to as pixels, pels, or picture elements. Therefore, image refers to a two- dimensional energy (mostly light intensity) function IMAGE [x,y] where x and y denote spatial co-ordinates and the value of function IMAGE at point (x, y) is proportional to energy level of the image at that point.

To produce a TV image it should be digitized to produce an array with a resolution of 512×512 picture elements and each element representing at least 256 gray level intensities. For acceptable intensity and detail the resolution, an average monochrome image must be represented by an array of at least 256 by 256 pixels. Each pixel should have at least 64 gray level intensities. However, algorithms can be implemented and tested even on an image of array size 64 by 64 with 5 bit (32 gray level) intensity.

8.6.3 Workstation for Image Processing :

The workstation suitable for image processing should have flexible architecture to allow easy extension of memory, inherent capability to produce high resolution graphics, and ability to handle large data arrays. The systems based on Intel 8088 or 80286 micro-processors, e.g., IBM PC, and PS/2 series and its true Compatibles, as well as Motorola 68000 series based Amiga and other systems meet this requirement.

8.6.3.1 Memory

The IBM PC or compatibles can support only 640 KB of memory under MS DOS operating system. However, for an IBM PC using Windows 95 (or 3.1), the Unix operating system or OS/2 limit of 640 KB is not applicable. Amiga systems do not have such memory restrictions and can address multiple mega- bytes, enabling manipulation of large arrays in the memory. In case of PCs with DOS, arrays larger than 64KB are difficult to manipulate. This restriction, wiii not apply to systems based on Intel 80386 or higher processors working under Windows or OS/2.

8.6.3.2 Backup Storage

A minimum of 270 MB of hard disk and a floppy disk is sufficient to meet the basic needs of image processing applications.

8.6.3.3 Image Source

An image can be obtained from a monochrome or colour camera. It can also be obtained by use of VCR. Some of the Graphic Controllers available in the market support such devices.

8.6.3.4 Pointing Device

A graphic tablet or mouse is used to capture, digitize and manipulate images.

8.6.3.5 Image Processing Hardware

The colour or gray scale values of the pixels of an image are mapped using look-up tables to make them compatible to graphic controller to present desired colors on the monitor.

Separate look-up tables are used to map image memory to display device. These tables output values to red, green and blue channels of a colour monitor, based on some input pixel values. A workstation can be converted into an image processing system by installing suitable hardware to facilitate image acquisition, provide image memory and look-up tables, and display device support on one board. Table 8.1 gives details of some of the hardware available in the market.

Table 8.1 Image Processing Hardware

No.	Device	Description
1.	EGA for IBM PC,XT,&AT and true Compatibles	640×350 6-bit pixels i.e., a pixel can depict only 64 fixed colors.
2.	VGA (Video Graphic Adapter)	640×480 pixels with 16 colors and 320×200 pixels with 256 colors.
3.	Super VGA	800×600 pixels with 16 colors or 640×480 pixels with 256 colors
4.	Matrox MGA	1600×1200 resolution 1280×1024 resolution with 16.7 million colors with 120 Hz. One can play back full screen video for Windows at 30 frames per second.
5.	TARGA (True Vision advanced Raster Graphics Adapter): Analog RGB Monitor is recommended.	This system can capture, digitize and manipulate real time images and is supported by TIPS (True vision Image Processing Software) from Island Graphics in California. RGB Palette of 32768 colors, 512 * 482 resolution, ability to overlay computer generated image on a video image, and image Capture rate of 1/30 second per frame.
	Video Source:	Camera, VCR, or Video disk that generates NTSC composite video or RGB signals.
6.	AT&T's Vista Video Graphics board Compatible, and Palette of more than	Supported by TIPS, multiple addressable resolution (from 1K*1K*32 bits to 2K*2K*8 bits), NTSC & PAL 16 million colors.
7.	Amiga Custom Chip	640 columns by 400 rows of 4 bit pixels,and a pixel can be mapped to any 16 colors from a palette of 4096 possible colors.
8.	VideoLogic for ISA and VL-bus PCI-Movie for PCI bus	supports full screen playback upto 1280 by 1024 pixel resolution with upto 30 frames per second on PCI.

8.6.4 Algorithms

Description of image processing algorithms is outside the scope of this book. However, an interested reader can see references [1 to 6]. A few basic techniques are briefly described to illustrate the power of image processing in the following sections.

8.6.4.1 Histogram of an image

The histogram of an image shows how many image elements occur in the image at each gray level. The histogram discards the spatial information in the image. It is unique for an image but the converse is not true. If we move objects inside an image the histogram of the image is not affected. Improper digitisation and low/high contrast in the image is depicted by the histogram.

8.6.4.1.1 Algorithm for drawing histogram of an image

IMAGE(P): Value of pixel P
Gray level range: 0 to G
Histo: Histogram Array
Step 1: Initialise HISTO [Z] for all values of $0 < Z < G$.
Step 2: For all pixels P of image do :
Begin
Step 3: Increment HISTO[IMAGE[P]] by 1
Step 4: End

End of Algorithm.

8.6.4.2 Point Operation :

A point operation maps the gray scale values of pixels of an input image to a new gray scale value such that

i) image sensor non-linearity with respect to light intensity is compensated.
ii) to suit an image gray scale to the contrast range of the output device,
iii) to show a feature of interest in an image into maximum visibility area or
iv) to divide image into disjoint regions based on gray levels.

Therefore, a point operation 'PO' can be defined as

Output pixel value = P0 [input pixel value]

where,

PO : modifies the gray level of an image pixel by pixel in a predefined way to produce processed image PRCIMAGE, i.e.

PRCIMAGE[x,y] = **PO** (IMAGE [x,y])

We now define linear point operation '**LPO**' as under:

Output Pixel value = **LPO** [Input pixel value]
= A [Input pixel value] + SHIFT

The effect of the **LPO** depends on value of A and SHIFT as described in Table 8.2.

Table 8.2 Linear Point Operations

Case	A	SHIFT	COMMENTS
1	1	0	Copy operation
2	>1		Contrast is increased
3	<1		Contrast is reduced
4	1	0	Scales gray level
5	<1	0	Maps dark area to light & light area to dark.

8.6.4.2.1 **Pseudo Coloring**

Point operation can also be used for pseudo colouring of images. For example, low medium and higher gray levels may be mapped into shades of red, orange and yellow respectively.

8.6.5 Procedure to run Image Program

Description : This is an interactive package and runs through a menu. Only histogram, and point operations have been implemented.

Program Name : Image.pas

Include Files : ditherplot . pas
rdimage . pas
wrtimage . pas
contrast . pas
hardcopy . pas

Picture files : Teapot . PIC size = 100
Donut. PIC size = 100
Sphere . PIC size = 100
Saturn. PIC size = 64
Airport. PIC size = 64
Chromosome. PIC size = 64

(Picture files teapot, donut, and sphere can be created in different views by using surface program given in Section 7.8.6.)

Run time interaction :

On giving run command following dialogue will take place :

Select Dither :- Enter 3 - for 3 x 3 and 4 - for 4 x 4

3

Enter PICTURE FILE NAME (A:/ B:/ C: FILE NAME)

Teapot.PIC <Ret>

Note : This file is created using surface program using Num_U and Num_V equal to 24 and rotation of 90 degrees about X-axis followed by rotation of 90 degree about Y-axis.

Size of the Image :

100 <Ret>

Action : At this stage 'Digital Image Processing Options' menu is displayed with following options:

0 - Exit Package
1 - Draw Image
2 - Histogram Enhancement
3 - Edge Enhancement
4 - List Image
5 - Hardcopy Image

An Item in the menu can be selected by pressing the space bar or the number on the left of menu item.

To select Option 1 :

Input : Press Number 1 key followed by <Ret>

Action : A ditherplot of the image and its histogram is shown on the screen. The gray scale is also shown on the top of the histogram.

Input : Wait for the caption 'Ditherplot of the Image' to appear below the image. Then Press any key two times.

Action :menu is again displayed.

To select Option 2 :

Input :Select item 2 either by pressing number '2' followed by <Ret> or through use of 'Space' Bar.

Action : Display will show original image and its histogram.

Input : Wait for the caption 'Ditherplot of the Image' to appear below the image. Then press any key two times.

Gray level in original ORGGMIN = 17 and ORGGMAX = 29

Linear transform : Input gray scale GMIN & GMAX

1 31 <ret>

Action : Display shows modified image & its histogram

Input : Wait for the caption 'Ditherplot of the Image' below the image to appear. Then press any key two times.

Action : Main menu will appear on the screen

Option 3 : Not implemented. Left as an exercise.

Option 4 : Select this option and press <ret>

The image is listed in its alphanumeric form on the screen

Option 5 : Select this option & Press <ret>

Original or Processed Enter "0" or "P"

p <ret>

Action: display shows processed image & its histogram and screen dump is obtained on the printer

Option 0: Selected to exit from the program
Input : Select this option & press <ret>
Press any key to return to Turbo Pascal
Input : Press any key
Action : Main menu of Turbo Pascal will appear on the screen.

8.6.6 Listing of Program

See instructions on how to get the floppy containing the source of the program.

Example 8.5: Figure 8.5 shows the picture of planet saturn and its histogram. The image matrix size is 64*64 and each pixel has 32 levels of intensity.

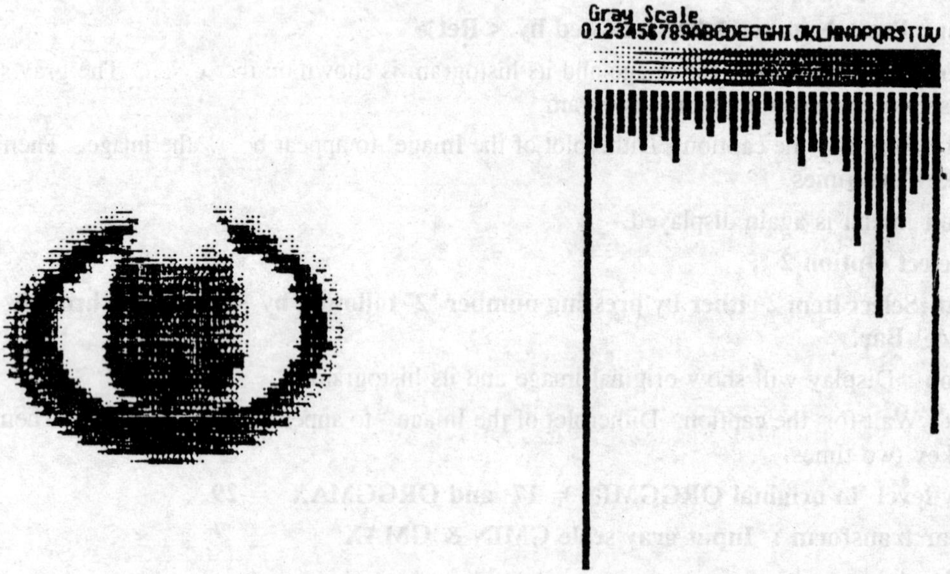

Ditherplot of Image using 4 X 4 Dither   Histogram of the Image

Figure 8.5 : Image of Saturn and its Histogram

Example 8.6: A picture of 'teapot' (see section 8.6.5) was created using the surface generation program given in section 7.8.6. The histogram of this picture shows that the minimum and maximum gray level intensities, 'Orgmin' and 'Orgmax' are 17 and 31, respectively after clipping histogram at count of 15.

The contrast of this picture is enhanced and the new range is defined by GMIN and GMAX. The pixel values of the processed image are defined by

[output pixel value] = A [input pixel value] + SHIFT

where A = (GMAX - GMIN) / (ORGGMAX - ORGGMIN)

and SHIFT = Gmin

Figures 8.6, 8.7 and 8.8 depict the original image, the enhanced image with GMIN = 1, GMAX = 31 and another image of teapot with Gmin = 10 and Gmax = 20, respectively.

Ditherplot of Image using 4x4 Dither

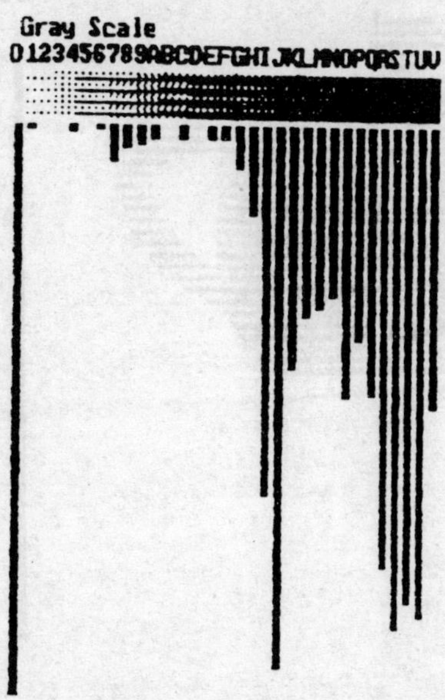

Histogram of the Image

Figure 8.6 : Original Teapot and its Histogram.

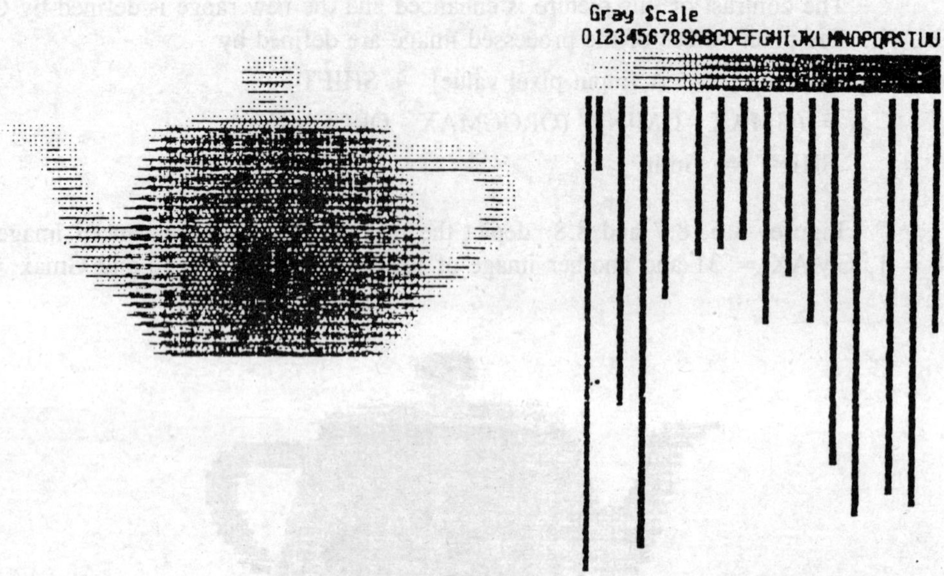

Ditherplot of Image using 4x4 Dither   Histogram of the Image

Figure 8.7 : Teapot with Stretched Contrast (Gmin = 1 and Gmax = 31)

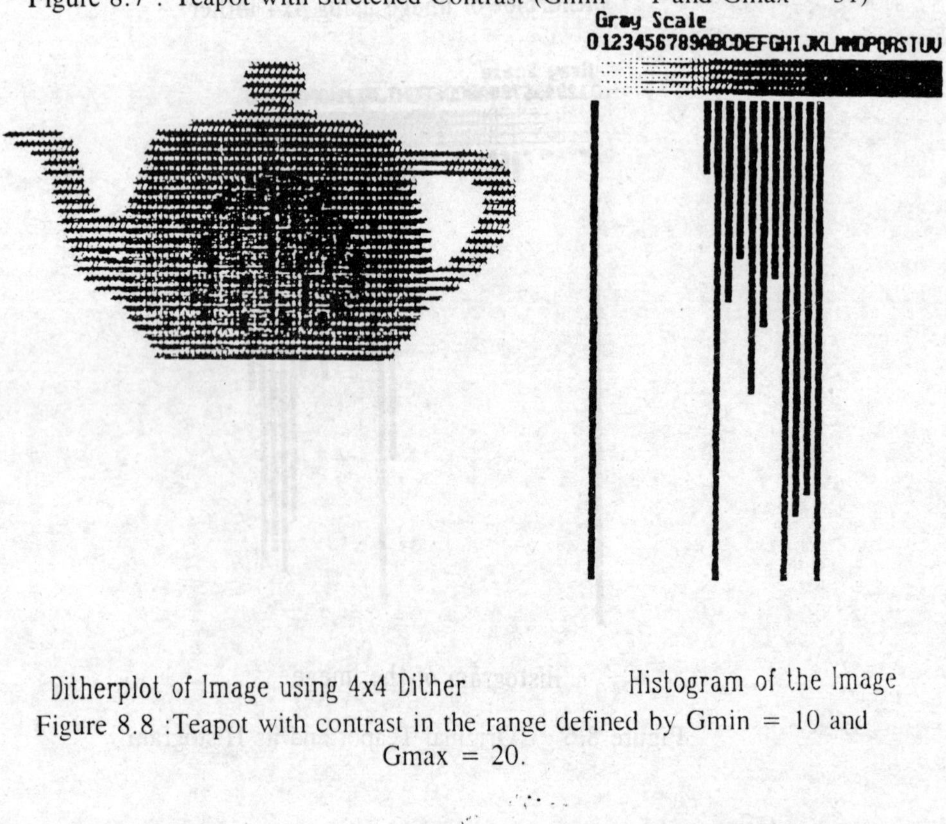

Ditherplot of Image using 4x4 Dither   Histogram of the Image

Figure 8.8 :Teapot with contrast in the range defined by Gmin = 10 and Gmax = 20.

8.7 ANIMATION

Animation, a sequence of still images, introduces a new dimension, time, for generating a sequence of frames to give the impression of motion. The frames consist of graphical images. Some examples are films made by photographing drawings, puppets etc., with only a slight difference in the contents of individual frames. When these are projected on to a screen in a sequence the impression of movement is produced.

An animated film/cartoon is designed through script writing and story-boarding. An artist creates components of animation by using generic materials from an artist's supply store to develop specialised components needed for the film/cartoon. These components are painted on a transparent acetate sheet. In case of computer animation one can take the analogy of a computer art supply store to a programmer's library consisting of graphic symbols. The graphic symbols can be taken as generic components to create specialised components, characters, scenery [7, 8], cartoons, tree, etc. [9]. This requires use of suitable data structures, together with interactive techniques and the concepts of 2- and 3-dimensional graphics described in the earlier chapters.

Computer animation and art are two applications of graphics which require not only technical expertise but also other talents.

8.7.1 Goals :

The following are the goals of animation ;

8.7.1.1. Motion :

Motion control for computer animation is becoming a rich area for new research. The animation system should possess intelligence to interpret the general description of the desired motion in such a way as to translate it into specific instructions that would result in the motion. Two types of controls are commonly used for animation of articulated bodies : Kinematic and Dynamic. A simple kinematic approach relies on user input facilitated by an interactive system. The user positions the articulated body at specified times and motion is interpolated between these positions for animation [11, 12]. This approach is referred to as 3-D key positioning as objects are placed in different positions and an interpolation method computes the in-between frame-to-frame parameter value. The result of this approach depends heavily on intelligence of the user to assign an appropriate path and rate of motion. Two-dimensional key-framing is not very popular because of its limitations [13,14] but three-dimensional object based key-framing is convenient and has become an accepted technique [11]. Dynamic motion is defined by dynamic equations consisting of relationship between forces, torques, and motion of masses [15]. The number of equations necessary to specify a system depends on its degree of freedom. Number of models exist which animate motion by using combinations of rotary joints. These joints can be controlled through choice of joint angles, key positions, and interpolation schemes. Most of these models assume a constant velocity of objects during each frame of the animation [16,17].

Much attention has also been given recently to the simulation of human motion [18] and other articulated bodies such as robots and animals. For example, the model of the human body used by TEMPUS [15] has 18 joints and 48 degrees of freedom. Attempts are being made to create computer generated human images which can be made to move appropriately in response to simple commands like 'WALK', 'RUN' or 'DANCE'.

8.7.1. 2. Photo Realism :

Photo realism has gained popularity in the production of commercial movies, flight simulators, architectural planning, meteorology, and graphical presentation of mathematical entities [9]. Environments can be created and animated to simulate such phenomena as sunsets, sunrises, fog, rain, smoke, fire. Other elements can be added to compose a desired scene. This technique is very effective in creating background scenery for actors in a studio. The background may consist of sequences of deserts, mountains, ocean and rivers. The scene will move realistically according to the movement of the actors. Thus, the need for creating an artificial set is reduced.

A seven-minute computer animated film entitled 'Rendezvous a Montreal' that brings Marilyn Monroe and Humphery Bogart back to life, was produced [10] to celebrate 100 years of engineering in Canada by researchers at University of Montreal. The synthesized characters were created and directed using Human Factory System (HFS) consisting of modules viz., object grasping control, body motion control, path planning control, and emotion and speech control. The sub-modules of the HFS are joint body control, hand joint control, facial expression control, object modelling , skin and hair creation, camera and light control, scene control, rendering control.

Animation is being used as an important tool in computer image generation to design Flight simulators [19] for pilot training to facilitate repetitive practice of landing and take offs, through presentation of 3D scenes of the airports, and view of cities for day and night landings to the pilots. The scenes change and present a view to the trainee with respect to the speed and position of the aircraft. Similar techniques are also used for training personnel for navigation of ships using ship simulators. Animation techniques are also used by television broadcast industry for vividly depicting the motion of clouds observed by a satellite.

The sequence of pictures created can also be used to educate or explain to people concept in other areas. This may need creation of realistic images of 3-dimensional objects.

8.7.1.3. Use of Holography for Animation

Manufacturers of automobiles are interested in the development of techniques for displaying crashes in 3-dimension to simulate accidents. For example, the holograph of a car may collide with the holograph of another vehicle to show how the parts of the vehicle will fly in a real crash.

8.7.2 Graphic Command Assembler (GCA)

To facilitate the description of a scene or an assembly based on primitives shapes or to create frames of animation containing a number of objects, a basic graphic command assembler may be described(see table 8.3). The arguments of a transformation command can either be assigned a numeric value or a symbolic name. Each symbolic name is assigned a numeric value. The symbolic names along with their values are stored in a file. This file is read by GCA. Thus, the program describing the scene need not have absolute values in the argument fields of the commands - a very useful feature while creating frames of animation.

In fact, one such file may define one frame of animation. To create dynamic graphics, motion can be described by changing parameters using equations of motion while the program is under execution.

This approach to animation relies on use of 3-D transformations of each part of every object in the scene.

Table 8.3 Commands used to develop a basic GCA.

Command	Mnemonic	Arguments	Comments
Scale	SCAL	SX, SY, SZ	Scaling factors
Translation	TRAN	TX,TY,TZ	Translation Factors
Rotation about X-axis	ROTX	ANGLE	-
Rotation about Y-axis	ROTY	ANGLE	
Rotation about Z-axis	ROTZ	ANGLE	
Perspective	PERS	ANGLE,ZNEAR, ZFAR	ANGLE defines the field of view
PUSH transformation matrix on the stack	PUSH	-	
POP transformation from the stack	POP	-	
OVER	OVER		Indicates termination of DRAW & DEF Commands
Exit	EXIT	-	End of program
Draw part	DRAW	see section 8.7.4.1	
Define Part	DEF	see section 8.7.4.1	Definition of a Part is between DEF and OVER command

8.7.2.1 Rules and Syntax :

1. Blank is used as a separator between commands and also it's arguments.
2. Command mnemonics, arguments, and partname can have a length of upto 7 alpha-numeric characters.
3. An argument value can either be a real number or assigned a symbolic name. If the argument value is symbolic, then its value is picked from a data file containing values for each symbol.
4. Every part defining an object is assigned a symbolic name. Each symbolic name is associated to a number. The symbolic part names and their values are stored in the data file.
5. Syntax of Draw Command :

DRAW partname
T1 arguments
T2 Arguments
...
Tn Arguments
OVER

where T1, T2, ..., Tn denote transformations such as scaling, translation, rotation, etc.

The expansion of DRAW command is as follows :

PUSH
T1 Arguments
T2 Arguments
...
Tn Arguments
DRAW Partname
POP

This structure permits positioning an object relative to a containing object. The draw command implies automatic execution of a PUSH and a POP command in the order shown above. The global homogeneous transformation matrix C is first saved on the stack. C is then used to concatenate other transformations and the resultant C is used to transform the object for display. By executing the POP command, the C matrix is restored to the values its elements contained before execution of the DRAW command.

6. Syntax of DEF Command :

DEF Partname
T1
T2
....
Tn
DRAW Partname 1 Tn+1, Tn+2 ....Tn+m OVER
Tn+m+1
...

Tn+m+p
Draw Partname 2 OVER
...
OVER

A part defined using DEF command can be used as a primitive by other definitions. For example, Partname 1 and Partname 2 are also defined by DEF Commands only.

8.7.3 Procedure to run animation program

The program 'Animate' implements the basic GCA and the technique of nesting transformations. A global 4*4 homogeneous co-ordinate transformation matrix (see section 7.2.1) is used for nesting the transformations.

Three main procedures, Support.Pas, Command.Pas and Traverse.Pas, are used to read the object description file, symbolic name and data file, for processing of commands, for insertion of part definition at each part instance, and to display an assembly or scene, respectively.

8.7.3.1 Program Name :

Animate.PAS

8.7.3.2 List of Include files :

Initial.Pas, Support.Pas {Consisting of procedures Error, CompareString, Convert, ReadString, and ReadConstant}, Command.Pas {Consisting of Procedures for Command lookup table and Command processing logic}, Viewport.Pas, Display.Pas, Creatput.Pas, Trans3D.Pas, Ditherplot.Pas, WritImage.Pas, HardCopy.Pas, Quadric.Pas, Dataseg.Pas, View.Pas, Cube.Pas and Traverse.Pas {generates expanded list (by replacing part instances by complete definition of the part) of commands for assembly of an object scene, and/or assembly}.

8.7.3.3 Data files

Butterfly description :	Fly . DTA
Frame for animation:	Flyfrm . DTA
Blobby Man description :	Blobby . DTA
Frames for animation:	Manfrm1. DTA
	Manfrm2. DTA
	Manfrm3. DTA

8.7.3.4 Initial Settings :

Same as Surface.Pas program, given in section 7.8.6

8.7.4 Listing of the program

```
PROGRAM Animation;
uses
  Crt, Dos, Graph;
{ World_Range   range of X_ and Y_   co - ordinates
```

```
{ Viewport_size  size of viewport for the ditherplot of image  }
{ Screen_Size    size of   screen  reserved  for  wire-frame  }
{ Num_U          number of iso-parametric lines in U- direction}
{ NUm_V          number of iso parametric lines in V- direction}
{ Shape   Order CP_Count  Patch_Count  Program Name   NAM_DTA  World_Range
  sphere   2     10        2            Quadric.pas    None     3.0
  Cube     -     -         -            -              -        3.0 }
Const
     { For Assembly }
     MaxCom       = 12;
     LenAlpha     = 7;    {Length Of Command}
     { For Transformation and display }
     World_Range     =  2.5;
     Viewport_Size   =  100;
     Screen_Size     =  250;
     Num_U           =  4;
     Num_V           =  4;
     Order           =  2;   { The degree of Bezier curve }
     CP_Count        =  10;  { Number of control points    }
     Patch_Count     =  2;   { Number of surface patches   }
     {data for Cube }
     PointCount = 8;
     EdgeCount  = 12;
     NAM_DTA     = 'teapot.dta'; {used only for bi-cubic surfaces}
Type
Alpha   = Packed Array[1..7] of Char; {defines assembly, part instance,name}
Alpha20 = String[20];
Ptr2  = ^Part;
Ptr3  = ^Constants;
Ptr4  = ^Trans;
Constants      =   Record
                ConsName: Alpha;
                 NextCons: Ptr3;
                 Value   : Real;
                End;
Command        =   Record
                Name    : Alpha;
                 Action  : Integer;
               End;
Trans          =   Record
                TransType    : Integer;
                 Parx         : Real;
                 Pary         : Real;
                 Parz         : Real;
```

```
            NextTrans    : Ptr4
           End;
Part        =  Record
           PartName : Real;
            NextPart  : Ptr2;
             NextTransPart :Ptr4;
           End;
 IMAG =  Array[1..Viewport_Size,1..Viewport_Size] of Integer ;
 Mat  =  Array[1..4,1..4] of Real;
 Stack = Array[1..10] of Mat;
 CP_Type           = Record X,Y,Z : Real; End;
 CP_Count_Type     = 1..CP_Count;
 CP_Array_Type     = Array [1..CP_Count] of CP_Type;
 Patch_Type        = Array [0..Order, 0..Order] of CP_Count_Type;
 Patch_Array_Type = Array [1..Patch_Count] of Patch_Type;
 {Declarations for Cube}
 PointType         = Record  x,y,z : Real ; End;
 PointCountType    = 1..PointCount;
 PointArrayType    = Array[1..PointCount] of PointType;
 EdgeType          = Record Point1,Point2: Integer; End;
 EdgeCountType     = 1..EdgeCount;
 EdgeArrayType     = Array[1..EdgeCount] of EdgeType;
VAR
 {Variables for interactive editing of assembly}
 Commands                        : Packed Array[1..MaxCom] of Command;
 InstanceName                    : Real;
 Ps2,P2,StartPartPtr,EndPartPtr    : Ptr2;
 Ps3,P3,StartConsPtr,EndConsPtr    : Ptr3;
 Ps4,P4,StartTransPtr,EndTransPtr  : Ptr4;
 ExitCommandFlag,DrawFlag,QuitFlag : Boolean;
 Tx                            : Alpha;
 DataSeg,ConsSeg                   : Text;
 {Globals for creation of primitive shapes : Sphere and Cube}
 CP                            : CP_Array_Type;{ control point data }
 Patches                       : Patch_Array_Type;{relates CP to patch}
 Point                         : PointArrayType;{ Vertices point data }
 Edge                          : EdgeArrayType;
 Prev_Scrn_X,Prev_Scrn_Y,Sel,Q     : Integer;
 Prev_Scrn_X1,Prev_Scrn_Y1         : Integer;
 WframeX,WframeY,VisibleX,VisibleY : Integer;
 Par_X,Par_Y,Par_Z,Z_pers          : Real;
 Ch,Ch1                          : Char;
 Min_Z,Max_Z,Scale,AspectRatio     : Real;
 Viewport_Array                    : IMAG;
```

```
MDASH,SurfaceType,Dith,Positive   : Integer;
F                                 : file of integer;
Flg,FlagAnimate                   : Boolean;
Data_Seg                          : Text;
NamDat,ConsDat                    : Alpha20;
Xasp,YAsp                         : Word;
{ Globals for Trans_3D Program}
C,TT,TS,TRX,TRY,TRZ,TP,M1,PMAT    : Mat;
TransStack                        : Stack;
{$R-}
{$K-}
{$I initial.pas}
{$I support.pas}
{$I Command.pas}
{$I viewport.pas}
{$I display.pas}
{$I creatpnt.pas}
{$I trans3d.pas}
{$I ditherplot.pas}
{$I wrtimage.pas}
{$I hardcopy.pas}
{$I quadric.pas}
{$I dataseg.pas}
{$I view.pas}
{$I cube.pas}
{$I traverse.pas}

Begin                { Main Program }
 writeln('Input file name w/o extention describing object to be animated');
 Readln(NamDat);
 NamDat := NamDat + '.dta';
 writeln('Input File name w/o extention containing symbolic constants etc.');
 readln(ConsDat);
 ConsDat := ConsDat + '.dta';
 Q :=0; WframeX := 425; WframeY := -50; VisibleX := 0; VisibleY := -40;
 DrawFlaG := False;
 ExitCommandFlag := False; FlagAnimate := True;
 DrawFlag := False;
 ReadConstant; { Read Value Of Symbolic variables for Animation}
 Close(ConsSeg);
 CommandLut;  { Read Command Look Up Table}
 CommandLoop;
 Writeln('HardCopyImage call should be commented if printer is offline.');
 Writeln('Num_U=',Num_U:2,' and Num_V=',Num_V:2,' :- for primitive SPHERE');
```

```
Writeln('Select Dither:- Enter  3- for 3 X 3 and 4- for 4 X 4');
Readln(Dith);
Writeln('Select Negatve - 0  or Positive - 1 image');
Readln(Positive);
InitViewport;
Initialize;
GetAspectRatio(XAsp,YAsp);
AspectRatio := XAsp/YAsp;
Flg := true;
OutTextXY(425,310,'Wireframe with hidden surfaces');
Traverse;
ScaleViewport;
DitherIntPlot(Viewport_Array,dith);
{ HardCopyImage(false,0);}
CloseGraph;
{wrtimage(ViewPort_Array);}
End.
```

Example 8.7.1: To illustrate use of graphic language described in Section 8.x.4 a simple butterfly has been animated. The description of butterfly in the graphic language is presented to 'Animate' program as a input file (FLY.PAS). The contents of this file are given below :

```
DEF WORLD
PERS FOV ZNEAR ZFAR
TRAN XSCR YSCR ZSCR
ROTX BACK
ROTZ SPIN
ROTX TILT
TRAN -XOBS -YOBS -ZOBS
SCAL 1.0 1.0 -1.0
DRAW BUTRFLY SCAL 1.5 1.5 1.8 OVER
OVER
DEF  BUTRFLY
DRAW LWING  TRAN -0.35 0 0.1 OVER
DRAW RWING  TRAN  0.35 0 0.1  OVER
DRAW SPHERE TRAN 0 0 0.1 SCAL 0.14 0.16 0.17 OVER
OVER
DEF LWING
ROTY LANGLE
DRAW WING OVER
OVER
DEF RWING
ROTY RANGLE
```

```
DRAW WING OVER
OVER
DEF WING
DRAW SPHERE TRAN 0 0 -0.425 SCAL 0.141 0.141 0.425 OVER
OVER
EXIT
```

PROGRAM TO ANIMATE A BUTTERFLY

The symbolic names representing arguments of commands, and various parts of butterfly along with their values are given below :

```
RANGLE 90
LANGLE -90
FOV 45
ZNEAR 5.17
ZFAR 10.7
XSCR -0.1
YSCR -1.6
ZSCR 7.9
BACK -90
SPIN 0
TILT 0
-XOBS 0
-YOBS 0
-ZOBS 0
CUBE 17.0
SPHERE 16.0
WORLD 15.0
BUTRFLY 1.0
LWING 3.0
RWING 5.0
WING 6.0
```

Symbolic names for FOV, ZNEAR,& ZFAR define the field of view and depth of field. The values of parameters XOBS, YOBS and ZOBS fix the position of the observer and values assigned to BACK, SPIN, & TILT, adjust the view about this point. Variables XSCR, YSCR, and ZSCR translate the point (XOBS, YOBS, ZOBS) on the screen. ZSCR moves the object away from the eye.

The left and right wings can be controlled by values assigned to symbolic names: 'RANGLE' & 'LANGLE'. Figures 8.9 and 8.10 depict butterfly for value of 'RANGLE' 90 & 120 and 'LANGLE' -90 and -120, respectively. The left and right wing angle can be changed to follow a pattern alongwith suitable translation to create an illusion of a flying butterfly by presenting a number of frames in a sequence. For real time animation, at least 30 frames per second should be presented to the observer.

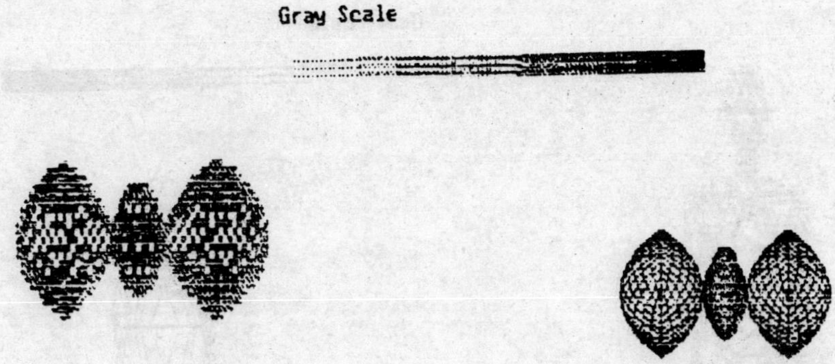

Figure 8.9: Animated Butterfly with RANGLE = 90 and LANGLE =-90.
Sphere with radius equal 2 units & Num_U = Num_V = 14 is used as a primitive.

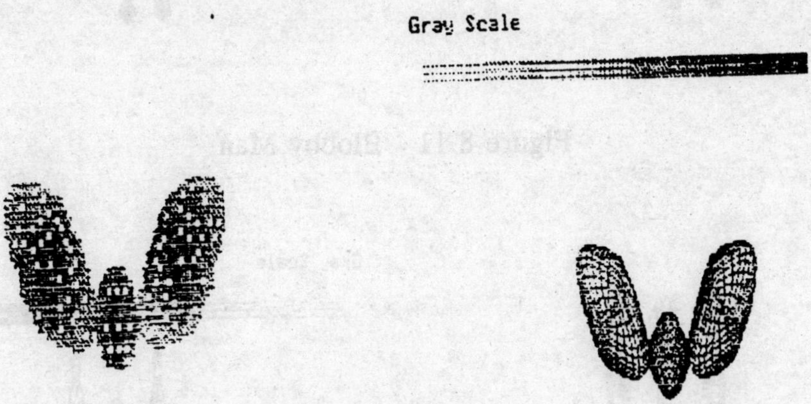

Figure 8.10 Animated Butterfly with RANGLE = 120 and LANGLE = -120.
Sphere with Num_U = Num_V = 4 has been used as a primitive.

Example : 8.7.2

The database for an articulated human figure called 'Blobby Man' [13] was used to create figures 8.11 to 8.13. A sphere (see program in section 7.8.6) of radius of 2 units is used as a primitive to create the figure. The time required to generate figure 8.13 on a 8.0 MHz PC/XT and 10 MHz PC/AT without floating point hardware is of order of 65 snd 26 seconds respectively. The primitive sphere was drawn with Num_U & Num_V parameter equal to 4. The time will increase witb the value of these parameters.

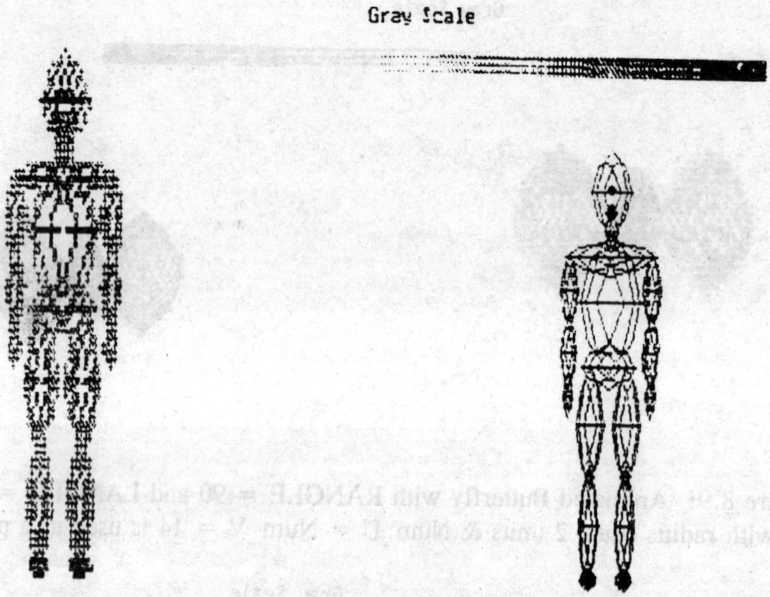

Figure 8.11 Blobby Man

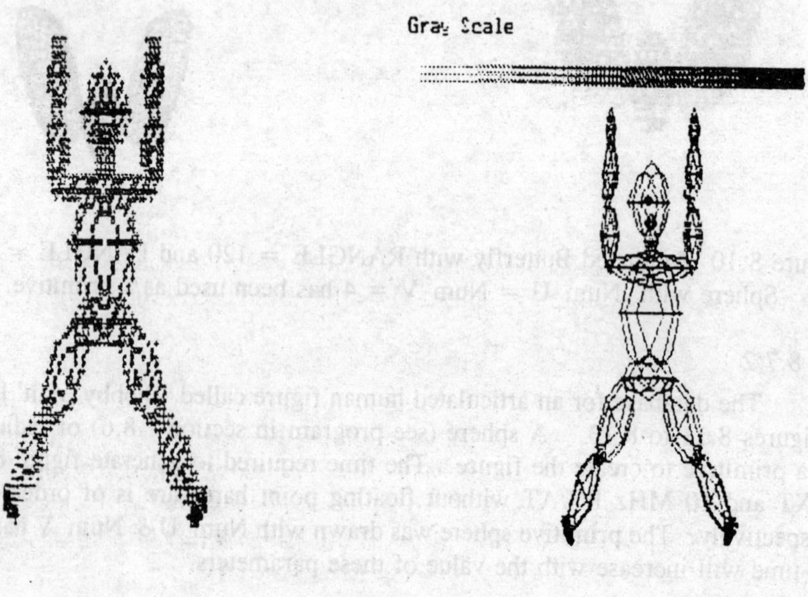

Figure 8.12: Blobby Man Exercising : Both hands up and legs spread out.

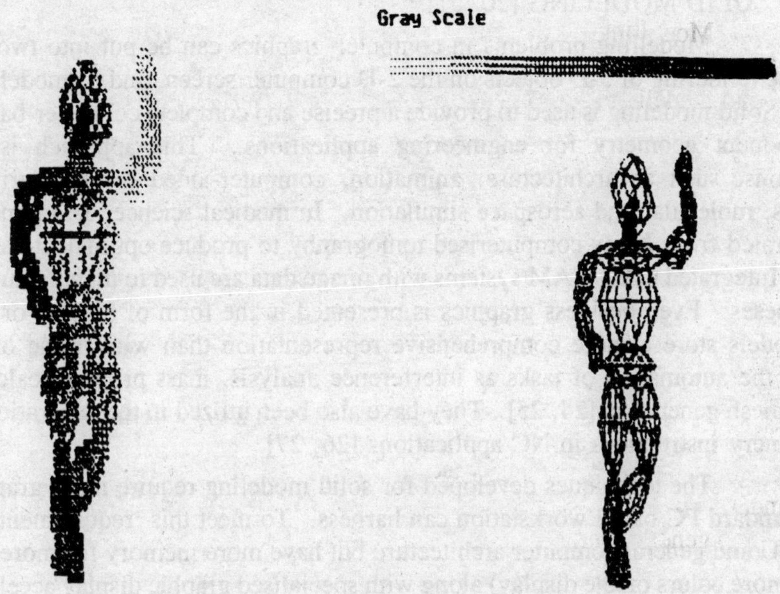

Figure 8.13: Blobby Man waving with legs in crossed position

Example 8.7.3 : In the file describing Blobby Man the primitive sphere has been replaced by a cube of edges of length of 2 units. The resultant 'Blobby Man' is shown in figure 8.14

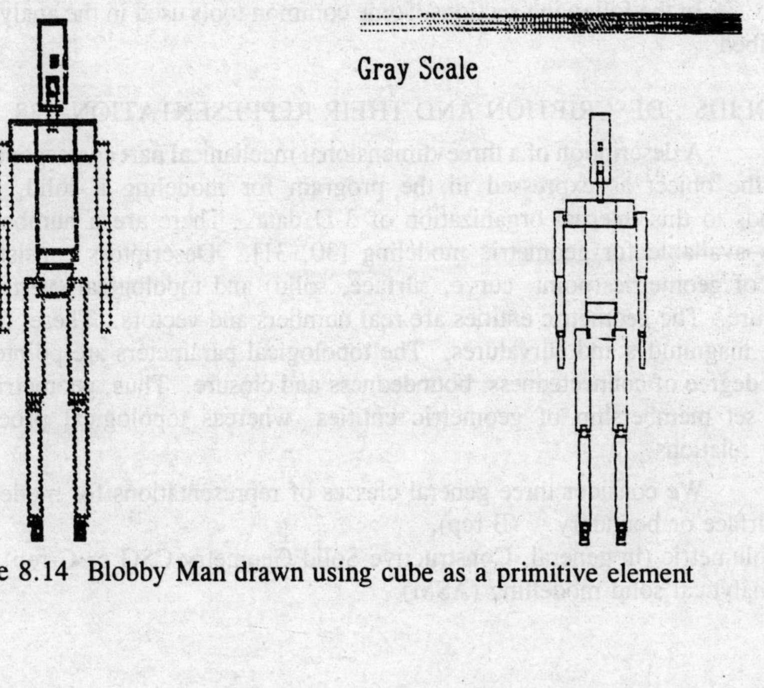

Figure 8.14 Blobby Man drawn using cube as a primitive element

8.8 3-D SOLID MODELING [20, 21]

Modelling problems in computer graphics can be put into two main catagories: i) realistic rendering of 3-D objects on the 2-D computer screen, and ii) modelling of shapes and motion. Solid modeling is used to provide a precise and complete computer-based representation of component geometry for engineering applications. This approach is used in several applications, such as architecture, animation, computer-aided manufacturing (CAM), fluid dynamics, molecular and aerospace simulation. In medical science, 3-D bone models [22, 23] are generated from X-ray computerised tomography to produce optimal fit stems for individual femurs. Integrated CAD/CAM systems with image data are used to manufacture structure model or prostheses. Even business graphics is presented in the form of blocks, or a solid pie-chart. Solid models store a more comprehensive representation than wire-frame or surface models, enabling the automation of tasks as interference analysis, mass property calculation and finite element mesh generation [24, 25]. They have also been utlized in the generation and verification of machinery instructions in NC applications [26, 27].

The techniques developed for solid modeling require more graphics horse power than a standard PC based workstation can harness. To meet this requirement systems have the same CPU and general computer architecture but have more memory for more bit planes (which provide more colors on the display) along with specialised graphic display accelerating hardware. Several engineering disciplines, such as fluid dynamics, finite element analysis and aerospace simulation demand high speed and high resolution graphic capability from the computer system. Earlier systems incorporated proprietary graphics engines and custom tailored graphic software. This created problem in the data interchange when different types of work-stations were connected. As a result of such inconveniences, concentrated efforts have been put to standardise the workstation graphic interface.

In the following sections, some common tools used in the analysis of solid models are described.

8.8.1 SOLIDS : DESCRIPTION AND THEIR REPRESENTATION [28, 29]

A description of a three-dimensional mechanical part corresponds to the designer's view of the object as expressed in the program for modeling a solid. A representation corresponds to this internal organization of 3-D data. There are a number of programming languages available for geometric modeling [30, 31]. Descriptors consist of operators and operands of geometric (point, curve, surface, solid) and topological (vertex, edge, face and body) nature. The geometric entities are real numbers and vectors. These quantities deal with locations, magnitudes and curvatures. The topological parameters are pointers or integers and deal with degree of connectedness, boundedness and closure. Thus, geometric processing deals with the set membership of geometric entities, whereas topological processing deals with adjacency relations.

We consider three general classes of representations for modeling rigid solids,

i) Surface or boundary (B-rep),

ii) Volumetric (in general, Constructive Solid Geometry CSG or C-rep), and

iii) Analytical solid modelling (ASM).

8.8.1.1 B-rep

A solid is represented by its enclosing surface or boundary. A boundary is made up of a number of faces; faces are represented by mathematical surfaces defined by edges and vertices resulting in polyhedron approximation of objects. Curved surfaces are represented using spline or bezier curves. A sphere may be thought of as having only one face. In fact, face has a clear definition only in the context of planar polyhedra. An explicit definition of vertices, edges, and faces makes representation of boundary quite useful in computer vision and graphics.

8.8.1.2 C-rep

In this technique, a solid model is represented by a combination of solid graphic primitives, possibly with different shapes and sizes, such as blocks, spheres, cones, cylinders and tori, instead of enumerating a huge number of spatial points. Each of the primitives is then described by its geometric parameters.. CSG represents an object as a binary tree (see figure 8.15) where each leaf represents an instance of a primitive solid with pointers to its geometry and each node represents an operation of its descendants. This representation is not unique since an object can be created by a number of possible combinations of primitives.

The most common method of structuring the solid model in the graphics database

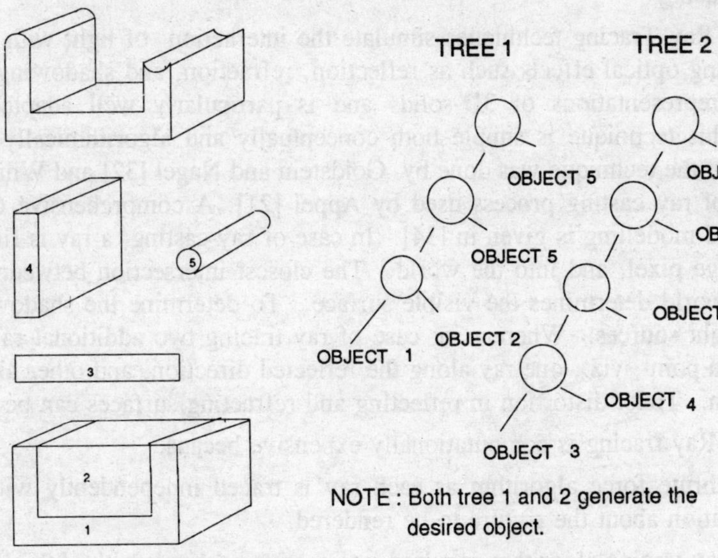

Figure 8.15 Composition of an object and its binary trees

is to use Boolean operations (set union, intersection and difference) which at the lowest level are 3D half spaces. Half space sets are defined by relations that partition space into two easily recognizable halves. For example, the membership of a point P is defined easily when F is the equation for a plane by substituting the coordinates of P in F

$$F(x, y, z) = Ax + By + Cz + D$$

If the value of F is positive the point P is in the half space, otherwise P is not a member of the half space but a member of its complement.

Although CSG representation covers most conventional, unsculptured solid objects, it fails to describe free form shapes and large class of sculptured objects.

8.8.1.3 ASM

Curves, surfaces, and solids in ASM are defined by parametric functions. Curves are represented by three component cubic functions defined over the unit interval. Surfaces are defined over the unit squares and solids are defined over the unit cube.

In case of CSG representation, the vertices, edges and faces on the boundary of the solids are not explicitly stored. A trade off exists between B- and C-rep in storage versus time, with a CSG type tree being more compact in storage and B-rep being faster in computation. However, some models use hybrid representation using both B- and C-rep. CSG and B-rep are the most important representation in CAD. The main drawback of using CSG in robot vision application is that surface evaluation is always needed as one can only see the surface of a object.

8.8.2 Ray Tracing

Ray Tracing techniques simulate the interaction of light with the environment, thus determining optical effects such as reflection, refraction, and shadowing. CSG is one of the classical representations of 3D-solids and is particularly well adapted to ray tracing algorithm. This technique is simple both conceptually and algorithmically. Early work in development of the technique was done by Goldstein and Nagel [32] and Whitted [33] and was an extension of ray casting process used by Appel [21]. A comprehensive description in the context of solid modelling is given in [34]. In case of ray casting, a ray is fired from the eye, through a image pixel, and into the world. The closest intersection between this ray and the object in the world determines the visible surface. To determine the shadows, rays are fired towards the light sources. Whereas in case of ray tracing two additional rays are fired from the intersection point, viz., one ray along the reflected direction, and other along the direction of transmission. Thus, distortion in reflecting and refracting surfaces can be modelled.

Ray tracing is computationally expensive because

i) it is a brute force algorithm as each ray is traced independently without using other information about the picture to be rendered,

ii) initial ray tracing algorithm required intersecting each ray with each object in the scene. Improvements incorporated in the algorithm subsequently [35,36] have tried to enclose objects into simple boundary boxes, thus reducing the need for more complex intersection calculation which are floating point intensive, and

iii such algorithms also have drawback of aliasing as we are intersecting an object with a ray (line) and are thus forced to point sample at the intersection point.

8.8.2.1 A Generic Algorithm for Ray Tracing

Let line R represent a ray, intersecting the bounding faces of an object O. The intersection points divide the line in segments with respect to the object. A generic ray tracing algorithm can be described by the following steps :

1. Compute the intersection of R with the bounding faces of O. This is to find out curve-surface intersection.
2. Sort intersections by increasing distance away from a reference point on R. The parametric equation of line is used and sort is performed in terms of parameter t of the parametric equation of line R.
3. Analyze the intersections in order depending on the intended application. For example, in case of image generation using a simple local lighting model, locating the first intersection of R is sufficient for an intensity, or colour of pixel based on surface reflectance property as well as on the number, type and position of one or more light sources.

8.8.2.2 Algorithm to find intersections of a ray and a quadratic or bicubic surface patch

1. Initialise the stack & push the test patch on the stack.
2. Pop test patch from the stack.
3. Divide patch into four subpatches. (see the quad tree algorithm described in section 7.7.1)
4. Compute the bounding box volume of each subpatch. A simple way to find the bounding box can be to take the minimum and maximum of the x, y, and z components of the control points to form a rectangular bounding box.
5. Test the bounding box for intersection with the ray.
6. If the ray hits the bounding box of a subpatch and patch is not smaller than a specified accuracy (maximum subdivision) then put the subpatch on the stack for processing. This proceeds in a depth first search order for the subpatches whose bounding boxes intersect the ray and which meet the desired accuracy criteria. The resultant patches represent the point of intersection.
7. Repeat from step 2 until stack is empty.

   The resultant patches (intersection points) specify

   i) (U,V) co-ordinates of the intersection point on the original patch, and

   ii) value of parameter 't' (see section 8.8.2.1) specifies the intersection point on the ray.

   More than one intersection point is found in cases where

i) ray intersection is close to the boundary between sub patches, or

ii) when the ray is parallel to and contained in a planar portion of the patch.

The selection of one intersection in such cases is carried out by either of the following methods:

i) Accepting an intersection point closest to the ray origin i.e., one with smallest value of 't'. However, if more than one point satisfies this criterion, any of such point can be selected,

ii) by computing the average of resultant intersection points.

8.8.3 Image Generation

This is an important analysis operation for modeling an object in an interactive solid modeling system. Display of objects as wireframes is a very common technique. The objects are represented by their edges. An edge may be drawn entirely or partitioned on the basis of a given view. The invisible edge or part of it may be drawn in a special mode (say dotted lines) or completely ignored. In case of B-rep models creating a display is a trivial task as details of edges are available in the data structure. However, in case of C-rep based models database describing bounding curves is not available, and it becomes necessary to evaluate boundary of objects before a wireframe display can be created.

The second technique for creation of images using shaded images of models is based on ray tracing. We describe generation of images using ray tracing technique in the following section.

8.8.3.1 Ray tracing approach for Image Generation

A scene containing an object and a source of light is shown in figure 8.16. A procedure using a local lighting model and a single light source is described below.

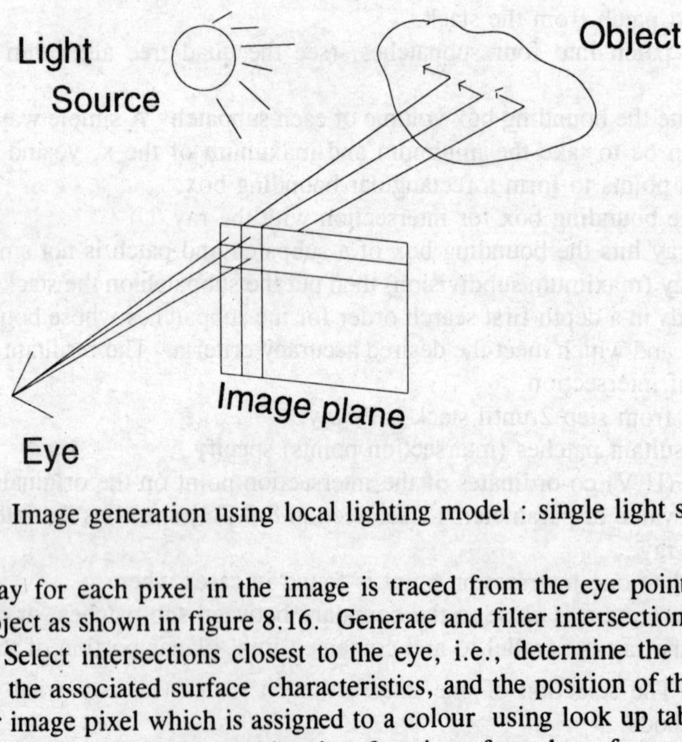

Figure 8.16 Image generation using local lighting model : single light source

One ray for each pixel in the image is traced from the eye point, through the image pixel to the object as shown in figure 8.16. Generate and filter intersections as described in section 8.8.2.2. Select intersections closest to the eye, i.e., determine the normal to the surface encountered, the associated surface characteristics, and the position of the light source to compute value for image pixel which is assigned to a colour using look up tables of display hardware. The time taken to generate an object is a function of number of rays which need to be traced to the boundary of given primitives and the time spent traversing CSG trees. The simplest technique which is used to minimise the computation on number of rays is the use of bounding boxes as described in section 8.8.2.2. A ray need not be traced to the boundary of a primitive if it does not intersect the bounding box. Some more techniques to minimise the number of rays to be traced and thus reduce computation time are described in [34, 37].

8.8.4 Computation of Mechanical Properties

Some mechanical properties such as volume, mass and moment of inertia are of interest in solid modeling. These and other properties can be computed by using the integral

$$\int F(x,y,z)\,dV$$

where F is collection of selected functions. For example, if F = 1, the integral will compute the volume of the object. Similarly if F = (density of material of the object) then integral will compute the mass of the object. One can see reference [38] for details of procedures used for computation of mechanical properties in the solid modeling environment. These approaches, however, are practical only for objects represented by B-rep and not CSG.

In case of CSG (or C-rep), mechanical properties are computed by extending the ray tracing approach used for image generation. A new line of sight is determined along with projection plane perpendicular to the line of sight. A grid is imposed on the projection plane. The grid defines a set of rectangular columns perpendicular to the projection plane. By tracing the ray through the complete solid it is possible to identify the columns inside or outside the object. The integral can, therefore, be computed by summing up the contributions of the portions of the columns of the grid in the solid. The coarseness of the grid determines the accuracy of the solution. An alternative approach using cell/solid classification is described in [39]. In this approach space is divided into small cells (see section on oct-tree in chapter 4). As expected, the accuracy depends on the size of the cell.

8.9 FRACTALS

In chapter 6 and 7, we have discussed methods to generate curves and surfaces. But many objects, such as mountains[50], water, trees[40,54], and clouds, landscapes etc. have irregular or fragmented features. Such objects can be modelled using the fractal geometry methods [40-54]. Fractals are geometric shapes. A number of shapes now recognised as fractals have been known for a long time. Books on fractal geometry [such as 45 ,48 ,49 , and 52] provide both descriptive and mathematical model for complex forms found in nature. Euclidean geometry fails to describe natural shapes such as coast lines, mountains, and clouds. These objects, however, have statistical shape similarity which essentially is a quality of fractals in nature.

The word fractal was coined by Mandelbrot in 1975 [52]. Fractals provide a platform where research in pure mathematics is connected with both the natural sciences and computing. Within the last 18 years, fractal geometry and its concepts have become very useful in the area of natural sciences, physics, chemistry, biology, zoology, and natural sciences. Graphic designers and film makers have also shown interest as fractals possess the ability to create new and exciting shapes and artificial but realistic looking worlds. In fact, the artificial planets shown in 'Star Trek II' movie also used fractals to create realistic looking shapes.

Fractal geometry now plays a key-role in the realistic rendering and modelling of natural phenomenon in computer graphics[43,50].

8.9.1 FRACTALS, SELF - SIMILAR AND SELF-AFFINE

Fractals shapes are self similar and independent of scale or scaling. Euclidean geometry provides concise and accurate descriptions of man made objects but is inappropriate for representing natural shapes. Fractals on the other hand simulate descriptions of many natural shapes and can create natural looking computer imagery. Euclidean shapes can be described by an algebraic formula, e.g., straight line by a formula ($y = mx + c$) and circle by equation ($r^2 = x^2 + y^2$). The fractal shapes, however, are described by an algorithm which often is recursive.

The main difference in Euclidean Geometry (EG) and Fractal Geometry (FG) can be summed up as follows:

i. EG is based on characteristic size or scale where as FG has no specific size or scaling.
ii. EG is suitable for creating man made objects where as FG can create natural complex shapes.
ii. Objects in EG are described by formula whereas fractals are generated using algorithms or procedures.

The property of self similarity is closely connected with a notion of dimension as explained in figure 8.17. An object like line segment is one dimensional - it is possible to divide it in number of equal parts. Each sub-division of a line segment is also a line segment. Similary, a square and a cube are 2 and 3 dimensional objects respectively and can be divided into equal parts, each of the smaller part resulted by the process of division also looks like a square and a cube only. As shown in figure 8.17, the property of shape similarity and dimensionality can be generalised, given a shape similar object of dimension D, divided into N equal parts and scaled by ratio S, as follows:

$$NS^D = 1$$

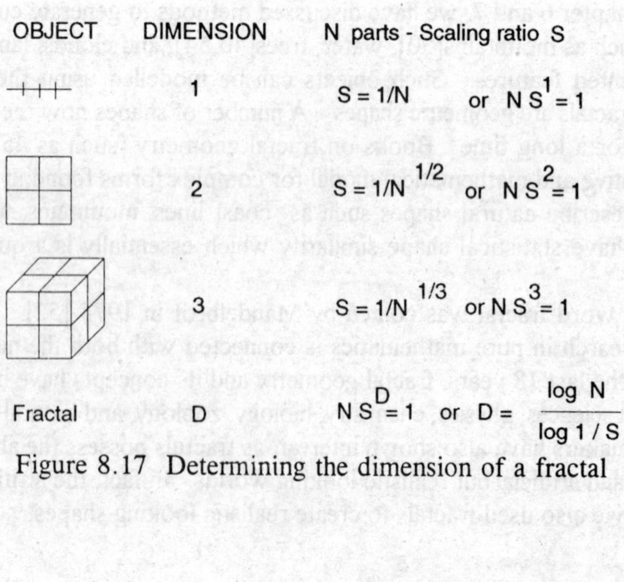

Figure 8.17 Determining the dimension of a fractal

Conversely, its fractal similarity dimension is given by

$$D = \frac{\log N}{\log \frac{1}{S}}$$

In fact, the fractal dimension as described above need not be an integer number. As an example, we analyse von Koch curve[52] composed of 4 sub-segments, each of which is scaled down by factor of 1/3 from its parent(see figure 8.18). Its fractal dimension can be computed as follows:

$$D = \frac{\log 4}{\log \frac{1}{1/3}} = 1.26$$

A self-similar fractal is a geometric shape in which each "larger part" can be subdivided into "small parts" in such a way that each small part is a reduced scale replica of the larger part. The fractal is composed by placing small parts as per a specified algorithm such that they do not overlap. The fractals used to model natural features such as mountains are not self similar but are self-affine, i.e., for a large part, it must be sqeezed horizontally in one ratio while it is squeezed vertically in a different ratio.

N = 4 S = 1/3

D = log (4) / log (3)

Figure 8.18 Dimension of von Koch snowflake curve

8.9.2 FRACTAL GENERATION THROUGH STRING RE - WRITING ALGORITHM

Recursive subdivision by midpoint displacement is the most widely used method for constructing fractals of every kind. For example, it is used to construct snowflake curves [52] and the reliefs [50]. String rewriting systems are also referred to as L-systems. In this method character strings are interpreted as lines, curves, and pictures. The string re-writing algorithm provides an elegant way to generate the classical fractals, e.g., Von Koch snowflake curve and the space filling curve of Peano and Hilbert. This method is designed, such that, it models the topology and geometry of plan including branching patterns of trees and bushes.

The string consists of letter of the alphabet or special characters, such as, '+' and '-', etc. The mapping between string and the display commands is established by a LOGO like turtle which interprets characters into graphic commands, such as, move, forward, turn left, turn right by an angle specified in degrees.

Figure 8.19 uses the following string to generate a fractal:

$$F \rightarrow F-F++F-F \tag{8.1}$$

This string is also referred to as a production rule. The interpretation of the string into graphical commands is carried-out as follows:

i.	'F'	-	draw a line forward. 'F' is called axiom.
ii.	'+'	-	turn right by 60 degree S
iii.	'-'	-	turn left by 60 degrees.

Looking at the production rule (8.1) from left to right following action is taken:

Step	Character encountered	Action taken
1	F	A straight line segment is drawn in the direction of the turtle.
2	-	turtle takes a turn left by 60 degree.
3	F	same as step 1
4	+	turtle takes a turn right by 60 degrees.
5	+	same as step 4
6	F	same as step 1

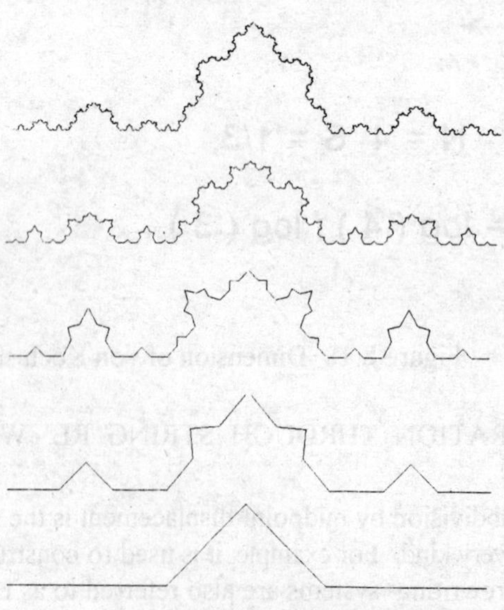

Figure 8.19: The first five stages in the generation of von Koch snowflake curve

Thus, we get the first stage fractal shown in figure 8.19. Stage 2 of the curve is created by replacing each occurence of 'F', the axiom, in production rule (8.1) by the string 'F-F++F-F'. The string generated for the second stage is

$$F \rightarrow (F-F++F-F)-(F-F++F-F)++(F-F++F-F)-(F-F++F-F) \qquad (8.2)$$

Similarly, third stage is generated by replacing 'F' by the string generated in (8.2). This procedure is repeated to generate the subsequent stages. This pattern is called Von Koch snowflake curve. Similarly, by using a production rule (8.3) given below

$$\begin{aligned} X &\rightarrow -YF+XFX+FY- \\ Y &\rightarrow +XF-YFY-FX+ \end{aligned} \qquad (8.3)$$

One can create space filling Hilbert Fractal as shown in figure 8.20 (it shows the first four stages only). Angle in this case is 90 degees and axiom is 'X'.

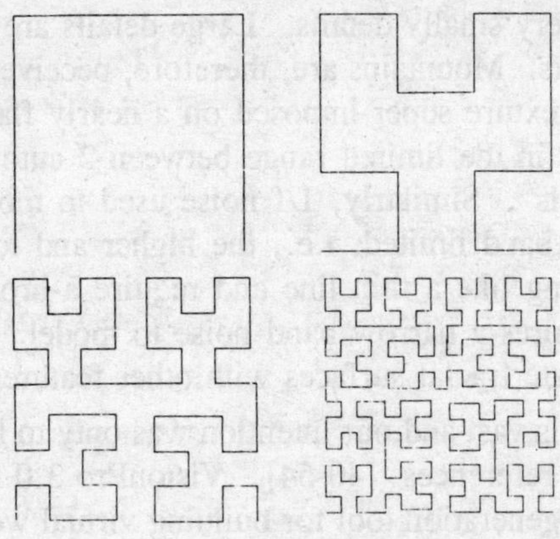

Figure 8.20 Space filling Hilbert curve

8.9.3 3 - DIMENSIONAL FRACTALS

Fractal surfaces can be described as objects with dimension between 2 and 3. Fractal surfaces can be generated using techniques similar to those used for curves.

To illustrate a simple way to create profile of a mountain, we take a triangle. A point is selected on each leg of the triangle. Then, random displacements are applied to each of the three points. The displaced points are joined by straight lines. Figure 8.21 (a)-(c)) shows this process upto three stages only. Figure 8.21(b) shows how by process of random displacement of boundary points the triangle is changed into four smaller contiguous triangles. This process is repeated for each of the new triangles formed at each stage.

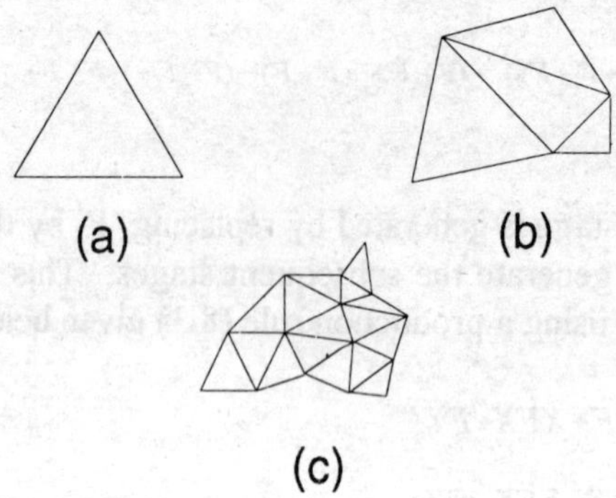

Figure 8.21 Generating a Fractal mountain from a triangle

It is very difficult to restrict one to create fractals which are strictly self similar because the existence of both infinitely larger and small parts is rediculous for natural surfaces and shapes, such as, real mountains and coast lines[50]. In fact, a mountain is never infinitely high and its relief does not include very smally details. Large details are fluctuant even more strongly in water then they are in rocks. Mountains are, therefore, peceived as a free - standing relief while ocean is perceived as a texture super-imposed on a nearly flat surface. It can be concluded that a factal is self similar in the limited range between 2 cutoffs, and it is lacking both very large and small level details . Similarly, 1/f noise used to model, irregularities of water as well as mountains, is also band limited, i.e., the higher and lower frequencies are cutoff. For example, mountains being like a thin line and require a broad band noise while water being like a rectangle and requires a narrow band noise to model. Many other type of transformations can be used to generate fractal surfaces with other features.

The subject of fractals is vast and our intention was only to briefly introduce this topic. Interested readers can see the references [40-54]. VisionPro 3.0 from Virtual Reality Labs is a fractal based 3D landscape generation tool for building virtual worlds. It comes with CD-ROM with scenes from Earth and Mars. The package comes with sample QuickTime (see chapter 10 on Multimedia) movies, music files and maps.

8.10 ANALYSIS OF ENGINEERING STRUCTURES

Computer-aided geometric design (CAGD) deals with the mathematical representation of geometric objects to facilitate computer assisted representation, analysis and display. Scientific visualization helps scientists and engineers to investigate physical systems through a process of geometric abstraction. Visualization is an interdisciplinary subject, drawing on numerical simulation, perceptual psychology, graphic arts, computer graphics, image processing, data management, parallel processing, distributed computing and various disciplinary specialities of science and engineering. Visualization is described as a structured process of data pre-processing, geometric abstraction and image rendering. After a discussion of the role of human perception in visualization, various techniques for displaying scalar, vector, and higher-order tensor fields are presented in [63].

Advances in both computer hardware and software technology have enabled engineers to solve very complicated practical problems by means of numerical methods on desktop computers. Meanwhile, finite element methods (FEM) are used increasingly for design and analysis of engineering systems and solution of vibration problems in structural dynamics[55-57]. We will highlight in this section the utility of graphical concepts useful for the analysis of structures.

8.10.1 VERIFICATION OF MODEL

FEM requires input data, such as, geometry of the structure, elements type, material property, boundary conditions, and external loads etc. Finite element data preparation requires great amoumt of time and effort. Because of the complexity of input data to finite element programs, the error in defining the models are very likely. Identification of errors, before the main analysis, reduces both time and money losses. One simple technique to verify, that all joints and elements(members of a frame) of given structure have been duly entered on a micro-computer, is by shrinking/enlarging the display of the frame on the screen. The area where members are missing appears blank and can easily be identified. Another method used is to draw the perspective view of the model and view it from different view points. This helps in identifying data input errors. Drawing perspective in transparent form becomes ambiguous for the complex structures. Thus, for all three dimensional analysis, it is preferable to take into account the opacity of the object by generating hidden line removed plots.

For the entry of two-dimensional data mesh generators [58-60] based on iso-parametric super elements are used to automate the process. These act as pre-processor for FE programs. The process requires the structure to be broken into simpler sub-blocks (super-elements) which are mapped into a unit rectangle described in terms of a convenient co-ordinate system. For generating three dimensional mesh[61,62], well proportioned tetra-hedral elements are used. However, these are difficult to visualize and are often replaced by hexa-hedrals. In another approach, models are build from from one of the two basic geometric families (parallelopiped and peripheral). Solids are generated from the composition of several of these.

8.10.2 PRESENTATION OF INFORMATION

A space framework is a geometrically stable structure (see figure 8.23), consisting of number of bars located in different planes and connected together by universal joints. There are three methods for stress detemination in statically determinate space frameworks:

- the method of sections,
- the method of bar replacement, and
- the method of reducing the structure to a series of plane ones.

Any of the above method can be used for the analysis of the structure. The next step is to show the results graphically for easy comprehension. We now desctibe a simple form of data structure for creating 3- dimensional structures as under:

Number of joints
Number of members(links) say n
Permissible stress limits
X,Y,Z co-ordinates of the first joint
X,Y,Z co-ordinates of the second joint
●
●
●
X,Y,Z co-ordinates of the last joint
Link 1 First joint Second joint Link attributes
Link 2 First joint Second joint Link attributes
●
●
●
Link n First joint Second joint Link attributes

Figure 8-24 shows a truss with 41 joints created using the above data structure. The attribute field consists of information such as area, elasticity, moment of inertia and weight etc. Colour Graphics can successfully be used to depict the members of structures in tension or compression, thermal stress plots, or any other attributes of members of the structures. Figure 8.25 shows a two dimensional view of a steel suspension bridge alongwith the stress levels in its members. Figure 8.26 shows the thermal stress distribution in a frame structure.

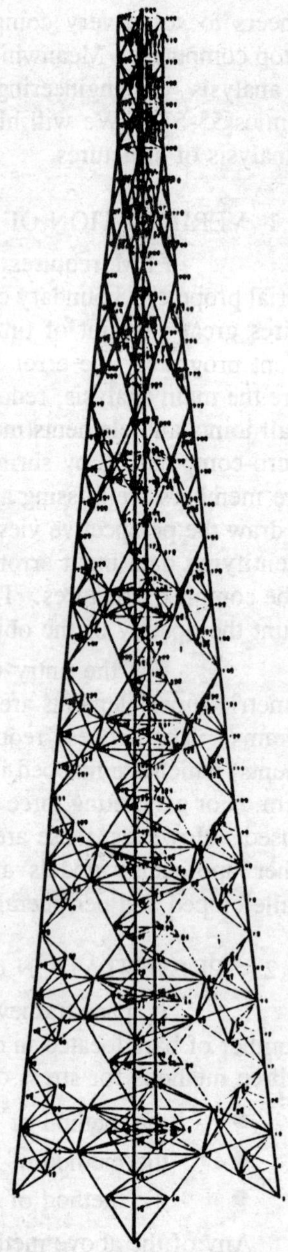

Figure 8.23 A tower

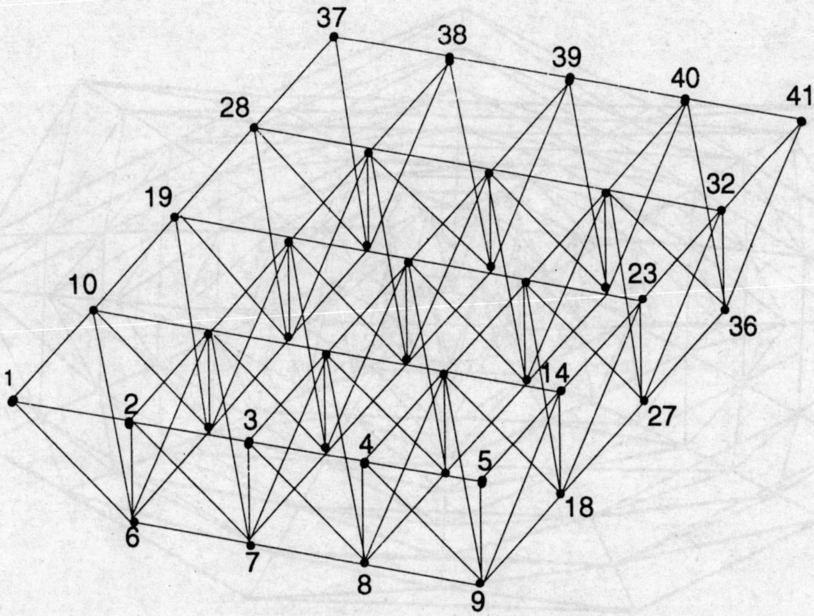

Figure 8-24 A truss with 41 joints

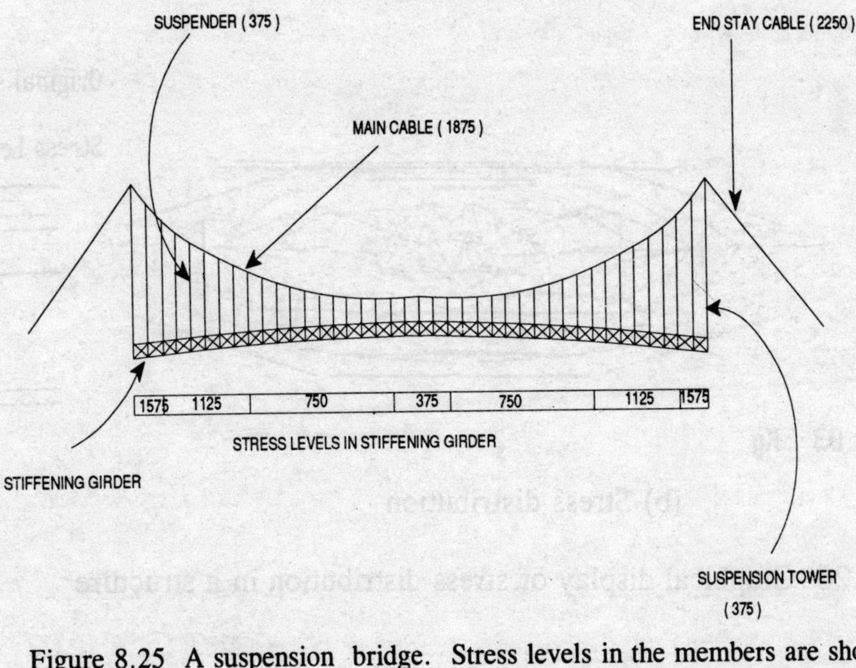

Figure 8.25 A suspension bridge. Stress levels in the members are shown in brackets. Stress levels in stiffening girder are given in the bar.

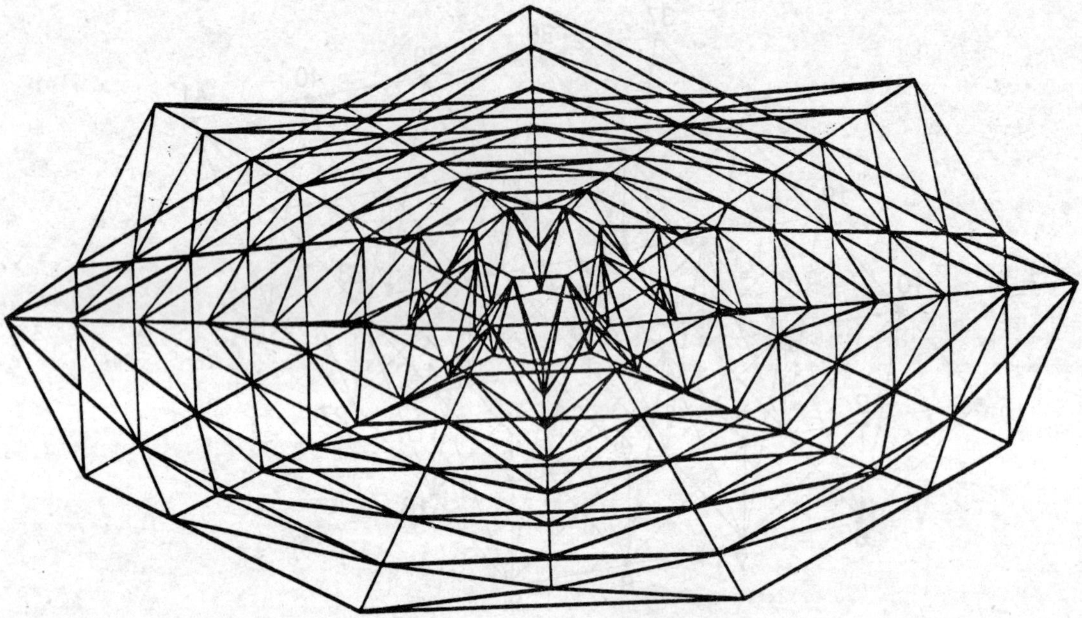

(a) The Structure

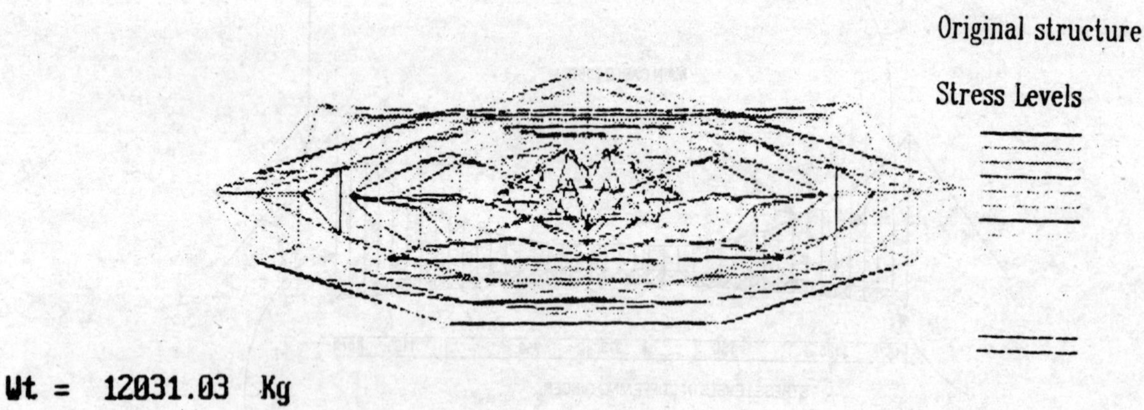

(b) Stress distribution

Figure 8.26 Graphical display of stress distribution in a structure

8.11 Software Packages for Analysis, Design and Drafting

8.11.1 CADAM 3D Interactive, CADAM Inc., California, USA

This package supports computer augmented graphics design and manufacturing. The main modules of CADAM are shown in figure 8.27.

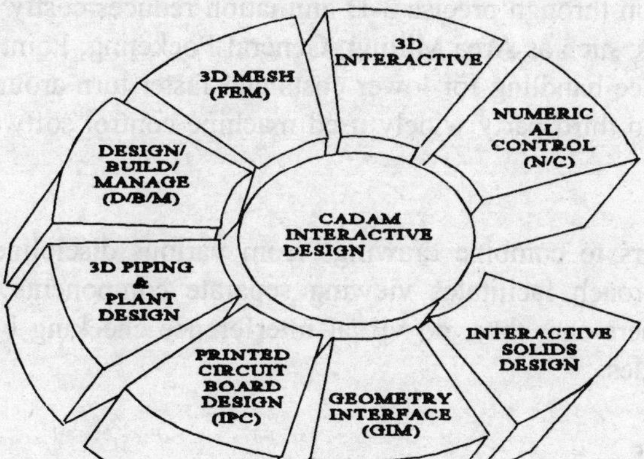

Figure 8.27 Modules of CADAM

A brief review of the main modules is given below:

- 3D Mesh

  Models created with 3D interactive can be used in the 3D Mesh. The data can be used to analyze finite element models for studies of heat transfer, air flow, stress, and mass properties. The key features are

  - 3D Mesh lets you move geometric data directly from the database into third party analysis software.
  - Simplifies mesh construction by allowing you to choose the construction method suitable for a given application. It develops automatically from 3Dsurface mapping, uses free-form 3D node creation or map mesh directly onto 2D sections.
  - It provides necessory interface with packages such as MSC NASTRAN (stress analysis), MOLDFLOW (Injection flow analysis for plastics), and ADAMS (mechanical design analysis).

- One can use standard libraries thus reduce the need of repeated analytical studies.

▶ Numerical Control

3-D Interactive generates simple as well as complex surfaces, which can be used in multiple axis numerical control programming. The key features are

- Extends CADAM capabilities to NC programming environment.
- Establishes relationship between 2-D/3-D part geometry and tool paths to assure faster, more accurate tool path definition.
- Visualization through precise 3-D animation reduces costly trial and error waste.
- Capabilities, such as Area Milling, General Pocketing, Point to point patterns and cycles reduce handling for lower costs and faster turn around.
- Interfaces to third party widely used machine control software.

▶ 3-D Piping

It enables designers to combine drawings from various disciplines into a multi layer model. This approach facilitates viewing separate components together as a single assembly. Designers can, thus, do visual interference checking by viewing the model from different angles.

▶ Geometry Interface

Helps in generating 3-D models automatically according to user defined parameters, or through interactively selected geometry. It also facilitates in writing programs to generate reports as per user desired format. Another use of this module is in reverse engineering. One can take digitized points from a 3-D model and load them into CADAM for 3-D surfacing.

▶ Design/Build/ Manage

One can use this to generate detailed 3-D models based on 2-D floor plans. Such models can be rotated for 3-D viewing, or for quick massing studies for evaluating structures in relation to their sites.

The advanced functions include features, such as color shading to enable designers to visualize plans into realistic color representations; off-plane construction using 3D splines to design objects like aerodynamically designed wing sections, turbine blades,.and other complex objects; hidden line removal capability to suppress hidden elements in 3D models and bring clarity; and general analysis features, e.g. popular surface types - including Bezier and Coons - to help in checking surface to surface interactions. The other useful programs are CADAM LATHE for lathe programming to generate tool path for roughing, drilling, finishing, and threading and copmputer aided dimensional inspection system.

8.11.2 Software Developed by Structural Engineering Research Centre, Madras, India

A list of a few software packages available from this centre for structural analysis is given below. We have described only the Interactive Frame Analysis program in some detail as other programs are of similar type.

► Interactive Frame Analysis

This program enables a user to interactively analyse two dimensional rigid jointed plane frame systems under different load conditions. The key features are

- accepts format free input
- interactive editing of data through query sessions
- Gives reactions and equilibrium checks
- Allows variation of member sizes interactively for redesign through queries
- Allows variations of nodal conditions to account for foundations interactively
- Allows analysis for nodal forces and moments in addition to member loads in the form of concentrated, uniformly distributed and trapezoidal load conditions
- Allows different end conditions for members like fixed hinged, hinged fixed and hinged hinged conditions for members so that truss and beam members can be combined

Inputs to the program are

- Name of the problem
- No. of nodes; No.of joints
- Nodal details:
  Node No; Condition; X,Y,Z, coordinates: X,Y, and Moment loads
- Member details:
  Member number: I[th] node; J[th] node; Member code (hinged or fixed); Area; Moment of inertia; Young's modulus
- Load details

Program outputs are:

- Input printed out first for verification
- Nodal deformations in X,Y, 0 directions
- Member forces and moments in local axis
- Reactions
- Equilibrium checks

A user can have interactive sessions to introduce changes in nodal conditions, properties and coordinates and study their affect . The order of these sessions is

- change of bounday conditions,
- change of connectivity,
- change of revisions of member properties, and
- change of coordinates of nodes.

► Interactive GRID Analysis

This programe allows the user to interactively analyse rigid jointed grid systems subjected to lateral loads.

- Space frame analysis
  The program allows the user to interactively analyse three dimensional rigid jointed space frame systems under static load conditions.

- Cylindrical shell analysis
  This program can be used to to analyze circular cylindrical shell roofs (Barrel shells) with or without edge beams for given uniformly distributed loads. It is based on classical procedure developed by Gibson.
- Folded Plate Analysis
  One can use this program to interactivly analyze simply supported folded plate structures under uniformly distributed loads, line loads, and moments.
- Tower Analysis Program System (TAPS)

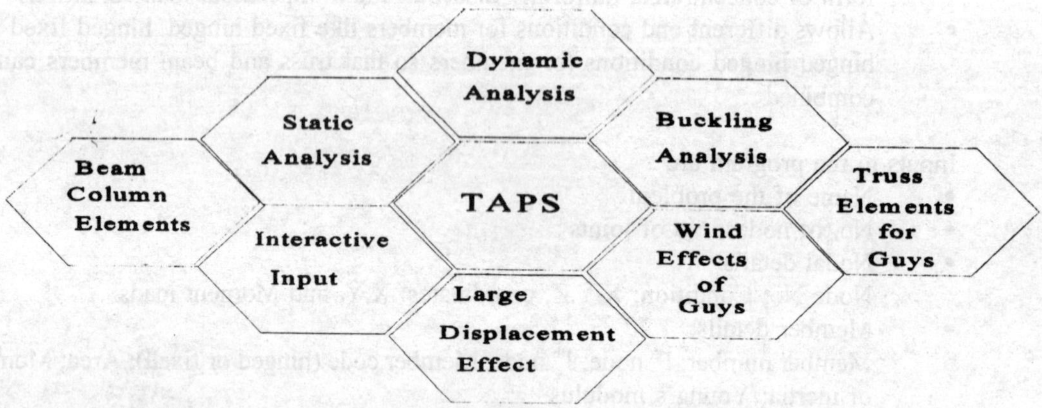

Figure 8.28 Main modules of TAPS

It is a finite element software package for nonlinear static, dynamic and buckling analysis of guyed towers. It runs on a PC and takes into consideration effects due to large deflections and rotations. It uses nonlinear finite iterative technique. The model supports 3D beam column elements for mast and 3D truss elements for guys. It utilizes a trilinear elasto-plastic stree-strain relation to idealize the material behaviour of guys.

TAPS accepts wind load as a distributed load or as pressure acting directly on the guys and mast. It uses Wilson's method of direct time integration of equations of motion for dynamic analysis. Displacement history at any selected node in dynamic analysis can be stored on file and retrieved. Buckling analysis is performed using load factor approach. The program automatically computes the buckling load to the desired level of accuracy. The typical output of TAPS include nodal displacements, member resisting forces at nodes, axial forces, and guy tensions.

In addition to the above software this centre has developed a number of programs for reinforced concrete slab, beams, columns, and footings design,

Structural analysis of

i. 2-D truss analysis
ii. 3-D truss Analysis
iii. 2-D frame analysis
iv. Grid Analysis

One can solve multistoreyed frames of upto 11 storys × 4 bays or 16 storys × 3 bays. Using symmetry double the number of bays can be solved.

All the above programs are written in FORTRAN language. The programs have been written in user-friendly interactive mode and eneble the designers to solve their design problems using PCs.

8.12 SUMMARY

In this chapter, we have studied many applications of computer graphics in engineering. Starting with the preparation of bar graphs and pie-charts, which are often used in presentation of reports, we studied a general program that can be used for plotting a graph of a function that can be input from the keyboard. Alternatively, the data can be read from a disk file. This was followed by an introduction to computer image processing, which has applications in many fields of engineering. Animation, solid modeling, and analysis of structures were also discussed briefly in sections 8.7, 8.8, and 8.10.

In section 8.8, some techniques used in analysis of solid models bounded by polygons, quadratic and bicubic surfaces have been described. In particular, we have reviewed representation of solids, basic ray tracing, and mechanical property computation techniques. One of the most important problems in solid modeling system is that the range of shapes generated is limited. Although it is easy to model a polyhedron, it is rather difficult to model free form and fillet surfaces. To overcome this problem and to promote wide use of solid modeling systems in the CAD/CAM area there is need to develop analysis algorithms to utilize the power and completeness of solid representations.

Algorithms commonly used in solid modeling are computationally expensive. With increase in complexity of models a user can either break models into simpler models or can use specialized hardware. Parallel computing in this area is also becoming popular because many algorithms for solid modeling are inherently parallel.

Fractals provide a descriptive and mathematical model for many of the complex forms and patterns in the nature. A brief review of this topic is given in section 8.9.

The programs described in this chapter are available both in Pascal and C languages on floppy disks. The C programs run on pull-down menus (see the Read.me file on the disk, whereas Pascal programs can be run as per the descriptions given in this chapter.

8.13 REFERENCES:

1. Gonzalez R.C. and Paul Wintz, Digital Image Processing, Addison Wesley Publishing Co. Inc., 1977.
2. Castleman, K.R. Digital Image Processing, Englewood Cliffs, Prentice Hall, N.J., 1979.

3. Rosenfield A. and A.C. Kak, Digital Picture Processing, Vol. 1 and 2, Academic Press, New York, 1982.
4. Pavlidis T., Algorithm for Graphics and Image Processing, Computer Science Press, Rockville, 1982.
5. Baxes, G. Digital Image Processing, Englewood Cliffs, Prentice Hall, N.J., 1983.
6. BYTE (Special issue on Image Processing), Vol. 12, No. 3, March 87.
7. G.A.Mastin, P.A. Waterberg, and J.F. Mareda, "Fourier Synthesis of Ocean Scenes," IEEE Computer Graphics and Applications, Vol. 7, No.3, March 87, pp. 16-23.
8. R. F. Vors, "Fourier Synthesis of Gaussian Fractals : IF Noises, Landscapes and Flakes," in State of the Art in Image Synthesis, Tutorial No. 10, SIGGRAPH 1983, ACM, NewYork, 1983.
9. N. M. Thalmann and D. Thalman, "An Indexed Bibliography on Image Synthesis," IEEE Computer Graphics & Applications, Vol. 7, No. 8, August 1987, pp. 27-38.
10. N. M. Thalmann and D. Thalman, "The Direction of Synthetic Actors in the Film Rendezvous à Montreal", IEEE Trans. Computer Graphics and Applications, Vol. 7, No. 12, December 1987, pp. 9- 19.
11. S.N. Steketee and N.I. Badler, "Parametric Keyframe Interpolation Incorporating Kinetic Adjustment and Phrasing Control," Computer Graphics (Proc. SIGGRAPH 85), July 1985, pp. 225-262.
12. D. Sturman, "Interactive Keyframe Animation of 3-D Articulated Models, "Intro. to Computer Animation, tutorial notes, SIGGRAPH 85, July 1985.
13. James F. Blinn, " Nested Transformations and Blobby Man, " IEEE Computer Graphics and Applications, Vol. 7, No. 10, 1988, pp. 59-65.
14. E. Catmul, "The Problems of Computer Assisted Animation," Computer Graphics (Proc. SIGGRAPH 78), July 1978, pp. 348-353.
15. N. I. Badler et al., Positioning and Animating Human s in a TaskOriented Environment, The Visual Computer, Dec. 1985, pp. 212-220.
16. J.Korien and N.I. Badler, "Temporal Anti-Aliasing in Computer Generated Animation," Computer Graphics (Proc. SIGGRAPH 83), Vol. 17, No.3, July 1983, pp. 377-388.
17. M. Potmesil and I. Chakravarty, " Modelling Motion Blur in Computer Generated Images," Computer Graphics (Proc. SIGGRAPH 83), Vol. 17, No.3, July 1983, pp. 388-399.
18. N.I. Badler and S. Smoliar, " Digital Representation of Human Movement," Computing Surveys, Mar. 1979, pp. 19-38.
19. Michael J. Zyda, el al., "Flight Simulators for under $100,000," IEEE Trans. Computer Graphics and Applications, Vol. 8, No. 1, Jan. 1988, pp. 19-27.
20. P. Quarendon and J. R. Woodwork, " The Model for Graphics," in Techniques for Computer Graphics, edited by D.F. Roger, and Rae, A. Earnshaw, Springer Verlag, 1987, pp. 39-63.
21. A. Appel, "Some techniques for shading machine rendering of solid", Proc. AFIPS JSCC, Vol. 32, 1968, pp. 37-45.
22. S.W. Granholm, et. al. "Computer Design of Custom Femoral Stem Prostheses', IEEE Trans. Computer Graphics and Applications, Vol. 7, No. 2, Feb. 1987, pp. 26-35.

23. M.L. Rohdes, Y. Kuo, L.G. Rothman, and C. Waznick, " An Application of Computer Graphics and Network to Anatomic Model and Prostheses Manufacturing", IEEE Trans. Computer Graphics and Applications, Vol. 7, No. 2, Feb. 1987, pp. 12-25.

24. Y.T. Lee, A. De Pennington, and N.K. Shaw, "Automatic Finite Element Mesh Generation from Geometric Models - A Point based Approach," ACM Trans. Graphics, Oct. 1984, pp. 287 - 311.

25. T C Woo and T Thomasma "An algorithm for generating solid elements in objects with holes," Advanced Topics in Solid Modelling, Course Notes, SIGGRAPH '86 ACM, New York 1986.

26. J.E. Bobraw, "NC Machine tool path generation from CSG part representation," Computer-Aided Design, March 1985, pp. 69-76.

27. U. Sungertekin and H.B. Voelcker, "Graphical Simulation & Automatic Verification of NC Machining Programs, " Proc. IEEE Conf. Robotics and Automation, 1986, pp. 156-165.

28. Dana H. Ballard and C. M. Brown, Computer Vision, Prentice Hall Inc., New Jersey, 1982, pp. 264-316.

29. A.A.G. Requicha and H.B. Voelcker, 'Boolean Operations in Solid Modeling: Boundary Evaluation and Merging Algorithm," IEEE Trans. Computer Graphics and Applications, Vol. 5, No. 1, Jan. 1985, pp. 30-34.

30. A. Baer, C. Eastman, and M. Henrion, "Geometric modeling : A Survey," Computer Aided Design, Vol. 11, No. 5, Sept. 1979, pp. 253 - 272.

31. A.A.G. Requicha, "Representation of Rigid Solids : Theory, Method, and System," ACM Computing Surveys, Vol. 12, No. 4, Dec. 1980, pp. 437 - 464.

32. R.A. Goldstein and R. Nagel, "3-D Visual Simulation," Simulation, Jan. 1971, pp. 25-31.

33. T. Whitted, "An improved illumination moving," IEEE Trans. Computer Graphics and Appplications, Oct. 1984, pp. 15-22.

34. S.D. Roth, "Ray Casting for Modelling Solids," Computer Graphics and Image Processing. vol. 18, Februaru 1982, pp. 109-144.

35. A. Glassner, "Space Subdivision for fast ray tracing," IEEE Trans. Computer Graphics and Applications, October 1984, pp. 15-22.

36. A. Fuginore, "ARTS : Accelerated Ray-Tracing System," IEEE Trans. Computer Graphics and Applications, April 1986, pp. 16-26.

37. W. F. Broonsvroot, J. J. Van Wijk, and F.W Jansen, " Two methods for Improving the efficiency of ray casting in solid modeling," Computer Aided Design, Jan. 1984, pp. 51-55.

38. H.G. Timmer and J. M. Stern, "Computation of Global Geometric Properties of Solid Objects," Computer Aided Design, Nov. 1980, pp. 301-304.

39. Y.T. Lee and A.A.G. Requicha, "Algorithm for Computing the Volume and Other Integral Properties of Solids," Comm. of ACM, Sept. 1982, pp. 635-650.

40. Aono. M. and Kunii, T.L., "Botanical tree image generation", IEEE Computer Graphics and Applications 4,5, pp.10-33, 1984.

41. Binning, G. and Rohrer, H., "The scanning tunelling microscope", Scientific American, August, 1985.

42. La Brecque, M., "Fractal Applications", Mosaic, 17, 4 pp. 34-48, 1986.
43. Carpenter, L., "Computer rendering of fractal curves and sufrfaces", *Computer Graphics*, 1980.
44. Dewdney,A.K.," Computer Recreations : Exploring the Mandelbrot Set," Computer Graphics 20, 4, 1985.
45. Falconer, K.J., *The Geometry of Fractal Sets,* Cambridge University Press, Cambridge, 1985.
46. Levejoy, S. and Mandelbrot, B.B. "Fractal properties of rain, and a fractal model", Tellus, 37A, pp.209-232, 1985.
47. Mandelbrot, B.B., "Self-affine fractals and the fractal dimension", Physica Scripta 32, pp.257-260, 1985.
48. Mandelbrot B.B., *The Fractal Geometry of Nature*, W.H. Freeman and Co., New York, 1982.
49. Mandelbrot B.B., *Fractals, Forms, Chance and Dimension*, W.H. Freeman and Co., New York, 1982.
50. Musgrave F.K. and Mandelbrot B.B.," Natura ex Machina", IEEE Computer Graphics and Applications, pp. 4-7, January 1989.
51. Norton, A., "Generation and display of geometric fractals in 3-D", *II Computer Graphics*, 16, 3, pp.61-67, 1982.
52. *The Science of Fractal* Images, edited by Peitgen Heinz-Otto, and Saupe Diear, Springer-Verlag, New York.
53. Reghbati H.K.," An overview of data compression techniques," *Compute Graphics*, 14, 4, pp.71-76, 1981.
54. Smith A.R.," Plants, fractals, and formal languages," *Computer Graphics* 18, 3, pp.1-10, 1984.
55. Bathe K.J. and Brezzi F.,"Studies of finite element procedures inf-subcondition, equivalent forms and applications", in *Reliability of Methods for Engineering Analysis*, edited by K. J. Bathe and D.R.J. Owen, Pineridge Press, Swansea, 1986.
56. Bathe K.J.,"Mixed finite elements - how useful are they in structural analysis?",Benchmark, pp. 17-18, Jan. 1990.
57. Bathe K.J., *Finite element procedures in Engineering Analysis*, Prentice Hall, 1982.
58. Martins P.A.F. and Marques M.J.M. Barata,"Model 3 - A three dimensional mesh generator",Computer and Structures, vol. 42, no. 4, pp. 511-529, 1992.
59. Buell W.R. and Bush R.,"Mesh generation - A survey", J. Engng. Industry, pp. 332-338, 1977.
60. Durochar L.L. and Garper A.,"A versatile two dimensional mesh generator with automatic bandwidth reduction", Computer Structures, vol. 10, pp. 561-575, 1979.
61. Pissanetzby Kubik,"An automatic three dimensional finite element mesh generation", Int. J. Numerical Methods in Engng, 17, pp. 255-269, 1981.
62. Caverdish J.C., Field D.A., and Frey W.H.,"An approach to automatic three dimension finite element mesh generation", J. Numerical methods in Engng., vol. 21, pp. 327-347, 1985.
63. Haber R.B.,"Visualization techniques for engineering mechanics", in Computing Systems in Engineering, Pergamom Press, vol. 1, no. 1, 1990.

CHAPTER 9

VIRTUAL REALITY

9.1 INTRODUCTION

Everyone has gone through the experience of seeing a dream - one remembers a few and forgets many. The dream world (figure 9.1) is a different world where inputs do not come through any of our senses but are generated by the mind internally - based sometimes on experiences and thoughts one has gone through during day time activities. All dreams comprise of characters, places and things culled from real life. The ingredients of dreams need not exist in real life as long as the person believes in them, e.g., ghost, fairies, monsters, dragons and so on. The unconscious in the human mind can construct visualization based on a rich set of cause-and-effect relationships stored in an internal model as required for building a dream plot. However, a person is so fully immersed that on suddenly waking up, it takes sometime to come out of the impact of the horrors/pleasures of the dream world. Let us compare this scenario with a soldier in a war with gun and tank fire all around. This is a real-life situation in which the soldier is fully immersed, fighting not only for his country but also for personal survival. He has to take action in real-time based on the inputs coming to mind through all his senses and cannot afford to make even a single mistake as it could be fatal. One thing is common, both dreams and many real life experiences cannot be repeated and rehearsed at will to improve performance. This technology promises to take one into a dream world (a computer generated environment) while in the conscious state of mind and repeat each experience as many times as one may wish. Thus, it is possible to perfect one's actions until command over the environment is obtained.

Figure 9.1: Dream World

The VR world is not bound to the two-dimensional realm of the graphical user interface but created from three dimensional graphical objects and audio elements. All avenues for exploration are available to the VR system designer to develop a man machine interface that defines computers' proper role and uses human intelligence. VR, as a new paradigm in computer applications, involves physical participation of a human in a three-dimensional synthetically generated realistic environment that can directly be manipulated through visual, auditory, and other stimuli in real-time with six degrees of freedom. A movie also places one in a synthetically generated environment but one gets inputs only through eyes and ears. However, the moment one sees beyond the movie screen the immersion, if any, is lost. The major difference is that pictures only produce a prerecorded playback whereas one becomes an integral part of the VR environment even to the point that one can touch virtual objects and have them react to one's actions.

VR has the potential to break the constraints of the real world. For example, a disability can be made to enjoy the same experience as when one may ski, or fly like a bird in the open sky. Thus, VR has the potential not only to take one to the dream world as many times as desired, but also to see and interact with objects as in the real world. The virtual reality tools can allow one to simulate and experience many real world situations, without incurring cost, risk, or danger, in the comfort of one's office. However, due to high cost, VR systems first came to high-risk areas like flight simulation, military applications, and chemical exploration.

In this chapter, we describe the common core systems, software and hardware requirements,and many applications including those which are not only enhanced by VR, but also made feasible only through use of VR technology. We also briefly describe a few programming toolkits available for developing VR applications. An interested reader can refer to several books [1-10] that are available in the market.

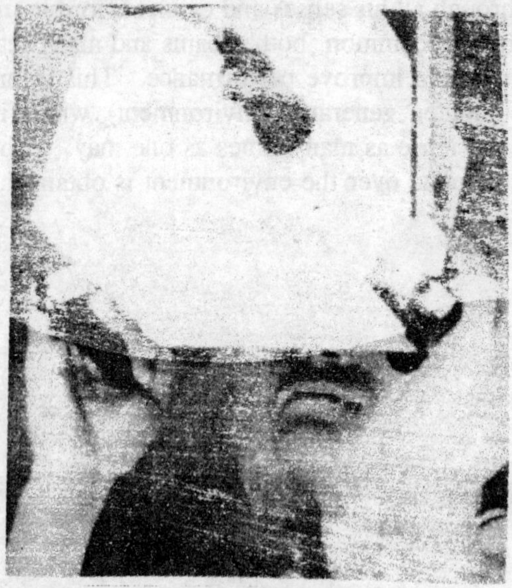

Figure 9.2: Head-mounted Display

9.2 REVIEW OF COMMON CORE SYSTEMS

9.2.1 HEAD MOUNTED DISPLAY(HMD)

A person's field of view is restricted by the size of the screen in a movie theater. Therefore, if one turns one's head and sees beyond the screen, the illusion of being a part of the motion picture is broken. IMAX wide-screen projection can extend the peripheral vision but the immersion in the scene is lost if a viewer turns his head. Disney's CircleVision 360 comprises of nine screens and surrounds viewers by putting them inside the scene. Each viewer watching a CircleVision movie can, therefore, see imagery as applicable as he or she turns head in any direction. Head mounted displays in a way are substitutes for a circular theater.

Evans and Sutherland were the first researchers to envision display as a window and designed the first head-mounted stereo display in 1965. HMD consists of small displays inside a head set placed on the user's head as shown in figure 9.2. As the user looks around, rotation of head is tracked by a computer and he sees on the display the imagery corresponding to the portion of the surrounding movie screens. Since the display is synthetic, i.e., generated by a computer, it is easy to present different 2-D views to the two eyes of the viewer. This approach produces a truly stereo display with illusion of depth so that objects in a 3-dimensional scene appear to be located with respect to the user's position.

Virtual I/O's i-glasses are a lowcost lightweight HMD. It supports both monoscopic (the left and right eyes are presented the same view) and stereoscopic modes.

9.2.2 STEREOSCOPIC SHUTTER GLASSES

In this approach, instead of looking at two small images in a head set, one looks at a computer monitor through the shutter glasses for a 3-D stereoscopic view. Shutter glasses are made by mounting liquid crystal shutters on plastic goggles. These shutters are controlled by the computer such that when the left eye shutter is open the display corresponds to the left-eye version of the image, and when the right shutter is open, the right-eye version of the image is displayed on the monitor. The effect is that only one eye sees an image that corresponds to it. Inside the glasses, the shutters run at a frequency that coincides with the multiplexed sequential field information displayed on the monitor. Synchronization of the alternating shutters with the corresponding alternating images is essential for creating pure stereoscopic effects as well to make the human brain believe that it is one image.

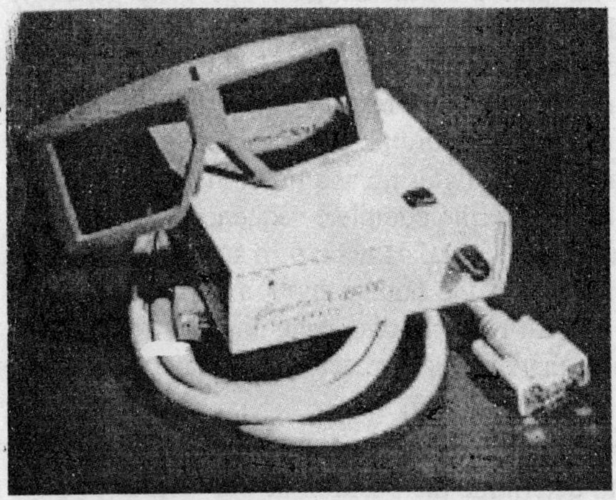

Figure 9.3: Steoroscopic Shutter Glasses

Shutter glasses are based on LCD shutters. These glasses turn a computer monitor into a VR system by enabling one to see stereo images that appear to float in front of your face, popping off the surface of the screen. Many persons can view single stereoscopic display while wearing LCD shutter glasses. A standard computer monitor runs on 60 Hz and can show stereoscopic images at a frame rate of 30 Hz for each eye. An SVGA monitor for PC runs on 72 Hz and can generate images at 36 Hz. Systems are available which can operate on a higher frame rate to provide smooth and clear illusion of depth. LCD shutter glasses are much cheaper than head-mounted displays. Products from StereoGraphics Corp. called CrystalEyes, and Crystal Eyes VR (See figure 9.3) follow this approach.

9.2.3 HAND TRACKING TECHNOLOGIES

The "Put-that-there" project[11] of Massachusetts Institute of Technology used the newly commercialized Polhemus 3-space tracking sensor to capture and transmit the user's hand position to the computer. The Polhemus works by radiating a pulsed magnetic field from a stationary source. Sensors attached to the hand can then identify their space position and orientation with respect to the source. MIT researchers attached the Polhemus sensor to the hand of a user and were able to identify the exact location where a user was pointing on a large wall display.

Three tracking technologies are used for tracking the location of the hand in the space and the orientation of the palm. These are based on optical, magnetic and acoustic tracking techniques.

9.2.3.1 Optical Tracking

In this technique, small markers are placed on the subject. These are generally either flashing infrared LEDs or small infrared-reflecting dots. To pick out the markers from their visual fields, two or more cameras are placed around the subject. This information is fed to the computer that computes the position of the markers with respect to multiple view points and uses information from the cameras to calculate the 3-D coordinates for each marker. In case of LED systems, the LEDs are sequenced so that only one lights up at a time. The performance of this system is dependent on the time taken to capture the complete sequence of the LEDs and to complete the analysis of the inputs obtained from several cameras. In an application such as computer animation such systems are used to record the human motion. However, such systems have limitations mainly since, (i) the need to perform two-stage analysis restricts the real-time capability, and (ii) the inability to resolve markers that are very close may restrict their use in tracking fingers of a person's hand.

The second method uses only one camera and captures the silhouette images of the subject. This silhouette image is analyzed to determine the position of the various parts of the body. Researchers have been using silhouette methods with custom hardware to analyze complex motion in real-time. This technique[12] successfully identifies parts of body such as hand, legs, arms and fingers.

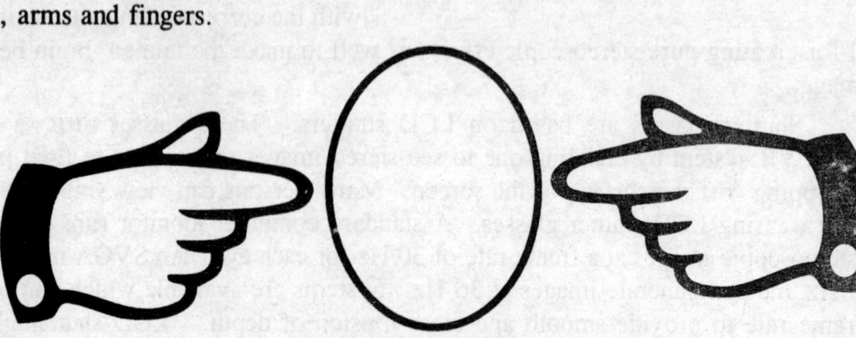

Figure 9.4: Control of Graphics by Fingers

Krueger [12] has developed many games and examples of interaction integrated in a system called Videoplace. In one example application, users can draw and modify shapes of figures with their fingers. When a computer identifies the outstretched thumb and index fingers of both the hands, it then draws a curve that inscribes the region between them. One can change the size and shape of the curve by moving fingers as depicted in figure 9.4. If one quickly withdraws one's hand from the curve, it fixes in place on the screen. Similarly, workers at Xerox EuroPARC have developed DigitalDesk, a normal office desk with objects such as papers and pencils. A computer can project on the desk electronic documents and applications, e.g., calculators or spread sheets[12]. A camera observes one's hands to see whether one is pointing to a real or electronic object. This approach enables one to interact with real as well as computer generated images with hands. Thus, we get an environment for freeform deviceless interaction with both.

The limitations of this method are: (i) low resolution of conventional video cameras; (ii) 30- or 60- frames per second conventional video technology; and (iii) difficulties in tracking as fingers and hands occlude each other sometimes and immature computer vision techniques in real-time. Thus, it is difficult to resolve fingers easily and track fingers as they often occlude each other and are also occluded by hand.

9.2.3.2 Magnetic Tracking

In this method, a source element radiating the magnetic field and a small sensor that reports its position and orientation with respect to the source are used. Systems from Polhemus & Ascension Technologies provide a number of multi-source multi-sensor systems. These systems can track number of points at up to 100 Hz and cover ranges from 3 - 20 feet. The accuracy of this system is generally better than 0.1 inches in position and 0.1 degrees in rotation. Metallic objects in the environment may distort the magnetic field giving incorrect reading. These systems also require cable attachment to the central device like optical systems. This technology is robust and is widely used for single or double hand tracking.

9.2.3.3 Acoustical Tracking

Acoustical tracking uses high frequency sound to triangulate a source within the work area. These systems send out pings from the source mounted on the hand received by microphones installed in the environment. Both Logitech and Mattel Power Glove use acoustical tracking for their operation. These systems can locate a source in space with an accuracy of a few millimeters but need line-of-sight between the source and the microphones. Acoustical systems are sensitive to acoustical reflections if surrounded by walls or other sound reflecting surfaces. Using different frequencies for using multiple acoustical trackers is necessary.

9.2.4 GLOVE-BASED INPUT

We use our hands for most of our everyday jobs. It will, therefore, be natural if computers can also capture data from hands without utilising devices like mice, joysticks or keyboards. The development of electronic gloves is mainly due to need to "read" a user's hands directly. Devices such as VPL DataGlove, Mattel Power Glove, 5th glove data glove and flexor strip (DFK) and cyber glove are already available as commercial products. Several research projects and applications are using these devices as interfaces to computer applications and computer controlled devices. These devices measure the shape of the hand as the fingers and palm flex. The cyber glove from virtual technologies is a high-end data glove with 18 sensors to track accurately every move of your hand would make. Although many such devices[13] are available but we are describing only a few of these in the following sections.

9.2.4.1 Sayre Glove

It was developed at University of Illinois, and is a low-cost and light-weight device for monitoring hand movements. It uses flexible tubes with a light source at one end and a photocell at the other end. These tubes are mounted along the fingers. The amount of light falling on the photocell is reduced as the tubes bend due to finger movement. The voltage generated by each photo cell is measured and it is proportional to the finger bending.

9.2.4.2 MIT LED Glove

This glove was developed by MIT Media Lab in 1980 using camera-based LED systems to mark body and limb position for real time computer graphics.

9.2.4.3 Digital Data Entry Glove

Digital glove was developed by Bell Telephone Labs in 1983. It used alphabets of hand signs [6] for data entry. The circuitry was designed to recognize 80 unique combinations of sensor readings.

9.2.4.4 DataGlove

DataGlove was developed by Thomas Zimmerman and others in 1987. It monitors 10 finger joints and 6 degrees of freedom of the hand's position and orientation [14]. It is a light weight lycra glove. The picture of a data glove is shown in Figure 9.5. Special optical fibers are mounted along the back of the fingers. The light transmitted through the fibers is attenuated when the fingers are flexed. The signal strengths from all joints are analyzed to determine the joint angles. This glove is light-weight, comfortable to wear, and unobtrusive to the user. It was commercialized by VPL Research and is used widely by VR workers.

The finger-flex accuracy of the data glove is rated at one degree joint rotation but practically flex accuracy is between 5 - 10 degrees. A data glove operates at a speed of about 30 Hz. This is not sufficient to capture rapid hand motions and is, therefore, unsuitable for time critical applications.

9.2.4.5 Power glove

Mattel toy company manufactured a low cost glove as controller of Nintendeo home video (**Fig** 9.3) games in 1989. This is a flexible molded plastic gauntlet with Lycna palm embedded in the plastic on the backs of the fingers are resistive-ink flex sensors. These sensors record the overall bending of the thumb, index, middle and ring fingers with 2 bits of precision for each finger. Acoustic trackers are put on the back of the hand to locate the glove accurately in the space with respect to the companion unit mounted on the television monitor. The trackers also provide 4-bits of information about rotation of the wrist of the hand. This is the cheapest and least accurate device available in the market. It works with Nintendo games and allows a player to hit, grab or throw a ball on a court imaged on the screen.

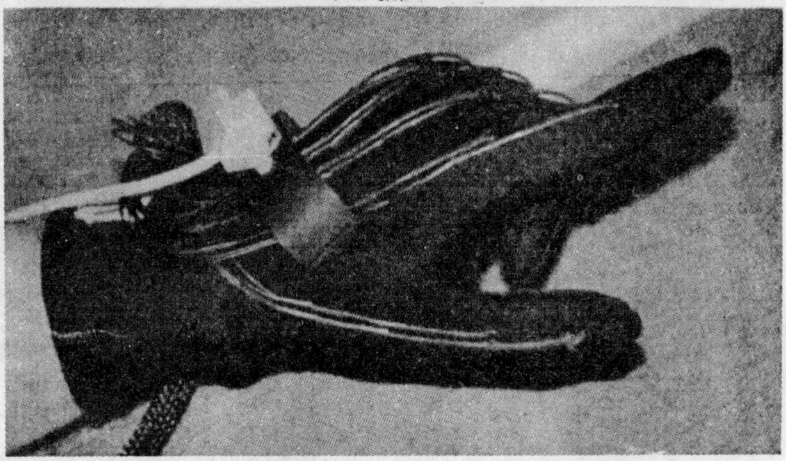

FIgure 9.5: Data Glove

9.2.4.6 Space glove[13]

W Industries had designed a glove called, "Space Glove." The glove is made of soft molded plastic that fits over the back of the hand. Rings around the fingers and strap around the wrist keep the glove in place. A 3-space magnetic tracker is mounted at the back of the glove. This glove is particularly responsive to finger bending and hand movement but is a little uncomfortable. Space gloves only works with W Industries products.

9.2.5 DISPLAY TECHNOLOGY

Displays used by many VR Labs have resolution of 200 horizontal by 150 colour pixels. Even expansive head mounted displays with 1024 by 1280 monochrome pixels provide low resolution as display optics has to extend the available pixels to the user's peripheral vision. Traditional displays mounted on long counter-weighted booms are also being used by some workers to solve the user fatigue problem. This allows a user to walk around an object without carrying the weight of the display.

The counterbalanced, CRT-based Stereoscopic Viewer System was developed by NASA in 1988 and the first generation BOOM device in 1990[15]. Both the systems were based on monochrome CRTs and had NTSC resolution. On a CRT, due to its very fine pitch, one can simultaneously display text information and computer generated graphics - a feature required in scientific visualization. CRT displays also provide high resolution and wide field of view. In addition, these displays also support most of the video signal standards.

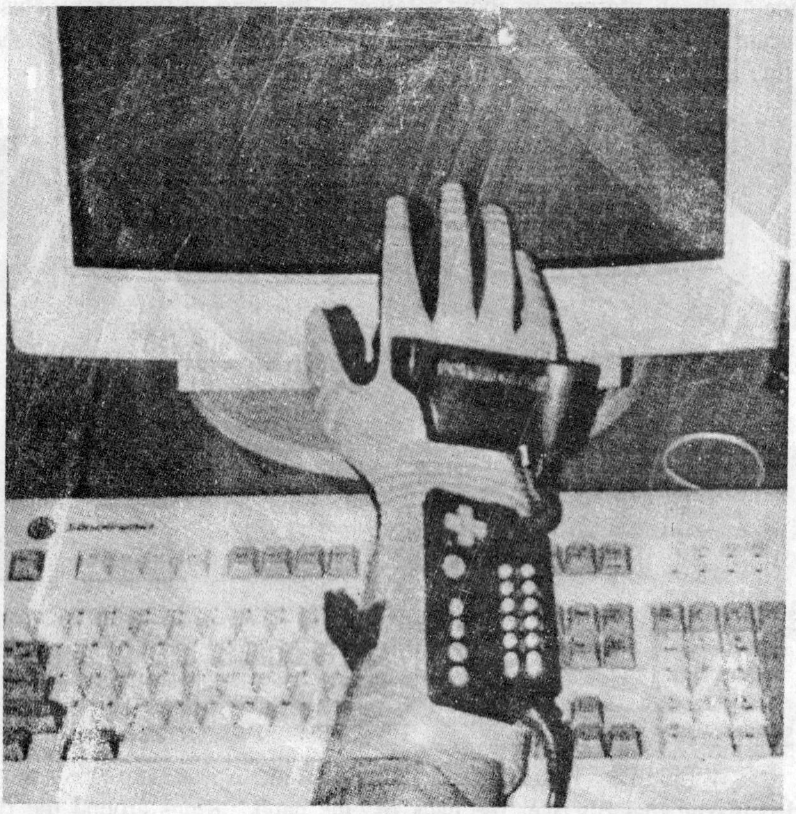

Figure 9.6: Power Glove - A low-cost glove for video games

Liquid crystal displays have two main problems. First, they have slow response time. Passive LCDs have response time about 200 milliseconds. The latest active matrix LCDs give 40 milliseconds response time but this also is considered quite slow as compared with the 16 milliseconds between 60 Hz frames provided by a CRT-based display. A slight cursor blur on a laptop/notebook computer is due to the slow response time of flat screen display. This blurring is not acceptable in a high end VR system as the view point is constantly changed in such a system.

The second problem is that an LCD cannot show many levels of shades. This is a critical requirement if a virtual world is to create an illusion of realism. The CRT gives contrast of about 100 to 1 as compared with LCD contrast ratio ranging from 5 : 1 to 20 : 1 [16].

9.2.5.1 Optical human factors

Counter balance displays provide a mechanical solution to problems of rapid access and fitting different head sizes. The lens option for the boom display is designed to work with eye glasses eliminating the need to adjust lenses for individuals. By changing the lens set, one can provide 30, 50 and/or 140-degree fields of views. This is considered adequate for medical applications, molecular modeling, and public viewing respectively.

9.2.5.2 Data and Video Interface

The Fakespace VLib software library produces a stereoscopic image from a single workstation via the standard RGB outputs. A user needs to possess only one workstation and can still display both a left eye and right eye image with more than one million pixels. VLib routines can easily be integrated with existing software, i.e., a programmer can quickly add VR compatibility to existing software. The boom system uses standard RS - 232 lines to the host computer and can, therefore, work with any computer system.

9.2.6 3-D SOUNDS

Sound infuses life into any 3-D world. One can identify number of objects not by seeing but by identifying sound generated by them, e.g., just by hearing the sound one can identify a truck or a car moving on the road. Similarly, one can hear an approaching aircraft in cloudy weather much before one can see it. Sound also provides knowledge about distance of the object. 3D sound seems to emanate from points in front of, above, below, and to either side of the listener. Thus, a listener perceives that sound is coming from some place other than the speakers or headphones.

Sound cards are designed to work with toolkits that help in building VR worlds. Crystal River Engineering's Alphatron works with most VR world toolkits. It interfaces through a C language application programming interface(API). It supports two or four simultaneous sound sources.

9.3 NAVIGATION AND MANIPULATION

A user can navigate through the virtual space by the aid of tracking technology. Trackers are devices that find your position and orientation in the real world and relate them to the virtual one. Devices used for tracking are rockers filled with mercury, radio waves, ultrasound, and laser tracking systems. Games normally use 3-D trackers. Most VR systems rely on the metaphor of moving a person through a space. HMD systems employ an instrumented glove that a person points in a direction he wants to move. This takes certain time to learn and may often tire the user. The Fakespace Boom provides a tracking

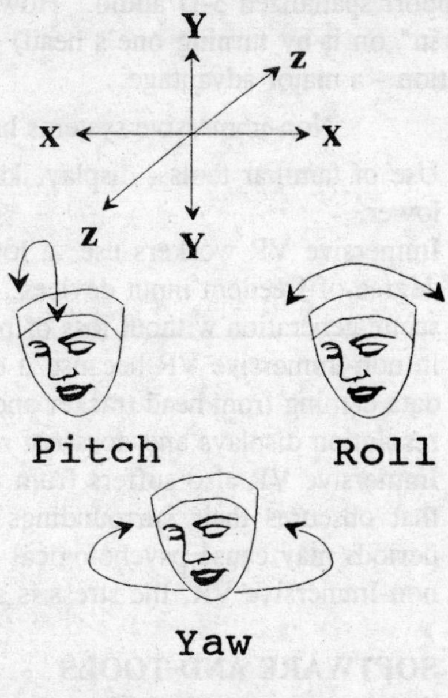

Figure 9.7: Six degrees of freedom - forward/back, up/down, left/right, pitch up/down, yaw left/right, and roll left/right

structure and buttons on the handles of the immersive display. Users' support small motions like walking in the virtual space with the Boom's tracking structure and large motions like flying through buttons. This opto-mechanical device is jitter-free, and is not disturbed either by CRTs, metal objects, or the line-of-sight problem as with magnetic and acoustic tracking systems.

A low cost tracking system called the Wayfinder-VR is available from Precision Navigation. It plugs into serial port of a PC. Trackers supporting 6 DOF (see figure 9.7) are also available.

9.4 IMMERSIVE AND NONIMMERSIVE VR

The common definition of VR includes systems that provide full immersion, i.e., users wear head mounted stereo displays and special gloves that allow a six-degree-of-freedom input. Thus, users get involved in full immersion and can directly manipulate the environment.

Another approach, called non-immersive VR, includes the use of conventional components, such as, graphics workstations, a keyboard, and a mouse. The scene incorporates the same 3-D depth cues, perspective view, hidden surface elimination, lighting, shading and shadows for both the approaches.

Although full immersion has major advantages, the same effect can be created with proper depth cues and interactive animation in many applications using conventional equipment. As one controls the animation and concentrate on the 3-D scenes, one gets into mental and emotional immersion in spite of lack of visual or perceptual immersion[17]. Non-Immersive systems do not suffer from display jitter and lag between the user's head or hand movement and the corresponding change to take place in the environment. Both types of VR can support spatialized 3-D audio. However, providing localized sound is possible (one can "home in" on it by turning one's head) in an immersive system as it has knowledge of head orientation - a major advantage.

Non-immersive systems have following advantages over the immersive systems:

(i) Use of familiar tools - display, keyboard and mouse and therefore the cost of set-up is lower.

(ii) Immersive VR workers use a lot of time for solving problems concerning lag in six-degree-of-freedom input devices, display jitters, and synchronizing machines for stereo scene generation without loss of performance. The problem of the display jitter is less in non-Immersive VR because it eliminates tracking devices, thus, eliminating noise in data coming from head tracker and by the neck muscles. Non-Immersive VR has higher resolution displays and does not require stereo vision.

(iii) Immersive VR also suffers from unwillingness of workers to put on special equipment that obscures their surroundings. Use of Immersive VR equipment for prolonging periods may cause psychological and mental stress that users may not like. In case of non-Immersive VR, the stress is similar to general computer use.

9.5 SOFTWARE AND TOOLS

Software is the most important element but no canned software option is available for creating the VR worlds like Lotus 1-2-3 for spreadsheet applications or Word Perfect for word processing. One needs the description and the use of the application along with the style of interaction and the level of the interface. Next step is to select the computing platform, input devices, compatible software to enable devices and computer to work together, and a 3-D object library to help to populate the virtual world. The following steps are required to create an interactive virtual world:

(i). Select an environment - that is to be modelled - and populate it with relevent visual objects and characters. Objects have characteristics, such as

- Geometry: It describes the shape of the object. An object is drawn on the computer display using a set of polygons which are logically connected. Once these polygons are assembled into the object's geometry, the object is rendered. Appearence: It comprises of parameters such as the object's size, color, texture, lighting, and shadows.

  Behaviour: It defines object's reaction to events and associates physical properties like gravity, elasticity, and weight of the objects. Dynamics controls interaction between objects, such as, collision and gravitational force. Other attributes of behaviour include sound generated by an object and how an object would react on occurence of a specified event during a simulation.

(ii). Acquire or develop program to carry out the following tasks.

- Render the objects. It involves color, light sources, and texture and produces life like or near realistic images. Rendering can be performed in wireframe, shaded, or textured modes. Texture mapping reduces the scene's complexity, provides depth, gives a real world like look, and produces a view with more details. In fact, a texture mapped polygon that rotates to face one whenever one changes the point of view can give illusion of being a 3-D object. However, one should not use too many textures to avoid slowing the application.

- ▸ Keep the number of polygons to the least as it would lead to better performance.
- ▸ Alter the view point and field of view and manipulate and cause the object to interact with other object(s).
- Capture inputs from various sensors and effectors and control on audio output devices.
- Objects in VR are more interesting if they respond to interaction and stimulate.
- Add collision detection, elasticity and gravity to objects.

(iii). Generate psychological depth cues to create illusion of 3-D space. These include

- Linear perspective: The size of an object becomes smaller as it moves away from the point of view. To speed up applications, one can also reduce the detail rendered as an object moves far away.
- Overlap: An object closer to the point of view covers part of object behind.
- Motion parallax: As one moves one's head, one sees different parts of the object/scene.
- Shading: Parts of an object perpendicular to the light source appear to be brightest and those at angle are dimmer. This property can be exploited to create illusion of depth and distance by fading the color of the object as it

moves away from point of view. Similarly, one can vary the object's opacity.

Two techniques for shading are generally used. First is flat shading. It renders each facing polygon by a single color that represents the amount of light interacting with that face. The second method is smooth shading. Two popular algorithms used are Gouraud shading and Phong shading. Gouraud shading makes surfaces look as if they reflect light diffusely. Phong shading allows addition of calculated highlights and it's effect can further be enhanced by incorporating surface properties such as wood grain, marble, steel and chrome etc.

- Shadows: These are caused when an object is placed between a light source and another object.

iv. Incorporate some animation and video. It is possible to import some animation in 3-D studio file format.

v. Incorporate sound in applications. Many development environment support sound . Sound libraries of music and effects are available in MIDI & .WAV formats.

vi. Make virtual world to look and feel realistic by ensuring that

- frames are played one after other at a rate so that motion looks smooth. Real-time VR systems also support changing the view point.
- Ensure that a participant receives visual and audio feedback which is consistent, i.e.
  a) if 3-D sound is provided it is also essential that sound sources move when the view point is moved. The sound should become louder when one faces an audible object and should fade if one turns away. One can gauge the distance of an object as sound also imparts depth cues.
  b) the virtual objects should also show similar dynamics as a real object would show in a given situation.

vii. Plan the complete simulation and properly sequence the events across each of the simulation frame.

The 3-D modelling software should have capabilities such as: (i) to create and export files in industry standard formats, for example, drawing interchange format (.DXF) developed by Autodesk; (ii) vertex editing - one can change each point which defines the object; (iii) spline modelling - to draw smooth curves; and (iv) to put a skin on the surface of the model in order to improve its appearance, for example, like putting wall paper on a wall.

There is a need for sophisticated debugging aids that allow one to alter an interaction while one is in it. The debugger should be able to introduce a simulated character which can repeat as many times as necessory a set of actions. This approach will facilitate a programmer to debug the program conveniently rather than he is a participant in the VR application.

9.5.1 VR SOFTWARE TOOLS AND PACKAGES

A VR application designer must create 3-D complex objects with any 3-D modeller that generates .DXF or 3DS files. After creating the world and its objects, one assigns tasks to the objects, links them to the sensors, assigns colors, suitable texture, and define collision detection between objects and polygons. The tools and packages described below facilitate a user to develop VR applications.

9.5.1.1 WorldToolKit (WTK) from Sense8(a California based company) is available on many platforms, viz., DOS, Windows(all versions), and Unix on workstations from HP, IBM, Sun, Digital and Silicon Graphics. It provides a *C* library of more than 400 functions which can be used with any Window based *C* compiler. It has support for VR style I/O devices such as Power Glove, 3-D sound systems, 6-D-O-F input devices and graphics accelerators. It offers real-time display of 3-D objects, rendered with wire-frame, flat-shaded, smooth-shaded and textured surfaces. It supports 16-bit texture maps in 640×480 16-bit color displays. It comes with some ready demonstrations.

Sense8's another product will use Micorsoft visual Basic as a scripting language. Thus, you will be able to change an object's behaviour on-line by dragging Basic code onto it.

9.5.1.2 REND386 is a freeware programming tool copyrighted by B. Roehl and D. Stampe. It requires Turbo C++ or Borland *C*++ and works on a PC with a 386 or higher processor, and with VGA display. It supports Power Glove and stereoscopic shutter glasses. It can create stereo images but does not have support for sound. The prerequisite for building a virtual world is knowledge of 3-D geometric data. REND386 generates fast, colourful stereoscopic graphics on a PC and supports mouse, joystick, keyboard, Power Glove, shutter glasses and head mounted display. REND386 allows one to define surfaces, and assign colours. It's animation features facilitate in creating objects that bounce and spin, and doors that swing open as one approaches. The Power Glove inputs to the system enable one to move and rotate objects in the world.

REND386 does not support texture mapping and permits limited object interaction. It does not have tools to help in creating complex objects or assemble a world.

9.5.1.3 Dimension International's Superscape software provides a set of tools to create and edit virtual worlds and objects. These include company's procedural SCL language, a bitmap editor for textures, a sound editor for .WAV files, and a keyframe editor for producing animation and morphs.

Superscape contains a library of intelligent objects and uses a physics-based interaction model to give these objects realistic properties (such as actions, rotations, gravity and elasticity), e.g. if one pushes a chair with a cursor, it rolls to the wall and bounces back slightly as a real chair would. One can quickly compose a scene comprising of thousands of intelligent objects, change it on the fly, control the objects in the scene through changes in the individual parameters of the objects or through a set of commands.

9.5.1.4 VRCreator from VREAM is a window-based software but has retained its original scripting language to ensure compatibility with earlier versions. It provides tools to create 3-D objects and the ability to assign actions, reactions, and connections to them without need to program in *C* or *C*++. It 's link feature helps to connect objects, actions and reactions. You open a Link dialog box, select an object or objects to link, select a condition, choose the object that will respond, select the response, and save the link. This makes the complete procedure simple.

9.5.1.5 CYBER SPACE Developer kit (CDK) release 2.0 for Window's NT and Window 3.1 from Autodesk is a C++ programming tool kit. CDK supports physical properties such as mass, gravity, springs, friction, and collision. It can support an animation produced in 3-D studio.

9.5.1.6 Open Inventor for Windows NT is a C++ toolkit. It is used from within the Microsoft Visual C++ environment and adds its own interface wizard to Visual C++. It provides object manipulators which let you alter shape, size and position of any object in the world in the run time. All information regarding virtual world is stored in an object oriented database called a scene graph. The attributes of the objects stored in the database include lighting, cameras, manipulators, events, shapes and actions. This toolkit does not support global behaviors.

9.5.1.7 It would soon be possible to navigate through on-line museums, libraries, and market places on the Internet through the use of a platform-independent standard called Virtual Reality Markup Language(VRML). Version 1.0 of VRML is based on a subset of Silicon Graphics' object-oriented OpenInventor 2.0 3-D scene and graphics description file format. It may be noted that VR on Internet does not require VRML. Using inline graphics one can view graphics in the middle of a mosaic page. At present, VRML does not support HMD's and lacks support for assigning interactivity attributes to the 3-D objects..

9.5.2 IMAGE GENERATION

VR Graphics is at present limited to several thousand polygons in a scene. A PC-based system can draw 3,000 to 5,000 polygons per second, whereas a high-end workstation can draw from 300,000 to 600,000 textured and anti-aliased polygons per second. The rate of update is generally 20 frames per second. Texture mapping is used to to paint patterns, such as wood grains, and scanned photographs onto the polygons.

To create stereoscopic images, it is essential to provide two images showing views as applicable for each of the eye. This is achieved by utilising two frame buffers(holds 8-bits for each pixel) to draw one set of picture while displaying another set. This allows the system to switch between two versions of the same picture and update picture while it is not in view. This could be achieved by dividing the bit planes of a 8 bit frame buffer into two four bit buffers. Although, this will enable to display fewer colours but would display stereoscopic image pairs.

The computer graphics cards must alternate between the two frame buffers atleast 30 times per second to have 3-D viewing of static images. The shutter glasses switch each time the monitor reaches the vertical blanking time, thereby reducing the flicker to create double buffered stereoscopic animation. Four system buffers are required to create double buffered stereoscopic animation - two buffers are used for displaying an image alternatively and other two for writing images from computer. Suitable software is required to create stereoscopic images and drive the shutter glasses interface and a graphics card that supports page flipping.

REND386 helps in creating stereographics on PCs. It supports any VGA graphics card. Matrox Graphics' MGA ImpressionLite and MGA Impression Plus are low cost rendering cards support VR world building tools from number of vendors. Number of programmes are available which can convert 3-D Studio, AutoCAD & other .DXF files for rapid stereoscopic rendering with REND386.

9.6 VR SET UP

Figure 9.8 shows a typical set up for VR. The set up includes the following :

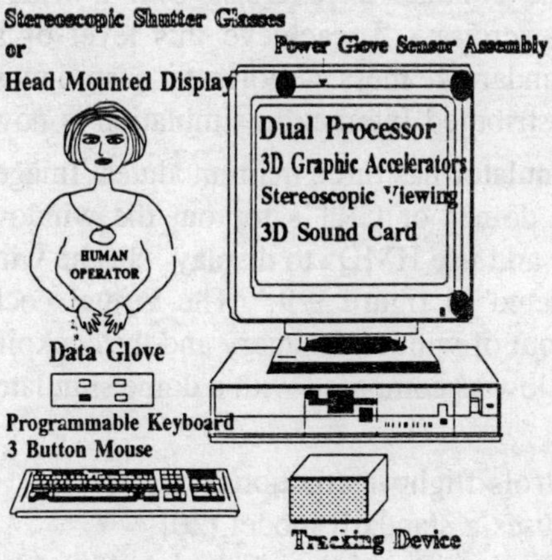

Figure 9.8 VR Setup

- Dual processors capable of handling multiple graphics cards.
- Two graphics cards are required so that your HMD/Shutter glasses can present you with stereoscopic view.
- Data glove to manipulate objects in the virtual environment.
- Head mounted display or stereoscopic shutter glasses to let you hear and see.
- hand held input devices like joystick or 3D mouse to enable you to manipulate movement in the environment.
- Tracking device to provide inputs to computer regarding your position and orientation in space.
- Graphics acceleration card(s) is a must for a PC based VR system as it facilitates to render objects in the virtual world with Gouraud shading and texture mapping.
- 3-D sound card to produce sound.
- Programmable keyboard to enable you to type in keyboard shortcuts.
- Keyboard to give text commands.

9.7 PROJECTS AND APPLICATIONS

Applications include items like training, simulation, concurrent engineering, tele-communications, telepresence, scientific visualization, education, medicine and entertainment.

Several companies have started looking at VR technology as a problem solving tool. The aim is to exploit this technology in assisting equipment operation by providing intuitive man-machine interfaces.

9.7.1 DISTRIBUTED INTERACTIVE SIMULATION[18]

Distributed simulation over a local or wide area network enables one to link heterogeneous collection of equipment, e.g., number of tank and flight simulators. You can add or delete systems and conduct a exercise over a wide area at a much lower cost as compared to a real life exercise. To achieve this level of simulation one needs to ensure database compatibility, standardize message formats, ensure message handling over network and many more facilities. Distributed Interaction simulation is now an IEEE standard [19].

A flight simulator has three main modules: Image display, image generation, and flight dynamics and uses domes or CRT's for out the window imagery. However, military simulators are very costly and use HMDs to display out the window imagery and have physical gauges and dials as depicted in figure 9.9. The virtual cockpit [18] comprises of virtual cockpit, uses HMD's for out of window imagery and the cockpit interior. Thus, the cost of such a simulator becomes very low as compared with a dome simulator. Virtual cockpit software does following functions :

- generates and controls flight instructions.
- flight dynamics - uses a standard model [20]
- generates out of the window view which involves database construction and database rendering. Virtual cockpit uses Software System's MultiGen polygon based modelling package and can generate stationary and dynamic objects. Virtual cockpit uses a multi processor Silicon Graphics Iris, a Polhemus Laboraratories HMD, Polhemus magnetic head tracker, and a hands on throttle and stick by Thrustmaster. Virtual cockpit can receive and send network distributed messages from other messages pertaining to current state of vehicles, i.e., location, orientation, speed, fire or damage if any.

Figure 9.9 Aircraft Cockpit with physical gauges and dials

9.7.2 THE RESPONSIVE WORKBENCH[21]

It provides virtual working environment. One can locate virtual objects and control tools on the real workbench. The objects are computer generated stereo images projected on to the surface of a physical work bench. The setting of workbench corresponds to the actual work environment say, a doctor's or an architect's office. A person can interact with the virtual environment while others can watch through stereo shutter glasses. The workbench can integrate input and output modules, such as motion, gesture and voice recognition systems. This approach is unique as it sets a new trend in man-machine design.

Workbench functions are implemented using powerful graphics workstations, tracking system, cameras, projectors and microphones. The user wears datagloves with Polhemus sensor mounted on the back. The user's interaction with the virtual world objects is processed by gesture recognition and collision detection algorithms, based on glove and Polhemus data. Software supports features such as changing geometry of objects by adding or deleting vertices and choosing and moving around objects. Another important aspect is of use natural language for interacting. Workbench supports spoken commands like 'zoom in', 'rotate' and 'transperancy' which the system interprets with a neural network running on a dedicated CPU for voice recognition. The system accurately tracks the eye position of the user to generate correct stereo rendering. To facilitate presentation of correct perspective view, the workbench reads the latest available Polhemus data reflecting the current head movement before the culling process starts. Experiments on workbench revealed the fact that

- tactile feedback via dataglove is most desirable;
- tracking head movement is necessary as it provides the visual feedback to generate perspective rendering;
- hand tracking and speech recognition are not real-time critical as delay of a few frames would not make difference; and
- multiple processors are required for application computations, culling, and rendering.

Presently workbench is used for applications in the areas, such as medical and architecture. Medical applications involve surgery planning and non sequential medical training based on a model of a patient. In a teacher/student scenario, it is possible to create a patient model whose skin becomes transparent making the arrangement of bones visible. Surgeon or student can pick a bone with a dataglove and examine joints of the world. One can also remove the body parts and study them in detail. Surgery can be planned using body's real datasets obtained from computed tomography (CT) or magnetic resonance imaging (MRI). Workbench can also be used to create architectural designs and make changes by moving buildings or objects such as trees in the virtual world. One can also set light sources through dataglove to simulate different times of day. An architect can allow a client to walk through the model in real time. Future applications on the workbench will be in the area of designing "virual windtunnel" for automobile design and the simulation of air and ground traffic at airports.

9.7.3 VR TRAINING PROGRAMME FOR DISABLED CHILDREN

Children born with disablity use wheelchairs for moving or being pushed from place to place. Oregon Research Institute is working on a feasibilty of a programme [22] to develop physical driving skills and a "danger sense" in disabled children through VR in wheelchair training. Virtual Worlds are created in Sense8's WorldToolKit and through 3-D sound. The programme can create either a flat checker-board world - to experiment with pure movement; or the one which depicts a big lawn alongwith various objects for the kids to drive around. This helps in developing their visual memory. Patches of mud and ice are also generated to teach children sense of danger. This experiment enables a seated person to maneuver a virtual wheel chair through a simulated building to see how good are its corridors for navigation, and how accessible are the light switches and shelves.

VR has the potential of breaking the constraints of the real world and allow a handicapped or even a normal person to experience surfing in the sea, or skiing as shown in figure 9.10 without leaving their home.

Figure 9.10 A handicapped person skiing

9.7.4 TELEPRESENCE

Telepresence is a combination of two technologies, VR and robotics.. It allows human beings to virtually go into hazardous areas such as nuclear reacter sites or burning houses. In a recent London VR trade show the University of Surrey in the UK demonstrated its active stereo head which provides a user with stereoscopic view of an environment even if it is miles away. The system contains of a robot with two cameras to act as its eyes. The robot is controlled by a servo-mechanism that moves exactly as a user does. Such a system can be of value in security and surveillance applications. In France, VR is being used for developing tools for safer nuclear reactor maintenance planning, including the reactor building, piping, duct work, control points and lifts between levels.

9.7.5 ENTERTAINMENT

In Japan, large scale applications are focused on games, where Sega Enterprises and Nintendo are the market leaders in home video and arcade machines businesses. In addition, Sega is also in the amusement-park ride market.

Figure 9.11 LegendQuest: A multiplayer VR game

W Industries now called Virtuality Entertainment Systems, U.K., produces VR games. It's adventure game LegendQuest, is quite different from usual driving, flying, or shoot-'m-up games (see figure 9.11). The player steps into a "pod", puts on a headset, and uses a joystick to manoeuvre through scenes, encountering virtual objects and engaging in sword fights with virtual creatures. The game allows multiple players to interact with the hostile environment. Players can take on Virtual characters as they not only have their customized tones(through voice synthesis) but also other personal characteristics.

9.7.6 VISUALIZATION

Scientific visualization aims to devise algorithms, methods and systems that transform massive scientific data sets into pictures and other graphic representations that facilitate comprehension and interpretation. We describe in the following sections some approaches which help users to share their data sets, simultaneously view visualization of data, and interact with multiple views by changing parameters.

9.7.6.1 The Cosmic Worm[23]

Cave Automatic Virtual Environment (CAVE) - virtual reality theatre is creation of the Electronic Visualization Laboratory (EVL) at the University of Illinois at Chicago. It is an immersive virtual environment developed at EVL. It consists of a $10\times10\times9$ foot cube with images rear projected on 2-3 walls and front projected onto the floor. Powerful Silicon Graphics workstations generate left- and right-eye images which users view through stereoscopic LCD shutter glasses. The head position and orientation of one participant, referred to as the driver, is tracked by Polhemus or Ascension electromagnetic sensors to give correct visual perspective. A wand device with three buttons provides six inputs: pitch, yaw and roll as well as the (X,Y,Z) coordinates. CAVE provides a complete sense of immersion. One uses projection devices to create the surrounings - e.g. a virtual sky as one looks up and ground as one looks down - one are immersed in VR.

Several persons can participate in the experience by wearing shutter glasses and using the menu provided with the system. Scientists can interact with simulation to analyse their data, initialize the simulation with new parameters or continue simulation to view ongoing evolution to the physical parameters. This simulator is being used to study astrophysical phenomenon, e.g., simulation of the formation of the early universe and therotical studies of gravitational waves which are important to physicists. These applications generate data in the range of hundreds of megabytes. Combination of VR and supercomputing opens doors to the interactive visualization of this data. At present the smallest volume that CAVE can handle is of the order of $32\times32\times32$ voxels. CAVE is aiming to become an interactive virtual reality tool to give complete sense of immersion and scientists can use it as freely as they use a computer today. To an immersed user, the hardware becomes transparent and helps in enhancing experience in the virtual environment.

9.7.6.2 Glyph based VR[24]

Glyphs are graphical objects whose attributes, such as position, size, shape, colour, orientation, etc. are bound to data and are useful in depicting discrete data. Glyphs owe their effectiveness to the human eye-brain system's ability to discern finely resolved spatial relationship and differences in shape. The first system developed using glyph was called Glyphmaker [25] and was not a VR system. The VR implementation of this approach was modified to include capability to provide a customized virtual environment without any programming effort, including laying different mode of interaction and the graphical representation of data variables. Thus, one can display and correlate several variables at once, e.g. two variables can be distinguished by binding them to the visually orthogonal representations of shape distortion and pseudo-coloring..

Furthermore, one can establish either one to one binding between data objects and glyphs, such as spheres, cylinders, cuboids, arrows, and cones or brtween many data objects to one glyph, e.g. surface. The user interface is provided through a virtual workbench with a drawer containing the basic glyphs and another with data file icons. Menus for the variables in the selected file and for visualization control float above the workbench in the virtual space. One can pick a glyph and resize and reorient it through the scaling handles and axes. By adjusting a selected glyph element and then dragging the smaller and bigger glyphs to the ends of the scale bar, one can choose a range for that element. One can then select the range for a previously attached data variable by adjusting the arrows below the scale bar, the variable range on the scale-bar is extended accordingly. Similarly, the right side sliders on the work bench control colour or transperancy ranges.

9.7.6.3 Data

vrTrader, a VR application from Avatar Partners, USA was developed using World Tool Kit and is a software which metaphorically turns financial data, stocks, markets, and trading activity into objects in 3-D space.

9.7.6.4 Architectural and Interior Design

In VR, an architect and a client can configure a space together by picking and placing machinery, office equipment, and movable wall systems. They can then walk through the model in real time and analyze different combinations of colours, textures and lighting. This approach to design minimizes cost as well devlopment cycles. Matsushita of Japan has a VR product to help homeowners in designing and visualizing new kitchens before ordering them by moving around components.

9.7.7 MEDICINE AND SURGERY

In this area, non-immersive technology is considered more useful as surgeons are trained to be intuitive observers. Presently, immersive interfaces are not only cumbersome to use but also give a feeling of isolation - a handicap for those surgical procedures that need teamwork. Surgeons would need to learn new skills in use of VR tools, e.g. recognising anatomical data obtained through magnification of body parts by miniature cameras.

The areas where certain capabilities for surgery and medicine have been developed include position tracking, endoscopic telemanipulation, treatment planning and training. The technology is yet not mature to present the internal organs of the body sufficiently well for users to interact with them in a realistic way. Current technology offers 3-D graphics, 3-D audio, tracking, collision detection and animation. Systems are platform independant and support multiple users over local or wide area network. Software is available to let users import geometry for CAD applications but it does not support medical geometries. The key problem is to define the physical model for simulating the visual and physical characteristics of organs.

ADAM system is currently used in over 200 medical schools in the US. It lets users peel back body layers to reveal the underlying structures as shown in figure 9.12 and extract organs for individual examination. The user can magnify any areas or organ of the body down to the histological level. This system is useful for training surgeons in anatomy before dissection and educating patients who are interested to know more about the procedure planned for them - without seeing any blood.

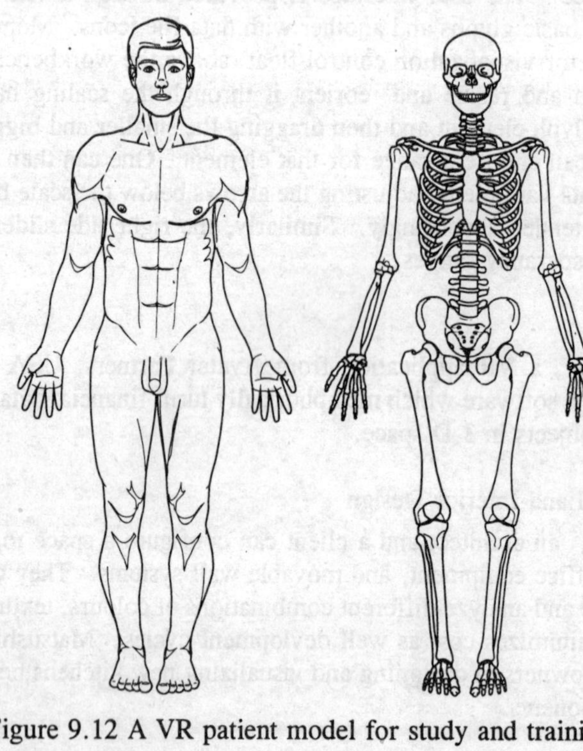

Figure 9.12 A VR patient model for study and training

An endoscopic training simulation has been developed in conjuction with medical school in London (U.K.) at the Imperial College.. The objective of this simulator is to improve the training in endoscopic procedures, particularly, as an endoscope is difficult to use and its controls are also not intuitive. Computer simulation can be helpful by providing opportunities for regular practise and exposure to even those problems that occur rarely. The simulator at present does not achieve total realism but the images are interpretable in 3D.

Other areas where progress has been made in the use of VR are telepresence and laparoscopic robots. There are three types of surgery robots: localisers, telemanipulators and nanorobots. Localisers offer precision and can assist in a number of operations such as drilling of bones etc. A telemanipulator provides an additional hand to a surgeon.

VR network, NSPNet IV developed by US Department of Defence, can train interactively upto 300 soldiers. Future application of VR envisages armed forces of the 21st century combat medical aid. The soldier's uniform can become a "Confirmational computer", sending data pertaining to the soldier's condition and relaying it to a medical and tactical centre. If a soldier is wounded, the uniform can transmit data about his vital signs. This approach will also help in deciding which soldier needs attention first. Medical vans with Telepresent surgery can pick up wounded soldiers and link up with the remote surgeon location. This of course is a futuristic scenario.

SRI, USA has done some impressive demonstration for laparoscopic surgery, where surgeon controls tiny instruments via a thin flexible tube inserted in the patient's body.

Health care is the largest growth area for training system after aviation, defence, energy and transport, since VR technology offers facilities for training and rehearsal of operative techniques without endangering patients. Robotics has been used successfully in prostate operations and ultrasound methods in treating kidney and gall stones.

9.7.8 GENERAL

9.7.8.1 Project Elysium has been taken up by IBM and Virtuality to develop an integrated workstation for immersive VR. It will facilitate development of VR software in the areas of engineering construction, medicine and entertainment. The system is expected to cost less than $50,000.

9.7.8.2 Project Virtuosi is a multi-user VR system for group work. It is being developed in the U.K. under a 3-year research contract. The software model would develop a VR form called "Blokies", simple embodiment of VR users moving around in 3-D space. The VR office will be constructed using T-shaped blocks and persons would move around in 3-D space. It is also planned to create office workers with pictures of users embedded on the heads of virtual "people" [26].

9. 7.8.3 A potential sleeper application area is augmented reality where computer-developed images are superimposed on the user's real world view, thus creating the illusion of realism. For example, electricians can walk around a building and see wiring behind the walls instead of deciphering blue prints.

9.7.8.4 The following applications, developed in Japan, in the area of health care, are of interest:

- A massage chair that uses VR images and sound to help relax users. It monitors parameters such as pulse rate and controls images and sounds to match the user's body condition and state of consciousness
- An exercise bicycle that presents a 3-D virtual world while a user is exercising.

9.8 SUMMARY

VR's main potential is in the ability to tightly couple the human mind with machine for problem solving. It enables a person to experience data rather than analyze it. Successful commercial applications are likely to appear but not quickly. Although the defense and aerospace industries invented VR, perhaps the entertainment will be the first to introduce it to the world and also pay for VR technology. CAD-CAM or office work is perhaps an unlikely market as people may not like to do their jobs putting on HMDs or gloves. However, this scenario may change as these devices become more user-friendly. The challenge to VR is to keep expectations of people to realistic levels in order to avoid what happened to Artificial Intelligence, i.e., boom and bust.

VR systems to-date have severe limitation due to display resolution, tracking and rendering. The hardware is at present inadequate to meet the demands imposed by VR. Although these limitations are likely to disappear with time, the development of quality software, debugging tools and training procedures will continue to be the primary areas of challenge. Modern programming techniques like neural nets, fuzzy logic and genetic algorithms will be used to tune the behaviour of the simulated characters and objects. Testing of such applications will be possible through the use of automated means rather than by humans who get tired and are often inconsistent. VR companies also have to worry about the impact on a human, such as motion sickness or nausea after using vehicle simulator or playing games, visual-vestibular mismatch or feeling that one is moving even though one is stationery.

VR needs, however, would outpace the ability of graphics hardware for the foreseeable future. VR will be used in the business environment to train workers to operate machinery safely as well as to perform complicated surgical procedures on virtual humans.

9.9 REFERENCES

[1] *The Art of Human-Computer Interface Design,* edited by Brenda Laurel, Addison-Wesley, 1990.

[2] *Virtual Reality,* by Howard Rheingold, Summit Books, 1990.

[3] *Cyberspace: First Steps,* edited by Michael Benedikt, MIT Press, 1991.

[4] *Artificial Reality II,* by Myron Krueger , Addison-Wesley, 1991.

[5] *The Metaphysics of Virtual Reality,* by Michael Heim , Oxford University Press, 1993.

[6] *Cyberarts: Exploring Art and Technology,* edited by Linda Jacobson, Miller Freeman, 1992.

[7] *Virtual Reality: Through the New Looking Glass*, by Kevin Teixeira and Ken Pimentel, Tab Books, 1992.

[8] *Garage Virtual Reality*, by Linda Jacobson, Sams Publishing, 1994.

[9] *Virtual Reality Now*, by Larry Stevens, MIS Press, 1994.

[10] *The virtual Reality Primer*, by L. Casey Larijani, McGraw Hill, 1994.

[11] Bolt R.A.,"Put-that-there: Voice and Gesture at the Graphics Interface," Computer Graphics(Proc. Siggraph), vol. 14, no. 3, pp. 262-270, July 1980.

[12] *Artificial Reality*, by M.W. Krueger, 2nd ed., Addison - Wesley, Mass., 1990.

[13] Sturman D.J. and Zeltzer D.,"A Survey of glove base Input", IEEE Computer Graphics and Applications, Vol. 14, No. 1, pp. 30-39, Jan. 1994.

[14] T.G. Zimmerman et al., "A Hand Gesture Interface Device," *Proc. Human Factors in Computing Systems and Graphics Interface,* ACM Press, New York, pp. 189-192, April 1987.

[15] Bolas Mark T., "Human factors in the design of an Immersive Display", IEEE Computer Graphics and Applications, Vol. 14, No. 1, pp 55-59, Jan. 1994.

[16] Jeff Oromaner, "Flat Panels Proliferate and Challenge the CRT," *Electronic Products,* Vol. 34, No. 8, pp. 21-24, Jan. 1992.

[17] Robertson George G., et al.," Nonimmersive virtual reality", IEEE Computer, pp. 81-83, Feb. 1993.

[18] McCarthy W. Dean, et al.," A Virtual Cockpit for a Distributed Interactive Simulation," IEEE Computer Graphics and Applications, Vol. 14, No. 1, pp. 49-54, Jan. 1994.

[19] IEEE Standard for Information Technology - Protocols for Distributed Interactive Simulation Applications, IEEE Press, New York, May 1993.

[20] Cooke J.M. et al.,"NPSNET: Flight Simulation Dynamic Modelling Using Quaternions," Presence: Teleoperators and Virtual Environments, Vol.1, No. 4, pp. 404-420, 1992.

[21] Krueger W. and Bernd Froehlich, “The Responsive Workbench, IEEE Computer Graphics and Applications, Vol. 14, No. 3, pp. 12-15, May, 1994.

[22] Karen Whitehouse, “Embracing VR as a Librator”, IEEE Computer Graphics and Applications, Vol. 14, No. 3, p. 90, May 1994.

[23] Goldman Jon, Trina M Roy, “The Cosmic Worms”, IEEE Computer Graphics and Applications, vol. 14, no. 4, pp. 12 - 14, July 1994

[24] Ribarsky W. et al.," Visualization and Analysis Using Virtual Reality, IEEE Compter Graphics and Applications, Vol.14, no. 1, pp. 10-12, Jan. 1994.

[25] Ribarsky W. et al.," Glyphmaker: Creating Customized Visualizations of Complex Data," IEEE Computer, Vol. 27, No. 7, pp. 57-64, 1994.

[26]] Check Martin,"Business waking up to virtual reality", IEEE Computer, Vol. 27, No. 12, pp. 8-9, Dec, 1994.

CHAPTER 10

MULTIMEDIA TECHNOLOGY AND ITS APPLICATIONS

10.1 INTRODUCTION

Multimedia technology [1,2, 5-9] facilitates integration of text, data, image, graphics, audio, video, animation in digital form in computers. While bringing audio-visual power to a desktop PC, requires just a sound board a CD-ROM drive but real-time exchanges of voice, video, images, and applications across WANs requires new ways to enhance the delivery of information. To facilitate creation and delivery of multimedia applications and titles, the need for multimedia computer systems and also of multimedia servers and associated software has emerged. This has been made feasible due to advances in computer and communication technologies - including inexpensive workstations, powerful PCs, high-speed local area networks (LANs) and wide area networks (WANs).

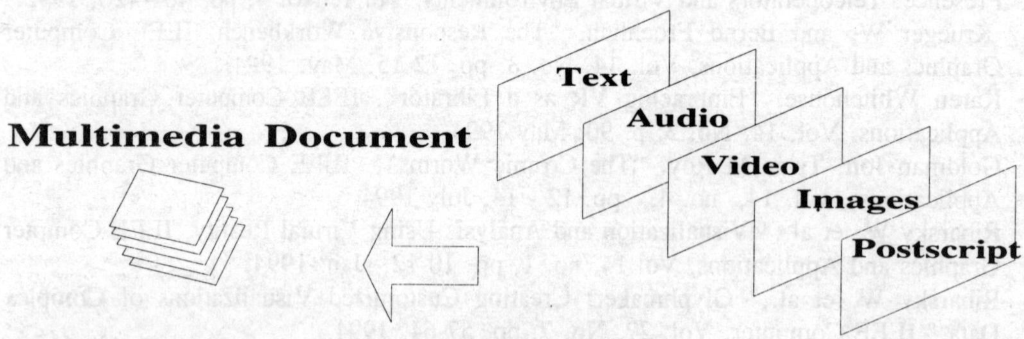

Figure 10.1 Multimedia Document

Multimedia authoring software provides tools for capture and creation of images, audio, video, animation and organisation of these into powerful and effective multimedia applications, documents and titles. Digital interactive video can be created by using technologies, such as, CD-I (for compact disk interactive) developed jointly by NV Philips of Eindhoven, the Netherlands and Sony Corp. of Tokyo, DVI (for digital video interactive), CD ROM-XA (Compact disc read only memory extended audio), and CD-TV(Compact disc television). Digital video is not new, it has been used in past by broadcast television studios to manipulate images and by tele-communication companies for tele-conferencing services. Studio equipment, however, is too expensive for a single user. For compressing sound and video, the DVI [1] and other technologies support CDROM. This medium offers a good trade off between performance features and cost.

In this chapter, we present a brief review of operating systems with multimedia capability, compression technology, and software codecs. To create interactive multimedia applications - from consumer education and game titles to in-house reference and training materials - a developer needs the right tools specifically designed for interactive media. The requirements for this includes a system with the necessary speed and power, audio/visual capabilities, and multimedia tools to facilitate development. We have included sections on configuring a multimedia system, multimedia servers, multimedia development tools, applications, and a list of popular CD-ROM titles available in the market to give the user a feel of the status of the technology as well to boost creativity and curiosity.

10.2 MULTIMEDIA OPERATING SYSTEMS

To meet the timing requirements of continuous media, the OS must use real-time scheduling techniques to support following considerations:

- The fault tolerance requirement for a multi-media system is less stringent than other real-time systems. A short time failure of multimedia system (say, delay in providing video on-demand) can be tolerated if the application is not critical like support of remote surgery.
- Among audio and video on demand, delivery of audio on-time is more critical as human ear is more sensitive to audio gaps than eye is to the video jitter.
- The real-time bandwidth requirement of a continuous media system can be adjusted dynamically as the quality of both video and audio can be regulated to the available bandwidth using different compression ratios.

Unix and its variants, Microsoft's Windows, Apple's System 7, and IBM's OS/2 are the most popular operating systems with multi-media capabilities. SVR4 Unix scheduler is a real-time static priority scheduler in addition to a standard Unix time sharing scheduler. Only through trial and error, one can tune the scheduler to find an acceptable combination of priorities and scheduling class assignments that will work for a given multimedia application set.

A new Windows technology called *Surround Video* can create a full 360-degree graphics environment. A user first creates background images with existing production techniques (e.g., 360 degree photography). *Surround Video* blends the image together to form an endless loop, correcting image distortion through remapping algorithms. Blue screen keying superimposes overlay images or motion video on top of the background. The view from within the interface extends right or left in a full circle. *Surround video* also incorporates authoring tools and scripts for designating a sequence of scenes, including other panoramas. Hot spots link to DIBs, AVI (Audio Video Interleave) movies, audio files, or other launchable components.

A new file type, called a striped DIB, stores scan lines as vertical strips (4 pixels wide). When one scrolls to a new scene, the engine loads enough vertical strips to fill the viewable area. In this way, the entire file is never read into memory - only the initial 640- by 480- pixel image is; a full 360-degree image is typically 4000 by 480 pixels. To improve display performance, two sets of stripes - those making up the view directly to the right and the left of the current view - are loaded into memory. When one pans left or right, the corresponding stripes are presented on the screen.

Microsoft has done a lot of work to make Windows 95 a multimedia OS. The success of this initiative will depend on the stability and robustness of the platform. Windows 95 provides an integrated multimedia architecture along with 32-bit versions of the Indeo and Cinepak codecs. It, therefore, has the potential to become a multimedia OS, but it is not designed to run optimally on low end systems. For true multimedia applications, we need powerful system to take advantage of the architecture's scalable design. Windows 95 has software for full motion video clips, a media player for playing video and any animation file. We can use the CD player for music CD's also.

OS/2 multimedia presentation manager - the multimedia extension to OS/2 - uses device driver as process manager approach and implements OS extensions as physical device drivers (PDDs). In this approach, a high resolution timer is used by a real-time scheduler to activate a process (or a thread) manager to run as PDDs. In other approach, each real-time task is assigned to a thread running in the time critical priority class. Each such class has 32 priority levels. A thread is interrupted if another thread with higher priority needs service. Noncritical applications run as threads in the regular class, which also has 32 levels of priority. Thus, second approach controls and coordinates all time critical threads through a system scheduler - a higher level instance. The third approach uses meta-scheduler as process scheduler. In this approach, the normal priority driven system scheduler schedules all tasks. A meta scheduler then assigns priority to the real-time tasks.

Apple's new operating system 8.0 codenamed Copland when released will offer features such as limited preemptive multitasking, concurrent I/O, memory protection and scalable user interface. It will be a good multimedia OS as it would provide almost all the features that windows 95 has but will also support hardware abstraction a feature only supported by Windows NT.

10.3 REVIEW OF COMPRESSION TECHNOLOGY

10.3.1 Standards

A brief summary of multi- and hyper-media standards is given in table 10.1.

Table 10.1 Summary of multi- and hyper-media standards

Name	Official Name	Standards Group
JPEG MJPEG	Digital compression and coding of continuous-tone still images that achieves very high compression ratios with some loss of quality.	Joint Photographic Experts Group
H.261	Video coder/decoder for audio-visual services at p×64 bps and overISDN lines	Specialist Group on Coding for Visual Telephony
MPEG	Coding of moving pictures and associated audio for adding animated video sequences to any software using JPEG compression.	Motion Pictures Experts Group
MHEG	Coded representation of multi-media and hypermedia information	Multimedia and Hypermedia Information Coding Expert Group
HyTime	Hypermedia/Time-Based Structuring Language	Standard Music Representation Work Group.

The JPEG standard defines image compression for still images and the MPEG standard is for moving image compression. Both JPEG and MPEG have been accepted by the industry. When applied to video, JPEG is also sometimes referred to as Motion-JPEG(MJPEG). JPEG compression hardware can compress incoming video stream by a factor of 60 : 1 with hardly any display image degradation. This makes it possible to store video sequences and digital data on the computers disk drive. JPEG comprises of baseline system that is a must in all implementations and a set of extended systems that are optional. JPEG compression scheme compresses each frame in isolation and cannot take into consideration the temporal redundancy in the video stream.

MPEG standard was cooperatively developed by more than 70 companies and institutions worldwide including Sony, Philips, Matsushita and Apple. MPEG can be applied to CD ROM, digital audio tape, Winchester and writable optical discs. MPEG addresses the compression of video and audio signals at 0.9 to1.5 M bits per second and 64 to 192 K bit per second per channel respectively. It also covers synchronization and multiplexing of multiply compressed audio and video streams. The MPEG video compression algorithm is based on two fundamental techniques: motion compression for interframe (temporal) redundancy and DCT (Discrete Cosine Transform) based compression for intraframe (spatial) redundancy. MPEG compression is irreversible because it uses DCT which is lossy. Figure 10.2 shows the MPEG coding scheme.

In addition to 32-bit versions of Cinepak and Indeo, Microsoft has provided MPEG support to enhance video playback under Windows 95. Windows will not include an MPEG codec in the box, but the MCI (Media Control Interface) command set will incorporate MPEG codecs from other vendors (e.g., Mediamatics or Xing Technologies) through MCI and manipulate the video just as one would an AVI file. Of course, DCI will directly access hardware MPEG decoders, when available, or otherwise launch MPEG decompression in software.

MPEG lets developers "scale-up" video playback. Under Video for Windows, video frames are simply dropped to keep audio and video in synchronism. To avoid dropped frames, developers often choose a frame rate according to the "lowest common denominator" hardware of the targeted audience. This approach results in a major problem - a video title captured at, say, 15 frames per second plays the same on a 486/33 computer as it does on a high-performance PCI based (Peripheral Component Interconnect) Pentium machine.

MPEG can dynamically adjust playback to meet the performance capabilities of the hardware. MPEG inserts key frames at configurable intervals. Intermediate frames look ahead and back to these key frames (i.e., bidirectional interframe compression), pointing to blocks of similar data to reference during compression and decompression. MPEG can adjust the media stream dynamically, perhaps running only key frames on a slower machine or sampling audio at only 11 kHz. On a hardware assisted system, the same MPEG stream could run at a full 30 fps with 44 kHz audio.

The JPEG and MPEG standards describe the content of the information object only and fail to cover the interrelationship between the different pieces of a multimedia presentation. MHEG will define the representation and encoding of multimedia and hypermedia objects interchanged within or across applications or services, by any means of interchange, including storage devices, telecommunications or broadcast networks. It also incorporates features that suit real-time interchange of multimedia data in a networked heterogeneous computing environment.

10.3.2 Compression Technology

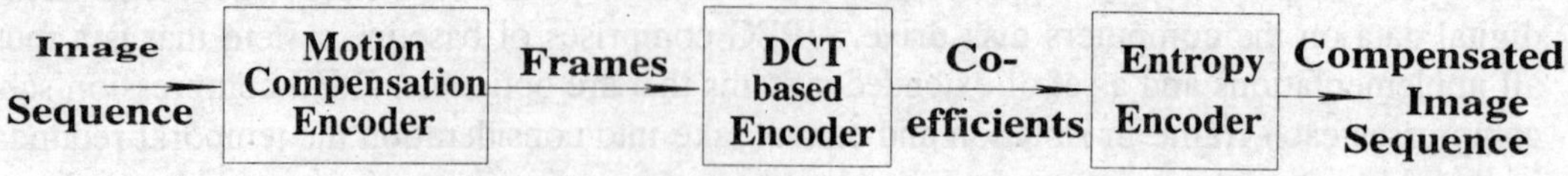

Figure 10.2 MPEG coding scheme

PC multi-media operating systems have functions to input a digital moving picture and to edit and play it with software alone. Moving pictures data compression/decompression tools (Codecs) are now available from number of vendors. These can mainly be grouped into two categories.

i. Produce video streams that desktop computers can decode and display without any special hardware. These are referred to as software only codecs. However, this approach offers only limited software image quality. A software codec can process frames of 320×240 at about 15 frames per second on a 486 or a 68040 CPU running at 33 MHz. This scenario will change with the introduction of more powerful CPUs.

ii. The hardware based codecs with MPEG algorithm provide better image quality than software based codecs. These codecs run on digital signal processors (DSPs) with limited instruction RAM and data RAM.

The quality of a video codec is assessed by image fidelity, bandwidth or data rate, playback performance, memory requirement, coding/decoding asymmetry - the length of time it takes to compress a given number of frames versus the time it takes to decode the same number of frames with same computing resources, scalableness, numerical complexity of the algorithm (significant, particularly for a software codec) and delay in presentation of video to the user. The steps involved in playback are decoding the compressed video stream, colour conversion operations and transferring decoded and colour converted video data from system RAM to the video RAM. Scalableness refers to the capability of the codec to decode and display a compressed video stream on a range of different computers at different quality levels (by adding finer details) and/or frame rates so as to exploit the available computing power without compromising performance. To ensure scalableness, we need to ensure that the video codec algorithm compresses the video in multiple frame resolutions, multiple sets of frequency bands, or multiple representation of pixel colour depth, and organises video information in hierarchical form. One simple way to assess a codec algorithm is to compare image quality after compressing an image to a required bandwidth.

A compression algorithm divides a video frame into blocks. It then looks for redundant data in the blocks. This is known as *interframe* analysis. The redundant data is dropped to reduce the size of the video file. Although this procedure compresses the video, it cannot recover the original file from the compressed file. It is, therefore, said to be *lossy* compression, and is used by all the major video codecs.

Codecs may be either *symmetric* or *asymmetric*. For real-time video capture in applications such as video conferencing, we need to use a symmetric algorithm - taking an equal amount of time for compression and decompression. Asymmetric codecs take more time in the compression stage but carry out decompression much faster. Such codecs are suitable for presentations or CD-ROMs.

Once a codec saves the nonredundant data, it statistically processes the arrangement of pixels in an image and encodes pixel patterns with an RLL encoding scheme or an equivalent. In fact, repetitive data patterns are assigned with shorter codes. Commonly used methods are *DCT* (discrete cosine transform) and *VQ* (vector quantization). Each frame is divided into blocks, generally 8 by 8 pixels each. All operations are performed on the individual blocks.

DCT[18] converts pixel intensities to a frequency-based equivalent. The transform yields a series of numbers that represent ever-finer detail in a pixel block. Compression is obtained by truncating the series after ceratin length. The result is a loss of fine detail. MPEG codecs use DCT. VQ uses vectors to select predefined equations. Codecs can tune quantization so that block colour and intensity are handled differently on a discreet basis and in relationship to the surrounding image values. VQ algorithm is based on a table comparison process to provide fast performance on high-end 486s and Pentiums.

The result of the transform process is then compressed using RLE (run-length encoding). Codecs compress these bit strings even further by scanning the patterns at a different angle and converting the values to RLA (run length/amplitude) tokens. Huffman coding then converts the most frequently occurring tokens into the shortest bit strings.

Fractal-image compression, a proprietary technology developed by Integrated Systems, is suitable for compression of data pertaining to irregular shapes. An enhancement of the still image JPEG standard called MJPEG (motion-JPEG) produces stream of individual frames compressed by JPEG - every such frame has high image quality. MJPEG is completely scalable, and at ratios less than 10:1, compression produces little or no degradation.

A brief review of the software only and hardware based codecs is given in the following sections.

10.3.1 QUICKTIME 1.5 and 2.0

QuickTime is Apple's software architecture that takes media rich content beyond the Macintosh. QuickTime is an enabling technology that supports the integration of media such as sound, video, and animation in a consistent, seamless fashion to personal computers. QuickTime is available for Macintosh, Windows and FM-Towns machines from Fujitsu.

Apple computer introduced their latest Codec software named compact video processor. It can play a 240×180 - pixels moving picture at 15 frames per second on a 20 MHz 68030 machine. On a Macintosh (with higher performance CPU), it can reach 24 frames per second with 320×240 pixels images. The salient feature of algorithm is that it enhances image quality by spending more time on image data compression and takes between 30 to 120 seconds to compress a single frame of moving data.

QuickTime 2.0 allows for the creation of a new generation of more compelling CD-titles and applications. Now, users have the ability to view full-size video on their monitors at faster frame rates, without the addition of video boards, closely resembling what viewers see on television screen today. The faster video and data in/out represents a 300% speed increase over the previous version of QuickTime. QuickTime 2.0 also supports music as well as interactive television. Music tracks, including a library of sounds licensed from Roland Corporation, are much smaller than that of standard digital audio formats allowing disk space to be conserved. Music movies are also MIDI-compatible.

In order to support Apple's future interactive television efforts, QuickTime 2.0 also supports MPEG video compression scheme for both development and delivery. The modular architecture of QuickTime will allow it to also support the MPEG2 standard, when it becomes available in the near future. MPEG2 is expected to become the digital video standard for CDs, cable television, direct satellite broadcast, and high-definition television.

QuickTime VR is software that enables a user to view a photographic or rendered representation of a scene in 360 degrees. Users can zoom in or out of a scene, navigate from one scene to another, and even "pick up" objects. As the user changes their view of the scene, correct perspective is maintained, providing the effect of being at the location and looking around.

Apple expects QuickTime VR to be widely adopted by CD-ROM title developers, architectural and engineering application developers, and game manufacturers. QuickTime for Windows and QuickTime for the Macintosh support Indeo, Cinepak, and MPEG decompression boards. QuickTime for Windows files and Video for Windows files aren't compatible.

10.3.2 Video for Windows: Software DVI

Windows supports Intel, Indeo and Microsoft Video. These codecs were designed primarily for natural moving pictures. Intel's Indeo takes between 10-30 minutes to compress one minute moving picture data. It is used on a i486 machine or with a accelerator card in system with an 80386 processor. It can play 160×120 pixels images at 15 frames per second on a 16 MHz 80386 machine, or 24 frames per second on a 33 MHz i486. Video1 was jointly developed by Microsoft and Media Vision, Inc. It can handle 24 bit per pixel gray scale and full colour video.

10.3.3 LIVEMOVIE - Compression by reducing color

The personal computers - FMTOWNS from Fujitsu have an integrated software Codec which includes LiveMovie and TownsGear digital moving picture editing software. These codecs can play a 160×120 or 80×60 - pixels moving picture at 7.5, 10, 15 or 30 frames per second. The compression techniques supports 4 modes of operations:

- low quality high compression - executes compression within CD-ROM (double speed), transfer speed 150 KBytes per second;
- standard quality mode compression - transfer speed of 80 -100 KBytes per second;
- high quality low compression mode - for hard disk drive and double speed CD-ROM drives, transfer rate 300 KBytes per second; and
- high speed compression mode - transfer speed is 800 -1000 KBytes per second. It takes only 3 - 4 seconds per frame on 16 Mhz 80386 machine.

In this system while compressing, the number of colours is first reduced from 32,000 to 256. The background and specific blocks in the picture are coded in further reduced colour. It may be mentioned that the compression rate comes mainly from the colour reduction process and the rest from sub-sampling.

10.3.4 ULTIMOTION

IBM's ultimotion software codec is a standard in MMPM/2. This codec can play 320x420 pixels images in 256 colours at 15 frames per second on a 16 MHz 80386 machine. It uses the digital video media control interface (DV-MCI) - the same application program interface (API) as that of Video for Windows. It will also support Intel's Indeo with its command set.

Ultimedia tools series (UTS) architecture provides a consistent and corporate set of multi-media tools for developing multi-media applications under DOS, OS/2, and Windows to look and act as similar as possible. Microsoft's video for windows consisting of two tools VidEdit (for editor) and VidCap (for capture) form the heart of video for windows. The recommended platform for running these tools is 486 based desktop. Windows support a video open technology for video through media control interface (MCI). It includes compression/decompression tools (codecs) that automatically recognize and play. Indeo (Intel's Codec for playing DVI) as well as Microsoft run length encoding (RLE), are good formats for running on less able platforms like 286s. Apple has QuickTime which runs video at reasonable animation rates. Apple figured out a way to subtract information from frames as necessary so that sound and animation are synchronized on playback.

10.3.5 Hardware Codecs

Hardware Codecs have one key advantage over software codecs - speed. With a MPEG board, we can decompress a video at the same rate and achieve video quality as that of a VCR tape. Hardware-assisted compression is now affordable enough to be considered and can capture 30 fps at 320-by-240 resolution. The boards now support Indeo (main vendors : Creative Labs and Intel) and motion JPEG (main vendors: Alpha Systems Lab, Diamond Multimedia Systems, Orchid Technology, and VideoLogic). A brief review of current status is as under:

- Hardware-Assisted Compression is now affordable enough to be considered viable. In the year 1995, several boards were designed using Intel's new clock doubled i750 chip (e.g. Intel's Smart Video Recorder Pro) and C-Cube Microsystems' CL-550 (on Cardinal Technologies' SNAPplus-VL).
- Analog to digital conversion is critical to a high-quality video-capture process. A board having the latest chip video decoder from Philips (the SAA7196, minted in 1993) is likely to give better quality.
- A motion JPEG chip such as LSI's L64702, is necessary if we want to avoid the daughter card, otherwise, the boards use the Zoran chip.
- Hardware assisted video playback continues to advance steadily. Matrox' Marvel II software-only capture board offers a glimpse at the future of video playback with the incorporation of Microsystems' C-Cube CL450 MPEG playback chip.
- S-Video improves capture quality. While standard or composite video input from a camcorder using RCA jacks can be acceptable, better capture quality can be achieved with an S-video input port.

- The new features introduced are VGA to NTSC encoding. We can now generate a NTSC signal from a capture board and record a digital video project on video tape.

The Smart Video Recorder Pro is based on Intel's clock doubled i750 capture chip set and supports Indeo 3.2 format. It captures 30 frames per second. It can also process images encoded with the JPEG standard. It can decode a 640×480 JPEG encoded image in less than 1second. Intel is planning to introduce Indeo 4.0 soon which will produce better than MPEG quality at data rates ranging from 38 Kbps to 800 Kbps.

The boards produce high bandwidth which corresponds to good color quality by using one of the following approaches:

- lossy-compression chips compress RGB data as it comes in at a rate of about 3.4MB per second;
- hardware assisted systems perform an on-line space conversion of the data from YUV (analog signal format) to RGB. Thus, these boards strip out two third of the bandwidth and this corresponds to incoming data rate of 1.2 MB per second. This leads to dropping too many frames and hence deterioration in the ultimate video quality.

The capture results[17] show that only three boards, viz. Creative Labs Video Blaster RT300, Diamond Videostar Pro, and Intel Smart Video Recorder Pro drop zero to negligible number of frames while capturing 10-second/15fps, 20-second/30fps,or 2-minute/30fps video

10.4 SYSTEM CONFIGURATION SUITABLE FOR MULTIMEDIA

For multimedia application we need a PC which can talk, sing and playback video in real-time. Most sound boards available in the market, create sound by manipulating instrument sounds stored in ROM or on a hard disk. FM synthesis is replaced on high-end boards by more authentic wave- table synthesis. All sound boards are capable of playing back the MIDI and digital .WAV files.

The Creative Labs 16-bit and 32-bit sound boards are suitable for games and serious users respectively. The 16-bit boards support only FM sound and have software based .WAV file player. The 32-bit boards support Q-sound technology, thus, delivering 3D spatial sound effects. However, only Turtle Beach Multisound boards provide the true CD-ROM quality sound. The Turtle Beach boards are not compatible to the Sound Blaster board, thereby may not run many games. These boards are good for business and edutainment where sound quality is the prime consideration.

The other high sound quality board is Antex Z1e from Antex Electronics. It gives very high quality sound and MPEG sound compression enabling authors to compress files while retaining broadcast quality sound. Figure 10.3 shows sound board and devices which can be interfaced with it. An interested reader can see [16] for a detailed study of the features supported by variety of the sound boards in the market.

We can use either hardware or software codecs along with Windows accelerator that incorporates on-chip motion video acceleration.

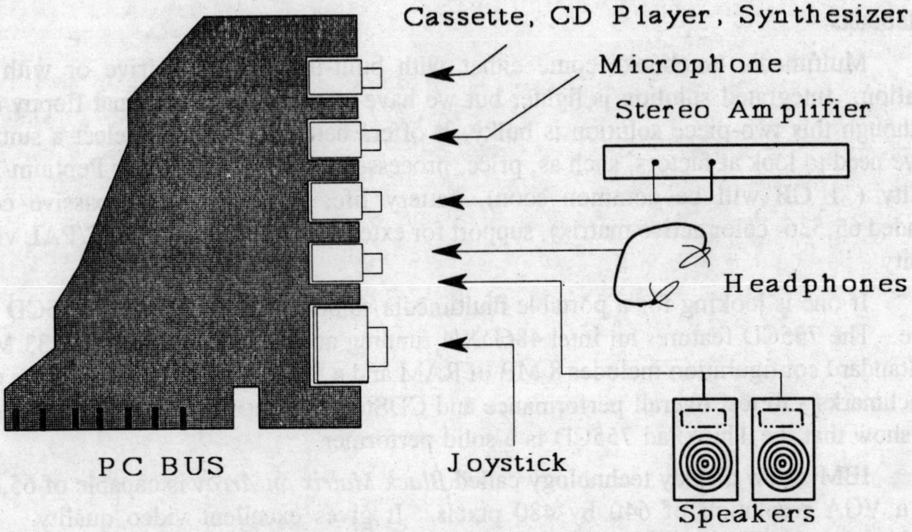

Figure 10.3 Sound board and devices which can be interfaced to it

10.4.1 Desktop

A typical configuration of the computer system with associated hardware and software requirement for running multi-media is as follows:

- An IBM PC or compatible computer with at least a 486 DX2 66 Mhz processor (Pentium recommended as Intel is going to stop manufacture of 486 chips in early 1996), at least 8 MB but preferably 16 MB of RAM.
- Minimum 540 MB hard disk (1 GB is preferable and upto 4GB for a video capture station is recommeded).
- A VGA or SVGA display controller and non-interlace colour monitor.
- A mouse
- DOS, Windows or OS/2 and Multimedia development software Audio and video sources - camera, VCR, and audio systems
- CD-ROM drive
- Desirable - Removable optical read-write drive and cartridge of storage capacity of 2 GB or more
- An authoring tool such as MacroMedia Authorware.

Macintosh machines serve as an excellent platform for multi-media applications. Recommended configuration includes 8 MB memory, at least 80 MB space on the hard disk drive, 13" colour monitor, videotape and laser discs as media sources, and multi-media hardware for video/audio capture and software.

10.4.2 Notebooks

Multimedia notebooks come either with built-in CD-ROM drive or with the docking station. Integrated solution is lighter but we have to trade off an internal floppy disk drive. Although this two-piece solution is bulky, it offers better sound. To select a suitable notebook we need to look at factors, such as, price, processor power (DX4/100 or Pentium/75), disk capacity (1 GB will be common soon), battery life, active/dual scan/passive color (recommended 65,536- color active matrix), support for external monitor, and NTSC/PAL video out capability.

If one is looking for a portable multimedia solution, IBM ThinkPad 755CD is a good choice. The 755CD features an Intel 486DX/4 running at 100 MHz internal and 33 MHz external. Standard configuration includes 8 MB of RAM and a 540-MB hard drive. On the new BYTE Benchmarks - to test overall performance and CDStone to test CD-ROM performance - the results show that the ThinkPad 755CD is a solid performer.

IBM's new display technology called *Black Matrix on Array* is capable of 65,536 colours at a VGA resolution of 640 by 480 pixels. It gives excellent video quality. The ThinkPad also has a port to connect an external monitor. It has not only a built-in CD-ROM and wavetable-synthesis sound into a 8.2 pound package but also has infrared transceivers and a 14.4-Kbps fax modem with telephony capability. Another notebook for multimedia applications is the TI TravelMate 4000M DX4/100 TFT with multimedia Docking Station.

The double speed CD-ROM meets MPC Level-2 specifications. On the CDStone tests, it posted respectable numbers for a double speed drive. The CD-ROM is spring loaded, rather than motor-driven, mechanism opens only when the ThinkPad is on - a smart feature that prevents accidental opening while the computer is stored.

Notebooks suitable for multimedia applications are available from number of other vendors, e.g. Toshiba's T4900CT has 75-Mhz Pentium Processor, 10.4 inch SVGA active color matrix screen, 772 MB hard disk, and a built in sound system for multimedia presentations. Acer's Multimedia note book AcerNote 950 has 75- or 90- Mhz Pentium Processor; dual battery; built in 16-bit speakers for livelier presentation, built in audio system with connectors for external audio device such as microphone and amplifier speakers; EasyTouch touchpad in the centre of palm rest and accessible to both left and right hand users, a docking station that serves as a powerful office or home computer base and drive bays - for 3.5" 1" high hard disk, two 5.25" half high (1.6") external and accesible drive base for CD-ROM player or tape backup.

10.5 MULTIMEDIA SERVERS

Client server computing uses the graphical and processing capability of the local stations (clients) through application oriented graphic user interfaces and makes transparent to the user its interaction with remote database server and data repositories. The user need not worry about the location and address of the database server having the desired information on the network. Multimedia servers will be designed to offer services like video on demand, interactive games, catalog shopping, and educational programming. These servers will support the needs of a community comprising of hundreds to thousands of families and would, therefore, be required to support number of full motion streams simultaneously in a cost-effective manner. To meet such high bandwidth/throughput demands, designers are studying the implications of extending Asynchronous Transfer Mode (ATM) to LANs and the desktop to bring this high bandwidth and uniform cell switching technology to multimedia applications. ATM supports constant bit rate, variable bit rate, connectionless and connection-oriented framing, multiplexing and transport services and thus is ideal for moving multimedia computation to the client-server paradigm.

The salient factors that would determine the architecture of the multimedia servers, therefore, are (i) evolution of IC and microprocessor technology - leading to increased processing speed; (ii) storage media - its type, size, and bandwidth; (iii) network technology such as, synchronous optical network (SONET), ATM, bridging, routing, and gateways; and iv. the client-server technology - to integrate computing power of multiple processors as one resource and make it available to the end user. The client-server model is leading to servers designed for community or enterprise serving using mainly ATM and support of multimedia through seamless integration of local area networks (LANs) and wide area networks (WANs). In the ATM protocol structure, the physical-medium dependent layer for use in B-ISDN is a SONET running at 155 and 622 Mbps. The next higher layer is called transmission convergence layer and it adapts other physical layers for transfer of ATM cells.

Multimedia servers need a large storage capacity across different storage media, such as disk storage, tape library, and expanded storage (ES) comprising of RAM modules. Disk storage capacities are increasing every year at a rate of 60-80%. However, the speeds of data transfer between storage and memory is still a bottleneck and the trend is to increase the level of parallelism and increase the bandwidth of the connecting network. One such technology is providing Redundant Array of Inexpensive Disks (RAID) - provides parallelism as well redundancy on the storage side. A designer needs to consider the changing demand of the video based on viewers interest, e.g. most of users may like to see a popular movie at the same time, thus necessitating higher bandwidth support from the storage device which may have copy of that movie. On the other hand a cold movie may be required to be shown only a few times in a year.

In a traditional multimedia system input/output devices will be connected to a workstation bus and the workstation would be interfaced to a network. In the ATM-based multimedia approach[14] the processor, memory, storage, network, and the peripherals will be connected to the ATM switches to provide the performance, scalableness, and reliability challenges of the multimedia systems.

Single switch topology connects the processor, memory, storage and the network sub- systems by a single ATM switch. The major problem in this approach is in the concurrent operation. The switching load of one system affects the switching bandwidth available to the other systems. This architecture is not scalable as a single switch has limited number of ports and we cannot add processor, memory and/or storage when the switch capacity is utilized. This approach has limitations in the areas such as speed, reliability, and in supporting different traffic patterns.

The Medusa project at Olivetti Research[13] provides a networked multimedia environment and supports many streams of multimedia data simultaneously. The hardware includes a collection of ATM direct peripherals (cameras, audio systems, multimedia storage servers, LCD displays, and television as well as ATM networked workstations (see figure 10.4). Each direct peripheral has a built in processor and runs an in-house micro-kernel called ATM

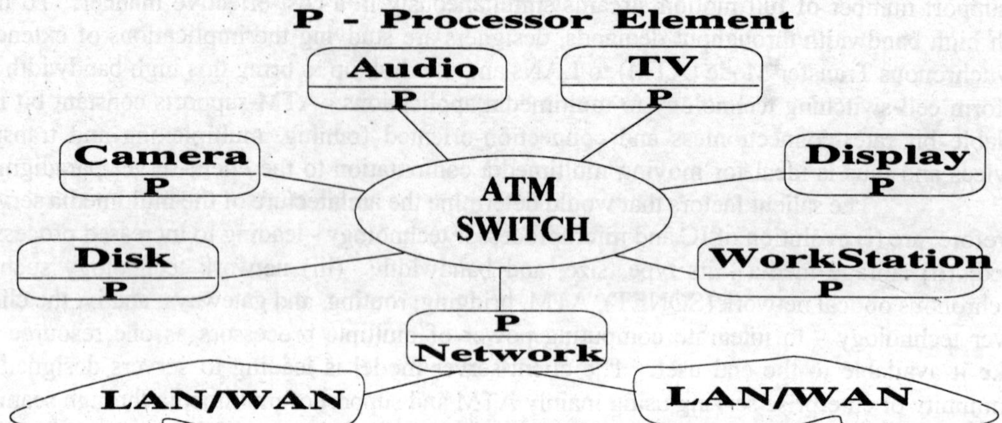

Figure 10.4 Single switch topology - allows many diverse pieces of hardware to share a single switch and interwork effectively.

operating system (ATMOS) - designed for networked, embedded, real-time systems. In another project called Desk Area Network (DAN) at Cambridge University[15], the workstation itself is being divided into separate ATM components, with CPUs, memories, microphone and video cameras all directly connected to the ATM network. DAN assumes that mass storage devices will be connected to a I/O system such as SCSI and not be fully integrated within the system.

Another approach [14] is to provide multiple cascaded and hierarchical switches (shown in figure 10.5 and figure 10.6) - each supporting processor-memory, network and storage. The advantages of this approach are

- Subsystem independence and concurrency
  Each switch can be designed to meet the requirement of the system it serves, e.g. input and output port rates and buffering strategies can be customized.
- Scalableness
  Each subsystem can be expanded independently with the least impact on the performance of the other. If a particular cluster gets saturated, another cluster can be added.
- Reliability
  Failure of one switch may not affect the total system, e.g. the failure of the processor-memory switch may not disrupt the operation of the communication and storage services.

In the hierarchical approach, the intercluster switch is a bus, it can, therefore, support synchronization and broadcasting across clusters.

Vunet - a distributed multimedia research project at the Massachusetts Institute of Technology - is a gigabit per second DAN based on ATM. It consists of a set of ATM switches which interconnect workstations, video and audio capture hardware, and image processing system.

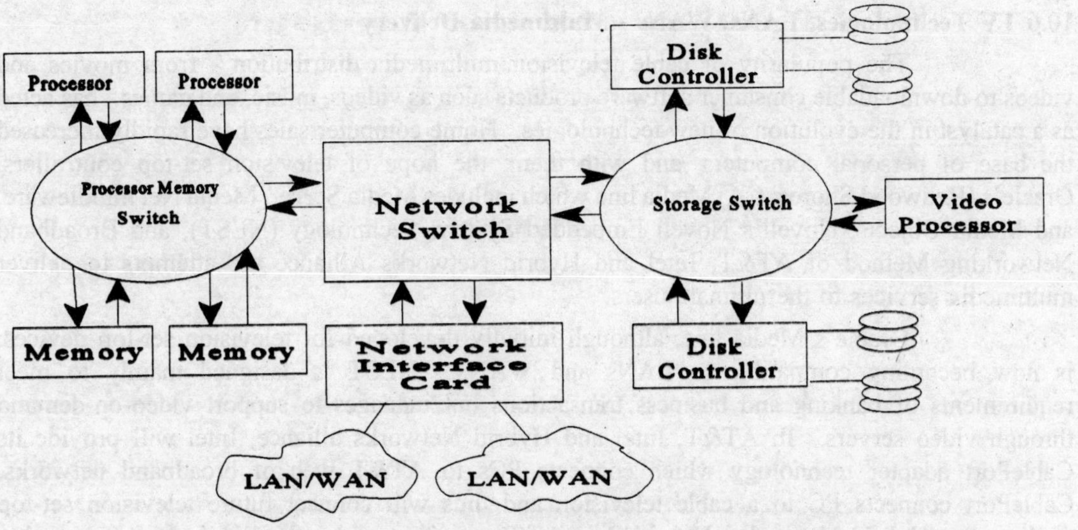

Figure 10.5 Multiple cascaded switch topology

The salient feature of the approach is to handle real-time data, such as video and

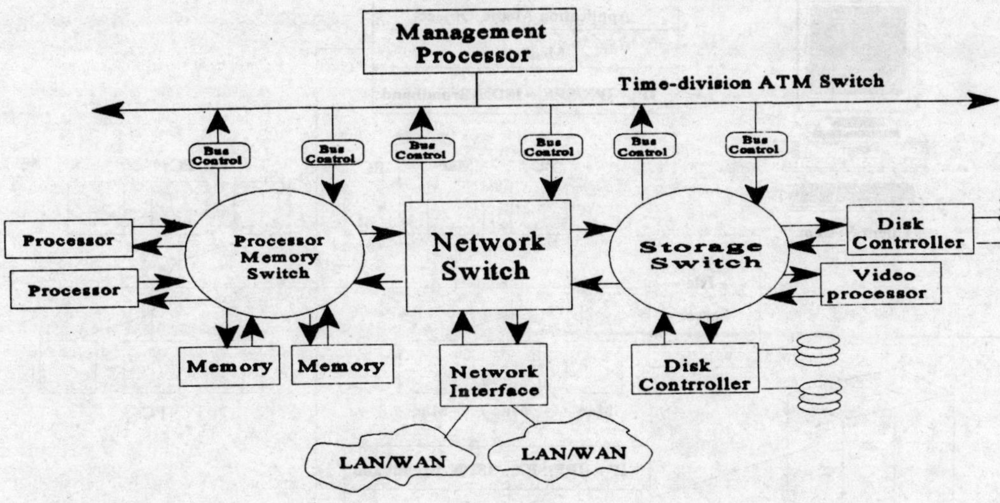

Figure 10.6 Hierarchical switch topology

audio from the network and deliver it to the network. The primary goal of this project was to study the use of ATM to connect multimedia peripherals to the workstation, therefore ATM was not extended into the workstation.

10.6 TV Technologies, LANs, WANs - Multimedia Delivery

The popularity of cable television multimedia distribution - from movies and videos to downloadable consumer software products such as videos, music, and games - has acted as a catalyst in the evolution of new technologies. Home computer sales have rapidly increased the base of personal computers, and with them, the hope of television set-top controllers. Oracle's (Redwood Shores, CA) Media line which includes Media Server, Media Net middleware, and Media Objects, Novell's Novell Embedded System Technology (NEST), and Broadband Networking Method of AT&T, Intel and Hybrid Networks Alliance are attempts to deliver multimedia services to the ultimate users.

Oracle's Media line, although initially developed for television set-top devices, is now becoming compatible to LANs and WANs. NEST is designed mainly to meet requirements of banking and business transactions but manages to support video-on-demand through video servers. In AT&T, Intel and Hybrid Networks alliance, Intel will provide its CablePort adapter technology which connects PCs to AT&T web of broadband networks. CablePort connects PC to a cable television and thus will connect future television set-top appliances. Hybrid Networks' Hybrid Point of Presence provides the link between the cable system equipment and the content providers.

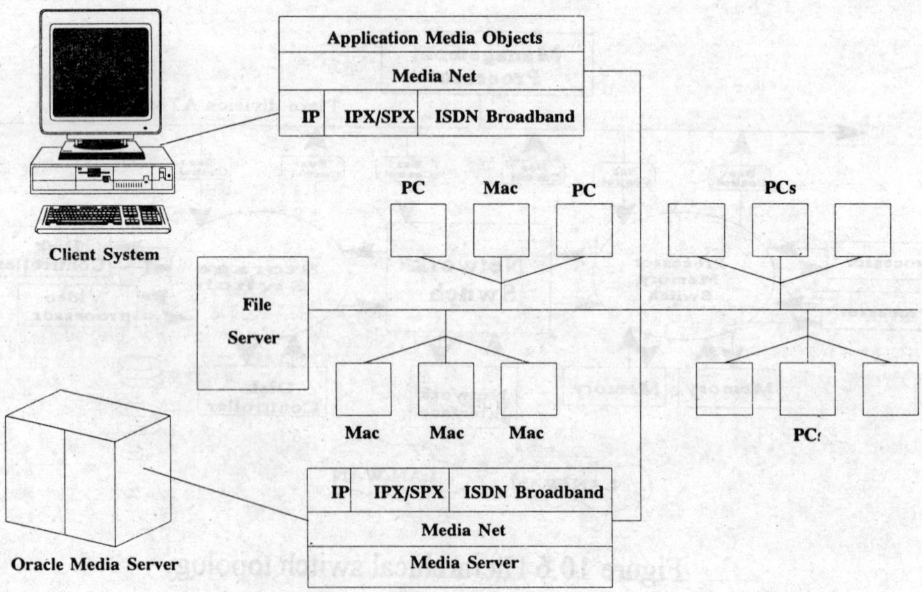

Figure 10.7 Oracle's Media System

A few years ago, the relational database management system (RDBMS) could barely store raw data exceeding 64KB (even a passport size black and white pictures needs more than 100 KB) in a field. That has radically changed. Oracle Media Server (see Figure 10.7) uses the Object Management Group's (OMG) Object Request Broker (ORB) to move data from the Media Server through Media Net to an application requiring multimedia objects.

Media Objects, in turn, are similar OMG-standards-based programming objects. They provide applications developers with a set of APIs and Remote Procedure Calls (RPCs) similar to a foundation class library. The objects contain multimedia data as well as information about that data and its characteristics.

Media Net middleware, a set of applications that sits between client applications and the database server, was designed to take advantage of multimedia data distribution through a variety of routes. These synchronous or asynchronous routes include common protocols such as Novell's IPX/SPX, TCP/IP, and WAN connectivity methods, from low-speed ISDN through DS1's 1.554Mbps and faster public/private data networks.

Today, the primary Media Net delivery mechanisms are broadband networks - the same kind that cable television uses to distribute its signals. In a recent technology demonstration [see Interoperability - A supplement to LAN Magazine, Nov. 1995], Oracle and Intel displayed an application in which the Media Server and Oracle Objects served as the video equivalent to a voice mail server. In the demonstration, a video conference using Intel's ProShare 200 was recorded, along with several concurrent participants, video feeds. The feeds were then used as mail objects that could be accessed by icon.

10.7 MULTIMEDIA TOOLS

It is an established fact that multi sensory input is more powerful than a mono-sensory input. We all know the aphorisms that

- One remembers 30% of material read;
- One remembers 60% of material read and heard;
- One remembers 90% of what one reads, hears and sees.

As mentioned in chapter 1 of this book that a picture is worth many thousands words, multimedia further enhances the comprehension by providing synchronized text, audio and video inputs. An authoring tool enables a developer to enrich his application by incorporating multimedia content in all forms as appropriate. It provides an application development environment which employs visual programming techniques including multimedia objects to enable quick prototyping and implementation of sophisticated multimedia applications. The authoring tool provides a complete object level paradigm to enable authors and professional publishers to build complex interactive desktop video projects from a rich set of objects. It includes text, data, image, animation and full motion video.

10.7.1 Benefits of using Professional Tools

Multimedia tools provide the power to incorporate text, graphics, sound, animation and video to create dynamic applications for learning, reference, simulation, merchandising and entertainment. A few benefits of the tools are listed below:

- One can structure the information as we see fit, skip certain areas and carefully study other areas, as desired.
- The use of video, sound and animation can bring a concept to life and make it highly memorable.
- Significant long-term cost savings in corporate training and educational applications can be achieved.
- Users can cost-effectively create CD-ROMs for reference and entertainment purposes.

10.7.2 MACROMEDIA

10.7.2.1 ACTION - Multimedia Business Presentations

MacroMind Action enables us to create multimedia presentations instantly by quickly and easily combining sound, motion, text, graphics, animation and interactivity creating professional quality presentations.

We can assemble a presentation scene by scene using the built in drawing and text tools, or import from Windows graphics, spreadsheet or paint packages. We can add motion and sound to the objects (we have created), access sound from CD-ROM player and include interactive buttons to link scenes together.

It includes more than 100 multimedia templates to use as building blocks for presentations, as well as a *ClipMedia* Library of sounds, graphics and animations that we can use to put life into our applications.

We can use it to add sound and motion to existing slide presentations or to create new impressive presentations. We control the timing and flow of the presentation with timeline, instant links and buttons and an easy to understand, VCR like control panel. The presentations can be printed to video tape for wide distribution with optional hardware.

10.7.2.2 *MAGIC*-Animated Multimedia Productions

With *Magic* and the Macintosh, it is easy to animate text and graphics, add sound and create buttons that can play transitions like *QuickTime* movies or take us to any point in our production. The other fast option is to customize one of the included templates and have a complete multimedia production in minutes. *Magic* facilitates in creating multimedia reports, kiosks training materials, storyboards, animatics and the like. *Genie*, the consumer information service from General Electric has used *Magic* to turn what was once a static presentation about their various services into a dynamic interactive kiosk, for use at Epcott Centre in Florida as well as at variety of trade shows and customer group meetings.

Magic makes full use of the theatre metaphor because of its theatrical qualities. It refers graphics and text as actors and the presentation area as stage and actions occur in distinct scenes. Actors can have custom costumes colours or patterns and can enter and leave with transitional effects.

Magic allows us to create text and graphics in a draw type environment with a familiar tool palette. The tools for creating a path of motion and animate an actor are the same. We can import the text and graphics created elsewhere into the Magic environment. *Magic* enables us to play animations or capture video clips as movies by using *QuickTime* or *QuickPICS*.

10.7.2.3 AUTHORWARE PROFESSIONAL *for Macintosh or Windows*

It is an authoring system used to create interactive multimedia applications. It uses visual mapping approach to enable even non technical experts to build applications without scripting. Eleven design icons provide full authoring functionality as well as a simple and powerful development platform. Each icon opens to reveal setting and tools for working with both multimedia elements and application logic.

The icons used for authoring are identical for the Macintosh and Windows versions. *Authorware*'s iconic approach to authoring leads to ease of use as an application can be created by placing iconic objects on a flowline, therefore, no scripting is required.

10.7.3 IBM's Multimedia Software

10.7.3.1 Ultimedia for AIX on RS/6000

It enables a user to:

- playback audio and video files received from the Internet or other sources;
- add voice navigation control to an application;
- use microphone input to record and edit comments to annotate a spreadsheet, document, data file, or office mail,
- add audio or video help to complement current training programs;
- edit and merge current audio or video files to update old material or create new material
- use the power of an editor to consolidate and organize audio and video archives;
- share movies or audio files in a mixed environment or workstations and PCs;
- Control playback of audio CDs;
- display and manipulating PhotoCD images;
- convert audio and video files from one format to another;
- monitor and capture live video information for video conferencing, video archives, training and annotation; and
- invoke multimedia players with C or C++ commands to add multimedia support to existing software.

IBM offers video adapter options for Micro Channel and PCI bus RS/6000 workstations. In addition, many third party adapters support specialized video operations, such as TV tuning, video, monitoring multiple windows, video scan conversion, and output.

10.7.3.2 Storyboard Live!

Based on *Storyboard Plus*, *Storyboard Live!* brings several new capabilities to the DOS multimedia environment, including:

- Video and audio playback without special hardware adapters,
- design and edit animation sequences,
- create and edit story lines via a mouse without programming, and
- create full motion video sequences with any supported video motion adapters.

10.7.3.3 ActionMedia II

- It helps in improving user productivity due to more natural ways of using personal computers. Supports all DVI Technology compression formats and a baseline JPEG still-image algorithm.
- The all digital DVI multimedia technology fits into existing information technology environments and, with suitable applications, becomes operable over LANs and data communications networks.
- Offers configurations to suit most personal computer platforms with configuration options to grow with applications demands.

10.7.3.4 IBM LinkWay Live! Version 1.0

LinkWay Live! is a multimedia-enabled version. In addition to providing a low cost application development environment, IBM LinkWay Live! enables the simplified creation and use of multimedia applications and supports DVI Technology using the Personal System/2 ActionMediaII(*) Display Adapter and IBM Personal System/2 ActionMedia II Capture Option.

10.7.3.5 Multimedia Presentation Generator (MPG) Version 1.5

MPG is a LinkWay application which functions as an authoring system for the DOS platform that allows an end user to create an application using objects. The software allows users to fully control their multimedia resources through a user friendly interface. It fully supports a variety of video sources as well as many IBM multimedia products such as the M-Motion Video Adapter/A.

10.7.3.6 Microsoft Multimedia Windows Extensions 1.0

It provides Multimedia accessories that enable an easy user interface. The *Music Box* accessory lets the user control the playing of audio compact discs on a CD-ROM drive. *Music box* is easy to use, with controls similar to those used by the home CD players. The *Media Player* accessory lets the user play various kinds of media files using different kinds of hardware. It can play animation, sound, and *MIDI* sequencer files. The *Sound Recorder* accessory makes it easy to play and record sound files. As the sound plays, it is graphically displayed in the *Sound Recorder* window.

In addition, the Multimedia Control Panel provides the standard Windows Control Panel applets and a series of new applets to allow adjustment of certain multimedia options.

- The *Display* applet changes display modes between high resolution color, and low resolution color, and grey scale.

- The *Driver* applet installs multimedia drivers for new multimedia devices and configures existing drivers.
- The *MIDI Mapper* modifies the mapping of MIDI output channels, standard instrument patches, and percussion key assignments.
- The *Screen Saver* applet allows the user to select a screen saver to display when the system is idle for a specified period.
- The *Sound* applet assigns sounds to specified system events, for example, indicate that a bell sound be played whenever starting Windows.
- The *Joystick* applet calibrates the joystick, if the system has one.

10.7.4 Multimedia from Apple

10.7.4.1 *QuickTake*

The Apple *QuickTake* 100 digital camera for both Macintosh and Windows lets users take 24-bit, high-quality colour pictures and quickly load them into a Macintosh computer or Windows based PC. This affordable digital camera needs no film. Users can shoot 32 standard resolution images or 8 high resolution images at a time, and then - using the included serial cable and software - load the images into a Macintosh computer where they can be displayed on a monitor in more than 16 million colours.

AppleDesign Powered Speakers can enhance the user's multimedia experience on the computer, or add excellent stereo sound to the multitude of personal electronic products or televisions in today's home. Magnetic shielding reduces interference, so customers can use them near their monitor and peripheral devices.

10.7.4.2 Apple Multimedia Kit for Macintosh

The new Apple Multimedia Kit for Macintosh is ideal for users who want to bring an enhanced multimedia solution to their Macintosh. In addition to Apple's new external CD-ROM player and new AppleDesign Powered Speakers II, the kit includes Apple Headphones, Compton's Interactive Encyclopaedia for Macintosh all required cables, set-up software, and the customer's choice of up to three free CD-ROM titles from a list of more than 30 top-selling discs. The Apple Multimedia Kit upgrades existing Macintosh computers - including Performa and Power Macintosh - into complete multimedia systems.

10.7.4.3 Multimedia Kit for Windows

PC owners can also benefit from Apple quality Multimedia Kit for Windows. The kit includes the AppleCD 399i Plus - an internal version of the CD-ROM player, AppleDesign Powered Speakers II, Apple Headphones, Compton's Interactive Encyclopaedia for Windows, a MediaVision 16-bit sound card, all required cables, set-up software, and a few CD-ROM titles.

10.8 **Databases and Multimedia**

A multimedia file can comprise of static images, such as bit map - .BMP, JPEG - .JPG, or Graphics Interchange Format - .GIF) files; video images, such as Video for Windows (Audio Video Interleaved, or .AVI) and QuickTime - .MOV or - .QT files; and sound files, usually stored in .WAV or Musical Instrument Digital Interface - .MID format.

Traditional PC-based databases are designed to be run on a standalone system or as a multiuser system with shared data files on a LAN file server. Client-server DBMSs are designed to run on a database server, with users accessing the database through various front-end applications provided by DBMS vendors or other third-party front-end vendors. Front ends can either be custom-written using a standard programming language or a client-server application development package.

PC-based DBMSs typically use one of the following methods to integrate multimedia files into a database:

- *Organization Method*

  In this technique, we do not integrate multimedia. We can still use database to organize our multimedia files. This method is adequate if the only information we need is the content and location of our multimedia files. A multimedia tracking database makes it easy to find the files when we want to use them in another application.

  The major advantage of this approach is that we can use any DBMS; it does not have to have built-in multimedia capabilities, so we are not restricted to a GUI-based DBMS.

  The drawback is that we know only the location of the file using this method. We cannot use a file browse function to find the file and enter the file name and path name into the database. We need to remember the file's location, then open another application in which to call it up. One way to circumvent this limitation is to create a database with at least three fields: one to hold the file name and location, another for the file type, and a third for the description and preferably also a fourth field for keywords about the file to make searching the database easier. We can create an Index on the Keywords field to speed up searches.

- *External File Method*

  In this technique we use a special data type which acts as a pointer to the multimedia file residing elsewhere on the disk. This approach is more commonly used with static images, where the DBMS can display the image using internal recognition and display routines.

  Superbase uses the EXTERNAL data type to store the information about the file. Superbase 3.0 has support for sound (.WAV and .MID) and video (.AVI) files. Superbase can directly display most popular image types, including .BMP, Emulated PostScript (.EPS), .GIF, .IMG, .PCX, Targa (.TGA), Tagged Image File Format (.TIF), Windows Metafile (.WMF), and .JPG files. It includes optional filters to display Computer Graphics Metafile (.CGM), .CHT and .CH3, .DRW, .DXF, .PCT, and .WPG files.

- OLE or *Linking Method*

  It is the most popular method of providing multimedia capabilities in a database, and given the current state of technology, perhaps the best method as well. In this method we use the GUI's data integration capabilities to link the multimedia file to the database. This approach is most commonly seen in Windows-based DBMSs, which use

OLE to link to the multimedia file (or any other file type that supports OLE) and to launch the appropriate utility to display or play the file.

With OLE main advantage over the external file method is that we are not limited to using only multimedia files the DBMS supports. In fact, it does not limit us to any particular file type at all. For as long as an application supports OLE, the database can link to that application files and use OLE to load the application and the file when we access the record containing that file.

OLE linking and the external file method have a common problem - they can't display the linked file if not found. It is the user's responsibility to ensure that the database can access the file, either from the local hard disk or a shared network directory.

- *BLOB Method*

It is used by client-server databases and some PC-based databases. It involves a special data type designed to hold large amounts of binary data. Its generic name is Binary Large Object, or BLOB. Many DBMS vendors have their own name for this data type, such as Oracle's LONG RAW and Microrim's R:Base VARBIT.

Use of BLOBs and embedded OLE objects increases performance. The database can quickly load the image from its own data file instead of having to search for it on the disk. This increases the size of the database file, but that's acceptable considering the potential problems.

Microsoft's Access, which was designed from the ground up as a Windows DBMS, uses OLE method. It has a data type called OLEOBJECT, which stores both linked and embedded OLE objects. Windows .BMP files can be stored and displayed directly in the OLEOBJECT field. Other OLE objects are displayed as an icon representing the object. FoxPro, Microsoft's other DBMS, uses the GENERAL data type to store linked or embedded OLE objects. FoxPro also lets us convert some types of OLE objects (.BMPS) to static images, which are automatically displayed in a form and can't be edited. Lotus uses the PICTUREPLUS field to store static images and OLE objects. Static images can be pasted directly into the field from .BMP, EPS, .GIF, .PCX, .TGA, .TIF, and .WMF graphic files.

Both the Windows-based DBMSs (dBase for Windows and Paradox for Windows) of Borland support OLE. dBase uses both the OLE and the BLOB approach. .BMP, .PCX, and .WAV files can be stored directly in dBase BINARY data type fields, and can be displayed using the built-in image viewer or played with the built-in sound player. Paradox for Windows supports two BLOB data types as well as an OLE data type. The OLE data type displays either an icon or an image of the object. The GRAPHIC data type is used to hold static images from .bmp, .pcx, .tif, .gif, or .eps files. Like the dBase BINARY fields, GRAPHIC fields can't be edited.

BLOB-like data types are common in the client-server DBMSs. For example, Oracle Server 7.0 has the LONG RAW data type that stores upto 2GB in binary data. The Microsoft and Sybase versions of SQL Server have the IMAGE data type. The IMAGE data type stores upto 2GB of raw binary data; other database servers have equivalent data types.

In a client-server system, the front-end application determines what data is in the BLOB field and how to use it. The front end must know what kind of data the BLOB field holds so it can properly manipulate or display that data. One approach is to store only a known type of multimedia file in a particular BLOB field. That way, the application will always know what to expect when it accesses the data. Illustra Information Technologies has developed an object-relational DBMS called Illustra database. Illustra builds object-oriented capabilities on top of both the relational model and SQL. It uses the standard relational capabilities to provide data integrity and performance and supports current ANSI SQL standards. Object-oriented capabilities are also added through a number of extensions to both the relational model and SQL, including user defined Abstract Data Types (ADTs) and user defined functions (UDFs).

10.9 MULTIMEDIA APPLICATIONS [2,3]

Multi-media environment is distinguished from existing technologies like television by the inter-activity it gives users. Currently, the only true form of video-on-demand many of us have involves our VCR. We can always make a quick trip to the video store and pick a movie, but, more importantly, if we can't view programming at its original broadcast time, we can tape it to view at our leisure. Multimedia allows users to affect selection and sequencing of story elements and to retrieve elements in multiple contexts. In brief, multimedia is user directed story telling with most natural resources like synchronised audio and video. A few representative applications have been quoted in the following lines.

In the area of advertising, multimedia will bring major change in the way it does business. It will allow free-lance agencies to produce inexpensive rough cuts and prepress clips, thereby, significantly reducing the dominance of the larger advertisement agencies.

The engineering industry will be able to store and use multimedia to call up typical designs from the storage, customise the design to meet the requirement of the job, visualise the design in 3-D, prepare a video clip, and forward it to the client.

The third major area multimedia technology will affect is education. In the near future hand-held machines for the study of various subjects will emerge. It is yet to be seen how effective and acceptable these machines will be as it will change the method of teaching and primary rules of schools and teachers. However, this technology will enable students to learn at their own pace. In the present system of imparting education, it is necessary for students to cope-up with the class - this situation will change. The quality of education can also be standardised and it will no more be function of the quality of teaching which varies from school to school.

The fourth upcoming application is multimedia databases. This is about huge databases from Oracle, Sybase, or many others that will be needed to manage the huge libraries of films delivered to homes via cable, as well as to process viewer input as consumers order from online catalogues.

It is possible now to give a tourist a walk through a tourist spot to facilitate him to plan his/her itinerary. Developer of such an application will need to visit the spot and do outdoor shooting to collect video for all possible paths. An effective way for doing this is to take still photographs at a interval of about one metre along each path on the tourist spot. This provides approximately one frame of video for each step we walk. At a resolution of 256×240 pixels, a CD ROM can hold compressed video for more than 40 km. of walking. When the still frames are displayed in a sequence of 10 frames per second, a viewer gets a feel of being there and walking down the path. The viewer can control the speed and the direction of the movement and hears sound appropriate to the background of the site. It is also possible to take panoramic view from the vantage points using proper lens in the camera. With the availability of full motion video (30 frames per second capture) at 320-by-240 pixel resolution on the PC and 4X and 6X CD-ROM instead of 2X (double speed), we reach very close to realism. While capturing Video it is advisable to

- Compress at the highest rate to which our system can playback without dropping frames
- Capture at the highest rate and then compress to the target rate
- ensure that hard disk can provide sustained data rate of 6 Mbps

- Compress with Indeo 3.23 for software only playback
- Use MPEG if the system supports MPEG playback

Electronic reading environment will not be limited to text, line art, and still images but would include sound, video sequences, and computer produced animations. MediaView developed on a Next workstation makes it possible to produce such a document.

There are many areas in which multimedia could be used. The potential is unlimited. As a more natural way to interface to the computer, it could be the front end for virtually any application. The following is only a brief list of some of the applications that can utilize the capabilities of multimedia:

- Marketing
  - Information Directory
  - Reservations
  - Buyer Guides
  - Product/Sales Promotions
  - Kiosks
  - Advertising
  - Interactive Catalogs
  - Merchandising - Point of Purchase

  Information kiosks[see figure 10.8] in public places, such as trade show floors, museums, employee information centres, lobbies of hotels, airports and corporate buildings is a good way to disseminate information.

Figure 10.8
Information Kiosk

- Diagnostics and Guidance
  - Equipment Diagnostics
  - Equipment Service
- Education and Training
  - On Line Job Assistance
  - Classroom Education (Schools and Universities)
  - Personal Training
  - Equipment Setup and Operation
  - Presentations

  Electronic courseware can be used for interactive corporate training or education.
- Desktop Video Conference - Video Electronic Mail

- Electronic Publishing - Digital Books and Libraries
- Video Editing - Content Creation
- Process Control and Monitoring
- Tourist Assistance and Information

  Computer demonstration disks and guided tours.
- General
  - Commercial "titles" on CD or floppy disk, in areas like entertainment and reference, or "infotainment"
  - Front-ends to databases and electronic information systems.

10.8.1 Interactive TV

We descibe below a few existing Interactive TV networks under trial that provide movies, sitcoms, video games, and shopping over the network right to our home.

Among the first deployments of interactive television was a trial launched by Time Warner Cable Full Service Network (FSN) in December 1994[20]. The Maitland, FL-based division of Time Warner Entertainment is providing movies, video games, and home shopping services to about 4,000 customers in the suburban Orlando communities of Wekiva, Sweetwater, Lake Brantley, and Spring Lake Hills.

The Orlando area was chosen for this trial for several reasons, including the considerable amount of fiber cabling that was already available. Furthermore, central Florida is Time Warner Cable's second-largest division, with more than 484,000 customers in the region.

To provide continuous and simultaneous streams of video to thousands of customers requires more than a powerful file server with multiple processors. Hewlett-Packard's Video Communications division designed its MediaStream Server to meet the requirements of video-on-demand applications. At the heart of the server resides HP's Video Transfer Engine (VTE), which was created to economically and efficiently move large amounts of data, but not to compute it. The VTE consists of a Unix-based control subsystem, an ATM switch, a video output processor, a master video stream controller, and a data source.

The data source, based on a Unix-style read-time operating system called HP-RT, is linked to the MediaStream Applications Server (MAS), software based on HP-UX that initiates delivery of real-time data from the VTE. With this configuration, the only processing required is response to interrupts that come through the network and set up the switch. While other servers may need more CPUs to increase speed and bandwidth, the MediaStream needs more data sources. MediaStream Server can be scaled to accommodate 75 to 10,000 concurrent video streams.

Further, Sybase intends to port its intermedia products to the MediaStream Server as well as set-top boxes to build and deliver interactive applications. The Intermedia family consists of Intermedia Server, which is based on Sybase's SQL Server; and Gain Momentum, which allows developers to create multimedia applications; and Gain Interplay, which allows interactive applications to run on set-top boxes and Pcs.

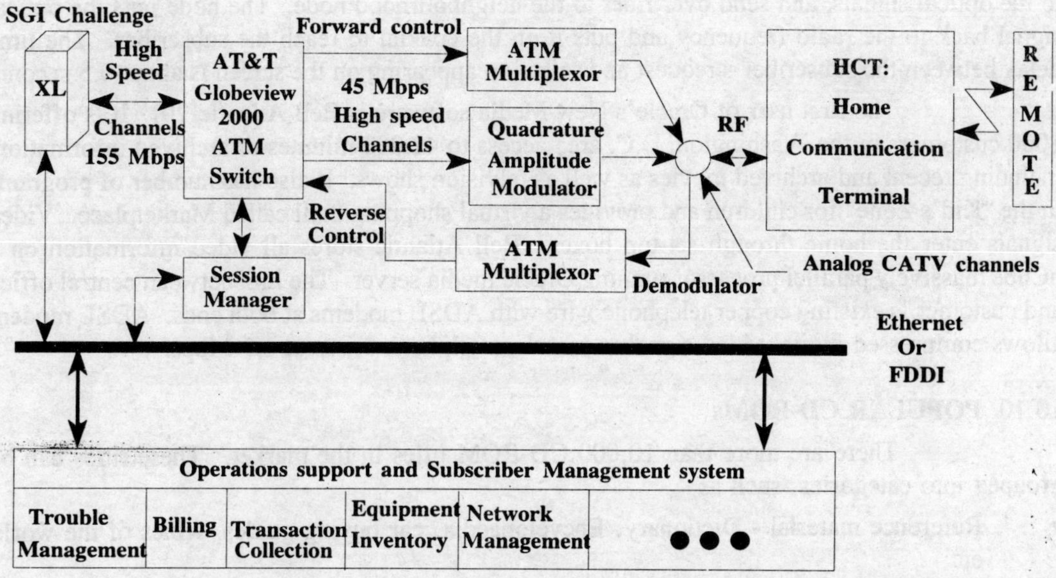

Figure 10.9 The Time Warner Cable Full Service Network (FSN)

When customers order a movie, they interact through a three-dimensional interface called Carousel Navigator (gateway to network offerings). With a remote control, subscribers send signals to a Home Communications Terminal (HCT) - similar to a set-top box. The HCT was developed jointly by Scientific-Atlanta, SGI, and Toshiba. The boxes, which contain a MIPS RISC processor from MIPS Technologies and Indy technology from SGI, form ATM packets into a data stream, decompress the video, and play the movie on the television set. Subscribers are provided a remote control, a optional HP Printer to print coupons and menus, and an Atari Jaguar game unit.

A request by subscriber's HCT travels on coaxial cable to one of the 16 nodes in the trial area. All the nodes are connected to the Network Operation Center (NOC) throgh fiber and receive signals at DS1 data rate of 1.5 Mbps. The Hitachi multiplexor combines the DS1 signals into a DS3 signal that runs at 45 Mbps to the ATM switch capable of routing packets upto a speed of 20 Gbps (see figure 10.9).

The SGI Challenge Media Server receives all requests from the ATM switch. It locates the appropriate program from an archive of MPEG compressed digital video from within it's terabytes of storage based on the request of the subscriber. The storage on the network at the end of 1995 was about 3 terabytes.

A movie once located by the media server is sent to the ATM switch in form of ATM packets of 48 bytes of data with a 5 byte address header. These packets travel from server to the ATM switch at OC3 speeds of 155 Mbps. These packets from the ATM switch go to Quadrature Amplitude Modulator (QAM) at 45 Mbps. QAM puts digital information onto radio frequency or broadband transmission to move throgh the network.

The digital information is superimposed onto the standard TV signal, converted to the optical signals, and send over fiber to the neighbourhood node. The node puts the optical signal back to the radio frequency and puts it on the coaxial to reach the subscriber. The time delay between the subscriber's request and selection appearing on the screen is about 0.5 second.

The first user of Oracle's New Media software is Bell Atlantic[20]. It is offering 1000 customers in the Washington, D.C. area access to 42,000 minutes of archived information, including recent and archived movies as well as telvision shows. It also has number of programs in the "Kid's Zone" for children and provides a virtual shopping mall called Marketplace. Video signals enter the home through set-top boxes. Bell Atlantic stores all video information on a nCube massively parallel processor running Oracle media server. The link between central office and customer is existing copper telephone wire with ADSL modems at both ends. ADSL modem allows compressed digital video signal to travel on telphone wires at 1.5 Mbps.

10.10 POPULAR CD-ROMs

There are more than 10,000 CD-ROM titles in the market. These titles can be grouped into categories, such as

- Reference material - Dictionary, Encyclopaedia, car buying guides, wines of the world etc;
- Home - home improvement, gardening, and leisure activities such as travel planning;
- Culture - Art gallery, cinema, and Opera guide;
- Science and Nature - Human anatomy, whales, astronomy and so on;
- History,
- Games,
- Education and other material of interest for children.

Given below is a list of few popular CD-ROMs[11,19]:

- 4 Paws of a Cab - A cook book Thai recipes, Live Oak Multimedia Inc.
- Cinemania, Microsoft - contains summary of 19000 films from contemporary to classic.
- Computer Select, Ziff Communications - contains full text of 28 computer magazines and abstract from 110 other periodicals.
- Compton's Interactive Encyclopaedia for Windows, Compton's Learning Company.
- Highway 61 Interactive, Graphix Zone - A Bob Dylan multimedia museum.
- Mayo Clinic Family Health Book, IVI Publishing - helps us understand anatomy, diseases, and health issues.
- McGraw Hill Science and Technical Reference Set, release 2.0, McGraw-Hill
- Microsoft Bookshelf, Microsoft - Comprises dictionary, thesaurus, World Almanac, Atlas, Encyclopedia, and dictionary of quotations.
- Encarta, Microsoft - Interactive Multimedia Encyclopedia - covers subjects such as Physical Science and Technology; Life Science; Geography; Social Science; History; Religion and Philosophy; Art, Language and Literature; Performing Arts; Sports, Hobbies, and Pets.
- Myst, Broderbund Software - A fantasy game.
- Star Trek: The Next Generation Interactive Technical Manual, Siman and Schuster Interactive - lets us explore the starship Enterprise and the entire federation.
- Taxi, Middlegate - lets us create personalized city maps of important American cities.

It also includes ratings of hotels and restaurants.

- Wines of the World, Multicom Publishing Inc.
- Disney's Animated Storybook: The Lion King, Disney Software.
- Multimedia Business 500 Release 2, Allergo New Media - Information on 500 leading U. S. Companies.
- Home PC Library, Allergo New Media - information to computer users interested in learning more about hardware and software.
- Memphis Math: Treasure of the Tombs, Novell Corp. - kids 8 - 14 can unravel a mystry that takes them to the Sphinx, the Pyramids at Giza, and the Mortuary Temple of Hatshepsut -- all while they are learning about decimals, fractions, and percentages.
- Sports Illustrated Multimedia Almanac, 1995 Edition, Star Press Multimedia - gives summary of all sports events of last 18 months.

10.11 SUMMARY

In the area of multimedia, the data requirement tends to be high and the time taken for retrieval of data is important. Methodologies and technologies will need to be developed not only for efficient storage of data but also provide sustained higher throughput rates. The hardware based multimedia solutions are comparatively expensive and for this reason software codecs are emerging which offer acceptable quality video which is adequate for many applications. The cost of codecs which are used to compress/decompress images will control the proliferation of this technology to different areas. Microsoft and Apple, with Video for Windows and QuickTime, respectively, influence the compression world, although they do not specifically provide their own codecs. The AVI (Audio Video Interleave) format in Video for Windows provides a standard file format for developers. Video for Windows includes Cinepak, Indeo, and Microsoft's RLE and Video 1.

One serious problem encountered by multimedia workers is that transferring files from system to system can result in slide services producing slides with colour that differs distressingly with what original creators saw on their screens. Standards for colour will need to be formalised as these are still in flux.

The opportunities for application of multimedia technology will continue to grow rapidly as CD-ROM technology advances, and other delivery media, such as "on-line" services over telephone and cable networks evolve. As the delivery technology advances, the content and the user experience will evolve as well, moving from a passive experience, involving text-oriented information to a more interactive experience, containing "richer" media such as video, sound and animation.

CD-ROM technology is only the first step in multimedia delivery and storage. A PC or workstation based architecture cannot meet the performance, scalableness, and reliability challenges of the multimedia processing and community/enterprise serving. We have discussed in section 10.5 the advantages and feasibility of using ATM protocols as the interconnect mechanism for a subsystem based multimedia server. As technology for storing and distributing media-rich data improves, large media servers will become widely available. These servers will allow such information to be distributed via network based computer systems. In the future, as the networking infra-structure evolves, media storage is likely to move to a more traditional client/server architecture, much like the data storage servers we see today.

10.12 REFERENCES

1. Arch C. Luther, *Digital Video in the PC environment*, Second Edition, McGraw Hill, New York, 1991.
2. Arch C. Luther, *Designing Interactive Multimedia*, Bantam Professional Books, Holms 1992.
3. Mark J. Bunzel and Sandra R. Morris, *Multimedia Applications Development using DVI Technology*, McGraw Hill, New York,1992.
4. IEEE Computer, *Special Issue on Multimedia Information Systems*, October, 91.
5. Pang H. Ang, Peter A. Ruetz, and David Auld, "Video Compression make big gains", IEEE Spectrum, pp.16-19, October 1991.
6. IEEE Computer Graphics and Application, *Special Issue on Multimedia*, July, 1991.
7. IEEE Transactions on Consumer Electronics, February 1992.
8. IEEE Computer, *Special issue on Multimedia Information Systems*, October 1991..
9. Communications of the ACM, *Special Issue on Digital Multimedia Systems*, April, 1991.
10. *Digital Video*, edited by Jurgen Ronald K. in IEEE Spectrum, pp.24-30, March 1992.
11. BYTE, *Best books and CD-ROMs*, p. 92, Sept. 1995
12. Steinmetz Ralf, "Analyzing the multimedia operating system," IEEE MultiMedia, vol. 2, no. 1, pp. 68-84, Spring 1995.
13. Stuart Wray, Tim Glauert and Andy Hopper, "Networked Multimedia: The Medusa Environment," IEEE Multimedia, Winter 1994, vol. 1, no. 4, pp. 54-63.
14. Rooholamini R. and V. Cherkassky, "ATM - Based Multimedia Servers," IEEE Multimedia, Spring 1995, vol. 2, no. 1, pp. 39-52.
15. Hayter M. and D. McAuley, "The desk are network," ACM Operating Syst. Rev., vol. 25, no. 4, Oct. 1991, pp. 14-21.
16. Quain John R., "An earful of sound boards," PC Magazine, Vol. 14, No. 6, March 28, 1995, pp. 167-217.
17. Ozer Jan, "Digital Video Shot by Shot," PC Magazine, Vol. 14, No. 7, April 11, 1995, pp. 104-163.
18. Bryan John, " Compression Scorecard," Byte, Vol. 14, No. 6, May 1995, pp. 107-112.
19. Top 100 CD-ROMs, Cover Story, PC Magazine, Vol. 14, N0. 12, June 27, 1995. Pp. 102-165.
20. Karve Anita, " Channel Surfing," Interoperabilty - A Supplement to LAN, Nov. 1995, pp. 46-50.

APPENDIX I

Graphics functions available in Turbo Pascal 7.0, Turbo C++ and Borland C++ version 4.5

The various graphics functions available with Turbo Pascal version 7.0 are listed below.

Category	Function Name	Function description
Graphic System Control	CloseGraph	Shuts down the graphics system.
	DetectGraph	Checks the hardware and determines which graphics driver and mode to use..
	GraphDefaults	all graphics system variable are reset to their default settings..
	_graphgetmem	Allocates graphics memory; hook for defining user routine.
	_graphfreemem	Deallocates graphics memory; hook for defining user routine.
	GetGraphMode	Returns the current graphics mode.
	GetModeRange	Returns the lowest and highest valid graphcis mode for a given driver.
	InitGraph	Initializes the graphics system and puts the hardware into graphics mode.
	InstallUserDriver	Installs a vendor-added device driver to the BGI device driver table.
	InstallUserFont	Installs a new font file that isn't built into the BGI system.
	RegisterBGIdriver	Registers a valid BGI driver with the graphics system.
	RestoreCrtMode	Restores the original screen mode before graphics is initialized.
	SetGraphBufSize	Changes the size of the buffer used for scan and flood fills.
	SetGraphMode	Sets the system to graphics mode and clears the screen.
	SetWriteMode	Sets the writing mode (copy or xor) for lines drawn by DrawPoly, Line, LineRel, LineTo, and Rectangle.

Category	Function Name	Function description
Drawing	Arc	Draws a circular arc from start angle to Fillingend angle using (x,y) as the center point.
	Circle	Draws a circle using (x,y) as the center point.
	DrawPoly	Draws the outline of a polygon using the current line style and color.
	Ellipse	Draws an elliptical arc from start angle to end angle, using (x,y) as the center point.
	GetArcCoords	Allows the user to use coordinates of the last arc command.
	GetAspectRatio	Returns the aspect ratio (Xasp:Yasp) of the current graphics mode..
	GetLineSettings	Returns the current line style, line pattern, and line thickness as set by SetLineStyle
	Line	Draws a line from a (x1, y1) to (x2, y2).
	LineRel	Draws a line to relative distance from the current position (CP).
	LineTo	Draws a line from the current position to (x,y).
	MoveTo	Moves the current graphics position (CP) to (x,y).
	MoveRel	Moves the current position to (CP) a relative distance from its current position.
	Rectangle	Draws a rectangle using the current line style and color
	SetAspectRatio	Changes the default aspect ratio.
	SetLineStyle	Sets the current line width and style.
	Bar	Draws a bar using the current fill style and color.
	Bar3D	Draws a 3-D bar using the current fill style and color.
	FillEllipse	Draws a filled ellipse using (x,y) as a center point and XRadius and YRadius as the horizontal and vertical axes.
	FillPoly	Draws and fills a ploygon,
	FloodFill	Fills a bounded region using the current fill pattern and fill color..
	GetFillPattern	Returns the user defined fill pattern.

Category	Function Name	Function description
Drawing	GetFillSettings	Allows inquiry about the current fill pattern and color. or PieSlice Draws and fills a pie slice, using (x,y) as the center point and drawing from start angle to end angle
	Sector	Draws and fills an elliptical sector..
	SetFillPattern	Selects a user-defined fill pattern
	SetFillStyle	Sets the fill pattern and color.
Manipulating the port	ClearDevice	Clears the action page screen.
	SetActivePage	Sets the active page for graphics output.
	SetVisualPage	Sets the visual graphics page number.
	ClearViewPort	Clears the current viewport.
	GetViewSettings	Allows inquiry about the current viewport and clipping parameters.
	SetViewPort	Sets the current output viewport f o r graphics output.
	GetImage	Saves a bit image of the specified region to memory.
	ImageSize	Returns the number of bytes required to store a rectangular region of the screen.
	PutImage	Puts a previously saved bit image onto the screen
	GetPixel	Gets the pixel color at (x, y).
	PutPixel	Plots a pixel at (x,y).
Text Output	GetTextSettings	Returns the current text font, direction, size, and justification as set by SetText Style and SetTextJustify
	OutText	Sends a string to the output device at the current pointer (CP).
	OutTextXY	Sends a string to the output d the specified position.
	RegisterBGIfont	Registersa linked-in or user-loaded fonts.
	SetTextJustify	Sets text justificat ion values used by OutText and OutTextXY.
	SetTExtStyle	Sets the current text font, style, and character magnification factor.
	SetUserCharSize	Lets you change the character width and height for stroked fonts.
	TextHeight	Returns the height of a string in pixels.
	TextWidth	Returns the width of a string in pixels.

Category	Function Name	Function description
Color Control	GetBkColor	Returns the current background color.
	GetColor	Returns the current drawing color.
	GetDefaultPalette	Returns the palette definiton structure.
	GetMaxColor	Returns the maximum color value that can be passed to SetColor.
	GetPalette	Returns the current palette and its size.
	GetPaletteSize	Returns the size of the palette color look-up table.
	SetAllPalette	Changes all palette colors as specified.
	SetBkColor	Sets the current background color using the palette.
	SetColor	Sets the current drawing color using the palette.
	SetPalette	Changes one palette color as specified by its arguments
	SetRGB Palette	Modifies palette entries for the IBM 8514 and the VGA drivers
Error Handling	GraphErrorMsg	Returns an error message string for the specified ErrorCode.
	GraphResult	Returns an error code for the last graphics operation.
State Query	GetArcCoords	Gets coordinates of the last Arc command.
	GetAspectRatio screen.	Returns the aspect ratio of the graphics
	GetBkColor	Returns the current background color.
	GetColor	Returns the current drawing color
	Getdrivername	Returns name of current graphics drivers.
	GetFillPattern	Returns the last fill pattern set by a call to SetFillPattern.
	GetFillSettings	Allows inquiry about the current fill pattern and color.
	GetGraphMode	Returns the current graphics mode.
	GetLineSettings	Returns the current line style, line pattern, and line thickness .
	GetMaxColor	Returns the highest color that can be passed to SetColor.
	GetMaxMode	Returns the maximum mode number for the currently loaded driver.

Category	Function Name	Function description
State Query	GetMaxX	Returns the current *x* resolution
	GetMaxY	Returns the current *y* resolution.
	GetModeName	Returns a string containing the name of the current graphics mode.
	GetModeRange	Returns the lowest and highest valid graphcis mode for a given driver.
	Getpalette.	Returns the current palette and its size.
	GetPixel	Gets the pixel value at (x, y).
	GetTextSettings	Returns the current text font, direction, size, and justification.
	GetViewSettings	Allows inquiry about the current viewport and clipping parameters.
	GetX	Returns the x-coordinate of the current position (CP).
	GetY	Returns the y-coordinate of the current position(CP).

Borland C++ version 4.5

Given below are the Borland C++ library routines available to 16-bit DOS applications. The main difference is that function names in C are only in lowercase letters. Library routines are composed of functions and macros. These can be called from within both C and C++ programmes. The DOS specific applications use static run time libraries (OBJ and LIB). These graphics routines let a user create on screen graphics with text. The graphics routines available with C++ are similar to those described above for the Turbo Pascal. A list of routines contained in graphics.h is given on the following page. They are not described in detail as they are similar to the corresponding routine in Turbo Pascal, and in most cases the names themselves indicate the functions.

Graphics Routines available with Borland C++ version 4.5

arc
bar
bar3d
circle
cleardevice
clearviewpoint
closegraph
detectgraph
drawpoly
ellipse
fillellipse
fillpoly
floodfill
getarccoords
getaspectratio
getbkcolor
getcolor
getdefaultpalette
getdrivername
getfillpattern
getfillsettings
getgraphmode
getimage
getlinesettings
getmaxcolor
getmaxmode
getmaxx
getmaxy
getmodename
getmoderange
getpalette
getpalettesize
getpixel
gettextsettings
getviewsettings
getx
gety
graphdefaults
grapherrormsg
_graphfreemem
_graphgetmem
graphresult
imagesize
initgraph
installuserdriver
installuserfont
line
linerel
lineto
moverel
moveto
outtext
outtextxy
pieslice
putimage
putpixel
rectangle
registerbgidriver
registerbgifont
restorecrtmode
sector
setactivepage
setallpalette
setaspectratio
setbkcolor
setcolor
_setcursortype
setfillpattern
setfillstyle
setgraphbufsize
setgraphmode
setlinestyle
setpalette
setrgbpalette
settextjustify
settextstyle
setusercharsize
setviewport
setvisualpage
setwritemode
textheight
textwidth

APPENDIX II

COMPARISON OF PASCAL AND *C* LANGUAGES

	PASCAL	*C*

Basic program structure	Program name
	Uses clause
	Const decl
	Type statement
	Variable decl
	Procedure or functions
	begin
	Main prog statements
	end.
		Include files
		#define
		Typedef statements
		Variable & function decl
		main()
		{
		Main prog statements
		}
		functions

Case Sensitive	No	Yes
Varaiable Intilization	No	Always Zero
Comments	(* or {)* or }	/* */
Begin End	begin end;	{ }
Assignment	:=	=
Exit from program	Halt	exit
Exit from block	exit	break (Which is exit from loop)
Include File	{$I <filename> }	#include <filename>

<table>
<tr><td>Constants</td><td></td><td></td></tr>
<tr><td></td><td>< var > = < value >;</td><td>#define < var > < value ></td></tr>
<tr><td>Type</td><td></td><td></td></tr>
<tr><td></td><td>< name > : < type >;</td><td>typedef < type > < name >;</td></tr>
<tr><td>Procedure/
Function</td><td>Procedure fname (par decl) or
Function fnane (par decl): < type >;
local declaration
begin
    statements
end;
Name := < value return ></td><td>void fname(par decl) or
< Type > fname (pardecl)
{
    local declaration
    statements
}
return(< value return >)</td></tr>
<tr><td>Operators</td><td></td><td></td></tr>
<tr><td>Relational</td><td>=
< ></td><td>= =
! =</td></tr>
<tr><td>Logical</td><td>not
and
or</td><td>!
&&
||</td></tr>
<tr><td>Boolean</td><td>not
and
or
xor</td><td>~
&
|
^</td></tr>
<tr><td>Shift left</td><td>shl</td><td>< <</td></tr>
<tr><td>Shift right</td><td>shr</td><td>> ></td></tr>
<tr><td>Arithmetic</td><td>Div
Mod</td><td>/</td></tr>
<tr><td>Set</td><td>+ for union
- for difference
* for intersection
< = subset
> = superset
= same
in member of</td><td>No such opearators</td></tr>
<tr><td>String</td><td>+ for concat
= or < >
< =, <
> =, ></td><td>use concat function
use strcmp or stricmp func</td></tr>
<tr><td>Data types</td><td></td><td></td></tr>
<tr><td></td><td>char [0-255]
byte
integer, longint</td><td>char [-128 127]
unsigned short
short , int , long</td></tr>
</table>

	real	float double or long double
	String (S : string[N])	Array of char (char S[N})
	represented as '	as "
	boolean	not available
		to be declared using enum type
		enum boolean = (false, true)
Pointer		
	intptr^	*intptr
	Nil	NULL
	New	malloc
	Dispose	free
	<name> : ^<Type>;	<type> *<name>
	<name> := <value>	<name>= <value>
Array		
Declaration	<Name>:array[<low>..<High>] of <type>;	<type><name>[Size];
Index	1 to Size	0 to (Size -1)
Records		
Declaration	<name> = record <var name> : <type>; end	typedef struct { <type> <var name> } <name>
	File of record exist	No such file
	With statement	No such statement
Object		

Declaration	<name> = object
	<var/fnc name> : <type>;
	end
		class <name> {
		<type> <var/fnc name>
		public:
		fnc name(s)
		}

Read/Write		
	read & readln	fscanf , fgets ,gets
	write & writeln	fprintf
File operations		

	Pascal	C
Declaration	<name> : <type>	FILE *name
	assign & reset & rewrite	fopen
	close	fclose
	flush	fflush
	seek	fseek
	erase	remove
	eof	feof
	filepos	ftell
If		
	if <exp> then	if (<exp>) {
	<Statements>	<statements> }
	else	else {
	<statements>	<statements> }
While		
	while <exp> do	while (<exp>)
	begin	{
	<statements>	<statements>
	end	}
repeat-until		
	repeat	do
	<statements>	<statements>
	until <exp>;	while (<exp>);
case		
	case <exp> of	switch (<exp>) {
	item : <statements>;	case <item> :
		<statements>;
		break;
	else	default
	<statements>;	<statements>;
	end;	}

In case of *C*, the switch statement is executed from the case till end of switch or till break statement is reached.

	Pascal	C
for		
	for <index> :<start> to <end> do	for (exp1;exp2;exp3)
		{
	<statements>;	<statements>; }
		exp1 is initilization
		exp2 is condition of exit
Library differences		
	Readkey;	getch
	UpCase	to_upper

	Chr	putch
	Int	floor
	Frac	modf
	Str	itoa
	ln	log
	Sqr(x)	x*x
	Val	atoi
	Random	rand
	Length	strlen , strnlen
	concat	strcat , strncat
	copy	strcpy
	delete/insert	not available
	pos	strstr
Ordinal functions		
	Ord	not available
	Dec	
	Inc	
	High	
	Low	
	Odd	
	Pred	
	Succ	
Integer division	no truncation	decimal is truncated.

APPENDIX III

STANDARDS

AIII.1 Introduction [1-5]

Standards can be grouped into three categories :

- Industry accepted but not formally approved by accredited standards making bodies;
- formally approved but irrelevant; and
- data sets used to test graphics system, e.g., see teapot in chapter 7.

The principle idea of developing graphic standards initially was to make main body of software device independent. The software should (i) interface with any device through a handler which, however, will be device dependent; (ii) be portable from one graphic system to another one of a different type; and (iii) not only be portable but even programmer should also be portable.

The device independent software was grouped into one for the construction and the other for manipulating an object followed by creating views of the object. Thus, two co-ordinate system emerged, the world co-ordinate system in which object is constructed and device co-ordinate system to display the object. These efforts led to 1979 Siggraph 'Core Standard' and many vendors developed compatible systems. It was, however, never adopted as a standard. In 1979, West German standards organisation forwarded the Graphical Kernel System (GKS) to International Standards Organisation. GKS differed from core graphics system proposed by ACM/Siggraph in a number of ways. For instance, initially GKS was 2-D only while core was 3-D system with a compatible 2-D subset. GKS adapted a workstation concept, which attempted to further device independence while exploiting power of hardware. GKS does not use concept of current position and contains language binding. Fortran binding was part of the initial standard and binding for other languages was in the offing GKS-3D standard is 3-dimensional extension of GKS.

A procedural or programming interface standard covers an active interface, providing for the exchange of both data and instructions between software packages running simultaneously. A data exchange interface specifies a means of moving static data between software not at the same time. GKS and Computer Graphics Metafile (CGM) are examples of procedural and data exchange standards respectively..

A number of graphics standards as briefly described below have emerged :

i. Initial Graphics Exchange Specification (IGES) was approved in 1981 as ANSI standard Y14.26 M. It was originally meant for the transfer of drawing data but eventually evolved into exchange of graphics databases among CAD/CAM systems. French standard SET and the German VDAFS cover automobile surface data exchange. IGES 2.0, 3.0 or 4.0 have been used as the reference for the design of most commercial processors. CSG solid representations are included in IGES 4.0 and incorporation of B-reps is scheduled in the next version.

ii. North American Presentation Level Protocol (NAPLPS) was accepted by Canada and ANSI in 1983. It uses sequences of bytes in ASCII code and code extensions to describe graphics and text over a low capacity communication link.

iii. Graphical Kernel System(GKS) emphasized on device independent programming. (GKS 3-D) is extension of original GKS.

iv. Computer Graphics Metafile (CGM) - data exchange standard.

v. Programmers Hierarchical Interface to Graphics Standard (PHIGS) - It is an updated, expanded, dynamic, 3-D version of core that will function at the same level as GKS. PHIGS has now been adopted by ANSI and ISO. Work on PHIGS+ has also started;

vi. Virtual Device Metafile (VDM) - It is a device independent format for computer graphics.

vii. Virtual Device Interface (VDI) operates at same level as VDM, VDE is two way communication protocol. It is the interface between device independent software and device dependent code.

AIII.2 Abbreviations of Graphic and Other Relevant Standards and Accredited Organisation

ANSI	American National Standards Institute
BNF	Bacchius-Naur form
BSI	British Standards Institute
CAX	Computer-aided … system
CCITT	Consultative Committee for International Telephone and Telegraphy
CEN	Comite European de Normalisation
Cenelec	Comite European de Normalisation Electronique
CGM	Computer Graphics Metafile
CIM-OSA	Open System Architecture for CIM
CMIT	Mixed Commission for Transmission of Television and Sound
DIN	Deutsches Institute fur Normung eV
EDIF	Electronic design interchange format
GKS	Graphical Kernel System, an international graphics standard
IEC	international Electrotechnical Committee
IGES	Initial Graphics Exchange Specification
ISO	International Standards Organisation
MPEG	Moving Pictures Experts Group
PDES	Product data exchange using Step.
PHIGS	Programmers' Hierarchical Interactive Graphics System, an ANSI standard
PHIGS+	Surface rendering extensions to PHIGS
SET	Standard d' Exchange et de Transfert
SMPTE	Society for Moving Picture and Television Engineers
Step	Standard for the Exchange of Product Model Data
VDAFS	Verband der Deutschen Automobilindustrie-Flachenschnittstelle
X	X Windows server and protocol.

AIII.3 Portability Standards

AIII.3.1 Operating-system services

- Kernel operations. Portable Operating System Interface for Computer Environment (Posix), FIPS 151-1.
- Commands and utilities. IEEE P1003.2 (Posix shell and utilities), proposed FIPS.
- System Administration IEEE P1003.7.

AIII.3.2 User-interface services

- Client-server operations. X-Window System, FIBS 158.
- Presentation. Extensible Virtual Tool kit.

AIII.3.3 Programming services

- CAINS X., 159 (1989)
- Fortran. FIBS 069-1
- Pascal. FIBS 109

AIII3.4. Data-interchange service

- Documents interchange. Office Document Architecture/Office Document Interchange Format, ISO 8613, proposed FIBS; Standard Generalized Markup Language, FIBS 152.
- Graphics-data interchange. Computer Graphics Metafile, FIBS 128.
- Product-data interchange. Initial Graphics Exchange Specification, planned FIBS; Standard for Exchange of Product Model Data, draft ISO standard.

AIII.3.5 Graphics services

- Graphical Kernel System, FIBS 120.
- Programmer's Hierarchical Interactive Graphics System, FIBS 153.

AIII.4 Multimedia[6]

- JPEG:Joint Photographic Experts Group - Digital compression and coding of continuous-tone still images that achieves very high compression ratios with some loss of quality. Digital compression and coding of continuous-tone still images that achieves very high compression ratios with some loss of quality. See chapter 10 for details.

- MPEG: The Moving Picture Expert Group were given the mandate to develop standards for coded representation of moving pictures, associated audio and their combination when used for storage and retrieval on digital storage media. The resultant work carried by the committee led to development of coding up to 1.5, 10, and 40 Mbps – were nicknamed MPEG - 1, -2, and -3 respectively. The MPEG-3 was dropped in 1992, as the scope of MPEG-2 made it redundant. The MPEG-2 is now at the International standard stage and is evolving in two directions - i) DSM-CC, 10bit video coding and non-backwards- compatible (NBC) audio coding; ii) the MPEG-4 work item, approved in July 1993 for audio-visual coding at very low bit rates.

- MHEG (Multimedia and Hypermedia Information Object Expert Group): defines classes of objects, the design of which relies on analysing their common behavior and the common properties among object categories.Digital compression and coding of continuous-tone still images that achieves very high compression ratios with some loss of quality. See chapter 10 for details.

AIII.5 References

1. Blyth D., Boldyrefee C., and Tetteh - Larty - N., "The case of formal methods in standards", IEEE Software, pp.65-67, Sept. 1990.
2. Kroszynski Uril, Palstroem Bjarne, Trostmann Erik and Schlechtendahl E.C., "Geometric Data Transfer between CAD Systems : Solid Models", CG&A, pp.57-71, Sept. 1989.
3. Mchover Cart and Myers Ware, "Interactive Computer Graphics", IEEE Computer, pp, 145-161, Oct 1984.
4. Wilson P.R. " Standards : Port Tense Future Perfect", CG&A, pp.44-48, Jan. 1991.
5. Wilson P.R., "A Short history of CAD data transfer standards", CG&A, pp.64, June, 1987.
6. Liu Pieya, " MPEG: A Technological Basis for Multimedia Applications," IEEE Multimedia, Vol. 2, No. 1, Spring 1995, pp. 85-89.

APPENDIX IV

Glossary

3-D Graphics	Computer-graphics representations of 3-D objects. Usually this term implies that the objects themselves are mathematically defined in the computer, as opposed to digitized photographic pictures of real 3-D objects.
A/B Roll	Video that is compiled from two sources in video-editing software, a scene editor, or video construction window often provides two tracks, sometimes called track A and track B, for one video. Additional special effects (F/X) and superimposition tracks allow you to combine, overlap, and move between video clips with sophisticated transitions.
Abbreviated button	A button that is displayed as a small square with a glyph inside the border.
Abbreviated menu	A menu button that is displayed as a small square button with a hollow triangle inside the border. The points downward when the menu is displayed below the menu button, and to the right when the menu is displayed to the right.
Ab initio design	From the beginning (Latin). Used to describe design processes in which the designer inputs his or her ideas without constraints directly into the computer.
Access time	In mass storage devices, the time from issuance of a command to read or write a specific location until reading or writing actually begins location.
Additive Color model	Red, green, and blue are called the additive or primary colors because various intensities of these three colors can be added together to form any other color.
Affine map	Any map that is composed of translations, rotations, scalings, and shears.
Algorithm	A group of processing steps that perform a particular operation, such as drawing a line, or compressing a digital image.
Aliasing	In sampling, the impairment produced when the input signal contains frequency components higher than half of the sampling rate. Typically produces jagged steps on diagonal edges. See anti-aliasing.

American National Institute Standards (ANSI) — A standards-setting institute. ASCII and ANSI-standard C was set by this institute.

Anaglyphic Stereoscopy — The art of making 3-D images by wearing goofy looking but fun red/blue glasses and displaying a red image for one eye and a blue image for the other.

Anaglyphs — Pictures made to be viewed with red/blue 3-D glasses.

Analog video — Video in which all the information representing images is in a continuous-scale electrical signal for both amplitude and time.

Animation — Simulating motion by displaying a sequence of images in rapidsuccession.

Anti-aliasing — The process of reducing the visibility of aliasing by using gray scale pixel values to smooth the appearance of jagged edges.

Application Programming Interface (API) — Defines a standard way for a programmer to use functions of an operating system (such as Windows) in his or her own programs.

Application Window — In Windows, the main screen window for a program.

Approximation — Fitting a curve or surface to given data. As opposed to interpolation, the curve or surface approximation only has to be close to data.

Arc — A part of a circle.

Artifact — In video systems, something unnatural or unintended observed in the reproduction of an image by the system.

Artificial Reality — As defined by Myron Kreuger, "An artificial reality perceives a participant's action in terms of body's relationship to a graphic world and generates response that maintain the illusion that his or her actions are taking place within that world."

Aspect ratio — The ratio of the width to the height of an electronic image. For broadcast television, the standard aspect ratio is 4:3.

AutoCAD — A popular computer-aided drafting program from Autodesk, Inc. It is the source of the .DXF file format.

Automatic Disk Compression — The process of removing extra spaces and repetitive patterns from data as it is written on a hard disk, and restoring the data to its original form when it is read from the disk. Programs such as Stac Electronic's Stacker and Microsoft's DoubleSpace can do disk compression automatically.

Audio-Video Support System (AVSS)	In the DVI runtime software, the data structure which contains the parameters for how graphics operations are to be performed.
Automatic scrolling	When not all of a file is visible in a window, the view in a pane automatically shifts to follow the movement of the pointer as users press SELECT and wipe through the data.
AVI (Audio/video Interlaced)	A video format that interleaves alternating video and audio data. The format is easily compressed and decompressed.
Axis	A dimension, often represented by a line passing through the zero-point on another perpendicular axis.
Backface Culling	A hidden surface removal technique that eliminates facets that face away from the screen.
Background	An underlying area on which objects, such as controls and windows, are displayed.
Basic pointer	A pointer that shows the mouse position on the workspace.
Bernstein polynomials	The basis functions for Bezier curves.
Bezier curve	A polynomial curve that is expressed in terms of Bernstein polynomials.
Bezier polygon	The coefficients in the expansion of a Bezier curve in terms of Bernstein polynomials are points connected according to their natural numbering, they form the Bezier polygon.
Bitmap	Bitmapped graphics render an image as a pattern of dots. The program records the position of each dot. The bitmap is an array of values in the frame buffer for a certain image.
Bitmap Brush	A drawing tool (within Windows and other graphics systems) that uses a bitmapped pattern to fill in a region.
Bitmap font	A special format of a text font that contains pixel values for each text character.

Bitmapped Graphics	Computer graphics images that are stored pixel-by-pixel, as they appear on the screen (in contrast to *vector graphics*).
Bits per pixel	The number of bits used to represent the color value of each pixel in a digitized image.
Blending Functions	Functions used in free form Bezier and Spline curves and surfaces to control the weighted influence of control points.
Blobs	Quadratic fluid objects that can deform each other by attractive or repellant forces.
Blur	The process of averaging adjacent colors in an image to make it look blurry.
BMP	A Microsoft Windows bitmap (can be used for Windows wallpaper)
bpp	See bits per pixel.
Bilinear patch	A patch that is ruled in two directions on a hyperbolic paraboloid.
Bit plane	In digital video display hardware which has more than one video memory array contributing to the displayed image in real time, each memory array is called an image plane; however, if the arrays have only one bit-per-pixel, they may be called bit planes.
Blocking window	A window that does not allow input to any other window of the application except itself.
Bounding box	A rectangle that is displayed on the screen to define a region for selection.
Breakpoint	Same as a knot.
Brightness	The apparent lightness of an image or part of an image or part of an image.
Browser	A hypertext reader for accessing the World Wide Web. Mosaic and Lynx are commonly used browsers.
Brush	A shape used to draw with or used to fill a region.
B-spline	A piecewise polynomial function. It is defined over a knot partition, has

	local support, and is nonnegative. If a spline curve is expressed in terms of B-splines, it is called a B-spline curve.
Bulletin Board System	Computer system connected to a telephone line that allows online users to send and to receive messages and files.
Bump Mapping	A rendering technique for producing the illusion of a three dimensional bumpy surface by modulating the surface normals with a two-dimensional "bump map".
B-spline polygon	The coefficients in the expansion of a B-spline curve in terms of B-splines are points. Connected according to their natural numbering, they form the B-spline polygon.
Busy pattern	A standard pattern displayed in the header of a window or within the border of a button to show that the application is temporarily performing a function and cannot accept input.
Busy pointer	The pointer that is displayed by the system when an application is busy and cannot accept input at the pointer location.
Cable	The scrollbar cable represents the total size of the data that users can view in the pane. The elevator moves up and down the cable to show the position of the view into the data.
Cache	High-speed memory stored on or near the microprocessor to improve data retrieval efficiency.
CAD	Computer-aided drafting, or computer-aided design. Sometimes called CADD, to mean computer-aided drafting and design.
CAGD	Computer Aided Geometric Design.
Cathode Ray Tube (CRT)	The name for the display technology used in most computer monitors and televisions.
CD	See compact disc.
CD-I	See Compact Disc-Interactive.
CDR	CorelDRAW vector drawing file.
CD-ROM	See Compact Disc-Read-Only Memory.

CD-ROM XA | A compact-disc ROM extended architecture that specifies an encoding format (adaptive differential pulse code modulation) for storing audio information in a digital format.

CDTV | Commodore Dynamic Total Vision, a multimedia system.

CGM | Computer graphics metafile, another ''universal standard'' that never caught on. The Windows metafile is a more well-known variation on the same theme.

Channel separation | It is simply the degree to which left and right channel signals remain distinct from one another. Ideally, channel separation should be infinite - meaning that no signal leaks from one channel into the other. Crossover in excess of 50 dB would likely mask the beneficial effects of stereo imaging.

Check boxes | A nonexclusive setting that shows a check mark in a square box when the setting is chosen.

Chroma-Key | A video process that allows one image to be selectively superimposed into another only in pixel regions where the color is a special hue.

Chrominance | The color dimension of a video signal.

Click | To press a mouse button once and release it without moving the pointer beyond the damping factor.

Client Area | In Windows, the region of a window where the application is allowed to draw.

Clipboard | The means for keeping track of data that is cut or copied.

Clipping Plane | In 3-D rendering, objects beyond the clipping plane are considered to be behind the viewer's head and are not displayed.

CMYK Color Model | Cyan-Magenta-Yellow-Black color model, used when printing on paper. The opposite of the RGB color model.

Coding | The process of representing a varying function as a series of digital numbers.

Color Balance | The relative intensities of red, green, and blue in a computer image, or cyan, magenta, and yellow in a printed picture.

Color bars	A test pattern of composed rectangles of different colors: white, yellow, cyan, green, magenta, and black.
Color Cycling	The process of rapidly rotating the values in the palette (color look up table) to animate the entire screen at once.
Color Look-Up Table (CLUT)	Also referred to as a palette or color palette, it is used in video systems where only 8 bits or less are available for each pixel, and an 18-bit or 24 -bit color value is stored in the CLUT, which determines the actual color of a pixel on the screen.
Color Plane	Colors are usually stored as red, green, and blue component values. The collection of all the blue component values is called the " blue color plane," and so forth.
Color Resolution	The number of colors that can be displayed on the screen at once. For example, standard VGA has a maximum color resolution of 256 colors, which requires 8 bits per pixel to store the color number.
Color Space	It represents an abstract 3-D space where the three dimensions are red, green, and blue (or cyan, magenta, yellow; or hue, saturation, lightness, depending on the color model chosen). The set of colors visible to the eye or displayable by a monitor can be represented as a region in color space.
Color Triangle	It represents a slice of color space, where each corner of the triangle represents red, green, or blue. The region within the triangle shows all possible mixtures of the three component colors at a particular light intensity.
Color Values	The actual numerical description of the intensities of red, green, and blue light to be displayed at a particular point on the screen.
Collision detection	A property programmed into a simulation that detects when objects come in contact with each other - a concept used in virtual reality and animation.
Collinear	Being on a straight line.
Compact Disc (CD-I)	An interactive audio/video/computer system developed by Sony Interactive and Philips for the consumer market.
Composite Video	A video format in which chrominance and luminance are mixed together into one signal. See S-video.

Compositing	A process in which a video is superimposed over another video and compiled into a single video file. Also called *superimposition overlay.*
Command window	A pop-up window that is used to execute application commands or set parameters.
Compact disk (CD)	The 12 cm. (4.75 in.) optical read-only disc used disk for storing digital audio, data, or video.
Compact Disc-Read-Only Memory (CD-ROM)	An adaptation of the Compact Disc for use with general digital data.
Component video	Three color video signals that describe a color image. Typical components systems are R, G, B; Y, I, Q; or Y, U,V.
Composite video	A color video signal that contains all of the color information in one signal. Typical composite television standard signals are NTSC, PAL, and SECAM.
Compression	A digital process that allows data to be stored or transmitted using less than the normal number of bits. Video compression refers to techniques that reduce the number of bits required to store or transmit images. Conic section The intersection curve between a cone and a plane or a projective image of a parabola.
Control polygon	See Bezier polygon or B-spline polygon.
Controls	Objects in a control area, a pane, or on a menu that are used to perform an action. buttons, items on menus, exclusive and nonexclusive settings, sliders, gauges, text fields, and check boxes.
Control Points	Points in any graphics or CAD image that allow a user to control some part of the image with the mouse.
Coons patch	A patch that is fitted between four arbitrary boundary curves.
Coordinate	A numerical location along an axis.
Convolution	A mathematical technique for image processing.
Convertibility	Capability of being converted to and from existing standards.
Copy	Command to duplicate selected text or graphics onto the clipboard.

CSG	Constructive Solid Geometry, a method of defining complex objects where solid volumes are added or subtracted together.
Cursor	The little icon that shows where the mouse or text editing point is on the screen.
Current item	An active item in a scrolling list.
Cut	To remove selected objects from a window and store them on the clipboard.
Cyan	The color obtained by mixing equal intensities of green and blue light. It is also the correct name for the subtractive primary color usually called "blue".
Cyber	See *cybernetics*
Cybernetics	Coined in 1948 by Norbert Wiener; from the Greek *kybernetes*, or "helmsman," + -ics. A science dealing with the comparative study of the operations of complex electronic computers and the human nervous system.
Cyberspace	Science-fiction author, William Gibson used this term to describe a shared virtual environment whose inhabitants, objects, and spaces are comprised of data that is visualized, heard, and touched. W. Gibson, in his book entitled, *'Neuromancer'*, described it as "a consensual hallucination experienced daily by billions of legitimate operators in every nation . . . a graphic representation of data abstracted from the banks of every computer in the human system."
Curve	The path of a point moving through space.
Data Compression	Algorithms such as RLE and LZW that encode and decode data so that it can occupy less memory or disk space.
DCX	A bunch of PCX images all crammed into one file.
Decimal	The ten-valued numbering system we normally use for counting money and almost everything else.
Decode	To read a file and translate the data back into the original form it had before it was stored in the file.
Depth Cues	Visual information that helps the brain translate two-dimensional images

into a mental image of 3-D space.

Data rate	The speed of a data transfer process, normally expressed in bits per second or bytes per second.
DataGlove	A gesture recognition device that enables navigation through a virtual environment and interaction with 3D objects within it. DataGlove has fibre-optic cables along its fingers and wrist and an orientation sensor for navigation and virtual object manipulation. DataGlove is a trademark of VPL Research.
Data Stream	The incoming stream of data when reading a file from a disk.
Device Context	Windows programming jargon meaning the state the display (or another device) is in.
Device-Dependent Bitmap	Windows storage format that stores images in a format similar to the way they are stored on the PC.
Device Driver	A small software program to interface with a physical piece of hardware.
Device independent	In computer graphics software, an interface specification that does not depend on the characteristics of any particular graphics device. Also used to refer to a similar independence in any software, not just graphics.
Device-independent Bitmap (DIB)	Windows storage format that stores images in a form that can be used on any type of computer.
DFT	Discrete Fourier Transform, a mathematical technique used in image processing.
Diffuse Digital video	Video where all the information representing images is in a digital form, which can be manipulated and displayed by a computer
Digitizing	The process of converting an analog signal into a digital signal. With images, it includes scanning and analog-to-digital conversion.
Discrete cosine	A form of coding used in most of the current transform current image compression systems to reduce the number of bits that must be transmitted.
DLL	Dynamic Link Library, a code file containing routines that can be shared by multiple programs or instanced multiple times.

Drag	To press and hold down any mouse button while moving the pointer - and the object under the pointer - on the screen.
Drag Area	The area in the middle of the scrollbar elevator or slider.
DRAM	Dynamic RAM, read/write random-access memory. This is the standard type of RAM used in personal computer main memory. Dynamic RAM requires a periodic refresh operation in order to retain its data.
Driver	A software entity that provides a software interface to a specific piece of hardware. For example, the CD-ROM driver provides software access to the data stored on it.
DXF	Data exchange format, the common file format used by many CAD and rendering packages.
Dynamic Link Library	See DLL.
Dynamic range	It is the difference, expressed in dB, between the highest signal a device can handle and the lowest signal (discernible) from the residual noise.
Edit decision List	A list of video editing instructions, sometimes generated by video editing software. It includes time code stamps, duration, trim marks, sequencing, and transition effects information, and it can be read by high end analog video equipment.
Edit-Level Video (ELV)	In DVI technology, the video compression/decompression technique which operates in real time using the DVI system itself. It provides picture quality suitable for application development purposes, but it will normally be replaced by Presentation Level Video for the final application.
Embossing	The process of coloring edges in an image so that the picture appears to be made up of 3-D layers of metal or stone.
End boxes	Rectangular buttons on a slider that are used to set the minimum or maximum setting.
End condition	In cubic spline curve interpolation, one can supply an extra condition at each of the two endpoints. Examples of such end condition: tangents or zero curvature.
Encode	To compress or otherwise process an image while saving it to disk.

Elevator The part of the scroll bar that has up and down arrows and a drag area. The elevator scroll bar cable and shows the position of the view in the pane relative to the total data available.

EPS Encapsulated Postscript file, which can be printed or read by most Postscript compatible programs.

File standard A standard for access of file-oriented data objects on a storage medium. For a CD-ROM, the file standard is specified by ISO 9660.

Flat-shaded A method of coloring facets that covers the entire facet with a single shade.

Flicker Any visible or subliminally visible shimmering or flashing caused by repeatedly erasing and redrawing images.

Flythrough See *walkthrough*.

Fonts Typefaces; the actual shapes that are displayed or printed to represent characters of the alphabet, numbers, and punctuation.

Force feedback See *tactile feedback devices*.

Forceball A 6DOF trackball style input device that enables object manipulation or movement of perspective. One applies force to this device to navigate or interact with the virtual world. For example, to move a pointer on-screen, one pushes the ball in the direction one wants the pointer to move.

Foreground The controls and the pane of a window.

fps Frames per second

Fractal Image File (FIF) A file format for highly compressed images stored as fractals.

Fractals Infinitely detailed shapes; each part of a fractal resembles the whole.

Fractal geometry Provides both a description and a mathematical model for many of the complex forms found in nature.

Frame A single complete picture in a video recording, film, animation, or simulation.

Frames Bordered screen regions (or object containers) that can contain application-specific objects. Borders are not necessarily visible.

Frame buffer	A temporary storage device that gathers all the data for an image frame from the graphics processor, which runs at a certain rate, before releasing it to the display system, which runs at a different rate.
Fourier transform	A process which determines the frequency domain parameters of a series of data points.
Frame	The result of a complete scanning of one image. In motion video, the image is scanned repeatedly, making a series of frames.
Frequency interleaving	In the NTSC or PAL television systems, the technique of choosing the color subcarrier frequency so that the chrominance frequency components of the signal fall between the luminance frequency components.
Frequency response	It indicates how well a board or speakers reproduce sounds ranging from deep bass to high treble. Ideally, the components should handle all frequencies from 20 Hz to 20,000 Hz uniformly.
FTP	File Transfer Protocol - A method of sending binary or ASCII data files from one Internet site to another.
Full-motion video	Video reproduction at 30 frames per second for NTSC-original signals or 25 frames per second for PAL-original signals.
Gamma Correction	The process of changing the balance of red, green, and blue light in an image to correct for the sensitivity of our eyes to different colors, or to correct for the ability of a monitor or printer to show different colors.
Gauge	A read-only control that show the percent of use or the portion of an action that has been completed.
Geometric continuity	Continuity properties of a curve or a surface that are more general than its order of differentiability.
IF	CompuServe Graphics Interchange Format compressed bitmap.
Glyph	A picture or graphic representation of an object.
Gopher	A client-server linked database system accessible via the Internet.
Gopher Space	A term for the combined database of all Gopher sites in the world.

Gouraud shading	A method of coloring facets in which a user applies smooth gradations of color over the facet's surface.
Graphics Accelerator	Hardware to take on some of the graphics calculations normally done by the CPU, thus speeding up the display of complex graphics.
Graphics Interchange Format (IF)	A standard for compressed image storage.
Graphics Kernel System (GKS)	A popular graphics programming system on UNIX platforms.
Grab handles	The small squares that are displayed at the corners and midpoints of the region that defines a selected graphic object.
Head Mounted Display	An output device based on a helmet or goggles containing one or two tiny video monitors. Often coupled with audio headphones, the HMD currently is the most popular device for entering the virtual worlds.
Hidden Surfaces	Surfaces that would not be visible while looking at a real 3-D object, but that need to be purposefully hidden when displaying a computerized rendering of a 3-D model.
Highlighting	A visual indication that an object is in a special state. In monochrome implementations, indication is reverse video. In color implementation, users can set the selection highlighting color.
HMD	See head mounted display
Horizontal	The specification of resolution in the horizontal direction, meaning the ability of the system to reproduce closely spaced vertical lines.
Horizontal Resolution	The number of pixels across the screen in the x direction.
Horizontal Scroll Bar	At the bottom of a Windows window, the bare that allows a user to move the window view back and forth horizontally.
Hue	The "color" of a colored point, as red, green, yellow, violet.
ICO	A Windows icon file.
Icon	A small pictorial representation of a base window. Displaying objects as

icons conserves screen real estate while keeping the window available for easy access.

IDE — Integrated Development Environment A programmer's work place for editing, compiling, and testing programs without returning to the command line or Program Manager window.

IGES — Initial Graphics Exchange Specification A standard file format for exchanging drawings and images between CAD programs.

Image — A still picture, or one frame of a motion sequence.

Image Buffer — The memory where an image is stored.

Image file — A file of data which represents an image.

Image plane — In digital video display hardware which has more than one video memory array contributing to the displayed image in real time, each memory array is called an image plane. See also bit plane.

Image processing — Techniques which manipulate the pixel values of an image for some particular purpose. Examples are : brightness or contract correction, color correction, changing size (scaling), or changing shape of the image (warping).

Immersive — A computer-mediated experience that involves inclusion or partial immersion (only the hand, for instance) in a virtual world.

In/out markers — Notations that are placed on digital video and audio files to denote where they begin and end.

Industry Standard — The expansion bus in an AT compatible computer Architecture (ISA) Almost all PCs have ISA buses.

Input area — The place on the screen that accepts keyboard input.

Intensity — The amount of light, or the amount of a particular color.

Interlace — In scanning, the technique of using more than one vertical scan to reproduce a complete television, 2:1 interlace is used, giving two vertical scans (fields) per frame; one field scans odd lines, and one field scans the even lines of the frame.

Inter modulation — It is the amplitude ratio (expressed in percent) of the distortions to the test

distortion	signal.
Inflection point	A point on a curve where the tangent intersects the curve. Often corresponds to points with zero curvature.
Insert point	The specific location in the input area where keyboard input is displayed.
Interactive	Involving interaction.
Intersection Point	A point on a surface that has been struck by a reflection ray, a refraction ray, or an eye ray.
Interpolation	Finding a curve or surface that satisfies some imposed constraints exactly. The most common constraint is the requirement of passing through a set of given points.
Items	Menu controls that initiate actions. Also, choices found in a scrolling list.
Jaggy	Having jagged edges.
Jittering	A method of simulating greater resolution or dynamic range by modulating intensity data with noise.
JPEG	The Joint Photographic Experts Group - defined by JPEG, an image file compression standard that achieves very high compression ratios with some loss of image quality.
JPG	Highly compressed format design by the Joint Photographic Experts Group (JPEG).
Julia Set	A type of fractal, similar to the Mandelbrot set.
Junction point	A spline curve is composed of segments. The common point shared by two segments is called the junction point. See also knot.
Kernel	(1) The central, essential part of anything. (2) The array of numbers that defines the effect of an image-processing convolution.
Keyboard accelerator	A key or sequence of keys on the keyboard, or multiple clicks of mouse buttons, through which users can quickly perform specific menu or application functions without using a menu.
Knot	A spline curve is defined over a partition of an interval of the real line.

	The points that partition are called knots. If evaluated at a knot, the spline curve passes through a junction point.
Layer	Windows and icons that overlap one another on the workspace.
LCD	Liquid Crystal Display
LED	Light Emitting Diode
Light Buffer	A depth buffer containing pointers to objects illuminated by a light source; a technique used to compute shadows with local illumination models.
Lines	Often used to mean visible approximations, of line segments.
Linear precision	A property of many curve schemes : if the curve scheme is applied to equidistant points on a straight line, that straight line is reproduced.
Light Emitting Diode	An optoelectronic device that uses electrical energy to generate light. LEDs are used for numerical displays in electronic test equipment, digital watches, and so on. On the sensor assembly of the Matter Power Glove red LEDs illuminate to indicate when it senses glove motion.
Liquid crystal display	A device commonly used on digital watches, calculators, and miniature televisions. A liquid crystal is sealed between two pieces of glass and polarisers, then activated by an external source. Electric current toggles the crystal between transparent and opaque.
Local Bus	The synchronous bus between a microprocessor and its memory.
Local Illumination Model	An illumination model that simulates only direct illumination such as Gouraud and Phong shading. No reflected light is taken into account.
Lofting	Creating a ruled surface between two given curves.
Lossless compression	Any data compression technique that does not lose any of its original data, such as Run Length Encoding (RLE).
Lossy compression	Any data compression technique that loses some of the original data in the process of compression, such as JPEG.
LUT	Look Up Table - An array of values, used in image processing applications to obtain intensity or color values from a spectrum.
Luminance	The brightness of a video sign.

Magenta	The color obtained by mixing equal intensities of red and blue light. It is also the correct name for the subtractive primary color usually called "red".
Mandelbrot Set	A famous mathematical fractal popularized by the French mathematician Benoit Mandelbrot. Most of the fractal pictures seen in magazines, with the pretty colored spirals within spirals, are parts of the infinitely detailed Mandelbrot set.
Menu	A rectangle containing a group of items/ controls. Menus are displayed in two ways: from a menu button with choices appropriate to the menu button label (button menu) and from any place on the screen that is not a control (pop-up menu). The pop-up menu displays choices appropriate to the pointer location.
Menu Bar	In Windows (and most commercial programs for DOS these days), the area at the top of the screen or window where the menu choices are.
Menu button	A multiple-choice control. A menu button always has a menu mark and is used to display a menu.
Menu group	A menu and its associated submenus.
Menu item	An item on a menu with a menu mark pointing to the right that is used to display a submenu.
Message	Information generated by an application that informs users about the status of a process.
Message Loop	The part of a Windows program that checks for messages and takes the appropriate action to deal with the messages it receives.
Minimize Box	In Windows, the little square that turns the window into an icon when one clicks the mouse button at it.
MIDI	See Musical Instrument Digital Interface.
MIPS	Million Instructions Per Second.
Mnemonic key	A key that represents the First letter of a command and is, thus, easy to remember.
Morphing	Tweening; gradually metamorphosing a shape into another shape.

Motif	A graphical user-interface for UNIX systems, championed by the Open Look Foundation.
Motion video	Video which displays real motion. It is accomplished by displaying a sequence of images (frames) rapidly enough that the eye sees the image as a continuously moving picture.
Mouse	An electronic or mechanical device that is used to select and manipulate information on a computer screen.
MPEG	The Motion Picture Experts Group's MPEG video compression technology, a standard for adding animated video sequences to any software using JPEG compression.
MPG	File extension for an MPEG file.
Multi-click	Clicking a mouse button rapidly a specific number of times.
Multimedia	Descriptive of the delivery of information that combines different content formats (motion video, audio, still images, graphics, animation, text, and so on).
Multi-tasking	In a computer, a technique that allows several processes to appear to run simultaneously even though the computer has only one CPU. Multi-tasking is done by sequentially switching the CPU between the tasks, usually many times per second..
Musical Instrument Digital Interface (MIDI)	A serial digital bus standard for interfacing of digital musical instruments.
Neural Network	A mathematical technique of pattern matching, originally inspired by efforts to simulate the behaviour of brain cells.
NTSC	Acronym for "National Television Systems Committee", the standardizing body which in 1953 created the color television standards for the United States. This system is called the NTSC color television system.
Object	In programming, a procedure that contains its own data and responds to messages telling it what to do with that data. In 3-D graphics, a mathematical model of a real object.
OpenGL	A portable 3-D graphics interface, developed by Silicon Graphics, independent of platform of GUI.

PAL — Acronym for "Phase Alternation Line", which is the key feature of the color television system developed in West Germany and used by many other countries in Europe. This system is called the PAL system.

Palette — When used with color look-up tables, the range of colors from which the table colors can be selected.

Pane — A bordered rectangle in a window where the application displays its data.

Panning — A method of scrolling in which users directly drag the contents of the pane instead of using the scroll bar.

Parametrization — Assigning parameter values to junction points in spline curves. Also used with a different meaning : the function that controls the speed of a point traversing a curve.

Paste — To insert data from the clipboard into a window. Selected data is placed on the clipboard with the COPY or CUT key.

PCI — A processor-independent bus architecture developed by Intel.

PCL — Hewlett Packard Printer Control Language (for LaserJet-compatible printers).

PCT — Apple Macintosh PICT format bitmap (sometimes given the PIC extension).

PCX — ZSoft's PC Paintbrush bitmap format.

Patch — Complicated surfaces are usually broken down into smaller units, called patches. For bicubic spline surface consists of a collection of bicubic patches.

Pel — IBM's goofy word for pixel.

Pen — A pointing device that looks like an ordinary desk pen but contains electronics allowing the computer to tell where it is relative to the screen or a digitizing pad.

Pentium — The name Intel chose for their next CPU chip when they found out they could not buy all worldwide rights to the digits 5, 8, and 6.

Perspective — The effect that makes distant objects look smaller than closer objects.

Perspective Distance	The simulated distance between a user's eyes and the object the user is rendering in 3-D.
PEX	A portable 3-D graphics interface that augments X-Window.
PHIGS	An old UNIX graphics standard.
Phong Shading	A local illumination model that accounts for specular and diffuse light by interpolating vertex normals to calculate surface intensity.
PhotoCD	Kodak's attempt at mass marketing a service to digitize 35mm film photos and put them on a CD-ROM for a user.
Pixel	An abbreviation for picture element, the smallest unit that can be displayed on a computer screen.
Pointer	Any graphic representation of the location of the mouse on the screen.
Pointing device	A mechanical or electronic device used to manipulate the screen pointer.
Pop-up menu	A menu that users access by pressing MENU on any area of the workspace that is not a control.
Pop-up window	A window that pops up to perform a specific function and that is then dismissed.
Postscript	A computer language specifically designed to describe graphics images and text fonts. Unlike most languages, Postscript is usually interpreted by a processor in the printer, not the CPU.
Position tracker	A system that tracks the movements of parts of the body and sends information about position and orientation to the computer for processing. Typically, a position tracker is attached to the head-mounted display.
Power Glove	This controller for the Nintendo Entertainment System game machine was adapted from VPL's DataGlove.
PC (personal computer)	A software-controlled system containing general purpose computer functions and intended for use by one person at any time.
Pixel	An abbreviation for picture element, the smallest unit can be displayed on a computer screen; or A single point of an image, having a single pixel value.

PLV — See Presentation-Level Video.

Point — A location in space. If one uses coordinate systems to describe space, a point is represented as an n-tuple of real numbers.

Potential gain — It is the maximum amplification, in dB, that the preamplifier can achieve. In order to accommodate sound sources with various output levels and record them at constant volume, high potential gain a low voltage input is desired.

Primitives — Basic objects (lines, spheres, cubes, cones, and cylinders) employed by two-dimensional and three-dimensional graphics systems used to compose more complex objects.

Presentation-Level Video (PLV) — In DVI technology, the highest quality video compression process. PLV requires the use of a large computer for compression.

Primary color — In a tri-stimulus color video system, one of the three colors mixed to produce an image. In additive color systems, the primary colors are red, green, and blue. In subtractive color systems, the primaries are cyan, magenta, and yellow.

Raster — The pattern of motion used in scanning, usually left to right, and repeated over the image from top to bottom as a series of horizontal lines.

Raster Operation — A way of combining the color of pixels to be drawn with the pixel colors already on the screen. The most commonly used "Raster-operations" are OR and simple replacement, sometimes called SET or PUT.

Ray Tracing — The act of using a ray tracer; or the calculations that the ray-tracer carries out.

Reflection — The effect one sees when light bounces off of something and the image of the surrounding environment appears in that thing. This is easy to simulate on a computer with ray tracing.

Refraction — The bending of light as it passes through a transparent or translucent object.

Render — To draw an image as it actually appears, rather than in schematic or outline form. The rendering process removes an image's hidden surfaces and jagged edges and defines the image's characteristics, such as color, lighting, and texture.

Resize corner	Areas that provide an unconstrained resizing boundaries of the window, without changing the scale of the contents of the windows that can be resized have resize corners.
Resize handles	Handles on the sides of a pane that can be adjusted; they are displayed when users select the pane.
Resolution	The ability of an image reproducing system to reproduce fine detail. In television, it is specified as lines per picture height, which is the total count of black and white lines that can be reproduced in a distance equal to the picture height.
RGB	Acronym for red, green and blue. A type of computer color display output signal composed of separately controllable red, green & blue.
RGB Color Model	The method of describing colors by specifying the intensities of red, green, and blue light to be added together.
RISC	Reduced Instruction Set Computing - A microprocessor design that calls for fewer instructions and more registers. RISC processors design offers considerable performance advantage over CISC processors.
RLE	An old CompuServe bitmap from before IFF was invented. A Microsoft Windows run-length encoded bitmap.
Ruled surface	A surface containing a family of straight lines. Obtained as linear interpolation between two given curves.
Run Length Encoding (RLE)	A way of compressing image data that replaces long sequences ("runs") of identical values with a code followed by the number of times the value is repeated.
Secondary Colors	Cyan, magenta, and yellow. See CMYK Color Model.
Self-Similar	Having parts that resemble the whole.
Scale	The ratio by which the size of each element in an image is altered.
Scaling	A process for changing the size of an image.
Scanning	The process for changing the size of an image.
Scroll bar	A control that is used to move the view of the data displayed in the pane.

Scrolling	Moving through data that cannot be viewed entirely in a pane.
Scrolling button	An abbreviated button with a solid triangular arrowhead inside the border that is used for scrolling.
Shadows	The darkness cast by the light. Each day hides a small patch of night.
SECAM	Acronym for Sequential Coleur Avec Memoire (sequential color with memory), which is the color television system developed in France and used in certain other countries.
Seek time	In a mass storage device, the time required to position the red head over the track containing the desired data.
Simulated object	A virtual-world entity that might have an appearance and/or a behaviour. Sometimes called an *object*.
Signal-to-noise ratio	It is the ratio, in dBr, of the maximum undistorted output of the board (the signal) and the inevitable electronic noise - mostly hum and hiss - generated by the board's own circuitry.
Six degrees of freedom	A sensor's capability to track movement of spatial position (x-, y-, and z-axes) and orientation (pitch, yaw, and roll).
Slider	A control used to set a value and give a visual indication of the setting.
Shutter Glasses	Glasses that have LCD panels in each eye opening. By alternately blocking each eye opening 30 times a second and simultaneously flipping between left and right eye views on a computer monitor, the shutter glasses allow a user to see color stereo pictures.
Solid Modelling	The description of objects that are bounded by surfaces.
Space	The collection of all points.
Spreadsheet	A program that lays out a grid of numbers and text, allowing one to enter formulas instead of a number for any square in the grid. It's handy tool for simple number-crunching and accounting tasks.
Spline curve	A continuous curve that is composed of several polynomial segments. Spline curves are often represented in terms of B-spline functions.
Status message	Information generated by an application that informs users about the progress of a process.

Stereo Pairs	A left-eye view and a right eye view of the same scene or object. These are often placed side-by-side for viewing.
Stereo Vision	The ability to judge the relative distance between objects from the differences between what one sees with the left eye and what one sees with the right eye.
Stereoscopic	Involving stereo vision.
Stereoscopic glasses	A wearable output device used for viewing in stereo to look at computer-generated, 3-D graphics that appear to float in front of one's eyes.
Submenu	A menu that displays additional choices under a menu item on a menu.
Subdivision	Breaking a curve or surface down into smaller pieces, usually recursively.
Super-VGA	Any video adapter with higher resolution than VGA's 640x480 by 16 colors, specifically, a 800x600 by 16-colors, or 640x480 by 256 colors.
Super VGA+	Video adapters with resolutions beyond 800x600 and/or more than 256 colors.
Surface	The locus of all points of a moving and deforming curve, or, the image of a region in 2-space under a continuous map. A surface is often broken down into patches.
SVGA or SVG	See Super-VGA
S-Video	A video format that separates the chrominance and luminance values of video into two separate signals.
System Fonts	The standard typefaces that come built into an operating system.
Tagged Image File Format (TIFF)	See TIFF
Targa	A high-end line of graphics hardware manufactured by TrueVision, Inc. See TGA
TGA	Bitmap format originally created for Truevision Targa boards.
Tactile feedback /force-feedback devices	Output devices that transmit pressure, force, or vibration to provide the VR participant with the sense of touch. Tactile feedback simulates the sensation applied to the skin. Force feedback simulates weight (or

resistance to motion.

Text field	An area in a window into which users type text from the keyboard.
Texture mapping	The processes of imbuing a computer reflection graphics image with the appearance of lifelike texture (smooth, rough, rippled, and so on) and light reflections and other characteristics.
Three-dimensional	Used in computer-aided design and the modelling creation of virtual worlds to geometrically define the shape of an object.
Three-dimensional (3-D) Sound	Reproduced sound that seems to emanate sound from points in front of, above, below, and to either side of the listener.
TIF	Three-letter extension for TIFF files.
TIFF	Tagged Image File Format used by many graphics programs.
Time codes	Time stamps that appear like page numbers on frames of a video clip. Each frame is stamped with a time code, which facilitates locating frames and measuring the duration of a clip.
Title	The name of the application or function that is displayed at the top of a window or a pop-up menu.
Title Bar	In Windows, the very top part of a window, which contains the title of the window.
Tool kit	A set of programming components used to build applications.
Total Harmonic distortion plus noise	It is the total of all spurious harmonic frequencies (plus the noise) generated within the board's electronics. It is expressed as a percentage of the undistorted output signal strength.
Transform	In data compression, a process that converts a block of data into some alternate form that is more convenient or efficient for a particular purpose.
Triangular patch	A patch whose domain is a triangle.
Tweening	The process of automatically calculating several images between key frames in an animation.
Validate	To have the application verify that the contents of a text field are appropriate to the function.

VESA	The Video Electronics Standards Association - a standard-setting consortium made up of big graphics hardware and software companies, the Super-VGA modes standardized by VESA, the local bus specification proposed by VESA.
VESA Local Bus	A 32-bit bus architecture developed by VESA that allows adapters to interface synchronously with the microprocessor.
VGA	Video Graphics Array The current low-end standard for color graphics hardware on the PC. It is capable of 640x480 with 16 colors or 320x200 with 256 colors.
Video	Electronic representation of images; both natural (real) or computer-generated.
Video Capture	The ability to digitize video and store it on a computer.
Video Cards	Computer graphics adapter hardware (not necessarily capable of dealing with video capture or digital video).
Video for Windows	A new standard for displaying digitized motion pictures within Microsoft Windows. It uses a tiny 160x120 pixel window for speed.
Video Co-processor	A separate CPU for video functions, operating in parallel with the main system CPU.
Viewpoint	The point in space where the observer or camera is located when computing a 3-D rendering.
Virtual reality (VR)	As generally agreed, virtual reality refers to technology that presents data visualizations or simulations in the form of computer-generated and computer-mediated three-dimensional "worlds" or environments that one can "enter", manipulate, and navigate using appropriate input and output devices.
Virtual Reality Softwarre	Software that supports real-time 3-D rendering, preferably with stereoscopic display. Most VR software allows a user to create a virtual world and then interactively explore it.
Virtual Worlds	See Virtual Reality Software.
Visual Simulation	Modelling something in a way that makes its essential components visible while the dynamics of the system do their thing.

Visualization	The visual representation of complex or abstract data, usually in the form of a computer graphics model.
VRAM	Video RAM. A variation of DRAM which has two ports - the usual random-access port for access by a CPU and a separate serial port, which can output a serial stream of data at high rates, independent of the activity on the random-access port.
Voxel	A volume element, the three-dimensional equivalent of a pixel. It is used in medical imaging and volume rendering.
.WAV Windows Wave form file	It is the standard audio file format of PCs.
Walk-through /fly-through	A complex, three-dimensional model of a building, structure, or other environment through which a user can move the viewpoint as if walking or flying through it.
Window	A rectangle containing application elements.
Windows NT	The newest version of Windows, which can run on several different types of computers and does not require DOS.
Window background	The area outside any panes, including the header, footer, and sides of the window.
Workspace	The background screen area on which windows and icons are displayed.
World Wide Web	A linked client-server database that uses hypertext information and requires a browser program.
WPG	WordPerfect vector drawing or bitmap image.
X-Window	A user interface and graphics operation protocol for UNIX developed at MIT.
Yaw	To pan (side-to-side movement around an axis).
YUV color system	A color-encoding scheme for natural pictures in which the luminance (Y) and chrominance (UV) are separate.

APPENDIX V

BÉZIER CURVES

V.1 INTRODUCTION

In computer aided design, it is often necessary to find a functional form for a curve or surface that is given graphically. Usually it is done in an interactive manner by a user trying various parameters with the help of a graphics terminal until the resulting functions appears satisfactory. Bézier developed a method for doing this while working on computer-aided design systems for Renault and Citröen in France. This method has now become a major tool in computer graphics. For a good introduction, the interested reader is referred to the book by Bartels, Beatty and Barsky [1].

We shall start by studying a simple set of functions called **Bernstein basis functions** in the next section.

V.2 BERNSTEIN BASIS FUNCTIONS

Assuming that all data is given in the range $a \leq x \leq b$, the i-th Bernstein basis function is a polynomial of degree n, defined as

$$B_i^n(x) = \binom{n}{i} \frac{(b-x)^{n-1}(x-a)^i}{(b-a)^n}, \quad i = 0, \ldots, n \tag{AV.1}$$

Here the notation $\binom{n}{i}$ represents the binomial coefficient

$$\binom{n}{i} = \frac{n!}{i!\,(n-i)!} \tag{AV.2}$$

For example, the four cubic Bernstein basis functions for $n = 3$ are given below:

$$B_0^3(x) = \frac{(b-x)^3}{(b-a)^3}$$

$$B_1^3(x) = 3\frac{(b-x)^2(x-a)}{(b-a)^3}$$

$$B_2^3(x) = 3\frac{(b-x)(x-a)^2}{(b-a)^3} \tag{AV.3}$$

$$B_3^3(x) = \frac{(x-a)^3}{(b-a)^3)}$$

For actual computation of these functions, it is better to use the following iterative algorithm, which reduces the growth of round-off error.

$$B_0^0(x) = 1, \quad B_{-1}^n(x) = 0$$

$$B_i^n(x) = \frac{(b-x)B_i^{n-1}(x) + (x-a)B_{i-1}^n(x)}{b-a}, \qquad 0 \le i \le n \tag{AV.4}$$

$$B_{n+1}^n(x) = 0$$

Since each Bernstein basis function is a polynomial of degree n, so is the linear combination

$$P_n(x) = \sum_{i=0}^{n} p_i B_i^n(x) \tag{AV.5}$$

Hence, we can try to find the coefficients p_i such that P_n interpolates the given data at $n+1$ points, $y_i = P_n(x_i)$ in the interval $a \le x \le b$. This can be done by solving a set of $n+1$ linear simultaneous equations. This would be similar to the use of Lagrange interpolation, except that we are using a different set of basis functions. In the case of Lagrange polynomials, it is possible to make a curve of degree n pass through exactly n given points, but this curve tends to be oscillatory in between these points [2]. On the other hand, the use of Bézier curves allows a designer to interactively make the interpolating curve smooth and as close to a given set of points as desired. This will be discussed in the next section.

V.3 INTERACTIVE FITTING OF BÉZIER CURVE

In general, it is rather difficult to guess the shape of a curve represented by a high order polynomial by simply looking at its coefficients. For the polynomial $P_n(x)$ given in equation (AV.5), however, the first and last coefficients, p_0 and p_1 are simply equal to the values y_0 and y_n, respectively. This follows simply as $B_i^n(a) = 0$ if $i > 0$, and $B_0^n(a) = 1$, so that $p_0 = y_0$. Similarly, $p_n = y_n$. It is interesting to note that the remaining coefficients p_i are related to the data point y_i almost as simply. This fact can be utilized to guess the shape of the interpolating curve, and can be exploited in an interactive manner.

For this purpose, we associate each p_i with a point in the plane (t_i, p_i), called a *control point*, where

$$t_i = x_0 + i\frac{(x_n - x_0)}{n} = a + i\frac{(b-a)}{n} \tag{AV.5}$$

so that t_i are equally spaced in the interval of interest. Note that although $t_0 = x_0$ and $t_n = x_n$, the remaining t_i are not necessarily equal to x_i.

From each trial set of control points we can form the Bézier polygon, starting with (t_0, p_0), connecting the successive control points by straight line segments and finally connecting (t_n, p_n) back to (t_n, p_n).

It can be shown that this polygon provides a rough idea of the shape of $P_n(x)$. In addition, $P_n(x)$ lies entirely within the convex hull formed from the control points. (A set S is said to be convex if a straight line joining any two points in S remains within S. The convex hull is the smallest convex set containing all control points.) Often the convex hull is the same as the region enclosed by the Bézier polygon. Thus moving a control point up or down has a direct and intuitive effect on the shape of the curve generated by $P_n(x)$.

In practice, the number and location of control points is not known in advance, but only decided by the minimum number of points required to obtain a satisfactory curve. A designer can interactively select the number of control points and move them so that a curve of the desired form is obtained. Several commercially available graphics packages generate Bézier curves after a user has set the control points. Thus, a "good" interpolating curve can often be obtained after a few trials.

V.3 REFERENCES:

1. R. Bartels, J. Beatty and B. Barsky, *An Introduction to Splines for use in Computer Graphics and Geometric Modeling*, Morgan Kaufmann, Los Altos, California, 1987.
2. G.J. Lastman and N.K. Sinha, *Microcomputer-based Numerical Methods for Science and Engineering*, Saunders College Publishing, New York, 1988.

INDEX